FUTURISTIC FICTION, UTOPIA, AND SATIRE IN THE AGE
OF THE ENLIGHTENMENT

HISTORIES IN MOTION

PEOPLE, IMAGES, OBJECTS, IDEAS (15TH-19TH CENTURIES)

VOLUME 2

Futuristic Fiction, Utopia, and Satire in the Age of the Enlightenment

Samuel Madden's Memoirs of the Twentieth Century *(1733)*

by
GIULIA IANNUZZI

BREPOLS

D/2023/0095/161
ISBN 978-2-503-60602-6
eISBN 978-2-503-60603-3
DOI 10.1484/M.HIMO-EB.5.133594

Printed in the EU on acid-free paper.

This book is dedicated to the memory of
Salvatore Iannuzzi

Contents

Part II
Samuel Madden, *Memoirs of the Twentieth Century*

List of Illustrations

Figures

.

Acknowledgements

I would like to express my sincere gratitude to J. S. D. Madden for his unique kindness and availability. I am deeply indebted to Giovanni Tarantino for his guidance and for the encouragement he gave me while I was working on this project. My heartfelt thanks go to Turtle Bunbury and Tom Jones for their help and suggestions on issues related to George Berkeley. I would also like to extend my special thanks to the anonymous reviewers whose advice helped a great deal to improve the manuscript.

This project has benefitted immensely from the interlocutors who have listened to seminar papers presenting portions and early versions of this research. For the stimulating discussions on my work in progress I thank the organisers of and participants in the 2021 International Society of Eighteenth-Century Studies early career seminar on *Credulity and the Age of Reason*, and the British Society for Eighteenth-Century Studies postgraduate and early-career seminar series.

I owe a deep debt of gratitude to the incomparable kindness of Susan Odell Walker at the Lewis Walpole Library, Yale University, for her assistance. I am grateful to the many museum curators, librarians, and archivists whose help made this research possible. In particular I would like to thank the Beinecke Rare Book and Manuscript Library at Yale; the British Library, London; the Department of Archives and Modern Manuscripts at Cambridge University Library; the Department of Early Printed Books and Special Collections and the Research Collections — Manuscripts & Archives at The Library of Trinity College Dublin; the Huntington Library; the library at Ickworth; the Library & Archives of the Royal Dublin Society; the Manuscripts Department at the National Library of Ireland in Dublin; Marsh's Library, Dublin; the National Archives of Ireland; the Public Record Office of Northern Ireland; the Suffolk Archives at Suffolk County Council; The Warburg Institute, London.

The first and second chapters in the first section of this book develop reflections I begun to formulate in the article 'The Illustrator and the Global Wars to Come. Albert Robida, *La guerre infernale*, and the Long History of Imagined Warfare', that was featured in the journal *Cromohs*, 22, 2019. Publishing it there was a fundamental step in the genesis of this work: I am very grateful to the editors of the journal. Parts of the third, fourth, seventh, and thirteenth chapters appeared, in less detail, in *History of Historiography*, 77, 2020, monographic issue *Imperial Times:*

How Europe Used Time to Rule the World (XVIII–XIX Centuries), as part of the article '"This New and Unexampled Way of Writing the History of Future Times": The Rise and Fall of Empires and the Acceleration of History in Samuel Madden's Eighteenth-Century Memoirs from the Future'. I am grateful to the editors and the other contributors of *Imperial Times* for the productive discussions we had while working together on that project.

Introduction

Knowledge, Power, and Time in the Age of the Enlightenment

> Let such ignorant objectors therefore, that are buried
> in the present state of the earth, and think it will
> continue in a manner unimprov'd and unalter'd, let
> them, I say, look back, if they know any thing of it in
> former ages.
>
> Memoirs of the Twentieth Century, *508.*

The aim of this study is to assess the cultural significance of one of the earliest futuristic fictions known in Anglophone and Euro-American literature: *Memoirs of the Twentieth Century*, published anonymously in 1733. This chronicle of the future foregrounds an acceleration of history brought about by an increasing degree of global interconnectedness, and the exclusion of prophetism and astrology as credible ways to know the future. It is the work of Samuel Madden, an Irish writer and philanthropist of Whig sympathies, and consists of a collection of diplomatic letters composed in the 1990s, which the narrator claims to have received from the future. Through these correspondences, twentieth-century world scenarios are spread out before the reader, in which British naval power rules the waves and international commerce while the transnational scheming of the Jesuits threatens the independence of weaker European courts. The flash-forwarding projections in *Memoirs* are closely connected to the dramatic changes that geographical explorations, scientific discoveries, and international commerce engendered in the European understanding of the world. The letters offer a fine example of the emergence of a secularised future, constructed through logical extrapolations informed by a variety of rationales, from utopian achievements to ominous warnings, to the satiric mocking of the writer's present.

Through a case study of *Memoirs*, this research intends to contribute to a wider cultural history of time and speculative fiction. An extensive discussion of the history of imagination related to the future places this work of prose fiction against the backdrop of early futuristic literature and allows us to rediscover and assess it as an essential work in the proto-science fictional and utopian canon. The first two chapters of the first part of this volume provide an overview of futuristic imagery in early modern European culture, focusing on literary works of fiction, and contextualising cultural uses of the future within a broader cultural history of time. In particular, the eighteenth century is explored as a pivotal moment within longer processes of change in the conceptualisation of history and secularisation of the future. *Memoirs* is thus located within a multilingual corpus, which includes better-known milestones such as works by Louis-Sébastien Mercier and Condorcet. Madden's futuristic tale may also be understood within the history of utopian literature and thought: while its temporal construction of utopian inventions bears notable elements of originality, it may also foster a better understanding of the non-secondary role that diachronicity has played in earlier, founding works of utopian thought, in particular within the Anglophone tradition. The first chapter argues that conceptualisations of historical diachronicity have underpinned the construction of utopian polities since More, Bacon, and Harrington.

Memoirs may be read within this long-term history as well as within the cultural context of its genesis. The third chapter places the novel within the intellectual trajectory of its author, highlighting a range of interests and cultural circles whose influences run through the text in various ways. An inquiry into the author's personal and family libraries and their fate may also contribute to a cultural history of publishing, as well as to the reconstruction of the cultural context of this particular book. The fourth chapter gives an overview of the novel's structure, the twentieth-century world as it is imagined in the main body of the text, and the criteria and themes guiding its futuristic portrayal. The epistolary form is the textual representation of the network of international connections described in the novel's depiction of the future and it is essential for an appraisal of how a transnational knowledge is shaped and circulates, and how historical processes function. It also conveys to some extent a culturally estranged perspective on the part of the British ambassadors to the countries where they are stationed, and — by enabling comparisons between the British commonwealth and other cases — from the partially defamiliarised standpoint of British observers abroad. Nonetheless, the courts where the ambassadors are located betray a London-centric and Euro-centric perspective, and it is to London that knowledge and news flow to be processed, organised, and rendered useful to the British political and economic interests.

Memoirs touches a number of issues as regards historical time and its knowability, offering an apt observatory for the dubious space carved out in European culture by Pyrrhonist scepticism and by seventeenth- and early eighteenth-century debates on the nature of historical knowledge. The following chapters are devoted to an in-depth examination of these aspects, with particular attention paid to the problems that the narrative raises regarding the conception of the future and the negotiation of the boundaries between credibility and credulity, between verisimilitude and absurdity.

In three prefaces, the letters' (fictitious) editor calls attention to beliefs that are being excluded from a system of knowledge built on reason and empirical enquiry. These prefatory writings are replete with scholarly references, whose function may have been in part to add a sense of authenticity to the purported letters, but more importantly they serve as a safeguard against the author's satire being taken too literally. The fifth chapter is aimed at illustrating the voice of this narrator and his satirical purpose with regard to a series of early eighteenth-century manners, customs, and intellectual trends. Through the narrator's portrait, aspects of British politics and behaviours of the gentry are stigmatised, and elements of the occult and the supernatural are introduced ironically. The future becomes an arena in which Enlightenment epistemologies of history and time are tested. The novel launches a satirical attack on a wide range of beliefs denounced as superstitious, absurd, and fanatical, from astrological prophecy to the worship of relics and guardian angels. In so doing, it calls into question notions that were being excluded from a system of knowledge increasingly informed by rationalism and constitutes an exceptional example of Protestant religious enlightenment. The belief in guardian angels or tutelary geniuses is instrumental — argues the sixth chapter — in evoking an encyclopaedia of ancient and early modern references from which the author distances himself through antiphrastic and satirical mechanisms. Many of these tags are extracted from a pool of classical and early modern referentiality, and are used in a jocular manner, with a graduated sense of their actual relevance. They were not meant to be taken by contemporary readers as a serious elucidation of the writer's intentions: they rather reflect a cultural background through ironic lenses, by mocking specific topics and debates and, on a meta-textual level, using argumentative methods built on the accumulation of quotations and *auctoritates*.

The relationship between conceptions of time and space is explored in the seventh chapter, which argues that the secularisation of time, of which *Memoirs* is an expression, is deeply linked to the exploration and cognition of the globe as well as the perception of a world in which the circulation of knowledge, people, and objects was forging increasingly concentrated interconnections between remote places. Inventions in navigation technologies and scientific instruments such as the telescope bring about, in the tale of the future, the compression of a global space-time. By placing technological superiority at the root of the future British monopoly on trade in the Mediterranean, and conceptualising the Moon as the 'new New World', the epistolary narrative highlights a fantastical-utopian transposition of the mobility of information, people, and artefacts at the heart of the dynamics of European colonial expansion. A reflection on the epistolography, transnational relations, and cultural exchanges portrayed in the novel may contribute to a better understanding of the circulation of ideas in the early eighteenth century. The epistolary construction foregrounds the transfer, translation, and appropriation of knowledge across the Mediterranean, the Atlantic, and across a European space, both by thematising these dynamics in the letters' contents and by choosing a structure informed by them. The missive is portrayed as a material object able to record, codify, and transmit information across space and — through a movement that occurs within the narrative frame — across time. The narrative testifies, through its inventiveness, to the power of the trope of paper as a medium.

The eighth chapter is dedicated to exploring the novel's reflections on historical time, the concept of verisimilitude, and the relationship between history and fiction. It starts with a reflection on the genre labels employed by the author and subsequent commentators, and looks at the novel's peritext and meta-historiographical indications contained in the prefatory writings. The problem of the knowability of the future is then explored in depth in the ninth chapter, which is particularly concerned with outlining the cultural background from which Madden's fiction satirically distances itself, that is, those divinatory and prophetic practices that in Europe have characterised, since antiquity, the attempt to know and control the time to come.

The narrative device represented by the letters from the future and their publication is the focus of attention in the tenth chapter, which explores some of the intertextual references and the satirical implications of this particular narrative structure. The next chapter highlights another aspect central to the novel's satirical intentions: the anti-Jesuit polemic. Within a broader attack on various doctrinal and social aspects of Catholicism, *Memoirs* shows particular interest in the Jesuit order's ability to adapt its missionary work to different social and cultural contexts. The recurring descriptions of how Loyola's disciples, with their well-organised and centralised apparatus, use the press, and control the circulation of ideas betray a certain admiration while functioning as a warning to the novel's Protestant readers.

The problem of the relationship between power and knowledge informs many of the themes that run through this tale of the future and its narrative frame, and is furtherly explored in the twelfth chapter. Today's readers are taken to the heart of central issues of the Enlightenment project: the negotiation of what falls within the limits of credibility, the existence of irrational beliefs in the age of reason, issues of control over the production and circulation of knowledge, and the relationship between places of intellectual elaboration and society at large.

The peculiar, and to some extent mysterious, publishing history of the book, explored in the thirteenth chapter, presents elements of great interest with regards to placing it within contemporary debates and

understanding the limits of its fortune and influence on subsequent literature. The print run was almost entirely destroyed hot off the press — for
reasons debated by current scholarship, that this chapter aims to address
— creating a shortage of copies available today. All the more significant are
the vicissitudes of the surviving copies, which through collecting practices,
dedications, bookplates, and evidence of use testify to the power of the
printed book and its material characteristics to bear witness to complex
and stratified networks of relationships.

The last part of this book features a modern, annotated edition of
Memoirs. This edition is aimed at scholars, students, and readers with
interests in cultural history, the early modern age, and the European
eighteenth century, and in speculative and utopian literature. The editorial
choices made in the preparation of the text, discussed in more detail in
'A Note on the Text', were determined by the desire to include readers
unfamiliar with the conventions of textual philology, while ensuring that
the specialist can use this edition in combination with direct consultation
of the original and other primary sources. It is the author's contention that
this work of fiction is an exceptionally fascinating piece of early eighteenth-
century literature and an important — albeit hitherto rather obscure —
chapter in the history of futuristic imagination. Reading it today can thus
enrich our understanding of how the future came to be appropriated as
a fundamental dimension of speculative projection and creativity, and a
virtual laboratory to test and argue politically charged ideas. By looking
at eighteenth-century debates through the literary mirror of *Memoirs*, we
may foster a reflection on what gives our knowledge a solid foundation
as well as on an Enlightenment project that has left us with a world in
which problems of authority and credulity are still of pressing relevance
and where the scientific and rationalist paradigm of reality often seems
more fragile than ever, in so many spheres of European as well as global
society and culture.

PART I

Samuel Madden's Eighteenth-Century Memoirs from the Future

I. Where Was the Future?

The possibility of extra-terrestrial life and of interplanetary voyages, explorations of the Moon and more remote celestial bodies, and close encounters with distant civilisations, including the possibility of being visited by extra-terrestrials beings on Earth: the seventeenth century saw the flourishing of a speculative imagination in Europe in which the role of a spatial dimension has been highlighted by subsequent scholarship. The Copernican revolution opened up cosmic space as a possible home to other planets and civilisations. From Francis Godwin's *The Man in the Moone* (1638) to Cyrano de Bergerac's *Les états et empires de la Lune* (1657, *The States and Empires of the Moon*), from Charles Sorel's *L'Histoire comique de Francion* (1623, *The Comical History of Francion*), progenitor of the imaginary visits of alien humans in Europe, to Fontenelle's *Entretiens sur la pluralités des mondes* (1686, Conversations on the plurality of worlds), fantastic imagination in early modern Europe was rich in philosophical motives and in theological and spiritual interests.[1]

Cultural historians and scholars of speculative fiction have usually located the appearance of a temporal dimension exploited as a means of dislocation from the writer's reality and thus as a source of cognitive estrangement in the late modern period.[2] A watershed in the European

---

1 Here and henceforth, where titles of books in languages other than English are cited in the text, if a published translation exists, it is given in brackets, in italics. In the absence of a published translation or in the case of problematic traditions (for example multiple translations with different titles, titles that deviate widely from the original), a literal translation is given in the text in brackets, in roman type, and the published translations are indicated in the footnotes. Godwin, *The Man in the Moone*; de Bergerac, *Histoire comique contenant les états et empires de la Lune*; Eng. trans. *A Voyage to the Moon*; [Sorel], *Histoire comique de Francion*; Eng. trans. *The Comical History of Francion*; [de Fontenelle], *Entretiens sur la pluralité des mondes*; Eng. trans. *Conversations with a Lady, on the Plurality of Worlds*. For a partial yet extensive bibliography of early extra-terrestrial voyage fictional works: Nicolson, *Voyages to the Moon*; Roberts, *The History of Science Fiction*, pp. 25–83; Roberts, 'The Copernican Revolution'.

2 Suvin, *Metamorphoses of Science Fiction*, pp. 115–44. See also Parrinder, 'Introduction'; Parrinder, 'Revisiting Suvin's Poetics of Science Fiction'. Here I follow Parrinder in making use of the concept of cognitive estrangement as a kind of defamiliarisation originating in the narrative dominance of a *novum* validated by a cognitive logic, adopting Suvin's category 'in its ontological and epistemological aspects [...] a mode of thinking rather than a body of texts': 'Introduction', p. 6.

speculative imagination has been identified at the end of the eighteenth century between the use of fantastic spatial settings and temporal ones, and between utopias placed in remote imaginary lands and the temporal estrangement of uchronias. The future, it has been argued, gradually became a dimension by which authors might escape the limits of naturalistic plausibility, ever more cogent in a cultural landscape — that of the eighteenth and nineteenth centuries — shaped by positivistic paradigms of reality. A shift took place during the eighteenth century from a spatial-based to a temporal-based speculation.[3] While the year 1800 has been pinpointed as a conventional turning point by authoritative scholarship, arguing that the adoption of a temporal dislocation was favoured by the capitalistic emphasis on time as a fundamental dimension in which profits are acquired and by the consequences of this on the European mind,[4] the colonisation of the future by a fantastic imagination has earlier roots.[5] The conceptualisation of a future intimately linked to the present and pliable by human action can in fact be traced back to the emergence of new ideas about and sensibilities towards historical time, which matured gradually during the early modern age.[6] However, as will be discussed in more detail in the following pages, while it is possible to trace general trends in the early modern European imagination and identify significant shifts that occurred in the eighteenth century, the history of the future is anything but teleological. Conceptions and uses of the time to come are areas in which different paradigms have coexisted and competed. Secular uses of the future have characterised a number of human activities since antiquity, while religious and prophetic horizons have never ceased to inform cultural and social uses of time, alongside the maturing of a mercantilist and capitalist mentality.[7] Prognostications and forecasts were based, during the Middles Ages and the Renaissance as well as in earlier periods, on the idea of a future exploitable at multiple levels. Memoirs written for posterity, testaments, forms of birth control and family planning, demographic projections, and estimates concerned with political, commercial, and strategic-military activities all bear witness to attempts to build the

---

3 Alkon, *Origins*; Clute, 'Ruins and Futurity'; Vieira, 'The Concept of Utopia'.

4 Suvin, *Metamorphoses of Science Fiction*, pp. 115–44.

5 Alkon, *Origins*, pp. 91–92; cf. Clarke, ed., *British Future Fiction*, I, p. ix, here Clarke identifies a turning point during the nineteenth century but traces the first developments of a temporal imagination from the seventeenth century onwards, in consequence of which 'the geographies of utopian fiction evolved into the historiographies of a new literature'.

6 Koselleck, *Futures Past*; Koselleck, 'The Eighteenth Century as the Beginning of Modernity' and in general Koselleck, *The Practice of Conceptual History*; see also Corfield, *Time and the Shape of History*; Sayre Schiffman, *The Birth of the Past*; Toulmin and Goodfield, *The Discovery of Time*.

7 Le Goff, *Time, Work & Culture*; see also Cipolla, *Clocks & Culture*; Thompson, 'Time, Work-Discipline, and Industrial Capitalism'.

future according to specific aspirations and to control uncertainty and risk by means of prevision and planning. Long-term histories of the future dealing with these complexities have been written from the standpoint of intellectual, cultural, and social history,[8] and important contributions have been formulated by historians of scientific thought and economics, which have focused, for example, on the role of probability, chance, and different horizons of expectation.[9]

Literature constitutes a vantage point for enriching our understanding of the non-linear cultural processes that affected the way in which the future was conceptualised during the early modern age. An open and constructible future is the implicit condition through which utopian thinking and writing takes shape. The utopian imagination, even when primarily characterised by geographical alterity, tends to become meaningful within a certain timescale, which allows the formulation of prescriptions for good government and policies, and descriptions of the causal mechanisms that might usher in a better society. The utopian construct finds its *raison d'être*, if not in time as a thematised structural dimension, then in the possibility of influencing history and the choices that posterity might make.[10] In order to outline the history of futuristic imagination, we can look at the temporal premises of some of the founding texts of the utopian tradition. The eighteenth century could then be examined to find the dawn of narratives that explicitly thematise the future as the setting for their fictions.

Understood in all its semantic ambiguity as a thought device and literary genre, utopia is profoundly linked to history as a culturally constructed cognitive frame, home to cause and effect mechanisms. The utopian projection, far from consisting in the creation of a-temporal and immobile models, abstract and detached from diachronicity, is a conceptual construction intimately connected to processes of temporalisation and acceleration of history. Utopian texts offer a vantage point to lay bare assumptions about historical time that inform the reconstruction and narration of the past in the early modern European mind. The temporal dimension is inherent to utopias on many levels. The topographical dislocation exploited in early modern imaginary voyages may serve the purpose of constructing an ideal society untouched by the same historical processes experienced by the author's and reader's own polity, so that history as it is known by the writer and the reader constantly informs the

8 Burrow and Wei, eds, *Medieval Futures*; Brady and Butterworth, eds, *The Uses of the Future in Early Modern Europe*, Burke, 'Foreword: The History of the Future'; Hölscher, *Die Entdeckung der Zukunft*; Minois, *Storia dell'avvenire*.
9 Beckert, *Imagined Futures*; Gigerenzer et al., *The Empire of Chance*; Hacking, *The Emergence of Probability*; Puttevils, 'Invoking Fortuna and Speculating on the Future'.
10 Baczko, *L'utopia*; cf. Jameson, *Archaeologies of the Future*, esp. pp. 10–21 on utopia as an enclave.

fiction as a negative presence, that is, by its absence.[11] Utopian societies may consequently be described as a result of different histories, sometimes underlined by the adoption of alternate calendars and time-computing methods, such as in *The History of the Sevarambians* by Denis Veiras (1677–1679).[12] The utopian project may serve the purpose of showing a different yet possible continuation of history, freeing society from its past to offer a new beginning, such as in Étienne-Gabriel Morelly's *Code de la Nature* (1755, Code of nature).[13]

Since sixteenth-century seminal texts, utopian inventions have been informed by a humanistic logic, postulating the possibility of using reason to influence reality and build what lies ahead, going beyond the acceptance of fate or the status quo. In this sense, utopian thought, by criticising the present or overturning it, always addresses a future public capable of accepting its indications and instigating changes in its reality. Located in a geographical elsewhere, the utopian construction, in prescribing measures for good governance and describing the causal mechanisms that lead to the realisation of a good society, is built upon a temporal dimension even when this is not thematised as a mechanism of narrative construction.

The great voyages of exploration that brought the Europeans of the early modern age into contact with places and peoples previously unknown to them, provided the cultural background for the literary plausibility of remote utopian places, as well as for the existence of civilisations whose history was different and alternative to that of Europe.[14] In Thomas More's *Libellus vere aureus nec minus salutaris quam festivus, de optimo rei publicae statu deque nova insula Utopia* (1516, Truly a golden booklet, as beneficial as it is cheerful, on the best state law and of the new island Utopia),[15] a founding text of the modern European utopian tradition, Raphael Hythlodaeus (Hythloday), the traveller who describes the island of Utopia to the character named Morus, is presented as a navigator who accompanied Amerigo Vespucci.[16] The removal of Utopia from the map of the 'Old World' is tantamount to its removal from the history

---

11 Baczko, *L'utopia*.

12 Veiras, *L'histoire des sevarambes*, critical ed. by Rosenberg, see here for a comprehensive bibliography of editions, translations, and criticism; Eng. ed. *The History of the Sevarambians*, ed. and with an introduction by Laursen and Masroori; Baczko, *L'utopia*, esp. pp. 159–63.

13 Morelly, *Code de la Nature*, critical ed. by Roza; on Morelly and eighteenth-century utopias as criticism of and projection into history, see also: Lemarchand, 'L'idéologie moderniste et l'utopie', pp. 26–28.

14 Jameson, *Archaeologies of the Future*, p. 18.

15 More, *Libellus vere aureus nec minus salutaris quam festivus de optimo reip. statu. deque nova insula Utopia*.

16 He may also be the epitome of the lying traveller, since his surname actually means 'peddler of lies', 'spreader of nonsense' — just one of the many fascinating open contradictions that inform the text of *Libellus*. More nuanced readings also propose 'skilled in pleasant speech'. Halpern, *The Poetics of Primitive Accumulation*, pp. 142–43; in general, on the contradictions

of Europe. The utopian place has not experienced the ills and vices that characterise the reader's society, it is the product of an alternative path. The 'topographical fracture also means a fracture in time',[17] just as it did for travellers in the modern era who visited places that were completely alien to the past and present of their home society — be they on the American continent, where it was debated whether the native people were also descendants of Adam, and whether there had been a further flood, subsequent to the universal one; or be they in Asia, where evidence of ancient forms of civilisation challenged the chronology of the world that relied upon the Bible.[18]

In More's text, perhaps most familiar today under the title *Utopia*,[19] the people of the island of Utopia had diligently kept records of their history over the last 1700 years. More is interested in the issue of the origins, the genesis of the ideal society, which is the result of an act of foundation by a legislator, Utopus,[20] who gave Utopia its laws — among which the abolition of private property and the death penalty have had notable consequences in the subsequent reception of the work.[21] Originally a peninsula in the 'New World', Utopia became literally isolated: Utopus transformed it into an island by excavating and submerging a strip of land, so that the historical-geographical isolation from the rest of the world known to Europeans complemented the good order pursued in the establishment of the Utopian society (Figure 1). No foreigner could come to the island unless guided by a Utopian. This original isolation was also marked by a change of name: the island of Utopia was previously a peninsula called Abraxa.[22] And perhaps it is because of an even earlier name change that the location of Utopia is unknown to geographers and cosmographers (while misfortune has it that a cough prevents Morus from hearing the exact coordinates during the traveller's account of his visit).

---

in the text, the use of forms of irony and litotes: Bruce 'Introduction'; Jameson, *Archaeologies of the Future*, pp. 22–23.

17 Baczko, *L'utopia*, p. 159.

18 On the utopian projection as an element in travel narratives: Manuel and Manuel, *Utopian Thought in the Western World*, p. 435; on the crisis of biblical chronology: Tortarolo, 'L'eutanasia della cronologia biblica'.

19 Neologism combining the prefix *ou-* and the word for place, *topos*, in the privative sense of 'no place', but ambiguously also in the sense of 'very good place'.

20 Bruce, 'Introduction', pp. ix–xlii.

21 An eloquent example is Kautsky, *Thomas More and His Utopia*; for a recent overview, see Papke, 'The Communistic Inclinations of Sir Thomas More'; on freedom and connected issues: Greenblatt, *Renaissance Self-Fashioning*, pp. 40–41; Jameson, *Archaeologies of the Future*, pp. 22–41.

22 A term of uncertain derivation, which according to some commentators is from a-*brakae* (i.e. *sans-cullottia*), and to others is a variant of *abrochos* (*without water*) with possible reference to the transformation from peninsula to island.

Figure 1a. Peter Giles, woodcut in More, *Libellus vere aureus nec minus salutaris quam festivus de optimo reip. statu deque nova insula Utopia* (1516). Illustration representing the island of Utopia. Copy at Bibliothèque nationale de France, via Gallica, free for scientific and academic use.

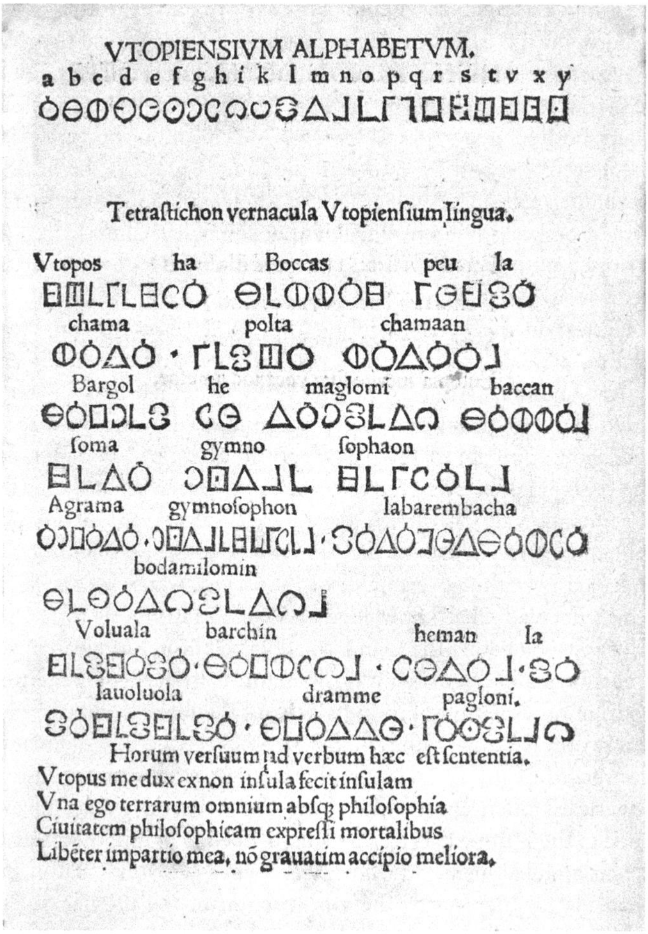

VTOPIENSIVM ALPHABETVM.
a b c d e f g h i k l m n o p q r s t v x y

Tetraſtichon vernacula Vtopienſium lingua.

Vtopos   ha   Boccas   peu   la

chama   polta   chamaan

Bargol   he   maglomi   baccan

foma   gymno   ſophaon

Agrama   gymnoſophon   labarembacha

bodamilomin

Voluala   barchin   heman   la

lauoluola   dramme   pagloni.

Horum verſuum ad verbum hæc eſt ſententia.
Vtopus me dux ex non inſula fecit inſulam
Vna ego terrarum omnium abſcp philoſophia
Ciuitatem philoſophicam expreſſi mortalibus
Libéter impartio mea, nó grauatim accipio meliora.

Figure 1b. Peter Giles, woodcut in More, *Libellus vere aureus nec minus salutaris quam festivus de optimo reip. statu deque nova insula Utopia* (1516). Illustration representing the alphabet and some verses in the language of the island. 'Vtopos ha Boccas peula / chama polta chamaan / Bargol he maglomi baccan soma gymnosophaon / Agrama gymnosophon labarembacha bodamilomin / Voluala barchin heman la lauoluola dramme pagloni'. The Latin translation reads: 'Utopus me dux ex non insula fecit insulam / Una ego terrarum omnium absque philosophia / Civitatem philosophicam expressi mortalibus / Libenter impartio mea, non gravatim accipio meliora'. The 1556 English translation by Ralph Robinson is: 'My king and conqueror Utopos by name, / A prince of much renown and immortal fame, / Hath made me an isle that erst no island was, / Full fraught with worldly wealth, with pleasure and solace. I one of all other without philosophy / Have shaped for man a philosophical city. As mine I am nothing dangerous to impart, / So better to receive I am ready with all my heart'. Copy at Bibliothèque nationale de France, via Gallica, free for scientific and academic use.

In Francis Bacon's *New Atlantis* (1626),[23] the ancient king Solamona bestowed upon the island of Bensalem the edicts that would regulate its life in perpetuity. Bensalem was also located in an unspecified point in the Pacific Ocean to the west of the Peruvian coast. It was kept inaccessible to foreigners, both for geographical reasons — its location and very existence were kept secret — and by law — in the founding edicts the inhabitants were forbidden to bring in unauthorised foreigners (a measure that in the narrative prompts an interesting comparison with China).[24] A deeply Christianised utopia, Bacon's island also experienced its own revelation of the divine word.

A key text in the Western utopian tradition, *New Atlantis* seems, at first glance, a model of what the traveller should methodically record, a practical implementation of what Bacon had theorised in his essay 'Of Travel' (1625): travel as a tool programmatically employed to amass ordered knowledge about the world's societies.[25] A closer look reveals that the problem of secrecy, the relationship between science, power, and the dissemination of knowledge played a central role in Bacon's project, exemplified by the College of the Six Days Works, the scientific society that presided over the government of the island, whose work was secret and which decided what knowledge and which inventions to use or disseminate and which not. The island isolated itself from European history in a unidirectional and calculated way: it kept its existence completely secret, hidden from other nations, but to its citizens the history and current state of the rest of the world were well known. Indeed, the Bensalemians kept a better record of the European and American past than the Europeans and Americans themselves. One of the first things that the inhabitants explained to the European travellers who happened to find their way to the island, was a global history of the earliest times, a history that in Europe had been lost to memory.[26] The construction of the utopian society in Bacon is based on a temporalised idea of civilisation. Bensalem is explicitly presented as the result of a given historical process and precise causal relations over time. It provides a privileged perspective on the history of the globe, making it possible to grasp a deep connection between systems of exchange and processes of historical change.

During the eighteenth century, travellers believed they could find the hypostatisation of past moments of European development in distant countries. By that logic, the indigenous peoples of America or Africa could become, so to speak, 'primitives' — paradoxical contemporary fragments of the past — and in the 'Old World' it was debated whether the people

---

23 Bacon, *New Atlantis*, in Bruce, *Three Early Modern Utopias*, pp. 149–86.
24 Bacon, *New Atlantis*, p. 166.
25 Bacon, 'Of Travel'; Bruce, 'Introduction', p. xxviii.
26 Bacon, *New Atlantis*, p. 163.

in America were the product of the same creation and thus progeny of Adam and Eve, or whether instead they were descendants of one of the lost tribes of Israel.[27] Against the backdrop of these geographies of time traced by travel accounts, philosophical treatises, and encyclopaedic compilations, writers could imagine that there were civilisations to be found on the globe that represented the future of the European one, i.e. that were more advanced politically, philosophically, or scientifically, or that were the result of independent histories, mirrors through which travellers could reflect on their home societies. Through a process of geographical disenchantment, which located utopia in a spatial elsewhere that was permeable and vulnerable to history and human nature,[28] Jonathan Swift's *Gulliver's Travels* (1726) exemplifies a body of narratives in which fantastic civilisations were still to be found just beyond the geographical horizon of the known.[29] In a world where Australia was not yet known to Europeans, and large areas of the globe were not yet mapped, Laputa could be imagined east of Korea, Lilliput northwest of the Sunda Strait, and Brobdingnag as a peninsula on the Pacific coast of North America. Geographical location was the spatial counterpart of otherness in a cultural and historical sense: these fantastic countries were the result of histories that were different and independent from the European one. In this way, they offered a satirical way to comment on the mechanisms that governed the writer's society.

Drawing on theories of the earth's internal structure such as the one proposed in Athanasius Kircher's *Mundus subterraneus* (1665) and astronomer Edmond Halley's hypothesis in the 1690s to explain the existence of the earth's magnetic fields, the historical-geographical otherness of lost races meant they could equally be imagined as dwelling underground.[30] In the eighteenth century, novels were published in a number of European languages that imagined extraordinary journeys to subterranean realms. Narratives such as the anonymous *Relation d'un voyage du pole arctique au pole antarctique* (1721, Report of a journey from the Arctic to the Antarctic Pole), *Nicolaii Klimii iter subterraneum* (1741, *The Journey of Niels Klim to the World Underground*) written in Latin by Ludvig Holberg, Norwegian by birth and Danish by adoption, *The Life and Adventures of Peter Wilkins* (1751) by Robert Paltock, and *Icosameron* (1787) written in French by the Italian Giacomo Casanova, to name but a few, were based on

---

27 Gliozzi, *Adamo e il nuovo mondo*.
28 Pearl, *Utopian Geographies and the Early English Novel*.
29 Swift, *Travels into Several Remote Nations of the World*.
30 Bleiler and Langford, 'Hollow Earth'; Fitting, ed., *Subterranean Worlds*; Standish, *Hollow Earth*.

these scientific notions.[31] These subterranean worlds — sometimes entire universes lodged in the centre of the earth — functioned as socio-political experiments, as well as, in many cases, backdrops for incredible adventures. The European protagonists encountered peoples that, imbued with certain values, characters, or laws functioned as demonstrations of given philosophical and socio-political theses, in a utopian or dystopian sense, or as an ironic commentary on the travellers' home society. These were civilisations whose origins sometimes preceded known history, and which had developed independently of the rest of the world, demonstrating the pliability of history and suggesting to readers what the consequences of given choices made in the present might be.

In eighteenth-century novels, utopian reflections tended to find new inner or domestic spaces, such as the female community imagined in Sarah Scott's *Millenium Hall* (1762),[32] in which an ideal female community located in rural England presents elements of isolation and secrecy consistent with an enclave, together with an inherent programme of replication and expansion of its social experiment.[33] Demonstrating the anything but teleological nature of the story we are tracing, tropes such as those of the hollow earth, the lost world, and the lost race did not wane, and were put to new uses. They tended to lose their connotations as philosophical mirrors and functioned increasingly as adventurous devices, pivots of fantastic tales of exploration, discovery, and conquest, sometimes charged with esoteric connotations, as in Edward Bulwer-Lytton's *The Coming Race* (1871).[34]

---

31 *Relation d'un voyage du pole arctique au pole antarctique par le centre du monde*; [Holberg], *Nicolai Klimii iter svbterranevm*; Eng. trans. *A Journey to the World Under-Ground*; [Paltock], *The Life and Adventures of Peter Wilkins*; [Casanova, credited as translator], *Icosameron, ou Histoire d'Édouard et d'Élisabeth qui passèrent quatre-vingt-un ans chez les Mégamicres*; partial Eng. trans. *Casanova's 'Icosameron'; or the Story of Edward and Elizabeth*.

32 [Scott], *A Description of Millenium Hall*.

33 Johns, *Women's Utopias of the Eighteenth Century*.

34 Bulwer-Lytton, *The Coming Race*; Csicsery-Ronay Jr., 'Science Fiction and Empire'; Rieder, *Colonialism and the Emergence of Science Fiction*, pp. 34–60; Langford, Pringle, Stableford, and Clute, 'Lost Races'; Pringle, Stableford, Nicholls, and Langford, 'Lost World'; Everett F. Bleiler with the assistance of Richard J. Bleiler, *Science-Fiction: The Early Years*; Everett F. Bleiler with the assistance of Richard J. Bleiler, *Science-Fiction: The Gernsback Years*, esp. *sub voces* 'Hollow earth', 'Lost race', 'Lost worlds'.

II. When Was the Future?

When can we pinpoint an explicit use of the future as a motivating horizon, as a backdrop to fictional narratives? When did the first colonisations
of time to come appear in the European imagination? A debate on when
and where the origin of futuristic fiction should be placed exactly — in
which linguistic-cultural area, or in precisely which text — is more useful
to contemporary interests competing within the scholarly field than to our
understanding of the complex and multifaceted processes which shaped
cultural and literary traditions. It might be more fruitful to resist any
teleological temptation to judge authors and ideas *ex postero*, preparing
subsequent stages in a retro-constructed historical evolution of ideas, and
instead consider changes to futuristic imagination as non-linear processes,
reading each text in its historical context.[35]

Anglophone and francophone literatures offered extrapolations of
near-future scenarios as early as the beginning of the seventeenth century.
Early examples had used ominous depictions of future invasions and
scenarios of armed conflict to argue in favour of specific political options
in texts whose primary aim was to influence the political debates of the
day. A play such as *A Larum for London* (published anonymously in 1602)
implicitly suggests that a Spanish sack of London might replicate the
horrors of 1576 Antwerp.[36] John Dryden's *Annus Mirabilis* (1667, Year of
wonders) imagines London reborn after the Great Fire.[37] *Épigone, Histoire
du siècle futur* (1659, Epigone, history of the future century) constructs a
parodistic allegory of heroic fiction, set not only in imaginary countries,
but also in the future.[38] Political prophetism feeds a work such as *Aulicus
his Dream of the King's Sudden Comming to London*, a 6-page pamphlet
written by Francis Cheynel and published anonymously in 1644 to encourage his readers to act upon the terrifying image of Charles I gaining

---

35 Rieder, 'On Defining SF or Not'.
36 *A Larum for London*; Stephenson, 'A Mirror for London'; Cahill, *Unto the Breach*, p. 166.
37 Dryden, *Annus Mirabilis*.
38 [de Pure], *Épigone, histoire du siècle future*; it is frequently attributed to Jacques Guttin, but
   for de Pure's authorship: McKenzie Richmond, 'Deux œuvres rendues à l'abbé de Pure';
   Épigone, histoire du siècle futur ed. by Leibacher-Ouvrard and Maher. On the political role and
   ironic use of the future see: Leibacher-Ouvrard, '*Épigone, Histoire du siècle futur*'.

the upper hand against Cromwell and his Parliamentary forces.[39] The future is home to a model society towards which the English Parliament is invited to work in *A Description of the Famous Kingdome of Macaria* (1642), attributed to Samuel Hartlib.[40] These narrations offer possible and counterfactual histories used to make a point about the politics of the day, whether through ominous predictions, practical indications, or — in the case of *Épigone* — as the backdrop to adventurous plots.[41] Squibs, satires, or exotic romances, these texts represent a step towards a secularised history and conceptualisations of a future that their late modern and early contemporary descendants would come to embody, without yet constituting a genre, nor focusing their inventions and extrapolations on those techno-scientific wonders that would only later take centre-stage.[42]

These literary forms appeared in a context already rich in textual uses of the future. The history of prophecies, predictions, and divination includes examples from biblical texts and rabbinic literature, as well as a number of occurrences and practices in the ancient world, including in Near East, Mesopotamian, Greek, and Latin literature and historiography.[43] Throughout the medieval and early modern period, understanding and depicting the future as a place of prophetic fulfilment remained common within the Christian context.[44] One significant example in the seventeenth century is *A Brief Description of the Future History of Europe, from Anno 1650 to An. 1710* published in 1650.[45] This text summarises the late sixteenth-century prophetic works of Paul Grebner in an editorial form — 38 pages in quarto — quite different from the Latin manuscripts preserved in the library of Trinity College, Cambridge. Popular publications such as astrological almanacs proliferated between the sixteenth and eighteenth

---

39 [Cheynel], *Aulicus his Dream of the Kings Sudden Comming to London*; Clarke, 'Future-War Fiction', p. 387; Roberts, *The History of Science Fiction*, p. 75.

40 [Hartlib], *A Description of the Famous Kingdome of Macaria*; Webster, 'The Authorship and Significance of Macaria'. On the possible contributions by others in Hartlib's cultural circle: Cagnolati, 'L'utopia al potere'. For an alternative attribution to Gabriel Plattes: Matei, 'Gabriel Plattes, Hartlib Circle'. On Hartlib see also Major, ed., *Literatures of Exile*, pp. 27–28.

41 Leibacher-Ouvrard, '*Épigone*'.

42 On science and technology in earlier utopias: Manuel and Manuel, *Utopian Thought*, p. 175, see also pp. 371 on Sevarambia; 8, 14 on the role of new science in seventeenth-century utopian thought; 19, 205–21 on the concept of *pansophia*.

43 Good entry points in an extensive bibliography are: Beerden, *Worlds Full of Signs*; Bohak, *Ancient Jewish Magic*; Wilson, 'The Prophetic Books'.

44 Burrow and Wei, eds, *Medieval Futures*; Wisniewski, *Christian Divination in Late Antiquity*; Koselleck, *Futures Past*, pp. 11–17.

45 *A Brief Description of the Future History of Europe, from Anno 1650 to An. 1710*; Alkon, *Origins*, pp. 59–60; Bross, *Future History*, p. 25; see Bross also for a discussion of Thomas Gage's *A Brief Description of the Future History* (1648) and Henry Jessey's *Of the Conversion of Five Thousand and Nine Hundred East Indians* (1650).

centuries.[46] At the dawn of the eighteenth century a myriad of clairvoyants and practitioners of various divinatory techniques competed for the public's attention and confidence as regards knowledge about the future, promoting themselves by means of advertisements in the periodical press and other publications. In 1710s–1720s London, Duncan Campbell — a soothsayer and peddler of talismans and miraculous medicines — became an object of curiosity and the subject of biographies and promotional writings.[47] From these eschatological, exegetical, and divinatory genres, literary works such as *Memoirs* aimed to distinguish themselves methodically, by introducing overtly fictional and fantastic elements into their futuristic imaginings.

The great explorations and the Copernican and scientific revolution contributed to create the crucial conditions thanks to which imagination first became capable of working outside the temporal horizon of Biblical time.[48] While the cultural history of a secularised future includes long-lasting processes spanning from the medieval and early modern to the contemporary age, a critical moment of change took place during the eighteenth century. The rise of a positivistic mindset might have nurtured the projection of fantastic scenarios into the future not as a way of escaping the close confines of its own paradigm of reality, but for quite opposite reasons. Positivism might have fostered a new colonisation of the future precisely because it permits a new understanding both of historical time as a linear continuity and of the causal mechanisms informing its flow.

In this respect, the imaginary realm of the future is intimately connected with the intellectual reverberations of the explorations of the globe, not least because the comparative systematisation of human diversity that European travellers encountered in remote parts of the world was the ground from which ideas of history as a process of linear development grew, and where the shape of things to come was conceptualised as the natural continuation of what had been. The expansion of the Western powers introduced techno-driven globalisation processes at an increased speed,[49] generating remarkable consequences in the development of a globalised consciousness, and of ideas and imageries deeply rooted in new knowledge concerning remote areas of the globe and their inhabitants.

---

46 Braida, *Le guide del tempo*; Braida, 'Les almanachs italiens du XVIIIᵉ siècle'; Capp, *Astrology and the Popular Press*.

47 [Bond], *The History of the Life and Adventures of Mr Duncan Campbell*; *Mr Campbell's Packet for the Entertainment of Gentlemen and Ladies*; Haywood, *A Spy on the Conjurer*; *The Friendly Daemon*; Bond, *The Supernatural Philosopher*; Campbell, *Secret Memoirs of the Late Mr Duncan Campbel. The Supernatural Philosopher* is a new edition of *The History of the Life* preceded by *Mr Campbell's Packet*.

48 Hölscher, *Die Entdeckung der Zukunft*, pp. 19–54; Roberts, 'The Copernican Revolution', p. 9; Toulmin and Goodfield, *The Discovery of Time*, pp. 125–52.

49 Headrick, *Power over People*.

The observation and representation of other cultures was nourished by a proto-ethnographic curiosity for the variety of social, political, and cultural forms, and led, in some European observers, to the adoption of an estranged gaze and forms of problematisation of their home society.[50] Yet, in the historical-philosophical systematisations elaborated in the 'Old Continent', the availability of sources deriving from geographical explorations contributed to the momentum gained by comparative and universal history during the late modern age, and to the growing influence of Enlightenment ideas of progress and conjectural histories, organising civilisations according to subsequent stages of development.[51] Notions regarding examples of radical 'otherness' from remote parts of the globe conceptualised as remains of the common human past and instances of humanity in its infancy were decisive in fostering ideas of historical time as a dimension of progress. Ideas of degeneration and stagnation applied to other societies implied the use of European civilisation as a standard against which others might be evaluated, and engendered reflections on historical time as a framework of causal relations between phenomena and human actions.[52] New knowledge and reflections on non-European cultures and the efforts made towards their comparative systematisation into a consistent framework provided, during the eighteenth century, the premises for new geographies of human diversity,[53] as well as for their disposition on a scale of historical development. In ideas of a linear and irreversible historical time lies the — insufficient but necessary — precondition for the hierarchisations of societies and humans that would later characterise a mature imperialistic phase.[54]

Against this backdrop the ruin functioned as a device of fantastic estrangement used to bring out and problematise these conceptualisations of historical time. The fantastic and pseudo-scientific use of the ruin and the idea of an archaeology applied to past futures have matured in the European imagination since the early modern age, and since the eighteenth century in particular.[55] Used to thematise heliotropic conceptions of civilisation, the ruin aroused the interest of writers, historians, and painters and was profoundly connected to ideas such as those of development and decadence, modernity and crisis applied to human organisations. In the eighteenth century, the idea of a history *magistra vitae* and a cyclical course

50 Iannuzzi, *Geografie del tempo*.
51 Rabasa, Sato, Tortarolo, and Woolf, eds, *The Oxford History of Historical Writing*; Iggers and Wang, with contributions from Mukherjee, *A Global History of Modern Historiography*, pp. 19–32; Woolf, *A Global History of History*, pp. 280–343.
52 Cazzola, Jones Corredera, Iannuzzi, and Beduschi, *Imperial Times*.
53 Minuti, *Una geografia politica della diversità*.
54 Lorenz and Bevernage, eds, *Breaking up Time*.
55 Clute, 'Ruins and Futurity'; for general background also: Macaulay, *Pleasure of Ruins*; Stewart, *The Ruins Lesson*.

of civilisations were premises for an application of history as a method to the future, and for the aesthetic appreciation and poetics of the ruin. This yearning for the ruin took on futuristic connotations, inspiring some of the earliest speculations about the time to come. Contemplation of the remains of the past made the idea of a future observer contemplating the ruins of the present synecdochically possible. A collection that appeared in London in 1780, attributed to Thomas Lyttelton, proclaimed to contain the letter of an American traveller from 2199, who wrote from the ruins of Saint Paul's porch to a friend in Boston, the capital of the western empire, including his poetic compositions about the remains of the once prosperous city of London.[56] Constantin François Volney's *Les Ruines* (1791, *The Ruins*) encapsulates the trope of the present as the site of future ruins through the writer observing the remains of Palmyra in Syria.[57] At the end of the eighteenth century and throughout the nineteenth century, the idea of radical changes to come increasingly incorporated the possibility of disasters, catastrophes, and extinctions: one thinks of the 'last men' imagined by Jean-Baptiste Cousin de Grainville and Mary Shelley.[58] Twentieth-century science fiction and fantastic archaeology start from similar assumptions to invent hyper-evolved terrestrial or alien civilisations set in the distant past.[59]

With the Enlightenment, ideas of progress and secularisation of historical time found their literary and programmatic reflection in diachronic utopias.[60] Ideas of history as progress fostered new forms and functions of the utopian imagination, intimately connecting it to images of different societies situated in the future.[61] Louis-Sébastien Mercier's *L'An deux mille quatre cent quarante* (The year 2440) might be considered a landmark in this process.[62] Mercier's novel is a futuristic fiction in which the protagonist falls asleep and wakes up in the same place, in Paris, but centuries later (Figure 2). Thus, although the narrative frame leaves a degree of ambiguity between reality and dream as regards the nature of the character's experi-

---

56 *Poems, By a Young Nobleman*; for the attribution to Lyttleton: *The Critical Review*, 49 (1780), pp. 123–27, see also Cannon, 'Lyttelton, Thomas'.

57 Volney, *Les ruines*.

58 Grainville, *Le dernier homme*; Shelley, *The Last Man*; Alkon, *Origins*, pp. 158–60; Kupiec, '"Le Dernier Homme" de Grainville'; Petitier, 'Le dernier homme et la fin de l'histoire'; Roberts, *The History of Science Fiction*, pp. 121–23.

59 Feder, *Frauds, Myths, and Mysteries*, pp. 159–215.

60 Pohl, 'Utopianism after More', p. 74.

61 Baczko, *L'utopia*, esp. p. 157.

62 [Mercier], *L'An deux mille quatre cent quarante*; Eng. trans. as *Memoirs of the Year Two Thousand Five Hundred*; Vieira, 'The Concept of Utopia', pp. 4–9; Darnton, *Libri proibiti*, pp. 120–40, esp. p. 124.

Figure 2. Mercier, *L'an deux mille quatre cent quarante* ([1801–1802]), I, p. 12. The protagonist reads the date on a plaque mounted on a pyramid column: 'Year of grace 2440'. The edicts posted on the walls confirm that he has slept for more than six hundred years, he is now seven hundred years old and finds himself in a Paris where everything has changed. Courtesy of the John Carter Brown Library, under Attribution-ShareAlike 4.0 International (CC BY-SA 4.0) licence.

ence, the novel is one of the first utopias set in a different time but not in an imaginary place.[63]

Mercier's work represents a critical point in the history of a temporal imagination not least because it compelled the authorities of the *ancien régime* to face up to the subversive potential of such a secularisation of utopia, and contributed to the codification of a new genre, thanks to an unprecedented editorial success across Europe.[64] Notwithstanding the circulation and impact of Mercier's best-seller, the eighteenth century saw a progressive colonisation of the future by speculative and utopian litera-ture through works chronologically preceding *L'An deux mille quatre cent quarante*, including Madden's *Memoirs* and the anonymous *The Reign of George VI* (1763),[65] in which military triumphs (of England over France) are part of the success of a Bolingbrokean monarch in the year 1900.[66]

Other significant futures malleable by human action are to be found at the turn of the century, in revolutionary plays written — if not always put on stage — in 1789 France. One example is Rétif de la Bretonne's *L'an 2000, ou la Régénération* (1789, The year 2000, or regeneration), which takes a look at the revolution already *ex post facto*, during a com-memoration that takes place in the year 2000, when the stabilisation of revolutionary laws and traditions has created a social utopia. Individual rights and interests have finally been subordinated to the collective good, and there is even room for an enlightened Lewis XXIII.[67] Thanks to the extremely long life of two of the characters, the memory of 1789 is still only two generations away in the past. Sylvain Maréchal's *Le jugement dernier des rois* (The last judgement of kings) had its stage premiere on 17 October 1793, the day after Marie Antoinette's execution.[68] Set in the future, the first act opens with an old man keeping note of the days on a home-made calendar. Banished to a remote island, he is measuring out the duration of his exile, imposed by an unjust tyrant. He is soon liberated by a group of sans-culottes from all over Europe, where the French revolution has been followed by many others. Kings, queens, and the Pope will be deported to the very same isle, only to be cast down into the depths of the earth when the local volcano erupts. The old calendar gets burnt.[69] These scenarios work as propaganda machines and bear clear signs of utopian

---

63 Alkon, *Origins*, pp. 4, 19, 23.
64 Alkon, *Science Fiction before 1900*, pp. 21, 60–61; Darnton, *Libri proibiti*, p. 120; Koselleck, 'The Temporalization of Utopia', p. 85; Baczko, *L'utopia*, pp. 42, 170–72.
65 *The Reign of George VI*.
66 Clarke, *British Future Fiction*, I, p. 2; Roberts, *The History of Science Fiction*, p. 112; Iannuzzi, 'Waging Future Wars'; Oman, 'The Editor's Preface', p. viii; see also *infra*, ch. 13.
67 Rétif de La Bretonne, *L'an 2000*; Aranda, 'Le Jeu des temporalités'.
68 Maréchal, *Le jugement dernier des rois*.
69 On calendar reformation in revolutionary France see Baczko, *L'utopia*, pp. 223–51; Shaw, *Time and the French Revolution*.

constructions, in which a movement towards the future is pasted onto the present of the revolution, thus undermining any possible teleology. Nonetheless, through the manipulation of time they attempt to metabolise the social changes brought about by the revolutionary years, including the construction of a point of view from posterity.[70]

Condorcet's *L'esquisse d'un tableau historique des progrès de l'esprit humain* (*Sketch for a Historical Picture of the Progress of the Human Mind*) is considered by Baczko the arrival point in the assimilation process between utopia and history as progress.[71] Not only does *L'esquisse* locate the perfected society it describes in a future historical time, it also presents its vision as a scientific forecast, based on the observation of the history of human societies in different past and present eras. The past, the present, and the future are connected by a global discourse about the progress of mankind, of which different phases and people are specific instances. The scientific method, allowing prediction based on universal and constant laws applied to human faculties,[72] provides utopia with a new conceptual foundation. In turn, historical unity is guaranteed precisely by the tenth epoch: only utopia allows for a definite interpretation of the precedent steps in terms of a unidirectional, secular progress (for example excluding cyclical, regressive, or decadent paths, and theological arguments).[73] *L'esquisse*, along with Mercier's *L'An deux mille quatre cent quarante*, may be considered the herald of a shift to uchronia.[74] Condorcet's idea of progress as a process of civilisation foresaw the development and assimilation of non-European peoples and cultures to European values.[75]

Between the French Revolution and the Napoleonic years, a handful of plays, tracts, and pamphlets envisaged a French invasion of Great Britain. 'At the height of the Napoleonic wars between Britain and France, the propaganda machine on both sides presented various scenarios of the potential outcome',[76] such as in *La descente en Angleterre* (1798, The raid on England) by Jean-Corisandre Mittié, in the advertisement for the (non-existent) farce 'The Invasion of England' (1804), and in 'The Armed Briton' (1806).[77] These narratives projected future scenarios in order to 'give a realistic edge to straightforward propaganda',[78] as did a

---

70 McCready, 'Performing Time in the Revolutionary Theater'; see also Clarke, 'Before and After', p. 34.

71 Condorcet, *Esquisse d'un tableau historique des progrès de l'esprit humain*; Baczko, *L'utopia*, p. 202.

72 Williams, *Condorcet and Modernity*, pp. 96–97.

73 Pons, 'Sur la Dixième époque'.

74 Manuel and Manuel, *Utopian Thought*, pp. 20, 415, 492–93.

75 Williams, *Condorcet and Modernity*, pp. 157–58.

76 Ashley, 'The Fear of Invasion'.

77 Mittié, *Descente en Angleterre*; 'Theatre Royal England'; Burke, *The Armed Briton*.

78 Clarke, 'Before and after', p. 35.

wealth of satirical engravings and caricatures, such as the series *Promis'd Horrors of the French Invasion* (1796) and *French Invasion* (1803) by James Gillray.[79] In fact, drawings and posters were the most popular media used to disseminate worries and fears about French armies invading England, after the Channel was crossed by hot air balloon in 1785.

It was during the seventeenth and eighteenth centuries that the future started to be explored as a dimension of possibilities, gradually entering the realm of a secular imagination. Expectations and fears in the socio-political scene and in military affairs saw the start of a mapping process involving these new imaginative territories. Ideas of a future pliable by human actions became part of narrative inventions, at a crucial moment in cultural history for the conceptualisation of time in general. As a result of the French Revolution, the emergence of Enlightenment ideas on history gained new momentum in terms of changes in the way the connection between the present and future is constructed, and matured into new notions of the secular and human dimension of manipulating of the course of history.[80] One can trace in the Age of Enlightenment the dawn of new negotiations and debates on the future as an object of scientific knowledge and utopian and speculative imagination, as well as humanity's relationship with it. The questions about the knowability and controllability of the future that arose during the early modern age, in their eighteenth-century forms in particular, reach all the way to the contemporary world, and still inform the reasoning about the different uses of the future that have emerged and confronted each other at different moments in the intellec-tual, political, and social history of the succeeding centuries up to the present.[81]

During the course of the nineteenth century, specific genres and sub-genres of speculative fiction clustered around the future used as a site of projection, of logical-fantastic extrapolation. Time travel — from the use of the dream mechanism in Charles Dickens and Edgar Allan Poe to the technology of the time machine codified by H. G. Wells[82] — and the setting of stories in near and distant futures are recognisable tropes in nineteenth-century science fiction, and will remain among the most recurrent throughout the twentieth century to the present day.[83] This vast corpus can also be read as part of a broader casuistry through which fictional narrative has continued to grapple with the problem of time more

---

79 Gillray, *Promis'd Horrors of the French Invasion*; Gillray, *French Invasion*.
80 Koselleck, *Futures Past*, pp. 3–4. On the time dimension in utopias set in the future see also Parrinder, *Utopian Literature and Science*, p. 4.
81 Andersson, *The Future of the World*.
82 Dickens, *A Christmas Carol*; Poe, 'A Tale of the Ragged Mountains'; Wells, *The Time Machine*.
83 Corfield, *Time and the Shape of History*, pp. 19–25; Nahin, *Time Machines*.

generally, and with various epistemological questions relating to history, its knowability and its narratability. Future, alternate, and counterfactual histories, asking in different ways and *at different times* the science-fictional question par excellence 'what if …?', have offered laboratories in which the understanding of causal mechanisms, of the relationships between historical processes and singular events and individuals, and of the tension between contingency and necessity were brought to the fore.[84]

Memoirs constitutes a case, within this history, that has remained relatively in the shadows.[85] Like a considerable number of literary works in the late seventeenth and early eighteenth centuries, it was published anonymously, in 1733.[86] Structured as a collection of seventeen epistles framed by three lengthy prefatory writings and a dedication, it was written by Samuel Madden, an Irish writer and philanthropist close to the Hanoverian court and loyal to Robert Walpole's Whig government. The fictitious narrator who signs the prefatory sections claims to have received the letters from the future. Through these epistolographic writings the world of the twentieth century is described. The minimal influence of *Memoirs* on the codification of later science fiction can be partly attributed to its particular publishing history, which, as will be seen in the following pages, penalised its circulation and reception among the author's contemporaries as well as in posterity. Intrinsic elements of the text, however, can also be called upon to explain its lack of popularity.

Memoirs is a complex text, in which the shaping of the future is governed by a multitude of different criteria. While parts of the novel satirise the politics and society of its day, its treatment of time also connects the perception of history speeding up with the idea of a new global interconnectedness, and dwells upon how the rise and fall of past empires should inform the reader's notion of historical verisimilitude as regards future scenarios. The novel offers a fine example of the emergence of a secularised future, constructed through logical extrapolations according to causal mechanisms and thus pliable through human action, but also includes utopian projections, dystopian elements presented to its readers as ominous warnings, and the satiric mocking of the writer's present. It therefore resists an unambiguous categorisation of its imaginative

---

84 Hellekson, *The Alternate History*; Gallagher, *Telling It Like It Wasn't*; Singles, *Alternate History*; see also Bode and Dietrich, eds, *Future Narratives*.

85 [Madden], *Memoirs of the Twentieth Century*.

86 Between 1660 and 1750 approximately 50 percent of the books of fiction published in England listed no author on the title page, and a further 20 percent were functionally anonymous, adopting a tagline or pseudonym; Orr, 'Genre Labels', p. 80; between 1750 and 1790 over 80 percent of British and Irish novels were published without attribution of authorship (on the title page or elsewhere in the text), although the absence of the author's name does not indicate that readers were necessarily unaware of his or her identity; Raven, 'The Anonymous Novel', p. 143.

mechanisms. The construction of British imperial projections overseas and of a transnational historical-political perspective, which tends towards becoming global in scope, shape and accelerate complex processes of time secularisation. Some elements — such as the idea of a globalised future world, home to scientific inventions and discoveries — can easily be read in connection with the later development of the genres of futuristic narrative. Other aspects need to be understood through their deep ties to the early eighteenth-century context of their genesis. The satirical components require today's reader to retrieve references to early eighteenth-century British and European current affairs. Furthermore, *Memoirs* constructs its narrative fiction against the backdrop of innumerable references to ancient and early modern European cultural elements: authors and works of Greco-Latin historiography and literature, patristics, rabbinic literature, religious controversialism, proto-ethnography and comparativism, correspondences and travel accounts, treatises on philosophy and natural magic. As will be discussed in more detail below, this cultural encyclopaedia is used with an ironic register, and it is not so much the result of serious and original studies on these subjects, but rather often drawn from secondary sources in comical imitation of the excesses of tagging that characterised so much previous and contemporary scholarly writing. The comical effect that this produces targeted, at the time of the novel's composition and publication, a learned rather than wide audience. Today, these elements are hardly part of the common background of a reader, with the exception of scholars specialising in aspects of early modern European culture. Yet it is also precisely within this background, whose historical distance is felt today, that the interest in a re-reading of *Memoirs* and its role in the history of futuristic imagination lies. The novel's ironic distancing of beliefs considered superstitious and absurd — angelic and demonic presences, divination techniques and astrological predictions, veneration of relics, magical and occult practices — today offers an exceptional testimony to the negotiation of the boundaries of verisimilitude and credibility within a religious enlightenment. The fact that this negotiation takes place in one of the first known futuristic novels in European literature highlights the role of the epistemological statute of time and of reflections on its knowability in the foundation of a rational paradigm of knowledge, and the ability of speculative fiction to enrich our understanding of deep cultural processes.

III. An Irish Whig between Philanthropism and Literature

To foster a better understanding of *Memoirs*, and critically assess its fortune in past and current scholarship, it would be useful to start with some information about the context in which the novel was conceived and its author's life. Writer and philanthropist, Samuel Madden (1686–1765)[87] was born in Dublin to John Madden (d. 1703/4) and Mary Molyneux (d. 1695). John was a physician and manuscript collector, who studied medicine at Trinity College, Dublin, obtaining a bachelor's degree in medicine in 1674 and a master's degree in 1682.[88] In 1680 he married Mary, grand-daughter of Daniel Molyneux. Educated at Cambridge, Daniel Molyneux had been appointed Ulster King of Arms and Principal Herald of the Kingdom of Ireland in 1597. His manuscripts researching Irish family history are today at Trinity College,[89] and it is possible that his antiquarian knowledge, amassed while carrying out heraldic and genealogical certification duties, influenced John's interests to some extent, whose collection of manuscripts partially follows similar lines.

In 1684, John was elected fellow of the Irish College of Physicians in Dublin (since 1692 known as King and Queen's College of Physicians in Ireland), where he subsequently acted as president three times.[90] In 1684 he also joined the Dublin Philosophical Society, one year after it was founded by his brother-in-law, William.

Shaped by interests in antiquarian studies, John's collection of manuscripts became one of the largest in coeval Ireland. It included material on genealogy, ecclesiastical history and the history of Irish religious houses. His compilations and notes, based among other things on James Ware's manuscripts, were to become a valued source for subsequent studies on English settlers in Ireland.[91] A significant section of John's collection

---

87 Essential sources for Madden's biography are: Ó Ciardha, 'Madden, Samuel Molyneux'; Cooper, 'Madden, Samuel'; Richey, 'Madden, Samuel Molyneux'; Welch, ed., *The Oxford Companion to Irish Literature*, p. 350.

88 Evans, 'Madden, John'.

89 On Daniel Molyneux: Clavin, 'Molyneux, Daniel'; Fraser, 'The Molyneux Family', p. 9; Dublin, NLI, Genealogical Office MSS Col., Visitations of Ireland, 1568–1648.

90 'John Madden', Royal College of Physicians of Ireland.

91 Fox, *Trinity College Library Dublin*, p. 77; Dublin, TCD, Genealogy, MSS 1212–1221.

consisted of the depositions relating to the 1641 Catholic uprising known as the Irish Rebellion. The papers had belonged to Matthew Barry, clerk to the Irish Privy Council.[92] Devotional works of note that were part of the collection included a fifteenth-century Hebrew psalter and a fourteenth-century Book of Hours from Bective Abbey (County Meath). Among other significant items were a sixteenth-century genealogical history of the Burke family of County Mayo (*Historia et genealogia Familiae de Burgo*), and an herbarium that John compiled with specimens probably collected at the family estate of Manor Waterhouse, which is today considered the earliest Irish example of its kind to survive.[93] The Maddenton estates (County Kildare, changed to Hilltown or Hilton around 1780)[94] and Manor Waterhouse (County Fermanagh) had been acquired by John's grandfather, who had moved to Ireland from Oxfordshire, although it is possible the family had distant Irish origins. During the 1641 Rebellion, the family fled the estate, returning in the 1660s.[95] John's interests in botany and agriculture, and his care for the family's considerable land holdings would be inherited by his son Samuel. A small octavo calf note-book contains Samuel's notes on plants and trees at Manor Waterhouse as well as the layout of the gardens.[96] Samuel's advocacy of careful and direct management of landed estates by landowners was articulated, years later, in *Reflections and Resolutions Proper for the Gentlemen of Ireland*.[97] Three levels of writing and reflection can thus be highlighted: in the manuscript notebook the author's direct experience is recorded, from which the later non-fiction writing distils a thesis of general interest, and the future history in *Memoirs* constitutes a hypothetical laboratory of that thesis, which demonstrates the validity of the author's ideas by imagining their application on a wider scale.

After John Madden's death, his collection was purchased by John Stearne, Dean of Saint Patrick's who had been his near-contemporary at Trinity, and was then bequeathed as part of Stearne's collection of manuscripts and ephemeral publications to Trinity College in 1741.[98] Other parts of Stearne's library, as well as some of John's — especially printed books and a few manuscripts — went to Marsh's Library in

---

92 'Librorum manuscriptorum viri praeclari Joannis Maddeni'; O'Sullivan, 'John Madden's Manuscripts'.

93 Nelson, 'A Late 17th Century Irish Herbarium'.

94 Belfast, PRONI, *Madden Papers*, p. 7.

95 Evans, 'Madden'.

96 Small full calf octavo volume, c. 1730–1798.

97 Madden, *Reflections and Resolutions*; see also Kelly, 'Public and Political Opinion in Ireland', pp. 121–22.

98 Abbott, 'Preface', pp. iii–iv; Fox, *Trinity College Library Dublin*, pp. 46, 60, 73–89; the collection was sold by John's second wife, Frances Bolton, whom he married after Mary's death in 1695; Sullivan, 'John Madden's Manuscripts', pp. 106–07.

Dublin.[99] In Marsh's Library, seven printed items, five of which are bound together as a sammelband, bear the stamp of Thomas Madden (d. 1640). Thomas was John's father, Samuel's grandfather, comptroller to Thomas Wentworth, Earl of Strafford and Lord Lieutenant of Ireland.[100] His books were inherited by John, who possibly also continued to use the same arms on volumes he acquired,[101] and some arrived at Marsh's Library as part of the Stearne bequest (perhaps some even earlier, since the five pamphlets composing the sammelband bear Narcissus Marsh's Greek motto on the title page, and so predate Stearne).[102] Thomas's books illustrate interests in the history and functioning of monarchical and parliamentary institutions, including for example Robert Cotton's 1642 *An Abstract out of the Records of the Tower*,[103] and in England's ancient laws and constitution, represented by the Latin 1610 edition of *Jani Anglorum facies altera*, in which John Selden — among the first English legal historians, and representative of a shift from medieval antiquarianism to a more modern approach of the use of primary sources in historical research — argued his interpretation of the English constitution as a mixed monarchy.[104] Other titles are related to antiquarian and historical research.[105] Although it is difficult today to distinguish between John Madden's original collection and Stearne's additions, it seems safe to assume that Samuel, seventeen years old at the time of his father's passing, was exposed to an extremely rich cultural environment during his early years, and that at home he had at his disposal a rare collection of manuscripts and printed texts, in which historical and antiquarian subjects occupied a central position. This tells us something about the family and cultural context in which the young Madden lived, but mere access or proximity to the family book collection should not be equated to an actual cultural influence. As will be seen in the following chapters and as is evident when reading his futuristic tale, while an attention to methodological issues concerning the study of the past and aspects such as genealogy can be seen at work in *Memoirs*, themes and references range over a number of different fields — from the history of magic to

---

99 Fox, *Trinity College Library Dublin*, p. 78.

100 'Madden, Thomas — 1640'.

101 Although the five sammelbands are bound with Thomas Madden's binding, two of them — Cotton, *An Abstract Out of the Records of the Tower* and Patin, *Travels thro' Germany, Bohemia, Swisserland, Holland* — also bearing Madden's stamp, were not published until after his death, which suggests that John may have continued to use the arms on his books.

102 Marsh's Library, *Catalogue*; Dublin, Marsh's Lib., communication with the author, 28 June 2021.

103 Cotton, *An Abstract out of the Records of the Tower*; Doddridge, *The History of the Ancient and Modern Estate*; *The Priviledges and Practice of Parliaments in England*; P. B., *The Priviledges of the House of Commons*.

104 Selden, *Jani Anglorum facies altera*.

105 Powell, *Direction for Search of Records Remaining in the Chancerie Tower*.

travel literature to religious controversialism. In compiling his work — many years after the sale of his father and grandfather's library — the author certainly followed his own interests and satirical goals.

One of Samuel's uncles on his mother's side, William Molyneux, was the author of an influential treaty 'advocating a federal interpretation of the regal union' from the perspective of the Protestant ascendancy,[106] which doubtless had some influence on Madden's own ideas. Samuel's brothers, John and Thomas, became respectively a fellow and professor of anatomy at Trinity College. John was also offered and declined the post of librarian in 1715,[107] and his cousin, Samuel Molyneux, was secretary to the Prince of Wales.[108] This important family background was followed by an education received at Trinity College: Madden began his studies in 1700, obtaining a bachelor of arts in 1705, and becoming a doctor of divinity in 1723.[109] Before graduating, Samuel inherited the family estate of Manor Waterhouse in 1703. He was ordained into the Church of Ireland and acquired the living of the nearby parish of Galloon. In 1709, he married Jane Magill (d. 1765), with whom he had five sons and five daughters. As a tutor to his children, he employed Philip Skelton, clergyman, scholar, and religious controversialist.[110]

In 1728, Samuel's cousin Samuel Molyneux was seized with a fit in the House of Commons and died some days later, after his friend and surgeon Nathaniel St André was called in to treat him. When St André eloped with the widow, Madden accused him of murder.[111] At the time, St André was already a somewhat controversial figure, thanks to his participation in sensational episodes such as Mary Toft's pretended preternatural birth of rabbits, portrayed by William Hogarth in a 1726 caricature (Figure 3). Although St André was cleared of murder, his reputation never recovered.[112]

---

106 William Molyneux's *The Case of Ireland's Being Bound by Acts of Parliament in England* (1698) had gone through ten editions by 1782; Goldie, 'The English System of Liberty', p. 55; on its influence on later American patriots in the 1760s, see also Eccleshall, 'The Political Ideas of Anglican Ireland in the 1690s', esp. p. 64.
107 Fox, *Trinity College Library Dublin*, p. 60.
108 Fraser, 'The Molyneux Family'.
109 Dublin, TCD, Adm. Rec., 1637–1725, MS IE TCD MUN V 23/1, fol. 237, *sub voce* 'Samueli Maddin'; *Alumni Dublinenses*, eds Burtchaell and Sadleir, pp. 543–44.
110 Lunney, 'Skelton, Philip'.
111 *A Letter from the Reverend Mr M--d--n [Samuel Madden].* The entry 'A Letter from the Reverend Mr M--d--n to the Hon. Lady M---n---x', in the National Library of Ireland catalogue notes that 'The surgeon Nathaniel St André eloped with Molyneux's wife following his death'.
112 St André, *A Short Narrative of an Extraordinary Delivery of Rabbets*; Hogarth, *Cunicularii*. See also Todd, 'St André, Nathanael'; Pickover, *The Girl Who Gave Birth to Rabbits*, p. 186 on Madden; Harvey, *The Imposteress Rabbit-Breeder*.

Figure 3. Hogarth, *Cunicularii, or, The wise men of Godliman in consultation*, etching (London, 1726). Below the image in the central column is the title and two lines of verse adapted from Hudibras's account of the magician Sidrophel: 'They held their Talents most Adroit./For any Mystical Exploit' (Part III, Canto 1, lines 365–66). On either side of the title there is a key to the characters, including A — The Dancing Master or Praeternatural Anatomist (St Andre) and F — The Lady in the straw (Mary Toft). Copy at National Gallery of Art, Rosenwald Collection, accession number 1944.5.115, under open access licence.

Madden's first literary work was the patriotic tragedy *Themistocles, the Lover of His Country* (1729),[113] staged successfully at the Theatre Royal in London.[114] Published anonymously, the printed version went through three editions in the first year. In 1730, he promoted a scheme to encourage of learning at Trinity through the awarding of prizes to the best students based on quarterly examination results,[115] to which he contributed with a generous donation.[116] The same idea is used in *Memoirs*, where a premium system is imagined at Oxford University.[117]

In 1731 Madden backed the foundation of the Dublin Society, in which his brother John, future Dean of Kilmore,[118] was more directly involved.[119] On his suggestion, a premium scheme was adopted by the Dublin Society to promote innovative methods in agriculture.[120] The idea and his subsequent contributions to it at the Dublin Society as well as at Trinity earned him the nickname of 'Premium Madden', and some notoriety among his contemporaries. During the 1750s, he was mentioned in local almanacs and gazettes for his philanthropic endeavours, as well as in a few treatises regarding the best way to foster innovation and wealth.[121] His name also circulated in the German-speaking world[122] and in Paris, appearing in the *Journal des Sçavans* in 1758.[123] A similar model was echoed in William Shipley's promotion of the English Society for the Arts,[124] which was created along the same lines as the Dublin Society in 1754. The correspondence between the two reveals how Madden had attempted to obtain the patronage of the Prince of Wales to help establish a fund in England, in favour of projects similar to Shipley's.[125] Despite Frederick Lewis's refusal, the episode evidences the good relationship

---

113 Madden, *Themistocles*.

114 Avery, ed., *The London Stage*, I, p. cxlix; II, pp. 1014–15.

115 Madden, *A Proposal for the General Encouragement of Learning*.

116 Dublin, TCD, MS TCD MUNI P /I/ 680, 30 March 1731, Bond, Madden [...] to Coghill.

117 Madden, *Memoirs*, pp. 150–51. Here and henceforth all page numbers refer to the original pagination, provided in square brackets in the second part of the present volume.

118 Burke, *Genealogical and Heraldic History*, p. 819.

119 The Dublin Society for Improving Husbandry, Manufactures and Other Useful Arts, renamed Royal Dublin Society in 1820; Berry, *A History of the Royal Dublin Society*, pp. vi, 46, 52–55, Berry dates Samuel's official affiliation to 12 April 1733, see p. 52; Long, 'The National Library of Ireland', pp. 3, 266–67.

120 [Madden], *A Letter to the Dublin-Society*.

121 Plumard de Dangeul, *Remarks on the Advantages and Disadvantages*, p. 116; Nelson, *An Address to Persons of Quality and Estate*, p. 87.

122 'Aus Ireland'.

123 'Nouvelles Littéraires'.

124 Turpin, 'The School of Design', p. 243.

125 Allan, *William Shipley*, pp. 16–17, see also p. 135 n. 45. Allan quotes the letter RSA, MS RSA/PR/GE/110/6/119, Madden to Shipley, 26 November 1757, in which Madden writes about an episode occurring sometime in the past (before 1751, the year of Frederick Lewis's death).

between Madden and the Prince of Wales (a note useful to bear in mind, as we shall see, for the correct interpretation of the dedication in *Memoirs*).

Another relationship that was significant in terms of Madden's interests and inclinations was that with George Berkeley. They had been at Trinity College together: Madden had joined one year after Berkeley (who was awarded his BA in 1704 and his MA and a fellowship in 1707).[126] In the late 1720s, Madden was certainly in contact with Berkeley[127] and his intellectual circle — which included Thomas Prior and John Percival — and he played a role in the publication of *The Querist*.[128] Berkeley's correspondence with Prior credits Madden as the editor of *The Querist's* first three parts.[129] Many of Madden's ideas were clearly in agreement with Berkeley's, especially as regards the economy, including a belief in the advantages of close commercial collaboration with England. His essay *Reflections and Resolutions* published in 1738 offers ample evidence of these ideas.[130] Ireland's inclusion in Great Britain — the expression of a 'limited monarchy' — is seen here as a pre-condition for its advancement in commerce and the arts and sciences.[131] Madden's friendship with Prior was cultivated around the activities of the above-mentioned Dublin Society. Prior was the pivotal figure in the Society's foundation, and undoubtedly a close relationship linked the group of philanthropists responsible for the birth of the association in 1731. In December 1739 the board's minutes record that it was Prior himself — secretary at the time — who laid before the board Madden's proposal to increase the Society's fund and set up the aforementioned system of prizes for encouraging innovation and excellence in agriculture and the arts.[132]

Notwithstanding his Whig sympathies, Madden was on friendly terms with Jonathan Swift. The Dean of Saint Patrick's kept a copy of *Reflections and Resolutions* in his library,[133] and between the 1730s and the 1760s, Madden's name was on the list of subscribers to some of Swift's editions

---

126 Jones, *George Berkeley*, p. 83.
127 Berkeley, *Life and Letters of George Berkeley*, ed. Campbell Fraser, IV, p. 150.
128 Jones, *George Berkeley*, pp. 82–83; Sale, *Samuel Richardson*, pp. 107, 155, 130; Kelly, 'Berkeley's Economic Writings', pp. 339, 357–59; Chuanacháin, 'Utopianism', esp. p. 123; Berry, *A History of the Royal Dublin Society*, p. 32; Berkeley, *Life and Letters of George Berkeley*, ed. Campbell Fraser, IV, pp. 242–43.
129 Berkeley, *Life and Letters of George Berkeley*, ed. Campbell Fraser, IV, p. 247; Jones, *George Berkeley*, p. 83.
130 Madden, *Reflections and Resolutions*; see also Kelly, 'Public and Political Opinion', esp. pp. 121–22.
131 Madden, *Reflections and Resolutions*, reprint (1816), p. 2.
132 Dublin, Dub. Soc., 13 December 1739, copy, quoted in Berry, *A History of the Royal Dublin Society*, pp. 54–55.
133 Landa, '"A Modest Proposal" and Populousness', p. 165 n. 18.

printed in Dublin by George Faulkner.[134] To paraphrase George Birkbeck Hill,[135] he also cultivated a 'poetical friendship' with Samuel Johnson, to whom he entrusted the revision of his *Boulter's Monument: A Panegyrical Poem* (1745).[136]

Hugh Boulter, the Bishop of Bristol, appointed Archbishop of Armagh in 1724, and to whom Madden's panegyric was addressed, was a Whig loyal to Robert Walpole. Within the Church of Ireland, he represented the current of opinion most committed to the defence of British interests. This current, of which Madden was also a part, has to be seen within the complex context of the Irish political stage of the 1720s and 1730s, where loyalty to the House of Hanover did not necessarily rule out advocacy in favour of Ireland's interests.[137] Boulter also had ties with the moderately Whiggish, progressive publication *The Freethinker* (1718–1722), where he often wrote on issues related to education, to which Madden similarly devoted considerable energy in his writings. From 1731 to 1742 Boulter also served as vice president of the Dublin Society.[138]

Madden's political positions between the 1740s and the 1750s are further illuminated by his correspondence with Philip Stanhope, fourth Earl of Chesterfield, Lord Lieutenant of Ireland and then briefly Secretary of State (and from 1732, playing an important role in the Whigs' opposition to Robert Walpole).[139] In the late 1740s their correspondence concerned, among other things, Madden's advocacy for procuring a Royal Charter for the Dublin Society, a project which saw Stanhope sceptical at first, for fear that having positions to fill, the Society might become a 'theatre for jobbers', but subsequently persuaded by the draft of the Charter shown to him.[140] It was in all likelihood Stanhope's experience as ambassador to the Netherlands that inspired one of the fictional correspondents in *Memoirs*, the diplomat in Constantinople called Stanhope. The Chesterfield family

---

134 Swift, *Volume VI of the Author's Works*, n.p. but p. 14; Swift, *The Works of the Reverend Dr Jonathan Swift*, I, n.p. but p. 36.

135 Birkbeck Hill, 'Notes on I', in Swift, *Unpublished Letters*, p. 8.

136 Madden, *Boulter's Monument*. On Johnson's editing: Birkbeck Hill, 'Notes on XXXIV', in Swift, *Unpublished Letters*, p. 147; Boswell, *The Life of Samuel Johnson*, I, p. 137; Clark, *Samuel Johnson*, p. 172 n. 31; Richey, 'Madden'. Johnson, 'Swift', pp. 208, 215; Johnson, 'Addison', p. 455. See also DeMaria Jr., *The Life of Samuel Johnson*, pp. 110, 285.

137 Holmes, 'English Whigs and Irish Patriots'.

138 Berry, *A History of the Royal Dublin Society*, p. 380.

139 'Philip Dormer Stanhope, 4th Earl of Chesterfield'; Cannon, 'Stanhope, Philip Dormer'; Stanhope, *The Letters of Philip Dormer Stanhope*, III — *Letters, Political, and Miscellaneous*, pp. 188–90; Stanhope, *Miscellaneous Works*, IV, pp. 95–101. See also Stanhope, *Letters Written by the Late Right Honourable Philip Dormer Stanhope*, II, p. 16.

140 Berry, *A History of the Royal Dublin Society*, pp. 75–76.

bookplate appears on one of the rare copies of the book, presumably presented by the author to his friend.[141]

Madden was also familiar with the work of the actor and promoter of the elocution movement, Thomas Sheridan (d. 1788).[142] He shared Sheridan's ideas about public speaking being an element of civic development, and they were both advocates of a reform of education in which elocution was to play a central role.[143] In 1758, Madden's name figured among the participants at the first meeting of the Hibernian Society in Dublin, and he was part of the committee to which Sheridan explained his programme for reforming the education system. The Society then promoted its adoption in Ireland.[144]

In December 1765, not yet eighty years of age, Madden passed away at Manor Waterhouse.[145]

As for his fortune in subsequent studies, in twentieth-century historiography he is known mainly as an active proponent of agricultural, economic, and administrative reform in Ireland and for his philanthropic activities, especially through the Dublin Society. His literary works are seldom mentioned: there are only passing references in histories of English-language literature, and the role of *Memoirs* in the cultural history of time is rarely recognised.[146] A 1980s article by Paul Alkon located the novel within the history of speculative fiction, although his main concern was with the text's use of original literary devices.[147] Also, a PhD thesis by Deirdre Ní Chuanacháin about Irish utopianism in the eighteenth century offers an attentive reconstruction of the political context in which Madden was writing.[148]

---

141 Copy today at New York Public Library. For the bookplate identification see also 'Chesterfield, Earl of Stanhope — ex libris'. This copy is also one of those containing the folded portrait of Frederick Lewis, discussed later in ch. 13.

142 Bullard, 'Rhetoric and Eloquence'.

143 Madden, *Reflections and Resolutions*, p. 54; O'Shaughnessy, 'Staging an Irish Enlightenment', pp. 17–18.

144 *The Proceedings of the Hibernian Society*, pp. 5, 6.

145 'News', *St James's Chronicle*, dating the death 30 December; 'News', *Owen's Weekly Chronicle*.

146 Brief mentions are in: Brewer, *The Pleasures of the Imagination*, p. 663; Clarke, *The Pattern of Expectation*, p. 16; Crane et al., *English literature*, II, *1939–1950*, p. 384; Margolis, *A Brief History of Tomorrow*, pp. 27–28; Porter, *The Creation of the Modern World*, p. 425; Spadafora, *The Idea of Progress*, pp. 43–44, 56 n. 50, 72 n. 69; Vance, *Irish Literature*, p. 71; Wasserman, *Paradoxes of Time Travel*, p. 1 n. 2; Wilson, *The History of the Future*, pp. 141–42; *Memoirs* is also listed in Bleiler, *The Checklist*, p. 131; Gibson, *St Thomas More*, p. 368; McBurney, *A Check List*, p. 94; Negley, *Utopian Literature*, p. 90. Madden is left out from Jeffares, *Macmillan History of Literature*, as noted by Beckett, Review of *Macmillan History of Literature*, p. 685.

147 Alkon, 'Samuel Madden's "Memoirs of the Twentieth Century"'; reprinted in *Vintage Visions*, ed. Evans; with a few minor changes, this essay also constitutes the chapter entitled 'Formal Variations: *Memoirs of the Twentieth Century*', in Alkon, *Origins*, pp. 89–114.

148 Chuanacháin, 'Utopianism'.

The following chapters appraise Madden's tale of the future through the lens of cultural history, the history of speculative literature from a comparative perspective, and textual analysis, assessing its use of literary devices, as well as how it conceptualises history and an ever-increasing global interconnectedness. To fully appreciate the complexity of Madden's inventions, *Memoirs* will be read against the background of its original social, cultural, and political context.

IV. An Eighteenth-Century Twentieth Century

Like the tragedy *Themistocles*, *Memoirs* is dedicated to Frederick Lewis, Prince of Wales, first child of George Augustus (1683–1760), who was elector of Hanover, Duke of Brunswick-Lüneburg and King George II of Great Britain and Ireland (Figure 4). Frederick Lewis was heir apparent to the British throne from 1727[149] and Madden served as his chaplain from 1729 to 1751.[150] The hypothesis that the dedication might be ironic, already put forward by a contemporary commentator, is to be rejected.[151] It is dated 25 January 1731, which is before the deterioration of the relationship between the prince and his father George II, and in fact, also contains fulsome praise of the king and the queen.[152] Following the dedication, there is a preface, in which an ironically unreliable narrator takes centre stage and explains that the subsequent pages feature a collection of letters from the future (dated between 1997 and 1999), which he received in manuscript form from a supernatural entity, and of which he is merely the editor, responsible for preparing them for the press. The novel contains these letters, framed by two other writings by the editor — a 'Second' and 'Third Preface', respectively in between and closing the sequence of epistles. Alkon argued that *Memoirs* created a new 'absurdist mock genre: the future history',[153] and it is true that the 'curatorial' apparatus mocks the typical vices of contemporary historical treatises in its redundant organisation and its pedantic accumulation of quotes, references, and exemplifications. The choice of the epistolary form is no less significant,[154]

---

149 Kilburn, 'Frederick Lewis, prince of Wales'.
150 Lees, 'The Religious Retinue', pp. 94–95, 102.
151 Nichols, *Literary Anecdotes*, II, p. 699. Cf. the correct interpretation proposed by Gerrard, *The Patriot Opposition to Walpole*, pp. 56–57, and by Lees, 'The Religious Retinue', p. 95.
152 '[…] you are only considered as the Heir apparent of the best Man and Woman, the best King and Queen, that ever adorn'd a Family, or blest a Nation […]', Madden, *Memoirs*, p. v. Unless specified otherwise, all quotations retain their original spelling, punctuation, and italics; transcriptions of the long 's' have been silently modernised.
153 Alkon, *Origins*, p. 103.
154 *Memoirs* is in fact part of the comparative corpus under examination in Moshe Pelli, 'The Epistolary Story'.

Figure 4. *His Royal Highness Frederick Lewis Prince of Wales*, mezzotint created and published by John Faber Jr, after Jeremiah Davison (*c.* 1730). Paper size 395 mm × 255 mm. This folded portrait is bound into some copies of *Memoirs of the Twentieth Century* after the title page. Courtesy of The Lewis Walpole Library, Yale University.

and constitutes the textual representation of the network of international connections described in the novel's future.[155]

Madden's book was published some forty years before Mercier's *L'An deux mille quatre cent quarante*, and although Mercier's work was more successful and influential, being one of the earliest if not the first significant example of a novel in which the protagonist travels through time into a remote future (the narrator wakes up in Paris seven centuries after the year of writing),[156] *Memoirs* contained the first example of an object travelling in time (the letters) and bringing with it knowledge about the future.[157]

The letters are diplomatic relations sent by British ambassadors in Constantinople, Rome, Moscow, and Paris, to the Lord High Treasurer[158] in London, and include some of the latter's replies. The reports describe a network of international connections, through which the reader is able to gradually piece together the global state of affairs; more specifically, what might now be called the geopolitics of the day, but also religious beliefs and practices, laws and customs of different countries, the organisation of the military, systems of trade and taxation, and progress in the arts and sciences. The British ambassadors also take particular care to trace the *status quo* back to its causes and to analyse which mechanisms brought about certain phenomena and trends. By means of (fictional) essays referred to and books presented to the Lord High Treasurer, they highlight significant choices and events — such as reforms, policies, strategies — of the recent and distant past that transformed the state of affairs in the eighteenth century to those of the twentieth century. In a world in which 'trade and correspondence got wings by land, as well as by sea',[159] the epistolary construction is essential to the appraisal of how historical processes operate. Furthermore, by adopting the point of view of British ambassadors stationed in other countries, a defamiliarised perspective on British affairs can be built, fostering comparisons between the British commonwealth and other forms of political organisation and exercise of power.

A notable feature of the global scene in the 1990s is British commercial success, especially in the field of maritime trade, built on clever treaties, technical superiority in navigation technology, and military successes against France and Turkey in the 1870s. For their excellence in the arts

---

155 On the eighteenth-century epistolary novel: Beebee, *Epistolary Fiction in Europe*, esp. ch. 'Epistolary Defamiliarization', pp. 76–102, and here p. 86 on early eighteenth-century notable examples of culturally estranged perspectives on Europe, including Montesquieu's *Lettres Persanes* (1721).

156 Darnton, *Libri proibiti*, pp. 120–40, esp. 124; Koselleck, *The Practice of Conceptual History*, pp. 84–99; see also *supra* ch. 2.

157 Precedents to Madden's novel are, in some respects, the 'colonial fantasies' analysed by Bross in *Future History*.

158 A role akin to today's prime minister.

159 Madden, *Memoirs*, p. 512.

and sciences, prosperity in trade, the intelligent and profitable alliances, and the enduring allegiance of the American colonies, the British people have mainly to thank the enlightened policies and choices of the Crown and parliament. These are the more overtly prescriptive-utopian aspects in the construction of the future in *Memoirs*, to be read in the light of the aforementioned dedication to the Prince of Wales, and undoubtedly written with his future ascension to the throne in mind.

In this respect, Madden's account of the future contributes, to some extent, to a lively strand of coeval utopian writing. Although little studied by a scholarship focused on a canon consisting largely of sixteenth- and seventeenth-century bodies of work, the utopian imagination of the Age of Enlightenment gave rise to a variety of commonwealth models (as well as dystopias) in the Anglosphere, in which satirical elements and reform proposals were often deeply entangled.[160] Similarly to *Memoirs*, a number of works that are part of a utopian tradition within the British Enlighten-ment interpret (or ridicule) coeval debates about corruption, morals and manners, and dissolution and luxury, such as Bernard Mandeville's *The Fable of the Bees: or, Private Vices, Publick Benefits* (1723), and *The History of a Corporation of Servants* (1765, published anonymously by John Wither-spoon).[161] Madden does not place his work methodically within a utopian tradition, and indeed, in his tale of the future one cannot find, for example, the customary references to Plato, Thomas More, Francis Bacon, and James Harrington, nor does the novel comply with the narrative model established by More's seminal work.[162] The role attributed to science and technology (discussed *infra*) might point to Madden's knowledge of the *New Atlantis*, but an open reference to Bacon is made only *en passant* with regards to control over the weather.[163] Mentions of Plato do not include references to the *Republic*. Nonetheless salient aspects of the future depicted in the novel are extrapolated from the writer's present according to utopian and anti-utopian mechanisms of projection.

The remarks on the American colonies and their relationships with the mother country are particularly interesting and may be read against the backdrop of Madden's possible involvement in Berkeley's Bermuda

---

160 Claeys, 'Introduction' and in general Claeys, ed., *Utopias of the British Enlightenment*; Altaher, 'What Happened to Utopias in the Eighteenth Century?'; Pearl, *Utopian Geographies*; see also Pohl, 'Utopianism after More', esp. pp. 63–72.

161 [Mandeville], *The Fable of the Bees: Or, Private Vices, Publick Benefits*; [Witherspoon], *The History of a Corporation of Servants*; Claeys, 'Introduction'; see also Pohl, 'Utopianism after More'. Claeys includes *Memoirs* in his 'Chronology', p. xxx.

162 Vieira, 'The Concept of Utopia', esp. p. 6 for a discussion of approaches to the definition of the utopian genre based on textual adherence to More's model.

163 Madden, *Memoirs*, p. 73.

project.[164] In his reply to the British ambassador in Rome, the Lord High Treasurer writes from London that:

> The truth is, our colonies abroad have, and are likely to acquire still, such an increase of hands and strength, that the greatest care will be necessary to keep the strongest of them dependent [...] I am confident the new bishopricks founded among them by the piety and generosity of his Majesty's ancestors, as well as those of *Carolina*, *Barbadoes* and *Boston*, establish'd by himself, will greatly contribute to the reformation of manners and principles in our colonies, and to the keeping them firm in their allegiance to the crown.[165]

Years after the appearance of his futuristic fiction, the virtuous administration of the overseas colonies was once again uppermost in Madden's mind: in 1757, at a meeting of the Royal Society of Arts, a letter of his was read out praising Benjamin Franklin's initiatives to promote innovations in agriculture through the awarding of premiums. 'I am rejoiced at Mr Franklin's coming over with so good a Plan which to the shame of government has been overlooked such a number of years. If our Colonies be not properly modelled and protected nothing but Ruin and Disgrace can follow [...]'.[166]

Back in the late 1720s, it was clear that while he was writing his chronicles of the future, one of Madden's main concerns was the Vatican's influence over continental Europe: in the scenario depicted in the novel, by the nineteenth century the Jesuits' power has reached its zenith, with Paul IX's pontificate and a subsequent bull by Clement XIV in 1862 giving the Jesuits the monopoly on confession, inquisition, exorcism, and the authority to grant divorces. Financed by rich revenues from overseas territories under its control in Africa and in Paraguay, and by lucrative trade agreements with China, Rome is able to vastly expand its secular dominions in the 'Old World', and secure increasing influence over the weak French, Spanish, and German courts. By 1997, the temporal possessions of the Vatican form a 'vast Empire, which has risen these two last Centuries, like a huge Mountain, from the unnatural fires and eruptions in the bowels of the Earth'.[167] While politics at the European courts are characterised by divisions and quarrels, which undermine their effectiveness,

---

164 'his unsuccessful attempt to found a missionary college on the island of Bermuda, which brought him to America for three years beginning in 1728', Winkler, 'Introduction', p. 2 and passim; Bunbury, *Irish Diaspora*, ch. 'George Berkeley (1685–1753) — The "Irish Plato" & Bermuda College'; Jones, *George Berkeley*, ch. 10; on the 'New World' as home to eighteenth-century utopias see: Imbruglia, *The Jesuit Missions*, pp. 21–25; Pohl, 'Utopianism after More', p. 53.

165 Madden, *Memoirs*, pp. 374, 375. On the role of religion in shaping an early Atlantic and global imagination: Pestana, *Protestant Empire*; Bross, *Future History*.

166 Quoted in Allan, '"Dear and Serviceable to Each Other"', p. 250.

167 Madden, *Memoirs*, p. 260.

the Jesuits promote their interests on a truly transnational scale, helping and protecting one another, and putting their religious affiliation and belonging before their national origins. Against this cosmopolitan Jesuitism, the particularism of parliaments and nations, and the squabbling and plotting of courtiers leaves the European courts open to manipulation and corruption.[168]

To the East, it is the rise of Russia's economic power and international standing that causes concern among British observers,[169] despite the fact that Moscow 'indeed, has not forgot the fatal Blow we gave their Naval Power in the Baltick formerly, and the great Restraint we keep them under ever since'.[170] Even here, the Jesuits' schemes are in evidence: emissaries from Rome are busy gaining the favour of the Russian people with their innovations and improvements in the field of medicine, but they should not to be trusted. The British ambassador in Moscow notes that the true design of the Jesuits is 'to enslave those they pretend to serve, and establish the Empire of the *Vatican*, and all its superstitions and errors'.[171]

The decline of the Ottoman Empire was sealed by the extinction of the Ottoman line of succession after Mahomet IX, who was supplanted by the Tartars. The Jesuits are able to exploit the Tartars' tendency to give people more religious freedom: with far-sighted strategic ability, they begin a subtle propaganda initiative, firstly in the form of teachings compatible with Islam, then using the printing press to undermine the intellectual authority of the *hogies*[172] and scribes, traditionally founded upon the monopoly of written knowledge.[173] In 1997, a treaty is negotiated between Constantinople and London, by which British 'Trade shall be as much favour'd here, as [...] it has been in all other parts of the World'.[174] But the British had long before supplanted the Ottomans in the Mediterranean: 'their Trade which in the 18*th* Century was in so poor a Way, and yet before 1876 was in so flourishing a Condition, is now entirely sunk and fallen into the Hands of the Merchants of *Great Britain*'.[175]

---

168 Madden, *Memoirs*, p. 38: 'yet are there no longer Spanish, French or German Cardinals in the World, since whatever Nation they belong to, they are absolutely and solely Jesuits and nothing else'.

169 On Russia: Madden, *Memoirs*, pp. 52–73, 153–82, 338–65.

170 Madden, *Memoirs*, p. 54.

171 Madden, *Memoirs*, p. 350.

172 'Hogies' is a word meaning those who have completed a pilgrimage to the Mecca, one of the Islamic pillars, MacLean, *The Rise of Oriental Travel*, p. 92; the use of 'hogies' as a synonym of 'clerk of law' is not unusual in modern Europe: Percy, *William Percy's Mahomet*, ed. by Dimmock, p. 206.

173 On the Ottoman empire: Madden, *Memoirs*, pp. 1–27 (page numbers after the preface), 183–214, 308–38, 473–504.

174 Madden, *Memoirs*, p. 1 (page number after the preface).

175 Madden, *Memoirs*, p. 14 (page number after the preface).

From Constantinople and Paris, the British correspondents provide detailed descriptions and comments about taxation systems, the sloppy administration of public resources, and, especially in France, the excessive and peculiar luxury in which the nobility live.[176] French people pay ever-increasing taxes on everything — from land to houses, from livestock to marriages, baptisms, and deaths. Inability to pay has impoverished large sections of the population.[177] According to the ambassadors, the decline of France was inevitable: '[...] this great Kingdom, that for so many Years was still enterprizing on the Liberties and Dominions of her weaker Neighbours, and laying Schemes for the Ruin of *Great-Britain*, (as the main Step to the Empire of the World,) fallen now from the Object of our Fears, to that of our Pity'.[178]

Virtuous reforms, representing a hypothetical application of some of the proposals contained in *Reflections and Resolutions*, are mostly attributed to the British Crown and its government. These include measures to tackle poverty — such as the lending of small sums at the lowest interest by a public central bank — bills against corruption and political careerism, in favour of the good administration of land and justice — such as 'an Act to prevent any judge, Bishop, or Archbishop, to be preferred, or translated, from any See or Place to which they were first promoted', and an act 'taking away all privilege of Parliament, in case of Arrests for Debt, or Law suits, when the house is not sitting'.[179]

The interest in corruption and luxury, poverty and principles of social reforms that runs through the novel, makes it an excellent example of the potential relevance of utopia in our understanding of eighteenth-century political, social, and cultural transformations. Comparison with the same ideas argued in *Reflections and Resolutions*, makes clear the distinctive contribution of utopian (and dystopian) invention. 'The unique, extremely imaginative form of the genre permits normal social restriction to be dissolved more readily than in other, more realistic, types of fiction' (and all the more so with non-fiction genres of writing), allowing 'the expression of more extreme or implausible principles'.[180] While Madden does not put forward proposals of an egalitarian society, nor of a community of goods, *Memoirs* shares with other coeval utopian narrations an emphasis on charity, prohibition of idleness, help in providing employment, and

---

176 For an overview of the debates on luxury in France and Britain before 1748: Hont, 'The Early Enlightenment Debate on Commerce and Luxury'.

177 On France: Madden, *Memoirs*, pp. 74–97, 285–307, 447–72.

178 Madden, *Memoirs*, p. 90.

179 On England: Madden, *Memoirs*, pp. 132–53, 257–84 (here for legal reforms), 366–86, 421–46 (here 421–25 on premium systems and aid for the poor), quote 270. On corruption as 'the single most important political issue of the eighteenth century': Langford, *A Polite and Commercial People*, p. 716.

180 Claeys, 'Introduction', p. ix.

sumptuary restraints among other things. These are also recurrent features in other texts in which Christian principles underpin important elements of moral reformation that have been debated with particular reference to a Protestant and Quaker tradition and to the construction of republican model commonwealths.[181]

France is forced to give up all her Channel ports. In a pacified world, writes the ambassador to Constantinople to the Lord High Treasurer, 'your sacred Master's Cares and Yours, will now be almost solely confin'd, to the keeping the general Peace [sic] we are in with all Nations safe and undisturb'd, and to promote our Trade wherever our Industry and Profit can extend it'.[182] British naval power is the only thing keeping Rome in check:

> our prodigious Naval Force has kept all the Islands in the hands of their old Sovereigns, and both prevented the Venetians being entirely swallowed up, and holds the Pope, by the means of his Sea-Coasts, Ports, and Trade, in great awe; I do not despair, but we may be able to humble his aspiring hopes. The confirming *Civita Vecchia* a free Port, restoring all our Privileges, and declaring by his Bull that none of his Majesty's Subjects shall be liable to his Inquisitors, are great points gained, and also shew the fear he has of us, which I hope your Excellency will improve to weightier purposes.[183]

A particular role is played by the Royal Fishery and the Plantation Companies (established by Frederick I and George III). The first enables Great Britain to undersell her rivals, employ numerous poor who would otherwise be unproductive, and make immense profits. The Plantation-Company for the new Colonies in the West Indies is 'favour'd by great encouragements, as to all duties of exports and imports, and a grant of three millions of acres, to be laid out and applotted equally to all planters who shall settle there, and build new towns'.[184]

While British American colonies have been greatly extended, the rest of the continent 'is grown vastly populous, and the inhabitants for this last Century, by the help of the natives, have carried their colonies and plantations thro' the remotest provinces; it happen'd the Portuguese and Spaniards frequently met, and had furious contests and engagements, about the boundaries of their dominions'.[185] In the 1990s, these heated territorial disputes are far from having been extinguished, if for no other

---

181 Claeys, 'Introduction', pp. xviii–xxvi.
182 Madden, *Memoirs*, pp. 3–4 (page numbers after the preface).
183 Madden, *Memoirs*, p. 259. On the future of empires based on control of the seas and trade, as conceived in the early eighteenth century, see Pagden, *Lords of all the World*, pp. 115–20.
184 Madden, *Memoirs*, pp. 372–73.
185 Madden, *Memoirs*, p. 469.

reason than that the issue of longitude is still dealt with by way of astro-nomical observations.[186]

A fascinating complexity characterises the conception of historical temporality underlying the future imagined in *Memoirs*. On the one hand, the emphasis placed on causal processes and links clearly refers to a notion of linear and unidirectional time flow.[187] On the other hand, as will be discussed in the following pages, the text's publication is ironically motivated by the postulated existence of a close eschatological horizon, and, by mixing utopian, dystopian, and satirical aspects, the novel keeps temporal linearity and progress far from being one and the same.

---

186 Madden, *Memoirs*, pp. 331, 469.
187 On linear conceptions of history during the eighteenth century: Rabasa, Sato, Tortarolo, and Woolf, eds, *The Oxford History of Historical Writing*; Osterhammel, *Unfabling the East*, pp. 480–517; Sebastiani, *The Scottish Enlightenment*; Spadafora, *The Idea of Progress*.

V. An (Unreliable) Historian of the Future

What lies ahead in Madden's account of the future is linked to the author's present by a range of different kinds of extrapolations. Along with inventions clearly ascribable to utopian and dystopian imaginative mechanisms (for example the future success and prosperity being attributed to British power or to a menacing Vatican), the author's and the reader's eighteenth century is wide open to satire, and this is made abundantly clear in the first preface, especially in the autobiographical portrait of the (fictitious) editor. In the prefatory writings, the editor mentions a series of elements relating to his own biographical and intellectual development. These autobiographical notes, which are strikingly far-fetched and antiphrastic, obliquely convey sarcastic reflections on certain trends in coeval culture, politics, and customs. The unreliable and contradictory character of the editor's voice and the double-edged and mystifying intentions of the narrative frame constituted by the prefaces make the tone of the volume 'hove[r] between straight-forward seriousness and irony',[188] 'wave[r] between satiric and utopian',[189] thus requiring particular vigilance if one is to distinguish passages intended ironically and prescriptively, and thus grasp the intentions and critical positions of the real author.

Born under the most fortunate of astrological signs — mentioned with unmistakable self-irony — and from a wealthy family, the editor aims to distinguish himself 'from the common Herd of Mankind'.[190] To reach this goal quickly, he deems it best to drop out of university; meanwhile every art and trade seem to be beneath him, 'both as taking too much Time, Thought and Reading to master, and a deal of mean Art, or good Money to succeed in'. A much quicker way to rise above the crowds is to spend one third of his fortune travelling, ostentatiously despising his own country.[191]

---

188 Bosse, 'Introduction', pp. 5–6.
189 Alkon, *Origins*, p. 93.
190 Madden, *Memoirs*, 'A Modest Preface: Containing Many Words to the Wise', pp. 1–31, see p. 10.
191 Madden, *Memoirs*, pp. 11–12, see also pp. 287, 363. As regards travelling as a means of education, in *Reflections and Resolutions* Madden writes: 'another great mistake in the education of our Irish gentlemen, which I hope we shall less frequently fall into for the future, and that is sending so many of them to travel. […] we should send none to travel, that have not almost a certainty of growing wiser, and more serviceable to themselves and the community by their rambles among foreigners', pp. 58, 59. On travel as a means

The rest of the family fortune is depleted in attempting a political career: buying a seat in parliament and keeping up 'an extravagant Table and a Crowd of humble Admirers of my Eloquence to eat at it'.[192] He then retires to the country, 'to the Ruins of my Estate, of which I had sold two Thirds, to pay off the Debts these Schemes in Politicks had brought on me; and because I could not with Ease look back on the World, I resolv'd to look forward, and consider what might happen, since I abhor'd to reflect on what had'.[193]

After this sequence of failures, he starts resenting his country and the Crown, and hopes for a sudden calamity to disrupt the status quo, so that he can take advantage of it and get back what he was forced to sell to cover his debts. A Papist revolution would be most welcome: he would be ready to line up in favour of 'the Chevalier', 'The Old Pretender': James Stuart.[194] The narrator's unreliability and repeated political about-turns call for an antiphrastic interpretation, in which his and the real author's ideas are poles apart. Archival sources, albeit scarce, confirm this hypothesis.[195]

On the evening of 20 January 1728,[196] while the narrator is mulling over this longed-for Jacobite coup, a supernatural being appears in his room, claiming to be his 'good *Genius*'[197] and to be bringing him proof

---

of cultural education in eighteenth-century British culture: Fabricant, 'Eighteenth-Century Travel Literature'; Leask, 'Eighteenth-Century Travel Writing'.

192 Madden, *Memoirs*, p. 13. On patronage, electoral corruption, and the buying of parliamentary seats in early-eighteenth century England: Kramnick, 'Corruption in Eighteenth-Century English and American Political Discourse'.

193 Madden, *Memoirs*, p. 15.

194 James Stuart's father, the Catholic King James VII and II, was deposed in the Glorious Revolution in 1688. With Jacobite support, James Stuart claimed the crown, notably during the failed Jacobite rising of 1715, which may be alluded to in the idea of a 'Papist glorious revolution'. Gregg, 'James Francis Edward'.

195 Cambridge, The Cholmondeley Papers, MS 1507, Samuel Madden to Sir Robert Walpole, n.d. [after June 1729] and MS 3047, Samuel Madden to Sir Robert Walpole, 3 January 1740 (see also *infra*, ch. 13 on the dating of the first letter), partially quoted in Urstad, *Sir Robert Walpole's Poets*, pp. 114, 90. On the unreliability of the narrator's political stance our interpretation differs from Chuanacháin, 'Utopianism', p. 238.

196 The year is also prominently placed on the title page, declaring the letters 'Received and Revealed in the Year 1728'. Is the choice of a precise date — 20 January 1728 — meant to foster the impression of verisimilitude? Or does it imply a reference to something that happened that day? In 1728 Frederick Lewis Prince of Wales, to whom the work is dedicated, arrived in London (on 4 December): perhaps the date combines a tribute to his arrival with a reference to his date of birth, which corresponds to 20 January in the Old-Style calendar. Less likely seems an approximate reference to the end of Voltaire's English exile, since the author is not mentioned in *Memoirs*. A satirical jab at Benedict XIII's confirmation of the two-hundred years of indulgence accorded to all Christians every time they recited the litany of the blessed Virgin twice (first established by Sixtus V in 1587) would be consistent with the anti-Catholic spirit of the work, but it is a very specific reference, and it is not taken up or substantiated by other elements.

197 Madden, *Memoirs*, p. 18, and passim for subsequent quotes in the text.

Figure 5. Kircher, *Iter extaticum cœleste* (1660), frontispiece. Theodidactus, depicted with the traits of Kircher and a pair of compasses in his hand, is guided by the angel Cosmiel on a journey through the cosmos. Above the system of the planets is the tetragrammaton (Jehovah). Engraving signed F. Sc. (Johann Friedrich Fleischberger). Courtesy of the John Carter Brown Library, under Attribution-ShareAlike 4.0 International (CC BY-SA 4.0) licence.

of how the Hanoverian line will bring Great Britain, together with him and his descendants, new fortunes and glory. As evidence, the ethereal being presents him with some bundles of letters addressed to his great-great-great-great-great-nephew, who in the twentieth century, is destined to become Chief Minister under George VI, and assures our narrator that 'I might, with good Husbandry, raise a Fortune whereon to subsist my Family with Honour and Affluence'.[198] He immediately abandons his new-found political beliefs and starts an erudite disquisition about the future with his 'good *Genius*', an entity possibly modelled — by substituting a temporal dimension for a spatial journey — after Athanasius Kircher's angel in *Itinerarium exstaticum* (The ecstatic journey).[199] He learns that the world will come to an end after the political rise of his distant progeny. With a fascinating temporal short-circuit, against this eschatological backdrop, the publication of the letters is also aimed at doing justice to his descendant's fame: since there will be no time to celebrate and eternalise his offspring's undertakings, because there will be no posterity to posterity, it is only right for his progeny to be celebrated in advance and acquire a 'preventive prestige'.[200]

After recounting this dialogue, the mischievous narrator goes on to say that the pages that follow contain the original letters from the future, which he is sending to press exactly as received, except for translating them from the English of the twentieth century to the English of the eighteenth — the latter being far more illiterate — and of course, except for withholding from publication all those parts that it seemed safer to keep only for the eyes of the Crown and those of his family.[201] The first preface thus introduces the letters and provides a narrative frame, offering — through these ironic autobiographical notes — a satirical account of the contemptible habit of noblemen of giving up administering their land and estates to try to buy a seat in parliament.

Among the elements in the narrator's autobiographical portrait, several pertain to the occult and the supernatural:

> I must own that I am descended in a direct Line by the Mother's side, from a Son of that famous Count Gabalis, in the 17th Century, whose History is in every ones Hands, and whose Wife, as all true Adepts

---

198 Madden, *Memoirs*, p. 21.

199 Kircher, *Athanasii Kircheri e soc. Iesu Itinerarium exstaticum*; the *Memoirs'* author refers to the 1660 edition brought to press by Gaspar Schott, *Iter extaticum*, see *infra*, ch. 6; Madden, *Memoirs*, p. 225, see also p. 20; Alkon, *Origins*, p. 95.

200 The underpinning irony, the secular nature of the future described in the letters, and the primacy of trade and economic exchange in enabling the global projection of British power distance Madden's eschatology from the millennialism of the 1620s–1670s works considered in Bross, *Future History*.

201 Madden, *Memoirs*, pp. 22, 30, 235, 237, see also p. 507; see also *infra*, ch. 8.

know, had Carnal Knowledge of, and was Impregnated by a certain invisible Dæmon, that call'd himself Ariel.[202]

The Count of Cabala is the fictional character who gave the title to *Le Comte de Gabalis ou Entretiens sur les sciences secretes* (The Count of Cabala or talks on the secret sciences) published anonymously by Nicolas-Pierre-Henri de Montfaucon de Villars in 1670.[203] In five satirical dialogues, the Count spoke about spiritual beings, Paracelsian elemental theory, and Rosicrucianism. It had widespread influence on subsequent literature, as well as on esoterism and occultism, and it notably introduced sylphs into European literature.[204] The first two English translations appeared in 1680, and another in 1714.[205] The reference in the text to the Count's history being in everyone's hand acknowledges the work's success, evidenced in the same period by the comment made by Pope in the preface to *The Rape of the Lock*.[206] The editor claims to be related to the Count of Cabala, as being the descendant of the son his wife had not with him but with the demon Ariel (intercourse between humans and supernatural creatures was a topic discussed in de Villars's dialogues). The narrator then goes on to argue that the celestial origin of his work originates in his exceptional birth, which he places among a number of famed cases: '[…] Plato, Appollonius Tyanæus, the Earl of *Poitiers*, and other great Personages; and as the Mareschal *de Bassompiere* in his Memoirs, is so candid as to confess it also, of one of the Heads of his Family'.[207] Many legends surrounded a supposed supernatural origin of Plato for centuries after his death.[208] Supernatural abilities were also attributed by a long-standing tradition to Apollonius of Tyana, a Neopythagorean philosopher who lived during the first century CE. The biography written by Philostratus around the 220s, founded the legend of Apollonius being the reincarnation of Proteus and a son of Zeus, and claimed that his birth was heralded by omens.[209] The reference to the Earl of Poitier is in all likelihood from the *Romans of Partenay*, composed in middle English around 1500. The poem's protagonist is adopted by Amery, Earl of Poitiers, and goes on to marry a supernatural woman, Melusine, with whom he has ten sons, each with facial features reflecting

---

202 Madden, *Memoirs*, pp. 9–10.
203 [Villars], *Le comte de Gabalis*.
204 Latimer, 'Alchemies of Satire'; Seeber, 'Sylphs and Other Elemental Beings'.
205 [Villars], *The Count of Gabalis, or, The extravagant mysteries*; [Villars], *The Count de Gabalis: Being a diverting history*.
206 Welburn, *Power and Self-Consciousness*, p. 217 n. 15; Nagel, 'Marriage with Elementals', pp. 28–30 on the English translations and the reference in Pope, and pp. 31–34 for *The Count* and visual arts; Brückmann, 'Pope's Shock and the Count of Gabalis'.
207 Madden, *Memoirs*, p. 10.
208 Novotný, *The Posthumous Life of Plato*, pp. 223–24.
209 Rife, 'Apollonius of Tyana'.

his supernatural heritage.[210] François de Bassompierre (1579–1646) was a French courtier and diplomat who began his career at the court of Henry IV in 1598, and was created Marshal of France in 1621, for services to Louis XIII during the Huguenot rising. In his *Mémoires du Maréchal de Bassompierre contenant l'histoire de sa vie* (Memoirs of the Maréchal de Bassompierre containing the story of his life) published in 1665, he related the legend of three magical objects donated to the Comte d'Angerweiller by a fairy who had fallen in love with him, and which he distributed among his three daughters. One of these daughters married Bassompierre's ancestor.[211] Bassompierre was in England more than once, but the memoirs he wrote regarding his time at court in 1626 were translated into English only at the beginning of the nineteenth century, so one may assume that the author of *Memoirs* had read them in French or knew them via secondary sources. The topic of the editor's extraordinary birth is further developed. It is a theme that allows for an ironic attack on various aspects of astrology, with particular regard to predictions concerning the future, from planetary influences in horoscopes, to the circumstances surrounding childbirth read as signs of the fates to come:

> I was born also under the most fortunate of all Planets and to make my Nativity still more Happy, in one of the *Ember*-Weeks, and with a Cawl, or certain Membrane about my Head; both which as the learned Jesuit *Thyræus*, (an Order I particularly Reverence), observes, in his Tract *de apparitione Spirituum*, are Circumstances, that render such Children more likely than others, to gain the Acquaintance and Familiarity of the *Genii* design'd for their Conduct.[212]

Notions of astrology are mixed with popular superstitions, such as the reference to the caul — a fragment of the amniotic membrane covering the head at the moment of birth — to which numerous European and non-European folk traditions connected the possession of magical gifts.[213] Literary sources on these topics are called into question. The German Jesuit theologian and inquisitor, Petrus Thyraeus (1546–1601) published a number of tracts on demonological subjects. The reference in the text is to *De Apparitionibus Spirituum Disputatio Theologica*, where a chapter is dedicated to 'the times and places where, and persons to which the

---

210 *The Romans of Partenay*, ed. Skeat.

211 See Bassompierre, *Mémoires du Maréchal de Bassompierre*, tome I, p. 6; Garland and Garland, eds, *The Oxford Companion to German Literature*, sub voce 'Bassompierre, François de'; Croker, 'Sketch of the Life of Bassompierre'; on the legend: Gerschel, 'Sur un schème trifonctionnel'.

212 Madden, *Memoirs*, pp. 10–11.

213 Ginzburg, *The Night Battles*, pp. 6–7, 12, 15–16, 60–61; Forbes, 'The Social History of the Caul'.

human spirits, both good and bad, present themselves more often'.[214] The reverence for the Jesuit order will be ironically contradicted just a few pages later, and throughout the novel, in which the Society of Jesus is one of the main polemical targets, allowing *Memoirs* to be read as part of contemporary anti-Jesuit polemics.[215] As already mentioned, between the eighteenth and twentieth centuries, the Jesuit order expanded its economic and political influence on the global stage. The Jesuits are skilful in exploiting the power of the printing press, and with subtle propaganda initiatives they gain influence in the Ottoman world and in Russia.[216] Rather than foreseeing the expulsion of the order from various countries and the dissolution that would in reality befall it in the second half of the century, the novel projects into the future the likely developments of the Society's power as observed in the 1720s. Detailed descriptions of how Jesuits came to obtain their twentieth-century global success may be interpreted as ominous warnings, demonstrating the dire consequences of the failure to impede their rise.[217]

The influence of celestial bodies on human destinies is further invoked through a reference to Ptolemy:

> Nay, I was born under that Aspect of the Heavenly Bodies, which *Ptolemy* in his *4th* Book of his *Quadripartite*, and 13*th* Chapter, assures us, generally confers this inestimable Privilege, having had the Moon, that great *Domina humidorum*, in Conjunction with *Sagittary*, Lady of my Actions, not to mention, lest it should look too like Vanity, some others as favourable, tho' less credible Circumstances.[218]

Ptolemy's *Quadripartite*, written in Greek in the second century CE, has been available in Latin since the twelfth century and it greatly influenced medieval astrology. The treaty argues for the ascendancy of celestial bodies and their movements over human character and destinies; the fourth book is dedicated to the effects of planets on the life of individuals — for example on material fortune, marriage and children, friends and enemies, travels. In the thirteenth chapter of the third book, 'Of the Quality of the Soul', it is explained that new-borns 'are afflicted by demons and have water

---

214 Thyraeus, *A Theological Discussion of the Appearances of Spirits*, n.p. but p. 84, 'De temporibus locis, atque personis, quibus humani spiritus tam boni, quam mali, plerunque se exhibent'. On Thyraeus in England: Harley, 'Explaining Salem', p. 320 n. 62.

215 Worcester, 'Anti-Jesuit Polemic'; Pavone, 'Anti-Jesuitism in a Global Perspective'.

216 On the Ottoman empire: Madden, *Memoirs*, pp. 1–27 (page numbers after the preface), 183–214, 308–38, 473–504; On Russia: 52–73, 153–82, 338–65, see also *infra*, ch. 11.

217 Madden, *Memoirs*, p. 10 (after the preface), on the Jesuits' success in the Ottoman empire: '[…] had *Great Britain* continued her Care and Protection of the *Grecian* Church, with her true *Christian* Zeal, possibly we should have made as large an Harvest of Converts in *Turky* as by our Supineness and Negligence the Jesuits have done'.

218 Madden, *Memoirs*, p. 11.

on the brain when the maleficent planets are in this position and control the moon in phase, Saturn when she is at conjunction, Mars when she is full, and particularly in Sagittarius and Pisces'.[219] The earliest English translation recorded, based on the Latin version, was published in 1701.[220] *Domina humidorum*, literally 'mistress of liquids' or 'governess of moist bodies', refers to the Moon's influence over liquids and wet bodies.

To those who might suggest that this knowledge was procured by means of the occult, the narrator counters with another tongue-in-cheek denial: anyone who really believes he commands such powers would certainly be too afraid of those very same powers to accuse him. In any case — making the umpteenth, sardonic, about-turn — he cannot deny that he has indeed applied himself to various magical disciplines. He admits he has acquired a certain degree of familiarity with the more well-known arts of divination, as well as with the more obscure ones, such as 'the Gastromantia or divining by the Belly, the Hippomantia by Horses, and especially Hunters, Race and Coach-Horses; [...] not to mention the Copromantia, as the Greeks call it, or in plain English, the Art of divining from the Dung of Creatures [...]'.[221]

---

219 Ptolemy, *Tetrabiblos*, fol. 365ʳ.
220 Ptolemy, *Ptolemy's Quadripartite*; See also Jones, 'Ptolemy'.
221 Madden, *Memoirs*, pp. 245–46.

VI. A 'Good Genius' and the 'Scene of Things Below'

A crucial element in the narrative frame of *Memoirs* consists in the fact that the narrator receives a bundle of handwritten diplomatic letters from the 1990s. What makes this object travel through time is a supernatural entity, an angelic apparition whom he also calls his 'good genius'. In the first preface, the narrator recounts this encounter.

> I was surpriz'd to see my Door which was fast lock'd, and my Curtains which were close drawn, opening suddenly of themselves, and a great Light filling my Chamber, in the midst of which I saw a beautiful Appearance of something like what we usually imagine Angels to be.
> I began to fancy my self in the famous *Van Helmont's* Condition, who says, he once plainly saw his Soul in an human Shape, but, as he modestly speaks, without distinction of Sex; or like that *Pisander*, who, as a certain *Greek* Author tells us, was afraid of meeting his own Soul, which he apprehended would appear to him separated from his Body, and play him a scurvy Trick.[222]

Once again, the narrator argues for the (antiphrastic) verifiability of the episode he describes by drawing a comparison between his own experience and learned sources, chosen from early European modernity and Greco-Latin antiquity. In his *Ortus Medicinae*, the Flemish philosopher, physician, and alchemist Jan Baptist van Helmont (1579/80–1644) contended that in a 'somnium intellectuale' ('intellectual Dream') 'vidi enim animan meam satis exiguam, specie humana, sexum tam discrimine libera', he had seen his soul 'small enough, in a human shape, yet free from the distinction of the Sex'.[223] The politician turned oligarch Pisander was ridiculed by Aristophanes in *Lysistrata* for his cowardice. In *Birds* he pays a visit to the necromancer Socrates, who conjures spirits, asking

---

222 Madden, *Memoirs*, pp. 18–19.

223 van Helmont, *Ortus Medicinae*, 'Confessio Authoris', pp. 13–16, quotes at p. 13. The reference in the text is possibly from the English edition van Helmont, *Van Helmont's Workes*, here see ch. 1 — 'The Author's Confession', pp. 8–11, quotes at p. 9 (the *Ortus* was first translated in 1662 as *Oriatrike or Physick Refined*). On van Helmont's philosophy, his conception of the soul, and the role of dream and vision in his epistemology: Hedesan, '"Christian Philosophy"'.

to see his soul which had deserted him while still alive.[224] The narrator compares the episode with the one described by the German Jesuit and scientist Gaspar Schott (1608–1666) in his *Physica Curiosa*, which is an encyclopaedic treatise on natural and supernatural knowledge notably including the 'Somnium Athanasii Kircheri'.[225] In the virtual encyclopaedia that the author assembles with references to everything that codifies contemporary credulity in the fantastic and marvellous, Schott's compilation — a conspectus of exotic, rare, supernatural, and curious beings and events — could not be left out (Figure 6). Schott studied at Würzburg under the tutorship of Athanasius Kircher (1602–1680). He edited a number of books by Kircher, including the 1660 edition of his *Iter extaticum*.[226] As elsewhere in the text, the layering of references creates a complex interplay. In this case, treatises from the 1500s and 1600s, which reveal the real author's opinion by way of ironic reversal, are accompanied by a reference to Aristophanes, which, as in the case of a previous reference to Horace to be found a few pages above, contributes to the construction of a gallery of the most famous prophets of antiquity, but significantly through the lens of coeval comedy and satire.

The narrator takes centre stage again in the second preface, about half-way through the book, using antiphrasis to direct a barrage of criticism against some of the more fashionable beliefs and opinions of the day. He sets out a whole series of arguments in favour of the credibility of his story and the existence of the seraphic entity from whom he claims to have received the manuscripts, with a massive deployment of erudite references. In unabashed imitation of the typical tools of historical-erudite treatises, he reels off a long list of ancient *auctoritates*, with examples showing how a belief in guardian angels, tutelar spirits, and geniuses is common to all peoples of the world and all the ages. The proposition is also supported by naming a multitude of modern authors, and by directly quoting the opinion of the infallible Catholic Church on the matter. In fact, the Pope is doubtless assisted in his high duties not just by a simple guardian angel but by at least a couple of archangels: '[…] I cannot but think', mocks the narrator, that 'these tutelar Angels, of his Holiness, must be wearied out of their very lives by such a vast variety of business, and

---

224 Aristophanes, *Birds*, pp. 224–27.

225 Schott, P. *Gasparis Schotti* […] *Physica curiosa*, liber III — 'Mirabilibus Huminum', caput XXV — 'De mira somniantibus', p. 524, 'Somnium Athanasii Kircheri'. The liber XXX referenced in a footnote of *Memoirs* does not exist in *Physica Curiosa*, which is divided into twelve books, this is most likely a practical mistake.

226 Kircher, R.P. *Athanasii Kircheri e Societate Jesu Iter extaticum cœleste*. On *Physica Curiosa* see Findlen, 'Jokes of Nature and Jokes of Knowledge'; on Schott's role in spurring the *Iter extaticum*'s composition and publication: Rowland, 'Athanasius Kircher's Guardian Angel', esp. pp. 253–54.

Figure 6. Schott, *Physica curiosa*, plate following page 762. Illustration of an episode in which marvels and natural wonders heralded remarkable future events. In 1661, a comet transiting between the constellations of the dolphin and the eagle announced a wave of bad weather. Copy at Smithsonian Libraries. Not in copyright, no known restriction for scholarly use.

multiplicity of Intrigues, Designs, and Interests, as they must have daily on their hands [...]'.[227]

The theme of guardian angels, which had a broad background in Protestant polemics against pre-Reformation religious forms,[228] like the veneration of relics and astrological predictions, prompted the collection of a number of sources and the questioning of their credibility. This encyclopaedia, to be read antiphrastically, places side by side traditions and authors towards whom the narrator professes his sarcastic confidence and admiration. An intellectual world of fantastic notions is thus outlined, whose credibility is called into question. The review starts with ancient authors. The concept of *daimon* in Greek thought and mythology was similar to that of a tutelary deity, a guiding spirit, or a supernatural manifestation and bearer of unexpected events in human life, depending on the author and the period. Hesiod (*c.* 700 BCE) introduced its use as the spirit of a deceased person from the Golden Age acting as the personal protector of a living individual. A specific passage from *Works and Days* (line 252) quoted by the narrator refers to the existence of immortal guardians watching, unseen, over mortals, and who 'take notice of all those who grind one another down with crooked judgments and have no care for the gods' retribution'. The narrator likens this idea to the Christian concept of a guardian angel.[229] He then includes in his review Pythagoras, Plato, and a number of Platonic and Neoplatonic authors.[230] The reference to the famous case of Socrates' *daemonium* — spirit guide or inner voice — stands out, about which *Memoirs* recapitulates the historiographic stratifications from Plato to Apuleius.[231] Socrates' *daimonion*, literally 'divine thing', translated also as 'inner voice' or 'genius', has been discussed by a number of ancient authors — listed in the text — as well as by later philosophers.

Non-Christian religious traditions, such as Islam and Judaism, are referred to and possibly known through secondary sources, universalist and comparative compilations, such as the famous *Religious Ceremonies* illustrated by Jean-Frédéric Bernard and Bernard Picart.[232] Written and lavishly illustrated by two French Protestants who had sought refuge in Amsterdam, and initially published in French, *Religious Ceremonies* was

---

227 Madden, *Memoirs*, p. 228.
228 Marshall, 'The Guardian Angel in Protestant England'.
229 Madden, *Memoirs*, p. 220; Hesiod, *Works and Days*, pp. 106–09; Wilford, 'ΔΑΙΜΩΝ in Homer'.
230 Madden, *Memoirs*, pp. 220–21; for an overview of the concept of *daimon* in Plato, in Middle and New Platonism, and in Stoicism, a good entry point is Versnel, 'Daimon'; see also Balaudé, 'Daimôn'.
231 Madden, *Memoirs*, pp. 222–24.
232 *Cérémonies et coutumes religieuses*; Eng. trans. *The Religious Ceremonies and Customs* (1731), and *The Ceremonies and Religious Customs* (1733–1739).

destined to be a great success in Europe and to have a profound influence on the debate on religious tolerance.[233] It constitutes one of the most recent bibliographical references cited in the pages of *Memoirs*.[234] Lists of angelic beings mentioned in biblical texts and rabbinic traditions similar to the one that appears in the prefaces are to be found in Giulio Bartolocci's *Bibliotheca magna rabbinica* (Great rabbinical library) and Gabriel Naudé's *The History of Magick*.[235]

The spurious *Heptameron* attributed to Peter of Abano,[236] and the treatises on natural magic by Cornelius Agrippa and John Dee, outline the early modern world of kabbalistic and Neoplatonic magical practices that crossed over into the religious, in heterodox Catholic and Protestant circles alike.[237] Regarding a polymath such as Girolamo Cardano, rather than aspects of mathematical or physical research, *De propria vita* (The book of my life) and *De rerum varietate* (On the variety of things) are mentioned, concerning the existence of tutelary spirits.[238] A reference to the nature of the dolphin dealt with in *De subtilitate rerum* (On the subtlety of things) is made within the discussion of a papal bull in the twentieth century authorising Catholics to consume wild fowl during Lent.[239] A topic apparently far from the main thematic focus of the novel, the problem of fasting imposed on the most fragile sectors of the population and the spiritual significance conferred on food is fully in keeping with the anti-Catholic spirit of the work, and rests on a broad tradition of Protestant controversialism. Criticism of the Catholic custom of abstaining from meat but eating fish during Lent had been recurring in Protestant circles since the reign of Elizabeth I.[240]

---

233 Hunt, Jacob, and Mijnhardt, eds, *The Book That Changed Europe*; Tarantino, 'From Labelling and Ridicule to Understanding'.

234 Madden, *Memoirs*, p. 217 n.

235 Madden, *Memoirs*, pp. 221–22; Bartolocci, *Bibliotheca magna rabbinica*, I, p. 213; Naudé, *The History of Magick*, p. 27; on Naudé see also Madden, *Memoirs*, p. 250. See also Reed, *Demons, Angels, and Writing* on the flourishing interests in angels and demons in ancient Jewish literature; for reference on single angels: Davidson, *A Dictionary of Angels*.

236 The *Heptameron, seu Elementa Magica* is a treatise on angelic magic, whose attribution to the natural philosopher, physician, astronomer, and astrologer Peter of Abano (c. 1250–1316) is considered spurious by modern sources; see for example Ventura, 'Pietro d'Abano'. The treatise is published in some editions of Cornelius Agrippa's *De occulta philosophia*, such as the one mentioned in Madden, *Memoirs*, p. 219.

237 Marshall and Walsham, eds, *Angels in the Early Modern World*.

238 Madden, *Memoirs*, p. 231; Cardano, *De propria vita liber*; Cardano, *De rerum varietate*, liber XVI, caput XCIII, pp. 629–30.

239 Madden, *Memoirs*, p. 407; Scaliger, *Iulii Cæsaris Scaligeri Exotericarum Exercitationum lib. XV*, 'Exercitatio CCXXIV. Quae Animalia cicurentur', pp. 704–06, see '2. An solus inter pisces spiret Delphin', p. 706.

240 Barnett, 'Reforming Food and Eating in Protestant England'.

As in other passages essential to the construction of the novel's cultural programme, many among the preferred polemical targets are internal to Christianity, and especially to a Catholicism accused of lapsing into superstition and absurdity. Here, too, the focus is placed — not exclusively, but with particular acrimony — on authors belonging to the Jesuit order. After a reference to Kircher's *Iter extaticum*, attention is turned to a successful devotional work written by the Jesuit theologian Francesco Albertini in the early seventeenth century.[241] Quoted in the timely Latin translation, which came out immediately after the vernacular version in Italian, the *Libellus de angelo custode* was composed after Albertini had founded a confraternity dedicated to guardian angels in Naples in 1611. Of several treatises that dealt with the subject after the Council of Trent, Albertini's was the first significant example written by a Jesuit, and is representative of the guardian-angel devotion as a consistent feature of Jesuit proselytism in the Counter-Reformation era.[242] The *Thaumaturgus Physicus* by Gaspar Schott, whose *Physica curiosa* the narrator has already recalled, is now targeted, the fourth part of which is dedicated to Saint Francis Xavier, to whom Schott prayed to watch over his intellectual labours.[243] Undoubtedly this tutelary spirit must exist, the narrator comments sardonically, because a Jesuit would never have dedicated a work to a non-existent creature, from whom he could not draw favours and benefits.

Should all these bookish arguments not suffice, mere reason suggests that the narrator would have no interest in pretending that his good Genius exists, since a much greater celebrity would await him if he had been able to predict everything described in the letters all by himself, based only on his knowledge and wisdom.[244] A second, perhaps more relevant, objection that the narrator anticipates regards the very possibility of predicting the future, even by a superior being. Again, the demonstration starts with a review of ancient and modern sources on prophecies and oracles from all the latitudes of the globe, and then proceeds to appeal to Roman Catholic authority. Since the Jesuits hold that 'evil Dæmons can foresee and foretell many things', it must be even more true that good spirits and angels possess the same ability. 'Nor indeed do they only foresee the rise and fall of Empires, and who will be the instruments therein; but also what the Means, Manner and Time will be, and the Causes and Consequences, and

---

241 Madden, *Memoirs*, p. 225; Albertini, *Libellus de angelo custode*; this is the Latin version of *Trattato dell'angelo custode*, of which there was also another Italian edition, printed in Naples in the same year; Caravale, *Forbidden Prayer*, pp. 234, 236–37; Pirri, 'Albertini, Francesco Maria'.

242 Johnson, 'Guardian Angels and the Society of Jesus', pp. 197–200, 208.

243 Madden, *Memoirs*, p. 226; Schott, *P. Gasparis Schotti* [...] *Thaumaturgus Physicus*, pp. 2–3.

244 'Would it not be much more to my honour, to foretell all these things (which will certainly in due time will be verified) by the force of my own Learnings and Wisdom, and a happy Foresight into future events?', Madden, *Memoirs*, p. 234.

even the minuter Effects that accompany them'.[245] Not bound by the limits of physical existence, these superior beings must be able to see ahead into the future, just as a person in a high-up place can see farther afield. Time lies, reified, before them, just as the material fabric of the world lies before a scientist ('physician'), or like the celestial bodies before the astrologer, who is able to observe their immense revolutions, and 'the wide train of consequences produced by them, in the vast rotation of Events, in this Scene of things below'.[246]

The narrator does not shy away from the problems that the predictability of the future entails in logical terms. In ancient philosophy, debates about the truth or falsity of future contingents — that is, predictions of actions, states, or events which are not impossible nor inevitable — dated back to Aristotle's *On Interpretation* and were complicated by arguments in favour of logical determinism on one side, and ideas of an open future on the other side. In the Christian tradition of the Middle-Ages, the problems of logic posed to theology by divine foreknowledge (that is, knowledge of future choices) and free will (and thus the moral accountability of men and women) were very close, from a formal point of view, to those regarding future contingents.[247] Our narrator swiftly resolves the centuries-old debate around future contingents by affirming that the truth of contingent statements about the future has been determined by he himself.[248] The passage reveals how the real author had contemplated the logical problems implied by the existence of a 'chronicle of the future', while opting for a solution that is obviously ironic in its pretentious hastiness, which is consistent with the satirical tone of the narrative frame. What is the ontological status of a future that can be accurately predicted? And what is that of foretelling? Elsewhere, the possible consequences of publication are in fact discussed in terms of the influence on the future that *Memoirs* foretells: in order to preserve the accuracy of their previsions, the letters are partly censored, lest the knowledge of the causal processes to come be used by someone to change the course of events to their own advantage or to the detriment of the state.[249]

Of course, the use of elements of the supernatural and superstitions in the narrative frame by no means implies that the real author is endorsing them: on the contrary, the demonstrations and lists of *exempla* and *loci* all bear the marks of an unreliable narrator, whose opinion often reveals the author's own by means of ironic reversal.[250] In short, *Memoirs* depicts

245 Madden, *Memoirs*, p. 242.
246 Madden, *Memoirs*, p. 244.
247 Øhrstrøm and Hasle, 'Future Contingents'.
248 Madden, *Memoirs*, p. 5.
249 Madden, *Memoirs*, p. 22; see also *infra*, ch. 9.
250 On this point, our interpretation differs from Chuanacháin, 'Utopianism', p. 244 n. 14.

a system of knowledge in which scientific disciplines coexist side by side with the occult and magical beliefs. Angelic beings, techniques of divination, forms of prophesying, and eschatology are mentioned in order to be made fun of, and in so doing, the author testifies to their persisting popularity in his own times.

VII. Empirical Science, Global Consciousness, and 'the History of Future Times'

The flash-forwarding projections in *Memoirs* are closely connected to the acceleration that geographical explorations and scientific discoveries have imposed upon history, and the dramatic changes they have brought about in the understanding of the world. In the above-mentioned second preface, where the narrator claims that the letters were given to him by a supernatural being, the credibility of the episode is argued also on logical grounds. The narrator would have had much more to gain from being not merely the publisher but the original inventor and author of the manuscript contents, 'of this new and unexampled way of writing the History of future Times'.[251]

When looking at the number and scope of all of the inventions in arts and sciences, and of all the factual scenarios described in the six volumes announced,[252] it is highly unlikely that he could have made everything up on his own:

> And indeed it would have requir'd such an unusual Fund of Imagination, to have struck out so many vast Inventions in all Arts and Sciences, and such infinite Scenes of Events, as are contain'd in the six Volumes I propose to present the world with; that I am sure this will serve as the fullest proof, (and a very modest and humble one) that I must have receiv'd them from the hand of a superior Being, since my talent that way, is so very confin'd.[253]

The implausibility of what the letters contain is the precise reason for their credibility, since — resumes the narrator in his third and conclusive preface — literary inventions would have required an Aristotelian elaboration of their verisimilitude: 'If they were mere fables invented to deceive, they would have been model'd [...] to the least disputed realities, and would have put on the dress of probability at least, in order to impose

---

251 Madden, *Memoirs*, p. 235.
252 Madden, *Memoirs*, title page and pp. 507, 509; references to the six volumes to be printed are to be interpreted ironically, with Alkon, *Origins*, p. 94, not to be taken seriously, with Bowyer in Nichols, *Literary Anecdotes of the Eighteenth*, II, pp. 31–32 n.
253 Madden, *Memoirs*, p. 237.

on the credulity of mankind'.[254] As Alkon duly noted,[255] the credibility of
what today would be defined as counter-intuitive is a product of that very
acceleration of history caused by new scientific notions regarding aspects
of reality hitherto unknown, and by that critical mass of new knowledge
about remote parts of the globe and their histories which explorers and
travellers have brought back to the 'Old World'.[256] Empirical science has
got people used to apparently incredible new truths, and has debunked
many old notions:

> [...] whoever are knowing and learning enough, to be acquainted with
> the infinite incredible verities in the World of science, the vast numbers
> of improbable and unimaginable truths, to be met with there, and
> the heaps of plausible errors and delusive falsehoods, that men are so
> usually led away with; will never consider the improbability of some
> relations in this work, as an argument for any thing, but their being
> more unfeign'd and genuinely true.[257]

From an historical perspective, the pace of scientific discovery accelerated
even during the author's lifetime, calling for a deep revision of epistemology. A few years had passed since astronomy was developed as a consistent and verifiable system, proven by practical demonstrations, and since
philosophy had finally started to be based on 'actual experiments, not
imaginary notions and opinions'.[258] Future discoveries accounted for in
the letters include the observation of the Moon through a telescope and
the unearthing on its surface not only of valleys, hills, rivers, and forests,
but also of cities, akin to terrestrial ones. The other planets are likely to
be 'not only habitable, but inhabited',[259] transposing on an interplanetary
scale that broadening of geographical knowledge that characterised the
European mind on Earth during the modern era. Though still to be
explored, the other planets are conceptualised as the 'new New World':
the inhabitants of the Moon '[...] must in many things resemble us pretty
nearly, and in all likelihood be not much more different from us, than
many Nations of the Indians, which the Ancients had discovered in *America*'.[260] The probability of the existence of civilisations on other planets,
such as Jupiter, is argued by the British ambassador in dialogue with the

---

254 Madden, *Memoirs*, p. 506.
255 Alkon, *Origins*, pp. 105–06.
256 Shapin, *A Social History of Truth*.
257 Madden, *Memoirs*, pp. 507–08.
258 Madden, *Memoirs*, p. 513. That these opinions expressed by the narrator are shared by
     the real author is made clear by their being taken up again in some letters by the British
     diplomats writing from Moscow and London, e.g. pp. 145–46, 344.
259 Madden, *Memoirs*, p. 136.
260 Madden, *Memoirs*, p. 319. On the telescope see also Kukkonen, *A Prehistory of Cognitive
     Poetics*, pp. 128–29.

Turkish Grand Seignior, also on the basis of religious arguments: it would be 'absurd to suppose that an infinite Creator would have such glorious parts of his Creation void and empty of proper classes of his creatures'.[261]

A critical increase in momentum has conflated together techno-scientific inventions and explorations, innovations in technology and military power, the rise of the printing press and of knowledge:[262] 'few years are past […] since the compass and the needle trace'd out the mariner's unerring road on the ocean, and war join'd fire to the sword, or muskets banish'd bows and arrows; since the invention of printing gave new lights and aids to the arts […]'.[263] This role of technology in propelling European expansion across the globe might be consistently read as an early example of speculative fiction as an expression of techno-scientific empires, through the theoretical framework suggested by Istvan Csicsery-Ronay's reflections on later science fiction and on a subsequent, mature phase of European imperialism (that is, the nineteenth and twentieth centuries).[264]

History, the unfolding of events in time, with its causal chains and unforeseeable accidents, and the variety of these accidents that an increased familiarity with the globe has shown, invalidate any objection to the veracity of this account of the future based on the unlikelihood of its contents:

> there is nothing foretold here, which will really seem so very improbable, to those who know the infinite power of the great Source of all events below; who have consider'd the vast operations of nature, the force of our minds when set on work by ambition and emulation, and the strange changes and chances, the revolutions, alterations and improvements, which attend all things here; as well as the vast fields of art and knowledge, which the new world hath brought forth among us, by the labours of different voyagers.[265]

References to the knowledge brought back by travellers is twice echoed at a structural level in the text: both in the choice of presenting it as a collection of diplomatic correspondences, being the form best suited to illustrate the history and geopolitics of the twentieth century, and in the comparative approach of the prefaces, which imitates the writing of

---

261 Madden, *Memoirs*, p. 332.
262 On the critical role of the printing press, see Madden, *Memoirs*, within the Ottoman Empire, pp. 6–9 (page numbers after the preface); at Oxford, 147; in Russia, 174; in France, 296. On the use of the press by the Dublin Society as a fundamental tool to spread useful knowledge, see Madden, *Reflections and Resolutions*, p. 170.
263 Madden, *Memoirs*, p. 512.
264 Csicsery-Ronay, 'Science Fiction and Empire'. On technological development as the precondition and driving force of imperialistic expansion and hierarchisation of human societies, see also Michael Adas, *Machines as the Measure of Men*; Headrick, *Power over People*.
265 Madden, *Memoirs*, p. 508.

a *historia* validated by ancient *auctoritates* as well as by the new evidence provided by travellers, with which to formulate and support new systematisations.

At a further level, travel accounts and correspondences are cited directly or used implicitly as a source of information on the customs and religions of societies around the globe. Anecdotes and details of everyday life in Constantinople are inspired by the correspondence of Busbequius, that is Augier Ghislain de Busbecq (1522–1592), a Flemish writer who served as Austrian ambassador to the Ottoman Empire. His *Itinera Constantinopolitanum et Amasianum* or *Legationis Turcicae epistolae quattor* (known in English as *The Turkish Letters*) were published in a number of Latin editions from the 1580s onwards and subsequently translated into many European languages, including English (1694) and French (1649, 1718, 1748).[266] In the letters there are several episodes concerning the Turkish fondness for birds, the use of keeping birds as pets, and the affection and loyalty that these creatures are sometimes able to show towards their masters, recalled by the British Ambassador to Constantinople. Emulating Busbecq's discovery and transcription of *Res Gestae Divi Augusti* (*The Deeds of the Divine Augustus*),[267] the British ambassador in the twentieth century unearths some lost Latin classics, restored to the commonwealth of learning thanks to Arabic manuscripts: Cicero's *De gloria* (*On Glory*), part of *De vita beata* (*On the Happy Life*), and Pompeius Trogus's history of the world.[268]

Among the proto-ethnographic writings known and used by the author, one of the most interesting cases is that of Johannes Scheffer's *History of Lapland*, which inspired the extensive treatment of a magical ritual performed by the Sami people ('Laplanders') to control the weather in one of the letters of the ambassador to Moscow.[269] Scheffer's *History* is a translation of his *Lapponia*, originally written in Latin and printed in Frankfurt am Main in 1673. The abridged English edition with a preface addressed to British readers enjoyed wide success thanks to the patronage of the Royal Society and Oxford University. Through this text, Sami cultural practices entered the discourse on the 'savage' in eighteenth-century British culture.[270] The treatise devoted ample space to religious and ritual aspects, with descriptions of magical ceremonies and sacrifices, including the use of the ritual drum (also the subject of a series of illustrations),[271] which *Memoirs* also discusses at length. The 'very strange things' that Lap-

266 Forster, *The Life and Letters of Ogier Ghiselin de Busbecq*, see I, p. 58, and II, pp. 284–91.
267 Güven, 'Displaying the Res Gestae of Augustus'.
268 Madden, *Memoirs*, pp. 205–06.
269 Madden, *Memoirs*, pp. 57–74; Scheffer, *The History of Lapland*.
270 Andersson Burnett, 'Translating Swedish Colonialism'.
271 Scheffer, *The History of Lapland*, pp. 48, 50–52.

landers believed they could achieve 'by the drum'[272] and by charms listed in the treatise included divination practices and the possibility of knowing the state of affairs in distant places. Other magical practices mentioned and discussed by Scheffer were aimed at controlling the winds and the sea.[273]

The English edition omitted the translation of extensive Swedish quotations, and the translator's preface portrayed Lapland as a realm of 'barbarity and darkness', where a new world has been discovered, rather than in America, 'and those extravagant falsehoods, which have commonly past in the narratives of these Northern Countries, are not so inexcusable for their being lies, as that they were told without temtation [*sic*]; the real truth being equally entertaining, and incredible'.[274] Through the Lapp ritual to entice sunny weather, *Memoirs* testifies to a contemporary fascination with Siberian shamanic culture especially related to mystical and magical aspects. A few years earlier, a biography of the well-known London-based soothsayer Duncan Campbell had, for example, boasted about his Lappish birth as a credential for his 'second sight', the ability to predict the future.[275] The Lapp case bears witness to a world of magic and superstition located on the fringes of European space. The British ambassador testifies to the effectiveness of the practice, emphasising the reliability of his own first-hand verification of the facts, where ambassadors normally represent more disenchanted and enlightened voices than the narrator. The case is significantly compared to one described by the Dominican theologian and author of influential accounts of witchcraft Johannes Nider (1380–1438) in his *Formicarius* (The anthill), which, printed in several editions between 1475 and 1692, was one of the first treatises on witchcraft ever written.[276] In contrast to the magic ritual witnessed in Russia, the possibility of accurately predicting the weather in twentieth-century Oxford rests on scientific, systematic study, with dedicated chairs at the university.[277] The ironic listing of the benefits that the Laplanders technique would bring to England also invites the reader to take a distanced perspective: 'How many fretfull uneasy Husbands and Wives, melancholy Lovers, and sullen Beauties, not to speak a Word of our gloomy Sectaries and sour Catholicks, discontented Courtiers that lose Places, and zealous Patriots that want them, would he recover to plain Sense and good Humour, by this lovely Cordial'.[278]

---

272 Scheffer, *The History of Lapland*, p. 54.
273 Scheffer, *The History of Lapland*, p. 58.
274 Scheffer, *The History of Lapland*, 'The Preface', n.p.
275 *The History of the Life and Adventures of Mr Duncan Campbell*, see also *supra*, ch. 2.
276 Madden, *Memoirs*, p. 72; Nider, *Formicarium*. Notably the *Formicarius* was an important source for the *Malleus maleficarum*, compiled by the Dominican inquisitor Heinrich Kramer and published in 1487; Bailey, *Battling Demons*.
277 Madden, *Memoirs*, pp. 143–45, see also *infra*, ch. 12.
278 Madden, *Memoirs*, pp. 69–70.

Other explicit references to travel literature include, to mention but a few examples, Joseph Addison's travels in Italy,[279] Joseph Pitton de Tournefort in the Levant,[280] William Camden's *Britannia*,[281] as well as major travel collections and comparative compilations such as the already mentioned *Religious Ceremonies*. The notes to the text in this volume identify several other accounts and histories, even if not openly mentioned, as likely sources of inspiration for specific passages.

The future takes shape as a direct consequence of how the past is viewed, deriving from the projection into the time to come of mechanisms observed in the study of history:

> Let such ignorant objectors therefore, that are buried in the present state of the earth, and think it will continue in a manner unimprov'd and unalter'd, let them, I say, look back, if they know any thing of it in former ages. Let them consider how absurd and incredible it would have appear'd, if a man, for example, at the building of *Rome* had (thus enlighten'd) foretold the vast growth of that Monarchy, the overturning all others by that embryo state, the majesty of the pagan religion there, the birth and rise of the Christian, the breaking of the Roman Empire into several little scraps and pieces, which are now miscall'd Kingdoms; the spreading conquests of the Pope and his Monks [...] Let them reflect, I say, if such a relation (or prediction) would not be receiv'd as more ridiculous and impossible, than those that are mention'd in these six volumes.[282]

What is the history of the world if not a constant scene of the most incredible and surprising changes? Along with the cataclysms that natural philosophy has brought to light, the upheavals that have characterised the prosperity and decadence of entire civilisations is today known: Greece, 'the seat of freedom and knowledge, philosophers and patriots, become a nest of slaves and ignorants',[283] 'the mighty *Rome*', 'once the chief nurse of the opposite virtues among men' has today become 'the mother of superstition, cowardice and cruelty'.[284] The transience of civilisations echoes on a macroscopic scale the mortality of the individual and of families and lineages on which the ambassadors dwell at various times.[285] Portraits of notable people now disappeared function in the letters as a *memento mori*, warnings against *vanitas*. These portraits are emblems intended to

---

279 Madden, *Memoirs*, p. 179; Addison, *Remarks on Several Parts of Italy*.
280 Madden, *Memoirs*, p. 511; Tournefort, *A Voyage into the Levant*.
281 Madden, *Memoirs*, p. 520; Camden, *Camden's Britannia*.
282 Madden, *Memoirs*, pp. 508–09.
283 Madden, *Memoirs*, pp. 510–11.
284 Madden, *Memoirs*, p. 511.
285 Madden, *Memoirs*, pp. 4 (after preface), 277–81, 304–05, 336–37, 364–65, 384–85.

stimulate contemplation of the mortality of things and the passing of time, following a fortunate trope in early modern literature and figurative arts, where in pictorial and sculptural compositions skulls and instruments for measuring time such as timepieces or hourglasses remind the viewer of the caducity of things and the ephemeral nature of human existence.[286]

Both in the letters and in the prefaces there are references to Greco-Latin historiography, including Livy,[287] Herodotus,[288] Pliny the Elder's *Natural History*,[289] Pliny the Younger's *Letters*,[290] Tacitus,[291] and Varro.[292] From the classical sources are taken episodes that the writer uses as terms of comparison to describe and explain future events, in other words that the real author uses as references or models for his narrative inventions. Underlying these discursive strategies is a concept of history as being potentially recursive and therefore of the didactic value of historiography. The futuristic projection, the extrapolation — logical and imaginative — of a distant state of affairs derived from the present is inspired not least by the analysis of the causal mechanisms that can be observed in the past, in what has already happened. Greco-Roman antiquity is also part of the ideological and rhetorical strategies used to represent British power in the islands and overseas.[293] Ancient history provides a repository of useful models for conceptualising and understanding cultural difference, for articulating an imperial discourse on its entanglements with ideas of monarchical power, colonial expansion, and civilisation, and not least, for anticipating developments to come. However, the relationship between narrative invention and ancient historiography is not univocal, it is not limited to comparisons between past and future, or to the use of a trope of *translatio imperii*. References to natural prodigies included by historians in their chronicles are cited with irony and resonate with the credulity of contemporaries. So, for example, if the Jesuits were to provide France with a rain of flesh such as that which Livy reports as having happened in 461 BCE in Rome, they would offer a remedy for the misery and hunger of the French people.[294]

---

286 Biedermann, *Dictionary of Symbolism, sub vocibus* 'death', 'hourglass'; De Girolami Cheney, 'The Symbolism of the Skull in *Vanitas*'.

287 Madden, *Memoirs*, pp. 85, 301, but see *infra*, in this chapter, for a discussion of the first reference.

288 Madden, *Memoirs*, pp. 79 (*The Persian Wars*); 240, 246 (*Histories*).

289 Madden, *Memoirs*, pp. 87, 240, 510.

290 Madden, *Memoirs*, pp. 278–79.

291 Madden, *Memoirs*, pp. 88 (*De Germania*); 129, 444, 527 (*Annals*).

292 Madden, *Memoirs*, p. 87.

293 Bradley, ed., *Classics and Imperialism in the British Empire*, here esp. Vlassopoulos, 'Imperial Encounters'.

294 Madden, *Memoirs*, p. 85; Livy, *History of Rome*, vol. II, book IV, pp. 34–35.

Memoirs reflects recursively on the rise and fall of past empires, looking both at the history known to the author, such as that of Rome and the commonwealths of Sparta and Carthage, and to the future past of the fiction, such as that of the Ottoman Empire, the Vatican, and the Tsar of Russia. The notion and the word 'empire' are used to refer to these historical-political entities. The concept of a 'British Empire' is not an ideological tool exploited by the author to describe British overseas dominions and transatlantic ties. This should come as no surprise from an author who is not especially concerned with political theory, and who is writing at a time (the late 1720s) when, as David Armitage has shown, the idea that the 'Three Kingdoms of Britain and Ireland and the English-speaking islands, colonies, plantations and territories of the western hemisphere were all members — albeit, unequal members — of a single political body known as the "British Empire"' was just being codified and was not yet common currency in British political debate.[295]

It is rather the idea of a British commonwealth that is being directly compared to past and present commonwealths and empires (of the future), to lay bare the distinctive nature of British power — international and principally commercial and maritime — and the British monarchy, which is limited in its authority. For example, when describing some commendable reforms carried out in the Ottoman Empire, regarding schools, the administration and hygiene of urban centres, and regulations as regards the production of wine, the British ambassador in Constantinople also criticises the harsh punishments envisaged for transgressors. Reflecting on the fate of absolute power in history, he goes on to comment:

> though it must be owned that there are some advantages in this absolute Monarchy, which ours, as a limited one, is deprived of; yet they are so trivial and inconsiderable, in comparison of the miseries that accompany it, that they deserve not to be mentioned. [...] no just and generous Man, would rather chuse to govern an Empire of Slaves, as this is, than a Nation of Subjects, as ours, merely upon the principle of ease and safety to himself, and security to his Family.[296]

Exploiting stereotypes of Ottoman power as tyrannical and despotic,[297] the ambassador further notes: 'Whoever looks into the History of this Empire, will be convinced by numberless instances of these truths, and will find in *them*, arguments sufficient to convince the most absolute Princes, that they would be happier in a more limited Government, and make them not only privately debate, like *Augustus*, how to moderate their tyranny, but

---

295 Armitage, *The Ideological Origins of the British Empire*, p. 8.
296 Madden, *Memoirs*, pp. 197–98.
297 Rolando Minuti, 'Oriental Despotism'; Minuti, *Orientalismo e idee di tolleranza*, pp. 1–7.

publickly set on foot so noble and generous a design'.[298] The loyalty of the Ottoman subjects is explained in part by forms of control put in place by the authority, and in part by the love for one's country inspired in everyone by 'domestick ties and relations, and by customs and languages'.[299]

How can the British Empire avoid what seems to be the fate of all great empires, namely to decline?[300] How can its fall be prevented? The search for lessons from the past, which will recur in later historians and political thinkers in the Victorian age,[301] and the delineation of a predetermined trajectory of rise, decline, and fall, appear to be ultimately counterbalanced in Madden's fiction by three elements. Firstly, the British Empire's specific maritime and commercial nature suggests its non-synecdochical position in relation to other past and present empires. Secondly, the extrapolation of future scenarios from present conditions is guided by a progressive stance, highlighted with reference to scientific and geographic discoveries. Thirdly, the presence of a utopian line of invention is particularly evident in the virtuous administration, and in the moderate, enlightened reforms for which the epistolary account of the future constitutes a virtual laboratory.

The comparisons between the (future) British Commonwealth and other coeval polities formulated by the ambassadors — and more in general the alternate montage of various political contexts provided by the epistolary structure — constitute in some respects an equivalent in prose of the visualisations of time as a linear continuum that during the eighteenth century were to be increasingly found in synoptic charts juxtaposing and synthesising the history of different empires, such as Joseph Priestley's 1769 *A New Chart of History*.[302] Thus, the causal chains of events taking place in disparate geographical settings are organised into a unifying narrative, that highlights the different speeds, asynchronous paces, and non-linear processes of change across the globe. The world is virtually observed from the capital of the empire. The courts where the ambassadors are stationed betray a London-centric and Euro-centric perspective: while Far East and Atlantic current affairs are sometimes discussed in relation to the balance of European powers, there is no letter coming from America, India, or China, to mention but a few remarkable examples. It is to London that knowledge and news flow to be processed and become useful to the British political and economic interests.

---

298 Madden, *Memoirs*, pp. 200–01.

299 Madden, *Memoirs*, p. 203.

300 Which notoriously takes place after around five hundred years of existence: Madden, *Memoirs*, pp. 282–83.

301 Bell, *Reordering the World*, esp. pp. 119–47. For a discussion of the *topos* of *historia magistra vitae* from Cicero to the modern era, in relation to the eighteenth-century temporalisation of history, see Koselleck, *Futures Past*, pp. 26–42.

302 Rosenberg and Grafton, *Cartographies of Time*, pp. 19–20, 112, 140.

Memoirs brought new ideas into play regarding a secularised future, in order to imagine different models of empire and transnational power. Madden's account of the future contributes to our understanding of how imperial times are shaped and function within a given historical context by providing evidence of how history as a cultural construction is moulded by imperial agencies, and by the adoption of a transnational and global horizon.[303] Furthermore, it exemplifies how imperial times might enter the realm of the imagination, allowing for the inclusion of contradictory and non-linear ideas of historical stratification, for the parody of historiographical issues, and for the use of the future tense.

---

303 Cazzola, Jones Corredera, Iannuzzi, and Beduschi, 'Introduction. Imperial Times'.

VIII. Blurring the Dichotomy between History and Fiction

Memoirs was not published as a 'novel', a label which only became common on the British publishing market near the end of the eighteenth century. Terms such as 'memoirs' and 'letters', which we find on our titlepage, were fairly widespread in the fluid nomenclature adopted for fiction at the beginning of the century. 'Memoirs' in particular was frequently used in the titles of works of fiction and readers may have recognised it as potentially referring to a fictional text.[304] In the present essay, the use of the term 'novel' as well as that of other expressions not found in either Madden's peritext or in the main body of his prose narrative, such as 'satire', 'utopia', or 'futuristic fiction', brings with it a relative degree of conventionality.[305] Of the commentators who have discussed *Memoirs* in more or less depth in the past, some have referred to it as a 'novel', others have avoided this term and have opted for alternatives. As we have already mentioned, Alkon, who falls into the latter case, hailed Madden's work as the founder of the (mock) genre of future history.[306] Alkon's contention highlights how the work's treatment of the future encourages a contemporary reading that locates it within a long-term history that goes beyond the text itself, that of futuristic and speculative literature. A number of other terms and periphrases have been used by existing scholarship to designate Madden's text, such as 'epistolary narrative', 'prose fiction', 'prose narrative' — sometimes tied to its speculative content — 'utopia', 'utopian satire', 'utopian anticipation', 'tale' or 'account' or 'chronicle of the future', 'futuristic fiction', 'future records'.

It is useful to begin a discussion of history and fiction in Madden's invention by observing this nomenclatorial proliferation for a number of reasons. First, it warns us against the retrospective fallacy that would result from the uncritical application of categories created later to an early eighteenth-century work: while it is clear that a given textual form may exist in the past before any name for it was coined and spread into use, keeping in mind the positioning of *Memoirs* in relation to its genetic

---

304 Orr, 'Genre Labels', esp. pp. 77, 80.
305 On the eighteenth-century novel: McKeon, *The Origins of the English Novel*; Watt, *The Rise of the Novel*; see also Berndt and Johns, eds, *Handbook of the British Novel*.
306 Alkon, *Origins*, p. 103.

context may help to understand which of the author's choices matched existing horizons of expectation and which took uncharted paths. Secondly, by paying attention to the variety of these labels, their study invites us to approach genres and modes of writing not as closed sets that a text can be included in or excluded from, but rather as repertoires of possibilities, both in terms of choices made by the author in the construction of the text, and of the intentions and interests determining the text's subsequent circulation, its critical appropriation, and its re-use in different historical moments.[307] Finally, the multiplicity of denominations that can be adopted brings out with clarity the protean and omnivorous nature of *Memoirs*, with its satirical commentary on the present, and its predictive, prescriptive, utopian, controversialist, erudite, and epistolary aspects. Its fluidity and self-reflexive quality in terms of genre serve its satirical pondering of the knowability of time.

A complexity, and possibly an unresolved contradiction, characterises the historiographic background of the novel. Madden undoubtedly places his literary work within the dubious space carved out by Pyrrhonist scepticism in seventeenth-century culture and by the debates that carry on well in the eighteenth century on the nature and reliability of historical knowledge.[308] The title page introduces the reader to the text with three epigraphs (Figure 7). The first one, the Euripidean maxim 'Μάντις δ' ἄριστος ὅστις εἰκάζει καλῶς' — 'The best prophet is the one who guesses well', is in all probability to be read, through Cicero and Plutarch, as a statement on how the rational, intelligent man — as opposed to prophets and seers — relies on verisimilitude and probability, and on how 'the correct methodology for prognostics [...] is founded on rationality and logical reasoning'.[309] Following the Euripidean quotation there is an apostrophe by François de La Mothe Le Vayer: 'Bon Dieu! que n'avons nous point veu reüssir des conjectures de ce temps là comme si c'eussent esté autant de Propheties?',[310] significantly chosen from a passage in the *Discours de l'Histoire* (Discourses on history) dedicated to explaining how history should *not* be written, and criticising Prudencio de Sandoval's *Historia de la vida y hechos del Emperador Carlos V* (*The History of Charles the Vth Emperor and King of Spain*, 1606).

The third and final quote brings together two passages from Seneca's *Naturales Quaestiones*, again focussing on temporal issues inherent in the

---

307 Rieder, 'On Defining SF or Not'.

308 Borghero, *La certezza e la storia*; Burke, 'History, Myth, and Fiction'; Matytsin, 'Historical Pyrrhonism and Historical Certainty', pp. 243–59.

309 For this translation and a general discussion: Simonetti, 'Who Is the Best Prophet?', pp. 350–51 and n. 3, quote p. 351. The Greek spelling and accents in the text follow Simonetti's transcription of the fragment.

310 The French spelling and accents, as well as the references to the volume and page, suggest the use of the 1662 edition: La Mothe Le Vayer, 'Discours de l'histoire', p. 267.

MEMOIRS

OF THE

Twentieth Century.

Being Original LETTERS of STATE,
under *GEORGE* the Sixth:

Relating to the moſt Important Events in *Great-
Britain* and *Europe*, as to CHURCH and STATE,
ARTS and SCIENCES, TRADE, TAXES, and TREA-
TIES, PEACE, and WAR:

And Characters of the Greateſt PERSONS of thoſe Times;

From the Middle of the Eighteenth, to the End of the Twentieth
CENTURY, and the WORLD.

Received and Revealed in the Year 1728;

And now Publiſhed, for the Inſtruction of all Eminent
Stateſmen, Churchmen, Patriots, Politicians, Projectors,
Papiſts, and Proteſtants.

In SIX VOLUMES.

VOL. I.

Μάντις ἄϱιϛΘ- ὅϛις εἰϰἀζει ϰαλῶς.   Eurip.

Bon Dieu! que n'avons nous point veu reüſſir des conjectures de ce temps
là comme ſi c'euſſent eſté autant de Propheties?
La Mothe Le Vayer *Diſcourſe de l'Hiſtoire*. Tom. 1. p. 267.

Hoc apud nos quoque nuper ratio ad certum produxit. Veniet tempus,
quo iſta quæ nunc latent, in lucem dies extrahat, & longioris ævi diligentia. Ad inquiſitionem tantorum ætas una non ſufficit, ut tota cœlo
vacet. Itaque per ſucceſſiones iſta longas explicabuntur. Veniet tempus, quo poſteri noſtri tam aperta nos neſciſſe mirentur, non licet ſtare
cœleſtibus, nec averti: Prodeunt omnia; ut ſemel miſſa ſunt, vadunt.
Idem erit illis curſus, qui ſui finis. Opus hoc æternum irrevocabiles
habet motus.   *Senecæ Nat. Quæſt*. lib. 7. cap. 25.

LONDON:

Printed for Meſſieurs OSBORN and LONGMAN, DAVIS, and BATLEY,
in *Pater-noſter-Row*; STRAHAN, and CLARKE, in *Cornhill*;
RIVINGTON, ROBINSON, ASTLEY, and AUSTEN, in *St. Paul's
Church-Yard*; GOSLING, in *Fleetſtreet*; NOURSE, by *Temple-Bar*;
PREVOST, and MILLAR, in the *Strand*; PARKER, in *Pall-Mall*;
JOLLIFFE, by *St. James's*; BRINDLEY, SHROPSHIRE, and SMITH,
in *Bondſtreet*; and GOUGE, and STAGG, in *Weſtminſter-Hall*. 1733.

Figure 7. Madden, *Memoirs of the Twentieth Century*, title page. Courtesy of
Beinecke Rare Book and Manuscript Library, Yale University.

future, and on the knowability of reality on the part of man. The excerpt, taken from the twenty-fifth chapter of the seventh book, which is dedicated to comets, invites the reader to consider how the knowledge of the natural world may take many lifetimes to acquire, and how, considering its progress, natural phenomena such as eclipses and celestial movements that remain unexplained by today's observers may seem obvious to their descendants tomorrow.[311]

The peritext thus synthesises some of the main issues as regards the nature of historical time and the conditions and methodologies of it its knowability, on which the prefaces and the epistles dwell extensively. There is a professed scepticism towards the epistemological standard used in our understanding of the past, which is mindful of Pyrrhonist debates, but it ought to be remembered that this is placed ironically within a literary work. Practices such as the use of footnotes and quoting and reproducing documents inserted in subsequent pages, support a text of fiction that, like many other fictional memoirs and historical novels between the late seventeenth and the early eighteenth century, finds inspiration in coeval and ongoing processes reshaping history as a discipline, while also exploiting the blurring of boundaries between written histories and works of fiction.[312] Against this backdrop, the epigraphs play up the novelty of the author's work: the projection into and onto the future of the object of the narrative invention and of the discussion of issues related to the reliability of evidence and methods of studying events that are outside the author's direct experience.

The first preface begins with two names: Miguel de Cervantes and Thuanus. 'I have been as much perplex'd how to introduce them [the letters] properly, by a Preface worthy of them', reasons the fictitious editor about his work 'as Cervantes himself, when he fell on that which stands before his inimitable Don Quixote, or as Thuanus was how to begin the first Sentence of his History'.[313] In the Quixote's prologue,[314]

---

311 'Among us, too, reason has only recently found a reliable answer to these questions. (4) There will come a day when the passage of time and the efforts of a longer stretch of human history will bring to light things that are now obscure. One lifetime, even if it can be wholly devoted to astronomy, is not sufficient for the investigation of such important matters. [...] So it will take a long succession of people to explain these matters. (5) There will come a day when our descendants are astonished that we did not know such obvious facts. [...] The celestial bodies cannot stand still or be turned aside: they all move forward; they proceed just as they first began. Their motion will end only when they do. The movements of this eternal structure are unalterable [...]', Seneca, *Naturales Questiones*, p. 130.

312 Burke 'History, Myth, and Fiction', pp. 277–78; see also McKeon, *The Origins of the English Novel*, pp. 25–89; O'Brien, 'History and the Novel'; Zimmerman, *The Boundaries of Fiction*.

313 Madden, *Memoirs*, p. 1.

314 Cervantes Saavedra, *El ingenioso hidalgo don Quixote de la Mancha* (1605–1612); Eng. trans.: *The Ingenious Hidalgo Don Quixote de La Mancha*, trans. by Rutherford, with an introduction by González Echevarría, pp. 11–17; see in this edition Rutherford, 'Translating

the narrator comments on the hardships of writing the preface, and on the opportunity of giving his book a learned appearance by adorning it with citations stolen from reference books. By presenting the novel as a pseudo-translation (that is, the translation of a fictitious original text) from an Arabic manuscript written by an unreliable author, 'Cervantes blurs the lines between history and fiction and turns the question of historical accuracy into something of a joke [...] The discourse of "history" thus opens itself up to the editorial comments of a second narrator'.[315] Perhaps less renowned today, Thuanus is Jacques-Auguste de Thou (1553–1617), a French statesman, magistrate, and historian, and a member of the Paris parliament during the Wars of Religion, who helped negotiate the Edict of Nantes. His unfinished *Historia sui temporis* (*History of His Time*), written in Latin, covered the years from 1545 to 1584, and it was published between 1604 and 1608. After his death, a complete edition was prepared for the press by Pierre Dupuy and Nicolas Rigault (1620).[316] His works may be regarded as an example of coeval conceptions of the utility of history and the didactic nature of historiography.[317] The first references in the preface eloquently juxtapose a model of erudite historical research and a founding work of the European novel and paradigm of Bakhtin's heteroglossia and comic carnivalisation.

In addition to the title, where the use of the term 'memoirs' adopts a common choice in the eighteenth century to persuade potential readers of the realism and authenticity of works of fiction,[318] other loci in the text thematise the problem of verisimilitude, blurring the dichotomy between history and invention. Verisimilitude constitutes a conceptual suture between a fictional construction aimed at gaining the temporary suspension of disbelief of its readers, and a reconstruction whose methodological marks — quotations and references, footnotes, *exempla* from the past — the author borrows from erudite writing and projects onto a chronicle of times ahead. In fact, after affirming that the preface is the result of his original work, as opposed to the subsequent letters which he received from the future, the narrator underlines the novelty of his operation, claiming to be the first historian venturing 'into the dark Caverns of Futurity, and discover[ing] the Secrets of Ages yet to come'.[319] While historical narration is verisimilar because it is veridical, fictional narration traditionally relies on the Aristotelian paradigm. As discussed above, the exponentially

---

Don quixote', for an overview of the earliest English translations starting with Thomas Sheldon's, published in 1612–1615.

315 Cascardi, 'Don Quixote and the Invention of the Novel', p. 66.

316 de Thou, *Jac. Augusti Thuani Historiarum sui temporis*.

317 On the utility of history and the didactic nature of historiography for de Thou and his contemporaries, and on the *Historia*'s sources: De Smet, *Thuanus*, pp. 201–62.

318 Raven, 'The Anonymous Novel', p. 142.

319 Madden, *Memoirs*, p. 3.

increasing pace of scientific discoveries radically changed the epistemological framework in which the narrator places his work, and he exploits
this theme to extol his own merits. While discussing the innovativeness
of his work, he unblushingly compares it to momentous inventions and
advancements in science, technology, and geographical knowledge, and
himself to 'those exalted Spirits [...] who discover'd the Antipodes, the
Circulation of the Blood, the use of Telescopes and Barometers, of Printing and Sailing'.[320]

---

320 Madden, *Memoirs*, p. 4.

IX. Satirising Past Futures

The title page of *Memoirs* promises the publication of six volumes (Figure 7), something which was taken at face value by more than one subsequent commentator, who described the work as unfinished, while the five volumes following the first are more likely to have been announced in mocking imitation of the excruciating length of learned treatises of the day. A passage in the first preface seems to substantiate this hypothesis:

> [...] I must indeed be greatly discourag'd by the World, if I suppress the Sequel of it [his work], which I propose by proper intervals to communicate to them, tho' I will not answer, how far their receiving this Book I now offer them, with Contempt and Disregard, may make me use the same Haughtiness the sacred *Sibyl* did to *Tarquinius Superbus*, and after burning all the remaining parts which I design'd for them, make them pay as high a price for this Volume, as on a contrary demeanour I design'd to allow them the whole for.[321]

The ironic narrator threatens to withhold from the press the subsequent volumes if the first one is not enthusiastically received, comparing himself to the Sibyl. The Sibylline Books were a collection of nine prophetic texts. They were offered for sale to Tarquinius Superbus, the last of the seven legendary kings of Rome (VI century BCE). When he refused to pay the price, the Cumaean Sibyl burned six of the books and sold Tarquinius the remaining three at the initial price she had originally asked for the full set of nine. They were then kept in the temple of Jupiter on the Capitol to be consulted for the welfare of the state.[322] The story is told by Aulus Gellius in the *Noctes Atticae*.[323] The narrator is thus comparing the letters he publishes with no less than perhaps the most famous prophetic texts of Latin antiquity. The reference introduces the issue of foresight in relation to the public good and inaugurates the construction of an ideal gallery composed of the prophets and soothsayers immortalised in Greek-Roman literature and historiography, appearing in the following pages. As for the narrator's ironically hyperbolic tone, subsequent comparisons are also

---

321 Madden, *Memoirs*, p. 6.
322 Madden, *Memoirs*, p. 519.
323 Aulus Gellius, *Attic Nights*, pp. 89–91. See also 'Sibyl'.

proposed between *Memoirs* and the Qur'an (*Alcoran*) and the Talmud.[324] Perhaps indicative of the vitality of English Islamic studies at the time, in 1734, just a few months after Madden's book was printed, the publication by George Sale of a new English translation of the Qur'an represented a landmark and became the new standard version until the twentieth century.[325] By the beginning of the eighteenth century Talmudic scholarship had produced an incredibly rich and sophisticated exegetical literature, and Talmudic studies, including casuistic approaches and discussions of the inner logic and literal meaning of the text, were cultivated during the century in intellectual circles throughout Europe.[326] By comparing his work to these sacred books of the Hebrew and Islamic traditions, the narrator is advocating that it be received in the same way as similar texts that are the object of extremely stratified traditions of scholarship. Moreover, the narrator justifies with these comparisons the fact of having counted and listed the number of letters, sentences, paragraphs, and syllables that compose his work and of making this information public in order to prevent manipulation and forgery. Knowing the number of characters and words that compose the six volumes as licenced by the author, readers will always be able to verify that nothing has been removed, added or modified.[327] While trying to discourage forgeries, counterfeits, plagiarism, and spurious writings of any kind, the editor graciously authorises the translation of his book into any language, and foresees that the book will be censored and included in the Roman Catholic *Index Expurgatorius*.[328] This thematisation of the narrative's textual nature can be traced back to the new critical spaces opened up by philological investigation in historical and religious studies. While the application of philological sensibilities and methodology to the biblical text had already characterised the Reformation and Christian humanism in the sixteenth century,[329] the acquisition of texts from other religious traditions in European Enlightenment scholarship paved the way for a possible proliferation of texts of apparently similar sacred value. Even if this should be interpreted, in our novel, in the light of a deliberately comic exaggeration, it can be seen as a fictional reflection of a relativisation or decentralisation of the Judaeo-Christian textual tradition in progress. The professed desire to protect one's own work from possible falsifications by using linguistic-textual tools calls into play the philological criticism of the text as part of historical research and thus, ultimately, also

---

324 Madden, *Memoirs*, pp. 30–31; from the Middle French *alcoran*, borrowing from the Arabic *al-qur'ān*, *alcoran* was the title used in French and English translations of the sacred book of Islam throughout the seventeenth century and at the beginning of the eighteenth.

325 Malcolm, 'The 1649 English Translation of the Koran': Holt, 'The Study of Islam'.

326 Feiner, *The Jewish Enlightenment*.

327 Madden, *Memoirs*, pp. 29–30.

328 Madden, *Memoirs*, pp. 520–22, on translations and censorship 523–24.

329 Cameron, ed., *The New Cambridge History of the Bible*.

the methods with which historiographic narrative constructs and defends its credibility.

The narrator argues for *Memoirs'* status as an authentic historiographical work — a philologically genuine edition of original letters, framed between the essayist structure of methodologically sound prefaces — by making fun of a variety of features typical of a historiographical knowledge undergoing processes of disciplinary specialisation. The apparatus of erudite sources is supplemented by elements that mimic the linguistic-textual aspects of research into the past, such as the focus on the genuine transmission of the text as produced by the original 'author'. Elsewhere, linguistic-translational aspects are at the centre of the narrator's mockery: twentieth-century English is very different from eighteenth-century English,[330] and the narrator claims to publish the letters exactly as received, without any changes, except those 'translating them into the English of these illiterate Times oblig'd me to [make]'[331] and with the exception of all those passages — paragraphs and even whole letters — which in the interest of the country should be reserved for heads of state, 'for the Use and Service of the Crown and my own Family, and not expos'd to publick view'. The assertion that the text received from the future was not subject to any alteration is, in short, comically contradicted by opposite assertions concerning the adaptation into the coeval diachronic variety of the English language, and the expulsion of an unspecified number of passages.

Again, the question of the credibility of the historical account of the future is addressed with reference to power relations in the construction of knowledge, where the recurrent polemical target is the abuse that the church of Rome perpetuates against the credulity of its followers. The celestial origin of the manuscript is not contradicted — the editor contends — by the 'alterations, interpolations, omissions, disguises, or mistakes, I necessarily, or possibly a little injudiciously, have been guilty of, in preparing it for the Press', no more than one can deny the divine origin of certain paintings and sculptures that the infallible Catholic Church worships as works of angels and apostles.[332]

The narrator becomes convinced that his work will be the object of 'the utmost Admiration and Reverence',[333] and that it is not necessary to threaten the withdrawal of the subsequent volumes, something that, as 'Apollo did on the ill Fortune of his unhappy *Phaethon*', would leave the world in darkness.[334] The best-known version of the myth of Phaëthon is told by Ovid in his *Metamorphoses*. Son of Apollo, god of the sun,

---

330 Madden, *Memoirs*, p. 269, see also *supra*, ch. 5.
331 Madden, *Memoirs*, p. 22 this and the subsequent quotation in the text.
332 Madden, *Memoirs*, pp. 256–57.
333 Madden, *Memoirs*, p. 7.
334 Madden, *Memoirs*, p. 8.

and of the nymph Clymene, Phaëthon asked his father to be allowed to drive the chariot of the sun for one day. When Phaëthon was unable to control the horses, the chariot came too close to the earth. To prevent the destruction of the earth, Zeus threw a thunderbolt at the chariot and Phaëthon precipitated into the river Eridanus. Apollo, saddened by his son's death, refused to drive the golden chariot, so the next day passed without sunlight, causing the darkness to which the editor refers. The narrator compares the absence of sunlight to the darkness he might cause by retiring his work from the world, should his papers be received without the appropriate admiration and reverence.[335]

The above-mentioned Sibyl simile is followed by a reference to another renowned prophet of antiquity. The narrator expects his revelations to be the target of the scepticism of many, and himself to be suspected as an impostor, akin to Tiresias being suspected by Ulysses in Horace's representation of their dialogue: 'Num furis? an prudens ludis me obscura canendo? O Laertiade, quicquid dicam, aut erit, aut non: Divinare etenim magnus mihi donat Apollo. Quid tamen ista velit sibi Fabula, si licet, ede'.[336] The Latin verses read: '[Ulysses] — Are you mad? or do you purposely make fun of me with your dim oracle? [Tiresias] — O son of Laertes, whatever I say will or will not be; for prophecy is great Apollo's gift to me. [Ulysses] — But what means that story? Tell me, if you may'.[337] To be noted is the ironic description of oracular utterances: 'quidquid dicam, aut erit aut non' — 'whatever I say will or will not be' — a ridiculing commentary on the factual reliability of prophetic prediction. In the fifth satire of the second book, composed sometime after 30 BC, Horace imagined a dialogue between Ulysses and the seer Tiresias, the 'burlesque continuation' — in H. Rushton Fairclough words — of the famous scene in the Odyssey where Ulysses in the underworld learns from Tiresias that he will be able to go back to Ithaca, but only after being reduced to poverty. The satire takes the form of a dialogue, hence the reference to this form. A mention of Tiresias, probably the most famous prophet in ancient mythology, was to be expected in the review of noble precedents in predictions and previsions featured in the first preface. To this end, the narrator choses a parody in which Tiresias, far from his traditional portrait as an august and solemn prophet, emerges as a shady character, advising Ulysses on how to easily enrich himself by seeking legacies.[338]

---

335 Ovid, Metamorphoses, lines 1–400.

336 Madden, Memoirs, pp. 8–9.

337 Horace, Satires, book II, v — The Art of Legacy-Hunting, pp. 196–207, lines 58–61. In the Latin text the modern reference edition reads 'Laërtiade' and 'quidquid'. 'Son of Laertes' is an epithet for Ulysses.

338 Fairclough, 'The Art of Legacy-Hunting' (editor's introduction). On Horace in eighteenth-century satire: Weinbrot, Eighteenth-Century Satire, pp. 21–33.

The Christian prophetic tradition — the object of laborious attempts to control it by the church of Rome during the Middle Ages — is also called into question.[339] The narrator compares the revelations of his own work to those of Saint Bridget of Sweden, inviting a thorough examination of their veracity. Birgitta Birgersdotter (*c.* 1303–1373, canonised in 1391) was a mystic and founder of the order of the Bridgittines. She first became known in Sweden as a prophetess, her *Revelations* were translated into Latin and were influential in the Middle Ages. Her *Liber celesti revelacionum* (The heavenly book of revelations) collected some seven hundred occasional pieces addressed to particular social or personal situations, while also offering messages aimed at the world at large, presented as a sign of the approaching end of time and the coming of the final judgement. Saint Bridget's prophesies have an articulated textual tradition, which includes their re-use in other texts by later compilers.[340] Like Saint Bridget's revelations, his work — the narrator suggests — may be scrutinised according to the severe criteria elaborated by 'Chancellour *Gerson*'.[341] Influential theologian, Jean Gerson (or de Gerson) (1363–1429) was a central figure in the conciliar solution to the Great Schism between the popes of Rome and Avignon (1378–1415) and at the Council of Constance (1414–1418). He was chancellor of the University of Paris in 1395, hence the reference to him as 'Chancellour' made by the narrator. He took part in a commission dealing with the canonisation of three Swedish saints, and in his extensive body of work *De Probatione spirituum* (On the discernment of spirits) he provided criteria to judge the veracity of revelations and expressed his doubts about Bridget of Sweden's prophesies — albeit without open attacks or denouncements.[342] The reference to Bridget and Gerson recalls the history of religious prophecy as a politically charged field, linked to moments of social instability in which predictions could concern events of a public nature and assume, in the eyes of political and religious institutions, a subversive potential. At the time of the papacy's transfer to Avignon in 1309, for example, Bridget predicted calamities if the pope did not resettle in Rome.[343] Among her prophecies, others concerned the misfortunes that temporal rulers such as Magnus of Sweden would cause if they did not conform their behaviour to Christian morality. However, more than these specific cases, not explicitly recalled in our text, the mention of the submission of prophetic revelations to investigation evokes the

---

339 Minois, *Storia dell'avvenire*, pp. 157–228.
340 Schier, 'Birgitta of Sweden'; on the *Revelations*: Ellis, '"Flores Ad Fabricandam … Coronam"'.
341 Madden, *Memoirs*, p. 9.
342 Hobbins, 'Jean Gerson'; on *De Probatione spirituum*: McGuire, 'Jean Gerson', pp. 249–50. See also Fraioli, 'Gerson Judging Women of Spirit'.
343 Minois, *Storia dell'avvenire*, p. 211.

problematic negotiation of credibility that, throughout the Middle Ages and beyond, took place between the institutional hierarchies of the church and figures and movements of prophetic and millenarian mysticism.

As in the disquisition on angelic presences and their ability to see into the future, the discussion of divination practices, with particular but not exclusive regard to astrological techniques, draws on intellectual spheres distant from the author in time and space, as well as on examples from late-seventeenth and early eighteenth-century British culture.[344] References to Greek and Roman historiography and literature are discussed together with examples from interpretations of the biblical text, from the church fathers, and from rabbinic and kabbalistic knowledge. The sources cited or alluded to regarding Jewish tradition significantly include Jacques Basnage's anti-Catholic *Histoire des Juifs*.[345] References to Renaissance and seventeenth-century astrology — from Peter of Abano to Robert Fludd — and to kabbalistic works of Christian authors such as Guillaume Postel, also draw on late seventeenth-century compilations such as those of Gabriel Naudé and James Gaffarel.[346]

Within the review of beliefs related to divination, conducted by the editor with the usual comical jumble of comparative references, a section devoted to almanacs and almanac compilers was an inevitable inclusion. The popularity of almanacs in early modern Europe was a multifaceted phenomenon. By touching, with their predictions, aspects of daily and public life, the astrological contents of almanacs and interpretations of prodigies were charged with political connotations, particularly at times of significant natural and public events, such as years between 1714 and 1716 (with, in close succession, a solar eclipse, the death of Queen Anne, George's accession to the throne, the visibility of the aurora borealis, and the execution of the Jacobite rebels).[347] The polemical targets of *Memoirs* include some of the most famous sixteenth- and early eighteenth-century issuers of astrological predictions and textbooks: Vincent Wing, who authored an almanac for the Company of Stationers from 1641 until his death, which shared coeval millenarian hopes, defended the influence of the stars on natural and human vicissitudes, including politics, and contributed to popularising astronomical knowledge; John Partridge, au-

---

344 Madden, *Memoirs*, pp. 238–53.
345 Basnage, *Histoire des Juifs*.
346 Naudé, *The History of Magick*; Gaffarel, *Unheard-of Curiosities*.
347 Burns, *An Age of Wonders*.

Figure 8. Hogarth, 'Hudibras Visiting Sidrophel': Hudibras and Ralpho visit the astrologer Sidrophel, attended by his servant Whachum, etching and engraving, *c.* 1721. The scene is set in a laboratory, a stuffed crocodile and bat hang from the ceiling and wall, on the floor there are a globe, books — one of which is about palmistry — and scientific instruments. An astrological chart is on the table. The plate has the number 11 in lower left-hand corner and in the right corner is written 'W: Hogarth Invt: et sc[ulpsit]'. This is the eleventh of the seventeen plates (a frontispiece and sixteen illustrations) of *Hudibras* designed by Hogarth *c.* 1721 and published in 1726, after the success of the series of twelve larger plates issued in that year. Copy at The Metropolitan Museum of Art, Harris Brisbane Dick Fund, 1932, public domain.

thor of popular almanacs made famous by Swift's hoax in the *Bickerstaff Papers*; and John Gadbury, one of the most successful astrologers in late seventeenth-century Britain, along with Partridge and William Lilly (Figure 8).[348]

---

348 Madden, *Memoirs*, pp. 252–53; Capp, 'Wing, Vincent'; Curry, 'Partridge, John'; Curry, 'Gadbury, John'.

X. 'Publishing' the Letters

Receiving revelations about the future relevant to public affairs and publishing them is compared in the first preface to the ancient custom as recounted by Artemidorus: '*moris antiqui suit, ut quicquid quisque de republica somniasset, illud vel Præconis voce, vel Pittacio, hoc est, tabula quadam descriptum indicaret*'. 'It is an ancient custom', the Latin quote reads, 'that a person who has received a dream concerning the state should make it public and describe its content either verbally by means of a crier or by means of a public notice'.[349] The quote, attributed to Artemidorus via Casaubon, is likely to have come from a commentary in the 1684 edition of *Suetonii Tranquilli Opera Omnia* (Suetonius Tranquillus's complete works).[350] Between the second and third century CE, Artemidorus authored *Oneirocritica* (The interpretation of dreams), a compendium of dream-divination, providing instructions on interpreting the prophetic meaning of dreams pertaining to a vast array of human, natural, and divine matters. The passage quoted in the preface relates to the fact that normally prophetic dreams concerning public affairs and society at large come to public figures, kings or emperors, not to ordinary people. However, the quotation — in which Artemidorus in turn referenced a passage from Homer's *Iliad* (book II, lines 80–82) — is intended to highlight the existence of exceptions to this rule, in which ordinary people receive prophetic dreams concerning the state. In such cases it is not wrong for the person who has received the dream to make it public. This is precisely the case with the narrator, maintains the preface, who prints the letters he received from the future.[351]

The publication of the letters is in fact meant to ensure Great Britain success and happiness in the centuries to come, contends the narrator, 'when the other Kingdoms of the Earth are to labour, as it were, in actual Convulsions, and be jumbled together, like the Mountains and Plains of

---

349 Madden, *Memoirs*, pp. 27–28, my translation.
350 Suetonius Tranquillus, *C. Suetonii Tranquilli Opera Omnia*, caput XCI, p. 220.
351 For Artemidorus' passage referenced here see Harris-McCoy, *Artemidorus' Oneirocritica*, pp. 54–55 and 425–26; for Suetonius' edition by Augustin Babelon (which is his only known work) and his use of Isaac Casaubon's (1559–1614) commentary see Léonard, 'Suétone'.

Jamaica in the dreadful Earthquake in 1692'.[352] The earthquake which occurred in Jamaica on 7 June 1692, destroyed half of Port Royal, one of the busiest harbour towns of the Caribbean, leaving a deep mark on British colonial culture. As with other large-scale disasters and 'wonders' between the end of the seventeenth and the early eighteenth century, it was discussed as a sign of divine judgement, but also as the result of geographic and architectural factors. Imagination and debates surrounding this episode indicate a knowledge and approach to the natural world that tended to disqualify a moral reading of events such as earthquakes. Many coeval histories and accounts, without challenging the interpretation of the disaster as an act of God, emphasised the role played by the physical environment, all the more so in the Jamaican context, where the threat of earthquakes was well known before 1692. The fact that his work is printed and made public, claims the editor, is intended to foster the happiness of England in a future where other countries will be shaken by unforeseen upheavals, just like Port Royal during its infamous earthquake. Underneath the obvious image of the earthquake as an event that disrupts the status quo, the simile uses the idea of the natural disaster as an unforeseen event and the prodigious 'wonder', the exceptional natural fact, as a cause for surprise. Thanks to the letters now published, the future will no longer be a source of unexpected and potentially damaging events. Readers will be prepared, just as — we may think — English settlers in the Caribbean at the beginning of the eighteenth century were increasingly prepared for earthquakes as routine events.[353]

On the other hand, foresees the narrator, 'many great Men will blame me as *Alexander* did *Aristotle*, for communicating too many of such hidden Mysteries, such *Arcana imperii*, to the Knowledge of the Vulgar'.[354] According to Plutarch, Alexander the Great reproached his old teacher Aristotle for publishing his work, and thus making public the acroamatic doctrines according to which he had instructed him in state leadership ('Arcana imperii', 'secrets of the state'), which were fit for oral teaching to chosen disciples only (to initiates, hence esoteric, as opposed to exoteric). '[F]or in what shall I surpass other men', lamented Alexander in a letter, 'if those doctrines wherein I have been trained are to be all men's common property?'.[355] The narrator has therefore decided to print his exceptional work, but only in fifty copies, a number which he calculates corresponds

---

352 Madden, *Memoirs*, p. 28.
353 On interpretations of 1682 at Port Royal: Mulcahy, 'The Port Royal Earthquake'; see also Hall, *Worlds of Wonder*.
354 Madden, *Memoirs*, p. 29.
355 Plutarch, *Lives*, vol. VII, see *Life of Alexander*, pp. 240–43, quote at 243.

to how many people in Britain are wise and honest enough to be told such important secrets.[356]

With a variation on Virgil's *Aeneid*, the narrator claims to be offering the letters to the printing press, and adds *uti digerit omnia Calchas*, 'So Calchas interprets the omens'.[357] In his narrative, Sinon attributes to Calchas, the mythical Greek soothsayer who took part in the Trojan War, the idea of the wooden horse as atonement for Pallas. Calchas's words, like the whole of Sinon's tale, were part of a fabricated hoax to convince the Trojans to bring the horse, within which the Achaeans were hiding, inside the walls of their city. Again, there is a subtle irony in the choice of a quotation that apparently refers to the vatication of a prophet but which in truth is relating a deceptive invention. Consistently, the proclamation of a faithful publication of the manuscripts is immediately and ironically contradicted by the announcement of the deletion of a number of passages which, the narrator states, are so sensitive that they should only be reserved for his descendants and the crown.

The first preface is concluded by two further learned references. The narrator says, like Saint Austin 'when he us'd to cut his Sermons into two, *Parcite mihi fratres, non dicam vobis quod sequitur*', 'Forbear to resent me, my brothers, if now I do not tell you what follows', an expression possibly taken from a secondary source, such as François Garasse's *La doctrine curieuse* (The curious doctrine).[358] The reader's indulgence is then asked when 'like the Adventure of the *Bear* and the *Fiddle*' the text breaks off 'a little abruptly'.[359] The reference is to Samuel Butler's *Hudibras*, a satire in three cantos published at the end of 1662. Modelled after *Don Quixote*, Butler's mock-heroic narrative featured knights chasing inheritances, charlatans posing as astrologers, disputes between Presbyterians and independent sectarians, academic pedantry, and hermetic philosophies. In the 'argument' (initial summary) of part I, canto 1 of the poem it is announced that 'Th' adventure of the *Bear* and *Fiddle*/Is sung, but breaks off in the

---

356 See also Madden, *Memoirs*, p. 519.

357 Virgil, *Aeneid books I–VI*, book II, pp. 328–29, line 182. Virgil's hemistich reads: 'Ita digerit omnia Calchas', our narrator's version, introduced by *uti*, may assume a more dubitative or open meaning.

358 Garasse, *La doctrine curieuse*, p. 731, my translation; the expression is commonplace, listed for example in Southey's *Common-Place Book*, p. 475.

359 Madden, *Memoirs*, p. 31.

middle'.[360] *Hudibras* was illustrated by William Hogarth in a series of plates printed around 1725, including *The Adventure of the Bear and the Fiddle*.[361]

The closing of the first preface thus takes place in the form of a juxtaposition of references to religious and satirical works. Once again, the use of tags and allusions is functional to an implicit meta-textual comment: here, the prophetic tone and profession of truthfulness are immediately counterbalanced by the adoption of a comic register. The publication of the letters triggers a reference to the public role of prophecy in the ancient world and thus to the political uses of prediction. In the *Memoirs'* fictional peritext, publication is understood in a twofold sense: the text becomes public both in the sense of being given to the press, disseminated through the book form, and thus exposed to public enjoyment and judgement, and in the sense of its finality for the public good, for the management of the state. In this way, the novel calls into question the future as an arena invested with a particular role in political planning, and draws a fundamental link between this theme and that of the circulation of information in society. As we shall see in the following pages, the utopian and dystopian inventions shaping the *Memoirs'* account of time ahead offer a penetrating representation of the interests competing in the production and dissemination of ideas, particularly in written form, testifying to the centrality that reflection on the public nature of knowledge has, in all the facets that the concept of public assumed in the Age of Enlightenment.

---

360 The gruesome entertainment of bearbaiting was banned by the Puritans during the midseventeenth century Civil Wars. The episode in Hudibras is likely modelled after the historical killings of bears by Puritan officers that took place after the prohibition, and it functions as the comic equivalent to an epic battle. For a discussion of the episode's context, and possible political allusions and identifications of the characters with prominent personalities living during Butler's time: Wilders, 'Introduction', pp. xxxvii–xxxviii.

361 Hogarth, *The Adventure of the Bear and the Fiddle*. On *Hudibras* in early eighteenth-century culture see: Higgins, 'The Politics of *A Tale of a Tub*'.

XI. 'This Prodigious Society': Anti-Jesuit Satire

Concerns over the success of Jesuit missionaries like those expressed by the British diplomats in *Memoirs* were not uncommon in eighteenth-century European culture.[362] The novel projects into the future an extreme version of the notion of accommodation — the adaptation of the Christian message and doctrine to the cultures of the native peoples to be converted.[363] Madden's futuristic tale testifies to the articulation and effectiveness of the institutional structure of the Society of Jesus and the central role that epistolography and written communication played in Jesuit activities from the first decades of their existence in the sixteenth century.[364] The unparalleled regulatory, bureaucratic, and administrative structure of the order had already, before the beginning of the eighteenth century, given rise to stereotypes of a hyper-efficient hierarchical machine. The normative collection *Institutum Societatis Iesu* (Institute of the Society of Jesus) in 1635 had brought together the norms and rules that governed the Society as a social body — norms of papal origin, internally promulgated *Constitutions*, decrees of the general congregations, as well as further *regulae* and *rationes* pertaining to specific aspects of the order's way of life and execution of specific offices.[365] The *Constitutions* had given the structure of the order some conventional and common elements — such as the division into 'provinces' on a geographical basis — and others considered particularly innovative and contested, including a high degree of centralisation of power and the very ample role of the Roman curia in all the affairs of the order at a global level. These are elements on which the novel dwells on several occasions.

While, like all Catholic orders, the Jesuits were subject to papal authority, in imagining a Jesuit monopoly of the papal throne — to which the letters return several times — the order's tendency towards hierarchical centralisation, and its trust in the authority of Rome is magnified. The

---

362 Madden, *Memoirs*, pp. 5–6 (page numbers after the preface) for remarks by the ambassador to Constantinople.
363 On accommodation within the Society of Jesus' missionary activities there is extensive literature. For a general introduction: Prieto, 'The Perils of Accommodation'.
364 Madden, *Memoirs*, pp. 45–47.
365 *The Constitutions of the Society of Jesus*, general ed. Padberg.

excessive proximity and privileged relationship with the papacy had been one of the recurring themes of anti-Jesuit polemics since the sixteenth century.[366] By replacing the Superior General with the pope as the apex figure of the Jesuit Roman curia, the novel's dystopic invention stages a future overlap between the power apparatus of the Catholic Church and that of the Society of Jesus, to the detriment of other orders and components of Catholicism. The case of the imagined twentieth-century disputes over the immaculate conception, in which the Jesuits unscrupulously use a theological dogma to eliminate their Dominican competitors, shows this very well. The Jesuit ascendancy is traced back to a number of elements internal to the Catholic ecumene — the assumption of a monopoly on a number of sacraments — and external — the influence on European courts.

The Society's construction of a network through which information — administrative, edifying, and related to missionary activities — flowed to the global hub in Rome relied significantly on letter writing. Written paperwork and governance were among the elements controlled by the *regulae*, and are an apt example of the robust long-term continuity that characterised the order's practices and organisational framework over the centuries, notwithstanding the introduction of novelties and reforms.[367] Thanks to this knowledge infrastructure, during the seventeenth and eighteenth century, Jesuit practices contributed in a significant way to the encyclopaedia of knowledge on the world that was available in Europe. The transnational nature of Jesuit power offers an exceptional representation not only of the global reach that characterised the order's activities, but of the high degree of awareness with which the socio-institutional apparatuses of internal governance were conceived as an instrument and cohesive element of this connectedness.

A passage in a letter from the British ambassador to Rome, evokes the Jesuitical infiltration of British society.[368] Reference is made to the centrality that educational practices and the founding and running of schools had in Jesuit activities, and to the place of the Society of Jesus within the dense and problematic interplay between religion and politics in late seventeenth- and early eighteenth-century Britain. The general backdrop to this discussion is the peak of anti-Jesuit sentiment in Europe, which was maturing during the eighteenth century, from the attacks of *philosophes* and Jansenists, to famous cases such as the trial of Jean-Baptiste Girard,

---

366 Worcester, 'Anti-Jesuit Polemic'; Pavone, *Le astuzie dei gesuiti*.

367 An extensive historiography has dealt with these aspects of the Society's history, a good entry point is: Županov, *The Oxford Handbook of the Jesuits*, here esp. Friedrich, 'Jesuit Organization and Legislation'; Nelles, 'Jesuit Letters'; and Rubiés, 'The Jesuits and the Enlightenment'.

368 Madden, *Memoirs*, pp. 47–48.

accused of witchcraft, seduction, and procurement of abortion in France in 1731, to the growing annoyance, also in the Catholic world, with an order seen as incompatible with state control over national churches. The first decades of the century saw a flourishing of polemical publications and resulted in the expulsion of the order from various countries, starting with Portugal in 1759, until the suppression of the order by Clement XIV in 1773.[369]

Memoirs slots in here in the long history of anti-Jesuit controversy in the Protestant world and in the British Isles in particular. In England, where the monarch was head of state and church, loyalty to the papacy of the Catholic clergy was perceived as a form of treason, not least from a political standpoint. Since the prohibitive measures and executions in the England of Elizabeth I and James I, Jesuit missionaries had often travelled in disguise, a practice alluded to in the novel's description of the activities that Loyola's disciples conduct under false pretences. 'If my Intelligence be good', remarks the correspondent from Rome, 'there are not less than 1300 quartered in different Places and Disguises; some of them as Tradesmen, *Valet de Chambres*, and Clerks, and not a few as Preachers and School-masters.'[370] Similar news also comes from Constantinople, where the Jesuits have made exceptional progress in evangelisation, operating under the disguise of '*Physicians, Mathematicians, Astrologers*', in the army, and in 'all kinds of the best sorts of Trades.'[371]

In staging a rivalry between Jesuits and Dominicans that even resorted to the physical elimination of opponents, the narrative invention is mindful of the strong competition between Loyola's order and the secular clergy as regards the ecclesiastical governance that had characterised Catholic missionary work in England since the late sixteenth century. These frictions had not subsided after the Society of Jesus assumed the stewardship of the English College in Rome (from 1579) and reached particularly virulent peaks in the seventeenth century. These included for example the argument in favour of the Jesuits' expulsion made by the dean and chapter of the secular clergy, after the promise of religious toleration made by Charles II with the Declaration of Breda (1660) had failed due to the opposition of the House of Commons. The disagreement over the nature of the authority of the vicar apostolic was a long-standing aspect of these disputes, up to the first half of the eighteenth century — a disagreement in which the Jesuits argued that their faculties depended directly on the pope, whose vicars the bishops were.

During the last years of James I's reign and then the rule of his son Charles I, the Jesuit presence in the British Isles was consolidated (with

---

369 Worcester, 'Anti-Jesuit Polemic', p. 32.
370 Madden, *Memoirs*, pp. 47–48.
371 Madden, *Memoirs*, pp. 5–6.

the creation of the English vice-province in 1619, then province in 1623).
The English Civil War, combined with the changing fortunes of Catholics
during the Thirty Years' War, and the order's reputation for meddling in
the politics and affairs of the gentry marked the beginning of a significant
decline. Charges of treason struck the order after the English Civil War,
and proliferated in connection with the so-called Popish Plot of 1678 —
with the accusation that a plan to assassinate Charles I in favour of his
brother was attributable to the Jesuits, resulting in six executions, a number
of deaths in prison, and many fleeing the country. Between 1685 and 1688
the Jesuits acted as preachers and royal confessors during the reign of
James Stuart, with one of them seated on the Privy Council, and eight
colleges were opened. The arrival of William of Orange and the deposition
of James II turned the fortunes of Jesuits and Catholics in England upside
down again. Charges of disloyalty recurred in the eighteenth century, especially during the 1715 and 1745 Jacobite rebellions. By the beginning of
the eighteenth century, the popular identification of Jesuits with treachery
and treason was a well-established trope.[372]

Confrontations between Catholic orders in the field of theological
controversy lead, in the novel's futuristic projection, to a solution to
the dispute over the immaculate conception exploited by the Jesuits to
prevail over their Dominican competitors.[373] The theological doctrine
of the immaculate conception had been debated in the Catholic world
since the twelfth century, and became the subject of particularly heated
disputes between many religious orders across Europe during the seventeenth century, after it became one of the topics addressed in Reformation
and Counter-Reformation debates. While Dominicans followed Aquinas
in maintaining that Mary was freed from original sin only after she was
conceived, Jesuits were among those orders supporting the dogmatisation
of the notion that the Virgin Mary was protected from all stains of original
sin from the first moment of her conception. The rivalry between the
different positions gave rise to treatises and references in sermons, to
processions, and to a rich production in figurative arts.[374]

Reporting evidence from different countries, the letters insist on the
ability of the Jesuits to control information and to adapt their communication and propaganda strategies to different political-geographical contexts,
and to different social groups. Anti-Catholic and anti-Jesuit arguments
on these matters generate a fascinating encyclopaedia of intertextual references. On the control of the press and book circulation in Italy, the
ambassador comments: 'This brings to mind, what *Pasquin* said on this
Occasion, that his Holiness had made his good Brethren the Jesuits, sole

---

372 McCoog, 'The Society of Jesus in the Three Kingdoms'; Wright, 'United Kingdom'.
373 Madden, *Memoirs*, p. 45.
374 Manning, *An Overview of the Pre-Suppression Society of Jesus*.

Spectacle-makers to the World; by which means they were impower'd to make all things in Print, appear dark or clear, fair or foul, great or little, as they pleas'd to represent them to the Eyes of others'[375] The reference is to *The Visions of Pasquin*.[376] This anticlerical, antipapist, satirical dialogue first appeared in 1544 in Celio Secondo Curione's collection *Pasquillorum tomi duo* (Two volumes of lampoons), then, in a revised version, enjoyed ample circulation in autonomous editions and translations.[377] In Celio's text, the metaphor of different spectacles used on different occasions embodies the corruption and nepotism of Rome: spectacles that make everything appear larger or smaller than it really is are used to evaluate and bestow positions and rewards, that are therefore inversely proportional to real merit. By monopolising the institution of censorship, control over the press, and the production of theological and historical knowledge, the Jesuits are, in *Memoirs*, the 'producers of spectacles' that are imposed on the whole of society controlled by the Vatican.

Another significant reference is to the *Monarchia solipsorum* (Monarchy of solipsists),[378] a seventeenth-century anti-Jesuit satire written in Latin under the pseudonym of Lucius Cornelius Europaeus and first published in Venice in 1645.[379] Printed in Latin in London (1680),[380] subsequently translated into German,[381] and, during the eighteenth century, into Italian and French,[382] the authorship of the text is debated. Hypotheses as regards the author have considered Giulio Clemente Scotti (1602–1669), writer of other works critical of the Society including *De Potestate Pontificia in Societatem Jesus* (On the Pope's authority over the Society of Jesus, 1646), and Melchior Inchofer (1585–1648), an Austrian Jesuit, among the experts in the Galileo trial (1632), who was tried himself and condemned in 1648 for the alleged authorship of the *Monarchia*.[383] The reference is significant not only because it recalls a precedent of anti-Jesuit satire with wide European circulation, but also because the *Monarchia* presents distinct utopian (or rather dystopian) aspects in its construction.

---

375 Madden, *Memoirs*, p. 44.
376 Pasquillus ecstaticus [Celio Secondo Curione], *The Visions of Pasquin*, possibly translated into English by William Phiston.
377 Simoncelli, 'Curione, Celio Secondo'; Biondi, 'A. Curione, Celio Secondo'.
378 Madden, *Memoirs*, pp. 47, 361.
379 *Lucii Cornelii Europæi Monarchia solipsorum*.
380 Simpson, *A Study of the Prose Works of John Donne*, p. 195.
381 *Deß Europäischen Lucius Cornelius Monarchia*.
382 In Italian under the title *Monarchia de' Solipsi* in 1710, later also as *Monarchia de' Solessi*; in French published in Amsterdam in 1721, 1722, and 1754, later also in Paris, 1824.
383 Beretta, 'Melchior Inchofer et L'hérésie de Galilée', p. 34; Pavone, *Le astuzie*, pp. 57–58 and n. 5, 190–98; Pavone, 'Between History and Myth', p. 64 n. 33; Reusch, 'Inchofer, Melchior'; Spini, *Ricerca dei libertini*, pp. 217–46. We have not been able to track down any copy of J. G. Kneschke's *Dissertatio de auctore libelli de Monarchia Solipsorum* (Zittau, 1811 or 1812), sometimes mentioned by secondary sources.

Interpreted by subsequent commentators as a satirical allegory or satirical utopia, it describes government, laws, customs, and society of a (fictitious) country 'unknown in our hemisphere', visited by an enlightened traveller — Lucius Cornelius Europaeus. In the prefatory letter, signed with the different pseudonym Timothaeus Cursantium, an equally fictitious editor states that he has received the manuscript of this treatise as a gift from Cornelius Europaeus and that he is now giving it to the press. Although the contrivance of the found or rediscovered manuscript recurs in more than one text at the beginning of the modern European novel, the narrative frame cannot but recall that of *Memoirs*. The *Monarchia*'s preface states that it is left to the dedicatee (and thus to the reader) to assess whether what is reported about this remote country is true or not, and whether the political and governmental system outlined is to be imitated or should rather be avoided.[384] This stated ambiguity resonates with the ambivalence *Memoirs* expresses towards the order, in which the observation of its abilities is a source of admiration as well as the basis of its dystopian portrayal. Among the elements of anti-Jesuit satire for which the *Monarchia* can arguably be considered a source of inspiration for *Memoirs* there are, for example, the absolute power and arbitrariness of the king — in the *Monarchia* an allegorical figure for the Superior General (*praepositus generalis*) of the Society — and the opulent sumptuousness of the palaces in the capital, the summer residences, and the churches. Also represented and barraged with criticism in the *Monarchia* are the subtleties and subterfuges with which young people are recruited and educated for several years in separation from the outside world, and the doctrinaire opportunism with which new beliefs and dogmas are adopted or abandoned — depending on the country — in order to gain the favour of the rulers and acquire more political power.

A tag used to comment on the distribution of favours, presents, and bribes with which the Society of Jesus secures the loyalty of its retinue and the courts of Europe, echoes a sentence from Manilius's *Astronomica* (Celestial phenomena).[385] A didactic poem composed in Latin at the beginning of the first century CE, *Astronomica* discusses astrological influences, zodiacal signs, their effects on human life and the world, and the calculation of the horoscope in its five books. The sentence *Omnibus una quies, Venter!* — 'all [the animals] alike have only sleep and food', from the fourth book, emphasises the material interests that the Jesuits leverage to

---

384 *Lucii Cornelii Europæi Monarchia solipsorum*, p. 4: 'Porro vere sint, an veri umbrae, et potius agendorum cavendorum in Politicis delineamenta, quae hic tradit, tu videris', 'it is up to you to judge whether what he reports is true, or a shadow of the truth, and whether he wanted to outline a political design, and teach us what should be done in a government, or what should be avoided'.

385 Madden, *Memoirs*, p. 39.

secure the alliance of powerful individuals.[386] Significantly, in Manilius the passage is to be found in the description of animals, from which man is distinguished by his ability to investigate and understand nature, and his being inhabited by the divine.

The anti-Jesuitic polemic thus exemplifies some of the central reflections that *Memoirs* develops on the negotiation of credulity and credibility and the relationship between religious institutions and society. The order of Loyola embodies, in a dystopian form, a deep understanding of the crucial role played in the construction of epistemic and spiritual authority by educational and pedagogical practices, by the relationship with the ruling ranks of society, as well as forms control over the written word and in particular over the dynamics of circulation associated with the press, at different geographical and cultural latitudes, as we shall further discuss in the next chapter. The order epitomises a negative model in which the institutional apparatus of a church and its ability to influence the production and dissemination of information are harnessed not to a spiritual end but to foster the growth of the temporal power of the ecclesiastical hierarchies, to which the spread of superstition and fanaticism in society is functional. The Jesuits constitute a distinct target of criticism, but — as we shall see in the following pages — the polemic against the order also becomes part of a broader discourse in which the novel combines satirical-dystopian elements with utopian-prescriptive inventions to reflect on the construction of a republic of knowledge, and on tolerance as an antidote to misplaced credulity and fanaticism.

---

386 Manilius, *Astronomica*, pp. 294–95, line 899.

XII. Whose Credulity, Whose Credibility

Memoirs develops a fascinating reflection on the problem of the production, control, and circulation of knowledge. In the letters from the ambassadors there are comments on the astuteness with which the Jesuits adapted their propaganda to different cultural contexts and social spheres, not least through the use of the press. The power of the printed word and the sharing of knowledge as a key to progress are also specularly portrayed in utopian terms, in the virtuous practices attributed to the British rulers of the future. A universal 'commonwealth of learning' is the ideal towards which the ambassadors work as they gather information in distant countries and, particularly in the Ottoman East, rediscover lost Greco-Roman classics through Arabic translations.[387] A reflection on the most suitable methods of sharing and disseminating scientific knowledge runs throughout the novel and emerges with particular clarity in the description of Oxford University and the connected Royal printing press.[388] Publication is a critical hinge in the advancement of scientific disciplines, and the two meanings of 'submitting to the press' and 'making public' are inextricably linked in the use of the concept. Weather forecasting is a particularly illuminating example: the accuracy of the estimates in the twentieth-century Great Britain imagined in the novel rests on disciplinary institutionalisation, systematic empirical observation, methodological soundness, up-to-date instrumentation, and the systematic publication of results. Those assigned the specific chair established in Oxford in the nineteenth century are required to fulfil specific obligations in the regular collection of data, their publication, and collaboration with colleagues across the Channel. The description of this Oxonian system can be read in contrast to the ritual for controlling the weather performed by Laplanders, recounted by the ambassador to Moscow.[389]

A number of passages whose relation to the main body of the novel may appear obscure to the contemporary reader may be understood in the light of a general argument for an empirical and rational foundation of social reform and humankind's relationship with the natural world as an antibody to superstition and fanaticism. This is the case with the digression

---

387 Madden, *Memoirs*, pp. 22, 204, 207, 297.
388 Madden, *Memoirs*, pp. 141–52.
389 See *supra*, ch. 7.

reserved for a papal bull reforming Catholic obligations during Lent by allowing the consumption of fowl meat. The innovation is discussed on the basis of religious and philosophical elements, but is also essentially motivated by the observation of an objective necessity for the survival and well-being of the less affluent and more fragile social groups, especially children, as well as the economic and commercial consequences, which are not neglected.[390]

A significant episode recounted by the ambassador to Moscow concerns a Jewish genealogist gone mad and imprisoned, who claims direct descent from Adam, thereby justifying a demand to own nothing less than the entire globe.[391] Genealogy and its uses to claim political, economic, proprietary, and social rights in early modern Europe was, at the beginning of the eighteenth century, far from obsolete.[392] *Memoirs* portrays its complex topicality in the context of a world where the rationalism that could exclude ancient systems of hereditary determinism was still far from prevailing in the structuring of societies. The novel addresses not only the use of genealogy in the shaping of social relations and identities, but also its noteworthiness in relation to the construction of knowledge of the past and of the methods of historical research, drawing on the cultural and bibliographical heritage to which Madden was possibly exposed in his family environment.[393]

The location of episodes such as this one in liminal spaces with respect to the geographical heart of a Europe seen through British eyes would seem to suggest an ousting from the European space of certain practices considered obsolete, absurd, or superstitious. The recurrent descriptions of fraudulent and fanatical practices in the Islamic religious world — such as the sect of the Bumicilli[394] — are also significant in this sense. However, all the more scathing are the attacks on polemical targets within the heart of Christianity. One of the most effective satirical passages in the entire novel relates to the auction of relics organised by the Jesuits in 1998, whose catalogue the British ambassador in Rome transcribes in its entirety.[395] The comical multiplication of heads, limbs, and bones, and that of sacred objects and cheeses made from the breastmilk of saints is accompanied by attestations of authenticity made by the papacy, and by justifications that, even in the case of manifest logical impossibilities, exploit arguments *de auctoritate* to speculate on the faith and credulity of potential buyers. In

---

390 Madden, *Memoirs*, pp. 402–11.
391 Madden, *Memoirs*, pp. 352–61.
392 Friedrich, 'Genealogy and the History of Knowledge'; Jettot and Zuñiga, eds, *Genealogy and Social Status*.
393 See *supra*, ch. 3.
394 Madden, *Memoirs*, pp. 209–13.
395 Madden, *Memoirs*, pp. 99–132.

the dizzying list, in this 'so hideous a Recital of the superstitious Dreams and Inventions of these formal Hypocrites',[396] culminates the denunciation of a religious authority bent on the production of falsified, unreliable knowledge, used to profit from the faith of the simple.[397] Criticism of the authenticity and veneration of relics had been a recurring theme in the Reformation since John Calvin,[398] and our author did not lack sources of inspiration and models in the Protestant religious controversies of the seventeenth and eighteenth centuries, as suggested by the notes to the text in this volume. The effectiveness of the satirical strategy is demonstrated by the intriguing reproduction of these pages in later printed libels, in which the catalogue was given different dates and revitalised in the context of anti-Catholic polemics by new, anonymous introductions stressing their anti-fanatical purpose.[399]

Prediction of the future is obviously a favourite topic in the discussion about credibility and credulity. Using the three prefaces to argue the trustworthiness of his story, the editor — who is a reader of Pierre Bayle's *Dictionnaire historique et critique (An Historical and Critical Dictionary)*[400] — calls attention to beliefs and uses of the future that were being excluded from a system of knowledge built on reason and empirical enquiry and by a religious experience free from fanaticism and superstition.[401] The demonstrations and lists of exempla on the supernatural all bear the marks of an unreliable voice, whose opinion reveals the author's own through ironic reversal. Through references to ancient and modern works dealing with the future the writer assembles a notable intertextual encyclopaedia,

---

396 Madden, *Memoirs*, p. 128.

397 Burke, *A Social History of Knowledge*, pp. 197–212.

398 Walsham, 'The Pope's Merchandise and the Jesuits' Trumpery'.

399 *A Catalogue of the Most Eminently Venerable Relicks of the Roman Catholick Church*; reprinted, with a different initial advertisement, ed. Josephus Tela. Note that Josephus Tela may be a pseudonym of Joseph Webb, to which the 1752 edition is attributed in many catalogues (*tela* means 'web' in Italian). The 1752 edition was reviewed in *The Monthly Review or Literary Journal*, and the reviewer noted that 'The titlepage of this pamphlet sufficiently shews, that its design is only to ridicule the church of Rome, in a ludicrous enumeration of the holy trumpery, by which she has been so unhappy as to bring an eternal disgrace and contempt upon herself, in the opinion of all who have sense enough to see thro' the folly of a superstitious veneration for inanimate substances, even if they could be proved to be really what they are pretended to be'. The catalogue was also reproduced as 'A Catalogue of the Most Sacred and Eminently Venerable Relicks' in the *Gentleman's and London Magazine* in 1784 and in *The Baltimore Literary and Religious Magazine* in 1837, also indicating 1 June 1753 as the date of the auction.

400 Madden, *Memoirs*, p. 517, see also editorial notes on p. 249; Bayle, *Dictionaire historique et critique*; on Bayle see Eusterschulte, 'Pierre Bayle's *Dictionaire historique et critique*'; Burke, *A Social History of Knowledge*, pp. 188, 200, 208.

401 The relationship between religions and the Enlightenment has been the subject of profound historiographical revision in recent decades. For an overview: Jacob, *The Secular Enlightenment*; Matytsin and Edelstein, eds, *Let There Be Enlightenment*.

and by mocking their trust in prophets and seers, he challenges the authority of his sources. The future becomes an arena in which Enlightenment epistemologies of history and time are tested. By throwing into relief the credulity of his contemporaries, the author documents a cultural system in which scientific knowledge coexists and competes with occult and magical beliefs.

The intertextual references that punctuate the novel form a rich historical, literary, theological, and philosophical encyclopaedic selection. What does this cultural background reveal about the ideal reader, the (real) author's intended audience? And how does the work conceptualise the problem of credulity? Many elements support the hypothesis that the intended reader is highly educated. In addition to the narrator's overly sophisticated style, there is an abundance of examples and quotations taken from works of Greco-Latin antiquity — often themselves replete with references, as in the case of satires works — and a wealth of mentions of early modern works written in Latin and French as well as English. The satirical transposition of and commentary on British international and domestic politics also point in the same direction, with allusions to fiscal and institutional reforms and colonial administration issues that would undoubtedly be opaque to a reader less than well informed about the recent past and current British political and parliamentary affairs.

The ridicule of astrological, prophetic, and divinatory practices presupposes a reader who is able to grasp the difference between what is expressed by the narrator and the real author's opinion, or, in other words, to unmask the unreliable nature of the narrator's voice and to draw amusement from it. In short, it is clear that the novel is not — or certainly not primarily — aimed at the gullible public of astrology, which constitutes one of its implicit satirical targets. Rather, the ideal reader of the novel is part of an enlightened elite, who has already metabolised the changes brought about by a new epistemology of reason in their paradigm of reality. The reader implicitly identified in the text is Protestant — they would appreciate the anti-Jesuitical polemics in the work — patriotic, and loyalist (Hanoverian and pro-Walpole). They are also disenchanted, do not lend their trust to the pedantry of the aforementioned *auctoritates*, are able to question the authority of the narrator, and grasp the ironic deception of a text that adopts and exaggerates the trappings of academic writing. An obvious target for satire is therefore, before and perhaps more than the uneducated and credulous elements of society who consume questionable knowledge, the producers of said knowledge, who make questionable claims to authority, and take advantage of the credulity of others. Untruthful sources claiming to possess information about what lies ahead, of which the narrator constitutes a caricature, undoubtedly including those who profess the validity of astrological and divinatory techniques. Of these John Partridge, satirised in Swift's *Bickerstaff Papers* (1708) and mentioned in *Memoirs*,[402] provided a famous example while the proliferation of astrological almanacs and divination manuals persisted in Europe throughout the eighteenth century.[403] The novel features, in common with Swift's satire, a game of identity in which the author assumes the *persona* of an astrologer. Furthermore, both works entertain a complex relationship with the problem of authority in relation to knowledge. In Swift a defence of established authority can be seen behind the choice of Partridge as a target — a Quaker shoemaker whose predictions reached a wide audience through their editorial success — as well as behind the attacks against 'abuses in Religion', fanatics and religious 'enthusiasts' — be they Catholics or Puritan sects — in other satirical works such as *A Tale of a Tub*.[404] *Mutatis mutandis*, both Swift's and Madden's works tackle the question of the relationship between authority, knowledge, and the public, and both choose to do so by employing a literary device and adopting a satirical mode.

The satirical element, designed to appeal at an emotional level in order to stimulate a critical disposition and rational judgement in its readers,[405] refers us to an essential question about the social and cultural history of the text and its uses, the answer to which clearly lies outside the text itself. It is therefore to the mysterious history of the material circulation of the book and its actual readers that we must turn in the next few pages.

---

402 Madden, *Memoirs*, p. 253, with the variant spelling (or possibly misspelling) 'Patridge', which is to be found in John Partridge's own *Prodromus* (signed as Patridge).
403 Braida, *Le guide del tempo*; Perkins, *Visions of the Future*.
404 Mueller, 'A Tale of a Tub and Early Prose'.
405 Phiddian, *Satire and the Public Emotions*.

XIII. Bookish Mysteries and an 'Alternate George VI'

Twentieth-century secondary sources on Madden and his tale of the future are substantially based upon eighteenth and nineteenth century ones.[406] Two twentieth-century editions of *Memoirs* did not result in any new critical efforts.[407] The laconic entries in encyclopaedias and biographical dictionaries testify to Madden's limited historical and literary fortune: they are short and often inaccurate, and the same mistakes are passed on from one source to the next. Some give the year of publication of *Reflections and Resolutions* as 1731, some as 1732 (probably confusing it with *A Proposal for the General Encouragement of Learning in Dublin College*), while others give it, correctly, as 1738. Similarly, the publication of *A Letter to the Dublin-Society* is dated either 1734 or 1739. As for Madden's role in the Dublin Society, some sources place him among the founders, others describe him as just as a member, while still others say he was an outside supporter.

The extend of available scholarship in assessing the treatment of historical time in the novel and the text's relationship with the author's present, along with the scant attention dedicated to its publishing history, originated widespread confusion as regards the history of the printing of *Memoirs* and the destiny of its print run. The publication was announced by the pro-Walpole *London Journal* edited by James Pitt,[408] by the influential and long-standing *London Evening Post*, a three-weekly paper whose pro-Jacobite position has been the subject of debates,[409] and by the *Fog's Weekly Journal*, a publication of Jacobite inclination but no stranger to accommodating Whiggism, heir to the *Mist's Weekly Journal*, and at the time

---

406 See for example [Jones], *New Biographical Dictionary, sub voce* 'Madden (D. R. Samuel)'; Nichols, *Literary Anecdotes*, II, pp. 32–33, 699; 'Art. IV: rev. Samuel Madden'; J. W. C., 'The Dramatic Writers of Ireland No. II [...]', esp. pp. 174–75.

407 Madden, *Memoirs of the Twentieth Century*, with an 'Introduction' by Bosse; Madden, *Memoirs of the Twentieth Century*, includes Gillick, 'Prevision'.

408 'On Monday the 9th of April will be Published', *London Journal*, 24 March 1732–1733.

409 'On Monday the 9th of April will be Publish'd', *London Evening Post*, 24 March 1733–27 March 1733; 'On Monday the 9th of April will be Publish'd', *London Evening Post*, 27 March 1733–29 March 1733; 'On Monday the 9th of April will be Publish'd', *London Evening Post*, 31 March 1733–3 April 1733; Harris, *A Patriot Press*, pp. 17, 55; Cranfield, 'The "London Evening Post"'; Harris, 'The *London Evening Post*'.

under the editorship of Charles Molloy.[410] The book came out between the end of March and the beginning of April 1733. The wages check book belonging to William Bowyer, one of the three printers of the volume, enables us to place the composing and printing between the beginning of February and the end of March. The first payment to composers who worked on the text is recorded on 10 February 1732 (old-style calendar year). The names of the compositors and pressmen who set the pages or sheets and their corresponding wages were recorded by Bowyer at intervals of 1–3 weeks; in this case the previous entry is dated 27 January, hence it can be deduced with good approximation that the composition had begun after 27 January, although an even earlier start cannot be ruled out entirely, since sometimes workers carried their claims over, beyond the usual time.[411] The date of the completion of the printing and delivery of the first copies on 24 March is recorded in both the customer account and the paper account.[412] The production, which took place at the same time as that of a number of other works Bowyer had in preparation, offers an example of the complexity of workflows that characterised the activities of an early eighteenth-century London print shop.[413]

Thanks to the ledgers and to a testimony by John Nichols — Bowyer's apprentice at the time and author of that exceptional source on eighteenth-century English publishing which is the *Literary Anecdotes* — it is known that out of the one thousand copies commissioned by the author, some nine hundred were eliminated fresh out of print.

> There is something mysterious in the history of these Memoirs, which are addressed, in an ironical dedication, to Frederick Prince of Wales. Only one volume of the work appeared; and whether any more were really intended is uncertain. One thousand copies of it were printed, with such very great dispatch, that three printers were employed on

---

410 'On Monday the 9th of April will be Published', *Fog's Weekly Journal*, 31 March 1733; 'On Monday the 9th of April will be Published', *Fog's Weekly Journal*, 7 April 1733; Harris, *A Patriot Press*, pp. 16, 45 n.; Molloy was born in Ireland and educated at Trinity College Dublin: Sambrook, 'Molloy, Charles'.

411 *The Bowyer Ledgers*, microfiche, ledger C1465–1469, esp. C1465 (wages check book); see also Maslen and Lancaster, 'Introductory Commentary', pp. xxviii–xxix.

412 *The Bowyer Ledgers*, microfiche, A296, P886. The printing of five hundred copies of an *errata* slip is also recorded in the customer account on 24 March. In the wages check book the remuneration for the printing of the *errata* is recorded on 11 April; since the previous entry is dated 24 March and since the pressman who worked on the *errata* — John Mazemore — was also present in the record on that date, the *errata* could have been printed immediately after the completion of the copies of the book, see microfiche, A296, C1468–1469. On the *errata* slip see also *infra*, this chapter and 'A note on the text'.

413 This may perhaps also explain the existence of slightly different impressions within the only existing print run, revealed by a pagination error (p. 523 incorrectly numbered) found in only a few copies.

it (Bowyer, Woodfall, and Roberts); and the names of an uncommon number of reputable book sellers appeared in the title-page. In less than a fortnight, however, 900 of the copies were delivered to Dr Madden, and probably destroyed. The current report is, that the edition was suppressed on the day of publication; and that it is now exceedingly scarce, is certain.[414]

In the final 'Additions and Corrections' to his *Literary Anecdotes*, Nichols then adds further details, consistent with what Bowyer's ledgers document (possibly the source he relies on):

> The extraordinary circumstances attending the printing and Suppression of these Memoirs have been already mentioned [...] but the reasons for it are not very evident. The whole of the business was transacted by Mr Bowyer, without either of the other Printers (Roberts and Woodfall) ever seeing the author. The book was finished at the press, March 24, 1732–3; and 100 copies were that day delivered to the Author. On the 28th a number of them were delivered to the several Booksellers mentioned in the title-page; and in four days after, all that were un sold were recalled, and 800 of them given up to Dr Madden to be destroyed.[415]

The participation of Woodfall and Roberts, the distribution to a number of the booksellers mentioned in the titlepage, as well as the delivery date of 24 March and the recall of copies on 2 April are registered in the printer's ledgers.[416] There is also the intriguing hypothesis that the destruction of 900 copies out of 1,000 is a legend deliberately circulated to increase the prestige of the work as a collector's item, and to contribute, with a discourse around the text, to the aura of exclusivity built up, as we have seen, in the preface, thus adding an element typical of media hoaxes to the story. Although the recall of copies documented in the printer's ledgers, and the impossibility of finding reviews or mentions in the contemporary press after its publication, including those newspapers that had announced its printing between March and April 1733 — such as the above-mentioned *London Journal*, the *London Evening Post*, and the *Fog's Weekly Journal* — would seem to be circumstantial evidence in favour of an effectively suppressed or very limited circulation. As for the book's rarity, until the beginning of the nineteenth century only three

---

414 Nichols, *Literary Anecdotes*, pp. 31–32 n.

415 Nichols, *Literary Anecdotes*, p. 700, the indication 1732–1733 follows the traditional computing of the year, beginning on 25 March, Lady Day.

416 *The Bowyer Ledgers*, microfiche, A296 (customer account), P886 (paper accounts, see here for delivery dates); see also Maslen and Lancaster, 'Checklist of Bowyer Printing', p. 152, entry 1920, for Nichols' reliance on the ledgers.

surviving copies were known about, by the 1980s four exemplars were registered in the United States,[417] while today at least eighteen copies are listed in catalogues of North American and European libraries. In the years following its publication, one copy was notably to be found in Horace Walpole's library.[418] The exemplar today at the British Library bears the bookplate Mark Cephas Tutet (approximately 1733–1785). Merchant, member of the Society of Antiquaries of London, and bibliophile,[419] Tutet was described by Thomas Dibdin as a renowned 'bibliomaniac' of good judgement and taste, owner of a 'cabinet of literary bijoux'.[420] Also part of a remarkable collection was the copy today at the Göttingen State and University Library, Georg-August-Universität Göttingen. It bears the bookplate of Christian Johann Sullow (1739–c. 1796), son of Caspar Süllow (c. 1687–1750), and chancellor (*Kantzley*) in the London office of the Hanoverian government between 1731 and 1749. Christian Johann may have inherited the book from his father, but as he was a collector he may have acquired it during his lifetime.[421]

Other exemplars bear the marks of affectionate owners: in eight copies the *errata* slip was mounted on one of the back endpapers, and in one copy the corrections indicated by the *errata* have been pencilled in at the corresponding points in the text.[422] In eight copies handwritten notes have been added on the preliminary leaves, commenting on the rarity of the book and the suppression of the print run, with or without an indication of Bowyer's testimony as a source, in some cases by hands which clearly came later — those of scrupulous librarians and cataloguers — in some cases likely coeval to the edition.

Bowyer's recollection of the circumstances of the print — transcribed by Nichols and picked up by many subsequent commentators — contains useful information but also generated more than one misreading. Some have attributed the elimination of the print run to political frictions with the Prince of Wales's entourage, misinterpreting the novel's dedication as ironic. The reference to six volumes in the titlepage was taken at face value by Bowyer and his tributaries, who described the work as unfinished, whereas the announcement of forthcoming volumes was more likely to

417 Alkon, *Origins*, p. 302 n. 11.

418 Horace Walpole's bookplate is in the copy at The Lewis Walpole Library, Yale University; see also Hazen, *A Catalogue of Horace Walpole's Library*, II, p. 550.

419 *A Catalogue of the Genuine and Valuable Collection*, see p. 4, entry 19.

420 Dibdin, *The Bibliomania*, II, p. 531, see also pp. 532–33. Tutet's copy was also mentioned by Nichols, *Literary Anecdotes*, pp. 32, 700.

421 Bühring, *Die Deutsche Kanzlei in London*, p. 78; Broadwell, 'Lions on the Clock II'. For the identification of the bookplate see also 'Wappen des C. J. Sullon' (here Sullon is a misspelling for Sullow).

422 Copy at The Lewis Walpole Library, Yale University.

have been written in mocking imitation of the excruciating length of learned treatises of the day.[423]

Bowyer's ledgers also confirm that the printing of the book was not commissioned and paid for by the twenty and more prestigious book-sellers and publishers listed in the colophon (Figure 7): the account was actually made out to Madden. As Keith Maslen aptly noted, 'imprints were not meant to reveal the background of a commercial transaction, and therefore may seriously mislead the modern scholar who reads them too literally'.[424] However, this does not necessarily mean that no relationship or collaboration took place between Madden and the names for whom the title page claimed the work was printed, especially since in a number of cases these were not only booksellers but also publishers, and we know that a number of copies were actually delivered to these firms on 28 March, immediately after printing.[425] Looking, for example, at the first names listed, Osborn and Longman were recipients of twenty-five copies. From 1724 Thomas Longman was no longer simply an apprentice to the book-seller John Osborn: he had acquired the shop, warehouse, and publishing business of John Taylor, had entered into partnership with Osborn, and was set to take over the activities on the latter's death (1734), not without the participation of Osborn's daughter Mary, whom he had married in 1731.[426] In Bowyer's ledgers, the two hundred copies delivered to Strahan stand out. This is George Strahan (not the today better-known William with the same surname, who was still an apprentice at the time),[427] whose name appears on a number of title pages of books printed by Bowyer between the 1710s and 1730s.[428] Batley (twenty-five copies), Shropshire (twelve), Millar (ten), and Jolliffe (six) also appear among the recipients of deliveries made between 28 March and 2 April.[429]

In any case, since the author himself commissioned the edition, it seems highly unlikely that the destruction of most of the print run was aimed at limiting circulation to a few close acquaintances — as at least two commentators have suggested[430] — something which Madden could easily have decided beforehand. Others, following Nichols, have interpreted

---

423 In a similar vein to that present in the text of the novel, see *supra*, ch. 6 and ch. 9, see also Alkon, *Origins*, p. 94.

424 Maslen, *An Early London Printing House at Work*, p. 101, see here n. 8 for references to Nichols' *Literary Anecdotes* and Bowyer's paper-stock ledger.

425 *The Bowyer Ledgers*, microfiche, P886.

426 Briggs, *A History of Longmans*, pp. 29, 37, 39, 45, 62 n. 108, 547.

427 Austen Leigh, 'William Strahan', p. 263.

428 *The Bowyer Ledgers*, 'Index of Names and Titles', *sub voce* 'Strahan, George'.

429 *The Bowyer Ledgers*, microfiche, P886.

430 Chuanacháin, 'Utopianism', p. 206; Moore, *The Novel*, p. 705.

Madden's action as being 'in deference to Robert Walpole'.[431] Ó Ciardha, for example, has put forward a similar hypothesis:

> it may have had something to do with the fact that the *Memoirs* went to press as the war of the Polish succession (1733–1735) was beginning, which considerably altered the political situation in Europe in favour of the exiled Stuarts. This, combined with the quasi-Jacobite activities of the hero and his indirect criticism of the church, may have seemed inappropriate in a book dedicated to Frederick and could explain why Madden destroyed the majority of the print run before the work could go into circulation.[432]

It is likely that the author feared that certain aspects of the work might be misunderstood, even if it would be incorrect to attribute to the real author the pro-Jacobite stance professed opportunistically by the novel's artful narrator, all the more so given the writer's friendship with Robert Walpole. Madden had discussed with Walpole the advisability of using satire against the government's opposition, around the same time as the idea for *Memoirs* was presumably taking shape. He had proposed launching a satirical counterattack against the Tories united around *The Craftsman*, founded in 1726 (Figure 9):

> Begin an attack against them in a method & manner entirely new & that there was no way so effectual to defeat them, as to turn their own Cannon against them & ridicule them; for besides that this is no reasoning age nor our People so fond of strong arguments as biting Jests, I was persuaded if once the laugh could be turn'd against them the mob would desert them & they must be undone.[433]

There is no evidence of a deterioration of Madden's relationship with Walpole around 1732–1733. He was never associated with those among his friends and acquaintances who followed Henry Bolingbroke into the Brothers Club, nor into the Scriblerus Club. His enduring commitment to the government cause is shown by the — admittedly limited but eloquent — documentary evidence: in 1740, he sent some of his latest writings to Walpole, including the first two cantos of the poem 'Bermuda Adventure', in which Walpole was 'often mentioned [...] with Honour & [...] the War with Spain makes a number of Passages very seasonable for these times'. The writer asked Walpole to read them through: 'to be publisht when & how you please, with whatever corrections those you entrust them with

---

431 Welch and Stewart, eds, *The Oxford Companion*, p. 350.
432 Ó Ciardha, 'Madden'; see also Ó Ciardha, *Ireland and the Jacobite Cause*, p. 246 and n. 41.
433 Cambridge, The Cholmondeley Papers, MS 1507, Madden to Walpole, n.d. [after June 1729]; see also Urstad, *Sir Robert Walpole's Poets*, p. 114; Holmes, 'Introduction', pp. xxxi and xl n. 123; Harris, *London Newspapers in the Age of Walpole*, p. 110.

think best [...] they & I are absolutely at your service, if such trivial things [Madden's writings] can be worth your notice'.[434]

The fact that some of the surviving copies have a folding plate with a portrait of Frederick Lewis bound after the title page and before the dedication to the prince (Figure 4), seems to support the idea of a circulation restricted to a small circle of friends and acquaintances close to Walpole's government. One of the copies provides further confirmation of this theory. It is a copy that the author presented to Lord Hervey soon after its publication, with a dedication penned on the flyleaf: '[...] this book is most humbly presented by the Author with the utmost deference for his approbation or Censure of it [...]'.[435] Hervey, courtier and writer, was a supporter and close political friend of Walpole, and from 1730 he was vice-chamberlain to the King's household and a member of the Privy Council. A member of parliament from 1725, his defence of the prime minister during the excise debate in 1733 earned him elevation to the House of Lords, in his father's barony, while in 1731 his liaison with Frederick Louis's mistress Anne Vane (d. 1736) and his close relationship with Queen Caroline estranged him from the Prince of Wales.[436] Incidentally, in 1733, Hervey began writing his own *Memoirs*, destined to become an essential source of knowledge about the court, politics, and power dynamics in Walpole's government between 1727 and 1737.[437] The publication of Hervey and Lady Montague's *Verses Address'd to the Imitator of the First Satire of the Second Book of Horace* in March 1733,[438] and the fact that he became Alexander Pope's satirical target certainly made Hervey the ideal reader of that satirical 'cannon' aimed in the opposite direction that Madden had described in writing to Walpole a few years earlier.

It seems that the *Memoirs'* ideological and political context leaves two viable hypotheses as regards the destruction of the print run. One possible scenario is that the protective veil of anonymity had somehow been lost and that the author, given his position as a clergyman in the Church of Ireland and his role at court, deemed it inappropriate to be associated with

---

434 Cambridge, The Cholmondeley Papers, MS 3047, Madden to Walpole, 3 January 1740; partially quoted in Urstad, *Sir Robert Walpole's Poets*, pp. 116, 90 (Urstad transcribes 'service' in place of 'notice', our transcription follows the original); on Walpole and pro-government propaganda in the early eighteenth century see also Tortarolo, *The Invention of Free Press*, pp. 38–40.

435 Copy at National Trust Libraries, Ickworth, UK.

436 Browning, 'Hervey, John'; Paglia, 'Lord Hervey and Pope'.

437 Hervey, *Memoirs of the Reign of George the Second*; Hervey, *Some Materials Towards Memoirs of the Reign of King George II*.

438 Donaldson, 'Concealing and Revealing'.

Figure 9a. Caleb D'Anvers [pseudonym used jointly by the contributors to *The Craftsman*, Nicholas Amhurst, Bolingbroke, and William Pulteney], *Corruption in the British Government under Walpole, and Its Opponents*, detail including the frontispiece to vol. 2 of *The Craftsman*. 'A harlequin of state', Walpole as harlequin sells the nation to the devil. Copy at Wellcome Collection, reproduced under Attribution 4.0 International (CC BY 4.0) licence.

Figure 9b. Caleb D'Anvers, *Corruption in the British Government under Walpole, and Its Opponents*, detail including the frontispiece to vol. 3 of *The Craftsman*. 'Hail typographic art': a compositor composing movable type in a composing stick to confound tyranny through the freedom of the press. Copy at Wellcome Collection, reproduced under Attribution 4.0 International (CC BY 4.0) licence.

a work of such open political engagement.[439] Supporting this hypothesis, in the closing remarks of the above-mentioned letter presenting his satirical plans in the late 1720s, Madden mentioned his appointment as first chaplain to the Prince, and his acquaintance with August Schutz,[440] 'from whom', the writer asked his powerful correspondent, 'if you acquire or give any directions about me I beg this design may be absolutely concealed.'[441]

Another plausible hypothesis, a possible concause along with the loss of anonymity of the work, is that, after the drafting had begun possibly in 1728 and certainly before 1732 — as the references on the title page and in the first preface as well as the date of the dedication suggest —[442] by the time of publication one or more of the political topics touched upon in the novel had simply become too sensitive with regard to current affairs. One example is Walpole's refusal to support Habsburg Austria in the War of the Polish Succession. In the novel, the British ambassador to Constantinople in 1997 remarks on the death of the Polish king, describing the monarch's personality as intemperate and overindulgent in eating and drinking,[443] comments which might have appeared unseemly, given the death of Augustus II of Poland in February 1733, just a few weeks before the book came out. Furthermore, the epistolary narrative refers to the Polish dynastic line as surviving until the twentieth century, describing future pretenders to the throne as mere puppets in the hands of various political factions; again, given what was going on in Europe at the time, the writer might have felt that such remarks were just too tactless.

As for contemporary events in Britain, in the novel, the Jesuits are attributed with introducing taxation on commerce in luxury goods, and giving tax relief for agricultural activities, measures which, according to the British ambassador to Rome, made it possible to avoid food shortages and

---

439 In favour of this hypothesis: Chuanacháin, 'Utopianism', p. 235. For a theoretical background on anonymity in eighteenth-century written communication: Braida, L'autore assente.

440 In all likelihood Augustus Schutz, George II's Master of Robes; Hunt, ed., The Irish Parliament, p. xvi; Beattie, The English Court, p. 64 and n. 2.

441 Cambridge, The Cholmondeley Papers, MS 1507, Madden to Walpole, n.d. [after June 1729]. While 1727 was written on the letter in pencil by another, posterior hand (presumably by looking at other correspondences preceding and following the letter in the same archival series), and it was adopted by secondary sources quoting the document, the reference to the appointment as Frederick's chaplain suggests that the letter may be dated sometime after June 1729, the date of Madden's appointment as reported by Lees, 'The Religious Retinue', p. 102, and by Bucholz, ed., 'Household of Frederick Lewis', p. 17.

442 Madden, Memoirs, pp. 18, x; see also supra, ch. 2. Four copies bear a handwritten correction of the year of the dedication, 1731, to 1733: Library of Congress, Washington, DC; The Lilly Library, University of Indiana, Bloomington, Indiana; Newberry, Chicago, Illinois; Private collection.

443 Madden, Memoirs, pp. 336–37.

famine.[444] In the spring of 1733, Walpole was facing rising opposition to his scheme of extending the excise on tobacco, and indeed, between March and April, a campaign against the excise led the *de facto* prime minister to withdraw the proposal from parliamentary discussion.[445]

Beyond the excise crisis, it is possible that Madden wanted to avoid getting caught in the middle of the political clash between Walpole and the Whig opposition, in which Stanhope had played a key role since 1732. In other words, it is possible that the writer did not want to jeopardise his friendship with either of them, perhaps fearing that the excellent relationship enjoyed by their fictional counterparts in the novel — the ambassador to Constantinople and the Lord High Treasurer in London — might have been seen as out of place. It is in fact possible that Madden's friendship with the fourth Earl of Chesterfield started before their known correspondence, in the 1730s, as the homonymous character would suggest, but as of today no documentation exists to confirm this.

In conclusion, there are no archival records to date that make it possible to establish in a decisive way why so much of the book's print run was destroyed. However, available documents read in the context of circumstantial evidence do make it possible to assume that, in terms of reasons linked to contemporary political events — whether these were related to the author's own sensitivities or to having been explicitly asked to do so by Walpole — there was no discord between the two.

One last clarification must be reserved for the erroneous, yet recurring attribution to Madden of *The Reign of George VI*.[446] This is a work of futuristic fiction published anonymously in London in 1763, and listed by numerous catalogues — including that of Trinity College Library —[447] as having been written by our author. Indeed, some secondary sources — including the *New Cambridge Bibliography of English Literature*, actually list it as a new edition of *Memoirs*.[448] A significant number of ideological, thematic, textual, and stylistic elements show that the two works were not written by the same pen, but oddly enough, these have never been exhaustively listed. At the level of narrative invention, the geopolitical scenarios imagined by the anonymous author of *The Reign* are radically different from Madden's work in all their main traits. In the future imagined in *The Reign*, the whole of Italy, except for Venice, has been unified by

---

444 Madden, *Memoirs*, p. 289.

445 Langford, *A Polite and Commercial People*, esp. p. 30.

446 *The Reign*, see also *supra*, ch. 2.

447 Trinity College Dublin, Library, items acquired by the Library before 1872. The erroneous attribution is currently (2023) repeated in a number of entries in the meta-online public access catalogue Worldcat, in the English Wikipedia entry, and in the metadata of two copies digitised in the Internet Archive. For a correct reference to the attribution being unfounded see: Clute, 'Madden, Samuel'.

448 Watson, ed., *The New Cambridge Bibliography of English Literature*, p. 993.

the Bourbons of Naples (and not under the Pope); France (and not the Jesuits) is the most powerful and menacing presence in Europe, a presence which George VI (and not one of his distant descendants) annihilates in the twentieth century; the Spanish monarchy (far from being weak) has taken over Portugal and extended her overseas dominions in Central and South America; Great Britain no longer has a base in the Mediterranean, and her internal affairs are troubled by the Whigs' constant scheming.[449]

The Reign and Memoirs have some similar details, such as the rise of Russia, the primacy of British naval power, and the attention paid to the American colonies in future balances of global powers. However, it still seems highly unlikely that the same writer would have taken such different positions on a number of key issues and have undergone a complete political turnaround, professing Tory ideas in The Reign, even in the light of the thirty years separating the two novels (and especially given the evidence discussed earlier of Madden's political consistency well into the 1740s). The two novels are also constructed in very different ways: unlike the epistolary and satirical nature of Memoirs, The Reign proposes a historical chronicle of the future starting in 1900, mimicking the structure and tone of a short treaty, with an introduction devoted to a didactic summary of British history from 1660 to the end of the nineteenth century.[450] Historical processes, chains of events, and interconnected political choices are at centre stage in Memoirs, while George VI is the exclusive protagonist of The Reign, in which 'the historian has confined himself to the actions of the Prince alone. And in the account of the exploits, he little more than names any principal Commander, directing his whole attention to the conduct of the King'.[451] The coexistence of utopian prescription and ominous prevision runs through Memoirs, while an allegorical roman-à-thèse reading with clear references to British current affairs and the Seven Years' War is transparently suggested in The Reign.[452] Moreover (though the list could be longer), the distinct interest shown in The Reign for (future) military history and polemological strategy is non-existent in Memoirs, and the stylistic patterns to be found in the respective introductions could not be more different — full of erudite circumlocutions in one, marked by rhetorical questions and emphatic repetitions in the other.[453]

In his preface to a late nineteenth-century edition of The Reign, the editor put forward a convincing argument for the probable Midlands

---

449 I explore The Reign's construction of the future in more in depth in Iannuzzi, 'Waging Future Wars'.

450 'Introduction: Containing a Review of British History A.D. 1660–1900', The Reign, pp. i–ix (after the preface).

451 The Reign, 'Preface', p. x.

452 The Reign, 'Preface', p. xi.

453 The Reign, 'Preface', p. ix.

origin of the anonymous author, by virtue of various internal references in the text.[454] It seems interesting, also for the purposes of future further investigation into the mysterious authorship of this chronicle of the future, that the bookseller to whom the printing is owed, William Nicoll, published other political pamphlets in the mid–1760s. These included libels intervening in the John Wilkes case after he was arrested for the inflammatory attacks on the Earl of Bute, the terms of the Treaty of Paris, and George III's speech commending the peace.[455] Other pamphlets published by Nicoll tackled the political shifts affecting the ranks of the Tories and conservative patriots, where loyalty to Pitt was coupled with growing concerns about the political radicalism of some of his allies.[456]

However, the presence of a 'George VI' both on Madden's title page and in *The Reign*'s main title, along with a futuristic projection not common among their contemporaries, were enough to generate confusion as regards the authorship of the two novels, which the rhapsodic nature of subsequent scholarly attention has not helped to dissipate.

454 Oman, 'The Editor's Preface', pp. xxiii, xxvi.
455 *A Letter to the Right Honourable Earl Temple.*
456 *The True Whig Displayed*; Vaughn, *The Politics of Empire*, pp. 174–79.

XIV. Concluding Remarks

The richness of the themes and rhetorical strategies at work in *Memoirs* locates it at the crossroads of a number of historical-cultural processes. The novel lends itself very well to being read as an expression of contemporary British satire — stimulating reflections on the adoption of ironic mechanisms in public communication — as well as being a part of the longer history of anti-Catholic and anti-Jesuit polemics. These aspects may contribute to a cultural history of satire and British society in the eighteenth century. The multitude of satirical elements in *Memoirs* need to be seen as being embedded in a cultural milieu which, in just a few years, saw the publication of a series of masterpieces parodying existing literary genres.[457] At the time, authors such as Jonathan Swift (*A Tale of a Tub*, *The Bickerstaff Papers*, *Gulliver's Travels*), Alexander Pope (*The Rape of the Lock*, *The Dunciad*, *Peri Bathous*) and John Gay (*The Beggar's Opera*), were busy giving exuberant expression to various types of formal experimentation, and were also making a mockery of prophetic-predictive beliefs (see, for example, *The Bickerstaff Papers* predicting the death of the astrologer John Partridge). In 1728, the year in which the novel's narrator claims to have received the letters from the future, *The Dunciad* and *Peri Bathous* were published and *The Beggar's Opera* premiered in London; Swift's *Gulliver's Travels* had been published just two years before.

Against this backdrop, Madden's history of the future represents a formal experimentation in generic conventions, and a satirical commentary on the methods and postures of historical writing. Its complex (and somewhat contradictory) semantic layers owe part of their richness also to the epistolary form, which functions as a formal correlative of a transnational historical-political perspective that tends towards being global in scope. However, the treatment of time in this futuristic narrative may not be fully appreciated if seen as the mere product of formal manipulation at the literary level. It may be better explained — as the previous pages have hopefully shown — as a specific manifestation of broader cultural processes of conceptualisation of historical time and the future, influenced by the pace and epistemological depth of the changes that accompanied the new scientific and historical-geographical knowledge

---

457 This is a benchmark in Alkon's interpretation, see his *Origins*, p. 103. A good starting-point on eighteenth-century satire is Quintero, ed., *A Companion to Satire*, part II.

Figure 10. 'Samuel Madden. Aetatis suae 68, 1755', *European Magazine*, 41 (April 1802), p. 264. Copy at Princeton University, via Google Books, no known restriction for scholarly use.

available in eighteenth-century Europe. Of course, this influence resulted in marked, post-Aristotelian shifts as regards verisimilitude and plausibility in fictional imagery, but also, at a no less important level, it changed the conceptualisation and rendering of history as being informed by a linear temporality and as home to chains of cause and effect.

It is the possibility for mankind to exert an influence on historical processes, or in other words, the pliability of the future, that essentially determines the contents of the letters 'published' in *Memoirs*, which devote a great deal of attention to describing the processes that brought about the current state of affairs. Some of these descriptions are to be read in a prescriptive sense, such as the good reforms undertaken by the British government, while others are to be seen as ominous warnings, like the dire consequences of the failure to impede the rise of the Jesuits.

The narrative frame and the letters juxtapose different strategies and argumentative aims. As shown by the close reading of the prefatory sections, the narrator is not only unreliable, but also fundamentally inconsistent. On the one hand, the reader is made aware of his unreliability by the glaring contradictions in what he says, for example, the opportunistic pro-Jacobite and anti-Jacobite about-turns, or his thoughts on the Jesuits at different points. At the same time, the narrator also expresses opinions in line with those of the British diplomats, and most certainly closer to those of the real author, for example when reflecting on progress and the acceleration of history. As in *Gulliver's Travels*, an important part of the satiric effect is achieved by the gap between what the narrator states explicitly, and what the reader is able to take in beyond the literal meaning of the narrator's words.

Likewise, the future geopolitical scenarios outlined in the letters have differing logical ties to the ideas we might attribute to the real author. Positive examples — mainly attributed to British strategies and choices — ought to be read as thought experiments, demonstrating, in the laboratory of a fictive history, ideas and policies expressed elsewhere in a programmatic form (for example in *Reflections and Resolutions*). Other predictions, such as the success of the Jesuits, or the decadent fate of France, show the unwelcome consequences that inaction or the wrong decisions may have in the future.

Admittedly, this lack of homogeneity in the novel's construction of the future makes its relationship with the genre of the encomiastic exhortation to the Prince more complex, but it also makes for a more fascinating and challenging read today. Most certainly, by tracing the connections between the imaginative feats and literary strategies of *Memoirs* and their location in coeval early eighteenth-century British and Irish political debate, or, in other words, by tracing the connections between the text and its cultural context(s), we gain a better understanding of its multiple extrapolation strategies, and a clearer idea of what the book contributes to a cultural history of the future and of speculative fiction.

Part II

Memoirs of the Twentieth Century

A Note on the Text

Copies of the original 1733 edition of *Memoirs* are extremely rare: eighteen are to be found in North American and European libraries, two others are known to exist in private collections. The exemplar owned by the British Library served as the basis for the text reproduced here. No manuscript copies have survived, and only one print run is known to exist. The present edition is therefore not concerned with collating textual variants, although some material characteristics of the surviving exemplars are pointed out to contribute to a history of the text's circulation and its intellectual and political significance.

No annotated edition of the text has ever been published. The 1972 edition with an introduction by Malcolm J. Bosse (New York: Garland) is a facsimile of the original with a five-page introduction that offers a brief outline of the text's content. The 2010 digital edition (n.p.: Halmos, PDF) is a transcription of the original without notes or other apparatuses, and includes a fourteen-page essay by Liam Gillick, which is not a commentary on Madden's text, but rather a creative exercise in futurology from the standpoint of a visual artist.

The editorial notes in the present edition are intended to provide information essential for understanding the text, without offering an exhaustive commentary on its contents or discussing possible interpretations. Notes gloss archaic and obsolete terms and borrowings from other languages that are no longer in use, provide the translation of quotes and expressions in languages other than English (notably Latin), and identify sources and references. Where possible, translations have been taken from modern editions of the cited texts. Translations are mine unless otherwise indicated. A number of the tags and references used in *Memoirs* are commonplace, drawn from a wealth of knowledge familiar to the author through secondary sources. In these cases, too, primary sources have been traced and indicated, highlighting where appropriate the derivative nature of the quotation, or its recurrence in later compilations familiar to the author. Other notes of an informative nature – on people, places, and events mentioned in the text, on historical and literary contexts, and indications of secondary sources – are kept to a minimum. An in-depth discussion of these aspects, as well as commentary on the content and its interpretation, is instead offered in the first section of the volume.

In giving access to the text, this modern edition is to some extent a recreation of it, since it obviously cannot incorporate the material characteristics of the original on which it is based. Nonetheless, some elements have been maintained which may seem unusual to today's readers, particularly those who are not familiar with early eighteenth-century print culture. In particular, the text retains the capitalisation, punctuation, and italics of the original edition. It also retains the original spelling, including obsolete, non-standardised forms (e.g. *deriv'd, Heroick, imprest*), variants and inconsistencies (e.g. *under-sell, undersell; Moscow, Mosco*), and a number of typos and material errors. These elements have not been normalised, and are offered to the contemporary reader as bearers of historical and authorial significance (such as diatopic and diachronic language varieties, idiolects), or as revealing of the circumstances in which the edition was produced (for example the hasty printing process mentioned by contemporary witnesses). Explicative notes have been provided whenever clarification was needed to facilitate the contemporary reader. As in other eighteenth-century texts, in the original edition of *Memoirs*, the 's' was rendered as an '*f*', except at the conclusion of a word. As this convention may be considered to have no specific semantic value or implication, transcriptions of the old style '*f*' have been silently modernised.

Original footnotes are set at the bottom of the page. The original edition employed symbols such as one or more asterisks and daggers to mark different footnotes on a single page. The system adopted in this edition does not reproduce the sequence of symbols of the original, as in some instances footnotes from two original pages fall on a single page or two or more footnotes originally on the same page fall on different pages. Editorial notes are presented as endnotes keyed to the page number in this edition, original page number in square brackets, and lemma or relevant point in the text.

The 1733 edition followed the common eighteenth-century practice of printing the first word of a following page immediately below the last word on every page, to aid the reader. These catchwords were not retained. Neither have type features such as leading section words being in all capital letters, with the exception of the half-title and title pages, which are type-facsimiles of the originals. Some typographic elements (repeated crowns or floral motifs) separated the title from the first letter (on page 1), some of the letters from each other (pages 28, 54, 74, 98, 132, 153, 284), the beginning and end of the second preface (215, 257), and the end of the work (527). These elements have not been reproduced.

Original page numbers are placed in brackets in the text at the beginning of the page. In the event a page break occurs in the middle of a word, the bracketed number is placed at the end of the word. The dedication page numbers retain the roman numerals used in the original edition. In the case of footnotes readers may derive the original page number by referring to the page number of the superscripted reference symbol in the text. The original edition contains two sets of page numbers 1–31: one for the first preface, and one at the beginning of the letters. Pages 155–60 and 324–27 are omitted in pagination but text and register are continuous. Page 271 is numbered 171. These anomalies have been retained in the indications in square brackets.

Extraneous space preceding or following marks of punctuation has been closed up. In the footnote on page 20 the erroneous duplication of the full stop after 'Lib.' has been silently amended. Some of the surviving copies contain an *errata* slip, which scrupulous owners have mounted on one of the back endpapers. The *errata* indicates fifteen amendments, which have been silently incorporated into the text:

> Dedicat. p. iii l. 3. for *have* read *has.*
> Page 33. l. antepenult. r. the *Priesthood.*
> 63. l. 13. for *Things* r. *Strings.*
> 68. l. 1. r. *June.* with a full Stop after it.
> 92. l. 10. for *has* read *have.*
> 116. l. 23. for *absur'd* r. *absurd.*
> 122. l. 24. for *Helina* r. *Helena.*
> 123. l. 22. for *Sebastion* r. *Sebastian.*
> 127. l. 16. for *Popalo* r. *Populo.*
> 137. l. 11. for *on Philosophy* r. *en Philosophe.*
> 204. l. 3. for *Saguntus* r. *Saguntum.*
> 207. l. 13. for *Godfather* r. *Grandfather.*
> 259. l. 6. for *her* r. *his.*
> 334. l. 10. dele *in.*
> 461. l. ult. for *Excuses* r. *Causes.*

Samuel Madden, *Memoirs of the Twentieth Century*

MEMOIRS
OF THE
Twentieth Century.

VOL. I.

MEMOIRS
OF THE
Twentieth Century.

Being Original LETTERS of STATE,
Under *GEORGE* the Sixth:

Relating to the most Important Events in *Great-Britain* and *Europe*, as to
CHURCH and STATE, ARTS and SCIENCES, TRADE, TAXES, and TREATIES,
PEACE, and WAR:
And Characters of the Greatest Persons of those Times; From the Middle
of the Eighteenth, to the End of the Twentieth CENTURY, and the WORLD.
Received and Revealed in the Year 1728;
And now Published, for the Instruction of all Eminent Statesmen, Church-
men, Patriots, Politicians, Projectors, Papists, and Protestants.

In SIX VOLUMES.

VOL. I.

Μάντις ἄριστος ὅστις εἰκάζει καλῶς.
Eurip.

Bon Dieu! que n'avons nous point vea reüssir des conjectures de ce temps là
comme si c'eussent esté autant de Propheties?
La Mothe Le Vayer Discourse de l'Histoire. Tom. I. p. 267.

Hoc apud nos quoque nuper ratio ad certum produxit. Veniet tempus, quo ista
quæ nunc latent, in lucem dies extrahat, & longioris ævi diligentia. Ad
inquisitionem tantorum ætas una non sufficit, ut tota cœlo vacet. Itaque per
successiones ista longas explicabuntur. Veniet tempus, quo posteri nostri tam
aperta nos nescisse mirentur, non licet stare cœlestibus, nec averti: Prodeunt
omnia; ut semel missa sunt, vadunt. Idem erit illis cursus, qui sui finis. Opus hoc
æternum irrevocabiles habet motus.
Senecæ Nat. Quæst. lib. 7. cap. 25.

LONDON:

Printed for Messieurs OSBORN and LONGMAN, DAVIS, and BATLEY
in *Pater-noster-Row*; STRAHAN, and CLARKE, in *Cornhill*; RIVINGTON,
ROBINSON, ASTLEY, and AUSTEN in *St. Paul's Church-Yard*; GOSLING,
in *Fleetstreet*; NOURSE by *Temple-Bar*; PREVOST, and MILLAR, in the
Strand; PARKER, in *Pall-Mall*; JOLLIFFE, by *St. James's*; BRINDLEY,
SHROPSHIRE, and SMITH *in Bondstreet*; and GOUGE, and STAGG, in
Westminster-Hall. 1733.

[i] To His Royal Highness
Frederick Lewis,

Prince of Wales, *and Earl of* Chester, *Electoral Prince of* Brunswick Lunenburg, *Duke of* Cornwall *and Rothsay, Duke of* Edinburgh, *Marquiss of the Isle of* Ely, *Earl of* Eltham, *Viscount of* Launceston, *Baron of* Snaudon *and of* Renfrew, *Lord of the Isles, and Steward of* Scotland, *and Knight of the Most Noble Order of the Garter.*

May it please your Royal Highness,

It would be highly proper even in a Stranger to Dedicate a Work, where the Growth of the Protestant Interest in Europe, *and the Happiness deriv'd to these Nations from your Royal House do so often occur, to that Prince who will one Day wear the Title of the* Defender of our Faith, *as well as prove the Ornament of that Crown he is to inherit; and that Succession of our Princes, which he is equally* [ii] *born to perpetuate and adorn. But in one that has so long liv'd under, so often admir'd and experienc'd the happy Influence of that Constellation of Virtues, (if I may so speak) which exalts you as much above other Princes, as your Birth does above other Men, it would be equally insensible and ungrateful to have applied to any other Patron.*

It is to be fear'd indeed, that the Work which I have the Honour to present to You, must seem less agreeable to you Royal Highness, who so frequently converse with the great Genius's of Greece *and* Rome; *to You, Sir, who do not only steal many early Hours from the Pleasures of the Court, to give to their Labours, but whose constant Practice it has been, like* Francis *the First, to spend some time every Night before you Sleep, in attending to a Gentleman, whose Office it is to read them to you then for your Amusement.*

But, as I have long observ'd, the Candour of excusing any unavoidable Errors is more agreeable both to your natural Temper and your settled Judgment, than the severer Delicacy of censuring them; so I must own I have with some Pleasure taken hold of this Opportunity of giving vent to the strongest Passion of my Heart, that Veneration or Admiration [iii] *rather of your Royal Highness, which my Personal Knowledge of your Heroick Qualities, has imprest in the most indelible manner on my Soul.*

Possibly I had been less liable to Censure, if I could have contented my self with paying You in private the secret Homage of my Heart, without giving any publick Testimony of that infinite Regard which I pretend to bear You.

Professions of this kind from a Subject to a Prince seem generally too Interested, to be very Sincere; and we may say of most of them, as well as of the false Patriot's Love for his Country, that, like some matrimonial Smithfield *Bargains, tho' much Affection is pretended, there is no more meant by it, than a good Settlement for one's Family.*

Nay in this case, the very Tribute of our Praise which we pay to such exalted Benefactors, is seldom taken by the World as current Payment, but is suspected to be mixt up with the basest Alloy. For Praise is so generally the common Incense offer'd up by the Idolaters of Power, that many Men are from the same Principle grown as perfect Infidels in matters of Panegyrick, as some pretend to be in Religion; who because they see so many false [iv] Gods set up for the publick Worship of the World, and ador'd with so much outward Profession of Zeal and Ardour; conclude, that all is but Mummery and Hypocrisy, that is paid even to the true One.

But if the Conduct of my Life cannot secure me from an Impeachment of this sort, your Royal Highness's uncontested Virtues so universally acknowledg'd by all, will surely stand as the strongest Proof, that the highest Professions of Veneration and Gratitude to such a Prince, may well be consistent with Sincerity of Heart, and unsuspected of the little Arts of fawning Sycophants.

And indeed, one may as well charge a Man with Hypocrisy, for professing the Religion of his Country, as tax him with Flattery who owns himself an Admirer of your Royal Highness. For certainly as the one is as universally given into as the other by all our People; if it be Flattery, it is the Flattery of a Nation, and should no more be objected to a particular Person, than the Anglicisms of our common Speech, and in the Mouths of all.

For who is there, Sir, in the most distant Corner of these Nations, that is so insensible [v] of his own, or the general Happiness, as not to regard you with the sincerest Love, when you are only considered as the Heir apparent of the best Man and Woman, the best King and Queen, that ever adorn'd a Family, or blest a Nation: As their Son, who have so frequently given us the most delightful Prospect this World can afford, the Joy of seeing that infinite Desire of doing Good, which has so remarkably distinguish'd their Lives, join'd to as unlimited a Power of exercising it, by contriving for the Happiness and relieving the Miseries of Thousands: As their Son, I say, who have by so many Proofs, taught their Subjects no longer to consider a numerous Family as an intolerable Burthen, while they see such repeated Instances of their Solicitude to lighten it by particular Bounties, so many Laws to provide in general, for the Ease and Maintenance of the poorest of their Subjects, as well as such a parental Tenderness for every Calamity that befalls the greatest of them.

Your Royal Highness appears in a most amiable view, even to every common Eye, that regards you merely as a Descendant from such Princes, who have made the Happiness of their People the solid Basis of their Throne; who have govern'd us so, as to be Examples to all [vi] good, and Reproaches to all bad Rulers, and in a Word, whose Love of Justice, and Benignity of Spirit, whose natural Goodness of Heart, and hereditary Hatred of Oppression, have secur'd the same Blessings to their Subjects who live under a despotical Government, which we enjoy from them under a free One.

But how infinitely dearer, Sir, must you be to those who are inform'd of your amiable Character from others, or are so happy to observe you at a nearer Distance, and are as it were grown familiarly acquainted with that Complacency of Manners, that Candour and Openness of Soul, that winning Condescension, that fearless Courage, that Elevation of Mind, and Generosity of Heart, join'd with that filial Piety and Sweetness of Temper, which have made you, like Titus, *the Delight of Humankind.*

With what Pleasure to myself, with what Joy to others, have I been able to produce a thousand instances of this Nature, and convinc'd the most Incredulous, that tho' you promis'd such prodigious things in your Youth, as would have bankrupt the Virtue of any other Prince to have made good; yet your Reputation, how glorious soever then, like the dawning of the Morning, was but the glimmering of [vii] *that Day, which is now hast'ning to its Meridian height of Splendour.*

'Tis the peculiar Happiness of your Royal Highness's Character, that there is nothing necessary to be concealed in it; and that, tho' there are few Princes, who must not have a Veil thrown over one half of theirs, in order to commend the other, who must not, like Hannibal, *be drawn in Profil to cover their blind side, there are no Deformities, or accidental Blemishes that need to be disguis'd in Yours. But if there were, your Royal Highness is so entirely in the Possession of the Esteem of Men, that your very Imperfections would appear not only pardonable, but even amiable; and indeed, as to behold You is sufficient to make You lov'd, so to know You perfectly is the surest Method to make You admir'd.*

And to speak the Truth, in what other Lights can we regard a Prince, who at an Age when others seem but to enter upon Life, has so happily emulated his Royal Father, as to have done more generous, more beneficent Actions, than he has liv'd Days; nay, more than would adorn the Annals of the longest Reigns? But I forget, that it is not allowable for me even to give the least hint to others, of those secret Depositories of your extensive Charities in this [viii] *World, which are entirely paid to him, who only can and will reward them openly in the next.*

I shall therefore stop my Pen, –– nor had I indulg'd it so far, had I consider'd how greatly what I have already said might offend that Modesty, with which you conceal the best Actions with the same Care that others endeavour to hide their worst; or to express the noblest Quality (which to my shame I recollect too late) in the meanest Poetry,

> 'Tis thy peculiar Grace, Great Prince, 'tis thine,
> Like rising Suns to blush because you shine!

I shall therefore turn the poor imperfect Tribute of my Praise, into what will become me more, my sincere Prayers for you; that you may so go on to copy all the Virtues of that best of Men and Princes, your Royal Father, that when worn with Cares and Years, God shall call him from that Crown he now adorns, to an eternal one, You may so fill his place, and so become in his stead a Father to your People, as to make his glorious Memory neither reproachful to You, nor too often honour'd with the Tears of your Subjects.

May You then reap the happy Fruits of all your Royal Virtues and his Majesty's prudent [ix] Counsels and perpetual Labours for the general good of his Kingdoms, and may they both concur to make us the happiest of Nations, and the best of Subjects under a race of Princes, against whom the little Clamours and Arts of Faction at Home, will be as impotent and contemptible, as the inveterate Malice of Rome, and the Enemies of our Peace Abroad.

In those Halcyon Days may God so bless your Reign as to give you no other object of your Cares, but to preserve to us those Blessings of Unity and Concord (the Seeds whereof are now so happily sown and growing up in our Land) and to encourage the Improvement of the rising Arts, and patronize the learned Sciences, till they gain new Life among us, and grow in proportion cultivated as our Manufactures, and extended as our Trade. In a word, may the Happiness of your People be then so universal and compleat, that your charitable and generous Spirit may search with equal Difficulty for distressed Families to relieve, as for Enemies to convert or pardon; and to sum up all, may you then so second the present pious Cares of your Royal Parents in combating the Vice and abandon'd Wickedness of a degenerate Age, that your Piety may shield us from the Vengeance of Heaven, if ever our Virtue [x] and Religion should sink to a lower Ebb than they are fallen to at present.

And thus in Virgil's noble Prayer for young Augustus, I commit your Royal Highness to the Protection of the Almighty.

Hunc saltem everso Juvenem succurrere seclo,
Ne, Superi, prohibete.

I am with the utmost Submission,
Your Royal Highness's

January
25, 1731.

Most Obedient
Most Devoted
Humble Servant

[1] A Modest
Preface
Containing
Many Words to the Wise.

Being about to deliver to the learned World in these Letters, one of the noblest Presents that ever was made to it, I must own, I have been as much perplex'd how to introduce them properly, by a *Preface* worthy of them, as *Cervantes* himself, when he fell on that which stands before his inimitable *Don Quixote*, or as *Thuanus* was how to begin the first Sentence of his History, which we are told, cost him so many painful Hours, before he could settle it to his Mind.

I question if *Malherb* who spent a Quire of Paper, in finishing his Simile of *Phillis's* gathering Flowers in a Garden; or the illustrious *Balzac* who us'd to take a Week to write a Letter in, for fear of the *French* Criticks; ever toil'd more than I have done, to give full Satisfaction in this Introductory [2] Discourse, to the profound Readers and Judges of these Times, who have the Glory and Advantage of being Witnesses to the birth of this admirable Production.

For, alas! People are so capricious, that as they often take good or ill Impressions of others at first sight, so they will frequently reject the most excellent Piece without looking into it, if the Preface be disagreeable to them. If therefore, I should stumble in the Threshold, and introduce this Work as injudiciously as *Ovid* is said to have done most of his, the consequences may be very untoward; and as I write this poor Prologue, without the least Assistance from that superior Nature, from whom I receiv'd the Volumes it ushers into the World, I am much perplext lest I should not appear equal to the task.

I will not say with the *Spaniard*, that I would willingly write it with the Quill of a *Peacock*, because it has Eyes in it, but I would rather express my Zeal and Concern for what I am here undertaking, in the words an Author, (who will appear before the Year 1739) paints the behaviour of a distress'd Suppliant in, that addresses to a severe and cruel Judge,

[3] — *her humble Prayer,*
And as a moving Preface dropt a Tear.

Be it as it will, I can only use my best Endeavours to convince the World, what a Treasure I have here offer'd them, and if they will not regard my fervent desire to serve them, but despise the labour I've been at, in bringing these first Fruits of a much greater Harvest to the publick use, I must acquiesce, and be content with the Honour and Misfortune, of being the first among Historians (if a mere Publisher of Memoirs may deserve that Name) who leaving the beaten Tracts of writing with Malice or Flattery, the accounts of past Actions and Times, have dar'd to enter by the help of an infallible Guide, into the dark Caverns of Futurity, and discover the Secrets of Ages yet to come.

I am sensible that all extraordinary Discoveries in their first Proposal, are lightly regarded and hardly credited, and I am prepared for it; yet, if Men will but be prevail'd upon to consider, of what uncommon use these may be, I hope I shall be able to say enough in their behalf, to procure them at least a candid Reception, it not the most generous Welcome.

[4] I expect this the rather, because I freely confess, that what I now publish, is but introductory to many other Volumes, so copious and full of matter, that they will almost deserve the name of the *History of the* XXth *Century*; and which I hope Persons of Taste and Judgment, will therefore receive with all that Regard, not to say Respect and Veneration, so prodigious a Work will appear entitled to.

Nor shall any slight Disappointments herein discourage me from Printing them; for how ungratefully soever the present Age, thro' Blindness or Envy may receive these vast Lights; yet, I shall be sufficiently comforted with the Consciousness, that my declaring the future Births of such great Events, will be regarded by the coming Ages, as my having in some measure sown the Seed of them, in the Bosom of a well cultivated, tho' an unthankful Soil: Besides, at the worst, I shall be as well treated by the World, as those exalted Spirits were, who discover'd the *Antipodes*, the Circulation of the Blood, the use of Telescopes and Barometers, of Printing and Sailing, the Loadstone and the *Indies*, who were so much despis'd at first, tho' so highly honour'd and regarded now.

[5] It is true as a mere Publisher, (which I only set up for) it may seem too arrogant, to rank my self with such illustrious Company; but if it is consider'd, that without my generous Benevolence to Mankind, these mighty Treasures and Discoveries I bestow on them, had never seen the Light, and that I have here convey'd to them the great Secrets of Futurity, in so plain and open a manner, that this Age may say, (tho' contrary to the receiv'd Axiom of the Schools) *de futuro contingenti est quoad nos determinata veritas*, I hope, I shall not appear too assuming. Nay, I have yet the merit of infinite Toil to plead, since I can fairly aver, that the translating this Work, form the *English* it was writ in, (*viz.* the *English* that will be spoke in the XXth *Century*) was a task so painful and difficult, that no unenligthen'd Mind could have perform'd, and which even I my self had miscarried in, without the superior assistance that my good Angel afforded me.

A Task so laborious! that besides this being the second Time of my Writing to the Publick,[*] which according to Cardinal *Berule*'s [6] Opinion,

---

* See my Works, three Volumes in *Quarto*, Printed for Mr. *Lintot*, 1720. *N.B.* There are some sets in Royal Paper for the Curious.

(who thought we should imitate our Saviour, who is never said to have writ but once before, and once after his answer to the *Jews*, who brought the Adulteress before him) is full enough for any good Christian; tho' I were more secure of receiving all possible Favour and Honour for my Toils than I am, yet I doubt whether I shall ever venture on a third Sally, in any other Performance, tho' my Modesty and Indolence should occasion ever so much Grief to Posterity.

As to this particular Work, I must indeed be greatly discourag'd by the World, if I suppress the Sequel of it, which I propose by proper intervals to communicate to them, tho' I will not answer, how far their receiving this Book I now offer them, with Contempt and Disregard, may make me use the same Haughtiness the sacred *Sibyl* did to *Tarquinius Superbus*, and after burning all the remaining parts which I design'd for them, make them pay as high a price for this Volume, as on a contrary demeanour I design'd to allow them the whole for.

But as I flatter my self, such Fears are very groundless, I shall say the less on that Subject. I shall rather hope, as these Papers [7] are design'd to enlighten the Nations of the Earth, they will be treated with the utmost Admiration and Reverence; nor need I from any unjust Imagination of their ill reception, threaten the World, as *Apollo* did on the ill Fortune of his unhappy *Phaethon*, to leave it hereafter in eternal Darkness, as a just mark of my Resentment, since I am persuaded all that have Eyes will see and applaud the Light I am lending to them. Naturalists tell us, that setting up a burning Torch in fenny or marshy Grounds, is a sure Method to shut up the clamorous Throats, and silence the Croaking of Frogs; and I hope the amazing Splendour and Brightness of this Work, will have the same happy effect on my envious Maligners, and quiet the noisy Tongues of dull Objectors.

Not that I expect to have it treated at first Sight, as well as it deserves; for as all who set up for extraordinary Discoveries that are reveal'd to them, ought to be receiv'd with Dissidence, and hearken'd to with Caution, I make no doubt, but many People may be ready enough to suspect me as an Impostor, in these I am communicating to them. And I almost imagine my self engag'd, with one of my Readers [8] of this Character, in such a Dialogue as *Horace* represents between *Ulysses* and *Tiresias*, who pretended to reveal Things to come.

> *Num furis? an prudens ludis me obscura canendo?*
> *O Laertiade, quicquid dicam, aut erit, aut non:*
> *Divinare etenim magnus mihi donat Apollo.*
> *Quid tamen ista velit sibi Fabula, si licet, ede.*

But as I am determined to give such Readers and all Men, so full, and fair, and convincing an Account of my self and that celestial Spirit I receiv'd these Papers from, and to answer all Objections so entirely, as to put

Ignorance, and even Malice it self to Silence: I am confident, the ingenuous and candid part of the World, will soon throw off such mean narrow spirited Suspicions, as unjust and ungenerous. I am willing the important matters reveal'd to me, may stand as publick and severe a Trial, as those of St. *Bridget* did before the Council, and have the Truth fully examin'd and search'd into, even by the strict Rules Chancellour *Gerson* prescribes for hers and all such Examinations, in this Treatise *de Probatione Spirituum*, where the most gravely and judiciously advises, that all Persons (Layman, Nun, Monk [9] or Friar) who pretend to Revelations of any kind, should give a satisfactory Account, 1*st*, From whence it is. 2*dly*, What it is. 3*dly*, Why it is. 4*thly*, To whom it is. 5*thly*, How it is, and 6*thly*, Whence, or from what place it is reveal'd.

To this end therefore, and that the Reader, my dear and kind and learned Reader, may the better understand the Nature and Value of the Present which I make him; I shall observe the following Method: *First*, I shall give some Account, both of my self and my good Genius, from whom I receiv'd it. 2*dly*, I shall mention the Reasons of my publishing it, and also my Care and Conduct about it. 3*dly*, I shall answer all kind of Objections, that are or can be made, against this wonderful Treasure I am putting into their Hands, and *lastly*, I shall give my Friends, (my great, wise and numerous Friends) the learned World, (the good, judicious and learned World) and Posterity, (our noble and excellent Posterity worthy of their admirable Ancestors) some Cautions about it, and so leave it to its Fate.

As to the first point then, I must own that I am descended in a direct Line by the Mother's side, from a Son of that famous [10] Count *Gabalis*, in the 17*th Century*, whose History is in every ones Hands, and whose Wife, as all true Adepts know, had Carnal Knowledge of, and was Impregnated by a certain invisible *Dæmon*, that call'd himself *Ariel*. I hope as this extraordinary particularity was the Case of *Plato*, *Appollonius Tyanæus*, the Earl of *Poitiers*, and other great Personages; and as the Mareschal *de Bassompiere* in his Memoirs, is so candid as to confess it also, of one of the Heads of his Family; it will not be consider'd as insolent or conceited in me, that I have own'd this Circumstance, especially since in all Probability, 'tis not a little owing to it, that I am able to enrich the World at present, with these Works, worthy of so celestial an Origin.

I was born also under the most fortunate of all Planets and to make my Nativity still more Happy, in one of the *Ember*-Weeks, and with a Cawl, or certain Membrane about my Head; both which as the learned Jesuit *Thyræus*, (an Order I particularly Reverence), observes, in his Tract* *de apparitione Spirituum*, are Circumstances, that render [11] such Children

---

* Cap. 14, Num. 346.

more likely than others, to gain the Acquaintance and Familiarity of the *Genii* design'd for their Conduct. Nay, I was born under that Aspect of the Heavenly Bodies, which *Ptolemy* in his 4*th* Book of his *Quadripartite*, and 13*th* Chapter, assures us, generally confers this inestimable Privilege, having had the Moon, that great *Domina humidorum*, in Conjunction with *Sagittary*, Lady of my Actions, not to mention, lest it should look too like Vanity, some others as favourable, tho' less credible Circumstances.

But to pass to more material particulars of my History: I came into the World Heir to a good Family and Fortune, as well as a deal of Pride and Ambition, to distinguish my self from the common Herd of Mankind. In order therefore, to gratifie this reigning Passion, after quitting the University, and determining any Profession to be below my regard, both as taking too much Time, Thought and Reading to master, and a deal of mean Art, or good Money to succeed in; I resolv'd as a shorter way, to raise my self above the thoughtless Crowd of Gentlemen, to spend one third of my Fortune in Travelling, and seeing and observing [12] something more, than my Country-Seat and Neighbours in Summer, and *London* in the Winter, could furnish me with. This I did for three Years, and came Home as perfectly improv'd as any fine Gentleman of my Time in an utter Contempt of *Tramontane* Barbarity, an absolute Aversion for my own People, Climate and Country, and a thorough Insight into all the little learned Cant of Priests and Religions of all kinds.

On these deep laid Foundations, I commenc'd a sage Politician and Patriot: I bought a Seat in Parliament at a fair Purchase, for a good deal of Beef and Ale for the Mob, and a round Sum of Money to the worthy Electors, and determin'd to grow great by Voting according to my Conscience, and as the best Arguments should be offer'd me in Favour of those two dangerous Monosyllables, *Yea* and *No*.

Accordingly all the Time I sat there as a *Senator*, I never gave a single Vote, without a substantial Reason of one kind or another for it, and endeavour'd to think a certain great Patron (I had devoted my self to) in the Right, whatever side of the Question he took, and shew'd a generous Violence in supporting all the Measures he pursued, [13] as the best and wisest in the World, and particularly while he distinguish'd himself as an Enemy to the Ministry, whom we were to overturn and succeed. But in spite of all the fortunate Constellations I was born under, being entirely disappointed in these glorious Hopes, it luckily happen'd my Patron fell in with the Court-Party, and got a very comfortable Post to live honest by; and as I found my self, by the sacred Ties of Love to my Country and my Family, oblig'd to turn with him; I us'd my humble Endeavours to second him, and to obtain some of those many honourable Employments, with good Salaries for doing nothing, which I was assur'd by my great Friends, I could not fail of.

To this end, I became as violent for the Court, as ever I had been against it, and to ingratiate my self the more with the Ministry, I kept up an extravagant Table, and a Crowd of humble Admirers of my Eloquence to eat at it, among whom I censur'd our Opposers as Fools or Knaves, rail'd at the Minority as Tools or Villains, and after confuting all their Arguments, to the Satisfaction of my Guests while they were eating, crown'd my daily Victories, with drinking Confusions of all kinds.

[14] On these excellent Foundations, I built up a World of Hopes, and askt for every thing I knew I deserv'd, making a Conscience of aiming at any thing further, and was happy enough to receive many fair Promises and good Looks, not only from my Patron, but my Patron's Patron's Patron, who was a very great Man indeed. I was trusted with several Secrets before they were in Print, and assur'd of succeeding to many tolerable Places, before they were vacant; and was so much consider'd, that I never askt for any thing, that I did not get a distant Promise of, or a very civil Excuse for being refus'd it. This kept up my Spirits, and quicknd my Zeal for several Sessions, till finding my Equipage and Table, my Elections and living like a Man of Consequence, had sunk another third of my Estate, I began to be so importunate for something, as soon as I found I had little or nothing left, that tho' I was willing to take any Place during good Behaviour, which by a fair Computation I might have purchased the yearly Value of in Land by half what I had spent in the Service, yet I found my self so utterly unsecure of any thing but sincere Promises, which I knew it difficult [15] to subsist my Family on, that I desperately broke with my Patron, and all my dear Friends the Courtiers, and set up once more for a good Conscience, on the other side. But, alas! I soon found this was the worst tim'd step I could have taken, for it both ruin'd my Character with the World, and my Tradesmen lost me my Election the next Parliament; and in a Word, left me to brood over my own Resentments, Disappointments and Despair.

Under these unlucky Circumstances, the Town not agreeing with my *Constitution*, I retir'd to the Country, to the Ruins of my Estate, of which I had fold two Thirds, to pay off the Debts these Schemes in Politicks had brought on me; and because I could not with Ease look back on the World, I resolv'd to look forward, and consider what might happen, since I abhor'd to reflect on what had.

The truth is, my dear Reader, tho' I blush to tell it, my Disappointments and Discontents wrought so violently on my Pride and Choler, which were the two chief Ingredients in my little carnal Tabernacle, that renouncing all my former Engagements in Favour of our civil and religious Rights, as [16] *Britons* and Protestants, I gave my self up Body and Soul, to a little sorry melancholy Faction, who only subsist themselves, like the *Cevennes* in *Languedock*, on a seditious Sermon now and then, and a few comfortable

Visions, Rumours and Hopes, of gratifying their private Resentments at the price of the publick Ruine.

Indeed I must own, I had some Scruples of Conscience at first, on this extraordinary Conversion that was wrought in me; but when I reflected on the Expences I had been at, to obtain Promises that were forgotten, and secure Places I now saw possest by others; when I compar'd the Ruins of my Fortune, with my old Rent-Rolls, my past Debtors with my present Creditors, and my former Hopes with my present Despair; I at once broke thro' all my Oaths of *Allegiance*, and thought my Revolt the less dishonourable, since I had taken them but about seven or eight Times, and I saw several Men of Honour, engag'd in this Faction against the Government, who had taken them on at least twenty different Occasions.

In a Word, my Resentment soon quieted my Reason, and I began to hope for a thousand Scenes of Confusion and Destruction to [17] my Country and the Royal Family, and to see their Labours to make us happy, luckily overturn'd by some fortunate Calamities, which might destroy their Interest with the People. By some such desirable Accident, I flatter'd my self, that by God's Blessing on our honest Endeavours, in bringing it about and improving it, we might all mend our Circumstances, and that possibly for my part, I might thus recover my Estate, from the Rogue who bought it, by turning *Papist* in some glorious Revolution in the *Chevalier's* Favour.

To indulge my Spleen and Melancholy the more, I gave my self up Night and Day to reading for several Years: And because I despis'd the little narrow beaten Paths of common Scholars, I studied all hidden Sciences, from Magick to the *Jewish Cabala* and the Philosopher's Stone, and particularly turn'd my self to Astrology with vast Application, in hopes to find some propitious Influence from the Heavens, to favour these reasonable Expectations, since I saw with Sorrow there was little to be hop'd for from the Earth.

I made a great Progress, especially in this last noble Science, and flatter'd my self, [18] that I had found out some favourable Conjunctions in the Planets above, that might be too strong for all the united Interests of the best Man and Prince and the happiest People among the Nations below. When behold one Night, which I shall never forget, and *Great Britain* must ever remember with Joy, (it was on the 20*th* of *January*, 1728,) as I lay in my Bed, agreeably soothing my Spleen, with these pleasing Prospects I had been contemplating in the Stars; I was surpriz'd to see my Door which was fast lock'd, and my Curtains which were close drawn, opening suddenly of themselves, and a great Light filling my Chamber, in the midst of which I saw a beautiful Appearance of something like what we usually imagine Angels to be.

I began to fancy my self in the famous *Van Helmont's* Condition, who says,* he once plainly saw his Soul in an human Shape, but, as he modestly speaks, without distinction of Sex; or like that *Pisander*, who, as a certain *Greek* Author tells us, was afraid of meeting his own Soul, which he apprehended would appear to him separated from [19] his Body, and play him a scurvy Trick. But I had not time enough for many Reflections, for while I lay silent with Wonder and Surprize, he instantly rais'd me up by the Hand, told me he was my good *Genius*, and was come to shew me nobler Prospects, that should be deriv'd to me and my Family, as well as my Country, from the present Royal Line and their Posterity, than those I was drawing from my mistaken Principles in Political Astrology. He assur'd me, if I would be directed by him, he would give me sufficient Lights to convince me, that there never could be a greater Blessing bestowed on a Nation, than these Kingdoms receiv'd when the Royal Line of *Hannover*, was by the Favour of Heaven plac'd on the Throne, to be the Source of a long Series of Prosperity, Wealth, Peace and Glory to us, if we would but be content to enjoy it with common Sense and Gratitude. He added much more on this Head, and concluded with promising to keep up a constant Communication and Correspondence with me; and to give me at once some little Intelligence of the great Events that would happen under their glorious Goverment, not only to my Country but even my own House and Descendants, he made me [20] a present of several large Volumes of these Letters, which, he assur'd me, would be writ by or to my Great Great Great Great Great Grandson, who would be chief Minister in the End of the Twentieth Century, and to deal plainly with me, as far as he could guess, in the last days of the World.

The Joy! the Surprize! the Transport! these Words gave me, is not to be exprest: And as a *Kircher* told *Schottus*,[†] he was cur'd of a deadly Disease, by dreaming he was made Pope, and receiv'd the Congratulations of all Kings and Nations, while he issued out Bulls and Decrees for new Laws, new Churches, new Saints, and new Colleges, with vast Joy, and awaken'd after a long and happy Reign perfectly recover'd; so I found in an instant all my Discontents in Politicks vanish'd and remov'd by these real Visions, my good Genius had communicated to me. I accordingly receiv'd this present, as an immediate Blessing from Heaven, and after assuring him in the most solemn manner how sincerely I renounced my former Principles, I enter'd into a long Dialogue with him, both as to the present and the future [21] state of Things, and learnt from him Secrets as important as the Ruine or Safety of Crowns and Empires can make them, and by the Communication of which, to the chief Ministers of such Princes as can gain my Esteem, and particularly of my own, he assur'd me, I might with good Husbandry,

---

* Chap. I. p. 9.
† *Gaspar Schotti Physica Curiosia*, Lib. 30.

raise a Fortune whereon to subsist my Family with Honour and Affluence, till my Descendant should be Prime Minister under *George* the VI. Every one may imagine, how eagerly I listned to all this, and how easily a Mind thus illuminated, with Views of so glorious a Change, in my own and my Family's future Circumstances, would lay aside its former Principles and Prejudices, as I immediately did, with a thousand Thanks to my good Genius, for all his Favours, and as many Entreaties for his future Correspondence, which both on my own Account, (as he was pleas'd to express himself) and my Relation to Count *Gabalis*, he kindly promiss'd, and has ever since often made me happy in.

He had no sooner left me, than I began to read over the Volumes he had given me, with all the Delight which I hope the World will receive from part of them, which [22] with his Consent and Assistance, and by the Advice of my learned and ingenious Friends, I have resolv'd to communicate to them, as a most inestimable Treasure. I have made no other Change or Alterations in them, than the translating them into the *English* of these illiterate Times oblig'd me to, except where the Secrets of crown'd Heads and prime Ministers, or the good or ill Conduct of the Friends or Enemies of my Country and some great People at home, made it necessary to leave out either whole Letters or particular Paragraphs, which shou'd be reserv'd in Secret, for the Use and Service of the Crown and my own Family, and not expos'd to publick view.

And thus having given my dear Reader, as full an Account as I judg'd proper, both of my self and my good *Genius*, and the Present he made me, (for of my constant Correspondence since with him, I shall say nothing here) I shall now proceed, to mention my Reasons for publishing this Work, and also my Care and Conduct about it.

And the first I shall assign is, that I really believ'd I should do an Injury to the World, to the Commonwealth of Learning, and above all to my Country, if being thus [23] enlighten'd, and having such wonderful Discoveries revealed and intrusted to me, I did not give them some Fore-tast of these surprising Scenes, which Fate is to open to Mankind, in future Ages.

Nor was this all, for to say the Truth, when I saw evidently in these Papers, that the World and my Descendant's Ministry would end together; I was the more willing to have my Fame and his laid open to the present Age, since it was impossible for future Times to do us Justice, by assigning us that shining place in History, which Printing these Volumes will so fully entitle us to. Those great Persons, whose Writings or Actions distinguish'd them so much in former Ages, have had a large recompence made them, by the Honour and Applause that has long been heap'd on them; but as my Fame had been entirely conceal'd, and his reduc'd to take up with the shortliv'd Applause of a few Years, in his old Age, the Dregs of Life, and the last Moments of the World, I resolv'd to be before-hand with the

Glory of my self and Family, and to enjoy some part of our Reputation before we had earn'd it. And while I make this sincere Confession, let me take this opportunity [24], to exhort those few great Spirits, who are thirsting after Glory, to redouble their Speed to perpetuate their Fame, and do greater and more glorious Things than have yet been attempted; that thereby they may the sooner obtain that reward of their Merit, and raise those Monuments to their Memories, which at best they see, must so suddenly perish in the common Ruine, and be left for ever in the general Destruction of all Things.

Another Motive I had for making these Papers publick was, that by magnifying the Glory of succeeding Ministers, I might sink and lessen the Reputation of those, that at present sit at the Helm, since they have been so regardless of all true Merit, as to do little or nothing for me or my Family. I saw it in vain to attempt their Ruin by downright Railing, throwing Dirt at random, and calling them at all Adventures Rogues and Knaves in Print; for they have so deluded the People, by the cursed Success of their Administration, that they will not listen any longer to general Declamations, to witty Insinuations or the boldest Satyrs, without some few real Facts to vouch them, and prove they are well grounded. Now as [25] I found this an insuperable difficulty, since they manage with such vile Art, as to keep all Proofs of that sort from our Knowledge, so I knew no better method to vilify their measures, and serve his *Majesty* and my *Country*, then shewing the World, that notwithstanding the popular Cry of the Prosperity of our Affairs, there will, some Ages hence, be much greater and more successful Ministers than they are, and who, by the by, may then remember to their Posterity, the little respect these Gentlemen pay one of their Ancestors now, whom (out of that Modesty so natural to all great Spirits) I shall not mention here.

Another reason, which, I must own, induced me to present the World with this Work, was, that the busy inquisitive Sages and Politicians of these times, may have some more Employment given to their restless Tempers. For as *Charles* II. by publickly setting up new Systems of *Philosophy*, diverted his unmanageable Subjects from disturbing the ancient Forms of Government, and by amusing them with searching into the Revolutions of the Heavens, kept them from contriving new ones upon Earth; or (not to grudge the Reader another instance of equal [26] force) as by settling our banish'd Felons in the new World, and employing them sufficiently there, we keep our selves pretty quiet at Home in the old one; so I hope that these ungovernable and satyrical Observers, who not content with censuring and decrying all that past in former Ages, turn themselves to ridiculing and contemning all that is done in this, may be kept from overturning the Peace of these our Days, by being employ'd on the Secrets of Times to come. Besides I find it is by no means sufficient, for the elevated *Genius*'s of this Age, to know all that *may be known:* This is too easy a Conquest for their superior Strenght, and they gloriously aim at being Masters of all that is *not to be known*. As I pay the highest Veneration to such exalted Spirits, I have done what Man could do, (aided by the Discoveries of my good Angel) to let them see all that is to be in Art or Nature, till the Dissolution of both, and have resolv'd to gratifie them with some considerable Hints of what will happen at the general Conflagration, when they, this Earth, and even Time, and all their learned (their exquisitely learned) Labours, shall be no more!

[27] I am sensible, an Author should observe as proper Seasons for his Productions, as the skilful Husbandman or Florist for their Seeds; and I am of Opinion, I could not have presented this curious inquisitive Age, with a Work more admirably calculated, to amuse and employ their vast Knowledge and deep Reserches, and divert them from less useful, tho' more dangerous Enquiries, which they are of late so profoundly taken up with.

In the last place, my dear Reader, when I consider'd that the great *Augustus*, as *Suetonius* tells us, neither neglected his own or other Mens Dreams, concerning himself or his Affairs, and consequently whatever related to his Country, or the whole World which was his Empire;* *Somnia neque sua neque aliena de se negligebat* are the Historian's Words when I read in the great *Artimedorus*, that it was the Custom of the Antients, that whatever any one had dreamt of the Publick, relating to the Commonwealth, he should publish either by the Voice of the common Crier, or by a written Table set up to the view of others;[†] *moris antiqui fuit, ut quicquid quisque de republica somniasset, illud vel Præconis voce, vel Pittacio, hoc* [28] *est, tabula quadam descriptum indicaret*, I thought it a criminal Action to conceal such important Discoveries as had been intrusted to my Care.

Besides, how do I know, but the bringing *these* to Light, may in some measure be a means to preserve our Country from all the Confusion and Madness, which the rest of the World will be involv'd in; and continue us in that happy Situation, and that Spirit of improving our Laws, Arts and Manufactures, which I have shewn we shall enjoy in the following Centuries, when the other Kingdoms of the Earth are to labour, as it were, in actual Convulsions, and be jumbled together, like the Mountains and Plains of *Jamaica* in the dreadful Earthquake in 1692.

As to my Care and Conduct in this Edition, I fear indeed how great soever it has been, Men will be displeased with me, as having bestowed much less on it, than so invaluable a Treasure will seem to have deserv'd. Some will censure me for having conceal'd and suppress'd many important Secrets, relating to our publick Affairs and Ministers, Peace and War, the Trade of the Nation, and the Conduct of the Throne; without considering

---

* In Augusto, Cap. 91.

† Lib. I. C p. 2.

the dangerous Consequences [29], of making such matters publick, as well as the particular Interest I may have, to keep them by me in *petto*, till proper Conjunctures.

On the other hand, many great Men will blame me as *Alexander* did *Aristotle*, for communicating too many of such hidden Mysteries, such *Arcana imperii*, to the Knowledge of the Vulgar. For my part, I have acted with the utmost Caution in suppressing or publishing any Particulars, and as it is to be fear'd, if after all my Care this Book should grow too common and be in every one's Hand, it may be applied to ill purposes, by letting the meanest of the People see, *uti digerit omnia Calchas*, I have given order to print but fifty Copies, which I compute will answer the number of Persons in *Great Britain*, who are *Wise* and *Honest enough* to be trusted with such a Jewel.

I have also gone further, and that Posterity may not be impos'd on, by any spurious Additions, Forgeries or Obliterations in this admirable Work, I have with great Labour number'd and reckon'd up the whole of what is in it, which is a safer and fairer Way than a Table of Contents, which our modern Publishers tack to their mangled Volumes [30]. I find therefore that there is in this Collection, (Publish'd and to be Publish'd) 28,967 Sentences that have meaning in them, 1,232,356 Words, 2,125,245 Syllables, 6,293,376 Letters, and thro' the Roughness of our barbarous Tongue, but 2,992,644 Vowels, (exclusive of *y* and all Dipthongs) as any careful Reader may find, who will cast them up with equal Diligence.

Possibly it may seem a little arrogant and conceited, that I should have taken such Pains herein, but if we consider, that the *Turks* have done as much for their *Alcoran*, and that the learned *Rabbies* among the *Jews* value their *Talmud* so highly, as to say, that mistaking a Letter in it, is enough to destroy the World; I hope, I may be indulg'd, if not applauded for my Care, in a Work in the *English* Tongue, where it may happen that the Loss a of Word in it, may be of vast Damage to our native Country, which all Men among us are so desirous to serve.

And now, after so candid an Account as I have laid before thee, one would think, my dear Reader, I might shut up this Preface, and have nothing more to do, than receive the tributary Thanks and Homage [31] of Mankind, for so glorious a Present as I here make them, for the common Good; but alas! I find the envious World, has cut out a deal of other Work for me, and that I must answer a Crowd of malicious Objections, which my learned Friends assure me, are levell'd against this unparallel'd Performance, by those who saw it in Manuscript.

But as this is Preface enough of Conscience for one Time, I must say with St. *Austin* when he us'd to cut his Sermons into two, *Parcite mihi fratres, non dicam vobis quod sequitur*; and beg the Reader to indulge me in a Liberty always allowed great Writers, of treading in unbeaten Paths, and for my Ease and his own, as well the Novelty and Boldness of the Stroke, to pardon me if, like the Adventure of the *Bear* and the *Fiddle*, I break off here a little abruptly, and (as I have resolv'd for a *Coup d'Eclat* to make three Prefaces to this glorious Work) send him for the Second and Third to the Middle and End of this Volume.

[1] MEMOIRS
OF THE
TWENTIETH CENTURY, & c.

To the Lord High Treasurer, & c.

Constantinople, Nov. 3, 1997.

My Lord,

I have, according to the Commands your Lordship honour'd me with by Captain *Milton*, by the way of *Vienna* in *September* last, so far press'd the Conclusion of the Treaty grounded on the new Stipulations, that I think it is as good as finished, and that our Trade shall be as much favour'd here, as by his Majesty's Authority and Influence and your Lordship's Care, it has been in all other parts of the World. [2] The only Difficulty that remains, proceeds from the 4*th* and 5*th* Articles, which the Grand Visier seems to think too highly honourable for our Nation, and derogatory to his own, judging it hard that their Ships of War, should in their own Parts and Seas, strike their Flag to ours and salute them, (as by the 5*th* Article is provided) with double the number of Guns.

However, these Points are so gently canvast by them, that I see evidently they design not to insist on them, and I make account, we shall in a little time mutually sign, and that our Cloath and Manufactures shall hereafter have no unreasonable Duties impos'd on them, as those of other Nations have; who must therefore vend theirs at great Disadvantages. I should be tempted to be exceeding vain on my happy Success herein, but that it is so evident my carrying all my Point here, is owing to no Dexterity of mine, but to the Wisdom and Courage of his Majesty's Measures, the Strength, Loyalty and Wealth of his Subjects, the Terror which his Fleet spreads over the Ocean, and the Care and Policy of his Ministers, and above all your Lordship, who now so happily preside over them.

[3] The long Intimacy and Friendship you have honour'd me with, as well as the Relation I have to your Noble Family, will prevent any Suspicion of Flattery, when I aver to your Lordship, that the News brought me by Mr. *Milton*, of your being declar'd Prime Minister and Treasurer by his Majesty in Council, was to me the most agreeable I have heard this twenty five Years that I have resided here. At the same Time I can say with Truth, that the Satisfaction this gave me, took not its rise from any private Views as to my own Interests, which I neither want nor desire to encrease in the World, but from the assured Hope I have, that our native Country shall hereby be highly advantag'd.

It is a peculiar Felicity that attends your Lordship's Promotion; that it happens when our glorious *George* VI. hath by the Success of his Arms oblig'd his Enemies to accept the Terms he was pleas'd to prescribe them, and that after having humbled *France* so far, as to oblige her to give up all her Ports in the Channel, even *Dunkirk* and *Calais* it self into our Hands, and taught all the Powers in *Europe* the Respect and almost Dependance they owe us; your sacred Master's [4] Cares and Yours, will now be almost solely confin'd, to the keeping the general Peace we are in with all Nations safe and undisturb'd, and to promote our Trade wherever our Industry and Profit can extend it.

But your Lordship is too usefully employ'd with such Cares, to listen to my awkward Compliments how sincere soever, and therefore I shall leave them; and since you are pleas'd to think I am capable of giving you some Light into the State of Things here, which by my long residence I must have some tolerable Knowledge of, I shall obey our Commands herein with the small Abilities I am Master of.

I shall not trouble your Lordship with any historical Events relating to these People, since the *Ottoman* Line was extinguished in *Mahomet* IX. and the *Tartar* Race succeeded. This was many Centuries since foretold, as well as the Decline of this great Empire, and that a *Mahomet* would be the last of that Family, as it has really happened. *Juxton*, the laborious Writer of the 19*th Century*, has given us so full a Detail of their Affairs, that they are known to all the learned World as well as your Lordship; I shall therefore only [5] dwell on such Facts and Alterations as are of a later Date, and confin'd within the Year 1949 and this present Time, which are worth your Curiosity; and which the *Memoirs* of my two Predecessors in this Post, which have fallen into my Hands, and my own Experience have given me a fuller Acquaintance with.

Your Lordship is no Stranger to the vast Alterations which the coming in of the *Tartar* Line has produc'd, and above all in Matters of Religion. For as the *Mufties* and all the Heads of their Clergy, have been still the *Grand Seignior*'s Countrymen, as fearing to place natural *Turks* in so high a

Trust, the Zeal to the *Mahometan* Religion and Discipline, has been thence greatly slacken'd, both in their Priests and People, which was anciently so hot and violent. By this means there succeeded in its stead a dead Palsy in their Faith, which has almost been destroyed betwixt *Christianity* and *Deism*. It is incredible, my Lord, what an Harvest *Christian Missionaries* and *Jesuits* have reap'd thereby among this People. For being disguis'd as *Physicians, Mathematicians, Astrologers*, nay, as *Janizaries* and *Spahies*, as well as under the appearances of all kinds of the [6] best sorts of Trades, (and some of them even by the *Pope's* Connivance circumcised and acting the part of *Turkish* Priests,) they got so throughly both into the Knowledge and Confidence of all Kinds and Ranks of People here, and especially the better sort, that under pretence of proposing their own Doubts, they soon overturn'd the establish'd Religion, in the Minds of all Persons eminent for their Posts or Learning.

They conceal'd the *Christian* Truths at first under the pretended Name of *Serabackzi* or *Enthusiasts*, till at length their Doctrines got Admission into the *Seraglio*, by the means of the *Renegedo Vizier Ibrahim*, in 1955 or 56, who they say, to make amends for his Apostasy, gave this Sect (whose Designs he was not only fully acquainted with, but also conducted) all possible Countenance and Encouragement. By his means it was, that so many *Printing-Presses* were dispers'd thro' the whole extent of the *Ottoman* Empire, thereby supplanting and almost extirpating the infinite Crowd of *Scribes* and *Hogies*, who liv'd by writing the Books of the Law and the heaps of Comments on the *Alcoran*, and consequently were the hottest Zealots for the Glory and Honour of *Mahometism*.

[7] With the same Views he put down the *Minarets* and order'd all to be called to the *Mosques* at the Hours of Prayer, by founding their wind Instruments and beating of Drums. By this means he oblig'd the *Missionaries* by silencing the blasphemous Proclamations of the *Muezins* or Criers from the *Minarets*, who us'd to call the *Turks* to their *Naama* or Prayers; and also made the People less zealous and furious, for the Honour of their Prophet and his Religion, who us'd to have their Ears still dinn'd, and their Zeal inflam'd with the proclaiming their *Mahomet* for the Prophet of God.

With the same subtle management, he confin'd to their own Towns all the vagabond *Dervices*, who us'd to run thro' the Provinces possest with the hottest Spirit of *Mahometism*, and turn'd many of the Monasteries of those lazy *Drones* (who had all the Zeal and Ignorance of our worst kind of Monks in them) to *Caravanseras* or Inns for Travellers, or else into *Timariots* to maintain such a number of Soldiers.

He sent such Orders thro' the Empire and appointed such faithful Ministers to execute them, (many of whom were disguis'd *Christians* and even Jesuits,) that the open Profession [8] of *Christianity*, was so far from being *penal*, that under pretence of the *Christians* being useful for the Arts and Sciences, the Trade and Plenty they brought with them wherever they came, they were even respected and regarded, provided they were not natural *Turks* or converted *Renegadoes*. Nor was this Work less subtilly carried on by the free Trade for all sorts of Wines, thro' the Dominions of the *Grand Seignior*; the Drinking of which was so universally conniv'd at, that in the open Taverns in every Village, the *Turks* would be seen all Day carousing and fuddling in defiance of their *Alcoran*. Nay, some of them have been heard in the Freedom of their Cups, to speak contemptuously of the stupid Prophet, who thought, (they said) by the blind Hopes of an imaginary Paradise above, to deprive them of the only Heaven Men could enjoy below, a cheerful Bottle, and an openhearted Friend.

But what help'd to introduce the *Christian* Religion still further, was the Custom he establish'd during his Ministry (almost as long as the two great *Kuperlies* in the 17th Century joined together) and which has been kept up ever since, of sending Ambassadors to all the Courts of *Europe*; these were accompanied [9] with a great Train of the Sons of the *Bassa's* and chief Men in the Empire, who return'd Home improv'd indeed, but often by the Address of the *Missionaries* (who waited still on the Catch for them) so prejudiced against *Mahometism*, and so in Love with the noble Arts forbidden by their Prophet, as *Painting, Sculpture, Architecture*, and above all the delicious *Vine-Press*, that it is incredible how far the secret Infection is spread, and how likely suddenly to break out into a violent Distemper in the State.

The Translation of select Parts of the Bible with useful short Notes licens'd by the Pope, and also the number of *Arabick* and *Turkish* Books which the *Printing-Presses* disperst among them, help'd on the *Missionaries* marvellously; for they were so subtilly compos'd, as to shake and under-mine the false Religion, and secretly to prepare the People for op'ning their Eyes to the Truth. Indeed, as to outward Profession *Mahometism* still shews its Face, but 'tis just like the *Pagan* Religion under *Julian* the Apostate, the Religion of the State but not of the People; one third of whom are either secretly or avowedly *Christians*, another third *Deists*, and hardly as many sincere *Mahometans*. What adds to the [10] wonder is, that all this has been effected chiefly by the Means and Management of the *Roman* See, who tho she has almost renounced the Faith her self, yet out of political Views labours to encrease her Converts here.

This is an odd Scene of things, my Lord, and yet as true as 'tis surpris-ing, and I doubt not in a few Years we shall see, that as the old Empire of the World forsook *Rome* to settle in *Constantinople*, so Religion possibly before this *Century* expires may do the same; and as the *Pope* is almost turn'd *Pagan* or *Turk*, the *Mufti* will set up for *Patriarch* of the *Eastern* World, and the great Head and Father of the *Christian* Church here.

What the Consequences of so prodigious a Revolution may be, I shall not presume to hint, to so exquisite a Judge of such things, as your

Lordship is confessedly allow'd to be; and therefore leaving them to your own judicious Reflections, I shall only observe, that had *Great Britain* continued her Care and Protection of the *Grecian* Church, with her true *Christian* Zeal, possibly we should have made as large an Harvest of Converts in *Turky* as by our Supineness and Negligence the Jesuits have done.

[11] But leaving this for another Occasion, I shall proceed to give your Lordship some Account of the State of their Army and Soldiery, their Trade and Revenue, their Laws and Customs at present; since the said Period of 1949, to which my Predecessors *Memoirs* and my own little Experience necessarily confines me.

It is certain then, my Lord, that both the Spirit and Courage, as well as the Discipline of their Soldiery, has been sensibly declining ever since the coming in of the *Tartar* Race, and especially within this last 150 Years, provided we always except the small Interval of Vizier *Ibrahim*'s Administration.

This has been chiefly owing to their taking in all sorts of People (and especially natural *Turks*, married Men and Tradesmen) for Money into the Body of the *Janizaries*; who us'd formerly to be compos'd of *Christian* Children taken Captives, and bred up in the strict Discipline and School of the *Seraglio*, in all manly and warlike Exercises.

It must be confest also, that the secret spreading of *Christianity* among their People and the Soldiery, has not a little contributed hereunto; for as the Success of their [12] Arms has ever been the great Source of the Propagation of their *Faith*, it is not to be wonder'd at, if those who had privately made a Defection from this last, did not fight with the utmost Resolution and Obstinacy, for the Power and Glory of a *Mahometan* Emperour.

But the dreadful Custom of giving the Soldiery such perpetual Largesses, and as it were, rewarding their Seditions whenever they resolved to depose one and set up another Emperour, (and confirm or destroy the Grand *Viziers* and Principal *Bassa*'s, as the Fancy took them) absolutely overturn'd what little Spirit, Virtue or Discipline was left among them. Let us join to this abominable Insolence, the horrible Licence of daily guzling Wine in the Streets, and almost the very *Mosques* of *Constantinople*, and their Debaucheries of all kinds that accompany'd it, and we need not seek for any other causes of their surprizing Degeneracy.

Some indeed, have also accounted for it from their frequent Defeats in their Battles with the *Germans* and the *Poles*, and their being so often vanquish'd by both the *Muscovites* and *Persians*, who have all of them strip'd this Empire of some of its strongest [13] Fortresses and richest Provinces. But it is plain these were not the Causes but the Effects of their decay'd Valour and Discipline, by which they have by degrees lost all their Conquests in *Persia*, and their Territories round the *black Sea*, together with the greatest part of *Transilvania, Moldavia* and *Wallachia*, and almost to the Gates of *Adrianople.*

Nor is it their Land Forces only that have thus declin'd, for their naval Power which was anciently so formidable is now so prodigiously sunk, since the Defect of their Fleet by the *English* Squadron in 1876, and in the Sea-fight with the *Dutch* ten Years afterwards, that besides their losing both *Crete* and *Cyprus* to the *Pope* and *Venetians*, they have lost all Interest and Influence, with their old Dependants of *Tunis* and *Algiers*. Nay, the very Knights of *Malta*, have since so often burnt and taken their greatest *Galeasses*, that their few Gallies and Ships of War that remain to them, dare hardly sail now out of sight of the *Dardanelles*, to collect the little Tribute of the neighbouring Islands, which are every Day revolting to them and the *Venetians*, and refusing the Payment of their old *Capitation Tax.*

[14] After mentioning this I need not add that their Trade which in the 18*th Century* was in so poor a Way, and yet before 1876 was in so flourishing a Condition, is now entirely sunk and fallen into the Hands of the Merchants of *Great Britain*. For a great while indeed, they applied themselves to it with more than ordinary Vigour, and by being Masters of the best Ports in the *Mediterranean*, and by the Assistance of their Harbours in the *Red Sea*, open'd an easier and quicker Passage to the *East Indies*, than the *Christians* could have, who are forc'd to sail to them by the tedious and hazardous Navigation of the *Cape of Good Hope*. It was easy with such Advantages to have engross'd the whole Trade of the *East*, and under-sell both the *British* and *Dutch* Merchants in the *Mediterranean*; but the Unskilfulness of their Mariners, the Weakness of their Vessels, with the natural Indisposition of the *Turks* to long Voyages, and the Toils and Hazards of the Sea, prevented their carrying these Designs so far as they might have done. But besides this, our visiting them with our Squadrons, and shutting up the *Dardanelles*, and at last our falling on their Fleets and destroying some [15] of them, soon made them surrender up their Pretensions to that Branch of Trade, and indeed all others into our Hands; where I hope they will long continue to improve, and especially if this Treaty be once agreed to in all its Articles, as I doubt not, it will very suddenly.

I have but little to say of the Revenues of this vast Empire, since I propose not to write to your Lordship, what is to be found in every printed Account of them, but only such Alterations as are of more modern Date, and little known in *Europe*. It is certain within this last forty Years, they have applied themselves much to raise them, even beyond the excessive Bounds of the late Emperours, who seem'd to strive to make up by new Taxes, the lost Revenues of their old Provinces, torn from them on every side.

They have laid immense Excises on all Eatables and Drinkables, and excessive Customs on all Imports and Exports except our *British*

Manufactures, on all Mills, Taverns, and every Trade, not only subservient to the Pleasures but the Conveniences and even Necessaries of Life. They have besides loaded their Lands with great Impositions, and laid [16] Taxes on every Acre plow'd or dug, on every Cow, Horse, Bullock, Sheep, Goat, Ass or Camel throughout the Empire. Besides this and the *Pole-Tax*, every House, Boat and Ship, and every Marriage pays so much to the *Grand Seignior*; the Births indeed are Tax-free, to encourage them to breed; neither do they pay for their Burials for a very good Reason, the *Grand Seignior* being Heir in effect to every Man that dies in his Dominions. There are also Taxes on Paper and Leather, and in one Word, on every thing necessary to Health or Ease, or even Life it self, and if it were possible, I am persuaded, they would Tax the only Blessing they enjoy here, their Air and Sunshine. Yet with all this grinding the Face of the miserable oppress'd Subject, these Revenues are so ill manag'd, and the Officers employ'd in the Collection of them, such wicked Stewards to their cruel and rapacious Masters, that hardly one half is brought into the Treasury of what is paid them. Indeed if it were not for the vast hereditary Revenue, the *Bassa's* are obliged to pay in from their several Provinces, over and above all these Taxes, and the immense Wealth that the dayly Forfeiture of their Heads, to their [17] Master's Avarice or Jealousy brings in, this unweildy dispirited Empire would almost sink, for want of vital Nourishment.

Under all this Oppression, there is not one found who dares even lament his own and Fellow-subjects Misery, or who will not pretend at least to Glory, in calling himself the *Grand Seignior's* Slave, and owning that he has no title either to his Life or Liberty, his Lands, House or Substance, but from the sole Will of his mighty Emperor. A Reflection which I cannot make, but with the honest Joy every *Britton* must feel, who sees himself secur'd by Laws of his own making, in his Liberty, Life and Property, above the Reach of the highest Power and the strongest Arm; and in Peace and Security under his own *Vine* and *Fig-tree*, enjoys from the best of Constitutions, and (the usual and natural Consequence thereof,) the best Princes, all the Blessings Men can ask for as *Freemen* and *Christians*.

O Fortunati nimium, sua si bona norint, Angligenæ!

I shall detain your Lordship no further, than with two or three Words, as to some [18] considerable Alterations of late Years in their Laws and Customs, by which they have endeavour'd to retrieve the Virtue and Majesty of this falling Empire, and which they owe chiefly to the Skill and Ability of the Renegado Vizier *Ibrahim*, who flourish'd in the middle of this *Century*. Many of them I sincerely wish with some Alterations could be transplanted into our Country and Constitution, and, if that Excess of Liberty we abound in would allow it, I doubt not we should find our Account in them.

The first I shall touch upon is the Method he took to cure the Defects of their Discipline and Courage, which he found so low, and endeavour'd to raise so high. To effect this, he divided all the Troops into Battalions and Squadrons of about 1000 or 1500 Men. Each of these Bodies were raised from one particular Province, whose name they carried, from whence alone their Officers and Recruits came; and consequently whenever they fought, the Glory or Disgrace of the Country to which they belong'd, and where they were born, was directly concern'd. By this means both Men and Officers fought still with the greater Emulation and Desire of distinguishing [19] themselves and their Country by their Valour; and also Recruits were more cheerfully and willingly rais'd, being sure to be sent to assist their own Country-Men and Acquaintances.

Nor was there any Danger of such Bodies uniting in Seditions in their own Province, being never disbanded; nor yet abroad in the Field, where their Strength was so small and inconsiderable, in respect of the whole Army, and their Country still answerable for their Conduct.

In the next place, (besides the popular Tenets of the *Turks*, that every one's Fate is writ on his Forehead, and is inevitable, and all who die in the War go strait to Paradise) he took care to breed up a contempt of Death or Danger in them, by remitting the half of all Taxes to the Widows and Children of the Slain, and by doubling the Pay of all that were wounded in Battle, as well as by allowing an annual Stipend for Life, to all who lost their Limbs, Eyes, or were any ways disabled. This he settled according to the following Table; for one Eye 5 *l.* a Year of our Money for Life, for both Eyes 12 *l.* for the right Arm 5 *l.* the left 3 *l.* for both 12 *l.* for their Hands something less, but with little [20] difference. For one Leg 2 *l.* 10 *s.* for both Legs 6 *l.* and the same for a Foot or both Feet, or with a very small Disproportion, according to the Danger and Suffering of the Soldier. Nay, so careful was he of Men so disabled, that if any one offered to wound, hurt or even strike a Soldier thus maim'd in the Service of the Empire, he was instantly sentenc'd to lose his Hand for the Offence; which was a severer Penalty than he incurr'd, if he had struck an *Iman* or a *Cady*; as they call their Priests and Judges.

By this means, my Lord, it is incredible for a while, with what Zeal his Troops us'd to rush into the Battle despising Wounds; or rather wishing for them, as the very Road to Preferment and Reward. Nor did his Care end here, for out of the choicest and best Troops, he form'd two great separate Bodies of *Infantry* and *Cavalry* of 5000 Men each, of the bravest *Veteran* Soldiers, who receiv'd double Pay, and were sworn on the *Alcoran* never to turn their backs in Battle, till they had Orders to Retreat, or that two Thirds of them were kill'd, and then to yield and be immediately ransom'd, with twice the Number of the Enemies Troops. To keep them in this severe Discipline [21], all Officers of his Forces both *Janizaries* and *Spahies* were intirely chosen out of these two Bodies; which were in like manner ever recruited out of those Men who had serv'd longest and distinguish'd themselves most, in every Provincial Corps in the Army. A method which had he liv'd to have kept up, (for it fell with him) might have bid fair for the Recovery of all the Territory and Glory, they had lost before in so many unsuccessful Battles, and had probably cost the *Christian* Powers, infinite Blood and Hazards to have surmounted. After all, my Lord, the Oath those Troops took was still less than the *Roman* Gladiators obliged themselves to perform, who us'd frequent to sell, not the Hazard but the certain Loss of their Lives, for smaller Advantages.

Till this great Man found a Remedy for it, the *Turkish Cavalry* were generally of little Service, for tho' their Horses were fine and beautiful to the Eye, they were light-limb'd and so thin-bodied and Fleet, that they were still ready to yield to the Shock of the *European Cavalry,* and to trust to their Speed to save themselves; but by banishing those sort of Horses, and obliging them only to use the largest and weightiest that could be [22] found, he taught his Troops to trust no more to the Swiftness of their Horses, but their Strength and the Weight of them, and their Swords, to the infinite Service of the Empire.

Another Method he took to improve the Soldiery, was frequently imploying them to shoot at Marks for Rewards, whence he made them excellent Marks-men with their Guns, when employed against their Enemy; saying often to them, "it was ridiculous a Soldier should not shoot as well as a Fowler, since the one shot for his Life, and the other only for his Diversion or a little silly Gain". Nay, he carried this even to his *Cannoniers,* who by this means in his time, us'd to shoot as true, as with a *Harquebush* or *Musket.*

Nor were his Cares and Skill in Civil Affairs less considerable than in Military Matters, for to him alone are owing those excellent Regulations (which the *Christian* World would be happy in) as to the Proceedings and Decisions of all Judges, who presided in Law-suits and Processes, in their judicial Courts.

By them, a Bribe being fully proved to be taken by any Judge, was Death without [23] Remission, and Forfeiture of all his Substance, half to the *Grand Seignior,* and half to the *injur'd Party.* Nay, whenever Judges decided any Controversy, they were obliged by him to give their Reasons on which they grounded their Judgment, to both Parties in Writing; and as there was still an Appeal allow'd to a *Cadelisker* at *Constantinople,* appointed solely to receive such Decrees; if there was found either great Ignorance, or the least evident Fraud or Malice in the Decision, the Judge was instantly summoned and examin'd, and if guilty condemned to pay the whole of the Value he had given his Decree for. A Precedent, my Lord, I fear we dare not hope to see follow'd, no more than that he establish'd concerning Perjury, by which all false Witnesses were for the first Offence condemn'd with forfeiture of Goods for ten Years to the *Gallies*; and for the second Offence, to be torn in pieces by Horses tied to their Limbs. He also forbid all Persons but the Soldiery, to carry any Weapons about them by Night or Day, on pain of Death; by which means Robbery and Murders were in a great measure prevented, or the Malefactor more easily detected; and, which was still more useful, [24] he made an Intention to Rob or Murder, if fully and evidently proved, equally penal with the having put the design in Execution. Nay, so far did the rigour of Justice carry him, that any kind of Fraud or Collusion, to cheat or deceive another, or even denying or avoiding artfully a just Debt, was made as punishable, as if the Offender had actually attempted a Theft of equal value.

He went further yet, and with the Spirit of the ancient *Spartans*, if any Person could justly impeach another of evident Ingratitude, he gave up the Offender to him into Slavery, for so many Years as might bear some proportion to the Heinousness of the Offence he was Convicted of. Besides, he inforc'd that excellent Law which had grown obsolete, that every *Turk* should effectually learn some Trade, by which he might preserve himself from Want, which he established with such Vigour and Care, as was never before seen in this Empire. A Law, my Lord, which if it were past in *England*, as to the Children of the ordinary People, would deliver us from those Shoals of Beggars, Thieves and useless Idlers, which are the greatest Curse of our Country.

[25] The late Emperour *Achmat* made also some Laws, (how ineffectual soever they proved) that deserve our Notice at least, if not our Imitation; as that, by which, for his short Reign, he effectually cur'd the growing, Crime of *Suicide*, by Forfeiture of Estate and Goods, and ignominiously exposing the Bodies of the Deceas'd unburied to the publick View. He also ordered the substituting perpetual Slavery, as the Penalty of most Crimes formerly punish'd with Death, not excepting even Theft and Adultery; and prohibited all Playing (which spread prodigiously among the *Turks*) either at Games of Hazard or Skill, on pain of the severest corporal Punishment.

'Tis to the same Emperor, that they owe those excellent Laws against Drunkenness, that occasions so many Quarrels and Murders, and destroys so many Families by Poverty and Disease; as also the appointing Clerks of the Market in all Places of the Empire, to prevent Extortion of Prices from the Poor, and to seize on such Meat for their use, or condemn it to the Fire, which should be found unwholsome or unmerchantable. It was he also, who sentenc'd all owners of Houses, which happen'd by their neglect to [26] be set on Fire, to make good half the Damage they bring on their Neighbours; and that all Slaves who by Negligence endangered and House by Fire, (tho' it should be extinguished) shall be branded on both Cheeks with a red hot Iron, and their Noses cut off as a Mark of perpetual Infamy.

It is certain, my Lord, many of these Laws seem too severe; but indeed, that is no more than what is necessary in *Turky*, both from the Nature of the People, and also because such numbers of them are now no ways restrain'd by the Injunctions of their Prophet, (which they consider no longer as the Commands of God, but the meer Inventions of Men,) and must therefore be the more severely watch'd over by the Hand of Justice, and the most sanguinary Laws. A Reflection which while I am making, I can't but turn my Eye and Thoughts, with Grief and Shame on the *Christian* World, where I fear the same Necessity will call too soon for the same Severity; while we behold so many Miscreants, slighting the Restraints of our holy Religion, and deriding the Faith and Principles, that us'd to Influence the Piety of their less corrupted Ancestors.

[27] But I detain your Lordship too long, with these unimportant Matters, to which I could add much more of the same Nature, if I durst flatter my self that they deserved your Attention.

In the mean Time, as I have the Fortune to be much in the good Graces of the *Grand Seignior,* and am often sent for to entertain him with Accounts of *Europe,* and the Advancement of *Arts* and *Sciences* there, which he Admires without understanding them; and as I have particularly made great Impressions on him, in behalf of our *Astronomy*: I must beg you will send me one of the best new Telescopes you can possibly procure, for I see it will be matter of infinite Delight to him.

When I have the Honour to receive your further Commands, I shall venture, if you desire it, to proceed to continue your Trouble in Reading, and the Pleasure I take in Writing any thing, you will vouchsafe to peruse.

In the mean Time I humbly take my leave, beseeching your being persuaded of my managing [28] the Treaty, with my best Care and Abilities, and my shewing my self with the utmost Zeal and Respect, both to my *King,* my *Country,* and your *Lordship,*

a most faithful Subject,
        Friend and Servant,

                                                        Stanhope.

To the Lord Treasurer, &c.

Rome, Nov. 7, 1997.

My Lord,

Your second Express which followed close on the Heels of the first, found me here just settled in a most handsome and convenient House, assign'd by his Holiness a Day or two after my first Audience, on the 3*d* Instant, which past to my entire Satisfaction. The *Pope*, to say Truth, how heartily soever he wishes our Destruction, as the great Bulwark of the *Protestant* Cause and Interest; yet is so sensible of his Majesty's Wisdom and Power, and the vast Ascendant his Fleets and [29] Arms have procur'd him, over all the Affairs in *Europe*; that he shews the greatest Readiness to comply with all our Demands, and puts the best Mien on it he can. He has already confirmed *Civita Viechia* a free Port for us, and restor'd all our Privileges in the *Adriatick*, and has engag'd that after the next Consistory he holds, which will be in two or three Days, no *British* Subject shall be liable to the *Inquisition*. A Bull is to be publish'd accordingly; and in a Word, he has complied with all the less important Articles I was commanded to insist on.

Matters standing thus, I see nothing to hinder our Squadron, to sail directly from *Leghorn* according to their Instructions, and have signified as much by this Express to Admiral *Mordaunt*; being persuaded that there will not be the least Objection or Obstacle arise in these Affairs, from the *Roman* See.

In the mean Time, I shall use my utmost Industry to observe my Instructions, to get the best Intelligence possible, of all the dangerous Intriegues of this overgrown State; and give the fullest Lights, and use the fittest Means I can reach to, to enable his sacred [30] Majesty, by your Lordship's wise Counsels, to disappoint and overturn them.

Tho' I am settled here but a few Weeks, I have not been asleep, but pursuant to the 5*th Article* of my Instructions, have applied my self where I was directed, as well as to the *Imperial* and *French* Ambassadours here. I live already in no small Degree of Intimacy and Confidence with them; as they assure me, they have in Command from their Masters to do, on their parts with me, and which your Lordship well knows their own Interests tie them to.

By their Informations and my Intelligence from the other Quarter, I hope to be able to observe your Directions, and answer your Enquiries concerning this tow'ring See, or rather this new Empire of the *Vatican* as they universally, and too justly call it here; which is risen of late to so prodigious an height, that it seems not only to rival, but out-grow the most extended Limits of old *Rome*, in the fullest Glory of its Strength.

I shall therefore endeavour to lay before your Lordship's discerning Eye, the whole Plan of this *spiritual Monarchy*, and the Pillars on which it is built; which we shall find subsists no longer, as Cardinal *Sancta* [31] *Croze* told *Thuanus*, (*Aulæ nostræ Majestas stat tantum famâ & patientiâ hominum*) but on the deepest and best laid Foundations Men can lay, by vast Riches, incredible Policy, and the greatest armed Strength in *Europe*.

When I have done this to the best of my poor Capacity, I shall, as your Lordship directs me, examine whether his Holiness still pursues his prodigious Views, in Case of the present Emperour's Demise; and what reasonable Hopes his Majesty may entertain, openly to thwart or secretly to undermine them.

Your Lordship's Knowledge of the Affairs of *Europe* in the 19*th Century*, as well as the present Times, is too extensive, to allow me to dwell long on those terrible Wars and Divisions, between the *Emperour, France* and *Spain*; which with the unhappy Dissensions here, gave the Jesuits so far the Ascendant in the *Conclave* at that time, as to blind the Eyes of the Cardinals, to take that fatal and deplorable Step, of placing *Paul* IX. a Jesuite on the *Papal Throne*.

Nor is your Lordship less appriz'd of all the dreadful Train of Consequences that follow'd, to the infinite Increase of the Power [32] of that aspiring Order, and thro' their means of the *Roman* See. Hence it came that after they had by degrees made themselves Masters one way or another, both of *Savoy, Naples,* and *Tuscany* in less than fifty Years; they brought even *Venice* it self with all her Policy, to be with her Territories but a sort of *Ecclesiastical Fief* to the *Empire* of the *Vatican*.

In a little Time they actually tore from them, *Brescia, Crema,* and *Bergamo* with their Dependencies, as having been anciently united to the *Millanese,* which they were long possess'd of, by the Cession of the Emperour *Charles* IX. in 1845. The *Polesin* they wrested out of their Hands, in the Wars that broke out soon after, between *Innocent* the XV. and the *Senate*; who after the fatal Battle of *Verona*, had like to have lost all their Dominions on the Continent, if they had not sav'd them by that infamous Peace, which has in a manner made them Vassals to this See ever since.

These are Events which fill the Histories of those Times, and all that read them, with Amazement; tho' I doubt not but your Lordship's Wisdom considers them, [33] but as the natural Consequences of the Power of that Church, which being entitled to seize or purchase every thing she can lay her Talons on, and unable to alienate any thing she has once possess'd, must necessarily have been foreseen, (if Men had Eyes) to be secure in a few Ages of becoming Mistress of the World, as she has now in a manner made her self, by enslaving *Italy*. A Truth, which even the Blindness of the last Age, might have discern'd with half an Eye, tho' the *Pope* had not been believ'd by them, to have the Keys of Heaven and Hell absolutely in his Disposal. For this Privilege alone as it tied all pious scrupulous Minds fast to *Rome*, so the other as to this World, where her Power must be ever necessarily encreasing, could not fail to join strongly to her, all daring and ambitious Spirits, by the Riches and Possessions, she could tempt them with, to her Interests. The Policy of this See had, for many Ages perpetually employ'd her *Ecclesiasticks* to preach up to the People in all parts of the Earth, the vast Superiority of the spiritual Office of Priesthood, above that of the Temporal one of a worldly King. They advanc'd the Priesthood, as taking care of the immortal [34] Part the Soul, infinitely above the Prince, who only had Authority over their Bodies; and as they had persuaded them that the poorest Friars, were the *Moses* and *Aarons* sent and commissioned by Heaven to be as Gods to Kings,* (who were really but the *Pharoahs* of the World,) they had gain'd a much greater Influence over the Minds of Men, than their Governours. On these deep Foundations the Jesuits took care to build the prodigious superstructures of Wealth, Territories and Power; and join'd to that notional Empire, which ties down Mens Minds and Consciences, those additional Strengths and Buttresses, that might prop it up, when length of Time and encrease of Knowledge should threaten it's Fall; and by every worldly Motive, secure Mens Hands and Passions, and earthly Interests to support and keep it standing.

But there are Reflections which lie too open to your Lordship's Mind, to allow of my dwelling long on them, and it will be sufficient to say, that as they have ever since had the ablest Hands and the wisest Heads to employ them; they have so far establish'd their Usurpations, during the Distractions [35] of *Europe* and *Italy* which they artificially fomented, that they have taken such Root, as will probably keep them secure from tumbling in the greatest Storm.

But let us carefully view the several Steps and Measures they have made use of towards the maintenance of this Power they have arriv'd at; and your Lordship will soon see the Apprehensions of the deep rooting of their Strength, to be more than probable.

And in speaking to this matter, I shall not once touch on that prodigious Authority which they have ever claim'd, of disposing of the Crowns and Empires of the World, as they find good for the Service of the Church and their spiritual Kingdom below: This they have exerted these two last *Centuries* in all the Plenitude of their Power: And I shall only dwell on such worldly Schemes and Methods, which have rais'd this Order to be Masters of the Earth; without which power of the Sword, that of the Keys (in these Days especially) would have signified little.

And first then, they are not only Masters of *Italy*, excepting *Piedmont* and that part of *Savoy*, which *Geneva* and the *Swisse Cantons* conquer'd

---

* Exod. Ch. VII. Ver. 1.

and keep in spite of them, [36] to the great Joy of the *Christian* Princes; but they are Masters of it more strongly fortified, better furnish'd with Magazines, and better guarded with a standing Force of near 130000 *Veteran* Troops, than ever the World yet saw it. But besides this, with the Forts and Hands of *Italy*, they have by the *Pope*'s Authority amass'd together, all the Wealth of it's Churches, the Hoards of it's Convents and Monasteries, and all the votive Plate, Images, Jewels and Riches of *Loretto*. These, under Pretence of saving them from the Fury of he Wars, and the Plunder of Hereticks, they have treasur'd up in the Castle of St. *Angelo*, to the Value of near 150 Millions, as Men generally compute it. A Fund which in such Hands, and under the Management of such artificial Craftsmen, is able not only to keep up an invincible Army as they perpetually do, but even to buy off the venal Faith and Forces of half the Princes of *Europe*, to their side.

Along with this immense Treasure, the Pope and this Order (for they are but one and the same Body and Interest) have from their Provinces in *Africk*, their Territories or Empire rather of *Paraguay* in *America*, [37] and their Revenues from *China*, a Fund so prodigious, that it exceeds all Belief, or even Computation; the neat Produce from *Paraguay* alone, after all Deductions, amounting to near three Millions. To add to these, the Computation of all the Revenues of *Italy*, and their vast Estates in the different Parts of *Europe*, would be a needless Labour; since every one may see, as plainly as your Lordship, that they are already Masters of a Treasure, sufficient to carry on the largest Designs, that their Ambition or even their Religion (as they have drest up Religion) can prompt them to.

But they have Forces still unmentioned, that are equal to their Riches, for my Lord, you, who know the Courts of *Europe* so intimately, can vouch, that there is hardly a great Person in them, who has not a Jesuite for his Confessor, nay his Director. How few of its crown'd Heads are there, whose Prime Minister is not either a Cardinal Jesuite or so absolutely under the Influence of the *Pope*'s Nuncio, that they may be said to be entirely govern'd and directed by them, and the perpetual Couriers and Councels that are sent hourly from *Rome*, where the Nephew or Cardinal *Padrone* dictates [38] measures to *Europe*, as if he were a fifth *Evangelist*.

By these means it is, that they have entirely excluded all Princes from intriguing in the *Conclave*; for tho' they sometimes leave the Nomination of fit Persons to the sacred Purple (provided they are Jesuits) to crown'd Heads; yet are there no longer *Spanish, French* or *German* Cardinals in the World, since whatever Nation they belong to, they are absolutely and solely Jesuits and nothing else. Thus by confining the Cardinalship and Popedom to their own Order, they have been able to avoid two Rocks, namely, long and factious *Conclaves*, and short Reigns. For it is not now as it was formerly, that he who went in there *Pope*, came out *Cardinal*, but even during the *Pope*'s Life, they settle by Agreement the next Successor, without Violence and Party-Feuds, and enter the *Conclave* for a few Days for Form's sake, and generally take care to chuse a middle-ag'd and healthy *Pope*, by which they are the more enabled to execute their Schemes and build up their Power.

Nay, so indolent are the Princes of *Europe* grown and so little jealous of their old Rights, or at least so conscious are they of [39] their want of Power to influence Elections, that 'tis grown a common Maxim with them, that *Popes* resemble Houses, which 'tis better generally to buy ready made, than to be at the Expence and Care in making and raising them, when the top Stone is plac'd on the Building. And here indeed, is the great Source and Fountain of their Strength, for chiefly by this Canal (the Popedom) that feeds their lesser Streams, are the great Promotions, Rewards and Preferments, not only in their own but all other Courts, deriv'd to the Friends of the Society; and by them are the smaller Rivulets supplied, and the Land water'd and enrich'd, by their wise and artful Distribution. Thus are all kept in awe by hopes of Preferment of one kind or another. *Omnibus una quies, Venter!* All that stick to them zealously and serve them faithfully, being secure of Rewards and Advancement, whatever Profession or Employment they follow.

From such plain Facts as these, it is, my Lord, that most People are convinc'd, that over and above the Crowds of great [40] Men, that are lifted openly in this Society, there are still a much greater Number, who are secretly Jesuites in private, and *ex Voto* as they call it. Nay, the World is much deceiv'd if they have not, by this subtle Method as many Generals at their Devotion, in the Service of other Princes, as they keep in their pay in *Italy*, and their Territories abroad.

With such incredible Assistances, is it any thing wonderful, that they have been able to divide and distract the *Protestant* Powers, to corrupt and pervert some of them, perfidiously and atheistically to break thro' Oaths, and the most solemn and sacred Engagements, and to embrace the *Romish* Communion; and purchase off the poor distress'd Branches, of the *Greek* and *Armenian* Churches, to submit to their Authority, and obtain their Protection at the Price of their Faith.

For my part, my Lord, when I see them posses'd of such Power and Policy together, when I see all the Cardinals, Fathers, Prelates, nay, all the Orders of their Church, all the Ministers of their Princes, (not to say the Princes themselves,) absorb'd and sunk into this one prodigious [41] Body; I cannot but admire at their Prudence or rather the Providence of Heaven, that keeps them from being as absolute Masters of this World, as they give themselves out, (and are believ'd) to be of the next; in spite of their flagitious Actions, and the open and flagrant Wickedness of their Conduct.

These Articles, my Lord, which I have been insisting on, are the great Engines by which this vast Machine has gain'd, and now continues to exert its Strength; and let me now hint some others as useful, tho' seemingly more weak and contemptible, which this Church makes use of by her inferior Dependants.

And First then, there is not an Art so mean, which these Jesuits do not stoop to, if it can be of use to them. With this View, besides their being the general Bankers and Traders of the World, they have unjustly, and by the vilest means engross'd all the Schools and Colleges of *Europe*, and the sole Education of the Youth there. From among those, they pick and garble all the choice Spirits and promising Genius's; whom by Places in their Universities and Preferments [42] when they leave them, and every Allurement that suits their natural Temper and Dispositions best, they tie fast to themselves, either as Friends or Members of their Society.

But they stoop lower yet, for as they alone, or such as they license, are allowed the Privilege of being Confessors, (that is Spies over all Mankind) by the *Bull* of *Clement* XIV. in 1862; so they do not only thus keep an infinite ascendant, over the Minds of Princes and all in Authority, but they even preserve their Empire with the lower Ranks and Degrees of Men; to the poorest Tradesmen, the common Soldiers, and the very Porters and Rabble of the Streets, who are all oblig'd to Confession at least once a Month, or to be Excommunicated and Outlaw'd.

In the next place, my Lord, as by the same *Bull* they are constituted sole *Inquisitors*, and thereby have intirely routed their old Rivals the *Dominicans* and secular Clergy; they have thence got an unbounded Power, of ruining the Fortunes and destroying the Lives, of all that offer not openly to oppose, (which were vain) but even to [43] censure them. For as by their Arts they have turn'd the holy Office of the Inquisition (as they style it,) into a meer Engine of State, to take off under Colour of Heresy, all of whom they, or the Prince conceive the least Jealousy; so the Awe which by this Method they strike their Enemies Minds with, can only be equal'd by the Hopes and Encouragement, they give their Friends both Laity and Clergy, by espousing and serving their Interests and Advancement, *per fas & nefas*, Right or Wrong.

By the same *Bull* they alone are privileg'd to Exorcise the Obsest, which gives them an huge Appearance of Sanctity with the Crowd, as if none but they among the Regulars, were able to combat with, and overcome the Rage and Fury of the Devil; and what adds not a little to their Veneration, tho' others are allowed to marry People, which they never do (possibly as fearing they may gain more Enmity and Curses, than good Will and Thanks by it) yet they alone are empor'd to examine into, and grant Divorces where they see cause, which makes them not a little consider'd and applied to.

[44] But as tho' these were but small Honours, which the holy See has heap'd on them, they are constituted also sole Licensers of Books, by which means nothing appears in Publick, but what is season'd to their

Palate, and dress'd up by their spiritual Cooks so skilfully, as to please their Society and the relish of the World. And it is worth your Lordship's Notice, that since 1862, there has not one Book either in Divinity or History (for on other Subjects they are very indifferent) which has seen the Light, but what have been wrote by the publick Professors in those Faculties; so that both present and future Times, must either take up with the false Lights they present them with, or search out Truth from a few private conceal'd Manuscripts, which it will be difficult, if not impossible to come at.

This brings to mind, what *Pasquin* said on this Occasion, that his Holiness had made his good Brethren the Jesuits, sole Spectacle-makers to the World; by which means they were impower'd to make all things in Print, appear dark or clear, fair or foul, great or little, as they pleas'd to represent them to the Eyes of others.

[45] But to preserve and maintain their Power yet further, as all other *Ecclesiasticks*, are but little Agents and under-work Men to them, so the Cures in remote places are ferv'd by such; while the crowded, and most frequented Pulpits are still filled with Fathers of the Society, who are the popular Preachers admir'd and ador'd by all. Nay, to insinuate themselves the more with the Crowd, they affect to appear the Champions and De-fenders of their darling Doctrine of the Immaculate Conception; in favour of which a *Bull* was at last procur'd for them, in spight of the *Dominicans* Opposition. By this means they pretend to be so peculiarly favour'd by her, as to receive particular Revelations from Heaven, nay, to work miraculous Cures and Conversions, and to be enabled as it were, to inspire the dullest Children with Learning, by her Blessing on their Prayers and Labours, all which extraordinary Gifts none of the other Orders have dar'd to set up for, or rival them in this last *Century*, whatever they us'd to do in the former ones.

Nay, so peculiarly does she protect them, (as 'tis generally said) and believed, that if any great Sinner enters into their Order, he either [46] dies by her Means, or amends his Life perfectly in six Months; and as there has not these fifty Years, been one Jesuit accus'd of any Crime whatever, so it is well known, that for fifty Years before, none were accus'd who were not acquitted, and whose Accusers did not die some violent or sudden Death, by her vengeance and the judgment of Heaven; tho' Hereticks, like your Lordship, may impute it to another cause.

In the last place, their Numbers and political Correspondence are of vast service to them, for tho' there are computed to be near 170,000 known Jesuits in *Europe* alone, all of whom by their Friends and Relations strengthen their Party; yet are matters so regularly order'd, that each Member once a Week, gives an Account of his Conduct and Observations to his Rector, and he to the College, each College to the Provincial, each Provincial to the *Nuncio*, and each *Nuncio* to the *Pope*, who is always General of the Order. Their Numbers are also as exactly distributed, as the regular Forces of a Prince, and even in *Great Britain*, if my Intelligence be good, there are not less than 1300 quartered in different Places and Disguises; some of [47] them as Tradesmen, *Valet de Chambres*, and Clerks, and not a few as Preachers and School-masters, among our unhappy and unreasonably dived Sectaries.

I send enclos'd a List of 75 of these Traytors Names and last Places of Residence; and I need not caution your Lordship, not to be impos'd on by Proofs of their being zealous *Protestants* in their general Conversation, or keeping no Fasts, nor regarding *Lent*, &c. for they have full Dispensations for these useful Acts of *Hypocrisy*.

And thus, I shall shut up this tedious Account, of this prodigious Society, which I believe will be found to have fully deserv'd the Title, so long since given it, of the *Monarchia Solipsorum*. Sure I am, this vast Encrease of Power, has done as much harm to the Health, not to say the very Being of the *Christian* Church, as the Swelling and Over-growth of the Spleen does to the Human Body, which wastes and consumes in proportion to the Size and Excess of the other.

After what I have laid before your Lordship, I fear it will appear, that there is too much Ground for my being sent hither; and to apprehend that his Holiness will [48] be able to pursue, (tho' I hope unsuccessfully,) those prodigious Views which the Imperial and *French* Ambassadors are so much alarm'd with; and both establish the *Inquisition* in *France*, and in case of his Imperial Majesty's Death, endeavour, if possible, to be chosen Emperour. This last is the more to be fear'd, because he has so far influenc'd the Electors already, as to refuse to chuse a King of the *Romans*, and it is by all agreed here, that as *Charles* V. one of the ancient Heroes of the 16*th Century*, actually laid his Schemes to be chosen *Pope*, tho' he could not carry it; so the *Pope* could not do better for the good of *Christendom*, if he made Reprizals, now when it is more than probable he may not be disappointed.

Of the eleven Electors, the two last of which were made entirely by the Intrigues of this Court, it is certain he has the five Ecclesiasticks at his Devotion, both as they are all Jesuits, and also as they expect the Purple for their Attachment to him; and tho' the other six seem determined to oppose him, yet alas, what a weak Security is a little *German* Truth and Virtue, when tempted by all the Arts, and Wealth, and [49] Power of this See. The Imperial Ambassador assures me, that he has actually offer'd the Electour of *Bavaria* to make him a King, and be acknowledg'd as such by all the crown'd Heads in *Europe* that are *Catholicks*, if he will Vote for a Person he shall propose, and with some Assurances that it shall be a *German*. But how far this, and especially the last Particular, can be depended on, and if true, how far his Electoral Highness's Virtue may outweigh his Vanity, which has so long thirsted after this airy and empty Title, we must wait on that great Discoverer *Time* to unriddle.

However, amidst all our Apprehensions, it is some Comfort that his Imperial Majesty's Health rather improves than declines; and tho' the strong and hale Complexion of his Holiness, bids fair to survive him, yet it is possible the Goodness of Heaven may interpose, for the Peace and Liberty of *Europe*, which if this terrible Intrigue should succeed, would be greatly endangered. It is most sure his *Britannick* Majesty is consider'd here, as the greatest Obstacle to all these Schemes of the *Papal* Ambition; and how far the daily Terror of our [50] Fleet on this Coast, and his Majesty's Arms, Conduct, and personal Bravery, (hereditary to his House) may intimidate and cool the Ardour of his Hopes, is not easily to be imagin'd. In the mean time, as to the other Particular, this Court seems resolute in setting up the *Inquisition* in *France*, and has actually sent an Express last Week, by the way of *Lyons*, to order the *Nuncio* to make the most pressing Instances, that it may be no longer delay'd; and if this be complied with, the Slavery of that unhappy Nation is compleated, who long since have had no other Remains of their ancient Liberty left them but the Freedom of their Tongues; whereas this infernal Office, like *Satan* who invented it, will accuse them for the very Guilt of their Thoughts too.

A Proceeding so much the more ungenerous and unjust, as it oppresses a Nation, to whose Valour and pious Assistance, the State and Grandeur of this *See* is so highly indebted; but as the great *Cornaro* said once, *that Ingratitude is the Vice of Priests*, so this will be but one of many Proofs, that it is a Crime that descends *ex traduce*, and is hereditary to the *Popedom*, if I may use such an Expression of an elective Kingdom.

[51] The Study of Antiquity which is the reigning Passion of this Court, has put his Holiness on an extraordinary Project, which is, to cut a new Bed for the *Tiber*, by a vast Canal from its old Channel, thro' the deep Valley hard by the *Poute Molle*. As it is expected, (besides, the Convenience of raising the Banks of the River, and securing it from future Inundations) that prodigious Quantities of Antiquities of all kinds will be found by this Method, and much more than will answer the Charge; they propose to spare no Expence, in executing the Design with Care and Expedition, before the great Heats endanger the Health of the Inhabitants, from the Stench of the Filth and Slime of the River.

I forgot to mention to your Lordship, that I was shewn here Yesterday, an old Gentleman, who is actually the lineal Descendant of one of our ancient Kings, who abdicated his Throne thro' a violent Aversion to the Northern Heresy, and his Zeal to this See; and yet, so grateful are his good Patrons the Jesuits, that he is no farther consider'd here then as a Piece of Antiquity, which they keep to [52] mortifie themselves with in *Lent*. They allow him 2000 *l.* a Year, and a beneficial Place, of first *Valet de Chambre* to his Holiness. He seems to be a grave heavy Man, and very constant at his Breviary, neither he, or his Father ever took the Title of King on them; he is near Eighty, and has a very bad Aspect. He keeps no Attendants but a few Highland Gentlemen, and has such a saturnine melancholy Severity of Manners, that he converses with none but a Rabble of *Scotch* and *English* Jesuits, and now and then an *Italian* Painter or Fiddler. He is certainly Great Great Grandson, to the Person who is once or twice mention'd in the Histories of the glorious Reigns of *George* II. and *Frederick* I. under the Name of the Pretender. He was never married but has five illegitimate Children; two Sons, one of whom is Bishop of *Como*, the other is a Colonel in the *Pope*'s Service, (but I know not whether Horse or Foot,) and three Daughters, who are Mother Abbesses to three *Nunneries* of very large Revenues. I saw him at the *Opera*, for he is a great Lover of Musick, and we conversed together near an Hour in *Italian*, having no *English*.

[53] *So fall the Idols and the Slaves of* Rome.

I am asham'd to have detain'd your Lordship so long and so unprofitably, and therefore shall only add, that as I shall faithfully pursue my Instructions here, so I hope my Zeal for my Country, and Attachment to your Lordship, stand in need of no Professions, and especially from one, who has so often sacrific'd his Fortune and Interest to the little Services he has been so happy to render to both, and to the Honour of being

My Lord, your Lordship's, &c.

Hertford.

I write this with Mr. *Secretary*'s Cypher, having unhappily mislaid the one you order'd for me.

[54] *To the Lord* High Treasurer, &c.

Mosco, Nov. 29, 1997

My Lord,

In my last of *September* 25, which carried my sincere Compliments on your happy Advancement, and being declar'd *Prime Minister* and *Treasurer*; I sent you the fullest Accounts I was able of the State of Things here, and the good Condition they stand in, by our last Treaty of Commerce. This Court indeed, has not forgot the fatal Blow we gave their Naval Power in the *Baltick* formerly, and the great Restraint we keep them under ever since; yet, as they see there is no hope of bettering their Affairs, by living on ill Terms with us, they seem determin'd to try to gain upon us, by all the Friendship and Favour they can shew us in our Commerce here. I shall omit no Opportunity, to improve this good Inclination towards us according to my former Instructions, and your Lordship's Commands; and as this People are [55] vastly improv'd every way, have made great advances in all polite Arts, as well as the learned Sciences, and are grown considerable in the World, by their Arms, Conquests and Riches; I doubt not but we shall find our Account, in keeping up a constant Intercourse of Friendship and Amity with them. The great Caravan for *China* went off Yesterday, with near twenty *British* Merchants in their Company, all provided with sufficient Pass-ports, and allowed the same Privileges with the *Czar's* Subjects; and I hope in time, to see this Branch of our Commerce turn to greater Account, than it has been represented to the Commissioners for Trade in *London*.

Your Lordship, who is so well acquainted with the vast Encroachments, this powerful Empire has made, on all her Neighbours round her, both on the side of *Turky*, *Poland*, *Sweden* and *Persia*, and how dangerous an Enemy, and useful a Friend she may prove, to the Affairs of *Germany*; can never want Inclination to tie the *Czar* to our Interests, by all ways and methods that in good Policy we can make use of.

All the crown'd Heads in *Europe*, except *Sweden* who is at War with them, have [56] Envoys of Ambassadors constantly here to this end, tho' some of them, as *France* or *Spain*, have little or no Trade with them, and therefore your Lordship's Resolutions to keep a constant Resident here, which has been so much neglected of late Years, is certainly extreamly necessary. Your Informations of the great Influence the present *Pope* and his Jesuites have gain'd here, are but two well grounded, and I make no doubt, but in a little time, if they go on as they have of late Years, by bribing the leading Clergy and Nobility, by Places and Promises of Preferment, and by keeping up a constant Body of *Missionaries* to disperse their Opinions among the People and lower Clergy; but this Church and her Emperour and Patriarch, will be more obedient Sons to the triumphant *Latin*, than they were to the militant *Greek* Church.

I have nothing more to add to my last Dispatches, but to shew my Obedience to your Commands, in procuring you as exact an Account as I could, of the Affair which you say has made so much Noise in *London*, to wit, the *Laplanders* Sun-shine. It is certain then, my Lord, that this matter, which begun about twenty Years ago, near *Novogorod*, [57] is spread to several Parts of *Muscovy*, and is likely to grow in Fashion at Court.

It took it's rise from the *Knez Peter Kikin*, who living near *Novogorod*, about the Year 1971, hir'd a Couple of *Laplanders* that were Brothers, for Servants. As their Master was fond of Gardening, and had got a *Gardener* from *Moscow*, he put one of these *Laplanders* to work there under him;

and the *Gardener* often complaining of the Climate, the Fellow told him if his Master would give him Money to bear his Charges, he would bring him a *Laplander* that with his Assistance, would make Sunshine for him. This he averr'd so frequently and so positively, that at last it was told his Master; who after examining the Fellow, and knowing it was usual with the *Laplanders* to sell Winds, resolved to make a Trial of this Method, tho' new to him. In a Word, he sent and had the Person hir'd and brought from *Lapland*, who perform'd all that his Countryman and Assistant undertook for him, and even exceeded his Masters fondest Imaginations. Tho' *Novogorod* lies in the Latitude of 56 Degrees, yet by the perpetual Sunshine these [58] Creatures produc'd in his Gardens, he had in Time as Choice Peaches, Nectarines, Figs, and Grapes, nay Pine-apples (as I am assur'd) as could grow in *France*, at least in the more Northern Parts of it. Nay, he got some of the tenderest Plants and Flowers which before he never durst venture out of his Green-House till *June*, to thrive and flourish in the open Air from *March* till *November*; which is longer by much than they dare keep out their Orange Trees at *Versailes*.

This look'd so like a Fable, that I could scarce give it Credit, till I enquir'd of several Persons of the greatest Worth and Honour here, who all agreed in averring it to me; and that several *Muscovite* Noblemen had actually got *Laplanders* by the Means of this Fellow, who by their amazing Art of making Sunshine (for I know not what other Term to use) had as fine Gardens for choice Fruit, Flowers, and exotick Plants, as any Gentleman in the Neighbourhood of *Paris*. They nam'd at least a Dozen to me, that made Use of this wonderful Method, so that there was no Room to doubt of the Fact; and being resolv'd to give your Lordship the fullest Satisfaction I could, I set out [59] the latter End of last Month, to see the Seat and Gardens of *Knez John Petrowisky*, who has two of the most famous *Laplanders* in all *Muscovy*.

I was receiv'd there with much Civility, he being prepar'd for my coming, and as the *Knez* spoke *French* very well, I enter'd into a long Dialogue with him on this surprizing Affair, of which I shall now relate to your Lordship the chief Particulars. The *Laplanders* are extremely reserv'd, in communicating the least Circumstance of their Art to any one; nor will they allow any Man, no not the least Child, to be in the Garden while they are about their Business, so that there was no talking to themselves upon it. The *Knez* told me that with great Difficulty he procur'd his *Laplanders* to leave their Country. That he was forc'd to allow them Cloaths, Brandy, Rain-Deers dry'd Flesh, and Marrow, (their favourite Dish) which he brings yearly from *Lapland*, besides Tobacco and ready Money, to the Value of at least 90 *l.* Sterl. by the Year. That there must alway be two of them, neither of which can perform the Operation alone, and that they will not leave their Country without bringing [60] a Wife with each of them, so that it is extremely expensive to get them or keep them. They are also excessively humoursome, and will neither eat with others, or let any but their Wives dress their Food for them, and upon the least Ill-humour they will leave the Garden without Sunshine for several Days, nay a whole Week; but by that Time the Fit is generally over, and they fall to Work readily of themselves. That about three Years ago being disgusted for not having Rain-Deers Flesh in sufficient Plenty, they left his Gardens without Sun for near a Fortnight, in the midst of a terrible Season of Frost and Snow, and the Wind all that while in the North. That he had like thereby, to have lost most of his foreign Plants and Flowers, several of the tenderest of which actually died; and the rest had followed, but that he got his *Laplanders* in good Humour and recovered them, by giving them fine Weather for several Weeks, and pruning away all that was decay'd of them.

He told me his Men generally made three Acres of Sunshine in a Day, but that few others could come up to that, and many not over one or one and a half. That by [61] their Contract they oblig'd themselves, to continue the Sunshine for seven Hours each Day, and when they were not lazy, would often give them eight or nine Hours; but in very foggy or rainy Weather, and especially, if accompany'd with great and high Winds, they would often toil for the whole Morning, without any tolerable Benefit. He said he had an hundred Times, seen them at Work from the Windows of his Apartment, and that they did all by the Beating of a Drum, and burning some particular Herbs, and especially wild Moss and Mint, and singing some odd Kind of Songs, which he knew not what to make of, but he believ'd they were no Psalms. He concluded with saying, that he would not prevent by an ill Description, the Pleasure of my seeing Things with my own Eyes, for if I would stay there that Night I should survey every Thing next Morning, as soon as I pleas'd.

I very cheerfully accepted the Offer, and tho' I rose before it was clear Day-light, I was hardly dress'd till he call'd me into his Bed-Chamber, and plac'd me with him in the Window, to behold this astonishing Scene. There I saw at about a hundred Yards Distance the two *Laplanders*, who seem'd to [62] be at their Prayers, for they were both on their Knees. He assur'd me they were every Morning, an Hour and an half before Sunrise constantly employ'd thus, murmuring something in a low mournful growling Tone, (which I heard, tho' faintly from the Window,) and reeling their Bodies back and forwards, and often beating their Foreheads violently against the Ground. He told me that the Place in the Garden, was a little Circle in one of the Walks, which they had planted round with their own Hands with Sun Flowers, common Daffadills, Marygolds, and red Daisies; under the Roots of which, they had buried many Skeletons of several Kinds of Birds, and that they allow'd no Body by their good Will, to walk or sit down in it, and much less to dig or break the Ground.

In a little Time, I perceiv'd they begun to alter their Motions, and heard a Noise of a Flint and Steel in striking Fire, which he told me they were now busy about, and preparing their Moss and Herbs and stretching their Drum. In some Minutes I plainly saw it was so, by a little Smoak arising form a small Heap, they had made in the Garden Walk; and no sooner did the Smoak appear, but they both fell a singing with a [63] low hoarse Voice, one of the vilest Songs for Words and Musick I had ever heard. One of them who held the *Kannus* or Drum, all the while beat on it, first low and softly, and then by Degrees louder and quicker, and again with all his Force, till at last a little Blaze began to appear; upon which they got on their Feet, stamping so violently on the Ground, that I could hear them to the Window, and dancing and singing as furiously, as if they had been distracted. They then fell to running in a Circle round the Fire, and still the Fellow who had no Drum threw something in the Flame; they seem'd to be Strings with Knotts on them, bawling lowder than ever, every Handful he cast on it, while the other still beat the Drum higher and fiercer.

This was all I could perceive they did, for above an Hour by my Watch, and then they both drop'd down beside the Fire, which went out of a suddain, and there they lay as if they were dead or asleep; and the *Knez* assured me the Operation was over, and bid me wait and see the Success. It was a dark cloudy Morning, as generally at that Time of the Year (the End of *October*) the Mornings are here, and as little Appearance of the [64] Sun, as if it had not risen that Day; and yet in less than half a Quarter of an Hour, I perceived the Clouds break into a little small Aperture, as regularly as if one would draw the Curtains of a Bed, and a lovely Gleam of Sunshine burst on the Garden, as bright and as fair as if it had been in Summer. Immediately I perceived the *Laplanders* get up and rub themselves, as Men would do after a severe Sweat, and then they retired immediately out of the Garden, whither I went down with my *Muscovite* Landlord.

I was not a little amaz'd at the Novelty and Surprize of the Thing, and had no great Inclination to go into the Sunshine, which I look'd on as the Devil's making, and could not help thinking of the *Spanish* Proverb of *going out of God's Blessing into the warm Sun*. But my Landlord laugt at my Superstition so heartily, and pull'd me into it so merrily, that I was ashamed of my self. I look'd round me and surveyed the Ground on which the Sun smote with remarkable Warmth; and to the best of my Judgment I verily believe there were about three Acres thus enlightned, while all the rest of the Garden about them, as well as the whole Country, was [65] covered with a dark misty Fog; and what amaz'd me above all, and convinc'd me there was something supernatural in the Matter, it continu'd so all the rest of the Day.

I spent some Time in it with my good *Muscovite*, who was very industriously shewing me his choicest Trees, Flowers, and exotick Plants, and telling me whence he had got them, and how well they throve with him; tho' I only answer'd him with a few Monosyllables now and then, so much was my Mind taken up, with what I had seen those Devils of *Laplanders* perform. He perceived my uneasiness, and tho' he laughed heartily at me, he was so civil as to take me into the House to breakfast with him. There I found his Lady and Family, who fell on talking as familiarly of their *Laplanders*, and how happy they were in them and their Sunshine, as if they had only been commending their dry Wood, and the Fire which was blazing finely in the Chimney.

I threw off my Surprize by Degrees as well as I could, and heard all their Discourse of the *Laplanders* and their Way of Living; and above all their Drum and the Herbs they made use of, both which my [66] Landlord undertook to steal me a Sight of, tho' there is nothing the *Laplanders* are so jealous of, as that any should see or handle either, and above all their *Kannus* and the Hammer they beat it with. However, to oblige me he sent for the poor Creatures, and by giving them a great Cup of Brandy apiece, he got them to speak to me and served as Interpreter between us. But the Truth is, they were either so reserv'd, or so stupid, that I could learn nothing from them, but that their Names were *Undo Marki*, and *Riconi Norki*, and that their good Master had brought them out of their sweet Country, and gave them good Brandy, Money, Tobacco and dry'd Rain-deer, for making his Sunshine. I ask'd them how they made it, and they laugh'd just as a Dog grins, and said *Kannus, Kannus*, meaning their Drum, and that was all I could understand from these *Deep Adepts* in Sunshine, who in a little Time thought fit to retire, to sleep off their Brandy. They were low, swarthy, ill-looking Creatures, very lean, and stooped much, and hardly ever took of their Eyes from the Ground.

[67] In a little Time my good *Muscovite* followed them, and was not long away, till he returned with a World of Joy in his Face, and their Herbs, Drum, and Hammer in his Hand, which he had stole from them while they were sleeping. I look'd at them and examined all very curiously. The Herbs seemed to be chiefly Mint, Rosemary, Lavender, and wild Thyme, mix'd with a good deal of Moss and some Feathers, and all appear'd to be sprinkled with Blood, probably of some poor Birds they had murder'd, with a great deal of Injustice, to strengthen the Charm. The Drum is oval, about sixteen Inches one Way and twelve the other; and there were pained on it several Figures of Men and Beasts, two or three Sorts of Birds, a great many Stars, and the Moon in the Middle of them, and at least a Dozen Representations of the Sun, all very ill-favouredly painted, and seem'd to be drawn on the Skin of the Drum with Blood.

The Hammer was of Bone, and about seven Inches long, and something like a *Roman* T, or rather like the young Branches or Sprouts, of the Velvet Head of a five or six Year old Buck, with us in *England* in [68] *June*. Both of them seem'd exactly to answer the Description *Scheffer* gives of them in his History of *Lapland*, which is too curious a Book, not to be well known to your Lordship, for the many rare and uncommon Accounts of that Country, which are contained in it. I am persuaded upon reading over his Work, that this Drum, and those described by him, are much the same, except the Painting of it; and besides their Manner of beating on it, seem'd to have a pretty close Resemblance with that he describes.

I was so free with my obliging Landlord, as to ask him if he did not think it was a Sort of Magical Incantation that his *Laplanders* us'd, and if he believed it was by the Assistance of the Devil they made their Sunshine, or suppos'd it lawful to make Use of such Helps in obtaining it? But he answered me only with a loud laugh, and assuring me he believ'd there was no such Thing in the Matter; and tho' for his Part he had other Thoughts, yet most of the Noble *Muscovites* in that bad Climate, had such a Passion for Gardens and good Weather, that they would almost be oblig'd to Magick for them, rather than want them.

[69] In short, my Lord, I left him in his Sunshine very happy and contented, and took my Leave much indebted for all his Civilities, and set out for *Moscow.* I fell to considering all the Way of this new Method of making Sunshine, and what Uses it might be applied to, if ever our industrious Merchants, should ship it off and with a fair Gale purchas'd in *Lapland*, sail directly for *England*, like *Ulysses* carrying all the Winds in his Bags. What Gardens should we see rising up on every Hill under the Direction of these lovely *Laplanders*, with all the Fruits, Trees, and Flowers of *France* and *Spain*, and even the *East* and *West Indies*. How many Cures might our *George* the Sixth make, by setling a few Acres by the Year on our Hospitals for the Sick, and our Mad People in Bedlam; and how many of our fair Ladies, and nice peevish fine Gentlemen, would be set free from their Spleen and Vapours, by setting out a reasonable Proportion for St. *James's* Park and the Mall, not forgetting his own Royal Gardens and amiable Family. How many fretfull uneasy Husbands and Wives, melancholy Lovers, and sullen Beauties, not to speak a Word of our gloomy Sectaries and sour Catholicks, discontented Courtiers that [70] lose Places, and zealous Patriots that want them, would he recover to plain Sense and good Humour, by this lovely Cordial.

If he would settle an Acre or two on our Professors of Astronomy, what clear Accounts of our Eclipses should we have for the future, without the old lazy Excuse of dark Days and bat Weather; not to mention a Syllable of the clouded Brows, and the silent splenetick Tempers of our University Men, that would be finely clear'd up by it.

In short, my Lord, I begin to be reconcil'd to this Affair, and tho' the Devil should have a little Hand in it, we might easily get an ingenious Jesuit to bring us off that Scruple, by two or three learned Doctors Opinions, and a few good Distinctions with Probability in them. We should by the Help of these honest Drummers, be able to make our Air and Weather above Stairs as easily and as conveniently, as those ingenious underground Philosophers the *Miners*, can below Stairs; who by mere Perflation and Ventilation, as they term it, that is by letting Air in and out as they find proper, produce a kind of actual Circulation of it, and make it thicker or thinner, as they find best for their Business.

[71] I must take Leave to be merry on this Subject with your Lordship, to make Amends for the Fright it gave me; and if we once fall to Dealing with these admirable Fellows, we shall soon be no longer satisfied, either with the Earth, or Sun of our Forefathers, but by the Help of their Improvements in our Fields and Gardens, we shall get, as it were, *new Heavens, and a new Earth*, as St. *Peter* speaks. We shall certainly have the Advantage of the good Catholicks, in taking up with this Scheme, for they will probably be fearful of dealing with these same Lords of the Air, *propter metum Judæorum*, and left the Clergy and Inquisition talk to them about it in private. Besides, they will probably stick to their old Way of Weather-making by Processions, and carrying about the Shrines and Relicks of their precious Saints, which we all know by Experience, never fail to produce Rain or Sunshine on all publick Occasions, as the Priest and People desire them; and may with proper Regulations, be made Use of in the Way of Gardening, for the Service of private Gentlemen, that have strong Faith and large Fruiteries.

[72] The Ancients keep a great Noise with their Witches charming down the Moon, and the Priest of *Jupiter Lycæus* causing Rain when he pleas'd, by dipping a Branch of Oak in a certain Fountain, whose Name I've forgot. The *Jews* boast as loudly of *Judha*, that by unloosing one Shoe, brought a heavy Rain down in a Drought; and that had he untied the other, it would have caus'd a second Deluge; but none of them could come up to these same *Laplanders*, that make the Sunbeams brighten the Face of Nature, where they direct them.

The famous *Swedish* Priest and Inquisitor, *Joannes Nider*, tells us, indeed, (in his 4*th* Chapter of his Tract about Witches,) that the learned Judge *Peter Stadelein*, condemn'd an old Witch for causing Tempests; who confest, on the Torture, that she did it, by invocation of the Devil in the Field, and sacrificing a black Cock, and throwing it up to him in the Air, which when the Devil seiz'd, he immediately began the Storm. This was extraordinary enough, my Lord, but to oblige him to give us Calms, and as bright glorious Seasons in the Night of Winter, as others enjoy in the Morning or Noon of Summer, is an honest [73] Sort of Magick that deserves publick Premiums, instead of Punishment, and excels all that ever yet appeared in the World. Even our learned Countryman, *Roger Bacon*, tho' he declares he could undertake to raise artificial Clouds, and cause Thunder-claps to be heard, and Lightning to flash in our Eyes along with them, and then make all end in a Shower of Rain, could never pretend to any Thing like these extraordinary Gentlemen; and therefore, my Lord, I leave it to your prudent Consideration, whether I had not better treat with a Colony of *Laplanders*, to come and settle with their Drums in

England, than spend my Thoughts and Time, with keeping fair Weather with these bustling blustry *Muscovites*.

But I must grow serious when I speak on so important a Subject as our good Agreement with *Muscovy*, which in so many Views, is of the highest Consequence to *Great Britain*. But as it becomes not me to dictate to your Capacity and Experience, and as I have Reason to hope, you think the same Way that I do on this Occasion, I shall not trouble you with a long Detail of Reasons and Motives, to persuade us to cultivate the *Czar's* Friendship. It becomes me better to say, that [74] whatever Commands your Lordship honours me with at this Court, I shall labour to perform with all my little Strength and Ability; as being conscious I am serving the best of Princes, the most generous and disinterested Minister, and where they are well govern'd, the wisest and bravest Nation, that ever gave Laws to the Earth and the Sea. I am, with the greatest Respect,

My Lord, Your Lordship's, &c.

Clare.

To the Lord High Treasurer.

Paris, Dec.
16, 1997.

My Lord,

Your last Dispatch of the *8th*, found me just return'd from visiting our Sea-Ports, and their Garrisons in this Kingdom, all which I left in perfect good Order. The new Works at *Calais* to the Seaward, have much improv'd that Port, and in the lowest nepe Tides at *Dunkirk*, our Ships of War of forty Guns can go out and come [75] in without any Hazard; the Benefit of which I need not mention to your Lordship.

Indeed if the eager Zeal of our Ancestors, had not with so much Industry ruin'd this Haven, while it was in the Hands of *France*, we might have sav'd a vast Sum in Repairing it now; and with half the Expence made it a better and safer Port, than at this Time can be hop'd for. All the *British* Garrisons, both Men and Officers, are in perfect good Health and Order, well fed, cloath'd, and paid, and made a fine Appearance; especially when compar'd with those of the *French* in the Towns I past thro', which were as naked and lean as Beggars. This is certainly very impolitick in this Crown, for when Troops are so ill paid and fed, they will never have Heart and Spirit in Time of Action; and tho' 'tis peculiar to the *Turkish* Soldiers, to carry a Spoon tied to their Swords, as Travellers assure us; yet in Effect all Soldiers do so, and never fight well for a Prince that feeds them ill, and neglects to keep them well. *France* and *Spain* have a long Time been remarkable for this Mismanagement, and have paid dearly for their Neglect, by so many terrible Losses as they have met [76] with for these last fifty Years, and yet the *French* seem no way industrious to reform it.

As to the wretched State of Things here, which your Lordship is pleased to demand an Account of from me, it is almost as bad as their greatest Enemies can desire. For these many Years past, partly by the Ravage which both Famine and the Plague made with them, their unsuccessful Wars with *Germany*, and our Ruining their Naval Affairs and cramping their Trade, they have been much on the Decline. Besides the Quarrels *Lewis* the nineteenth and his present Majesty have had with the Papal See, (when the *French* Kind would fain have acted the Part of *Henry* the Eighth in *England*, and renouncing the Pope's Authority, seized on all the Wealth and Revenues of the Abbies and Monasteries) ended so disgracefully for this King, and their Holinesses have held so severe an Hand over him ever since, that his Affairs have gone very untowardly. He was forc'd to give up his Patriarch of *Paris*, (which as your Lordship knows he set up as our Metropolitan of *Canterbury*) into the Pope's Hands, who as he had been the prime Contriver of the Scheme was burnt for an Heretick; and in short, the Clergy and People [77] joining with the See of *Rome*, cut out such Work for him, that he was sufficiently humbled, and glad to buy his Peace, with giving up the Regale and the Loss of two or three strong frontier Towns in *Dauphine*, which the Pope keeps as Keys to enter the Gates of *France* from *Italy*, now that most of *Savoy* is his own.

Nor on the Side of *Spain* are the Affairs of this Crown any Thing better, for tho' in the last Wars between the Crowns, both made a mighty Noise of their Advantages, singing *Te Deum* for every little Village they took on either Side, just like the *London* Prize-Fighters, that with Drums and Trumpets proclaim each little Cut they give each other; and tho' *France* especially pretended, that the *Spaniards* were not able to stand before them, yet on the upshot of the Matter, when they made the Peace that has lasted ever since, *Spain* forc'd them to very inglorious Conditions. Your Lordship is perfectly well appriz'd, that they are as ill circumstanc'd on the Side of *Flanders and Germany*, where they have lost both *Lisle, Mons* and *Doway* to the *Dutch*, and *Strasburg* to the Emperor; so that all their Conquests in the 17*th* and 18*th* Centuries, that cost them such vast Sums, and such [78] Numbers of Men, are vanish'd into Smoak and gone, and the Pope is now the entire Object of the Fears of *Europe*, instead of the conquering *French*. The Truth is, this Nation does not seem form'd for Empire, and tho' they've often made mighty Efforts, and great Conquests, they never preserve them. They seem to traffick for Provinces, as *Busbequius* tells us the *Turks* do for Birds, to take them and buy them, just to let them go again, and that they may thank them for their Liberty. His present Majesty, *Lewis* the twentieth, does not seem sufficiently resolute, or able, to mend the ill Posture of his Affairs; and if he were, his Clergy and People seem no ways desirous to disoblige the Pope, by strength'ning the Hands of their Prince; and what is worse, they are jealous the King would take a severe Revenge for their joining with *Rome* against him, if he should once recover his former Power.

Besides, tho' the King is not fifty, he is grown a little crazy, and leaves his Affairs to his Ministers, who are more desirous to manage Things well at home, and remedy the Disorders that cramp their Administrations, than quarrel with their Neighbours who use the Nation ill. Thus it is with [79] great Difficulty, we have been able to influence them, to think of coming to an actual Rupture with the Pope, tho' he treats them so ill, and tho' we pay them such high Wages for it. As the King also has been always a very weak Prince, and extremely amorous, and entirely under the Management of one Mistress or another by Turns, so he is now more so than formerly, which is a dead Weight on his Government. Every reigning Mistress introduces a new Set of Ministers and Officers; and this has often occasion'd vast Convulsions at Court, where the Fall of every Favourite brings on the Ruin of all his Dependants; which is but a Sort of Copy of the Custom *Herodotus* tells us the *Scythians* had, where when the King died, all his chief Officers were of necessity to be slain, and accompany him to his Grave.

Judge, my Lord, if the natural Consequence of this must not be, That his Majesty will be very ill serv'd, and have only mercenary rapacious Ministers to manage his Affairs, when he neither shews Prudence in chusing, nor Constancy in supporting them; and indeed the *French* Nobility have plaid their Game accordingly. The whole [80] of their Endeavours, under several Administrations, for two Thirds of his Reign, has been to pillage the Kingdom, whether Affairs went well or ill, being like some Mills I have seen on the *Seine*, that will grind and get Toll both with Flood and Ebb.

In the Mean-time this unhappy Kingdom has been paying severely for these Mismanagements; tho' every Ministry, in their Turn, have been applauding their own Conduct, and on every little Occasion crying up their happy Times, and striking Medals to the Glory of their King. And certainly if future Historians were to plan out their Chronicles of these Days from such Vouchers, they would represent Writers (if they impartially represent the Distractions of his Councils, the Defeats of his Troops, the Loss of his Provinces, and the Cries and Sufferings of his opprest Subjects) must paint him a weak, unfortunate, and contemptible Tyrant.

It is true, indeed, Mr. *Meneville*, who is a wise and able, tho' a corrupt Minister, and those who are at present at the Helm with him, (and depend on Mrs. *Duvall*, the reigning Mistress) as they seem to have an absolute Ascendant over him, and are likely [81] to keep it, have manag'd him and his Affairs, these last four Years, something better than their Predecessors, and are endeavouring to bring Things into tolerable Order. However, after all, they have chiefly aim'd at keeping the Clergy a little humbler, and calming the Parties and Factions in the Kingdom; and by stopping the Mouths of the boldest and most seditious Leaders by Preferments, making every one pay more Submission to the King's Decrees and Authority.

Tho' this has not sufficiently quieted the Provinces, yet at Court they have taught them all, to speak entirely the King's Language and Senti-ments; where (as in *Copenhagen* every body's Clock and Watch is set to go exactly with the King's great Clock the Palace) all are ready to answer his Majesty and his Ministers as submissively, as *Menage*, an ancient *French* Writer tells us in his Time, the Duke *D' Usez* did the Queen Regent, who when she ask'd him what Hour it was, answer'd, Madam, what Hour your Majesty pleases.

This great Work, tho' it be but half done, would never have been brought about barely by Preferments and Places; for I can assure [82] your Lordship, it has cost immense Sums too, which they have been forc'd to fleece the People for, to buy off their Demagogues, so that they whip the Subject with Rods of their own making. And indeed the *Ratio ultima Regum*, which us'd to be plac'd as the Motto on the Cannon of this King's Predecessors, ought to be taken off and plac'd around his Coin, as the chief Specifick of the present Times, for Submission and Obedience to the Authority of the Crown.

Their great standing military Force, has also with the Help of these Lenitives, gone of late a good Way to re-establish Peace and Order, in the Room of their former Confusion and Distractions. By the Means of so considerable a Body of Troops as they keep up, they at once over-awe their Enemies and the *Pope*, from attempting new Disturbances; and also silence the loud *Orators* whom he prompts, from thundering in their Pulpits to stir up the People, as effectually as *Lewis* XIV. us'd to drown the Speeches of the *Huguenots* at the Scaffold and the Gibbet, with the Noise of the Drums, left their Words should make too strong Impressions on the Crowd, by representing how Religion and its true Professors were injur'd.

[83] Such miserable and destructive Measures is Tyranny, and its detestable Advocates forc'd to make use of, to support its own Violence, and chain down that natural Desire, which the great Author of Mankind has plac'd in every Breast, to weaken or overturn it. Whereas, if Princes would act with the Spirit of our glorious King, or his Royal Ancestors, and make the Laws of the Land, the Rule of their Government and the People's Obedience; nay, if they would act barely as honest Men, with a common

Regard to Conscience and Justice, how happy would Mankind be? What would then become, my Lord, of Generals, Officers, and Soldiers; of Infantry and Cavalry, Artillery, Powder-Mills, Gun-Smiths, Sword-Cutlers, Spies, Informers, Jesuits, and Assassins?

But Sycophants and Flatterers, that are ever buzzing about the Ears of great Princes, knowing it is impossible otherwise to support themselves, and the desperate Measures they put their Masters on, are still persuading them they can never reign effectually, but when they tyrannize absolutely. To this End it is, that they so immensely encrease their Troops, to tie the Subjects Chains [84] and Bondage so fast, that 'tis dangerous at last even for the Prince to unloose them, if Pity and Humanity should encline him to it. Thus they strain the Cords of Government, so far beyond their natural Strength, that sooner or later they break of themselves, and end in the Destruction of those Sycophants; who, while they push on Princes to aim at enlarging their Power, (just as the Devil deluded our first Parents) by telling them they shall be as Gods on Earth, turn them into Devils, and occasion their irretrievable Ruin.

The Misery of this poor People, that groan under so many Burthens, is inconceivable; they pay Taxes for all that they eat or drink or wear, to an excessive Degree, even to their Salt and Bread; nay, they pay for every Beast that they keep, even to plow their Land, for every Arpent (equivalent almost to our Acre) when plow'd, and for every Mill that they grind their Corn in, for the Houses, or Cottages rather, they live in, and the very Fires in them which they warm themselves by; and also for every Marriage, Christening, and Burial in their Families. These Taxes are every Year encreasing, and indeed, like *Virgil*'s Torrent, [85] the longer they run, the more they swell and enlarge, till at last they lay waste whole Counties, like an Innundation, sweeping away both the Substance, Houses, and Inhabitants of the Land.

By this Means the Poverty, especially among the lower Sort, is so excessive, that they want even the common Necessaries of Life; nor is it possible, in some Provinces, to prevent a general Desolation, without a Remission of many of their burthenous Gabells, unless some of those miraculous Showers should be procur'd them by the Jesuits, which *Livy* tells us were sometimes sent the *Romans* by their Gods, that rain'd down Corn and Flesh and Milt among them.

In the midst of this Misery, the Luxury of the Nobility and Gentry is increas'd beyond all Bounds, as if they were not only insensible of, but even rejoyc'd in the publick Calamities of their Fellow-Subjects. Their Tables are cover'd with such Profusions of Expence, in all Sorts of Delicacies, that it exceeds the Riot and Revelling of *Greece* and *Rome*, flush'd with the Glory of their Conquests, and corrupted with the Wealth and Spoils of the World. The stated [86] Hours of dining and supping are absolutely laid aside, and thro' a silly Affectation of mimicking their Princes, People of Distinction oblige their Cooks, to have a Dinner still ready at all Hours when they call for it, thinking it only fit for Tradesmen and Rusticks to dine at set Times. Nay, I can assure your Lordship, some are grown to such Excess and Folly, as to buy no Flesh of Beeves or Sheep for their Tables, that have not their Hair and Wool close shaven off, and curried with Pumice-Stones, to make the Meat sweeter and higher relish'd.

Nay they have, in Imitation of the Ancients, brought into Fashion, the sowing and cultivating the famous *Silphium* of the *Persians*, with which they feed these Sheep, and make them extremely fat and high tasted; and many mingle *Assa Fœtida* with their finest Sauces, which they reckon gives them a more exquisite Flavour, than the Spices and Ambergreace of their Ancestors. They have in all great Houses also, several different Sorts of Cooks, that preside over the particular Provinces of Luxury; as Cooks for Soops, Cooks for roasting, Cooks for boiling, Cooks of the Fishery, as they call them here, Cooks for Ragooes and Fricassies, Cooks for bak'd [87] and stew'd Meats, Cooks, Confectioners, and Cooks of the Pastry. They have carried this wretched Pleasure of their Palates so far, that there are few Noblemen who do not, like *Fulvius Hirpinus,** keep an *Escargatoire,* or Snail-House, where they feed their Reservoirs of Snails, all the Year, on the choicest and finest Herbs, Fruits, and Flowers, for making their exquisite Ragoos, which this Nation is so ridiculously fond of; and have even brought the Breed of Pullets from *Malabar* to *France,* because their Flesh is reckon'd prodigiously sweet and delicious, tho' the outward Skin and the Bones are as black as Jet, as dr. *Frier* tells us in his Travels. One would think, my Lord, after indulging themselves in such amazing Extravagancies this Way, they would not give into any other; and yet the violent Passion for Gaming, in both Sexes, runs so high, that the Honour and Modesty of the one, and the Fortune and Ease of the other, are entirely sacrificed to it. It eats up even their State, and their belov'd Equipage; and devours their favourite Embroidery and Jewels. The only Resource the Ladies have, under the dismal [88] Ravage that attends this bewitching Madness, is to prostitute their Persons to the fortunate Conqueror, and at the dreadful Expence of all that should be dear to them, to prevent the irreparable Destruction that must otherwise consume, like Fire, their domestick OEconomy, and the Fortune of the Family. A Practice which I fear spreads too fast in some Countries, as well as here, and puts me in Mind of what *Tacitus* says† of the *Germans* Love of Gaming in his Time, that when they had plaid away all their Money, they then set their Liberties and their Bodies at Stake, which became the Property of the Conqueror. The Men indeed have sometimes the happy Consolation, by turning Villains and Sharpers, to repair the Ruins of their Estates, by preying on the Ignorance

---

* Vid. Pliny, L. IX. C. LVI. & Varro, L. MI. C. XIV.
† De mor. Germ. C. 24.

and Inexperience of others; but surely, to an honest and ingenuous Mind, there is no Ruin can befall a Man equal to this, where the Repairs of their Circumstances are owing to the Sale of their Reputation?

I know not, my Lord, whether it be an Alleviation of the Crime, or an Aggravation of it, that this fatal Luxury and immense Extravagance is not so much owing to the Humour of the People, as the Policy of the [89] Court; but certain it is, that this is the main Fountain of all the sad Disorders. Frugality and OEconomy are the great standing Fences against the shining Temptations of ambitious Princes and designing Ministers, and therefore there is a Necessity of breaking thro' them, by rendring them unfashionable, and consequently ridiculous. The great *Machiavels* in the Art of Ruling, know too well the Force of this Reasoning; a luxurious Gentry must be expensive, if expensive needy, if needy they must run in Debt, and if indebted, they must either give up their Pleasures, or take Places and Preferments to support them, that render themselves Slaves to the Will of their Master, who is thereby Lord at once of their Honour and Liberty, and in them a fair Purchaser of that of his People.

Behold at once, my Lord, the fatal Market of the Freedom of this Nation, and all their boasted Parliaments Rights and Privileges, which they once enjoy'd in as full a Proportion, as our own happy Countrymen. But while we lament their miserable Conduct, let us rejoice at our own, and the Blessings that, under Heaven, we owe to that glorious Race of Heroes, under [90] and by whom we still possess those invaluable Blessings, which the false Ambition of our neighbouring Princes, and the thoughtless Vanity, Pride, and Folly of their Subjects, have extirpated.

But I have detain'd your Lordship too long with these grave Reflections, and shall therefore reserve any further Accounts of this People, and the Conduct of the Ministers here, who seem desirous of improving the present State of Things, till the next Dispatch I have the Honour to send you. Possibly in case what I now send be not disagreeable to you, I may be able, in my next, to entertain you better on this Head. In the mean Time, it cannot fail to give your Lordship some Satisfaction, to see this great Kingdom, that for so many Years was still enterprizing on the Liberties and Dominions of her weaker Neighbours, and laying Schemes for the Ruin of *Great-Britain*, (as the main Step to the Empire of the World,) fallen now from the Object of our Fears, to that of our Pity.

I am sensible, your Lordship's great Wisdom and Experience, knows all these Things that I have wrote on this Subject, or that I am able to write on it or any other, infinitely [91] better than do. But you will be so just to consider, that I have herein rather obey'd your Commands, than follow'd my Inclinations, being sensible I have as little Desire as Ability, to speak or write on such weighty and difficult Matters, but when I am enjoin'd it by your express Direction.

I send herewith two little manuscript Treatises, remarkable for their Oddness and Novelty, and more to gratify your Curiosity, than please your Taft. One of them is wrote by Monsieur *Perault*, first Surgeon to the King; it is entitled, *An Essay on Circumcision and Embalming*. On the first Head he endeavours to prove, that it is vastly serviceable to Health, in many Respects, especially in warm Climates, and particularly that it is a great Extinguisher of Lust, and chiefly for that Reason enjoin'd the *Jews*, and therefore advises the Renewing that Usage now. In the other Treatise, he shews the Satisfaction it would be for great Persons, instead of throwing their Friends and Relations, to rot and corrupt in Vaults and Graves, to keep them in a decent Repository, where they might survey the very Persons and Features, of the whole Race of their [92] Ancestors, as little disfigur'd as an *Ægyptian* Mummy. He undertakes to do this in the greatest Perfection, and proposes it to the Publick for their Encouragment, tho' his Friends have, with much ado, prevail'd on him not to publish it. Your Lordship sees, however, these Gentlemen are not satisfied with the Work we cut out for them, which our Debaucheries and Luxury have made but too considerable; but they are for beginning with us from the Birth, and following our wretched Carcasses, even after our Death.

The other Manuscript is a short History of, about, an hundred Men, remarkable for their great Wealth in this last Age, in *Paris*. He first gives a severe, but seemingly an impartial Account, of the vile Arts by which they obtain'd their Riches; of their several Cheats, Extortion, Oppression, sordid Avarice, slavish Toil, and mean Drudgery; their flattering the great, or ruining the Poor, by which they had risen in the World. He there shews the Pain and Uneasiness they went thro'; the Undutifulness of Children; the ill Conduct of their Wives or Widows; the Deaths of their favourite Sons, or their dying Childless, and [93] Strangers possessing their Substance; or at least an extravagant Heir squandring it faster in base Methods, than they rais'd it. In the Conclusion he shews how few of their Families or Fortunes remain at this Day, and how much fewer of them had the Honesty or Virtue to leave, even the twentieth or fortieth Part of what they had, to publick Uses, or the Poor.

The Book is rather an useful Subject, than a well writ Treatise; but I wish it were translated into *English*, and ten Thousand of them presented to the rich Men of our Age; who, with so little Regard to the publick good of their Country, or thinking of making generous Foundations of their own, or contributing to those of others, go on continually in those beautiful Expressions of the *Psalmist, to heap up Riches which they cannot tell who shall gather*. It is not to see the Light here, it being dangerous to publish it, for fear of provoking the Resentments of some Persons, whose Relations are hardly treated in it, tho' I am told, with great Justice. 'Tis writ by Father *Meron* a *Capuchin*; but this I tell only to your Lordship. The

Jesuits are severely satyriz'd in [94] it, for their Avarice, which makes it dangerous for the Author to own the Writing it.

When I have obey'd your Commands, as to giving you some Account of the poor Duke *D'Aumont*'s Fate and Character, who has been so differently represented to you, I shall put an End to this tiresome Letter. It is certain, he died the first of this Month at his lovely Retirement in the Country, but not of Poison, as your Lordship mentions, but of a Fit of the Apoplexy, which took him off in a few Hours.

He was unquestionable a Gentleman of the most uncorrupted Integrity, the greatest Abilities, and the most universal Genius, of any Minister of State this Nation ever bred, not excepting that Hero of the Antients, Cardinal *Richlieu*. With all these Advantages, he carried himself in so haughty and arbitrary a Manner, with his late Majesty, who favour'd him, and his Enemies that envy'd him, that he made his Merit and great Qualifications almost useless to his Country. His Honesty had the Appearance of Ostentation and Insolence, (tho nothing was further from his Heart) and his Capacity and Knowledge, seem'd to wear an assuming and supercilious [95] Air. He affected a Sincerity and Severity, that continually alienated the Hearts of the Courtiers from him. Not content to be unblameable himself, he thought to brow-beat Corruption and Immorality, in all that had any Thing to do in the King's Affairs; by reproaching them openly with any ill Conduct in their Lives and Manners. He was not satisfied in excelling all Men in the greatest Talents for the Camp, or the Cabinet, for Books or the World; unless he could drive Ignorance or Insufficiency from the Court, by severe Upbraidings of the Weakness, or Mistakes, the Folly, Incapacity or Vices of many in the Crowd of Pretenders there to Place and Power.

It was easy, my Lord, to see the Consequence of such a Conduct must be the Ruin of him who gave into it. And indeed tho' Heaven seem'd for some Time to declare in his Favour, against the Malice of the World, and to labour for his Establishment, by many Successes abroad; yet, on the first Turn of the Tide, by the Loss of the Battle at *Strasburg*, the whole Kingdom, or in other Words, all that was vicious and bad in it, seem'd, with one Voice, to cry out against him, and call for his Destruction; and even [96] *Lewis* the Nineteenth, his Master, tho' he esteem'd him, was so sick of his intolerable Virtue, that he readily abandon'd him to the publick Hatred.

He was turn'd out of any share of the Administration, banish'd the Court, and confin'd to his Country Seat for Life, where he gave himself up, with infinite Relish, to a few worthy Friends and his Studies; and where he writ those Memoirs of his Time, which I sent your Lordship, and which alone will be a lasting Proof of the Virtue and Capacity of the Man. It is certain, if he could have pardon'd his Master's and his Courtiers Vices and Follies, or his Enemies evil Arts to defraud the Crown, by the Mismanagement of the Finances, and the usual Corruptions in the Officers of the Army, he might have rul'd the one, and triump'd over the others; but he was too much in hast to do good, and too violently virtuous to reform a corrupt World, which he profess'd to abhor. I remember a great Man one Day speaking of his Vigilance, Dexterity, and his equal Zeal and Capacity to serve his Master, and clear the Court of such troublesome Vermin; compar'd his Fate to the Duchess of *Chevreuse*'s Cat, who having broke her Leg, [97] by a Fall in the Cellar, was the next Night bit to Death, and almost devour'd by the Rats, she had so often been labouring to destroy.

I am impatient for your Lordship's next Dispatches, and doubt not but this Court will oppose, with Vigour, the setting up the Inquisition, in spite of the Intrigues of the Nuncio, and his humble and pious Masters, the Jesuits; in which, according to my Instructions, I have and shall continue to express his Majesty's and your Lordship's zealous Concurrence and Assistance, by all proper Measures, and am, with the highest Deference and Esteem,

My Lord,
Your Lordships's, &c.

Herbert.

[98] *To the Lord* High Treasurer.

Rome. Jan. 7, 1998.

My Lord,

By the last Courrier, my Dispatches carried you a full Account of the fair Prospect of Success I have for all my Negotiations here. The Bull mention'd therein, ordaining that no *British* Subject shall any longer be jugd'd liable to, or hereafter be seized by the Inquisition, having past the usual Forms; has delivered already many of our Countrymen from the Harpies of that Court, and secur'd them from it's terrible Judicature for the future. The Emperor's happy Recovery, has, at present, pretty much suspended all our design'd Proceedings, to prevent the Intriegues of this See, in order to place his Holiness on the Imperial Throne; and above all, as the Elector of *Cologne* has luckily broke with this Court, I hope we shall have Time to take such Measures, as shall effectually secure in *Europe* from so terrible a Blow.

[99] In the mean Time, I hasten this by a very worthy *English* Gentle-man, Mr. *Lumley*, which brings you an Account of as extraordinary an Undertaking, as this Court has ever attempted, tho' it seems to be the natural Soil and Climate for Projects of all Kinds. In short, 'tis nothing less than selling by publick Auction all the vast Collection of Relicks, which were brought hither many Years since, at different Times; and particularly, when the Treasures of *Italy* were heap'd up in the Castle of St. *Angelo*.

This amazing Event, of selling publickly those venerable Remains, which the Bigottry and Zeal of their Ancestors had so long held sacred, is entirely occasion'd by the Avarice and Prodigality of the Cardinal *Nephew*; whose Expenses are as unbounded, as his Passions and Extravagancies, which this Sale is design'd to supply. It is palliated indeed with the Pretence of dispersing such holy and precious Things, thro' all Christian Nations, to encrease their Devotion and Piety, which might otherwise sicken and flag, for want of such extraordinary Incentives, but I have told your Lordship the true Cause.

[100] It is generally believ'd that this Design will bring in vast Trea-sures to the Cardinal *Nephew*'s great Relief and Comfort; and as the Pope's managing Temper, and the rest of the Cardinals high Regard for strict OEconomy, prevent his squandring the Treasures of the See; they have complied with this Project, to raise a large Sum out of this holy Trumpery, which they were sick of, and which they found the Devotion of the *Italians* growing very cold to. I remember to have heard, that in the Beginning of the 16th Century, *Vergerius*, who was afterwards the Pope's Nuncio in *Germany*, was employ'd by the Elector of *Saxony*, to buy up for him many Relicks of the Saints in *Italy*. Accordingly he bought several, but before the Relicks had been sent to *Germany*, *Luther*'s Books and Doctrines began to fly about, and lessen'd the Value of such delicate Wares so far, that the Elector order'd him to sell them with great Loss, and possibly that is one Reason that occasions the present Sale, since *Italy* begins to despite them.

The Catalogue is not yet printed, but I have procur'd the Original from the Imperial Ambassador, who designs to lay out great Sums on them, and what follows I [101] have copied and translated very faithfully from it, adding some few Notes of my own, in Hopes it will both surprize and entertain you.

I can venture to assure your Lordship, that whether the Relicks in the Catalogue be really genuine or no, there are none in it, which have not actually been maintain'd, by the gravest Writers of this Church, to have been preserv'd in the Places, from whence they are said to be brought, and which were not religiously venerated, not to say, ador'd there. Indeed the good Jesuits may have falsified some of them, to make their Collection more glorious, and raise the larger Sum; yet I have Faith enough to believe they are fully as authentick, as most of the Originals, which these poor

Catholicks, in different Places, preserve so religiously, and attribute so much Sanctity, and even Miracles, to.

But I will detain your Lordship no longer from perusing the Catalogue, than to say, I omit the Preface, because it only contains a fulsome, affected Declamation on the Veneration due to Relicks, on the vast Preference these deserve above all others; the pretended Reasons of their being exposed [102] to Sale, in order to disperse them more equally thro' the Christian World, and the unquestion'd Authority these ought to have, with all good Catholicks. For these, my Lord, are all voucht (as the Preface speaks) by the Pope's authentick Inspection and Direction, confirm'd by his annex'd Bull, (which I also omit) and verified before the Consistory of Cardinals, by the due and legal Proof, of having past untouch'd and undamag'd, in the Trial by Fire. ---- But I hasten to the Catalogue, which follows. -- -- A Catalogue of the most sacred, and eminently venerable Relicks, of the holy *Roman* Catholick Church, collected by the pious Care of their Holinesses the Popes, the most august Emperors, Kings, and Princes, Potentates, and Prelates of the Christian World, and several of them brought to *Rome*, by the vast Care and Expences of the most Reverend Fathers, the Jesuits. All which are now to be dispos'd of by Auction, for the general Benefit and Emolument of the Christian World, at the Church of St. *Peters* at *Rome*, on *Monday* the 25*th* of *April* 1998, from Nine in the Morning till eight at Night, and to continue till all be fold. *N.B.* The whole of these said most precious Relicks, [103] with their proper Vouchers and Certificates of Verification, and his Holiness's Bull for their being true authentick Originals, may be viewed and examined, (but not handled) at the Church of St. *Peter's* aforesaid, by all Ambassadors, Prelates, and Persons of Quality, and proper Credit, Condition, and Character, till the Day of Sale.

The Ark of the Covenant, the Cross of the good Thief; both somewhat Worm-eaten. *Judas's* Lanthorn, a little scorch'd. The Dice of the Soldiers play'd with, when they cast Lots on our Saviour's Garment; from *Umbriatico* in *Calabria*. The Tail of *Balaam's* Ass, that spoke when she saw the Angel. St. *Joseph's* Ax, Saw, and Hammer; and a few Nails he had not driven, a little rust eaten. St. *Christopher's* Stone-Boat, and St. *Anthony's* Mill-Stone, on which he sail'd to *Muscovy*. The Loaves of Bread turn'd into Stone by St. *Boniface*, on a Soldier's denying him a Piece of them when he was starving, for which he suffer'd Martyrdom, as a Sorcerer. Our B. Saviour's Teeth, Hair, and *Præputium* (*Emptum Charovii*) another *Præputium* (*Emptum Aquisgrani*) brought thither by an Angel from *Jerusalem*. *N.B.* In all such Cases [104] of Duplicates equally well vouched and verified, it is left to the Faith of the Buyer, which deserves the Preference; but the *Præputium* vouch'd by Cardinal *Tolet*, to be kept at *Calcata*, in the Church of St. *Cornelius* and *Cyprian*, and that other of *Podium*, as well as that preserv'd at *Antwerp*, and vouch'd by *Theobald* Archbishop of *Bisonti*, *John* Bishop of *Cambray*, and confirm'd by Pope *Eugenius* and *Clement* VIII. since they are all three also approv'd by Mir- acles, are left uncensur'd to the Piety and Veneration of the Faithful; it being certain, that the same Power that maketh his Body to be and exist, at the same Time in different Places, may exert it self in like Manner, as to this most precious and holy Relick. Several Drops of *Christ's* Blood, on different Occasions, as his Circumcision, bearing his Cross, and his Crucifixion, purchased at a vast Price, and brought by the Fathers, the Jesuits from *Rochel*; several small Phials of it from *Mantua*; larger Vessels of it from St. *Eustachius's* in this City of *Rome*. Mix'd with Water, as it came from his Side, from St. *John Lateran* in this City. His Cradle and Manger very old. *Ditto*, a Pale full of the Water of *Jordan*, where he was baptiz'd, [105] fresh and clear to this Day (*emptum Cassini.*) The Water-Pots of the Marriage at *Cana* in *Galilee*. N.B. These are not the Pots shewn at *Pisa* (*Cluniaci & Andegavi)* but the true original ones. Crums of the Bread that fed the 5000 (*Romæ ad Mariæ Novæ.*) A Bough of the Tree carried by *Christ* entring *Jerusalem* in Triumph, the Leaves almost fresh still; from *Spain (ad Salvatoris.)* The Table on which *Christ* eat the last Supper, a little decayed; at *Rome* St. *John Lateran*. Some of the Bread which he broke then; from *Spain ad Salvatoris*. The Cup he then drank out of and gave to his Disciples (*ad Mariæ Insulanæ* near *Lyons*.) The Sacrament of his Body and Blood (from *Brussells*.) I assure your Lordship, this is neither more nor less than a plain small Ivory Ball. The Towel with which he wip'd his Disciples Feet, very rotten, (*Rome*.) Part of the Money paid *Judas*. *Malchus's* Lanthorn, some of the Panes crack'd, and the Door quite decay'd, from St. *Denis*.

The following most holy and precious Relicks were brought to *Rome*, by the blessed Father *Francis Visconti*, by Order of the Pope, from *Aquisgranum* or *Aken*. Part of [106] the Wood of the Cross, a little decay'd, and a Nail of the same. Some of the *Manna* in the Wilderness, and of the Blossoms of *Aaron's* Rod. Part of the *Sudarium*, of the Reed, and Spunge of our Saviour. A Girdle of our Saviour's, and another of the Virgin's, little worn. The Chord with which *Christ* was bound at his Passion, very fresh. Some of the Hair of St. *John* Baptist. A Ring of the Chain of St. *Peter*. Some of the Blood of St. *Stephen*, and the Oyl of St. *Catharine*. The Arm of St. *Simeon*, ill kept. The Image of the blessed Virgin, drawn by St. *Luke*, the Features all visible. The Relicks of St. *Spes*, or St. *Hope*. Some of the Hair of the Blessed Virgin. One of her Combs, brought originally from *Basançon* in *Burgundy*, and twelve Combs of the twelve Apostles, all very little used, originally from *Lyons*. The *Indusium* or Shift, of the Blessed Virgin, when our Saviour was born. The Swathes in which our Saviour was wrapt the Night of his Nativity. The holy Linnen-Cloath upon which St. *John* was beheaded, wants new Hemming and Darning. The Cloath with which our Saviour was cover'd, when he hung on the Cross. The Brains of St. *Peter*, from *Geneva*. Note, these are the individual Brains [107] which that Arch-Heretick *Calvin* declar'd were a mere Pumice-Stone, sinning against God, the holy Apostle, and his own Soul.

The following most venerable Relicks were bought at, and brought from *Prague* to this City, by the Reverend Father *Priuli*, Jesuit commission'd and authoris'd by the Pope. The Head and Arm of the blessed *Longinus*. Some Relicks of *Abraham. Isaac*, and *Jacob*, very old. The Arm and some Part of the Body of *Lazurus*, ill kept and smells. Two Pieces of two Girdles of the Blessed Virgin. A Part of the Body of St. *Mark*, and a Part of his Gospel, of his own Handwriting, almost legible. A Piece of St. *John* the Evangelist's Coat. A Piece of the Staff of St. *Peter*, and another Piece of the Staff of St. *Paul*. A Part of St. *Peter*'s Chain. A Finger of St. *Ann*. A Part of the Blessed Virgin's Veil, as good as new. The Head of St. *Luke*. It is true, there is also another in this Catalogue, but both are so amply verified, nay avouch'd by daily Miracles, that his Holiness leaves it undecided; betwixt God and the Buyer be it. Some of the Relicks of St. *Catharine* of *Alexandria*. The Head and Finger of St. *Stephen*, 'tis suppos'd to be his middle Finger, but that is doubtful. Here endeth the Collection of [108] Relicks from *Prague*. The Staff deliver'd by our Lord to St. *Patrick*, and with which he drove all the venemous Creatures out of *Ireland*. Eight *Veronicas*, or holy Handkerchiefs of our Lord's, one from *Turin*, another from St. *John de Lateran*, and a third from St. *Peter*'s in this City, another from *Cadoin* in *Perigort*, a fifth from *Besançon*, another from *Compeigne*, a seventh from *Milan*, and another from *Aix le Chapelle*. It is as impossible as unjust, to decide which has the best Title to be the real one, since they all have been received from Age to Age by the Faithful: but as that of *Cadoin* hath fourteen Bulls in it's Favour, and the rest but one or two, (tho' that of *Turin* produceth four in it's Behalf) we leave it undecided. This we do the rather, as the Prayers and Devotions of the Pious have probably sanctified them all equally; and moreover, it is possible that they have been miraculously multiplied by the Goodness of God, for the Support and Aid of the Faithful, as the Loaves and the Fishes were to the hungry *Jews*. The most holy Fore-Finger of *John* the Baptist, with which he pointed to *Christ*, saying, *Behold the Lamb of God*, &c. brought from *Jerusalem* to *Malta*, by the Brothers [109] of St. *John*'s Hospital, and since to this City. The holy *Sindon*, or Linnen, in which *Christ*'s Body was buried, from *Turin*. The Dish in which *Christ* eat the Paschal Lamb, made all of one Emerald, from *Genoa*. A Nail of our Saviour's Cross, fix'd formerly on the Church Roof of *Milan*, and brought hither: Another, being one of those which the Empress *Helena* order'd to be wrought up into the Cheek of a Bridle, for the Emperor *Constantine*; and a third which was thrown into the *Adriatick* Sea in a vast Storm, to appease it, as it actually did. Taken up since in a Fisherman's Net, and brought to this City. The Stone upon which *Abraham* offer'd to sacrifice his Son; and another Stone on which our Lord was plac'd, when he was presented in the Temple. The Top of the Lance with which *Christ*'s Side was pierc'd. The Smock of St. *Prisca*, in which she was martyr'd 1700 Years ago, something decay'd. A Thorn of that Crown of Thorns which was put on our Saviour's Head. The Head of the Woman of *Samaria*, who was converted by our Saviour, decay'd, but plainly an Head still. The Arm of St. *Ann*, Mother of the Blessed Virgin; and the Chain of St. *Paul*. [110] *Scala Sancta*, or the twenty eight Steps of white Marble which *Christ* was lead up in his Passion to *Pilate*'s House, and on which visibly appear the Marks of his Blood; sent by *Helena* from *Jerusalem* to the Emperor *Constantine*. A Picture of our Lord, said to be begun by St. *Luke*, and finish'd miraculously by an Angel; or (as others say) St. *Luke* preparing to draw it, and falling to his Prayers to God, that he might draw his Son aright, when he arose, he found the Picture finish'd. The holy Crib of our Saviour's. The Pillar at which he was whip'd, the first of these very old and tender.

Here follow some most venerable and precious Relicks, brought hither from *Venice* by the aforesaid Father *Francis Visconti*.

Some of our Saviour's Blood, gather'd up at his Passion, with the Earth it was spilt on. A Thorn of the Crown of Thorns. A Finger of St. *Mary Magdalen*. A Piece of St. *John* Baptist's Skull. A Tooth of St. *Mark*, a little rotten; also one of his Fingers, and his Ring with a Stone in it. A Piece of St. *John* Baptist's Habit. Some of the Virgin's Hair. The Sword of St. *Peter*, very rusty and old. A Piece of *Christ*'s white Robe when he was set at nought by [111] *Herod*. One of the Stones wherewith St. *Stephen* was stoned. Some of St. *Joseph*'s Breath which an Angel enclosed in a Phial, as he was cleaving Wood violently, which was so long ador'd in *France*, and since brought to *Venice*, and from *Venice* to this City. The Head of St. *Denys*, which he carried two Miles after it was cut off under his Arm, praising God all the Way, and saying, *Glory be to thee, Lord*. The Rock which *Moses* struck in the Wilderness, with the three Holes in it of the Diameter of a Goose Quill, out of which the Water issued for the 600000 *Israelites* and their Cattle. Here endeth the List of the Reliques from *Venice*.

A Piece of the Rope *Judas* hang'd himself with, from *Amras* near *Inspruck*. Part of the Crown of Thorns from *Paris*. Several single Thorns from different Places, *Compostella*, *Tholouse*, and this City, to be sold separately. The Reed given our Lord for a Scepter (*Romæ* St. *John Lateran*.) His Holy Cross, a great Part of it from *Jerusalem*, more of it from *Constantinople*, more from *Paris*. A large Crucifix made of the Wood of it (*Rome*.) Several Nails belonging to it, two of *Rome*, two from *Venice*, [112] one from *Colen*, two from *Paris*, one from *Sienna*, one from *Naples*, one from St. *Denys*, one from the Carmelites at *Paris*. *N.B.* We say in this as aforesaid, Which are the right Nails, he only knows, whose Body they pierced; but the Vouchers and Certificates for all are to be seen, proved, and examined, let the Purchasers determine according to the Truth. The Title fastned to the Cross, fair and legible, and thought to be *Pilate*'s Hand Writing, from

Tholouse. The Spunge that was dipt in Vinegar, and given to our Lord; *Rome.* From *Cassini* another. The Point of the Launce, three of them, one originally of *Rome*, another from *Paris*, a third form *Xaintonge*, all properly voucht and evidenc'd. The Church herein decides nothing, but modestly faith, *Caveat Emptor.* The Footsteps which our Lord left in the Rock on his Ascension; *Rome.* The Marks of his Seat made on the Rock by his resting; from *Rheims.* Four Crucifixes, whose Beards grow regularly, seven that have spoke on several proper Occasions; ten more, that have wept often and bitterly upon *Good-Frydays*, and the Success of Hereticks, in their Wars with Catholicks. Five other [113] that have stirred and moved on different Accidents, four of them equal to any in the Christian Church; six more that have groan'd, smil'd and nodded, all voucht authentically, very little inferior to the former, except the freshest being the last made. Another Crucifix, which having had it's Leg broke by accident, stunk so grievously, that all in the Church were forced to hold their Noses for the Stench, till proper Remedies being applied, the Bone knit again, tho' the Place where the broken parts join'd, is still visibly thicker and larger, and that Leg near two Inches shorter than the other. Another Crucifix from *Trent*, under which the Synod was sworn and promulg'd, and which bow'd it's Head to testifie the Approbation which it gave to the learned Decrees of that Holy Assembly. *N.B.* As no Man could ever tell what this Crucifix was made of, so it is much doubted by the Faithful, if ever it was made with Hands; it worketh unheard of Miracles. Another Crucifix from St. *Dominick the greater* in *Naples*, which spoke one Day to St. *Thomas Aquinas, Thou hast well written of me,* Thomas. Another from the Church of the *Benedictines* in *Naples*, [114] which held twice two long Conversations with his Holy Vicegerent, Pope *Pius* V. of blessed Memory; and another of St. *Mary* of the *Carmelites* of the same City, which bowed it's Head at the Sight of a Cannon Bullet which was shot at him in 1439, (when *Don Pedro* of *Arragon* besieg'd that City) and only struck off the Crown. *N.B.* To cover his Head, being very bald, there is a Peruke of the Hair of the Virgin fitted to it, to be taken off in hot Weather. An Image of *Christ* made by himself, and sent to King *Abgarus* from St. *Silvester*, in the Field of *Mars* in this City. Another made by Angels, from the Chapel of the *Sancta Sanctorum* in this City, and a Crucifix which was begun to be painted by *Nicodemus*, but finisht by Angels; from the Cathedral of St. *Martin* in *Lucca. N.B.* All these Crucifixes have wrought incredible Miracles within these last fifty or sixty Years. Large Parcels of the Blessed Virgin's Hair, all of one Colour, from *Paris* and several Places less known, and much of it of this City. Great Quantities of her Milk gathered from many Places. Some Butter and a small Cheese made of it, that never decays or corrupts, from *Mexico* in *America* [115]. Her Slipper, and one of her Shoes. *N.B.* This is the original Shoe, which the famous *Rivet*, in his Apology for the Virgin (*Lib.* II. *Chap.* IX.) was possest of, and had the Figure of it grav'd, and publisht with

Licence; and in the middle of the Sole this is written, *The Measure of the most Holy Foot or our Lady*; and then follows, *Pope John* XXII. *bath granted to those who shall thrice kiss it, and rehearse three Ave Maries with Devotion to her Blessed Honour and Reverence, that they shall gain 700 Years of Pardon, and be freed from many Sins*. I must add here, my Lord, what all the learned, and even those who have only seen the Cut of it publisht by *Rivet*, know to be true, that the exact Measure of this blesses Shoe, is just seven and a quarter of our Inches; which I hint to your Lordship, because some well-shap'd Catholick Ladies, may be much rejoyced in case their Feet should tally with this Measure. Her Needle, Thread, and Quasillum, (*Halæ*.) Her Picture by St. *Luke* (*Romæ ad Mariæ Inviolatæ*.) Another by the same Hand of that Holy Evangelist (*Romæ ad Mariæ novæ*.) A third from *Cambray*. *N.B.* Tho' some Catholicks maintain St. *Luke* only painted [116] one, yet as these are each of them unquestionably voucht, and that allowing St. *Luke* was a Painter, as well a Physician, it is but reasonable to suppose he should have painted more than one; his Holiness, by the annext Bull, has thought is expedient to warrant them all for Originals, of the same divine Pencil. St. *Michael's* Dagger and Buckler (*magni Michaelis apud Carcassonenses*.) St. *John Baptist's* Face, very little the worse for the keeping, (*Cambiis ad Joannis Angelici*.) The Hand, and part of his Head, without a Face, from *Malta*. Others *ditto*, from *Nemours*. His Brain very well dried and preserv'd (*Novii Rantroviensis*.) His whole Head (*Rome*, from the Convent of St. *Silvester*.) As to these two Heads, the pious Reader is referred to the foregoing Apology for the two Heads of St. *Luke*. It is true, *Gregory Nazianzen* has declared that his Bones were burnt by the *Donatists*, so that nothing remain'd but a Piece of his Skull; but 'tis *absurd* to compare the Authority of him, or one Hundred such Fathers, with the Authority of the Church, and her sacred Traditions. At the same time, far be it from the Modesty of the Holy See to maintain he had two, but [117] both are so amply voucht and verified, that 'tis presumptuous to decide for either. Let us say rather with Cardinal *Baronius* in the Sentiments of a truly pious Mind, allowing a Mistake in such cases, *Quicquid sit, fides purgat facinus*. It is not the Head of the Saint we adore, but the Faith for which he died. Behold, my Lord, what a delicate Plaister of Faith here is for the Wounds of Idolatry. A second Fore-finger of St. *John Baptist*, with which he pointed at our Saviour, and said, *Ecce agnus Dei*, &c. from *Tholouse*. As good an one from *Lyons*. Another from *Florence* wants the Nail. Another from *Genoa* mightily damaged. *N.B.* Tho' there are not maintain'd to be Forefingers, yet they are indubitably the real Fingers of the Saint, and be they anathema and accursed who say otherwise, wounding the Sides of the Church thro' these her blesses Reliques. His Ashes (*Rome* St. *John Lateran*.) More of them from *Genoa* very safe and dry. Some of the Blood of our Saviour as he hung on the Cross, gathered in a Glove by *Nicodemus*, which being thrown by him into the Sea, for fear of the *Jews*, was cast up after many Ages on the Coast of *Normandy*, and found out by a [118] Duke of that Country as he was Hunting, by the hunted Stag and Dogs all kneeling quietly about it. From the Abbey *du Bec* in *Normandy*, which the Duke built for it, and where it was kept till now, and the said History recorded. St. *Peter* and St. *Paul*'s Bodies mixt together, one half belonging to St. *Peter*'s, the other half from St. *Paul*'s at *Rome*, both equally weigh'd and divided by Pope *Silvester*. *N.B.* That Moiety at St. *Peter*'s (with some other precious Reliques) is not to be dispos'd of to any Person whatever, but to remain to the Church. Both their Heads, from St. *John Lateran*, (*Rome*.) A Toe, a Finger, and a Slipper of St. *Peter*, all in good condition (*Rome*.) His Episcopal Chair wants a Foot. His Vestments want mending and darning greatly, but dangerous, the Cloth is so sadly decay'd. His Rochet, which he always us'd to say Mass in, and especially in this City, when he was here, much torn and greatly damag'd by Time, (all at *Rome*.) Another Chain, and another Sword of this blessed Apostle's when in Prison, (all at *Rome*, from St. *Petri ad Vincula*.) A Shoulder of St. *Paul*'s (*Rome*.) St. *Bartholomew*'s Body. Three of them, [119] one from *Naples*, another fully as well saved from St. *Bartholomew*'s in this City, and a third from *Tholouse*, very tender, and not well dried, but plainly his own. *N.B.* These different Bodies are as hard to have any thing determin'd about them, as the Duplicates aforesaid. They are well voucht by ancient and unquestionable Tradition, and all proper Depositions and Certificates; and it suits better with good Faith and good Manners, to leave such perplext Difficulties in suspense, as the Holy Church, and our Religious Ancestors have deliver'd them down to us, (however ambiguous and incomprehensibly obscure) than that the Temerity of these Days should overturn the Piety of the former. Let the Buyers examine and judge to the best of their Faith and Knowledge, and remember as they are blessed who believe tho' they saw not, so much more blessed doubtless are they, who believe piously and candidly, even against that which they do see. The Skin which was flay'd off this blessed Apostle, in a sad condition, and something rotten; from *Poitiers*. Another of them, probably from one of the aforesaid Bodies, but wants the [120] Buttocks, tho' better preserved by a great deal (*Rome*.) St. *Matthias*'s Head (*Romæ Petri ad Vincula*.) His Rib, Shoulder, Arm, one Foot, and a Piece of another, all of them moist kept, and strong scented (from *Paris Aquæ Sextiæ*, and other Places of equal credit.) Another Skin of St. *Bartholomew*, in all human probability flay'd off one of the Bodies aforesaid (from *Pisa*.) His Head, and another Member, but hard to say what it is, 'tis so much disfigur'd by Time, and the zealous Devotions of pious Pilgrims and Visitants (from *Pisa* also.) St. *Mathew*'s blessed Bones (*Treviris*.) His left Arm (from *Cassini*.) His right Arm (*Romæ ad Marcelli*.) Another Arm (*Romæ ad Nicolai*.) We have said enough on these Duplicates already. The compleat Body of St. *Anne*, the Blessed Virgin's Mother (*Aptæ oppido Provinciæ*.) Her Head (*Treviris*) another. Other Heads (*Tureni apud Juliacenses*.) A third

(*Annabergæ oppido Thuringiæ.*) We have said above, what is abundantly sufficient to ease the Minds of truly pious, tho' scrupulous Christians, concerning these δυσνόητα, these vextious Difficulties. The [121] faithful and sincerely religious Person will ask no more hereupon; and to Schismaticks, Hereticks, and Unbelievers, we speak not, as gangren'd Members cut off from the Body of Holy Church, to their eternal Destruction.

St. *Magadalen*'s Body (*Vessali prope Altissiodorum.*) Another Body of hers; but as this is not well voucht, having but twenty Depositions, and those no fully confirm'd by oral Tradition, and the constant Testimony of the Church, and the Devotion of her faithful Sons; we candidly and ingenuously declare, our not being perfectly satisfied in this particular Relique, which yet we would not cast out, lest we should scandalize the devout Catholicks who have so long venerated it; (*apud San. Maximinum oppid. Provinciæ.*) Her Head, and the Mark of the Blow, given her by our Lord on the Cheek when she would have toucht him, when he said, *noli me tangere*, the Blow very plain still. The Head out of order. Great Quantities of her Hair, near twenty Pound from many Places. *N.B.* Tho' this Quantity is large, there is nothing therein to give the least Offence to the Faithful; for on all [122] dead Bodies, and much more on those of the Saints, the Hair, even after Death, grows most exuberantly, by which means probably these Quantities have been produced. The holy spousal Ring with which the Blessed Virgin was espoused to *Joseph*, for which the *Clusians* and *Perusians* waged such Wars here in *Italy*, as History mentions; (from *Perusia*.) The Bodies of the three Kings, or Magi, *Melchior*, *Jaspar* and *Balthasar*, all perfectly fresh and fair, and good liking from *Colen* or *Cologne*. Three other Bodies of the same Kings, fully as fair and as well preserv'd, except the Nose, the right Eye, and a part of the left Foot of King *Jaspar*; (from *Milan ad Eustorgii.*) We shall be altogether silent on these six Bodies belonging (that is, universally agreed by infallible Tradition to belong) to these three Kings; and shall content our selves with referring the Pious Reader, and especially if a Purchaser, to the foregoing Apologies. Blessed be the pious Care of the Empress *Helena*, to whom we and the Christian Church are indebted for these precious Reliques, by her sending them to *Constantinople*; and surely it is much better to have [123] six Bodies disputing for this Honour than none at all. The Knife used at the Circumcision of our Lord; (from *Compendium.*) The Stone on which St. *Peter*'s Cock crew, and the Column which was cleft asunder, from top to bottom on the Day of the Passion, and the Stone on which *Pilate*'s Soldiers cast Lots for *Christ*'s Garments; all from St. *John de Lateran* in this City.) St. *Stephen*'s Body (from St. *Stephen* at *Rome*,) Several Parcels of the Bodies of the Innocents from *France*, *Germany*, and *Italy*. *Testiculi eorum* (from *Friburgh* in *Brisgaw*.) St. *Lawrence*'s Body (from his Church in this City) together with a Vessel full of his broil'd Flesh, and another full of his Fat when broiling on the Fire (from the same.) The Gridiron on which he suffer'd Martyrdom, and the Coals wherewith this blessed Martyr was broil'd to death for the Faith, (from St. *Eustachius's* in this City.) Four Bodies of St. *Sebastian*; one from St. *Lawrence's* in this City, another from *Soissons*, a third from a Town near *Narbonne* his native Country, and the fourth from *Pelignum apud Armoricos*. 'Tis not to be denied, these undistinguishable Duplicates do return [124] too frequently, but our former Defences, and the Confusion and too forward Zeal of those darker Times, must (and if he be Faithful and Pious) will content the Reader and Buyer. Let us only add, which is a Point full of Comfort, that the Prayers of the Church, and the Devotions of her Religious Children, have so far consecrated the Mistakes of their Forefathers, that all must allow, that each of these Bodies have wrought most prodigious Miracles, of which the proper Certificates remain with each of them. An Head of the same glorified Saint, at St. *Peter's* in this City. Another Head of his, belonging most certainly to one of the above Carcasses, (from *Magdeburg.*) A third Head of his, in like manner (as is to be believed) fever'd from another of the said Bodies, procur'd from the *Dominicans* at *Tholouse*, who recover'd it at the immense Expence, of a tedious Law Suit. Four of his Arms, one got from the *Dominicans (Andegavi.)* A second from *Tholouse (ad Saturnini.)* A third from the Town *Casedei* in *Avernia.* And a fourth from *Monbrison.* Serveral of the Arrows he was shot and cruelly martyr'd with. (*Lambesii* [125] in *Provincia.*) More of them, from the *Augustine Fryers* in *Poitiers.* Several Chests full, of the 11000 Virgins, from *Colen, St. Deny's*, the Monastery of Marcian in Flanders, and many other Places, where the Bodies of those wonderful Saints were disperst. The Bones of *Abraham, Isaac* and *Jacob*, very sound and well kept (*Romæ Mariæ super Minvervam.*) One of *Aaron's* Rods (*Paris ad Sacri Sacelli.*) *Solomon's* Candlestick, from *Prague.* Some of the Oyl of the Holy Sepulchre's Lamp, which every *Easter Sunday* blazes up of its self, before the Eyes of the truly Faithful, got from the Alter of St. *John.* The Ring of St. *Thomas a Becket*, the Blessed Martyr, who rebell'd against his Prince, to serve the Holy See and the Cause of Truth. His Rochet sprinkled with his Blood when murder'd, so as never to be washt out. His Hair Shirt, the same which *Gononus's Chronicon* assures us, the Blessed Virgin sow'd herself for him, and then hid it under his Bed; all from the Monastery of St. *Martin* in *Arthoise*, with an authentick Catalogue of Sixty Seven Miracles wrought by them. St. *Apollonia's* Head and Arm, one Jaw, [126] and several of her Teeth from two or three different Churches in this City. Her Mouth, Part of her Jaw, and one of her blessed Teeth, from *Volaterræ* in *Etruria.* Several more of her Teeth, and her lower Jaw, from *Bononia*, where they us'd to be solemnly venerated the 9*th* of *February* each Year by the Pope's Legate, or Vice-Legate. A Part of her Jaw from *Antwerp*, where frequent Miracles were wrought by it. A Part of her Tooth from *Mechlin* and several whole ones from *Flanders.* A remarkable Portion of her lower Jaw from *Artois.* Four other Teeth, a

Rib, another Tooth and her Shoulder-blade from *Colen*. Another Jaw from the *Carthusians*, a Tooth from St. *Maurice*'s Church, and another Lower Jaw from St. *Alban*'s, all in the same City. Another of her Teeth and some other blessed Reliques of her's, from the Church of St. *Roch* in *Lisbon*, and from *Placentia* in *Spain*, St. *Anthony*'s Beard from *Colen*, and a remarkable Part of his Head. His Tongue, blessed for ever, from *Padua*. *N.B.* This is the same Tongue which St. *Bonaventure* 30 Years after his Death, found in his Ashes still fresh and full of Juice and Blood; [127] which before the Magistrates, he reverently took up and kiss'd, saying, *O blessed Tongue, which always did bless God, and taught others to bless him; now it appears of what Merit thou wast*; and so deliver'd it to them to be laid up again with his holy Ashes, as the famous *Mendozius* tells us. The Hay found in the Cratch where our Saviour was laid, call'd the Holy Hay; (Brought from *Lorain*.) *Moses*'s Horns, which he had coming down from Mount *Sinai*, and the Tail of the Ass our Saviour rode on, got from *Genoa*; and a Pair of *Joseph*'s Breeches, very old and much worn, from *Aix*. The blessed Navel or our Lord, form St. *Mary del Populo* in this City, and the Skin or Pannicle, that came out of the most holy Body, of the Blessed Virgin with our Saviour, when he came into the World, from the Church of St. *Mary* the Greater, in the same City. The Stone, on which the same Blessed Virgin used to wash our Saviour's Linnen, brought from *Constantinople*. A Tear which *Christ* shed over *Lazarus*, enclos'd in a little Crystal by an Angel, who made a Present of it to St. *Mary Magdalen*. Another from the *Benedictins* Convent, at *Vendome* in *France*. *N.B.* This is the [128] very Tear, which the learned Pere *Mabillon* writ so admirable a Treatise in Defence of, to the Honour of God and holy Church.

But, my Lord, I propos'd to entertain you, and I am but tormenting you with so hideous a Recital of the superstitious Dreams and Inventions of these formal Hypocrites; whose Godliness is Gain, and who, under the Pretence and Cloak of exterior Sanctity, and an high Veneration of for such holy Trumpery, seek only Wealth, Ease, and Profit, and make a God of their Belly and their sacrilegious Gain.

I shall therefore leave the bulky Remains of this amazing Catalogue, till I know how your Lordship relishes this Taft of it, which I send you; and shall only mention to you, that from the Beginning to the End of it, on the strictest Examination, I don't recollect one Relique, the original of which at least, has not been actually venerated, and almost worship'd, this several hundred Years, by this blinded and deluded People; except that one of the Cheese and Butter made of the Virgin's Milk, which is said never to corrupt, and to have been brought from *Mexico*. Among all the rest, there [129] are but a very few, which I have not been at the Pains to search for, and have really, with these Eyes, seen in different authentick Lists of Reliques shewn at *Rome*, and other Places, and either mention'd by her own Writers, or Men of Honour and Truth, that assert they have seen them in their Travels. So that I can aver, there are few or none inserted in this List, which were not publickly known, and exposed to the Veneration of pious Catholicks. I have made bold, to add a few ludicrous Notes to several of them, that deserv'd much severer Remarks, on such horrible Impostures and Fables. For, alas, if all these Reliques, and the infinite Number of Miracles wrought by them, were fairly to be examined, and call'd to the Proof, before equitable Judges, as the Temples in *Greece* and *Asia*, who set up Asylums, were by the *Roman* Senate in *Tiberius*'s Time; how many of them would be oblig'd, either quietly to give up all their Pretensions, or to maintain them by some silly old Tale or other, as most of the Defenders of the Temples were forc'd to do, as *Tacitus* assures us in the Third of his Annals, *Cap.* 60, 61, 62.

[130] But if this were the Case, this jugling Church, which, like a true Quack, makes Use of Infallibility and Authority as a certain cure for every Sore, has provided a sufficient Remedy, tho' all her Reliques should be prov'd counterfeit; and that is by determining, that such superstitious Reliques may really work actual Miracles, because the good Intentions of those, who piously have Recourse to them, procures them that Blessing from God, as a Reward of their Devotion. She actually teaches this Doctrine, my Lord, which solves all Difficulties on this Point, and what is more, she is believ'd on it; her Confidence in deceiving, and the Credulity of her People in believing, answering like two Tallies, and makes one often remember the famous Axiom, *Homo est Animal credulum* & *mendax.* In the mean Time, what a Crowd of terrible Reflections, must this Scene of Things raise in every honest and ingenuous Breast, to see this infallible Church abusing the Purity and Excellence of our Faith, and the common Sense of Mankind, with imposing on them such an Heap of senseless Fictions, and silly Bawbles, not only for their Belief, but [131] even for their Veneration and Homage. With what Indignation! with what Resentment! with what honest Scorn! must every considering Christian, that has not blindly given up his Senses and Reason (the only Evidence to which our Blessed Saviour appealed for the Truth of his Miracles) to her groundless and usurp'd Authority, look on such horrid Trifling both with our Religion and Understanding?

Can one bear, without Grief and Torment of Heart, to see this Church of *Christ* exceeding in the Foppery and Folly of such Conduct, the greatest Absurdities of the *Heathen* and *Turkish* Superstition; and at the same Time, by infinite insidious Arts and horrible Treasons, as well as furious Persecutions and open Wars, attempting daily against the Authority of all Protestant Princes, and the Peace and Prosperity of their Subjects in this World, and giving up both of them in the next to eternal Damnation, for daring to question her Power, or dissent from her Opinions?

After saying this, can I add, (without lamenting the Blindness! the Meanness! the Dishonesty of Mankind!) that Popish Princes [132] will probably, for political Views and worldly Motives, never fail to combine together in supporting her Authority, tho' in their Hearts they may despise or renounce it; and consequently they will in all Likelyhood, by enlarging her Power, and joining in the Schemes of her infinite Policy, perpetuate their own unreasonable Slavery, and her rediculous Empire, to the End of the World, and this wretched Scene of Wickedness and Folly and Falsehood below! I am,

My Lord, Your Lordship's, &c.

Hertford.

I beg the Favour of your Lordship to transmit to me a regular List of the Temporal Peers summon'd to this Parliament, his Holiness having desir'd to see it.

To the Lord High Treasurer.

London, Chelsea, Dec. 19, 1997.

My Lord,

I had the Pleasure of your Dispatches, of *Nov. 3d,* some Days since, and am thus early in returning my Thanks, where I hold [133] my self so much oblig'd, both for your Care of the Publick and of me. Your Congratulations on my Advancement were very welcome, for from one so sincere and candid, as I have ever found your Excellency, even Compliments pass for Truths, and we think our selves oblig'd to give Credit to them. At the same Time, my Lord, you have not forgot *England* so much, by your long Residence at *Constantinople*, but that you must know, there can be no great pleasure to preside over the Councils of a People, that may almost be called a Nation of prime Ministers; that examine and suspect every Thing, and yet are never pleas'd or in good Humour, and least then, when they can find nothing to blame.

Your Accounts, of the State of Things in *Turky*, were most entertaining; his Majesty did you the Honour to hear your Letters read, and to express some Satisfaction in them; and therefore you must hasten to us the Remainder of your Observations, that we do not overpay for the Pleasure, by too long Expectation.

Mr. *Secretary* will, by this Night's Express, by the way of *Vienna*, communicate to you [134] his Majesty's Pleasure, in Relation to the Treaty, and the Approbation which all the Steps you have hitherto taken, have met with here. His Majesty has particularly order'd me to assure you, that the Bishops and Papa's of the *Greek* Church, shall be honour'd with his Protection and Favour; and all that are Needy and sincerely Scrupulous to submit to *Rome*, shall have proper Pensions to prevent their making Shipwreck of their Faith, and selling their Birthright, like *Esau*, for a little Food to sustain them. I think there has been an inexcusable Negligence, in the Ministry here (tho' I know not realy at whose Door to place it) in Relation to that unhappy neglected Church; which has neither had any Benefit drawn from our Protection at the Port, nor the least Care shewn, by sending Missionaries of our own, to prevent the Artifices of the Jesuits, and keep her steddy to her Principles, as a Sister Church, who has ever abhor'd to join in their Communion. This is a Defect, which all Protestant Churches have much fail'd in, and our own as much as any; with many other Irregularities, if Providence [135] shall be pleased to lend me Opportunity and Power.

I shall be much oblig'd to your Excellency, if you can inform me if Mr. *Biron* or Mr. *Pearson*, have recover'd any choice Manuscripts, either *Greek* or *Arabick*, or valuable Medals, or any Rarities or Curiosities in their Travels, which I procur'd his Majesty to send them abroad for, when I was only principal Secretary of State. I thank you for the Curiosities you sent me, and to engage you to this Kind of Traffick, I have given Orders to send you, by the *Turky* Fleet, an excellent Hogshead of *Carolina*, (our own Plantation White-Wine) and three or Four fine pieces of Damask, made of the Silk of that Country; both which we have brought to that Perfection there, as is of vast Advantage to *Great Britain*, as well as the Colony.

Since you think it will make the Grand Seignior encourage Astronomy, I have also sent you one of the compleatest largest and best reflecting Telescopes in *London*, which we make with such exquisite Skill and Contrivance, that they exceed tenfold all those that were used by the Astronomers in the last Age. Tho' it be but of a moderate Length, yet [136] it is altogether as good as the larger Ones; and the Expence of fixing it up, much less; and you may discern evidently with this, not only the Hills, Rivers, Vallies, and Forests, but real Cities in the Moon, that seem nearly to resemble our own, and what is still more, even Mountains and Seas in *Venus* and the other Planets. Nay some of our Astronomers have gone so far, as to aver, they could distinguish the Times of Plowing, and Harvest there, by the Colour of the Face of the Earth, and to specifie those Times, that others might make a Judgment of their Observation, and have maintain'd, that they have plainly seen in the Moon, Conflagrations, and the Smoak arising from them.

As I fancy there is more of Imagination than of Truth, in such Opinions, I would not have your Excellency quarrel with this I send you, if it does not perform all these Miracles. I will assure you, beforehand, you will find it magnifie to so prodigious a Degree, as will perfectly astonish you, as much as you are us'd to Telescopes; while it gives you such evident Demonstrations, that all the Planets are not only habitable, but inhabited. I shall desire you only, while you are enjoying those Pleasures, to remember, [137] that you are chiefly indebted for them, to the Bounty and generous Encouragement, with which our Royal Master contributed to the Project, for improving them so highly, without which, they would never have receiv'd the Perfection they have gain'd.

As Mr. Secretary will entirely take off my Hands, to Night, the Province of the Statesman and the Minister, your Excellency will pardon me, if I only entertain you very poorly *en Philosophe*, and as a Brother Virtuoso, with some small Accounts of what Improvements have been made here in the polite Arts; and also, how far our Trade, and both the Laws and Manufactures of our Country, are advanc'd and regulated within these twenty-five Years, since you left us.

That I may prepossess your Excellency in the best Manner I am able, in Favour of our Improvements here, I shall begin my Account with those elegant Arts, you have so long admir'd and cultivated, Painting, Sculpture, and Architecture; which, tho' greatly encourag'd by his Majesty's Royal Ancestors, have been shewn such extraordinary Favour and Protection, under this Reign, that there have not only Salaries been allow'd to Professors, [138] in each of them, but a Fund of 5000 *l. per Ann.* establish'd by Subscription of his Majesty, and the Nobility and Gentry, which is divided equally on his Majesty's Birth-Day, in *December*, to the three best Pictures, Statues, and Houses, that have been made in *Great Britain* in that Year. Tho' his Majesty subscribes 1500 *l.* a Year, he has but one Vote in determining who best deserves the Premiums; and that Parties and Factions may be excluded, and only Merit consider'd, all the Subscribers are engag'd, on their Honour, not to solicit any Member for his Vote, and as all is performed by Balloting, it is generally agreed, that nothing can be manag'd with greater Candour and Impartiality.

By this single Method, we have made *Great Britain*, the Seat of these lovely Arts, and have drawn hither, the first Masters of the World, to contend with Emulation for the generous Rewards, which our Country bestows on their Labours and Merit. I do assure your Excellency, it has such an Effect here, that I am confident, we have better new Pictures and Statues in *Great Britain*, than in all *Europe* besides; and perhaps *Italy* her self, will not, in a little Time, be able to [139] excel the Palaces we have built here, since this Scheme has taken Place. In Sculpture, particularly, we have so far excelled, that no Nation comes near us in cutting in Granite, Serpentine, or Porphyry; and we alone have the Art of Working in that hardest of Stones, the Bisaltes, by the Help of Emery, prepar'd in the new Method; and by having probably found out the Secret of tempering our Steel, after the Manner of the Ancient *Greeks* and *Romans*.

I am sorry to tell your Excellency, that we have gone as great Lengths as to Musick, but without assigning Premiums, and am afraid you will put me in Mind of *Cicero's* Maxim, in his Treatise *de Legibus, Mutatâ Musicâ mutantur Mores*, and the Rule he lays down for it, which is worth the Consideration of every Nation, *Curandum itaque est, ut Musica quam gravissima & sedatissima retineatur.* It was with this View, that several of his Majesty's Royal Predecessors, peremptorily drove the *Italian* Opera and Music twice from *Great Britain*, and forbid their acting in their Theatres, in St. *James's* Square and *Kensington*, as enervating our Spirits, and emasculating the *British* Genius. *George* III. would never [140] allow it to be us'd in his Troops, or by any Officers in them; and with Difficulty let it be remain'd in the Church Service, and Anthems. Some States have prohibited the Study and Practice of Musick; with the same Views; and the *Spartans*, your Excellency knows, made a Decree against *Timotheus*, for improving soft Musick, and yet we have run into a Passion for it, with that Violence, that it has not only thriven at the Expence of the good Sense, and, almost, the Valour of our Nation, but has, in some measure, supplanted our Ambition, and our Thirst for Wealth and Power.

The Fiddle, particularly, has so far got into the Hands of our Gentlemen, that, I fear, they will at last forget the Use of their Swords; and am jealous, they will set up, in Time, a new Sect of visionary Religionists amongst us, who will worship nothing but that ador'd Instrument, tho' at the same Time, every one knows, 'tis as rare to see a good Fidler without a poor Understanding, as it is in *Ireland* to see an Harper, that is not blind. It is certain, however, that they have brought the Improvement of it here to a vast Pitch; but your Excellency observes, that this is rather what I am asham'd, [141] than proud of, being heartily concern'd to see our brave People rivalling the Eunuchs of *Italy*, in so trivial an Excellence, to say no worse of it.

Let me lead you now by the Hand, into the Royal College of St. *George* at *Oxford*, which, tho' founded by his Majesty's Ancestors in the Eighteenth Century, has been so vastly improv'd, and it's Revenues so far encreas'd, by the King our Master, that we may almost call it his own Foundation. Your Excellency was well acquainted with it in your Youth, and therefore, I shall only mention to you, such Additions, and new Regulations, as have been made there of late Years. I shall begin with the great Square, all built by his Majesty, which he nam'd the College of the learned World. Here there are Apartments for Twenty-six Fellows, who must be learned Foreigners in Distress, chosen by the Votes of the Nobility, Bishops, and Heads of Colleges, signifying by a sign'd and seal'd Certificate, that the Person to be elected, is a learned Foreigner in Distress, whom they think best deserving the vacant Fellowship, which is worth 50 *l.* the Year, [142] and Diet, and is conferr'd on him who has the most Votes.

In the old Square, adjoining to this, there are Lodgings for four new Professors, who have each of them 150 *l.* a-piece *per Ann.* The First professes and teaches Agriculture and Gardening, and has (near the College) twenty Acres of Ground, which he employs in small Parcels, under the Plow and Spade, in different Methods and Experiments, in those two useful Arts; and has still a Number of Scholars, who are bred under him, to whom, in soul Weather, he reads Lectures; and in fair Day's he instructs them, in all the practical Methods necessary to the Improving the Culture of the Field and the Garden. They are to assist him in all his Experiments to that End, which he is oblig'd to publish each Year, with their Success or Failure, and the probable Causes and Reasons of both. The King's, and all Noblemen's Gardener's are bred here; and all young Gentlemen, who come to the Universities to learn nothing, are oblig'd, before they take any Degrees in Arts they are perfect Strangers to, to spend six Months under this Professor, in order to make them know something.

[143] The second is called the Weather Professor, and tho' this was established in 1840, yet as his Salary was trebled from 50 *l.* to 150 *l.* I reckon him with the others. He is oblig'd to keep exact Diaries and Indexes of the Wind and Weather, of all Storms, Drougths and Rains, and the antecedent concomitant and consequent Circumstances, as well as the Position of the Planets; and collect all other Symptoms indicative of the Changes of the Air and Weather, with Deductions and Conjectures as to all Dearths, great Crops, healthy Seasons, and epidemical Distempers, and the Causes and Remedies of Famines and popular Sicknesses. He is to enter his Observations in regular Calendars, and to add Dissertations on all, and particularly on the Causes of such Accidents, as are occasion'd by Heat or Cold, Rain, Frost, Snow, Lightning, Blasts, Mildews, biting Winds and scorching Suns; and to set down the probable Extents of Coasting Winds, Rains and Snows, and to keep three Clerks at three different Distances of at least Eighty Miles asunder to pursue the same Methods exactly. He is also to keep carefully, and observe constantly, his *Statical Hygroscopes*, as to the Moisture and Dryness of [144] the Air, how far full or new Moons, and the menstrual or annual Spring-tides, the Multitude or Fewness of the Solar *Maculæ*, the Approach of Comets, the Aspects of the Planets, their Eclipses, Conjunctions, &c. appear to affect our Atmosphere in this particular. He is to attend with the same Exactness his Weather Engines to express the Strength of the Winds, by their lifting up such and such Weights; and measure the Quantities of Rain that fall throughout the Year, the Thickness of the Ice, and Depth of Snow, the Length, Breadth, and Force of Earthquakes, as well in his Neighbourhood as by his Correspondents throughout *Great-Britain*, and the neighbouring Coasts of *France* and

Ireland, and whether they move as is supposed generally from East to West, or how otherwise.

Six Volumes in Folio of these Calendars have been publisht from 1840 to 1991, at the King's Expence lately, and it is incredible what a Certainty we are come to in these Matters, and the Advantage thereby, as to Sieges, Campaigns, Harvests, Journeys, Sailing of Ships, Inundations, and Tempests; it being certain from them, that every Revolution of *Saturn*, we have the [145] same Weather exactly, or with very small Variations. A Discovery, which your Excellency sees at one Glance the Importance of, tho' I fear, as 'tis probable the World will not hold out many Centuries longer, this will be like coming to a great Estate when one is past Seventy, and has no Hopes of enjoying it. The last I shall mention to your Excellency, are the two Professors of Trades, and Mechanical Arts. These divide all the most mysterious Trades between them, such as Dying, Weaving, Tanning, Turning, Carpenters, Masons, Painters, Brewers, Bakers, Spinners, Miners, Wheel, Mill and Ship-wrights, Printing, Glass-making, and such like; and are oblig'd to inspect into all possible or probable Methods to improve those in his Province.

Each Year they give in their Observations or Inventions to the Board of Trade, who, after examining into them, and consulting thereon with the Hall of Tradesmen in that Mystery, give Orders for its being followed and observed by them and their Apprentices, and publisht, if proper, for the common Good. The Professors must be Masters of Arts in one of the Universities, and well vers'd in Experimental Philosophy, and must [146] every seven Years, present his Majesty with an History of the several Trades in their respective Provinces, and the Improvements made in them by their Care and Inspection. I cannot detain your Excellency too long, or I could reckon up many prodigious Advantages the Publick has gain'd, by light'ning the Labour, short'ning the Road, removing old Mistakes, and supplying new Methods and Inventions, to the several Trades and Manufactures of these Nations.

Thus I have gone thro' the new Professors our Royal Master, following the Steps of his glorious Ancestors, has so generously and so happily establisht. The Queen indeed, who is the best of Princesses, and a second *Caroline* or *Elizabeth*, would have had his Majesty found a Professorship of Piety, since there was ne'er a one in either University; but he told her pleasantly, There were so many Professors of that Kind already in the World, and so few who put what they profest in Practice, that he would not hear of it, till that matter should be amended. But to shew your Excellency how much the learned World is indebted to his Majesty's Cares, I must describe to you the Royal Printing-house which he has erected and [147] endow'd, and which stand in the middle of the noble Square where your Excellency and I lodg'd. It is of *Portland* Stone, built on such vast massy Vaults, and with such an huge Profusion of convenient Offices of all kinds, and Apartments for the Printers, Correctors, and Servants, and makes all together so august and magnificent an Appearance, that *Sheldon*'s Theatre would appear but as a Cottage by it. There is 500 *l. per Ann.* issuable out of the Treasury to the Foundation, besides the Benefit of all Copies they print. They must use no Types or Paper but of the best kind, and they work Night and Day, relieving each other by turns, and are to forfeit 5 *s.* each for all Erratas, so that their Copies are reckon'd the most correct extant. Over the great Gate there is a large Inscription in a vast Marble Table, in which the Causes of the Foundation are declared to be, the Service of Religion, the Good of the State, and the Benefit of the Learned World. Then it goes on to say, that as the Number of Books is infinite, and rather distract than inform the Mind, by a mix'd and confused Reading, some being well writ, but ill Books, others good Books, but ill writ; some hudled up in haste, [148] others stinking of the Lamp; some without any strength of Reasoning, others over loaded with Arguments, half of which are insignificant; some Books being obscure through too affected a Brevity, others perspicuous through an unnecessary Redundancy of Words (like a bright Day at Sea, where yet there is nothing to be seen but Air and Water;) some treating on Subjects that thousands had handled better before, others publishing useless Trifles, because new and unthought of by others; some Writing as if they had never read any thing, others as if they writ nothing but what they read, and then borrowed; therefore his Majesty decrees, no Book should be printed within those Walls but the Works of the Ancients, and such only as should be voted most proper, by two thirds of the Colleges in his two Universities, and confirmed by the Lord Chancellor, and Arch-bishop of *Canterbury* for the Time being. I have dwelt the longer on this noble Design, because I had the Honour to propose it to his Majesty, and the Happiness to bring it to Perfection for the good of Mankind; and I must now lead your Excellency, to take a View of the noble Square that surrounds the Royal Printing-House [149], which is all new built since we lodged in it. It is divided now, besides a large House for the Provost, into twenty different Buildings, each of which belongs to a Fellow, and contains Apartments for twenty Scholars who are his Pupils, and live with him as in one House, of the Door of which he keeps the Key, as also of all their Chambers. By this Means, as none can go in or out but with his Knowledge, and by his Leave, so nothing can be privately transacted or conceald in their Chambers, which he enters by his Key at Pleasure, thereby shutting out idle Visitors, and Cabals; and to prevent all Intriegues with Women, none are allow'd to come into the House. This Rule extends to all Relations except Mothers, and to their very Servants, who are all Men.

To each Building there is a large Hall, where Morning and Evening his Pupils meet, and study under his Eyes four Hours, writing down his Lectures from his Mouth, or contracting the Authors he gives them;

and each *Saturday* they are examined the Repetition of the whole. For each Morning or Evening Lecture the Tutor is absent, there is treble the Sum due for each Day's Tuition [150] deducted, which ensures their Attendance. There are each Year four Examinations of the whole Body of Scholars in publick, divided into four Classes, and each Class into five Divisions. The Examination lasts two Days, four Hours in the Morning, and four in the Evening, each Day. The twenty Fellows are the Examiners, and return Judgments of each Scholar's Answering on their Oaths, and the five best Answerers in each Division are paid 5 *l.* each in Books, and their Names hung up in the great Hall for ten Days, and opposite to them the Names of the five worst Answerers. After four compleat Years they take their Degrees of Batchellors, except ten of the worst Scholars in each Class, who are constantly stopt for at least one Year more.

After taking their Degrees, their Studies are continued in like manner precisely, as when Under Graduates; when they are lectur'd and examin'd by the Professors, with equal Severity and Constancy, and not allow'd to idle in private. The first of *August*, each Year, if there are any vacant Fellowships, and are examin'd six Days, and eight Hours each Day, by the publick Professors, [151] who, upon their Oaths, nominate the best Answerers, and distribute in like manner 40 *l.* apiece of the Royal Annual Bounty to those who miss, but appear to deserve the Fellowship.

After eight compleat Years, they commence Masters, and are dismist the Society, if they desire it, with proper Testimoniums of their Behaviour and Scholarship; and if they continue in the Society, are allow'd 20*l.* a Year each, from the Royal Bounty, and are oblig'd to attend the Professors of Divinity, Mathematicks, History, and Civil Law, each of them, two Hours every Day at their publick Lectures for four Years, and then they are declar'd *Emeriti*, and honour'd with larger Testimoniums, betake themselves to their several Professions in the World.

This truly Royal Foundation, of which I omit many smaller Particulars, costs his Majesty about 3000 *l*, a Year, besides the Expence of a Regal Visitation every three Years, when the Morals, Learning, and Diligence of the Provosts, Professors, and Fellows, are severally enquir'd into, and all Offenders, either strictly caution'd, remov'd, or expell'd.

The Numbers of admirable Scholars that this Society has sent into the World, and their having deservedly obtain'd, a large Share of [152] all Preferments in Church and State, is the best and plainest Evidence that the Foundation is well modell'd, and will save you the Trouble of my enlarging further on it, unless I venture to add, that were the Discipline of our other Colleges proportionably strict, and the Premiums and Allowances more enlarg'd, it is impossible but a Nation so capable of exerting it's natural Turn for Letters, would send out more exalted Genius's, and excellent Scholars, than we have of late done.

But the Delight I take in this Subject, and my Desire that your Excellency should have your full Share in it, has run this Letter into an unexpected Length, especially from my weak Eyes and Hands. It has perfectly tir'd me, and as the Reader is generally sick, by the Time the Writer is weary, I shall cut off half the Trouble I propos'd to give you, in relation to our late Improvements, as to our Trade, Manufacturers, and Laws; and shall reserve those for the next Dispatch, I have the Pleasure to send you.

Since I wrote this, Mr. Secretary tells me he has drawn up his Majesty's Commands for you, in relation to the poor deserted *Greek* Church, and the State of all Affairs where you are; to which I have nothing to add, but my [153] best Wishes for their Success, and my earnest Entreaties for your Diligence and Vigilance, that nothing may disappoint the Hopes your Excellence has given us, and the kind Expectations I have ever had, of the skillful management of all Matters, that are to pass through your Hands. When you receive the *Carolina* Silks, and White-wine, pray let me know sincerely how you approve of them, for they are much admired here.

All your Relations in this Family kiss your Hands, and your good Lady's, and long for your return once more to them and your Country, where there is no Man more desirous, not only to see but to serve you, than,

My Lord, Your Excellencies most, &c.

N — M.

To the Lord High Treasurer.

Mosco, Jan. 27, 1997.

My Lord,

I Have the Pleasure of your Command by Mr. Secretary of *January* the 3^d, and am highly delighted that I have in some measure answer'd your Expectations by mine of the 29th of *November* last; and as I shall faithfully pursue my Instructions, and particularly the Hints in Cypher, so if any thing new arises, I [154] shall use my best Diligence to give the earliest Intelligence, and in the mean time shall act as my present Lights shall direct me.

I find your Lordship considers me as very little employ'd here, since you seem desirous I should explain to you, upon what Grounds the common Opinion hath prevail'd, that the *Muscovites*, who have so long adhered to the *Greek* Church, are now, as it were, with all their Sails, a Trip bound for *Rome*. You desire I should also inform you at large, by what Methods the Jesuits have been able to overcome, that violent Aversion which has so long been manifested, against them and their Communion here; and above all, what Alterations they have been able to bring about, in order to make the Doctrines and Rites of this Church, compatible with theirs.

I will make no Apologies for my Inability to perform this Task, since you have enjoyn'd it me; and shall endeavour to lay the whole of the Jesuits Plan before you, as I have been shewn it here by a very considerable Person, that you may gratify your Curiosity fully, and judge if I am right in my Conjectures, in saying *Venient Romani*, as the *Jews* said of old; and that the *Greek* Church will soon veil her Mitre, to the Pope's Triple Crown.

[161] It must be confest indeed, that the Jesuits herein have proceeded with their usual subtlety and caution, and have not hitherto attempted in an avowed manner the least publick step to oblige this Church to own her Subjection to that of *Rome*. As they know the general stream of the People's affection, as well as of the inferior Clergy, went violently against them; they have taken their measures accordingly, and have done all they could to remove that Aversion: while at the same time, they have by a thousand methods, secured to themselves the Czar's favour and protection, as well as the Patriarchs, the two Metropolitans, and most of the Bishops, and the Chiefs and Heads of the regular and secular Clergy.

They have managed this point so well, that they are more respected at Court than is easy to be credited, and have such interest with the Nobility, that no man can succeed with them, but as he is favoured and recommended by these pious and worthy Fathers. It is true, indeed, they owe this kind reception to the vast interest this Court finds they have all over *Europe*, and if that were weakened or overturned, probably they would soon sink here also; but as there [162] is little danger of that, and as they are on all occasions vastly serviceable to the Czar's affairs, both at home and abroad, it is certain their power will rather increase than lessen here.

In the mean time, they make the utmost use of what they have, to bring over more and more the whole body of the Clergy to their Party, that by them they may gain on the People, and by degrees prepare this Church to receive the Yoke on her neck, which she has so long, and so obstinately renounced.

To oblige the Clergy in the most sensible manner, they have persuaded the Czar to establish in different parts of the Empire, near two hundred Schools for the *Muscovite* Youth, and especially the Sons of the Clergy; and to settle the annual Præmiums on the several Universities, for such of them as distinguish themselves by their parts and diligence: and at the same time, they have those Schools, and Universities, and Præmiums, entirely under the management of persons solely dependant on them.

By this means, such principles are instilled, secretly and imperceptibly, into the Youth of the Empire, as necessarily beget a [163] horror of Schism, a love of Union, and a high veneration for the authority and doctrines of the Church of *Rome*.

But as these counterfeit Fishers of men are generally observed not to do their work by halves, they have taken measures yet more effectual, to oblige both the People and Clergy for ever. There are, my Lord, numbers of poor mortals in this Nation, who being able just to read the service of the Church in their own tongue, and a translation of St. *Chrysostome's* Homilies into it, to the People, get into Priests Orders, like the sons of *Eli*, to gain a piece of bread; and yet the provision made for them is so small, they are disappointed even in securing that, and are almost starving two thirds of the year. There are in the Czar's Dominions four thousand Parishes in these circumstances, where the priest was in this wretched scituation; and yet by his Majesty's personal contributions, and by a regular tax of the tenth penny on all ecclesiastical preferments, which they procured to be voluntarily laid on, by the Patriarch, Bishops, and richer Clergy, whose livings exceed a hundred pounds *per annum*, there is a fund raised, with so generous and christian a spirit, that their poor [164] brethren, who were daily in danger of perishing, and Religion with them, for want of support, are delivered from the contempt and misery of their condition, and have now full forty pounds *per annum*, settled for ever on each of their Livings.

While they thus provided for the poor and the ignorant, they have not forgot the richer and more learned Clergy; and as they have their spies and emissaries every where, whenever they find a man of real merit confin'd to a parish in some remote corner, out of the eye and notice of the Court, where he is obliged to waste his life in instructing his *Russes* (the most stupid of rational Creatures) like a second St. *Francis* preaching to the rocks in a desart; they take care, if they find him a friend to their Order, or can make him so, to have him removed to some happier scituation.

Judge, my Lord, what an influence this must give them on poor *Russian* Monks, who though they are regular enough in their lives, and are good men at their breviary; yet, I fancy, when they pray, may now and then, as Naturalists say of the Cameleon, look at the same time with one eye to Heaven, and with the other on the Earth, [165] where ease and convenience are pretty industriously sought after. Nay, they have even taken care of their interests, if I may so speak, after their death; and have obtained a Law, that their Widows, if poor, shall enjoy one year's full profit of their Husband's living, after his decease, or ten pounds *per annum* for life: So that here is another deep obligation laid on this powerful body, and by men that are little inclined to favour a married Clergy.

I shall continue, my Lord, a little longer, to make these Jesuits pane-gyrick (and certainly, if they did these good things to a good end, they would deserve a much nobler one than I can honour them with;) for I must confess, the Constitutions they have introduced into this Church, as to Bishops, are worthy the virtue and piety of the apostolick Age. For in the first place, they have obtained a Law, that no Bishop shall be capable during life, of being translated from the first See he is appointed to fill, (except when he is removed to be Patriarch) but he is married as effectually to his Church as to his Wife, and can never espouse another. The *Russian* Bishops formerly were still changing their scituations, and driving [166] about in their coaches, like the *Tartars* who lived perpetually in carts, journeying from one place to another for better grass, when they had eat the pasture bare where they had first settled; but they have taught them now, like *Issachar*, to know that Rest was good (at least in one sense) for them, and made them both remember and practise the good old Monkish maxim,

> *Si qua sede sedes, quæ sit tibi commoda sedes,*
> *Illâ sede sede, nec ab illa sede recede.*

By this Law they have obtained two good ends. First, that the Bishops shall not dangle perpetually after the Court, but shall be less slavishly dependant on the Czar, (who before used to manage them as he pleased, and set their tongues to go faster or slower, as we do our Clocks, as he found most convenient) and in consequence hereof, that hereafter they shall be more inclinable to the interest of the Pope, and his ecclesiastical Authority, when once it shall be established here. This was certainly a most impolitick step for this Court to make, but it is grown a maximum now in this, as well as most Governments in *Europe*, that [167] where the Jesuits are obliged, every thing is done with prudence; and this original error sanctifies all others that flow from it.

In the second place, by bolting the gate against all future preferments, they have effectually provided that the Sees shall be faithfully watched over, and constantly resided on, to the infinite emolument of the Christian Church, and the several Cures dependant on their Bishopricks.

This your Lordship will certainly allow to be an excellent regulation, and yet I have another to mention, nothing inferior to it, which is estab-lished by the same Law; and that is, that every Bishop shall on the death of any of his Clergy, before he gives away his Living, publickly receive the Sacrament in his Cathedral Church, and in the view of all his Congregation, solemnly swear on the Evangelists, that he will collate to that Living no Relation, nor be moved by any respects to solicitations of others, or blood or affinity, or any worldly regards, *nec prece nec pretio,* but the service of God, and his true Religion; and shall then and there (I am repeating the words of the Law to your Lordship) on the place name the person to whom he resolves to bestow it. A [168] security so strong and binding, to have piety, learning, and true merit only considered in such sacred preferments, that if it prevailed through the whole boy of the Popish Church, or indeed in any other, would soon give them strength and credit sufficient to baffle and overturn all their adversaries, and almost give countenance and authority to the worst and weakest Doctrines she could maintain. Behold here the noblest provision for learning and merit! but the difficulty that still remains, is to find either of them in *Russia*. My Lord, they have taken effectual care, even of this almost insurmountable evil; for besides the new Præmiums they have got established in the Schools and Universities, which are able to rouse and awaken the drowsiest natures, the Bishop is obliged to keep a constant Library (appropriated to, and belonging to the See) in good order and condition, for the use of his Clergy; and in their turns of seniority, to have six of them residing in his house for twelve calendar months, reading under his direction for at least eight hours every day.

By this means learning, that is, some reasonable degree of it, is become more general [169] among the Clergy who formerly could hardly read their Liturgies; and surely if this obtain'd in our Country, it would be of much greater service than our larger libraries are, which like armories have few or no arms kept for constant service, but are really more for shew than use, and to give an air of strength and superiority to our Neighbours and Strangers that visit them.

And because formerly the *Russian* Clergy like the rest of the *Greek* Church entirely neglecting preaching, never making Sermons but twice in the year, on the First of *September* when their year begins, and St. *John Baptist*'s day, they have by their influence and authority in many Diocesses prevail'd on the Bishops to oblige their Parish Priests to preach at least the first Sunday in every month, and to lessen their labour those days they have order'd them to abbreviate the tedious Liturgies of the *Greek* Church, and thereby prepar'd them for the shorter and much easier one used in the *Latin*. It is certain indeed, with all this care and reading the *Russian* Sermons are miserable Performances; for tho' they are kept by turns thus constantly poring in their Bibles and Comments on them, and [170] eternally turning over the best of the ancient Fathers of the *Greek* Church, they do not seem to relish, or at least to digest them well; and if I may be allow'd the levity of the expression, they drink Wine, but they piss Water.

But methinks, my Lord, I perceive an Objection ready to be offer'd here, and which yet I will undertake the good Jesuits shall effectually answer; and that is, that by these excellent Institutions they seem to have cut short their own power of providing for the Friends of their Society and

Faction. No, my Lord, never doubt them, they are not so short-sighted; for tho' they concern themselves less in the smaller Preferments, they industriously take care of all that are considerable, and particularly as to the Bishopricks they let no Man step into the poorest See of this Church, whom they cannot absolutely depend on as a Creature of their own.

There are in all Churches, and especially in this, a kind of very managing and manageable Divines, who pay their court to interest and power, wherever they find it, by a servile obsequiousness in prostituting their Pens and their Pulpits to defend or explode [171] all Tenets as they are convenient or improper for the present times, and the present views of their masters. They are a race of creatures who are still mighty sticklers for all seasonable local Truths and temporal Verities, and are too often found to be the use fullest tools that ever were set at work by the wise *Matchiavels* of the world: However the malice of some envious people nick-name them sometimes the Professors of the *Engastromythick* Divinity, and rail at them a little severely as teaching trencher Truths, and writing and preaching from that lower kind of Inspiration which has set so many great Souls at work, and fills the head from the fumes of the belly.

Out of this illustrious body these good Fathers fail not with infinite skill and care to garble such Spirits as they find entirely devoted to their service, and ready to act the part of meer machines, to be directed and managed as they shall find proper to employ them; and of this clay, thus temper'd and prepar'd, are the choice vessels of the *Russian* Church, her holy Bishops and Fathers constantly made.

[172] Next to this great circumstance (which is ever a *conditio sine quâ non*) there are two material considerations that have perpetually influenc'd their choice of fit Persons to fill the vacant Sees, both which deserve your Lordship's consideration.

The first is, that such as are of the families of the Nobility, and related nearly to the great Knezzes and Officers at the Court, or in the several Provinces, shall still be preferr'd to those that are meanly born, tho' superior to them in parts and learning; by which rule they tie down their relations to support their designs, and approve of that great revolution they have projected.

The second is, that unmarried and childless persons shall always be pitch'd on; because tho' they find it impracticable to introduce Celibacy among the inferior Clergy (who by the Canons of the *Greek* Church must be married before they take orders, and can never marry again being widowers) yet by this method they have sufficiently establish'd it among the whole Order of Bishops. Hereby they have brought them to conform to the *Latin* Church in a material article, and by being childless, made them less tied down in their families [173] and fortunes to the Civil Powers, and likelier and abler with their Wealth and Interest to support the Ecclesiastical Estate, to which they are so nearly related.

A rule, my Lord, which, if it obtain'd in the *Greek* and Protestant Churches, which allow marriage to their Clergy, would at least have this good consequence, that men of the greatest Talents, and bless'd with a spirit and genius fit for governing others, would live unmarried, and prepare themselves by times for such important trusts; and also the little stream of wealth which is yet left undrain'd and allow'd to feed the conveniences or necessities of their Prelates, would not so often be entirely sunk in filling up the private ponds and canals of a family, but be more generally dispers'd to enrich the face of their country, to the profit and service of the publick. But as these reflections are fitter for a different place, I shall dismiss them, to mention to your Lordship another maxim by which these good and pious Fathers prepare the way for the papal authority; and that is, by encouraging learning among the Nobility and Clergy of *Russia*.

[174] This would be a very unlikely Engine for them to work with, if they did not confine it in proper bounds and limits; but as there are few Printing-presses here, and most of them set up by themselves; and since they are in a manner the sole importers of books; they take heed, while they cherish and reward Scholars, to furnish them only with such Authors as are either secretly or openly conducive to these ends. Thus in *Russia*, as in many other places, Men read not to direct themselves in forming just thoughts and opinions of things, but to confirm them in those which they have already taken up, or in favour of which their Interest or their Passions are strongly engag'd. As to this people, it is beyond all question, the Jesuits could not have so effectually broken down (the main fences between the *Greeks* and *Latins*) the Zeal and Ignorance of the Laity and Clergy, as by this limited kind of learning; which is as different from true knowledge, as the light of a lanthorn that just directs us in the night in the path we desire to walk in, is from the light of the Sun that opens the whole face of the Creation to our view.

[175] Let us now pass from their management of the Clergy, to consider the mixt body of the people in general; and we shall find there three powerful causes, that are perpetually at work to bring about the ends which the boundless ambition of this society, and the empire of the *Vatican* are ever persuing.

The first of these is, removing a scandalous practice that prevail'd, as all historians tell us, for many ages in this country, of the landlords obliging all their poor vassals to work on Sundays as much as other days, to the intolerable burthen of their tenants, to the utter breach of the Laws of God, and the scandal of those of Men. Their remedy indeed has little regarded the former of these, but has entirely removed the latter, which was nearer their hearts; for by a new constitution of the Czar's, and a Canon of one of their Synods, they have ordain'd, that on Sunday no person shall be allow'd to labour, but shall spend the day, after attending divine service, entirely in sports and diversions of all kinds. As this was known to be their work, it is incredible what favour and respect they have gain'd by it among all the lower ranks of people; [176] who used to abhor the least communication and correspondence with them.

As this artifice takes in all the herd of the lower people, the second reaches to those who are easier in their circumstances, and endeavour by their industry to enlarge their fortune. To gain these, as the good Fathers are the great Bankers and Traders in the Catholick world, (where they have labour'd to supplant both the *Dutch* and us) so they have with great expence and gain establish'd trade and manufactures in the chief towns of this vast Empire, and have taught the *Russians* to extend their commerce and bring in wealth to their country in a surprizing manner.

How far this must endear them to all, is easily conceiv'd; and therefore I shall pass on to the last main cause that favours their designs, and that is the universal Deism that has infected such crowds of persons considerable for rank, power, and fortune in this nation. This epidemical plague has spread most unaccountable among them several ill-grounded and shameful causes, the falshood and folly of which we are not to examine now: but it has prevail'd so here, that even those who still [177] preserve some remains of respect for our holy Faith, indulge themselves in picking out of it and their particular fancies and prejudices, a mix'd Olio of a Religion of their own, which deserves to be compar'd to nothing so properly as that of their neighbouring *Tartars*, the *Morduites*; who are both circumcis'd and baptiz'd as *Jews* and *Christians*, and yet are absolute Pagans in their worshipping and sacrificing to Idols. Nay, I have known Great Men here, remarkable for more Learning than generally falls to the share of Noblemen in *Russia*, who were credulous enough to allow a thousand historical absurdities in Authors of credit on the slightest evidence, who believ'd, or affected to believe nothing in the Bible, tho' supported by the strongest.

Such an odd unaccountable way of thinking have some Minds contracted, that resemble the Dead Sea, as *Mandeville* describes it, on which Iron would swim, but a Feather would sink immediately. How far this deluge of Infidelity, overspreading and overturning the old Foundations settled here in this Church, may contribute and give opportunity to the building up the papal Authority amidst the ruins and destructions [178] of both, I need not observe to your Lordship, who have so thorough an insight in the dependance and consequences of such things. Thus far it is obvious to remark, that in so terrible a confusion, *Rome* and the worst of her corruptions will be preferred by the Clergy themselves, and all that have any remainder of Piety left, to no Religion at all; and even the debauch'd and immoral part of Men who have none, and find it necessary to keep up some outward profession in the world, will come into the change as the best and fittest they can find for their purpose. And indeed it must be confest, there is no Religion upon earth, where believing or doing so little, will so effectually serve the turn (if men will be silent and obedient) as that of the Church of *Rome*, and these good Fathers with their distinctions and absolutions.

But while I say this I would not be understood, my Lord, as if I gave credit to the reports that are spread here, as if the Jesuits secretly favour'd the growth of this devouring pestilence. Tho' we well know by sad experience in *Great Britain*, what horrible sects and heresies their emissaries sow'd among our ancestors, in the calamitous [179] confusions of the seventeenth Century, in hopes to overturn *our* Church and restore their own; yet I am unwilling to believe they can be posses'd with so infernal a spirit as that of *James Mora* the Surgeon and *William Platen* of *Milan*, who conspir'd to poison and infect the Citizens in the time of the Plague, in order to make themselves masters of their Fortunes, as an old Author tells us in his Travels.* However I think I may without breach of charity say, that they would rather even Deism or Mahometism should prevail, so they could at last establish themselves, than that the *Greek* Church should flourish in opposition to *Rome*, and keep their ador'd St. *Nicholas* in his post of Porter of the gates of Heaven, in contempt of St. *Peter* whom they have plac'd there.

And thus I shall put an end to this account of their Intrigues here, and their Schemes for obliging and serving the *Russian* Church and Clergy, in order to enslave them; and must own, there are some things they have done as to this last particular, that with proper Abatements I would rejoice to see copied in our own Kingdoms, whenever the [180] wisdom and piety of our excellent Sovereign should judge it convenient.

Where truth allow'd it, I have given them their due praises, and should be sorry to speak of them with any unreasonable bitterness and severity. I admire the great Talents, Learning, and Wisdom of that prodigious society as much as any man, where they are applied (as they ought solely to be) to the good of Mankind, and the glory of our Creator. But to see such excellent instruments turn'd to corrupt our Morals, to wound Religion, and raise Factions, Schisms, and Rebellions in the earth to serve their own ambition, must raise every one's indignation. 'Tis a detestable perverting of Wit and reason, and all the powers of the human mind, from the noble purposes they were given us for by Heaven, to the worst that can be suggested by Hell; and bears a near resemblance of their practice who make use of that soul of vegetation, and basis of nutriment, the Nitre of the Earth, to convert it into gunpowder for the destruction of their fellow-creatures.

It is true they pretend the good of mankind, and the peace of the Church, are the great views which all their toils and labours [181] are directed to; tho' they make use of such infernal methods to arrive at them,

---

* Addison's *Travels in Italy*, page 39.

as plainly shew 'tis the power and empire of *this* world they aim at. If they made a good use of their power where they are masters, Men would certainly oppose them with less violence than they do; but alas, they are perpetually employing it where they dare, to persecute and torment their Christian brethren for the least unessential differences in opinions: condemning them to dungeons and tortures, and delivering them up, as far as they are able, both to temporal and eternal fire. The savage nations in *America* indeed, are said to make war on their neighbours, who do not use the same customs and speak the same language; but these Gentlemen go a few steps further, and persue you to the death, nay beyond the grave, because you do not think as they do (a matter in no man's power) in speculative points of their own contriving and imposing. For after all, my Lord, they have not only made a perfect manufacture of this commodity, but a monopoly too, and have manag'd with their *Faith*, as to the world, as the *French* King has done with his salt as to his subjects. At first it lay ready in every [182] creek, a plain useful healthful commodity, which all that pleas'd had for taking up, till by his absolute power the King seizes it solely into his hands, makes it up his own way, and refines it as he thinks proper; and then orders every one, on pain of death, to take such a proportion of it as he thinks necessary for them, whether they want it or no, or whether they will or no; and forbids under severe penalties that any that's foreign should be imported, and punishes all that make use of any other (tho' ever so much better) that is privately brought in by strangers.

But my zeal to satisfy your Lordship's curiosity on this subject has made me go somewhat beyond my own intentions, and I fear a great way beyond your desires. I will not encrease my fault by a long apology, and how ill soever I may have executed this, I shall wait with impatience for some new occasion of obeying any other commands you have for me, and every opportunity of shewing my self with great respect and submission,

My Lord,
Your Lordship's, &c.

Clare.

[183] *To the Lord High Treasurer*, &c.

My Lord,

Constantinople, Feb. 25. 1997.

I Can never sufficiently thank you for the pleasure I received from your Lordship's of *Novemb.* 29. from *London-Chelsea*, and the agreeable accounts you gave me in it, that my little Services here are acceptable to his Majesty and your Lordship; and above all, that the King condescends to entertain himself with the imperfect accounts I am able to send from hence.

Your Presents were most welcome to me, and especially, the glorious Telescope you have honour'd me with, which I shall in a few days set up conveniently enough. The Grand Seignior has already heard of it, and has resolv'd to have it brought into the Seraglio for his entertainment; which I am much rejoic'd at, you may believe, for the reasons I gave you. When he has seen it, I shall write to your Lordship a full account of all passages. Your *Carolina* White-wine was admirable, and the Silks much applauded here.

[184] I hardly know which to admire most, your prodigious Prudence, that has so greatly improv'd that drooping Colony in so small a time; or your Goodness, that after so long an absence can continue to remember me in so obliging a manner. But tho' I have less share in it as to any pleasure or expectation of my own, your Lordship's most exact and minute account of all the surprizing improvements made in the politer Arts, and those noble marks his Majesty has given of his zeal for Learning, gave me the highest satisfaction: and I am confident, all who have any regard to what our Country owes him, will never fail to express a due sense of the blessings they receive from him, and to beseech Heaven to continue long to us a Prince, who seems born for the good of his subjects and the world.

I am glad I can now assure his sacred Majesty and your Lordship, that at last the Treaty is perfected in every article, as directed in my last instructions in Mr. Secretary's Cypher. The Grand Seignior order'd the Vizier to sign them last Tuesday, as he accordingly did; and by this safe conveyance I transmit them for your perusal, and doubt not but your Lordship will be pleas'd [185] to see our Trade here so happily establish'd, and that no weakness or inability of mine, has been able to disappoint the prudence and wisdom of his Majesty's and your Lordships's Measures.

I have spoke to the Patriarch and several of the *Greek* Papas or Priests in a body here, and they have assur'd me they will transmit their thanks in a particular Address to his Majesty. Their miserable condition made the mention of Pensions highly welcome; and indeed if some of our learned Clergy and Books could be sent hither, to concert measures with them, it might produce uncommon consequences in favour of our Church, and to the prejudice of the Papal See, who so ridiculously stiles herself *Catholick*, tho' her dominions are nothing equal to those of this Church in *Europe* and *Asia* as to extent, and very little superior as to numbers of people. And now, my Lord, I return with all submission to observe your commands, to make some additions to those imperfect Observations I had the honour to transmit you from hence relating to these people. But while you increase my desire, you almost take away the power of obeying you, by letting me know [186] I am writing every word under my royal Master's discerning eye. This over-awes and damps my mind: for alas! what am I able to write, that can be fit to be heard or consider'd by so great a Prince, by so great a Judge as his Majesty? But your Lordship's desires, which are to me in the place of the most absolute commands, oblige me too strongly, to admit of any excuse to disobey them: and therefore as I have already spoke sufficiently on the subjects of their Army, Navy, Trade, and Revenue, and have also touch'd on several new Customs and Laws establish'd among them of late years; I shall go on to take notice of some others, that as yet I have left unmention'd. And the first I shall point to, are several Regulations formerly quite neglected here (which possibly may not be be unuseful to our selves or neighbours here-after) in relation to the Plague.

Your Lordship, who is so perfectly acquainted with the customs and usages of all Nations, is by no means a stranger to the stupid contempt and indifference which this Court used to shew formerly on this occasion; and though they saw every year so many millions swept away, by the ravage of that epidemical evil, yet so blindly [187] were they given up to their prejudices of Predestination, and that every Man's Fate was wrote in his forehead, that they never took the least measures for the common good and safety of their Subjects. But as experience (the fond wife of Wisemen, and the scornful mistress of Fools) has sufficiently convinced them of their error, they have of late issued several Orders relating to this subject, that are not unworthy your Lordship's consideration, if ever the crying Sins and Immorality of our times should call down this severe chastisement on our Country.

I shall not need to take notice to your Lordship, that in all Countries, and especially in *Turky*, whenever that calamity falls on them, one fifth of the People generally perish, and consequently that this is a vast drawback on the strength of the Empire, and the increase of their Subjects, and therefore that the severest Laws are requisite to remedy so dangerous an evil. As they are fully convinced of this now, they have established such Orders throughout the Empire, as they judged most necessary to prevent the spreading of so fatal a Contagion, and decreed that the most severe [188] Quarantines must be observed in all Sea-Ports, whereby it shall be death for any Mariner or Passenger to come ashore, and sufficient rewards established for every person who ingenuously discovers the infection of any Ship, and the heaviest forfeitures in case of concealment. That all

Custom-house Officers shall have the same rewards, who discover any ship to be infected, and forfeiture of place and goods, if they connive at, or conceal such Infection: and that all ships where one fifth part of the crew are sick, shall be judged as infected, and perform the most rigid Quarantine accordingly.

Thus far they strive to shut out the danger by Sea, and at Land they have taken as great precautions, both to prevent its least approach, or, if it appears, to stop its course; and in case it spreads, to put all possible bounds to its raging fury. As to the first of these, the late Emperor *Achmet* ordered that the whole Quarter called the *Janisarchi* where the Linnen and Woollen Drapers, and the Druggists lived, (and where by reason of the moist earth near the Seashore, and the rotting of the vast heaps of drugs thereby, and the aptness linnen and woollen packs have to retain infectious qualities [189], the Plague generally first broke out) should be removed into different parts of the suburbs, and adjacent villages, in the best air, and only one of those Trades to be assigned to each street. The same order obtains as to all Apothecaries, Brewers, Bakers, Tallow-Candlers, Butchers, Dyers, and such trades, which are apt to infect the air, and injure the health of great Cities, and are therefore obliged to live at a convenient distance from *Constantinople*: which I wish heartily were observed in every Metropolis in *Europe*, as well as in *London*, since I am confident it would make them abundantly more pleasant and healthful. There are Clerks of the Market also settled, who watch carefully that no corrupted or unwholesome meat, fusty corn, or rotten or decayed fruits or roots, be sold to the People, under severe Fines; nay, they are obliged also to destroy and bury those hideous tribes of wild dogs that run about their streets; and have even laid a tax on all houses that keep cats in them (though this last is so great a favourite with the *Turks*) those creature being reckoned to contribute much to the spreading, if not the breeding, infectious distempers. Besides [190] these precautions, all common Beggars, Gypsies, and Dervises, who live on alms, are banished this City on pain of Death; their usual nastiness and distempers having justly rendered them suspected: and also all persons are obliged to bury their dead at least seven foot underground. Nay though they keep publick Scavengers to carry away all filth and nastiness, yet every Housekeeper is to have the street clean swept before his door, and in summer time sprinkled with water to cool the air.

But in the second place, my Lord, if the Infections break out, each district has publick Searchers appointed to attend it, who remove all the sick who are necessitous to publick Hospitals, where they are well looked after; and oblige the richer sick to live retired in the remotest part of their houses, under the care of the publick Physicians of that district, who are in sufficient numbers obliged to attend them, at the general charge of the Inhabitants, on pain of the Galleys. All sick houses are marked with black strokes, to the number of the sick in them, and two slaves set to watch them by turns night and day, and to bury all that die, in their yards or gardens ten [191] foot deep, with all their clothes and bedding, it being death to sell, or even conceal the least part of such goods, as they used to do.

In each district there are Cadies and publick Officers appointed to examine daily if the publick rules are observ'd both as to Physicians and Apothecaries, Searchers, Watchmen, and the Sick they are to attend; and to order all proper food and provisions for such houses as are shut up, and to oblige all such attendants on the Sick to carry white wands in their hands, that all may avoid them. It is true indeed they are under some difficulties to provide a sufficient number of Physicians for all districts, and the Physicians here are really very ignorant creatures; but then by their frequent experience in this epidemical distemper, and the general rules that are printed and dispers'd among them, every little Quack, Druggist, or Apothecary is able to discharge his duty tolerably in this point, tho' perhaps in no other.

Lastly, my Lord, if the Plague in spite of all this care spreads thro' the City, all publick concourse, even at markets or the mosques, is prohibited, and no person [192] allow'd to walk the streets without some strong-scented herbs in their hands to smell to, or tobacco in their mouths or noses, and all publick houses are forbid the sale of any thing within doors. No Magistrates whatever are to leave the City, but must assemble once every day, to issue necessary orders, and punish all Offenders without mercy. They are to keep guards of Janisaries in every proper post, and to make vast fires in all great streets and squares, to purify the air, and in a word, to see nothing omitted for the publick benefit.

By these methods, my Lord, it is incredible how many millions of his subjects lives this good Emperor has saved, many of which, if established as laws in *Europe*, would keep us from those disorders, and panick fears which attend us when this publick judgments visits us for our sins, as it has more than once this last Century. In this view I have troubled your Lordship with this tedious repetition of some of the most considerable of them, which have been practiced of late so successfully throughout this Empire.

It is certain, such care is more necessary in this age than ever, when Men and Women [193] are observ'd to grow barren, and to have fewer children than their Ancestors. Whether this proceeds from a detectable proneness to the unnatural Sin, or at least, to Whoredom, or from the waste and ravage which Luxury, Voluptuousness, and Debauchery of all kinds have made in our bodies, or the dwindling and decay of Nature, that is wasted and spent with its own labours, or, which is most likely, from all together; I leave to your Lordship to decide, and to the Governors of Nations to provide against: for as their Strength consists in the numbers of their subjects, so their Lives seem to want and deserve more care than usual.

But I shall quit this melancholy topick, to observe some more agreeable regulations which have obtained here, that might be of service to our Country, if introduced among us, either by Laws, or Custom, the strongest of Laws.

And the first I shall take notice of in this light, is one which has contributed to raise this City from its Ruins, and the obscurity of its dark, narrow, and irregular Streets, to the beauty and uniformity which appears in every quarter of it: and that is, that even [194] in its smallest streets, and much more in its larger ones and open squares, all houses whether great or small, must be built of one equal heighth and uniform model, as to doors, windows, and cornishes, according to the publick plan, settled by the Grand Seignior's Architect.

By this method the meanest streets are kept so even, straight, and with so regulated a neatness and proportion, for the poorest Citizens and the greatest, and are so properly suited to and matched with the adjoining dwellings, that they make a most pleasing prospect to the eye. I have often reflected, that if this had been settled but fifty years since with us, we should have by this time a very different City, and less of that shocking mixture of good and bad, high and low, old or new-fashioned houses, which deform our streets and squares, and look more like ill-sorted different sized Ships, of all burthens, and built by several Nations, when they lie at anchor in our Harbours, than Houses of the same City and People.

Another method I shall hint to your Lordship, is that of the publick Schools, which are used here of late for instructing [195] the youth in wresting, leaping, vaulting, swimming, riding, shooting, and fencing, which has prov'd of vast use in making them active, strong-limbed, and able-bodied. This is of such infinite service to Mankind in the various accidents of Life, that it were to be wished, we, who have so many schools for the improvements of our Minds, would have some to provide for the service of our bodies; and not leave such matters to chance, or the humour of Children, who seldom mind them or practise them, but with danger of hazard, for want of care and skill to direct them.

The next particular I shall mention, is a Law that obtains here as to houses already built, but extends not to future buildings, whereby all homesteads in every City, Town, or Village, where any house falls down, and continues four years in ruins, are immediately forfeited to the Grand Seignior, and sold at a low price to any Person, who will oblige himself to rebuild it. By this single rule they have kept their Towns from that Desolation which used to lay them waste; and if this were extended in our Country to forfeiture or fine, from the Tenant to the Landlord, and then in seven years to [196] the King, it might keep up at least our present

Tenements in repair, which are gone to ruin in so many of our Towns, to our great detriment.

I know not whether so abstemious and regular a person as my constitution and course of life have obliged me to be, may venture to mention another Custom which universally prevails here, since the use of Wine has been so general; and that is, that the *Jews* are entirely possest of the monopoly of Wine in this Country, who are found by experience to sell it pure and unmixed. This practice they give into out of principle, the Law of *Moses* strictly forbidding all mixtures; and as they scrupulously adhere to it, and dare not violate it, they are observed to keep it unadulterated, as it comes from the Vineyard. How far this might deserve to be encouraged in *Great-Britain*, where we consume so much Wine, and so abominably brewed and compounded, by the tricks and imposture of our Merchants; or how far at least, these Brokers of the World, who lie sucking the life-blood of our Trade, might be made useful in this branch of our Commerce, I leave to your Lordship's consideration, who know so [197] well how much the health and lives of the Subjects are concerned in it, as well as the Excise on the consumption.

I have but one thing further to offer to your Lordship, and I shall quit this subject for a while; and that is, the severe Penalties that every one is liable to, who is found in the streets of this City after one a-clock at night. I am very sensible this would be very disagreeahle to a Nation like ours, that glories in the very abuse and excesses of Liberty; but whether the consequences of such a regulation amongst us, by preventing Murders, Robberies, and Debaucheries of all kinds, would not make abundant amends for the restraint, I am more in doubt than possibly your Lordship may be, when you ballance the two Evils together.

I shall take the hint from hence to turn to another subject, and shew your Lordship that though it must be owned that there are some advantages in this absolute Monarchy, which ours, as a limited one, is deprived of; yet they are so trivial and inconsiderable, in comparison of the miseries that accompany it, that they deserve not to be mentioned. Nay, if I might trouble your Lordship [198] with my small judgment in Politicks, I am of opinion, that no sensible, not to say no just and generous Man, would rather chuse to govern an Empire of Slaves, as this is, than a Nation of Subjects, as ours, merely upon the principle of ease and safety to himself, and security to his Family.

For tho' Men here are such vassals to power, that, like the *Chæroneans* in *Bæotia* of old who worshipped *Agamemnon*'s sceptre, (as made by *Vulcan* for *Jove*, and brought from Heaven by *Mercury*) they make Gods of their Rulers; yet their History shews us how often they have served their Emperors whom they worship, as the poor Heathen did his Idol that he prayed to so long in vain to ease his miseries, that at last in a rage he broke it to pieces.

As on every little ill-success or ill-humour of the People, the heads of the Bassas are made a sacrifice to them, so on all greater misfortunes or misconduct abroad, we see how insolently and violently the rage of the Commonality and Soldiery breaks out against the Emperors themselves. They then depose one and set up another, according as their Passions or Caprice directs them, [199] and take a full revenge for their intolerable slavery, by usurping as unjustifiable a power to themselves. How often, my Lord, since I have been Ambassador here, have I seen the worst and lowest of the People demand and obtain the heads of the wisest and the best of the Bassas, on false and ill-grounded surmises? and this with such universal fury, that one would think the vengeance of Heaven fell on these Infidels, like *Moses's* great miracle on *Pharaoh*, when the dust of the Earth was turned into Lice that swarmed every where, crawling into the Palaces of Kings, and defiling and devouring the Princes of the Land.

It is true indeed, I have sometimes known these terrible Seditions of the People occasioned by real dangers of the State, which, like the Geese in the Capitol, they have saved by their noise and clamours, when those who should have been their best watchmen slept. But they have still been attended by such dreadful consequences to their Governors, as may make their Successors tremble to consider, that the rage of their Subjects, like the authority of their Emperor, is not circumscribed and bounded [200] by settled and regular Laws, but their own wills.

A reflection which more or less there is too much ground for in all absolute Monarchies, but especially in this; and must make every wise Man chuse to govern a People, who are bound by Rules they have freely consented to, and have no temptations to break through from their own interest, than to rule over them by an absolute authority, which must ever be precarious, in proportion to the People's temptations and advantages to overturn it.

Besides, though in the hands of a good Prince the People seldom suffer by a Despotical Government; yet this Virtue will be no defence to him, if this Arms prove unsuccessful abroad, or his Administration by unforeseen accidents prove unfortunate at home; neither of which opportunities are often neglected by his opprest Subjects, or left unrevenged by Civil Wars or Insurrections, which seldom end but in his ruin, or his Ministers.

Whoever looks into the History of this Empire, will be convinced by numberless instances of these truths, and will find in *them*, arguments sufficient to convince the [201] most absolute Princes, that they would be happier in a more limited Government, and make them not only privately debate, like *Augustus*, how to moderate their tyranny, but publickly set on foot so noble and generous a design. I am persuaded, were the Grand Seignior to travel over, as a private person, the wide depopulated Wastes of his Provinces, and with his own eyes behold the Cruelty, Extortion, Oppression, and Injustice, which, under the cover of his authority, his

Governors, Cadies, and Officers, make use of to enrich themselves, and plunder his wretched Subjects; his good-natured and generous temper would be affected in the tenderest manner by it. But while he sits in his Palace or Camp, surrounded by his great Bassas, he must hear with their ears, and see with their eyes, whatever is offered to his consideration; and to propose the least abatements of the misery of his People, would be regarded only as undermining his power, which at present rather wants props to support it.

In all absolute Monarchies where I have been, the inhuman treatment of the subjects had ever struck me in the most shocking manner; and surely, to see Wretches, [202] whom the Prince who tyrannises over them, calls his Fellow-creatures, and sometimes his Christian Brethren, us'd with less mercy or humanity than the beasts of the field; must fill every one, who has any bowels of pity in him, with horror. Indeed the lovely climates where Tyranny has generally seated herself in the World, seem to make some amends for the misery of those who groan under the burthen of such severe task-masters. But to behold it destroying the peace and happiness of the Northern Parts of the Globe, is to see upon Earth a lively image of Hell, that is, Woe, Punishments, and Misery in the midst of an uncomfortable gloom and darkness, without the least glympse of hope from the mercy of Heaven, or the smallest relaxation from their own complaints, or the weariness of their cruel tormentors, who must share in the tortures they are made ministers of.

Many people have wonder'd how such Governments find subjects to live under them, and have generally accounted for it by the love of one's Country, which runs thro' all. But can Debtors love their Goal, or Felons their Dungeon? No certainly, my Lord; and therefore it must be accounted [203] for, partly by the care these greedy shepherds take, that as few as possible of the flock they are to fleece stray from them; and partly, from seeing few of their neighbours much easier; and lastly, from their being teather'd up by little domestick ties and relations, and by customs and languages that are used by them, and thought barbarous by others.

I am assur'd, that about fifty years since the Inhabitants of the Isle of *Scio* found out a middle way (which few I doubt will dare to imitate them in) to put an end to their slavery under the *Turks*. For having severe new Taxes laid on them, and on being unable to pay them, finding their Wives, and Friends, and Children carried away for Slaves; they all, Men and Women, bound themselves by the severest penalties to make their Commonwealth, as *Florus* speaks, *Res unius ætatis*, and to put an end to their Slavery by having no more Children. It is certain they kept up this resolution so many years, that their Masters were glad at last to prevent the utter depopulation of the place, to remove their obstinacy and despair by abolishing the new Gabels. This was certainly a degree of resentment and resolution [204] greater than ever was known in former Ages, and infinitely beyond the generous Fury of the people of *Saguntum* the *Roman* Colony in *Spain*. For they only burnt themselves, their Wives, Children, and Wealth, rather than be taken and enslav'd by their Enemies; but these calmly and deliberately persisted in cutting off all their Race, and delivering themselves without violence or rage in a calm, quiet and regular method, from an insupportable Tyranny, which at last they conquer'd by a noble Despair.

But it is time I should take your Lordship from such disagreeable Scenes of the misery of these States, to acquaint you with the happiness of a Commonwealth, which, next to your native Kingdom, you love above all others; and that is, the Commonwealth of Learning. It is with the highest pleasure I send you two of the noblest Manuscripts which possibly the Spoils of the East or Western World could furnish me with, and which our Royal Master's generous allowance for searching out and buying up all choice Manuscripts throughout this Empire, has enabled me to lay now at his feet, through your Lordship's hands.

[205] They are both in *Arabick*, and as far as I can judge with my little skill in that language, wrote in a good style, tho' probably in the tenth Century. They are perfect and tolerably well preserv'd, though such Treasures deserv'd infinitely greater care. The first and smallest is a Translation of several of *Cicero's Tusculan* Questions, which we have already; and those two invaluable Books of his *De Gloria*, the original of which was preserve'd, as *Paulus Manutius* and several Authors tell us, till the sixteenth Century, in the Library of *Bernard Justiniani*; and probably stolen from thence by *Alcyonius* the Physician, who is said to have destroy'd them, and inserted a great many passages out of them in this Treatise *De Exilio*. If I had the good fortune to have *Alcyonius's* Work here, I could soon inform your Lordship if the Physician was indeed the Plagiary he was suspected to be: but as I want that Treatise, I must leave that disquisition to your Lordship's care.

Besides this, there is at the end of the Manuscript a Treatise of his *De Vita beata*, that seems admirable in its kind, but 'tis imperfect. I should regret this as a great loss, if the joy of recovering the rest allow'd [206] me; where tho' his admirable Style is still wanting, yet his manner of handling these noble Subjects, and the Reasonings and Images he adorns them with, is still preserv'd, and now happily restor'd to us.

But I hasten to the other larger and in my poor judgment a more desirable Treasure; which is a fine *Arabick* Translation, by one who calls himself *Abumepha Nezan Ali*, of that noble Historian *Trogus Pompeius*, who writ the History of the World in forty-four Books, in so elegant and admirable a style and manner, under *Augustus*. Your Lordship well knows, that this admirable Work was mangled and epitomis'd by *Justin*, and how that wretched Abbreviation occasion'd the loss of his noble performance; like *Pharaoh's* lean kine devouring the fat and well-favour'd ones of their own fort. The Translation seems well perform'd, and has some good Notes added to it, and seems to have been wrote in the ninth, or at least in the beginning of the following Century, by the hand and style, which answers that Age. I have look'd over it carefully, with what little judgment I have in such things, and cannot without indignation observe what Treasures of Antiquity [207] and History, as well as Geography; and what material Passages and Actions, untouch'd by all other Writers but the learned and judicious *Trogus*, his poor end unskilful Abbreviator has ignorantly and carelessly pass'd over unmention'd. This excellent and admirable Person, to whom History and the learned World were so much indebted (tho' they so ill repaid the debt, by suffering him to perish) was, as he tells us in his forty-fourth Book, a noble *Roman*, originally descended of the *Vocontii* in the *Narbon Gaul*, and whose Grandfather of the same name was declar'd a *Roman* Citizen by *Pompey* the Great in the *Sertorian* War. His Uncle commanded a Squadron of Horse in the War against *Mithridates* under the same General, and his Father serv'd under *Caius Julius Cæsar*, both as a Commander and his chief Secretary of State and War. Judge, my Lord, with what transport of heart I send you this incomparable Author, to be restored by you and our Royal Master's cares to the Commonwealth of Learning, which has too long mourn'd for his loss.

I beseech your giving the strictest orders to some able hand, to have him translated [208] into an excellent *Latin* Style; tho' it will be impossible to equal that of his own inimitable Elegance, which we have lost for ever.

I must in justice to the care and judicious conduct of Mr. *West*, who carries this and them, acknowledge, that 'tis to his industrious and unwearied labours, next to his Majesty's bounty, that we are indebted for the recovery of this invaluable Jewel. He found it, and the Tracts of *Cicero*, cover'd with dust and moldiness in the *Armenian* Monastery at *Etchmeasin* near *Rivan* in *Persia*: and on this and many other accounts I zealously recommend him to your Lordship's favour.

He assures me, Mr. *Pearson* is still in that Country on the same account; and gives me hopes we may yet be able to retrieve some other valuable Authors, among the old *Arabick* and *Persian* Manuscripts that lie dispers'd in the neglected Libraries of many Monasteries there, and in the Eastern Countries.

Will your Lordship forgive me, if I encrease the length of this tedious dispatch, by accompanying these ancient rarities with a modern one, that was perfectly so to me, [209] tho' I have so long resided here, and which I met the other day at a Cady's house in *Pera*, where I went on some business.

It was a Man of the famous *African* Sect of *Mahomeians* that are called *Bumicilli*, of whom I had heard so much from common report, and the Writings of Travellers, without every meeting one of them before. They set up for a very religious sort of people, who have a knowledge of, and conversation with aerial Beings, and are engag'd in perpetual war with the

Devils, who are still ranging about the Earth and the Air, in order to tempt and hurt Mankind by all the arts and methods they can contrive.

However, it is certain these Gentlemen of the *Bumicilli* Sect are at bottom but a sort of vagrant thieves, who go round this vast Empire under this pretence, and either beg or steal all the pence they can from the deluded people. I am assur'd they have by these means greatly enrich'd themselves, and their Society; who have by such collections thus gather'd, founded great Convents, and got large Possessions, to enable them to continue their constant wars with all wicked Spirits with vigour and success.

[210] Methinks, my Lord, one may see here, with half an eye, a perfect picture of that illustrious religious Society, who owe their rise to the holy *Loyola*, and who profess all kinds of labour and toil, both as Exorcists, to drive out evil Spirits, and to extirpate imaginary Heresies and Hereticks, and defeat all such emissaries of the Devil, who distract their infallible Church.

I saw this Creature from my window in the street, laying manfully about him with all his might, (for he was a tall strong black fellow) and beating the air like a Bedlamite, with a long Pike he brandished about his head, and frequently push's most furiously with; traversing his ground, now running forwards and shouting, and then giving back, and appearing sorely hurt; and anon, recovering himself, and seeming to fall anew on his foes. The people of the house told me he was a most holy Man, and had defeated all the Devils in that neighbourhood so fortunately, that they liv'd much happier and holier than formerly; and that it had cost them very little money for so great advantages. I found my self obliged to give them a paient hearing; and especially seeing all the teople [211] in the street seem'd to be of their mind, by the zeal and joy they shewed whenever their heroick Combatant appear'd to get the better of the imaginary and invisible Devil he was engag'd with: for I need not assure your Lordship, that whether he apprehended being oppress'd with numbers, or having foul play shewn him, or other reasons best known to himself, the Devil was so cowardly as never once to let himself be seen by us, who were gazing on this furious engagement.

After I had look'd on this fine battle, with equal amazement and delight, near a quarter of an hour by my watch, I saw our Warriour, to the great concern and trouble of all his religious Spectators, fall down on the earth as in a swoon. There he lay a long time, and the Cady, in whose house I was, being a very zealous and sincere Mussulman, ran out into the Street, with tears in his eyes, and with all the concern and care imaginable had him brought in. He made him be laid gently on a Sofa in the room where I was, and had two or three Slaves, sometimes throwing cold water on his face, and sometimes rubbing his limbs, and endeavouring to bring him to life.

[212] As sensible as I was that it would displease, I could not help asking the Cady in the ear, if it was possible he could think all this any thing but a meer cheat to get money from them; and indeed all the people before our faces (as the custom is on these occasions) had put money into the Combatant's bag which hung at his back. Notwithstanding all this, he lift up his hands and eyes at my infidelity, reproach'd me with our credulity as to miracles in *Europe*, and our false Church, tho' we would believe none in the true one; and to convince me of my mistake, and open my blind eyes (for so he call'd them with some fury) he made the slaves pull off the wretch's clothes, and shew me the black-and-blue marks he had receiv'd in the combat, and which appear'd plentifully all over his arms, back, and sides.

The truth is, tho' I well knew, and had been told, that their way is to make such marks by cords, and actual blows they give themselves in the night-time, in order to impose on the croud; yet finding the good Cady so violent, I was oblig'd to seem amazed and convinc'd, and to give my assent to a number of stories they told me of the [213] battles this holy Man had fought with unparallel'd success with a great many Devils, to the peace and comfort of all true Mussulmen in those parts. I was even under a necessity to applaud his courage and sanctity as the rest did; and at last, when they had recover'd their Warriour out of his counterfeit swoon, I very humbly sat down, and eat and drank with him and the Cady, listning attentively to his accounts of his long warfare with different Dæmons, and to shew my firm faith in all he related, and entirely appease the Cady, I gave him a Zequin for his further encouragement in so useful a method of serving his Prophet, and the good Mussulmen in *Turkey*.

Was this a wonderful scene or no, my Lord? and is there not matter here for fine reflections? However, my Lord, I shall cut them short, having so long trespass'd on your patience already, and shall leave you to make your own remarks on the wretched impostures, and the silly credulity of that noble, that wise, that rational creature Man!

I expect in some little time to be summon'd to the Seraglio to shew the Grand Seignior your admirable Telescope, of which, probably, I may give your Lordship some [214] account in my next; and in the mean time I must acquaint your Lordship, that I find two or three packs of some of our best deepmouth'd southern Hounds would be a most acceptable present to his Highness. If you would procure some able and skilful Physician to come and attend the Grand Seignior, I am empower'd to assure him of 30 Purses at least (or 15,000 Ducats) besides Presents, with all possible good treatment, and to be *Hachîm Bachi* or chief Physician. As this I find would be a most agreeable Obligation, I recommend it to your Lordship's care to procure such an one: and indeed the favour and complaisance that has been shewn to his Majesty's desires in our late Treaty, deserve all the returns we can make them.

I reserve my Compliments for another opportunity, and, if I may say so, for another sort of Man than your Lordship; to whom, and all your excellent Family, I and mine are,

My Lord, your Lordship's, &c

Stanhope.

[215] Preface
the Second.

It is not without a mixture of shame and sorrow, my dear Reader, that I am forced to take thee from the delightful Entertainment which thou hast been tasting in these admirable Letters, and the amazing Scenes of Futurity discover'd in them; to return to so insipid an employment, as my answering all objections against this Work. But there is no help for it; and since the World (as some ill Paymasters serve their Workmen) loves rather to rail at the performance and skill, of the wise Authors who labour for its service, than to pay them their wages; I must do my best to answer all its Accusations and Cavils.

[216] I shall not expostulate here against the ingratitude of such treatment. I shall take a nobler revenge, than upbraiding or reproaching them for it: and that is, by shewing the Folly, Stupidity, and Ignorance of all they are able to urge against me! Against me, did I say? against that exalted Spirit, that seraphick immortal Being from whom I receiv'd it!

The first Objection then, and which I find most insisted on, is, That there are no such Beings assign'd to attend Mankind, as good or bad Angels or Genii; and that therefore all I have said on that subject, must be meer Invention, that I may not use so vile a word as Falshood.

These Objectors are very violent, but altogether as blind and ignorant; and I may say of them as *Momus* did of the Bull, that he was a stout pusher, but he wanted an Eye in his horn, it being his way to shut his Eyes when he pushes, as one would think these poor people do.

For it has been the common opinion of all Nations, of all Religions, of all Ages, that every Man had a good Angel attending him. 'Tis true indeed, we must except a little Sect among the *Jews*, from this general [217] account: but till we are in danger of becoming a Nation of *Sadduces*, I hope we shall have little regard for their Error. All the *Pharisees* in the ancient *Jewish* Church, who were follow'd by infinitely the largest, and wisest part of that people, did not only maintain the existence of Angels, but many of them believed every Man had two assign'd him, the one good to protect him, the other bad to record his faults, and be his accuser. Nay, some of their Doctors made these Angels to resemble exactly those whom they thus attended; and asserted, that as it was *Esau*'s Angel, who wrestled with *Jacob*, it was for fear of being known, that he would fain have persuaded *Jacob* from keeping him till the morning, which however he could not succeed in, and so was discovered by the Patriarch.

Some of them carried this point so far, that I can produce proofs from their best Authors, (however some *Rabbies* may deny it) that they used to pray on all occasions, to their guardian Angels to protect them; and applied to them to this end, even in the very act of relieving Nature:* a time when [218] in every one's opinion, but *Thomas d'Aquinas*'s, the body is too much taken up, to leave room for pious Meditations, or Ejaculations of any kind, unless in case of painful costiveness, or violent fluxes.

The very *Turks* and *Persians*, and all the Heathens that overspread the Eastern parts of the Earth, acknowledge this great Truth; and tho' they shut their eyes against some of more importance, yet are asham'd to deny one so glaring and manifest as this; and surely my Adversaries will not have us shew ourselves greater Infidels than these, let things go ever so ill with some conceited Men among us as to believing. Nay, the *Mahometans* do not only allow two Angels to Men, to attend on them during their Lives, but even after their Deaths, they assign to each wicked person two black Angels, whom they call *Mongir* and *Guavequir*, to sit by him in his Grave, and torment him there till the Day of Judgment; or if good, two white Angels, one of which lays its arm under his head, and the other sits at his feet, and so protect him most quietly, till Domesday discharges these trusty Watchmen. It is true, we should not build too much on the *Turks* opinion herein, [219] the good *Mahomet* having been so very liberal of his Dæmons, as to assign an evil Angel, (a matter of Faith to all his Followers) to every single Grape. But tho' he may have overstrain'd that point a little, yet still he has but followed the general opinion of Mankind: for many Nations in different parts of the Earth, do not only allow Angels to Men, but even to the four Seasons of the Year, the four Gates of Heaven, the four Quarters of the World, the four Rivers of Paradise, the four Winds, the seven Planets, the twelve Months of the Year, the four Elements, the twelve Signs of the *Zodiack*, and the twenty-eight Mansions of the Moon. To the very Days of the Week, and every particular Hour of the Day and Night, they assigned a presiding Angel, as these ignorant Objectors might read (if they could read such things) in all occult Astrologers, and great Philosophers; and particularly in the *Elementa Magica* of † *Petrus*

---

* Vide *Ceremonies of a'l Nations, for those of the* Jews *Prayers.*

† *Apud Corn. Agrip de occulta Philosoph.* p. 342. Edit. *Lyons.*

de Abano, where their names are specified, and joined regularly to their several Offices.

Certainly therefore, as almost all the known Nations of the Earth, not excepting [220] the Atheists of *China* and *Siam*, have maintained this opinion, I might, had I wanted stronger proofs, fairly insist that it must be true; and lay it down as no ill axiom for these sceptical doubters, *Quod præscriptione valet, ratione valet*. But I shall argue more fairly with them, and shall undertake to shew them, first, that the learned Heathens, and some great Rabbies; and secondly, that many of the Fathers, and all the *Roman*, and truly Catholick Infallible Church, have ever maintained this doctrine; and shall give some known instances from learned Writers in both.

Among the first, both *Homer* in several places of his *Iliad* and *Odyssea*, and *Hesiod*, in his *Moral Poem*, appear plainly of this opinion; and the latter has even assigned the number of good Angels,* appointed to attend Mankind. In the little that we have of the Works of *Menander*, there is a full proof that he gave into the same sentiments; for in one of his fragments he asserts, that every one from his birth has a particular Dæmon assigned to take care of him. *Pythagoras*, who dogmatized in the sixtieth Olympiad, and whose school lasted to the [221] nineteenth generation; and *Plato*, who flourished above thirty Olympiads after him, (as *Diogenes Laertius* tells us†) and all their Disciples taught this; and especially among the *Platonists*, *Maximus Tyrius*, *Plotinus*, and *Jamblicus*. This was also the universal doctrine of the *Stoicks*, as one might easily shew by numberless proofs; but it will be sufficient to point out *Seneca's* hundred and tenth epistle to *Lucilius*, where this is abundantly made evident: and not only that they maintained that every man had his *Genius*, but every woman her *Juno* attending on her. All the greatest *Jewish* Rabbies of the three last Centuries, treading in the steps of the learned *Porphyry*, and more ancient *Jewish* Writers, held this doctrine; and have sown it so thick in their works, that a man knows not where to begin to quote them, or where to end when he has begun. They all agreed as one Man on this head, and to this day it is generally maintained by the few among them that have any learning. To go no farther than the Patriarchs, they believe that *Adam* was often conversant with, and governed by his Angel [222] *Raziel*; *Sem* by *Jophiel*; *Abraham* by *Tzadkiel*; *Isaac* by *Raphael*; *Esau* by *Schamael*; *Jacob* by *Piel*; *Moses* by *Mitraton*; and King *David* by *Michael*; as any one may see, that will but look into their Writings relating to these matters.

Nor are the instances in ancient Writers of Men who had such *Genii*, and conversed with them sometimes, infrequent. *Hermes, Socrates, Numa, Cyrus, Scipio, Marius, Scylla, Sertorius, Julius* and *Augustus Cæsar, Julian* the Apostate, and *Apollonius Tyanæus*, are often mentioned on this occasion;

---

* Vid. Hesiodi *Opera & Dies* ad lin. 252.
† In his Lives of *Plato* and *Pythagoras*.

as well as *Aristotle, Dion, Fl. Josephus, Plotinus, Galen, Synesius, Porphyry, Jamblicus,* and even *Brutus, Cassius,* and *Cicero;* though these three last indeed, had no communication with them, till a little before their deaths. It were endless to quote all the testimonies of Authors, that these great Men were allowed to have their *Genii,* who either appeared to them, or only assisted and watched over them privately: whoever reads their Lives or Works will easily acknowledge it, and save me much needless labour. But the evidence for *Socrates* having such an one, is so universal both among the Philosophers and the [223] Fathers, that I can't but mention it particularly. Some of the latter have carried it so far as to say, that from thence he had an actual prescience of our Saviour's coming into the World, and though darkly (as *Socrates* words are very dark on it) yet he foresaw both the necessity and advantages of his appearing among Men.

As to the Philosophers, both *Plato,*[*] and even *Zenophon,*[†] who was no friend to *Plato* (and would willingly have contradicted and opposed him, had he writ a falshood) agree in this fact, and are worth a thousand other Witnesses (for *Maximum Tyrius,*[‡] *Apuleius,*[§] *Antisthenes,*[**] *Diogenes Laertius, Cicero* and *Plutarch,* all agree in it) because both of them knew him intimately, and were Men of the highest veracity and honour. Nay, this was so uncontested a fact, that *Origen* shewing the virulence and rage of calumny, in Men of bad hearts and malevolent spirits, whom no innocence can escape, nor virtue silence; adds, that such People will even make a mock of the Genius of *Socrates,* as a vain thing.

[224] Now as this is so evident, as to *Socrates,* so a few quotations of the like nature, would make it as probable, that the testimonies producible for all the rest are as well grounded; and especially, when such undeniable Facts and Authors are brought for their vouchers: all which, however, to avoid confusion and a troublesome prolixity, we shall omit, and pass to the opinion of the holy *Roman* Church, and more modern instances of this sort among men.

It has been said already, and 'tis universally known and allowed, that several of the ancient Fathers were of this opinion, and (abstracted from proofs from holy Writ, which, I will own to my adversaries, is perfectly silent here) it was indeed a natural consequence from their being generally *Platonists.* There will be no need therefore, of appealing to quotations from their works, on this head; and for the same reason I shall pass by the Schoolmen, many of whom are so clear on this point; and content myself to shew, that some modern Divines and Philosophers have not deserted

---

[*] *Plato de factis & dictis Socratis in Theage.*
[†] *Lib. 4to memorabilium & alibi.*
[‡] *De Deo Socratis.*
[§] *De Deo Socratis.*
[**] *In vita Socratis.*

the Fathers here, but rather have gone as much beyond them, as truth and prudence could possibly allow them.

[225] Let us begin then (without mentioning *Kircher's* good Genius, who carried him through the Planets in his *Iter Extaticum*) with that grave and wonderful writer, the excellent *Franciscus Albertinus*. I shall introduce this Author first, both as he is a Jesuit, and on that account alone deserves to precede all others; and because in his admirable Treatise *de Angelo Custode*,* he has, on evident reasons, though too tedious to insert, peremptorily determined, that every Church, Temple, Monastery, and Family, as well as every Man, is allowed a Guardian Angel, not excepting even Antichrist himself, which, says he, is to keep him from doing greater mischief. Nay, he does not only assure us, on his own unexceptionable credit that the number of Archangels is greater than that of Angels, and that the crowd of these last, exceeds that of all Mankind: but to put it out of any possibility of being ever contested again, he has irrefragably proved it by a divine Revelation made to St. *Bridget*, whose words he quotes, *viz.* That if all Men that have been born since *Adam*, to the last Man that [226] shall be born in the very end of the World, should be computed, there would be found more than ten Angels for every single Man.

I will not urge here that all this wise and venerable Order, are so far from doubting of this great Truth, that they and their whole Church pray to them daily; (*Paul* the fifth having published *Officium Angeli Custodis*, with the Prayers to them) because my ill-natured Opposers may say, they pray to a number of Saints who never had, and who they know, as well as Mons. *Launoie*, never had a being. But I hope I may fairly insist on it, as a good proof, that the Jesuit *Schottus* must have believed their Existence, otherwise he had never dedicated his Book of Mathematicks to his Tutelar Angel, so solemnly as he did: for however a wise and learned Jesuit may pray, he would never dedicate his Writings (I speak as an Author) but to a real Being, from whose influence he might receive benefit and advantage.

But let us pass from these great Men, and their sacred Order, whose probity, humility, and piety, I ever honoured, to the learned *Cornelius Agrippa*; who in his third book *De occulta Philosophia*, and the [227] twentieth chapter, declares, that no Prince or Nobleman could be safe, or Woman chaste, or Man in this Vale of ignorance (so he speaks) able to serve God, but for the assistance of their good Angel. That great Divine *Bartholomæus de Sybilla*,[†] goes yet farther, and avers, a good Angel is assigned to every one of us, from the moment we peep into the World; because, as he wisely and judiciously observes, the minute we are in danger of sinning, the care of the good Angel is necessary to defend us from the

---

* Printed at *Cologne*, 1613.
† *Peregrinarum Quæst.* p. 436.

assaults of Satan; and that till we are born, we are sufficiently watched over by our mother's good Angel.

In another treatise,[*] he is so modest as to except our Saviour from this general rule, and determines that he had no guardian Angel: and though he proposes it as debateable, he gravely and learnedly maintains it, against all opposers, and overturns a seeming objection, of the Angel that appeared to him in the Garden, and shews that it was but a ministring Spirit, and not a guardian Angel: which last thought, as odd as it looks, was the opinion of no less [228] a man than St. *Jerome*. As the Devil when exorcised will sometimes witness to the Truth, so even one of the greatest Hereticks that ever appeared in the pulpit in *Great-Britain*, is forc'd to maintain the doctrine of good Angels very strenuously, in his sermon on the Feast of St. *Michael* the Archangel;[†] though he does not carry it so far, as that eminent writer *Joannes Eckius*[‡] does, in his seventh homily on the same festival. Indeed many grave Doctors of the holy and infallible Church of *Rome*, have ventured to assign to Men in high and publick Stations, not only an Angel, but an Archangel; and to the Pope, besides his Angel in ordinary, which he had a full title to from his birth, a couple of prime Archangels, to assist and direct him, having all of them enough to do, to keep him and his important affairs in tolerable order. And really to say the truth, I cannot but think these tutelar Angels of his Holiness, must be wearied out of their very lives, by such a vast variety of business, and a multiplicity of Intrigues, Designs, and Interests, as they must have daily on their hands, [229] for the good of mens Souls, and the service of the Church. Possibly indeed the two Angels, whom *Lactantius*,[§] with some ancient Fathers, asserts, God appointed to watch over Satan, might save them some trouble, and make their Province less burthensome to them. But the good *Eckius* is so bounteous of these spiritual Guardians, that he declares in that Homily, a Man of consequence may sometimes be allowed thirty or more Angels; and that he cannot think his Imperial Majesty (for whom he has a mighty regard) ought reasonably to be allowed less, his great cares and employments considered, than a single Angel for every Kingdom, Dukedom, or Province, over which he presides.

One would think the *Germans* were either flattered extremely by the Divines in this point, or supposed to have more enemies below, or friends above, than all other Nations, since they are more than the rest indulged in this affair by them. Nay the learned *Carlo Fabri*[**] has been also so careful of their interests, as to give us in the list of the Angels assigned to the several

---

[*] *De Angelorum Custodia.*
[†] Vid. *Tillotson*'s Sermons. vol. 3.
[‡] Vide *Ekium in dicto locol.*
[§] Vide *Lactantium*, lib. 2. chap. 15.
[**] *Carlo Fabri dello Scudo di Christo o vero di David.* lib. 2.

[230] Princes of the World, those who watcht over the seven Electors of the Empire, when he writ. He assures us, that the Angel *Michael* waited on the Archbishop of *Mayence*; *Gabriel* on the Archbishop of *Treves*; *Raphael* on the Archbishop of *Cologne*; the Angel *Uriel* on the Count Palatine of the *Rhine*; *Secaltiel* on the Duke of *Saxony*; *Jehudiel* on the Elector of *Brandenburgh*; and the Angel *Farechiel* on the King of *Bohemia*.

It is certainly an huge pity this same *Carlo Fabri*'s knowledge did not look forwards into future Ages, since by this means he gives us no account of the two Electorates of *Hannover* and *Bavaria*; so that unless Providence has issued new orders about them, they must be unluckily left destitute, of the care and superintendance of any good Angels; and must therefore necessarily cost his *Britannick* Majesty, and his said Electoral Highness, abundance of more Pains, Money, Troops, and Counsellors, to manage them, than any of the other seven can want, that have such preternatural assistances to aid them.

But as this is fully sufficient to shew, that the holy and infallible *Roman* Church declares [231] entirely for the opinion we have been defending, I shall not weary the Reader by quoting more Authors; and shall only name a few eminent Persons among the Moderns, who have been allowed to have had an intercourse with their Genii, as well as the Ancients.

And here I can't but begin with that famous Physician and Astrologer *Peter D'Apono*, because he had no less than seven entirely in his service, which also taught him the seven liberal Arts, as *Ludovicus Wigius** tells us. We shall place *Cardan*,[†] and *Scaliger*, those two great rivals, next to him, though they are both so modest as to own they had but one a-piece; which is the more humble in *Cardan*, because even his father *Facius*, as the son assures us,[‡] had one, which he conversed with about thirty years. *Boissard*, in his book *De Divinatione*,[§] tells us at large, that the renowned *Trithemius*, Abbot of St. *James*'s Monastery, had several Revelations and important Discoveries made to him by his good Angel; and [232] *Froissard*,[**] the Historian assures us, Count *Raimond* of *Gascony*, had a constant communication with his Genius, who informed him of all occurrences, and frequently gave him his advice, as to his conduct concerning them.

To these Gentlemen, besides *Paracelsus*, who 'tis disputable whether he had a Dæmon attending him, or was one himself, every one will agree to join the illustrious *Tasso*; who as his intimate friend *Baptista Manso*,[††] the Author of his Life assures us, (being a witness of one of his conversations

---

* *Dæmonologia*, Quæst. 16.
† *Cardan de vita propria.*
‡ *De rerum varietate*, lib. 16. p. 221.
§ P. 49, and 50.
** *Froissard Annal.* lib. 3. cap. 17.
†† See *Tasso*'s Life by *Manso* in *Italian*, and in *French* by D.C.D.D.T

with it) frequently had a communication with his good Genius. *Bodin* (to say nothing of his anonymous friend, of whom he gives the same account) is another instance among the Moderns of this sort; though *Guy Patin*[*] seems to insinuate, his conversation with his Guardian Angel went little farther than such hints as were lent him, by the chairs and stools in his room being moved by an imperceptible hand, whenever any thing was proposed to him that he ought not to agree to.

[233] But to omit many other Foreigners, who have been famous on this account, we might find several instances of the same nature among our own People, if the modesty of some Families, who would be offended to be named on this occasion, did not confine us to those which are already publick. Among these, the Manuscripts of the reverend Dr. *Richard Nepier* (with which Mr. *Ashmole* has wisely enriched the *Musæum* at *Oxford*) are plain evidences of his frequent conversation with his Angel *Raphael*, whose answers he has there regularly set down, not only as to several polemical points in Divinity, but (as he was a Physician as well as a Divine) as to his Patients and Prescriptions, their Diseases, and Cures.

This was an intercourse extraordinary enough, and yet it falls very short of that which another of our Countrymen, Dr. *Dee*, (the great Mathematician and Astrologer) is known to have had with his aërial Spirit: as Dr. *Meric Casaubon*, has with equal labour and zeal shewn, in his dissertation and preface before his large folio,[†] entitled, *A true relation of Dr.* Dee *his actions with* [234] *Spirits*; to which I would gladly refer the Reader.

With these evident instances therefore, I shall shut up this matter; and though I could name some great Men at Court, who it is impossible could have our hearts and affections so entirely devoted to them, if they had not more good Angels at their command than any I have yet named: yet being loth to insist too far on this point, and having sufficiently made good already, what I undertook to prove against my adversaries, I shall venture to leave it to the Reader's serious consideration; who I doubt not is fully convinced of the absurdity of this objection, that there are no such Beings as good Angels assigned to Men.

But were this less clearly proved, let me ask thee, dear Reader, what motives, what considerations, what reasons, could move me to say, I received this work from my good Genius? Would it not be much more to my honour, to foretell all these things (which will certainly in due time be verified) by the force of my own Learning, and Wisdom, and a happy Foresight into future events? Would it not be more glorious to my memory, that all Posterity should speak [235] of me in future Centuries, (when they see, with astonishment, the verification of all I have here

---

* *Patiniana*, p. 6.
† *London* Edit. 1659.

presented to them) as *Nepos* does of *Cicero*,[*] *Sic enim omnia de studiis Principum, vitiis Ducum, ac mutationibus Reipublicæ perscripta sunt, ut nihil in his non appareat; & facile existimari possit, prudentiam quodammodo esse divinationem: Non enim Cicero ea solum, quæ vivo se acciderunt, futura prædixit; sed etiam quæ nunc usu veniunt, cecinit ut vates?* Would it not endear me infinitely more to After-ages, that I was the original Inventor and Author of this new and unexampled way of writing the History of future Times, than that I was the bare Transcriber, or Translator of this prodigious work? Yes surely, and consequently nothing occasions this honest plain-dealing, and this ingenuous, this modest confession, but the infinite weight which humility and gratitude ought to have with all Men.

I am sensible the World has indeed been too frequently imposed on in these Matters. *Lycurgus* pretended his Laws were dictated to him by *Apollo*; *Draco*, and *Solon*, by *Minerva*; *Charondas*, by *Saturn*; and *Minos* [236], that his come from *Jupiter*, with whom he convers'd familiarly, nine years together, which was a pretty long Dialogue, for a Mortal to hold with a God. *Zaleucus* ascrib'd his Laws to *Minerva*'s Revelations; and *Numa* pretended to owe his to his close and intimate Conversations with the Goddess *Ægeria*, which he had with her in the Night-time; a very suspicious hour for her communicating such Favours in! But these were the little Arts and Contrivances of Governours of the People, set on fire with a poor ambition, of enlarging their power; whereas all I propose to publish, are a few naked Facts, which if they bring me any honour, when confirm'd by the event, I disclaim, as not belonging to me; and the disgrace of which, if falsified by time, I must entirely bear with Posterity, without any advantage at the present, but what I can reap from the envy and malice of an ungrateful Age.

Besides, what is it I set up for? I pretend not to entertain such hopes, from any correspondence with my good Genius, as *Kepler* did on *Tycho Brahe*'s death, that nothing new should happen in the Heavens, unknown to him! No! all I pretend to, is [237] to be the bare Publisher of just so much and no more, as he has been or shall be pleas'd to communicate to me: and if I do this candidly and sincerely, without obtruding any vain Fancies of my own on the world, I hope the least I can expect in return, is to be absolutely trusted and believed, in what I put into their hands. And indeed it would have requir'd such an unusual Fund of Imagination, to have struck out so many vast Inventions in all Arts and Sciences, and such infinite Scenes of Events, as are contain'd in the six Volumes I propose to present the world with; that I am sure this will serve as the fullest proof, (and a very modest and humble one) that I must have receiv'd them from the hand of a superior Being, since my talent that way, is so very confin'd.

---

[*] *Nepos in vita Attici.*

But this will be still further enforc'd, when my dear Reader perceives, that he finds so little in this Work, which ever was contain'd in Books and Authors, as being a subject entirely untouch'd and unthought of by mortal Man; and consequently he'll plainly discern things in every part of it, too transcendent for the little narrow roads and beaten, paths of such low groveling Creatures as I am; and only fit to be the produce of [238] that enlightned Mind, whence I fortunately receiv'd it.

But I hasten to another malicious Objection urg'd against this Work, which is, that allowing my Communication with my good Genius, it is impossible that he, or any such Being, could be able to foretell Events, which are so contingent and uncertain. But this Objection is very ill grounded; for first, it is against Matter of Fact, both in our own days and in ancient times: secondly, against the opinion of the holy and infallible Church of *Rome*: and thirdly, against Reason.

It is against Fact, even in our days; for, not to mention several uncontested proofs of the like nature in *Lapland*, the *East* and *West-Indies*, and many foreign Countries, we see at home here how common it is in *Wales*, to have the Death of particular persons evidently foretold, as well as the place of their departure and burial, by the means of those surprizing Apparitions, call'd Dead Men's Candles; which are as frequently seen walking their rounds in that Country, as our Watchmen are with their Lanthorns every night in *London*. Nay, we find in the Western Isles of *Scotland*, by the assistance of such aërial Spirits, not only Men [239] and Women, but even Children foretell things to come, with the greatest certainty; nothing being so universally known and practised there, as the learned Mr. *Martyn* has shewn the World in his History of those Islands; the veracity of which, no man has, will, shall, may, or can presume to question.

But secondly, it is against Fact in ancient times; in as much as we have the testimony of both the Historians and Philosophers, that the Oracles of the Ancients, in numberless places, for many Ages, did on all occasions, when regularly consulted, give such undisputed proofs of their sufficiency herein; that both *Greeks* and *Romans*, who were most capable of, and interested in discovering the cheat, if it had been one, entirely acquiesced in all they deliver'd; and found it still confirm'd by the Success. Nor was this perform'd only by the Heathen Priests and Priestesses, assisted by their *Dæmons*, at *Delos*, *Delphi*, *Thebes*, *Libadia*, *Milesia*, and a thousand other places; but if we believe *Callimachus* and *Pindar*, the famous brazen Bulls in *Rhodes*, on the Mountain *Æthobirius*, (probably directed and inspir'd by particular Dæmons and Spirits, like their [240] Oracles) used to give the *Rhodians* sufficient warning of all impending Evils, or remarkable Accidents.

It were easy to enlarge here, on many instances of the like nature, if there were occasion for them, and to bring in the prophetick Cow at *Memphis*, the Crocodiles at *Arsinoe*, and the Doves and Oaks at *Dodona*, mention'd by *Herodotus*; as well as the Ox *Apis* in *Ægypt*, whose oracular Faculties *Pliny*, and all the Ancients speak so much of. The *Teraphims* of the old *Chaldæns*, which used to foretell future Events to them, by the means of the informing Dæmon, is an evident proof herein, as well as their Telestick Science, which by certain Rites and Ceremonies, procured them the Conversation of their good Genii or Dæmons, at Mr. *Stanley** informs us. Even amongst the *Jews*, we see by all our accounts of them, this was a method of Divination or Prophecy, too frequently practis'd. The learned *Rabbi Kimchi* declares he believes *Laban's* Gods were of the same nature, and a kind of *Teraphims*, that by the means of their Dæmons, were endued with a prophetick Spirit.

[241] St. *Austin*† is of the same opinion, as well as our Learned *Selden* in his Tract *de Diis Syriis*; and *Philo Judæus* has the same sentiments, speaking of the *Teraphim* of *Michal* the Daughter of *Saul*. Nay, this last-cited Author does not content himself with advancing this as his opinion, but has confirm'd it in another place, by that remarkable History he has given us, of *Manachemus* the *Essæan Jew*, who he assures us foretold, by the assistance of his good Genius, that *Herod* (at that time an Infant) should become King of the *Jews*.

It was so generally known and believed among the Ancients, that all Dæmons were endow'd with this faculty, that *Homer* makes *Elpenor's* Soul in his 11th *Odyssea*, (*lin.* 69.) prophesy to *Ulysses*; and *Scipio* in *Silius Italicus*, *Tyresias* in *Statius*, *Æson* in *Valerius Flaccus*, and *Erichtho* in *Lucan*, are all introduced as consulting the Souls of the Dead on things to come.

The famous *Psellus*‡ gives us the precise manner, how they were to obtain exact Answers to their Demands from the Dæmons and Genii; and prescribes their manner of preparing the Alter, and sacrificing the [242] Stone *Mnizuris* on it, which had the power of evocation over them: all which abundantly proves, what we have asserted on this point.

Thus Fact is against my Objectors. But further, the Opinion of the holy infallible *Roman* Church is against them; which ought to silence these silly Reasoners.

All her Divines, and what is more, all learned Jesuits allow unanimously, that even evil Dæmons can foresee and foretell many things, not only as the Devil in *Samuel's* shape did, with regard to the impending Judgment of *Saul's* death, but of distant accidents, by interpreting the Prophecies in Holy Writ, more skilfully than even the Fathers, or Popes and Councils are able to do. Hence it was, say they, that the Devil foresaw *Alexander* the Great (who is darkly pointed at by *Isaiah* and *Daniel*) would conquer the World, and told him so by his Oracle at *Delphos*: and much

---

* *Vid. Stanley* of the *Chaldaick* Philosophy. *Ch.* 4, 5, *and* 6.

† St. *Austin* in *Genes.*

‡ *Psell. de Orac.*

more may we suppose Angels, and good Spirits, able to perform in the same way. Nor indeed do they only foresee the rise and fall of Empires, and who will be the instruments therein; but also what the Means, Manner and Time will be, and the [243] Causes and Consequences, and even the minuter Effects that accompany them. But if any one desires to be more fully satisfied in these matters, let him read *Eusebius de Præparatione Evangelica*,* and also St. *Austin*'s Treatise *de naturâ Dæmonum*, where they will find several reasons assign'd, for their being endow'd with such powers.

Lastly, Reason is also on my side; for as some by the advantages of greater knowledge, parts, age and experience, can see much further than other Men; as he that is placed on a heighth, has a more extended prospect and view, (especially if he has better Eyes and a sharper Sight) than he who is in the vale: since even wise Men, as the excellent *Marcus Antoninus*[†] observes, may by looking back on past times, and the changes of Empire, foresee in some measure what will happen for the future; since even the humble *Loyola*, as *Maffæus* tells us in his Life,[‡] was a remarkable instance of this kind, so much more can those spiritual Natures, who are unincumbred with bodily Organs, and have these and many [244] other advantages, to infinite degrees above us, be suppos'd to be endow'd with such powers, in proportion as they rise higher, in the unbounded Scale of celestial Beings. Who can say, what unimaginable helps they may borrow, from their intimate acquaintance, if not with the very Decrees, yet at least with the ways of Providence, (whose Agents and Ministers they frequently are, in the great Changes and Revolutions below) as well as from their perfect knowledge of the natural Byass of our Tempers, the Influence of Education and Principles, of our Humours, Appetites and Passions, and from the perpetual course of Causes and Effects, since the Creation. What assistances may they not gain, even as bare Historians, contemplating all the various Accidents of Time, lying naked and undisguis'd in one view, before their piercing Eyes; as Physicians, judging as it were of the Constitution of the World, by the feeling its pulse; or even as meer Astrologers, surveying the immense Revolutions of the celestial Planets, in their different aspects, and the wide train of consequences produced by them, in the vast rotation of Events, in this Scene of things below.

[245] But as this point is not worth insisting on further, I shall now proceed to an Objection, which gives me infinitely greater trouble, which is, (*horresco referens*) That it is entirely by my deep skill, in the worst sort of Magick, (or the Black Art, as the Vulgar speak) that I have attain'd to the amazing knowledge in Futurity, discover'd in this Work.

---

* *Lib. 6. Cap. 1.*
† *Lib. 7. Cap. 4. Gataker's Edit. with Dacier's Notes, Lond. 1697.*
‡ *Ignatii Vita per Maffæum, Lib. 3. Cap. 14.*

An Objection, which if my Adversaries themselves sincerely believ'd to be just, they would not dare to make, for fear of exposing themselves to my resentments, and that power and art they pretend I am master of; and which therefore, as I might content my self with barely denying, and they could never prove against me, so I shall only answer for the sake of Philosophy, as *Apuleius* speaks, *ut omnes apertè intelligant, nihil in Philosophos non modo vere dici, sed ne falso quidem posse confingi, quod non ex innocentiæ fiducia, quamvis liceat negare, tamen habeant potius defendere.*

I am not ignorant from what quarter this aspersion comes; and if it continues to spread, shall not fail to name my unjust Enemies, (as eminent and learned as they think themselves) to the world, and expose [246] them to the publick resentment, as wretches of a malign and envious spirit; who, like the people about Mount *Atlas*, as *Herodotus* tells us, curse the rising Sun, for the prodigious heat and splendour he lends them.

I well know the only grounds they go on, next to their envying the little Learning and Glory, which has fallen to my lot; and as *Furius Cresinius*, when accus'd at *Rome* of having by Magick drawn away the richness and fertility of his Neighbours Farms to his own, clear'd himself by bringing into Court his Rakes, and Spades, and Plows, which alone produced his large Crops; so I hope my sincere confession of the Celestial Source, to which only I owe this knowledge of Futurity discover'd here, will suffi-ciently overturn this wicked Objection, tho' I did not frankly lay before the Reader, as I am resolv'd to do, all that the malice of Men or Devils can contrive to urge against me on this head.

It is certain then, that in my retirement in *Yorkshire*, I did read the more innocent branches of Magick, and apply'd my self much to understand thoroughly all the mysterious Arts of Divination, practis'd by [247] the Ancients; and that I am in some degree skill'd in the *Anthropomantia*, or divining of Men, the *Cyathomantia* and *Oinomantia* by Cups and Wine, the *Chiromantia* by the Lines of the Hand or Palmistry, the *Arithmantia* or divining by Figures, the celestial *Astrologia* by the Stars, the *Cleidomantia* or Bible and Key, the *Stichomantia* by different kind of Verses; besides the useful Art of *Physiognomia* and *Metoposcopia*, by the mien and persons of Men: all which indeed I was not meanly vers'd in.

I got also a thorough insight in the *Gastromantia* or divining by the Belly, the *Hippomantia* by Horses, and especially Hunters, Race and Coach-Horses; the *Rabdomantia* by the Rods or White Staves, much used at Court, where I both taught and practised it, as many Great Men* can vouch for me; and which I think fully as valuable, the *Coskinomantia* [248]

---

* I appeal to my very good Lord the Earl of *R–*, my Lord *C–*, my Lord *L–*, and my Lord *G–* for the Truth of this Fact; and am content to let the Credit of this Work entirely depend on the report their Lordships, in their great Judgment and Goodness, shall give of my Abilities herein.

or Art of managing the Sieve and Sheers. I made also some moderate progress in the famous *Cubomantia* or *Aleatoria*, the Art of divining by the Dye, a Mystery which if well understood would prevent numbers of our Gentry and Nobility being daily stript and plunder'd with impunity, by those judicious and sagacious mortals, the Knights of the Industry; not to mention the *Copromantia*, as the *Greeks* call it, or in plain *English*, the Art of divining from the Dung of Creatures; a matter I wish from my soul, the sage inspectors of our Close-Stools, were a little better skill'd in, than our Weekly Bills of Mortality shew they are.

My Knowledge and Practice in these things, made a little too much noise; especially among the poor party I was then engag'd in, and who had little else to trust to, but a few monthly Predictions I dispers'd for them, and some good Prognostications once a year, from *Rome* and *Bologna*: But that my Skill, even in these little Outlines of Magick, went any further, than helping people to stolen Goods, calculating Nativities, or giving some small helps to Almanack-makers, as to Wind and Weather, and predicting a little Treason now and then, from a few Eclipses, Sextiles, Trines, Oppositions, and Conjunctions of the Planets, [249] pursuant to the Configurations of the celestial Bodies, and their mutual Radiations, or in the least border'd upon the infernal Branches of Magick, (which I renounce and abhor) I utterly deny.

There is nothing I do abominate more, or hold in greater detestation, than all evil magical Arts: and tho' I know the great *Hermolaus Barbarus* rais'd the Devil, to consult him, on the meaning of *Aristotle*'s unintelligible term, Εντελεχεια; and that the learned Jesuit *Cotton* had him examin'd, at the famous Exorcism at *Loudun* in *France*, on several abstruse points in Divinity; yet I must own, I cannot even think of such practices, but with the greatest abhorrence.

Far be it from me therefore, to deserve such horrid Imputations, as my envious Maligners would gladly throw on me: and if by any extraordinary insight into these deeper Mysteries of Divination, used by the learned Ancients, I have heedlessly given some seeming grounds for this malevolent Accusation, I hope this candid confession will largely attone for it, and set me right in the opinion of this honest and scrupulous Age. It has too often been the fate of the greatest Names of Antiquity for Virtue [250] and Knowledge, as *Naudæus* shews us, to be blasted with this vile and gross aspersion: and if such divine Persons (*Heroës celeberrimi nati melioribus annis*) could not escape it, I may the better despise this invidious Objection, in these evil days into which I am fallen; and possibly the next Generation may join my name with those illustrious Personages he has defended, in some future Edition of that learned *Frenchman*'s Apology.

There is another Objection, somewhat allied to this, which I shall now go on to consider: and that is, an Insinuation some people have whisper'd about, as tho' I borrow'd all the vast Scenes of future Events, from my understanding thoroughly the Celestial Alphabet, which many of the greatest Rabbies assure us* is wrote by the divine Finger of the Creator in the Stars, plac'd in the Heavens in *Hebrew* Characters, and which contain all the various accidents which shall ever happen below.

I am not so disingenuous to deny, that I have been very conversant with the works of several of the *Jewish* Doctors of note, as *Maimomides, Nachman, Chomer, Aben-Ezra* [251], *Kimchi, Jomtoss, Levi, Capor,* and *Abravanel,* who have strenuously maintained this opinion; and aver'd that a true Adept in this heavenly Science, may by it predict every change and revolution in Nature and Empire, in this inferiour World. I acknowledge, the learned Jesuit *William Postell,* has not only confest the truth and infallibility of this Science, but has also called his Creator, in the solemnest manner, to witness his having read in Heaven (in the Stars thus disposed in *Hebrew* Characters, which *Esdras* has given the Key of) whatever is in Nature. I confess, if that will satisfy my enemies, that *Picus,* the learned *Picus Mirandola* maintains, that several of the *Jews* hold this opinion as unquestionably true; and I own that even the illustrious Rabbi *Chomer,* embraced this Sect so far in the 17th Century, as to foretell the ruin of the *Turkish* and *Chinese* Empires from it. Indeed, the great *Origen* is justly taxed by *Sixtus Senensis,* in the sixth chapter of his *Bibliotheca,* with maintaining it; and every one knows, *Plotinus,* by thus foreseeig things, hindered *Porphyry* from killing himself: and the judicious *Flud,* whose Works I am so fond of, was [252] as deeply skilled in, and in all future accidents by it, as *Postell* himself.

Nay, that I may conceal nothing from the Reader, and as I love to bring all learned remarks as close to the eye of common observation as I can; I shall not deny but one of the most skilful and ingenious Writers of Almanacks among us, my honoured and esteemed friend Mr. *Vincent Wing,* has plainly given into the same opinion, as appears by that fine Lemma he prefixes to all his Almanacks;

> *The Heaven's a Book, the Stars are Letters fair;*
> *God is the Writer, Men the Readers are.*

But alas! does this prove that I am a follower of their Doctrines, and reduce them to practice, because I have been conversant with those Writers who hold them, and have foretold some few things by them? Is it reasonable, or indeed honest, to infer, that because I may perhaps be more than ordinarily acquainted with such Books, and have profest to esteem them, and the immense erudition of some of their Authors; that therefore I am tainted with all their opinions, and have given into the whole of [253] their Hypothesis? No, surely! and above all, since I truly

---

* *Vide Basnage's* History of the *Jews,* Book 3, ch. 25.

and sincerely aver, though I have seen and studied *Gaffarell's** Tables* of that celestial Alphabet, and his Explanation and Defence of them, yet I have not got the least assistance to this work from those Systems; and that what time soever I may have spent that way, which I candidly own has been too much, I have only been able to discover from them, that they know less of that matter than *Patridge* and *Gadbury* did, in their little way of star-gazing. Nay, I must go further, and declare that I have found such palpable errors in the whole of their Doctrines, as makes me entirely distrust and despise them; and tho' the reverence I had for the learned *Postell*, (whom still as a Jesuit I must ever honour) kept me a while in suspence about them; yet I soon abandoned both him and them, when I found him so intoxicated with Enthusiasm, that he was firmly persuaded a *Venetian* Religious, whom he calls Mother *Jane*, was sent into the World to save all Woman-kind, as every one may see in his famous Treatise (which for the sake of that blessed Order I blush to mention) called, *The most marvellous* [254] *Victories of Women*, printed at *Paris* in 12mo, in 1553.

This stumbling-block therefore, which malice would lay in my dear Reader's way, being thus happily got over, I shall proceed to mention another envious insinuation, which some, who by the indulgence of my friends perus'd this work in manuscript, have ungenerously spread against it. For, say these judicious Persons, if these Memoirs were indeed the performance of a Guardian Angel, they would carry unquestionable marks of their high Original, and the Style, and Matter, and Manner, would evidently shew something celestial in them, and above the stinted force and skill of human wisdom and learning.

It becomes not me, my dear Reader, nor that unexampled modesty I have shewn in these Prefaces, to expose the want of Taste and Judgment, that appears in this false, this groundless, this inhuman method, of attacking such a consummate performance. Let Men use me and it as they please, I am resolved to possess my Soul in patience, and smile at their malice; and especially since I know 'tis as vain and impotent, as if they laboured to tear down the Sun from Heaven [255], because their purblind eyes, dimm'd by this splendour, and unable to survey so glorious and Orb, pretend to discern a few spots in it. I shall therefore silently and quietly pass by the illiterate ignorance of such Barbarians; who thus resemble the Negroes of *Africk*, that murder all *Europeans* for the deformity of their white complections, and not coming up to the hideous standard of beauty which they have established. I shall; for my part, make no other return to the ignorance and ill-nature of such Cavillers, than my prayers for their reformation; and shall contentedly, in this matter, chuse to refer myself to the better informed Judgment and Taste of the learned World, and leave

---

* *Vid.* Gaffarell's *Curios. inaudita, c.* 12.

them to decide how unjust a surmise this is, which they bring to discredit these Papers.

This only I must say, which with all modest and candid persons, and especially all good Catholicks, must have great weight; That though there might appear some slight, some very slight grounds for this objection, yet the defects they are built on, ought to be imputed to the alterations, interpolations, omissions, disguises, or mistakes, I necessarily, or possibly a little injudiciously, have [256] been guilty of, in preparing it for the Press; and were even these faults to be imputed to my good Genius and not to me, yet I never heard it objected against the many Crucifixes and Pictures ador'd in the holy and infallible Church of *Rome*, as being made by Angels and Apostles, and such celestial hands, that they sell very short of the Works of many famous Sculptors and Painters among Men. It is enough that we are well assur'd of the Celestial Hands that produc'd them, and that single point ought in justice and modesty, to be sufficient to silence the silly criticisms and affected cavils, of such self-conceited Examiners, who could call them down to the common rules of Art and Science.

And thus having ———— But 'tis time to let the wearied Reader sleep, who when he has rested himself, may (after the delightful entertainment of the remaining Letters, and the vast scenes of future times contained in them) either read at the end of this volume what is to follow in my third Preface; or slight it and throw it by, like the fag end of a Cloth, which serves only to wrap up the rest of the piece, and preserve it from the dirt that would otherwise fall on it.

[257] My Lord,

London-Chelsea, Feb. 2. 1997

I Am ashamed to acknowledge so late, that through a load of affairs of importunate People, that engross my time and thoughts, I have so long referred you to Mr. Secretary, and am but now returning my thanks for two of yours Excellency's Letters from *Rome*, one of *November* the seventh, and another of *January* the seventeenth; for both which I am indebted to your care and goodness, beyond all possibility of repaying you.

The account you gave of your respectful and honourable reception there, is very agreeable to us in *London*; and as his Imperial Majesty's health is spoke of by the last Letters (as well as the disagreement of the Elector of *Cologne* with the Court where you are) in stronger terms than ever, I doubt not we shall manage our Negotiations so happily, as to secure the Peace of *Europe*, and defeat the astonishing ambition of the Empire of the *Vatican*.

[258] It is certain, we shall stand in need of our utmost efforts to accomplish this, because the rest of the Protestant Powers are far from being well united, through the artifices of this See ever watchful to divide us, and even buy off the venal Faith of some of them from our Communion to hers. Moreover though the Protestant Interest is greatly increased in *Europe*, and in spite of all her snares, stronger this last Century than ever; yet they are so distrusted by their jealous Neighbours, that all offers to humble the Papal Power, are but considered as attempts, to throw their Kingdoms into confusion and rebellion.

Besides, the Popish Princes have by their furious Quarrels and Wars among themselves (which this See has ever fomented) given the Pope great opportunities to raise his temporal Power, and spiritual Authority on their Weakness. Hence he has acquir'd such large accession of Subjects, Wealth, and Territory in *Italy*, that they are cow'd and over-awed by his prodigious Strength, and the interest he keeps up even in their own Kingdoms and Councils; and seem only desirous of good conditions, to become [259] as it were provincial Tetrarchs to this Lord of the Earth, and Vice-gerent of Heaven.

However, as this violent Jealousy of the Emperor, and the Scheme of introducing the Inquisition into *France*, are likely to unite us more than ever, in opposing his designs; and as our prodigious Naval Force has kept all the Islands in the hands of their old Sovereigns, and both prevented the *Venetians* being entirely swallowed up, and holds the Pope, by the means of his Sea-Coasts, Ports, and Trade, in great awe; I do not despair, but we may be able to humble his aspiring hopes.

The confirming *Civita Vecchia* a free Port, restoring all our Privileges, and declaring by his Bull that none of his Majesty's Subjects shall be liable to his Inquisitors, are great points gained, and also shew the fear he has of us, which I hope your Excellency will improve to weightier purposes.

Your accounts of the monstrous growth of this vast Empire, which has risen these two last Centuries, like a huge Mountain, from the unnatural fires and eruptions in the bowels of the Earth, have occasioned many reflections in my mind, on the blindness and folly of our Ancestors, who with [260] proper care, might have prevented the confusion and oppression this age labours under. If instead of dreading the *Bruta Fulmina* of *Rome*, they had opposed their cannon to her thunder, and instead of attacking her with a silly paper-war of Books and Writings, they had by resistance and arms contracted her power; if instead of increasing her Riches and Wealth, and loading her with the very Lands, and the Tribute, and Spoil of their Nations, they had kept her within her own bounds, humble, pious, and just; the Princes of the World, and *Italy*, had not worn her Chains, and groaned under her bondage now. We had not seen in these our days, her Armies and Forces under the command of Cardinals, and her Generals, that are Priests and Jesuits in secret at least, and *ex voto*, as they call it, haranguing her armed Troops, and turning the old word *Concio* (which signified the speech of a Commander to his Legions, to the Senate, or People, upon affairs of State or War) to its original signification again, and shewing themselves the true Sons of the old Soldier their Founder.

It is true, what our Ancestors did, proceeded from a laudable Piety; and the [261] Wealth and Possessions they poured into her lap, were paid by a sincere respect to their religion. But what has been the goodly consequence? only this, *Religio peperit divitias, & filia devoravit matrem.* The Christian Bishop has been entirely absorbed in the Temporal Prince; as the *Cæsars* of old sunk the *Pontifex Maximus* in the *Imperator*. In the mean while through a thirst to secure the Power of the latter, the holy Fathers have stuck at no Crimes or Wickedness, even of the blackest dye: And to hinder the Gates of Hell from ever prevailing against the Church, too many of her Popes, I fear, have gone thither, as eternal Hostages for her faithful alliance with it.

Your Excellency, who is so well read in her Historians before the ancient Reformation of Religion, is perfectly acquainted with many of the detestable Lives of these creatures, who stile themselves the Successors of St. *Peter*. A name they have no other title to, than that as *He* contradicted and shamefully opposed the truth, of what our blessed Saviour asserted twice, and afterwards denied him thrice; so they have ever since been acting the same part, and while they are openly renouncing him, have been violently making [262] use of the Sword, and shedding blood, under pretence of defending his cause.

I shall not rake in the filth of History, to mention to your Excellency the foulness of the Crimes, so many of them were confessedly guilty of. Your Excellency and the learned World, are but too well acquainted with them: and would to God, for the honour of Christianity, they were as fully amended as known! Indeed, since the family of the Jesuits have set up for the royal Line of this Empire, the crime of Whoredom has been less frequent among them; but they have so far excelled their Predecessors in all others, that it were to be wished we had such Popes again as *Paul* the third, *Pius* the second, and *Gregory* the eighteenth, who, with the best titles of all other to be called Fathers of the Church, were, with all their Bastards, much better Popes than these last ages have seen.

And yet these are the great pretenders to Infallibility, and to being directed immediately by the Holy Ghost; though surely common reason would allow a Man to believe as easily what a known Historian tells us (absurd and blasphemous as it is) in *Peter the Hermit's Crusade to the*

Holy Land, that a Goose [263] he kept was believed by the Crowd to be the Holy Ghost; or what the *Turks* say of the same nature of *Mahomet's* Pigeon; as that he speaks by the mouth of such vile and evil Popes, as these which the Jesuits have given us.

Certainly if your Excellency considers their lives and history, you will be of an opinion I have often maintained, that nothing has more fatally contributed to that dreadful Deism which has infected our Gentlemen, and so long sapt the foundations of our Faith, than the actions, or in other words, the Crimes of those holy patrons of it. For where Men of sense and figure evidently see, such flagitious wickedness daily practiced by them, under such sanctified professions, they enter into a distrust of their Religion, as some do of Physick, when they behold so many die by it: and as these last think the shortest way to health, is by plain constant temperance, so the others think the best and surest way to please God, is by a plain, honest, moral conduct, without regarding particular Systems of Revelation and Rules of Faith.

It were easy to prove the weakness of this way of reasoning, and to shew by experience [264] (to carry on the allusion) that both of them, when Age and Sickness overtake them, call for the Priest and the Physician: but this I need not meddle with at present, having only hinted at the cause, not the remedy, of that vile and infectious evil. The very Jesuits themselves are so sensible of this truth, that they trouble not their heads to persuade these Rulers and Pharisees to believe our blessed Religion, provided they are silent and quiet. They only aim to gain the Crowd and Rabble of mankind, and have calculated all their conduct, as *Terence* says he managed as to his Plays, *Id sibi negotii credidit solum dari, populo ut placerent quas fecissent fabulas.*

And indeed, what other management could be expected from the inferior Clergy, or opinions in the sensible Laity among them; when the Popes have on all occasions shewn, that they judged themselves under no obligations to keep the sacred Commandments of Christianity inviolably, whensoever they found the good, that is, the temporal interest of the Church, advantaged by breaking through them. It is true, some of the best of them, as *Gregory* the twentieth, and *Pius* the tenth, as Popes, were blameless [265] and worthy Men, and careful enough not to break through those sacred fences of our holy Faith; but even they, as Sovereigns, were seldom observed to regard them, where reason of State made it adviseable to distinguish between their private and publick Characters.

Whenever your Excellency, or any impartial judge, looks into the history even of their reigns; you will find their Religion, as Temporal Princes, to be a System in which they and their Predecessors have ever moved, like flaming Comets, each in its different Orbit, not to be reduced to any known certain rules by the best Astronomers.

Like them you will find them menacing in their progress, ruin and destruction to the wretched Sons of Men, and even seeming to be no otherwise influenced by God's Power, Laws, or Will, in the circle of their Lives, than Comets in their revolutions are by the Sun; which sometimes they approach so near as to be heated, and violently set on fire by its flames, but which generally they keep themselves at such a distance from, as to be not only cold and unaffected, by its beams, but even unenlightened by its rays and splendor.

[266] But this I write to your Excellency, not as the Statesman, and my Royal Master's Servant, but as your old Intimate and Friend. You may blame yourself for my dwelling so tediously on the subject, by the long detail you have given me of their Power and Arts to sustain it, which my heart has been too much affected by, not to let it overflow a little in my pen. Your catalogue of the Relicks, and their intended sale of them, has equally surprized and scandalized his Majesty; and he is pleased to direct you to purchase some few of the most remarkable, that will come cheapest, but not to exceed ten thousand pounds in the whole. He inclines you should employ some skilful and able hand in bidding for them; and take care to have all their pretended vouchers and certificates exactly preserved, and sent over with them, with the utmost care; that we may have here the strongest evidences, of the superstition and vile conduct of this See at the same time, and try if the drousy eyes of some of our zealous Catholicks, can bear so glaring a light, without opening them effectually.

I admire their usual caution and subtlety has not restrained them; from so manifest a [267] breach of all the Laws of decency, which they do not break for unimportant reasons; but I suppose, as your Excellency observes, the greatness of the gain this sale will produce, to supply the vast expence of the Cardinal-Nephew, has drawn them to these measures. For a small profit they would hardly have taken such a step; being like the Negroes in the *Guinea* Coast of *Africk*, who hold themselves obliged by their Religion, as *Bosman* tells us, not to eat a lean Fox, but that it is lawful to eat a fat one. I am confident however, it will strangely offend the *Italian* Gravity, and make them think on occasion of this Cardinal's conduct, of a certain proverb of their Country, relating to their good Lords the Popes, that *when God denies them Sons, the Devil sends them Nephews.*

Your account of their allowing no books in History or Divinity to be licensed, but such as are wrote by the publick Professors, is what I was no stranger to, nor the grounds of their policy in it; for 'tis plain, by this method, that the two great keys of Knowledge, as to the Will of God, and the Actions of Men, will be hung at their girdle. This they do under pretence of the love of [268] truth, and to prevent falshood; though in fact, 'tis but to impose it on the World their own way. I must own (*entre nous*) I am not fully satisfied, if it were to be wish'd as to History (for as to Divinity I am certain it is) that the truth of every thing was known;

for possibly, if the secret springs of the actions of some of our neighbour Kings of late years, the cabals of Ministers and Courtiers, and the trivial piques, humours, and passions, in those Princes, that occasion Wars, and the destruction of millions of their fellow-creatures, were nakedly and sincerely laid open to our eyes; I fear there could not be a readier way to turn the hearts and heads of Men, to hate or despise those that rule them.

But these are secrets only for your Lordship's ear; which as I believe I have pretty well tired on this subject, I shall return to one that will furnish us with more agreeable scenes of things, I mean our happy Country. As it is a great while since your Excellency heard from me on that subject, I think I may venture to tell you, as news, that about ten weeks since our Parliament was dissolved, and last week a new once called. Before their dissolution, after dispatching [269] the publick Business with all possible regard, both to his Majesty's affairs, and the interest of their Country, they past several Laws, which I cannot but congratulate you upon, as publick benefits.

The first of them was an Act for translating all our Writs from the old unintelligible *English* of the eighteenth Century, into our present modern Tongue; and also for the regulating and ascertaining the Fees of all Offices and Officers, Counsellors of Law, and Attorneys; and obliging these two last names, to swear, when they take usual Oaths on being admitted to practice, never to be concerned in any base, wicked, or evidently unjust Cause. The second was a Bill for establishing a publick Bank for lending small sums of money to the Poor, at the lowest interest, to carry on their trades with; such as the *Monte della Pieta* at *Rome*: but by this Act no sum larger than then pounds, or less than twenty shillings, can be borrowed, and it must be lent upon sufficient Pawns, or City-security.

The third was an Act for erecting the Bishopricks of *London* and *Bristol* into Archbishopricks, and enlarging their Revenues to five thousand pounds *per annum*; and [270] appropriating a fund to raise all the Parishes in *England* under thirty pounds, to fifty pounds the year. A fourth was the so much talk'd of Law, for new modelling, and farther confirming and enlarging the two Corporations of the Royal Fishery and Plantation Company, and their Rights, Privileges, and Præmiums, as established in the Reigns of *Frederick* the first, and *George* the third.

Another, was an Act to prevent any Judge, Bishop, or Archbishop, to be preferred, or translated, from any See or Place to which they were first promoted: and also one for the settling four thousand pounds *per annum*, for the founding a School and College, with proper Officers, for the advantage of Experimental Philosophy, according to the excellent scheme proposed by Mr. *Abraham Cowley*, the famous ancient Poet.

The last I shall mention (though several others were past) is an Act for explaining and amending an Act in the tenth of *Frederick* the second, and the eighth of *William* the fourth, for taking away all privilege of Parliament, in case of Arrest for Debt, or Lawsuits, when the house is not sitting. And indeed, the amendments made in this Law [171] are so favourable to the rights of the Subject, that it will endear the memory of the Contriver of it to Posterity; and will keep up that veneration for Parliaments with the People, which the burthen and abuse of Privileges, had too far undermined and supplanted.

I have not time to enlarge on the vast advantages, these several Laws will probably derive to Posterity; though indeed I could dwell on them with great delight, if I had more leisure, and were not writing to one of your Lordship's great discernment, and intimate acquaintance, with both the excellencies and defects of our Constitution in Church and State.

At your Excellency's request, I send you an exact List of all our temporal Peers, summoned to meet at this Parliament, to be held at *Westminster* on *Tuesday* the 25th of *March* 1997, which the old Act against creating more than one Peer in a Session, has contracted to a small number.

His Royal Highness George Prince of *Wales*. His Royal Highness *Frederick* Duke of *York*. *John Scrope*, Lord High-Chancellor of *Great-Britain*. *John* Earl of *N--m*, Lord High-Treasurer of *Great-Britain*. [272] *William Herbert* Duke of *Pembroke*, Lord President of the Council. *William Fitzroy* Duke of *Grafton*, Lord Privy-Seal. *Charles Seymour* Duke of *Somerset*, Lord Steward of his Majesty's Houshold. *George Sackville* Duke of *Dorset*, Lord Chamberlain of the King's Household. *Henry Lenox*, Duke of *Richmond*. *Charles Somerset*, Duke of *Beaufort*. *Richard Beauclair*, Duke of *St. Albans*. *John Pawlet*, Duke of *Bolton*. *George Wriothesly Russel*, Duke of *Bedford*. *John Churchhill*, Duke of *Marlborough*. *John Manners*, Duke of *Rutland*. *George Montague*, Duke of *Montague*. *Charles Graham*, Duke of *Montrose*. *William Ker*, Duke of *Roxburgh*. *George Hamilton*, Duke of *Hamilton*. *Frederick Pierrepoint*, Duke of *Kingston*. *William Holles Pelham*, Duke of *Newcastle*. *George Bentinck*, Duke of *Portland*. *John James Brydges*, Duke of *Chandos*. *George Campbell*, Duke of *Greenwich* and *Argyle*. *Charles Egerton*, Duke of *Bridgewater*. *George Compton*, Duke of *Northampton*. *Frederick Stanhope*, Duke of *Chesterfield*. *Robert Boyle*, Duke of *Burlington*. *John Slingsby*, Duke of *Warwick*. *John Davers*, [273] Duke of *Andover*. *William Bridgman*, Duke of *Guilford*. *Joseph Williams*, Duke of *Hargrave*. *Robert Halsey*, Duke of *Preston*. *John Bacon*, Duke of *Dunsmore*.

MARQUISSES.

John Stanley, Marquiss of *Derby*; *Henry Clinton*, Marquiss of *Lincoln*; *John Hales*, Marquiss of *Brompton*; *George Edward Turner*, Marquiss of *Allerton*; *George Walpole*, Marquiss of *Walpole*; *John Parker*, Marquiss of *Macclesfield*; *Edward Vaughan*, Marquiss of *Richley*; *John Coke*, Marquiss of *Hilton*.

EARLS.

Henry Howard, Earl of *Suffolk*; *James Cecil*, Earl of *Salisbury*; *Charles Sidney*, Earl of *Leicester*; *Basil Fielding*, Earl of *Denbigh*; *John Fane*, Earl of *Westmorland*; *Charles Finch*, Earl of *Winchelsea* and *Nottingham*; *Philip Stanhope*, Earl *Stanhope*; *Charles Tuston*, Earl of *Thanet*; *George Spencer*, Earl of *Sunderland*; *Frederick Mountague*, Earl of *Sandwich*; *Charles Howard*, Earl of *Carlisle*; *Henry Lee*, Earl of *Litchfield*; *James Berkeley*, Earl of [274] *Berkeley*; *John Bertie*, Earl of *Abingdon*; *James Noel*, Earl of *Gainsborough*; *Richard D'Arcy*, Earl of *Holderness*; *Frederick Lumley*, Earl of *Scarborough*; *Robert Booth*, Earl of *Warrington*; *Francis Newport*, Earl of *Bradford*; *William Zulestein de Nassau*, Earl of *Rochfort*; *George Van Keppell*, Earl of *Albemarle*; *Thomas Coventry*, Earl of *Coventry*; *George D'Auverque*, Earl of *Grantham*; *Sidney Godolphin*, Earl of *Godolphin*; *Hugh Cholmondeley*, Earl of *Cholmondeley*; *James Sutherland*, Earl of *Sutherland*; *Robert Leslie*, Earl of *Rothes*; *Robert Hamilton*, Earl of *Hadingtown*; *James Campbell*, Earl of *Loudon*; *Thomas Ogilvy*, Earl of *Finlater*; *George Hamilton*, Earl of *Selkirk*; *James Hamilton*, Earl of *Orkney*; *William Dalrymple*, Earl of *Stair*; *William Campbell* Earl of *Ila*; *Robert Hume*, Earl of *Marchmont*; *Charles Paget*, Earl of *Uxbridge*; *Frederick Bennet*, Earl of *Tankerville*; *John Mountague*, Earl of *Hallifax*; *Thomas Cooper*, Earl *Cooper*; *Robert Sherrard*, Earl of *Harborough*; *George Farmer*, Earl of *Pomfret*; *George Byng*, Earl of *Torrington*; *Charles Townshend*, Earl *Townshend*; *Henry Raymond* [275], Earl of *Raymond*; *Frederick Offley*, Earl of *Stafford*; *Edward Scrope*, Earl of *Avington*; *Harvey Westley*, Earl of *Newington*; *Joseph Milton*, Earl *Milton*; *John Temple*, Earl of *Beverley*; *Jacob Tilson*, Earl of *Westbury*; *Roger Richmond*, Earl of *Malmsbury*.

VISCOUNTS.

William Fiennes, Viscount *Say and Sele*; *Thomas Lowther*, Viscount *Lonsdale*; *George Obrian*, Viscount *Tadcaster*; *Frederick Temple*, Viscount *Cobham*; *William Boscawen*, Viscount *Falmouth*; *Robert Grosvenour*, Viscount *Grosvenour*; *James Wentworth*, Viscount *Wentworth*; *William Jones*, Viscount *Wandsworth*; *Robert Smith*, Viscount *Langston*; *Edward Wynn*, Viscount *Marston*; *Robert Dean*, Viscount *Hedesworth*; *Richard Wardell*, Viscount *Wardell*; *John Morecraft*, Viscount *Alston*; *Thomas Clerk*, Viscount *Dorington*; *Frederick Holmes*, Viscount *Rainsford*.

BARONS.

George West, Lord *De la War*; *Charles Fortescue*, Lord *Clinton*; *John Ward*, Lord [276] *Dudley* and *Ward*; *William Maynard*, Lord *Maynard*; *George Byron*, Lord *Byron*; *Robert Berkeley*, Lord *Berkeley* of *Stratton*; *George Carteret*, Lord *Carteret*; *Charles Waldgrave*, Lord *Waldgrave*; *William Ashburnham*, Lord *Ashburnham*; *Richard Herbert*, Lord *Herbert* of *Cherbury*; *Robert Gower*, Lord *Gower*; *Edward Boyle*, Lord *Boyle*; *Henry Windsor*,

Lord *Mountjoy*; *Charles Granville*, Lord *Landsdown*; *Henry Bathurst*, Lord *Bathurst*; *George Onslow*, Lord *Onslow*; *John King*, Lord *King*; *George Edgecombe*, Lord *Edgecombe*; *Charles Morgan*, Lord *Tredegar*; *Henry Hobart*, Lord *Hobart*; *William Doddington*, Lord *Gonvill*; *George Pulteney*, Lord *Heddon*; *William Bowes*, Lord *Stretham*; *Edward Child*, Lord *Wansted*; *Richard Dutton*, Lord *Sherborne*; *Thomas Bateman*, Lord *Bateman*; *Edward Monson*, Lord *Monson*; *Robert Coke*, Lord *Beverley*; *John Methuen*, Lord *Methuen*; *Thomas How*, Lord *How*; *Arthur Worsley*, Lord *Worsley*; *Henry Fortescue*, Lord *Borlace*; *Robert Davers*, Lord *Clifton*; *George Windham*, Lord *Windham*; *John Mowbray*, Lord *Danvers*; *Thomas Edwards*, Lord *Harston*; *Peter Strickland*, Lord *Ridgeway*; *Frederick* [277] *Bamfield*, Lord *Brereton*; *Joseph Lane*, Lord *Walton*; *John Pierce*, Lord *Rolston*; *Henry Hatson*, Lord *Elsington*; *George Gore*, Lord *Walford*; *Edward Beaumont*, Lord *Stoughton*; *Robert Bagot*, Lord *Cranston*; *Frederick Long*, Lord *Upton*; *John Pritchard*, Lord *Castleton*; *George Pitt*, Lord *Woodcote*; *John Stapleton*, Lord *Bromfield*.

I have been comparing this List, with the ancient ones that remain on record with us, and I am struck with the deepest melancholly, when I see so many great and noble Families, that once made such a figure in our Country, washed away by the devouring Flood of Time; without leaving any more remembrance of their vast Fortunes, stately Houses, and magnificent Equipages, than there is of the very Beggars, that in their days were refused the scraps and crumbs of their Tables. When they flourished, and distinguished themselves by their Wealth and splendid Living, and immense Estates, surrounded with Power and Interest, Relations and Children, one would have thought they must have lasted in their glory for ever; and yet, alas! in a few years of a Century or two, how are they and their Generation [278] swept away, like the Leaves of the Forest by the Winter's Storms.

It is true, indeed, some few among them have left Monuments of their merit and virtue by good or great Actions, that make their names dear to us, and will carry down their Memories with honour and esteem, to future ages. A few others, by the blessing of Providence on them, and their real services to their Country, have left Posterity behind them, that to this day reflect back part of the glory they receive from their Ancestors: but alas, your Excellency will perceive how few they are, to those whose Families and Fortunes have been hurried down the high and steep abyss of time. *Apparent rari nantes in Gurgite Vasto!* I am persuaded, that of near twelve hundred Families that have been ennobled since the Reign of *Henry* the first, to these days, there will hardly be found above eighty who were Peers before the great Revolution, in the end of the seventeenth Century. I cannot but put your Excellency in mind here, of our favourite *Pliny's* reflection on the like occasion, when he was surveying a vast Assembly of the highest Court of Judicature at *Rome*, in his old age, and comparing

[279] them with the same Assembly, when he had first appeared in it a young Man; and considered within himself the terrible ravage, which so great a tract of time had made, among them and their Fortunes. *Tantas conversiones aut fragilitas mortalitatis, aut fortunæ mobilitas facit. Si computes annos, exiguum tempus, si vices rerum ævum putes*: and then follows that noble moral reflection, *Quod potest esse documento nihil desperare, nullius rei fidere, cum videamus tot varietates, tam volubili orbe circumagi.*

There is something of Madness sure, in the passion that Men are generally possessed with, of spending their days in care and anxiety, to build up mighty Fortunes, and raise a Family by their toils and labours; (and too, too often, by the most flagitious actions, and the vilest, and the most dishonest conduct) in hopes that they and their Descendants shall last for ever, and at worst, enjoy their Possessions for many Ages. But they calculate that matter so ill, that generally all they are able to do, is to feed the extravagance and pride of two or three Descendants for a while, till Luxury and Debauchery have brought all the dwindled, sickly Race to the grave; as Gaming, Building [280] and Equipage, had put an end to their Wealth and Fortunes.

Now I am got into this serious way of thinking, what if your Excellency allowed me to carry it on farther, and observe to you, that even the great Empires of the World, that set the ambitious Spirits of Mankind on fire, are, in proportion, of as short-liv'd a duration, as these little private Families. For after all the Blood and Bustle, which they cost their mighty Builders and Founders to rear them up, we shall find five hundred years may be reckoned the grand Climacterick of most of them, as much as sixty-three to Men. In the Government of the Kings of *Judah*, beginning with *Saul*, the first Kingdom continued to the Captivity of *Babylon*, which was five hundred years, and pretty nearly the same space of time may be assigned from the Captivity, beginning at *Esdras*, and reckoning down to *Vespasian*, who utterly extirpated the *Jews* and their Empire. The *Assyrian* Empire in *Asia*, was of just the same duration: and the *Athenian* Commonwealth, from *Cecrops* to *Codrus*, lasted four hundred ninety years, and then was changed to a Democracy. The Commonwealth [281] of the *Lacedemonians* lasted about that time, under the Kings *Heraclides*, till *Alexander* the Great swallowed that up with many other States. The consular Government in *Rome* flourished about five hundred years, till *Augustus*'s Monarchy; and the same period is observed from *Augustus*'s reign, till the fall of *Valentinian*, the last Emperor of the *West*, and that then the *Western* Empire failed. The same number of years were remarked a little after, from the time that *Constantine* the great transported the Empire from *Rome* to *Constantinople*, until *Charlemain*, who restor'd the Empire to the *West*, having chased the *Lombards* out of *Italy*. I could easily produce many other instances of the like nature, to shew that five hundred years has been frequently the age assigned to Empires by Providence. It is true, many have hardly subsisted so long, and some of them have flourished somewhat longer; yet the first of these we must consider as being formed and produced with unhealthy Constitutions, and that had naturally in their first conception, such *mala stamina vitæ*, that they perished in their infancy, and were not able to live out half [282] their days: and the others we must look on as we do on men of hardy, athletick Constitutions, which are thereby enabled to outrun the common periods of life, that generally are assigned to their neighbours. Of these short-liv'd ones we may reckon that of the *Persians*, from *Cyrus* to the last *Darius*, continued but about two hundred thirty years: and the Monarchy of the *Greeks*, founded on its ruin by *Alexander*, and derived from him to the Kings of *Egypt* and *Syria*, lasted but two hundred and fifty, and then sunk under the *Romans*. In *France*, from *Syagre* the last *Roman* Proconsul, who was deposed, to *Clovis* the first Christian King, until *Pepin* Father of *Charlemain*, and then after until *Hugh Capet*, was but two hundred thirty-seven years; and so of many more. And on the other hand, the *Carthaginian* Commonwealth, when destroyed by *Scipio*, had lasted seven hundred years: and even the ruin of the *Roman* Liberties, if we reckon in the seven Kings (as we justly may) which was compleated under *Julius Cæsar*, continued full that time.

All I mean to deduce from this long detail of things, is a very plain and obvious [283] inference, which I am sure your Excellency makes before I mention it; and that is, what little, mouldering, tottering Cottages, these boasted Empires seem, which yet are the utmost efforts of human pride and ambition, with seas of Blood, and ruins of Wealth. After all, the building up noble Families, or founding great Kingdoms, are in the eye of reason as trivial performances, as the baby-houses and puppets of Children, in comparison of those generous schemes and foundations, Wealth and Power might provide, to relieve the distressed and the miserable, the poor, the sick, and the unfortunate part of Mankind, and to instruct the ignorant, or reform the savage, the brutal, or the wicked among Men. In short (for we may trust such a dangerous truth to a private Letter) all the empty noise, and pomp, and shew of Life, which Men aim at with such infinite expence and folly, is not worth one action greatly generous, humane, or honest.

Well! by this time I suppose your Excellency is willing, to give me a full discharge for the two Letters I was indebted to you, when I begun this, which I believe you think is never to end: for fear therefore of [284] enlarging too much, I will soon put all my excuses for it in a very short and a very sincere compliment; and that is, that as full as our Court is at present, I do not find there every day one like you, that I unbosom myself to, on such subjects with pleasure, being very much,

My Lord,
Your Excellency's, &c.

N----m.

I refer you for his Majesty's new Instructions to Mr. Secretary's enclosed Pacquet, which I see is above half of it in cypher; and which I heartily recommend to your care.

[285] *To the Lord High-Treasurer, &c.*

My Lord,

Paris, Feb. 8. 1997

My last from this place to your Lordship, was of *December* the six-teenth; and I have since, pursuant to your commands, given Mr. Secretary the trouble of two Letters, of the first and thirteenth of last Month. I now return, because you are pleased to have it so, to go on with the long account of Affairs here, since I have sufficiently answered all other particulars, relating to our Negotiations at this Court, in those two former ones.

When I broke off this subject in my last, I had acquainted your Lord-ship with the address of Mons. *Meneville*, and the present Ministers, in remedying the Disorders of their Predecessors conduct; and by Places, Preferments, and Pensions, to take off the edge of the factious Leaders of the People, and bring both the Clergy and Nobility, to the legal restraints of Duty and Allegiance to the King. I observed, that this had succeeded as it usually does, where Men mean nothing by their Clamours for the good of [286] their Country, but to build up their own Fortunes, and make themselves considerable: but I must add here, that this would have been doing their work but by halves, if they had not cut off all occasion for new Complaints and Patriots, by remedying the evil that occasioned them. As the great diseases they laboured under, were the want of Trade and People, and scarcity of Money, frequent dearths of Bread-corn, the defrauding the Kingdom in the accounts of the Publick Money, and the extream Debaucheries of the Gentry; they endeavoured to remove them all, by severe Edicts against the Causes of these Grievances.

As their Trade and Manufactures had suffered by an idle affectation in the Nobility, of wearing and using every thing that was foreign, high Taxes were laid on all Commodities not of the growth of the Kingdom: and as his Majesty set an example to his Subjects, by observing this rule himself, as to wearing Apparel particularly, so no Person that had any Office under him, or that ever appeared at Court, was allowed to wear any thing of foreign growth. By this single point of management, the tide of the fashion was turned entirely in a [287] new channel, to the great advantage of the *French* Manufacturers, and to the saving immense sums of the Cash of the Kingdom, which used to go out to feed the pride and folly of the People of condition, to the utter impoverishing of the Poor.

The same care was taken to redress an evil that had gained ground extremely among the *French* Gentlemen, of travelling abroad. This, by a severe Tax of the fifth of all their Estates, and by being also discountenanced by the King, in a little time was quite laid aside; and remittances of near a million of Money prevented, besides a destructive importation of foreign fashions and luxury. At the same time as the long Plague, their unsuccessful War, and the Dearths and Confusions of the times that followed them, had made a vast consumption of their hands, and made their People, and especially their Gentlemen, very averse to marrying, and taking such an encumbrance on their Pleasures and Debaucheries upon them; an Edict was passed, by which no unmarried Person, if past thirty and under fifty, could hold any profitable employment, or Pension whatever; and all of them were taxed a fifth part of their yearly Income, if [288] Gentlemen, and all others ten shillings a head. This was sufficiently strict, and yet the latter part of this Edict was more severe: for after remarking that it was unreasonable, he who ravishes a Woman, and only hurts her honour, shall be hanged; and he who debauches her by flattery, and ruins her Soul, shall be often admired by the Women, and envied by the Men, as a fine Gentleman; it enacts, That in all such cases, the Woman shall be entitled for life, on full proof of the fact, to the third part of the Person's Estate who debauches her.

Your Lordship may easily guess what a compleat alteration for the better this has produced in the *Beau Monde*, as well as the inferior People; and I am persuaded *France*, in half a Century, will owe one seventh part of its inhabitants to this cause; at least in conjunction with another Law, that soon followed it, by which severe Penalties were laid on all voluntary Abortions, or unwholesome Nurses; and freedom from several Taxes to all who had ten living Children, or a proportionable reward for all who had a smaller number, if above six.

[289] The next Evil they applied themselves to remove, was the frequent Dearths; which they also effectually remedied by taking off the Taxes on plowed Grounds, and laying them on all such Trades as are nourished by our Luxury, and prove unprofitable to the Commonwealth; as Perfumers, Confectioners, Embroiderers, Wig-makers, Vintners, Jewellers, Lacqueys, Lawyers, Toyshops, Foreign Lace, and gold and silver Lace-shops; by which means numbers were kept to Agriculture and Husbandry.

At the same time they kept publick Granaries in all considerable Villages; by which means, by borrowing and saving from the plentiful Crops, like *Joseph* in *Egypt*, they have now near two years provision before hand, to supply their necessities, and relieve the low condition of the Poor in times of Famine, whenever this Judgment of the Almighty happens to visit this Nation, in vengeance for their sins.

The last evil this Ministry has prudently remedied, was the preventing the continual Frauds in the managing the Finances, and over-reaching the King and the Nation, in the Receipts and Disbursements of [290] the Publick Money, and the Accounts of the national Taxes and Funds.

Judge, my Lord, what notions I must have, of his integrity and honour who is to read this, when I speak with abhorrence and detestation, of the vile arts these Financiers, and Bankers of the Treasures of the State, made use of to enrich themselves, and impoverish their Prince and their Country. For it is evident by the facts, that have since their disgrace been proved on them, and by the immense Fortunes they so suddenly raised, that there never were greater Robbers or Villains employed, under a careless and lavish King, and a cunning Ministry.

To prevent such base and dishonest management for ever, there was an excellent Edict passed, constituting seven Commissioners, with eighteen thousand Livres yearly Salaries to each of them, sworn to examine with the strictest care and fidelity, all publick Accounts of the Nation; and with their utmost industry, by their examining all Officers (from the highest to the lowest) on oath, to discover all errors. These Accounts, with all proper Vouchers annexed to them, they were obliged by the first of *March*, to publish and print annually for the [291] publick view; with their notes and observations upon them, and to mention all errors found in them, and the several Officers who had committed them, whether by fraud or mistake. All such sums so discovered, the particular Officers and their Securities, were to make good; and the Commissioners also, to have the entire benefit of such sums, paid to them by the said Officers and their Securities.

But this did not end here, for if after the publishing and printing the said Accounts, any other Person should prove and make out, any fraud or mistake omitted by them; then such Person was to be adjudged the whole of the said Sum, as a reward for his diligence, half to be recovered from the Commissioners, and half from the offending Officer, who by fraud or corruption had passed it over.

By this means, it is hard to be believed with what honest severity, regularity, integrity, and œconomy, the Publick Finances here have been managed of late: while in other Nations, whoever robs a private Subject of five shillings, is hanged, and those who can with dexterity rob their Country of a Million, are honoured and rewarded, if not ennobled for it.

[292] If we add to this the publick Registry, for all Conveyances of Lands and Settlements, and Deeds affecting the real Estates of this

Kingdom; I believe your Lordship will see in these Regulations, as great care and conduct shewn, to retrieve this People from all their misfortunes, as has been known in this Kingdom, since the days of *Richlieu* or *Mazarine*.

I shall now take leave of this part of my observations, and shall proceed to such others as I have not yet touched on; if possibly I can communicate any thing of this kind, that may deserve your notice.

And the first I shall mention is the low ebb of Religion in this Country, which is indeed in a very dead and languishing way, between the blind Infidelity of the Laity, and the cold indifference and want of Zeal in some, and the immoral and luxurious Lives of others of the Clergy.

As the first of these is greatly occasioned by the latter, so *that*, I fear, is too much to be charged to the conduct of the Court and the Ministry. For finding in the late contests with the Pope, that the Clergy universally preferred the interest of the Empire of the *Vatican*, to that of their own Country; it has been a constant maxim ever since, to sink their credit [293] with the People, by encouraging them in a want of Zeal for Religion, and a scandalous looseness of Life and Morals, and preferring either the most lukewarm or the most luxurious and debauched among them, to all Sees, Abbeys, &c. in the gift of the Crown.

By this conduct, their influence on the Laity and the State, is perpetually sinking: and as such heads will probably prefer Men like themselves, to the Cures of Parishes in their several Dioceses, the credit and interest of the Clergy, and consequently of the Pope, must necessarily decrease; and all that they lose, must as naturally revert to the Crown, as the Power and Estates of Rebels, that are forfeited for Treason.

It is grown so much the fashion here, to treat them with contempt on all occasions, and despise them, that the great Men shut them out generally from their conversations; and even at their Tables they have always a Page or *Valet de Chambre*, to say Grace, (which for fashion's sake some of them keep up as an old custom in their Families) that they may not be disturbed by the Priest or the Friar.

And indeed, notwithstanding the general decay of Learning and Virtue, in the Ecclesiasticks of this Century, I believe there can hardly [294] be found such notorious and flagrant instances of this nature, as in this Kingdom. Many of them are as nice and effeminate, as if, (as we read of the Clergy of *Formosa*, who are all Females,) they were entirely of a different sex from the Laity; or like the Prophetesses of *Caria* in *Asia Minor*, who, as *Aristotle* tells us, were bearded Women. But I am sure they live with such softness, nicety, and woman-like delicacy of manners, as shew their sense and notions of things, must be mean and sensual. Numbers of them are sunk and drowned, in the good Wine and Cheer of *Paris*; wallowing in the Bottle and the Dish, as the chief pleasure and joy of life, and are so given up to their bellies and gluttony, as if they thought our blessed Saviour was born at *Bethlehem*, because the word in *Hebrew* signifies, The House of Bread; and was designed to express thereby, that they should serve him chiefly on that account, and feed by him. Is it not a melancholy prospect, my Lord, to see the sacred repository of the divine Will, shut up from the eyes of the Laity, and confined to such despicable creatures, as stewards and dispensers of it to others?

[295] So far, indeed, they may be called faithful stewards of it, as they bestow its Treasures entirely on their neighbours, without keeping any share of it to themselves; being too often, and especially the Jesuits, in this case like Miners, who are perpetually employed to dig out the Riches of the Earth; for the use of the World, while they preserve not the least portion of it for their own service. The truth is, the pretended heads of this Church are not, as formerly, Men who by an eminence in Parts and Learning, and a Sanctity of Life and Manners, are chosen out as fit Overseers of the Christian Sheepfold, to increase their numbers, cure their disorders, and prevent their straying; but are picked out to disunite and disturb it, in hopes thereby to shake the foundations of the Papal Power. They are not, my Lord, so properly Archbishops of *Paris*, or Bishops of *Auvranches*, as Temporal Peers, and the Dukes and Barons of those places; who have these Preferments bestowed on them for life, as Pensions to oppose the Pope, and maintain the Quarrel of the Crown. How far true Religion can be served by such Creatures, or Learning, Virtue, and Piety, be kept up in this Kingdom, is [296] easily foreseen; and especially, when neither the outward decencies of publick Preaching or Praying, or even appearing in their Churches, unless on great Festivals, is made use of to palliate their irregular Lives, and corrupted Morals.

A reflection, which while I make with sorrow and anguish of heart, on the State of the Church here, I cannot without pleasure and transport turn my eyes on our own Church; where we are so happy to see the greatest purity of Faith, joined with a primitive simplicity and sanctity of Manners, and an eminency in both these, made the surest road to Promotion and Preferment.

Another point of policy which the new Ministers have put in practice here, in relation to the Clergy, and which deserves to be locked up *inter arcana Imperii*, is, forbidding all polemical Works from the Press, or Discourses of that kind from the Pulpit. For as such Disputes and Party-wars of the Pen, have been ever observed to heat, and keep up the zeal and spirit of the Clergy, above all other things; such stimulative and awakening Medicines are by no means judged proper by these State-Empiricks, for that Lethargy and drousy Stupidity, they [297] find it their interest to keep the Ecclesiasticks in.

It is certain, by this means the peace and quiet of the State, as well as the Church, is the more secured, and many eminent Genius's employed in nobler pursuits, to the great advantage of the Commonwealth of Learning. But at the same time, this introduces a sensible decay and indifferency in all points of Faith, that lie like the Fortifications of Towns, on the Frontiers of a Country, where we are secure to have no War; mouldering, and falling away daily, being neglected, and ill maintained, in too profound a Peace.

Along with this part of their conduct they have joined another, and left in any future disputes with the Pope, they should want able Pens to defend the Rights of the Crown; they have in several Universities, and especially in the *Sorbonne*, appointed Salaries for learned King's Professors of Divinity; though indeed their true title should be, Professors of the King's Divinity. These are the best Pens and the ablest Men they have, who are retained, like Lawyers, to plead the Cause of *France*, against the Usurpations of the Papal See, as they have [298] often done, though never so successfully, as when they have had the Armies of the Crown for their Seconds.

The truth is, they have taken up such an aversion to Learning here, from the mischiefs it has occasioned, in their disputes with the Pope; that I am persuaded I could not do them a more agreeable piece of service, than to contrive a Plan to model all the Schools and Colleges in this Kingdom a-new, in such a manner that they should be entirely employed in teaching Children Nothing, educating them to Nothing, and breeding them up to read Nothing. By this means, they might have the rising Generation, ready to receive any impressions they pleased, unbyassed by the reigning prejudices in favour of the Pope's Supremacy. If I set up this Scheme here, I must aim to introduce the famous *Chinese* Sect of *Bonzes*, who assemble their Followers in the Fields, where every one is furnished with a pair of Drum-bones between his fingers; and whenever the *Bonzes* learnedly prove to them, that all the Opinions, Pleasures, Sorrows, Hopes, and Fears of this World are *Xin*, that is, (in their Language) Nothing, which word ends every sentence; the whole Croud rock [299] their Bodies to an extasy of transport, and rattle their Drum-bones, crying out in confirmation of their beloved Doctrine, *Xin, Xin, Xin!*

I must also of a certainty send for some Professors, from the Academy *Gli Infecondi* in *Italy*, who write Nothing; and for crouds of *Spanish* Schoolmen, *German* Poets, *Dutch* Divines, *English* Politicians, *Muscovite* Sea-Captains, *Italian* Patriots, *Jewish* Rabbies, and *Turkish* Dervises, who have above all Men the happy art of amusing others, and employing themselves in that amiable mystery, of writing, and thinking, and doing Nothing. We should have some trouble in watching carefully over a few bustling, inquisitive tempers, who are possessed with that devilish spirit, of doing, thinking, or writing something. But the usual croud of the School or the College, might be left to the conduct of their gentle, easy Genius, and by the amiable inactivity of their Indolence, would naturally arrive at Nothing. By such a model as this, great things might be done here, to drive out the impertinence of reading and study; and in a few years we might see this Reign, rival that of *Lewis* the seventeenth, when Learning, and Religion [300], and Arts, were so happily banished that Kingdom; and

Infidelity united all its divided Schisms and Parties, in one general League of Irreligion and Ignorance, against Superstition, Pedantry, and Priestcraft, or in other words, Piety, Virtue, and Knowledge.

But it is time to present your Lordship with some observations of a different nature, as to the Humour and Temper of these People. I formerly took notice of the prodigious Luxury that reigns here, amidst the confusion of their affairs; which shews it self in all the amusements and diversions of the better sort, in such an infinite variety of things, that it is impossible to describe the half of them. It would be very entertaining to write an History even of the Fashions, for the last five years I have resided here, and I am confident it would make a little folio, to go thro' them in all their different reigns and seasons. High Stays, low Stays, no Stays, short-waisted, long-waisted Stays; short, mid-leg, all-leg, no-leg Petticoats; broad Lace, narrow Lace, *Flanders* Lace, *English* Lace, *Spanish* Lace, no Lace, Fringes, Knottings, Edgings; High-heads, Low-heads, three Pinners, two Pinners, one [301] Pinner; much Powder, all Powder, little Powder, no Powder; Mantua's with a Tail, want a Tail, false Tail; four Flounces, three Flounces, two Flounces, no Flounces; wide Sleeves, strait Sleeves, long Sleeves, short Sleeves; many Ribbons, all Ribbons, few Ribbons, broad Ribbons, narrow Ribbons, rich Ribbons, plain Ribbons, flowered Ribbons, stampt Ribbons, no Ribbons. Such a noble and important work as this, with the dates and rise of every Fashion, the Councils that decreed it, the Authors and Inventors, and the vast Revolutions it produced in the polite World; and dedicated to the lovely Dutchess of *Monbazon*, who is able, my Lord, to prescribe what Fashions she pleases, both to her own Sex and ours; would, I am sure, raise more Subscriptions here, than the Works of *Cicero* or *Livy*. I fancy an History of their Breakfasts at *Paris*, for these last thirty years, would be almost as diverting; for as the quickness and inconstancy of the fair Ladies Fancies, are ever on the wing for new Entertainments for us, it is comical to consider the various successions they have contrived, since the days of cold Meat and Wine of their Ancestors. How have these lovely Cooks rung the [302] changes with Tea, Coffee, and Chocolate, Chocolate, Coffee, and Tea, backwards and forwards, sometimes drinking their Tea infused long in cold water, sometimes in hot; and when they were driven off the stage, what new scenes have they furnished out, between Sweetmeats and Creams, Tysans and Sherbets, Milk cooked in twenty different methods, Bitters for the Stomach of a thousand sorts, Wine mull'd and brew'd in several shapes, Jellies and Fruits of all kinds, Broths and Caudles drest up in various disguises, and Possets, Syllabubs, and Gruels, in as many; till at last they have returned to Manchets and Butter, with fresh Eggs and Whey, or Milk from the Cow, which their Fathers used about three hundred years ago, in *Lewis* the thirteenth's time.

One of the reigning Fashions at present is, in all their Assemblies, or Visiting-days, to entertain their Company with Consorts of the best Musick, and to perfume all the Apartments but the Anti-chambers, which are at the same time adorned with the most exquisite Pictures *Great-Britain* or *Italy* can furnish them with. I take this to be the most natural and agreeable method of receiving great People with respect, that can be thought [303] of; for besides regaling you with many kinds of Wines and Sweetmeats, almost all the Senses are gratified at once, and the everlasting, unmeaning rhapsody of Talk, that prevails in mixt Conversations here, is removed; and the Ear, Eyes, Taste, and Smell, entertained in the noblest manner. If your Lordship will allow me to mention one reigning Fashion more, that seems established here, I shall detain you no longer on this subject; and that is, the keeping Mutes in all great houses, which they generally import from *Turkey* at excessive rates, and employ as *Valet de Chambres* and Waiters at Table. I fancy this humour is likely to reach some of their neighbours in time: and indeed, where half the World act, and the other half talk things, that ought to be buried in ever-lasting silence, I wonder it has not been introduced among us long since. In some Provinces of *France* this has obtained so far, that they as commonly cut out the Tongues of Infants, as in *Italy* they make them Eunuchs; and the prices for them run so high, these having the advantage of hearing, which many of those that are imported want, that it is probable in time, the number of Mutes among [304] Servants, will bear a higher proportion than they do in the letters of the alphabet. In the mean time, to encourage us to give into this practice in our Country, it is to be considered, we may furnish ourselves much cheaper with very tolerable Mutes from both our Universities; who besides, are generally happy in a more grave and sheepish Modesty than these Foreigners, and can sometimes also, on an extraordinary occasion, utter an odd monosyllable now and then, which is rather an advantage in my opinion, than otherwise.

I am sorry, my Lord, that I must lengthen this tedious Letter with two pieces of news, neither of which, I fear, will be agreeable. The one is the death of Mons. *Le Fevre*, whom your Lordship honoured formerly with managing some business for you here. He was a chearful, well-natured, honest Man, but he talked immoderately; and though he shewed a great deal of wit in his Conversation, he used to laugh so much at his own Jests, that his mirth was seldom accompanied with *Sarah*'s blessing, who said, *God had made her to laugh, so that all that heard her laughed with her.* I mention this the rather [305], because I was with him the day he died; and as he had raised his fortune from nothing, by your Lordship's bounty, so he spent it extravagantly, and died almost for want. He took notice of this rise and fall in his Circumstances, and desired me to tell your Lordship, he died your humble Servant; and that for the change in his fortune, it was but in the way of the World, and according to the old axiom in Philosophy, *Ex nihilo nihil fit.*

But I have another loss to acquaint your Lordship with, which will touch you more nearly; and that is the *Danish* Envoy here, Mr. *Plessenburg*, who died last night of an Apoplexy, as he sat at supper among a great many friends. He had no Will by him, to the ruin of a numerous Family; for his while Estate goes to his eldest Son, a Man not worthy even to inherit his Name. Your Lordship knew him personally so long, and lived so intimately with him, when he was Envoy at our Court, that I need not draw his Character. He served his Prince faithfully, and was an honour to his service, and a credit to his Country; and indeed, we may say in this case, that the Servant was greater than his Master.

[306] He was a most religious Observer of his Promise, of which he gave a glorious instance lately; when being pressed by the Nuncio to prefer a friend of the Society to a Troop in his Regiment, and put by one he had promised it to, he told him, he would not break his word to serve the true friends of Religion, and much less to serve its real enemies, the Jesuits. 'Twas an answer worthy of Mr. *Plessenburgh*, of whom I cannot say a greater thing, than that he had the honour of your Lordship's friendship, and deserved it.

In my last dispatch to Mr. Secretary, I gave so full an account of the state of my Negotiations here, and the high professions they make of their obligations to his Majesty, for interesting himself in the affair of the Inquisition; that I need not report a matter to your Lordship, which I know Mr. Secretary, with his usual care, has long since laid before you.

I expect very soon to have an Audience of the King, in which I hope to find their measures concerted and resolved on, pursuant to what I was instructed to lay before them, for their approbation. When it is over, I shall give your Lordship an exact account [307] of it, and what is likely to be the result of these counsels, which you so happily direct, and so worthily preside in.

By our last Letters by the way of *Vienna*, we have received fresh assurances, that his Imperial Majesty is so well recovered of his asthmatick disorder, that he had ventured out to take the air in the Park, and to see his Hawks, (which the Grand Seignior lately sent him as a present from *Constantinople*) kill two or three brace of Woodcocks. However this may be relished at *Rome*, I am sure it is very agreeable news at *Paris*, and I hope will be as much so at *London*; where I wish you all the Honour and Happiness you deserve, and am, with the greatest deference and regard,

My Lord,
Your Lordship's &c.

Herbert.

[308] *To the Lord High-Treasurer, & c.*

My Lord,

Constantinople, April 16, 1998.

In my former Letters I believe I gave you a sufficient surfeit of my political observations on this great Empire, and its present Condition, Laws, and Customs; and I shall now furnish another kind of entertainment for you, if any thing I can send your Lordship can be justly called so. I shall chiefly confine myself at present to give you some imperfect accounts of my Telescope's performances, and of several conversations I have had on it, with the Grand Seignior in person; in those secret recesses of his retirement, the Apartments of the Seraglio, and the lovely Gardens with which it is almost surrounded, to the very Banks of the Sea.

I have formerly told your Lordship, how extremely affable and courteous, not to say obliging and affectionate, I have on many occasions found the Grand Seignior to me; insomuch, that I am really considered here as the greatest Favourite, of any Ambassador that has appeared here from a Christian [309] Prince, for these many years. This, I believe, has been chiefly occasioned by my speaking the *Turkish* Language to some perfection, and by my studying to gratify, as far as I could, his great passion for such Curiosities, as I could furnish him with from *London;* such as Globes, Maps, Clocks of all kinds, and Watches; Dogs, Guns, Barges, Coaches, and, in a word, whatever I found him most desirous of.

It is certain, by these means I have ingratiated myself mightily with him; so that when he refuses Audiences to other Ministers, he often *sends* for me, and will make me sit in his presence, and discourse of *Europe* and my Travels, with a familiarity very unusual to this Court.

Since my last Letters by Mr. *Biron,* I received his commands to wait on him, and found him in one of his Gardens, after our *European* Models, with Grass, Gravel, Portico's, and Fountains, by the side of one of which he was reposing himself. He told me, he had heard of the wonderful Telescope your Lordship had sent me, and that he was impatient to see it, and try if it answered the surprizing relation the Grand Vizier had made him of it; and desired to [310] know, if it could be set up in that place immediately. I answered every one of his demands, in the manner I knew to be most agreeable to him; and as I had been prepared for it by the Grand Vizier, I told him, I had brought it by some of his Highness's Slaves, who, with my Servants directions, should soon set it up, and regulate it. As he expressed a great desire to make trial of it immediately, and as the Evening was very serene and cloudless, I gave my People proper directions, and with a very little time and trouble, the necessary Apparatus for it was set in order; and then, without delay, it was brought in, and made ready for using. All this time he employed in examining me about it, how much it magnified, and if it were possible we could discern Mountains, Hills, Seas, and Rivers, in the Moon by it.

I assured him I had tried it, and though in the last age few magnified more than two hundred, I found it magnified Objects many thousand times bigger than they appeared to the naked Eye; and that we could not only discern Hills and Rivers, but even objects like Towns and Forests in the Moon; and that, if the Inhabitants [311] there were as large as some great Astronomers conceived them to be, I doubted not in time, our Glasses might be so far improved, as to see even Men and their actions there.

He repeated all this after me with vast surprize; and after musing on it, he turned to me, and said with some concern, Seignior *Stanhope*, do you think there can be living Creatures, and above all, Men in our Moon? I told him, I had great and weighty reasons to be persuaded of it; and as he himself would see Hills and Woods in it, Clouds and Vapours surrounding it, though they are very thin and small, and also actual Waters, Seas and Rivers in it, I durst undertake he would be of the same opinion. For since she is found to resemble our Earth in all such Conveniencies, what is more natural than to suppose she must have Fruits and Herbs also, as we have; and if those, unquestionably Animals to live on them; and above all others, Men, since Nature does nothing in vain.

That it was absurd to suppose such a beauteous Work of God, should be so amiably and usefully adorned, and yet be furnished to no purpose, with such vast Conveniences [312], which might be so pleasant and useful an Habitation, for rational, intelligent Beings; who might there enjoy with so much happiness, the Beauties and Delights of the Place, and with due praise and gratitude look up to the excellent Author. That though our Eyes did not convince us by such evident appearances, that there were so many resemblances in the Moon, of what we see on our own Earth, yet it was absurd to suppose, the wise Maker would have formed such immense, solid, opake Globes, rolling by rules, and in Orbits he has prescribed them in the Heavens, as bare useless Heaps of Matter, and unwieldy Lumps of Rock or Clay, to no end, but to give an imperfect Light to our system, and to be looked at by the Eye. And if this is not to be imagined as to the other Planets, much less as to the Moon, who enjoys the Heat and Light of the Sun, to much greater advantage than several of them, and almost as well as our Earth. I said a great deal of this sort to him; to which he made several slight objections, that were easily got over: and perceiving our Telescope was by this time near ready, I presented him with the vast Map of the [313] Moon, which I had from *London*, with all the Seas, Rivers, Mountains, Hills, Valleys, Forests, and the supposed Towns that are so accurately laid down in it by the Selenographers; and especially by the *Savilian* Professor Dr. *Bertie*, who has divided it into its several Kingdoms and Provinces.

He examined it with abundance of care, and was delighted with the prodigious size, as well as the beauty and exactness of the Performance, asking me many questions on it; and appeared particularly pleased to see *Stamboul*, and his own Dominions (which I shewed him) set down in it. But by this time our Telescope being perfectly settled, I begg'd his Highness to let his own Eyes answer his curiosity better than I could, and to compare the Map with what the Telescope would shew him; the Moon being just at the Full, and the Heavens clear and serene.

He immediately set himself to make his observations, and with the greatest surprize and transport, one while applied his eye to the Telescope, and then to the Map, surveying all the different ranges of Mountains, Hills, and Valleys, the vast Surfaces of Seas, Lakes, and Rivers, in the Lunar [314] Globe, tracing out every thing with the greatest sagacity.

It is hard for your Lordship to believe the amazement that appeared in his Face all this while; and as the faithful Telescope represented every thing so plain and distinct, and brought the Objects he surveyed so clear and close to his eye, that he could not be more convinced of their existence, had he walked on the face of the Earth he was surveying, he would ever and anon break out into some expressions of admiration.

He seem'd, indeed, to doubt a little as to the darkness of the vast Plains of the *Pontus Euxinus*, the *Caspian*, and *Mediterranean*, and the *Baltick*, and *East* Seas, and the great Rivers that roll into them, by so many mouths; and supposed the Sea would rather appear with a lucid brightness, and even outshine the everlasting Snows and Rocks of Mount *Taurus*. But I soon convinced him, without troubling him with the philosophical reasons of things, with putting him in mind, that the Earth and Sea had just this appearance from the elevated heights, of his own Mount *Olympus*, where he so often had been. The only scruple that remained with him, was as to [315] the great *Hyrcanian* Forest, and the resemblances, to call them no more, of the several Cities, such as *Rome, Stamboul, Paris, Vienna,* and *London.* As to the Forests, I made him observe the vast difference there was between the appearance of the bright even flats and plains, and that dusky, brown roughness that swelled up in the middle of those extended fields; and that as all the higher grounds in the surface of the Moon's Globe wear a remarkable brightness, compared with those vast levels; it was impossible these being so dark, could be high Downs, or Hills, not to insist on the even Level that their tops appeared with, which hilly Countries never have.

That it is certain, besides all this, that allowing there are Woods and Forests in the Moon, (and such she must probably have, in so many different Soils as he saw there) they could appear no otherwise than they did here, because they imbibe the Sun's rays through so many apertures of their Boughs and Shades, and therefore cannot reflect them back, as the surfaces of hard, solid bodies would: and since it is plain, there must be Woods and Forests there, and if there, they must appear in the same manner [316] he saw them; it is most reasonable to call them, and suppose them such.

For the Cities, I must own, my Lord, I had not much to say; and though it is true, the running of Rivers close by them, the white circles that like Walls seemed to surround them, and the different heights and hollows, as it were Houses and Towers, and Shade and Lights, that reflect from them within those circles; and above all, that blackness, that like a thin cloud hung over the largest, and looks like a vast collection of smoke, such as we see about Cities here; all which make it possible, they may be what the Map calls them: yet I cannot but think, they may be rather white Rocks, shaded by Woods on them, or some neighbouring Hills, than real Cities. However I endeavoured to convince the Grand Seignior, that the resemblance was so strong, and agreeable to what one would imagine Cities would make to us, if they were built there; that one could not charge the composers of the Map, with over-great rashness or folly, for assigning such denominations to them.

The Grand Seignior seemed pretty well satisfied with what I said to him, and continued [317] some hours surveying and contemplating the beauteous Object he had before him, till the interposing of some clouds, and a little rain that fell, put an end to this agreeable amusement I had furnished him with. We retired from the Garden into the gerat *Kiosc*, or Summer-house, where he often spends the Summer Evenings, and the beginnings of the warm Nights, with his chief Favourites and Bassas, drinking Sherbets and Coffee, and smoking Tobacco. He made me sit down on the Sofa, and begun a long discourse with me, of the wonderful instrument I had brought him, which, as he expressed it, drew down the Heavens to the Earth, and made us as it were neighbours to those celestial Orbs, which the great Author of them had placed so remote from us. He asked me of the distance between us and the Moon, and when I told him it was generally computed by Astronomers, that her mean distance was about sixty semi-diameters of the Earth, he seemed astonished that our Telescopes could bring her so near us; but he was a great deal more so, when I acquainted him with the much greater distance, betwixt us and the other Planets of our system, some [318] of which I told him I would shew him, whenever he could have leisure for it; and, if he pleased, the next day about evening, if the Sky was serene and cloudless. He seemed much rejoiced with my undertaking, to procure him that satisfaction so soon; and telling me, he would not detain me any longer for that night, he in a very gracious manner dismist me, and left me to retire to my house, where I immediately hastened; much pleased that I had the honour, of being the first that had introduced the *Turkish* Moon, (the Arms of this Empire) into the acquaintance of her great Masters, that had oftener alarmed the World, with her appearance in their Standards, than ever she had been able to do, with all her Eclipses.

Early in the evening of the next day, I returned to the Seraglio before it was dark, the weather being very favourable, where I found the Grand Seignior attending my coming. He immediately began to tell me, that as he was convinced by what I had said, and what he had seen the night before, that the Moon must be inhabited, he had been considering with himself, what sort of Men they must be that were placed [319] there. I told him, that, was what no one could pretend to account for, but that probably they must in many things resemble us pretty nearly, and in all likelihood be not much more different from us, than many Nations of the *Indians*, which the Ancients had discovered in *America*.

But, says he, I am perplexed with a great scruple, that I know not how to get over; and that is, as we know of a certainty that *Mahomet*, in his passage to Heaven with the Angel *Gabriel*, touched there, I cannot conceive, had there been Men there, but he must have communicated his Law to them; and if he had done so, he must have mentioned it in that holy book his *Alcoran*, which he has left us. Now as he has not taken the least notice of so important a point, I am persuaded there cannot be such Inhabitants there, as you and your Philosophers have disputed for.

I saw the danger immediately, of touching on this point, and therefore shifted it off, by saying, that there were so many Worlds more, as thick planted with such Colonies as the Moon was, that it was probable he chose to leave them to themselves, since had he undertaken to visit them all, they [320] were so infinitely numerous, and so infinitely distant, it would have taken up many millions of years, to have gone through with them. Your Highness, continued I, will allow there is some weight in this reasoning, since it is as probable that every Star we see in the Heavens, and an immense number we cannot see, even with our Telescopes, are every one of them so many Suns, in the centre of as great and as noble a system, at this which we are placed in, all the Planets whereof have the same pretensions to be inhabited as the Moon. This, I observed to him, was a point which all Astronomers contend for, as in the highest degree reasonable; not only from the same arguments that evince the Moon's being replenished with living Creatures, and rational Beings, which I already touched on; but also because, in the first place, all the denser Planets are seated nearest the Sun, in regard that the denser matter requires more heat, to render it capable of natural Productions; and secondly because the nearer such Planet is to the Sun, the greater is the velocity of its motion, and consequently, the vicissitudes of its Seasons are rendered the quicker, as it is highly proper [321] they should be, in order to favour the productions of Nature in it, of what kind soever they are. And really the presumptions on these accounts, and many others, are so exceedingly strong in favour of this opinion, that I think we must leave the Astronomers, in possession of this favourite

Doctrine of theirs, till we can bring better arguments against them, than I have ever yet heard of. I perceived he was going to reply, and as I had a mind to avoid the dialogue, I told his Highness, if he pleased, we would leave those enquiries, to see what information we could get about it from *Jupiter*, one of the noblest Planets of our system; which, says I, (pointing to it) shines so brightly yonder, as if he had spruc'd himself out in order to shew himself to us, and entertain your Highness in the best manner, his great distance from the Sun and our Earth will allow him.

Accordingly, I immediately applied my Telescope to him, and as I had seldom seen him so bright, he made a very glorious figure, drest up with all his Belts, and Spots, and Satellites about him. I laid the fine Map your Lordship sent me of him, before the Grand Seignior, with the imaginary [322] Regions, Mountains, and Seas, which these admirable Glasses have furnished us the prospect of.

I pointed out all the most considerable tracts on his mighty Globe, and especially the bright Mount *Olympus*, and *Athos*, and the wide *Atlantick* Ocean, and *South* Sea on his *Western* Limb, and the vast Islands here and there disper'd in them.

I then made him turn his observations, to such of his Satellites as we were able to observe, and explained to him how these attendant Moons, served to enlighten the darkness of his Inhabitants, and to make him some amends, for their being so far removed from the warmth and splendor, of that sole source of light and heat in our system, the Sun. He attended to both their appearances, in the Map and the Heavens, and the explanatory hints I added to all, with infinite surprize and delight; every now and then crying out, how wonderful it all was, and what a pity, that so immense a Globe, should be confined to so dark and gloomy a scituation!

To remove his concern on this account, I told him, that though *Jupiter's* People, certainly received but the twenty-fifth part [323] of our light from the Sun, and that this days were but five hours long, yet it was plain, by the very brightness he now shone with, and by the splendor of so many attendant Moons, he had abundant light to make every thing agreeable, and pleasing to his inhabitants; who had probably more light and warmth than our Polar Regions, and were certainly so formed as Moles, Owls, and Batts with us, to take more delight in the gloom of the evening, than the dazling glare of the broad-day. That possibly in *Jupiter*, they measured not their days by sun-rise and sun-set, but by several successions of them, and called them only sun-hours, and moon-hours; after such a proportion of which, according to the strength of their bodies, they divided their times of rest and labour. * N.B. *There were here some new, and (in the Editor's and Translator's poor opinion) some beautiful hints given the learned World, in relation to* Jupiter, *and the rest of our Planets. But as several of our greatest Astronomers, whom I will not name, for fear of exposing them to the rage* *and resentment of Mankind, have been pleased to threaten, they would lay out all* [328] *their skill, in publickly opposing the new systems, which had been communicated to him, it has been thought proper to suppress them for the present. A method which the Translator has the more willingly complied with, for the sake of peace, and to prevent new Schisms, Feuds, and Factions, between great and learned Men; and especially, since such amicable methods have been proposed, that there is good hope all points may be so fairly adjusted, that these vast discoveries, in this new system of things, may, to the satisfaction of all parties, be communicated to the World in the subsequent Volumes. Accordingly, the Translator has modestly deferred his Publication of them, and in the mean time, has so carefully connected the paragraphs in this admirable Letter, that there will appear no material interruption in the sense.* But certainly, says he, how contented soever they may be with their Light, they must suffer severely by cold; nay, I am afraid their Waters are constantly frozen. I told him there was no fear of that evil, if we either supposed their Waters of a warm nature, like our mineral Springs, and Hot-Wells, or the [329] inhabitants so fram'd, as to delight in a cold climate, and abhor a warm one, as our northern nations do the heat of the Line; or if warmth, like ours, must be suppos'd necessary for them and their plant, &c. possibly as *Jupiter*'s Diameter is 20 times greater than that of our earth, and all of it bask'd in the sun's beams, the warmth of the sun might be greatly increas'd there by *Jupiter*'s so frequent rotation round its own axis, and by its acting on so much greater an extent of surface; which answer, however your Lordship may think of it, pass'd for very good reasoning at the Seraglio. But, says he, I fancy I am the more sensible of their being pinch'd by cold yonder, because I find the night air grow very uneasy; and as we have fully observ'd these wonders of the heavens for this time, let us retire to our former shelter in the Kiosc, and talk over our coffee of these amazing Discoveries.

We were hardly set down on our Sofa's, when he began to ask me, whether the Astronomers in *Europe*, or elsewhere, were often thus employ'd, and to what uses their labours-serv'd? I told him, unhappily Astronomy had been confin'd to *Europe* to its great disservice; having been banish'd *Egypt*, [330] and those regions in his Empire, that by their serene skies and air were fittest for her observations, and where she first appear'd, and for many ages flourish'd considerably. That in *Europe* our Astronomers were perpetually taken up in watching the Stars, Comets and Planets, adjusting their places, and observing their motions. That by their labours we both discover the harmony by which the immense works of the Creator are knot together in the great Universe, the motions of the heavenly bodies, the degrees of their magnitudes, light, heat and motion, and how they act on each other, their natural intercourse and regulated circulations, with their certain returns and periods. That by their observations on each and all of these, we are oblig'd to confess and adore the infinite magnificence, power and goodness of the great Mover and Former of them all; of which we could before have no true notions, till these his glorious works were thus reveal'd to us to our equal convenience and pleasure.

That besides these advantages, we also were indebted to the labours of Astronomers, for the clearing up the now establish'd system of all the Comets in their immense [331] Orbits, as well as the perfection of our Geography and Chronology; both which would be made up of mere fables and guesses without their assistance. Nay, that we owe to the same means, that our navigation is become so safe and secure thro' the vast seas and pathless oceans through which our commerce is extended. That his Highness might have some notion hereof by those very *Satellites* of *Jupiter* which he had been so long observing that night, the observation of whose frequent Eclipses alone, had ascertain'd the Longitude of many thousand places in our Earth, which before were utterly unknown; and had thereby made that noble Globe, I had presented him with from your Lordship, so admirably compleat, as I had often shewn to him.

That besides many other things, by the observations of their Eclipses, as I had explain'd them to him, men had demonstrated, by their being seen earlier when the Earth is nearer, and later than calculation when it is remoter from *Jupiter*, that Light was not propagated to us instantaneously, but by a successive motion; and that we can measure out its journeys from the Sun and the Planet to us, as by a stated scale, which [332] was about 500000 miles in a minute. We had a vast deal of conversation on these subjects, in which as I gave him accounts, that probably our Earth, by its smalness, had never yet been observ'd from *Jupiter*, and that *Jupiter's* Moons, to say nothing of *Venus's*, which are vastly smaller, were as large as our Earth, and that as their days were proportion'd to their revolutions round their Axes, so they were in some of them double, and in others 16 times as long as ours. We fell again into a long discourse, whether these vast Orbs, no ways inferior to the Earth in bulk, ought not to be allow'd inhabitants as well as our Moon. As to *Jupiter*, the very beholding him thro' the telescope with his seas and mountains, made it sufficiently probable to him: but tho' I urg'd to him, that is was absurd to suppose that an infinite Creator would have such glorious parts of his Creation void and empty of proper classes of his creatures, like an extravagant builder raising more edifices than he was able to place fitting furniture in, and used many arguments, which I need not repeat to your Lordship, I could hardly make him confess, that he thought it very probable that they must be inhabited.

[333] However, I had the pleasure to find that my hopes had not deceiv'd me, and that what I had said now and formerly of Astronomy's being driven out of *Egypt*, and those parts of his Empire, which Nature had, as it were, cut out for an Observatory for this lovely Science, had made great impressions on him. In short, before we parted, he order'd the Vizier to take care directly for chusing a fit place there, and building and

endowing an Astronomical College, as I should direct; and desir'd that I should send for some of the best Professors in *Europe* to settle there, with large and honourable provisions. I can assure your Lordship this is already settled so far, that a large quantity of ground near *Grand-Cairo* is set out, and by this time actually building; and as I am persuaded no delay or obstacle will arise from hence to compleat this noble design, I intreat your Lordship to give such orders, that some excellent Astronomers may be prevail'd with to set out with the next fleet for *Turky*, whose provision and protection to their full content, I do hereby, on sufficient warrant, bind my self to be answerable for.

Judge, my Lord, what progresses we shall be able to make in this noble Science, when [334] she is restor'd to her native Empire, and the serene and cloudless skies of *Egypt*, where neither rains nor vapours, nor the exhalations, mists and fogs of our Northern Climate shall once interrupt her divine Contemplations. What discoveries shall we not make in the Heavens of new Stars arising, old ones decaying, unobserv'd Comets, with new Suns and Planets in their several systems, arranging the thousands and then thousands of the yet undiscover'd hosts of Heaven, in the beauteous order and array of Glory, in which their omnipotent Creator has plac'd them in his infinite Wisdom and Power?

But I must leave this subject, my Lord, lest I run out into too great lengths on it; and tho' I have often since attended the Grand Signior, to shew him the rest of the Planets, and particularly *Saturn* with his Ring, and his Satellites, which he was infinitely pleas'd with; and had many farther conversations with him on their Eclipses, one of which I shew'd him; and also on the new discoveries and improvements in Astronomy, and the new College for its Professors in *Egypt*; yet as the repetition of them would be needless, after what I have [335] said on them here, I shall not trouble you with them.

On my return home from the Seraglio, I met your Lordship's dispatches of the 28th of *December*; but as my last of the 25th of *Febr.* effectually answer'd all their Contents, I shall make no other return to them here, than my humble thanks for the care you express so obligingly for me, and to make my compliments to Mr. Secretary for the huge Pacquets of *English* News Papers he was pleas'd to inclose to me. It was really a surprize to me, to see such a vast spawn of the productions of these insects, that thus float and feed upon the air we breathe, and have no appearance of existence but in their constant buzzing about, hearkening out, and attending and list'ning to the noise and motions of their neighbours. They seem to make their ears as useful to them, as the Pigmies which* *Pigafetta* tells us he saw in the Island of *Aruchet* near the *Moluccas*, who liv'd in dark high caverns

---

* Viaggio del sig. Ant. Pigafetta, & c. Racolti da Ranusio, *p.* 368. *Venet.* 1588.

(like the garrets, I suppose, of these Authors) and lay upon one ear as a bed, and cover't themselves by way of warm bedcloaths with the other.

[336] I send your Lordship, as a little return for all your favours, a very excellent statue of *Constantine* the Great, which was lately dug up near this city by some *Greek* masons, and with great difficulty preserv'd from the barbarous hands of the workmen, who maim all such statues as they meet with any where. It is the more curious, because it is represented with a cross to it; which (tho' the Ecclesiastical Writers assure us there were many such erected to him) is, I believe, the only one to be found now in *Europe*. Your Lordship will observe, that it perfectly agrees with the Medals of this Emperor that are stampt with it, of which I send your Lordship two very fair and well preserv'd. He is crown'd by a victory on the reverse with this In- scription, *In hoc signo Victor eris*; and I am rejoic'd I have got such a treasure to adorn that admirable collection you have made, and are daily increasing.

Every thing here continues on the same happy foot as when I last wrote, and our merchants are treated with the greatest favour and regard we can possible desire. As I have few correspondents, I have no foreign news worth sending your Lordship, unless the late death of his *Polish* Majesty, [337] who, after the most intemperate Life, died at (I think) near eighty. A great age for any one to arrive at, and especially a King; it being observ'd by historians, that of all the *Roman*, *Greek*, *French* and *German* Emperors, but four liv'd to eighty, and but five Popes; and none of those in any late Century.

He was so given up to his belly, one would have thought he could not have liv'd to fifty, unless the devil had kept him alive to procure credit to intemperance. He was a sowre, ill-natur'd man, but an excellent King; for it made him inaccessible to flatterers, and not to be practis'd on by favourites, and the skilfullest courtiers, who could neither lead or blind him. He had so little Religion, that he infamously gave up that which he was born in for his Crown; and us'd to say, as it was necessary to profess some kind or other, if he was not a Prince, he would have lik'd that of the *Jews* best, because it allow'd railing at all the rest, and was never believ'd or minded by those that profest it.

As that Crown is soon to be set to sale, I hear there are already as many new Kings set up among them, as ever were made on [338] a twelfth-night for diversion; and will probably have the same fate, and be unking'd again, when their parties that set them up are tir'd of them and their silly play, and sick of the poppets they created.

I beg the continuation of your Lordship's undeserv'd favours, and to believe me, with all possible gratitude, my Lord,

Your Lordship's, &c.

Stanhope.

To the Lord High-Treasurer, & c.

Moscow, March 8. 1997.

My Lord,

Since mine of the 29th of *November* and 17th of *January*, I have receiv'd but one short one from your Lordship of the 26th of *February*, in which you acknowledge the receipt of mine, and are so good as to desire the continuance of my correspondence, and to express some satisfaction in the accounts I have hitherto had the happiness to send you.

You are pleas'd also to desire the best information I can procure you, in relation to the Jesuits practicing Physick here with surprizing success; which, you are told, has [339] contributed to their interest in this Court, as much as any one method I took notice of to your Lordship, in relation to the prodigious growth of that Society in *Muscovy.*

As I have endeavour'd to prepare myself to obey your Lordship's commands on this head, I shall begin such accounts as I have been able to procure for you, with ingenuously confessing, that I quite overlook'd that particular; which was chiefly occasion'd by my considering them only as Ecclesiasticks, and omitting the disguises they wear here, and in all Courts, in every kind of profession that can give them interest and favour.

And indeed it must be allowed, that their great application to the study of this profession has been of infinite credit and service to them, by the prodigious success they have had in their practice at the Czar's Court, and throughout his Empire; and tho' this is ascrib'd, by common report, to the prayers of the Society, that bring a blessing down on all their prescriptions, yet I fancy I shall have no difficulty to persuade your Lordship, that 'tis owing to their employing some of the most learned and ingenious men of their whole body in the business of this profession. For as by the *Athenian* Law, all [340] mean, illiterate people, and slaves particularly were forbid to practice Physick; which, if put in force now, would exclude numbers of base, servile, mercenary creatures, who follow that employment, and would force them to turn Horse-farriers and Rat-catchers; so these Fathers have taken care that none of their body should study this branch of learning, who were either of mean parts or griping spirits. By this means, what between vast reading and a generous neglect of fees, as well as close attendance on their patients, and several new methods they have establish'd, it is hardly credible how few that have recourse to their medicines, have fail'd of being recover'd, where old age, or a weakness of nature, or a long course of intemperance and debauchery, did not occasion it. I have as little faith in the common run of Physicians as most people, but I must own I have alter'd my thoughts on that article, since I have seen such effects of their skill; and I fancy were the ingenious *Petrarch* now living, he would not write in the title page of his *Hippocrates*'s Aphorisms, as he did in his days that odd Axiom, *Nulla certior via ad salutem quam medico* [341] *caruisse*, for the reverse of it is now become true.

There have of late years prodigius genius's in physick appear'd in *Great-Britain*, who, like new stars, have enlightned the darkness of the last age, and have plainly shewn, not to say demonstrated, the reasons of the several virtues and operations, by means of which their prescribed Medicines produce such vast changes in our bodies. Nay, Dr. *Turner*, in his *Treatise de principiis rerum*, has found out evidently the fountain and first principle of life and action in all animated and vegetable bodies, which formerly appear'd such an unfathomable mystery to our Ancestors, who were wandering about and groping in the dark after knowledge; or, at most, wishing in the dawn of its morning for that bright and glorious Day that has since broke out upon us.

The Jesuits have studied the works of these great men with no small application, and by improving their hints, and introducing several new methods and rules, have been of vast service to the publick; some of these I shall now lay before your Lordship [342], as I have observ'd them my self, or have been appriz'd of them by others.

And I shall begin with that excellent one of prohibiting all Apothecaries to practice on the severest penalties. For besides the want of skill in a profession they can never be supposed masters of, it is certain those Gentlemen used to bestow their attendance on the poor *Russians*, merely with a view to be well paid for their drugs, (that would otherwise have rotted on their shelves) just as Vintners give a sunday's dinner to their customers, provided they pay for the wine they drink. After all, my Lord, there is methinks as good ground for this Law, as for one we have in *Great-Britain*, that forbids Drovers to be Butchers, it being unreasonable that the same persons who provide the cattle we are to make use of, should also have liberty to kill.

Another method they introduc'd here, and which produc'd a great care in the physician of his patient's recovery, was, obliging the Doctor to refund half his fees in case of the death of the sick person. This ingratiated them much with the people, as it shew'd a generous neglect of gain in the college that establish'd the rule, and [343] also spurr'd on all practitioners to do their utmost to serve their patients, or to pay a reasonable fine for their want of success.

In the next place, all that were licens'd to practice, were oblig'd to keep regular Diaries of every symptom in their patients from the least to the greatest, and to have the Friends and nurse-keepers that were about them write down all things observable in their absence, and to give copies (if demanded) of their prescriptions, in case the sick person died, to the censors of the college, where any ignorant or faulty conduct was fineable. By this means the hands of those dangerous animals, officious Physicians as well as ignorant ones, were severely tied up, and caution and judgment made necessary in prescribing.

But further, all were obliged to see their prescriptions made up themselves, and that right and good drugs were only used; by which means thousands of lives were sav'd, that us'd to be sacrific'd to the knavery of Apothecaries, who gave bad ones, or the ignorance of their apprentices, who often gave wrong ones; both which evils were thus effectually prevented.

[344] Another method they were oblig'd to observe, was, that each practitioner was sworn to report to the college and censors all such extraordinary cases as occur'd in his practice, and his observations on them, and at least three each year; out of which a choice collection was made, and annually publish'd for the service of the publick, with proper notes and reflections: and this occasion'd great helps to the advancement of the Science in general, and the improvement of each member of the college in particular.

In the next place, the Czar, at their request, gave the college the lives and bodies of so many condemn'd Felons as they pleas'd, to try all such experiments on, which they judg'd useful to improve their Science. By this means many thousands of such experiments were made, to the vast emolument of the world, and at the same time the lives of as many thousand honest *Russians* sav'd, that us'd to be sacrific'd to the folly, the curiosity, or rashness of their Doctors, by substituting Malefactors to be purg'd, blooded, and vomited, and to run thro' all the ordeal fire of experiments, in their room.

[345] But again, the college having divided all diseases incident to the human body into four parts, each member was oblig'd, after ten years practice, to confine themselves entirely to the list of such diseases, as they judg'd themselves best qualified to succeed in the cure of, and all the rest of their lives to meddle with no other distempers, unless in case of necessity. By this means their studies and experience being thus entirely apply'd to a narrower province, they grew in time so absolutely masters of all that lay within their own district, that they frequently perform'd cures in the most desperate cases, and were able to exert the whole force of their art in that particular branch which they apply'd their studies and practice to. And certainly, my Lord, it is to this regulation of the Jesuit Physicians in *Russia*, as much as any thing I have observ'd, that we have found out since the 19th Century so many wonderful specificks for the Jaundice, Bloody-Flux, Small-Pox, Dropsy, Green-Sickness, and Cholick, which otherwise would never have been discover'd, or at least not so soon. With the same sagacity they have introduc'd the use of scales into their practice, and the weighing Urine with greater caution than [346] Bankers do Gold; from whence in many cases what advantages have arisen, is known to all. Nor with less care and judgment have they brought Musick into use in particular disorders,

which before their cultivating this Science, was never once thought of any service, even in melancholy or phrenetick disorders themselves.

But I must not pass by unmention'd another singular method they have ever used this last forty years here, and that is, curing several disorders by milk of goats and asses, which they have brought to prodigious perfection by several methods that are reserv'd to themselves. One of these I know by experience, is dieting the animal whose milk they prescribe with particular kinds of herbs, whose juices and qualities they judge most efficacious and conducive to the circumstances of the distemper. The service, (the miracles, I may say) they have done in this way is perfectly prodigious; and indeed as they first introduc'd the skilful use of the admirable *Chinese* Root Ginseng with such success in most cases, so they are observed as much as pos- sible to deal in the simplest medicines, and frequently restore men to health with as much ease as *Asclepiades* did, who [347] only used cold water and wine in his method of cure.

This single circumstance in the practice of Physick is surely of vast importance; and as one of the prayers in the wise *Italian's* Litany, is, *Da Guazzabuglio di medici*; so certainly that terrible hodge-podge of drugs, powders, and a thousand compounded recipes we are obliged to swallow for a little ease or health, is a hazardous and as unpleasant a circumstance as I know in all their method of prescribing. I remember to have read in a great physician's works, that what naturalists assert, that whoever draws the root of *Moly, Cynospastus,* or Mandrake, out of the earth, will die soon after, is a meer vulgar error; but I wish he could as easily convince us, that those who take their roots and drugs inwardly, are not often seiz'd with death for their pains. And indeed there is nothing I admire more in their conduct, than their banishing those heaps of drugs which used to enter into the prescriptions of most physicians, and which formerly many of them were obliged to keep up, *propter metum Judæorum,* tho' thereby they sacrific'd our lives to the dishonest gain of those vermin [348] the Apothecaries, whom they were afraid to disoblige.

Their gentleness and caution to avoid violent courses, is much applauded also. Some physicians purge, bleed, blister and vomit with such haste and fury, that they may be said rather to murther the disease than to cure the man, who is left weak and spent may be for life; and, like a Country where the King gets the better by a bloody civil war, they save the man, by ruining the happy constitution he enjoyed before. This is what the Jesuits are remarkable for avoiding, unless where it is absolutely necessary indeed; which, as they manage matters, seldom happens.

There is another particular, which is entirely owing to them, and which has been very serviceable to these people, that I must not forget to take notice of. Your Lordship has often heard now epidemical pleurisies used to be here, and what numbers they swept away of the poor *Russians* every year, like the plague in *Turky*.

To remedy this, the Czar, at the instigation of the Jesuits, introduc'd the custom of using linseed-oil by the common people with all eatables, where olive or sallad-oil was formerly [349] used (on which last he laid great duties;) and by means of this medicinable kind of sustenance, they have so effectually removed this reigning kind of pestilence, as I may call it, that it is seldom known to make any ravage among them now. This was at once restoring the health of a nation, my Lord; there remain'd only to banish the gluttony and drunkenness of the Nobility and Knezzes, to have in a manner compleated the cure.

One would think, my Lord, I had reckon'd up enough of their performances, and yet I have one more to touch upon that is sufficiently remarkable, and that is, a pleasant Elixir which they have invented, a few drops of which, taken just going to bed, never fails to give easy rest, and, what is most extraordinary, pleasant dreams. You see, my Lord, their skill has contriv'd to reach to that half of our lives (which we give to sleep) that before lay entirely out of our power and theirs; and as they have invented a specifick, to make it not only easy but delightful to us, I think they almost deserve to have altars and monuments raised to them.

[350] But, my Lord, after what I have said to the advantage of these Gentlemen, I am sorry to add one reflection that overturns all their glory; and that is, tho' they have made the practice of Physick extremely laborious to themselves, and useful to others (beyond what it ever was known to be) by these methods and inventions; yet they have done it all with faulty views, to enslave those they pretend to serve, and establish the Empire of the *Vatican*, and all its superstitions and errors. Nay, my Lord, it is said, that they watch the sinking spirits and the dying hours of their patients, to screw from them, by their sollicitations and importunity, large legacies and considerable donations to their society; and, what is still more detestable, that they are as industrious and artful to dispatch their enemies out of the way, as they are to preserve the health and lives of their friends. It is certain, there have not wanted instances in this kind that have occasion'd such suspicions; yet they have entirely surmounted them, and beat down all opposition, by letting every one see it was in vain to contrive any remedy against their power; it being as useless an attempt (in *Caligula's* [351] words) as *Agrippina's Antidotum versus Cæsarem*.

But it is time to quit this subject, to acquaint your Lordship with something more material, and that is, the apprehension every one is in here, that the war between this Crown and *Sweden* is like to be carried on by both sides, with greater animosity and resolution than ever, this approaching season. They work night and day at *Petersburg* in their preparations to have their fleet in the *Baltick*, before the *Swedes* can be able to leave their ports; and indeed, if the frost were once gone, and the Harbours open, I believe we should soon see the *Muscovite* squadron at sea. They carry on their levies for their land forces with all possible application, and have made large remittances to *Poland* and *Germany*, to remount their cavalry; and tho' I am inform'd by a sure hand, that the *Swedes* are doing their utmost not to be unprepared for them; yet I am very doubtful they will not prove so good a match for them this campaign as they did last. How far his Majesty's mediation between the contending powers may be proper, your Lordship and the Kind are the best Judges; but I am privately assured, it would be very [352] useful to the *Swede*, and probably not unacceptable to this Court.

I know not, while the Princes of the Earth are contending for these little corners of it, whether it may entertain your Lordship, to give you a little history of an honest Gentleman here, one *Rabbi Abraham Abrabanel*, who has very fairly put in his claim to the whole* of it.

He is a mad enthusiastical *Jew*, who followed merchandize, and broke; and after travelling over most part of *Europe*, settled here at *Mosco*, and was employ'd at last by the Czar, as his first herald, and got a good deal of money by drawing up genealogies for the *Russian* Knezzes and Noblemen, whose pride he flatter'd, by tracing up the source of their families further than history or truth could carry them. He had a very numerous family, and as the *Jews* here paid him great respect, as being a descendant from the famous *Abrabanel* of the tribe of *Judah*, and the house of *David*; his pride and some losses in his fortune turned his head, and made him take up one of the oddest fancies that ever madman thought of, that [353] he is the direct descendant from *Adam* in a right line by *Noah*, and has a full title to his father's inheritance, the world. Tho' he hehaved very oddly in his family and neighbourhood, yet no one ever disturbed him, till he went one day directly to the Czar's apartments, and making way for himself thro' all the crowd, humbly acquainted him with his pretensions, and desired him to set a good example to the princes of the world, by resigning his Empire to him.

The Czar was so good as to compassionate the poor creature's disorder, which he soon perceiv'd by his appearance and gestures, as well as his speech, and very gently desired him to give him some time to settle his private affairs, before he resigned his crown; and promised him to have all possible regard shewn in the mean while, both to his person and remonstrances: But as he happen'd to smile in speaking these words, *Rabbi Abraham*'s passion was raised so high, that he called him a vile dissembling usurper, and ordered the guards to seize him. Your Lordship may easily imagine the consequence was, that they very basely neglected his commands, and convey'd him with less respect than became his station as Emperor [354] of the World, to the pnblick Bedlam where they confine madmen.

---

* *Vide Filmer*'s Patriarchal Scheme.

This affair has occasion'd much mirth; and as the Czar has order'd great care to be taken of him, I had the curiosity to pay him a visit yesterday along with the *Danish* Envoy here, to see if we cou'd make any tolerable terms for our royal Masters. We found him in a neat, clean room, where his wife was sitting by him weeping bitterly; but he was in no manner of concern, but writing a great many letters which lay in heaps before him. As he offends no body, we began to discourse with him of his affairs, and desir'd to know calmly what his pretensions were; because we were confident if the Princes of the World could be convinc'd of the justice of them, they would rather come to an amicable treaty, than dispute it with him against Conscience and Reason, by arms. As he knew us both, and our characters, by seeing us often at Court, he seem'd mightily pleas'd; and pulling a prodigious long genealogy out of his papers, he bid us read them there, and we should find he was the lineal descendant in the right line from *Adam*, and consequently had an undoubted title to every acre on the globe.

[355] We look'd over his paper with great respect, and told him we should represent the affair and his pretensions at our several Courts; but would be glad to know, whether he was not inclinable to compromise matters, and accept some kind of tribute, by way of acknowledgment of his title, and allow the present possessors to hold their Crowns under him as Fiefs of his great Empire. By the Crown of *David*, said he, it is a very fair proposal; and tho' I have eight sons who could fill the Thrones of *Europe*, to say nothing of the rest of the Earth, better than they have been for these five Centuries past, if your masters and the rest of their brethren will pay me 1 *s. per* acre, rough and smooth. I shall give them no farther disturbance, nor trouble my head with writing to my subjects on this dispute. It is true, says he, finding the Czar trifling with me, and putting off matters from week to week, I was drawing up manifestoes to all my vassals, and discharging them from owning their pretended masters any longer; and I have order'd all the inhabitants of the Earth to pay no further rents, taxes or customs to them; and if I can once cut off those supplies of their power and pride, I shall soon [356] humble them so far as to submit to me. The truth is, says he, taking me aside, and whispering me in the ear, I am under some perplexity what place to receive the money they bring me in; for having at present no one of my Territories in my possession, if they should pay it me here, this Usurper the Czar might be so dishonest and base, as to seize on it for his own use, and possibly might hang up some of my poor, faithful vassals for their loyalty to me.

I told him very freely as his friend, that his doubts were reasonable, and that he should first try to get into some one of his Kingdoms by the way of treaty, before he order'd any of his rents or subsidies to come into him, unless a few for his private occasions. He thank'd me very gratefully for my good advice, and told me he was resolv'd to follow it; and in the mean time, says he, I shall send four general manifestoes to the four quarters of the World, and circular letters to the several Princes and their subjects, acquainting them with my title, and commanding them to acknowledge it. After all, said he with tears in his eyes, God knows how far they may regard my remonstrances; but considering how few of them [357] can pretend the least title under my great Ancestor; and besides that defect in their titles, how much worse they govern my poor people than I should, I think they might in conscience either submit to me, or at least pay me a few millions of Rubles by way of an annual tribute. Besides, as I should be willing to take half those taxes and rents from my subjects which they extort from them, it is certain the poor people would gladly revolt to me if they durst, and if I had a tolerable army to maintain my just title.

I told him he spake very reasonably; but it was so difficult an affair, either to conquer his antagonists by force, or convince them by reason, that he must necessarily manage with the greatest caution and prudence to compass his ends. Sir, says he, you know not the circumstances of mankind as well as I do, who both from interest and inclination have so long consider'd their hardships and oppressions, and their uneasiness under their Tyrants, whose titles to their Empire are only founded in blood and violence, and a few sorry Laws which their swords have cut out for their own purposes. My people are torn in pieces by new Religions [358] of a hundred different cuts and fashions, by unjust Laws and worse Judges, by Poisons they call Physick, and Murderers they call Doctors, by Plunderers they call Landlords, and publick Villains whom they call Tax-gatherers. They have departed from all the good customs of their Ancestors before the flood, and after it; and have so far deviated from the right of succession in the lineal descendants, that I can maintain there is not this day in the world a single family that has the least title to the estates they enjoy.

There is no Prince in *Europe*, whose Genealogy I cannot trace up to people that were no later than 2000 years ago; either Pedlars or Tinkers, Lieutenants, Lacqueys or Lawyers, or at most menial Servants to several of my relations. There is not a Nobleman, Knight or Gentleman on earth, who is a lineal descendant from his own forefathers: I have search'd into their Genealogies, and I find them in their different successions the sons of Coachmen and Footmen, Soldiers and Courtiers, Priests, Friars, Jesuits, and Valet de Chambres.

Besides all this, they have confounded right and wrong, vice and virtue; they take [359] corruption for justice, hypocrisy for religion, falshood for truth, lust for love, brutal fury for courage, cheating and fraud for honest gain, prodigality for generosity, pride for greatness of spirit, ribaldry for wit, debauchery for pleasure, purchases for legal titles, cunning for wisdom, slavery for liberty, and irreligion and infidelity for strength of reason and zeal for truth.

Nay, they mistake the butchers of mankind for heroes, readers for scholars, bastards for heirs at law, soldiers for patriots, flatterers for friends, and honest advisers for open enemies; they look on atheists as moral men: and in short, their conduct in every view is so equally absurd and wicked, that I am no longer able to bear with them; and I see evidently I must take the government of them into my own hand, to be able to reform them as they ought to be. Neither in truth do I resolve on this from any interested views of power and profit to myself and children, but barely for the general good of mankind, being willing to sacrifice the unquestionable title I have to the Empire of the World, to their service, if I could otherwise contrive any way to work a proper reformation among them in this depraved state of things.

[360] I told him I very much approv'd his generous intentions to serve the publick, and be as instrumental as his high birth and station entitled him to be: but that I was apprehensive his setting up his title, how just soever, might occasion prodigious wars and commotions in the world, which must certainly be a great affliction to him. Dear Sir, says he, what you say would deserve my consideration, if I did not certainly know, that obliging men, even by force (if force must be us'd) to acknowledge my title, would still deliver them from much greater evils. For be assur'd, says he, (in a very important whisper) all the famines, pestilences, commotions, desolations and wars that have afflicted the world these last 40 Centuries, have fallen upon men by the vengeance of a just Providence, enrag'd to see the succession and claim of my family laid aside and neglected by a wicked and degenerate race of villains and traitors. He accompanied this with a flood of tears; and turning to his wife, My dear, says he, if your Majesty will reach me those papers I have written, I think this will be an excellent opportunity for dispersing them through my subjects, and Gentlemen, says he, as [361] you are the first of my vassals who have shewn a sense of your duty and inclinations to return to your allegiance, if you will send them to the several Princes they are directed to, and assist me to bring about the Revolution I have resolv'd on, I shall both consider your respective Masters, and (tho' I can't part with any of my dominions in *Europe*) I hereby promise them the best Territories in my *Asian* or *African*, or at worst in my *American* Continent. But by this time the farce grew too tedious; and therefore desiring a few weeks to consider of his demands, we thought fit to retire, and leave his Imperial Majesty to write his dispatches without the help of Secretaries or Counsellors. I am sorry I forgot to beg his Majesty to take care of his precious health, and to be on his guard against his mighty rivals for the Empire of the World the Jesuits, and the dangerous Monarchy of the *Solipsi*, who I fear are so jealous of all rivals in interest and power, they will be very apt, by fraud, or poison, or violence, to remove so dangerous a Competitor out of the way.

But I must make amends to your Lordship for this trivial amusement, by a present that is really worth your consideration and [362] regard, which I send you by this bearer; and that is no less than sixty volumes in *Folio* of the late Czar's travels thro' *Europe*, who, as your Lordship knows, never stirr'd out of his own Empire. He was a Prince of great natural genius and abilities; but as he did not approve of his own or any great Princes travelling, he employ'd a number of the most able and understanding men he cou'd procure, to take that trouble for him, and travel thro' the whole tour of *Europe*, accompanied with excellent designers, who at all proper stations should graphically design the face of nature, and the situation of rivers, towns, palaces, castles, mountains and plains, in the very manner the eye survey'd them on the spot. Besides this, they were oblig'd to take draughts of all the finest gardens and improvements, the most famous performances in Architecture, Painting and Sculpture; and even the very habits, the very looks, shape and air of the people of every country they pass'd thro'. Nay, they were to design the very cattle, fishes, birds; and, in a word, every thing that could deserve their notice in their journeys: all which they were to accompany with the best notes, remarks and observations possible. But this [363] is not the only treasure that has enrich'd these volumes; for here are all the rarities of the best cabinets in *Europe* for choice collections in all kinds, express'd to the life in admirable cuts, and explained by short judicious dissertations. In these, all the best statues, and their habits, medals, seals, intaglias and basso-relievos, inscriptions, vases, mausoleums, sacrificing instruments and vessels, sepulchral and other lamps, lachrymatory and sepulchral urns, idols, engines, and instruments of war; rings, symbols of cities and countries, instruments of musick, and the weights and measures of the ancients, are incomparably represented, as well as whatever relates to the temple and worship of their Gods; not omitting all the modern productions of art and nature in animals, plants, minerals, metals, and the manual improvements of the several Sciences. An immense profusion of all these, digested under their proper heads, are engrav'd on these copper plates in a beautiful and regular order, where we may at once form the clearest notions of all such things, without running the hazards of ill health, as well as the corruption of faith and manners, which travelling is generally accompanied with, and [364] have at least all the benefits that one can borrow from the eye in performing the tour of *Europe*. The Czar has about 1000 Copies made of them, which are presented as the greatest favours to those they design to oblige; and as I owe this I have receiv'd to your Lordship's friendship, by whose means I am fix'd here, I thought it a piece of justice to restore them to the hand, by whose mediation I became posses'd of it from the Czar's bounty.

If it were not for the Patriarch's death, who died here last week, I should have no news of any consequence to communicate to your Lordship. Tho' he was brought over, in the latter part of his life, to all the Jesuits measures in modelling this Church to submit to the Pope, yet he would have been an excellent Bishop but for one fault, which I believe few men were ever guilty of before him. He was a learned, sensible, pious man, and with the greatest zeal to serve the cause of Religion and Virtue, he had an utter contempt for that epidemical evil in the Christian Church, the building up a fortune, and making a family. But as he ow'd his advancement to the Prince *Dolhorouky*, thro' a false notion of gratitude to the end of his [365] life, he never ceas'd heaping preferments on every relation or friend, nay, on every dependant of that Prince, how worthless soever, (against all reason, nay, against his own) on the sole merit of their belonging to that family. This is a little obscur'd the lustre of his virtues, and might teach us (but, alas! we do not want the caution) that we should not be too violently grateful; which is almost as dangerous as being too violently in love, and distracts and biasses the judgment as much. But we may forgive his excellent Person this weakness, which was compensated by so many great and shining virtues; and besides, there is so little danger of his example being infectious, that I fancy he is the first man in this age, who (in his character) fell a martyr to gratitude. He is to be buried with a great solemnity, which the Jesuits are to have the management of, as well as of providing him an humble, docible Successor, who, 'tis said, will certainly be the Bishop of *Novogorod*. One very unfit for such a charge, being an old, weak, injudicious creature, without will, or even speech or passions of his own, but as he is inspir'd and mov'd, like a puppet, by the hands of these jugglers behind the curtain; and so [366] notoriously dull, that the *Knez Petrowisky* told him in a violent quarrel this winter, his head was so barren (he is very bald) that it would not even bear hair. Yet to these very defects, which ought to have prevented his promotion, it is that he owes his advancement: a thing, miserable and unfortunate as it is, that often happens in the world; these Jesuits being like those mungrel sort of curs, that would never find a master to own them, but for such poor blind wretches, who cherish and feed them, that they may lead and guide them in the ways of the world.

But I detain your Lordship too long with these trifles, and therefore will not increase their number by vain and useless professions of being on a thousand accounts, and by a thousand ties,

My Lord,
Your Lordship's, &c.

Clare.

London, Chelsea, Feb. 24. 1999.

My Lord,

I Had the pleasure of receiving yours of *December* the 16th and *February* the 8th, and have now the shame of answering them [367] together; but if your Excellency considers the multiplicity of affairs that have been on the carpet of late, and in which I have been more than ordinarily engag'd; you will not take it unkindly, if I am more dilatory in my answers, than my strong attachment to your noble family, and my personal regard and esteem for your merit and services, may justly demand from me.

In the mean time, I have not been wanting in my care, as to those negotiations you are charg'd with, as the dispatches from Mr. Secretary *Bridges* will witness for me; nor in my respects for your brother, who is now one of the two Secretaries for foreign affairs. It is true, the salary, by increasing the number of Secretaries to four, is not so considerable as formerly, yet the credit and honour of the place will be of greater service than a more lucrative employment.

His Majesty expects with impatience the resolutions of the *French* Court, as to the affair of opposing the Inquisition. As you have receiv'd his instructions on that affair from his own hand, you will do well to return as exact an account as possible of your next audience, and to shew your utmost dexterity to spirit them up to vigorous [368] resolutions on that matter, which may produce events of vast service to that crown and this, in humbling the exorbitant power of the empire of the *Vatican*. Your care in reviewing our *French* seaports and garrisons, and the works carrying on in the harbours of *Dunkirk* and *Calais*, gave his Majesty much satisfaction; and be assur'd, I shall endeavour to improve the impressions which your diligence and skill, in observing the state of things where you are, have made on him, to the utmost.

The ability and application of the *French* Ministers to retrieve the low condition a weak and unfortunate reign has reduced their country to, is very commendable; and as she can never recover strength enough in half a century to make her once more an object of our jealousy, it is our interest to support rather than distress her, lest she becomes a perfect province to *Rome*. *Cæsar* left her so, and there are many cowled *Cæsars* beyond the *Alps*, and in her own bowels, whose heads are as wise and bald as his, who would make her so again, if the pastoral staff and crosier did not want something of the force and vigour of his sword. Our accounts from *Rome* leave us no shadow [369] of doubt of this, as well as their deep designs on *Germany*; but I hope the recovery of the Emperor, and a vigorous opposing the establishment of the Inquisition, will give us both room and time to lay such invincible obstacles in her way, as she can never get over.

But Mr. Secretary has so fully enlarged on this subject to you formerly, that there is no occasion for renewing any discourse on it now to your Excellency, who are also so well appriz'd of the state of affairs in *Europe*; and therefore I shall only add my earnest desires that you may continue to do service to the King and your Country, and honour to the character you sustain, by observing and taking hold of every occasion that offers, of making his Majesty's cares for the service of the world more and more successful.

I observe with pleasure (to pass to another subject) that while your Excellency is thus sollicitous for the service of the publick, you are perfectly regardless as to your own interest here; and particularly, as to the Royal Fishery and Plantation Companies, in both which you have so large a stock, and are so deeply engag'd. As those corporations have been entirely new modell'd [370] by the act past this last sessions, and much improv'd from the state they have been in, since *Frederick* the first and *George* the third's establishing them, till now, I believe it will be a pleasure to you, if I acquaint you with their present circumstances.

I shall begin with the Royal Fishery, to which this act has assign'd six new ports to the ten formerly appointed, and obliges the company to keep at least 200000 hands employ'd, either as Coopers, Ship-wrights, Smiths, Cawkers, Sawyers, Sailors, Fishers, and Sailmakers; or else in making nets, baskets, ropes, dressing and spinning hemp and flax, and weaving poledavies. Of these hands, there are to be at least 1600 lame and 1000 blind people employ'd in ropes and net-making, and the hemp and flax articles. The company must keep at the least 1000 Busses employ'd, and one fifth of all their hands, boys from 11 to 16 years of age, and one third new men, who had never been at sea before, as a nursery for seamen; and are to furnish the royal nave, on forty days notice, with 4000 mariners. On these accounts it is enacted, that for the encouragement of the company, and those who enter into wages with them, and enabling them [371] who carry on the trade (tho' less gainful to private persons, yet more serviceable to the Nation than any other) to pursue it vigorously, the fourth of all the Profit of play-houses, shows, prize-fighters, operas, musick-meetings and gaming-houses, shall be paid to them for ever; and also the 200th part of all money or land recover'd at law, and the same of all immoveables that are sold. That all common beggars and vagabonds, and all foundlings, when eight years old, shall belong to the company, and be seiz'd by them, and kept in their work-houses for seven years, allowing them cloaths and diet, without wages. That no person shall have more than 10000 *l*. stock, nor less than one, in the company's funds, except his Majesty, who shall have 20000 *l*. embark'd therein; and that the tolls and customs for passage on the great canals cut by *George* III. and *Frederick* II. from *Bristol* to the *Thames*, from *Southampton* to *Winchester*, and from sea to sea from *Carlisle* to the *Humber*, be paid also to them. That for their further encouragement, each

Friday in every week no person shall eat flesh, on severe penalties nam'd in the act; and every [372] house in which are five inhabitants, besides children, shall be oblig'd to take from them one barrel of herring or other fish, at the market-price.

This is the main act, which by the nearness of our shores, and being furnish'd with all victualling and fishing necessaries within our selves, without the taxes the *Dutch* pay their masters; and being nearer the *Baltick*, and most foreign markets, enables us to undersell all our rivals in this trade, to breed up every year several thousand Seamen, and employ numbers of our useless poor, and import immense sums of treasure to our happy Island. But the great advantages this new model of the royal Fishery has procur'd us, are best seen by its stocks having risen above five *per Cent.* which your Lordship will be a great gainer by. The Plantation-Company for the new Colonies in the *West-Indies*, is by the same act favour'd by great encouragements, as to all duties of exports and imports, and a grant of three millions of acres, to be laid out and applotted equally to all planters who shall settle there, and build new towns. They have also large Premiums settled for such limited quantities of iron, pitch, tar, hemp, flax, silk, [373] indigo, wine or oil, as they shall import from them hither. This has rais'd their stock as considerably as the former, and will probably, in a few years, make us utterly independent of our neighbours in the North for all naval stores, which us'd to drain such immense sums from us.

I do not congratulate your Excellency on your particular advantage herein, but on the credit and honour you have gain'd, by being so zealous for the welfare of these two glorious companies, and the prodigious addition they are likely to give to the strength and wealth of our native country. They will not only enrich us vastly beyond any of our neighbours, (and they that are richest, will be able to carry on a war longest, and consequently tire out and subdue at last their enemies;) but they also vastly increase our naval strength, employ our starving poor, and will so far enlarge and extend our colonies on the Continent (greatly encourag'd by our former laws) that our trade will be every day growing more considerable. The very wine, oil and silk imported annually from them, is incredibly great already; and tho' in *Frederick* the first's and *George* the third's days, there [374] were hardly forty engines for throwing of silk in this nation, it is certain there are now above a hundred; and yet there are daily new ones set up by the company, which throw more silk with two or three hands, than by a vast number of workmen in the ordinary way. The demands for our goods and manufactures there, are within this last century (as I am assur'd) risen to double what they were before; and I doubt not but your Excellency will live to see our *Thames* like the famous River the *Tibiscus*, of which it was said, that one third of it was water, a second fish, and another shipping and boats.

The truth is, our colonies abroad have, and are likely to acquire still such an increase of hands and strength, that the greatest care will be necessary to keep the strongest of them dependent; and yet to provide that the weakest of them may not live on the blood and spirits of the mother nation, nor suck, if I may use the allusion, on her breast too long. I am confident as they will require, so they will well deserve, and fully repay this care. Besides the advantages of the commerce and navigation betwixt us, it is certain, they [375] generally in proportion produce greater, more sublime, and warlike spirits; as being compos'd of adventurous and daring people, or, at worst, of melancholy discontented men; which last, to say nothing of the other, (who must evidently be of service to us) are the best seed-bed for ingenious and inventive, as well as learned and judicious heads. It may indeed be objected to our foreign plantations, that they are in part made up of the filth and purgings of the nation, as felons and robbers; but we all know *Rome* it self built up all its courage and virtue on no better a foundation: and after all, even such offenders have often such resolution, subtilty, strength, sharpness and activity, as make their posterity, (by these qualities they derive from them,) sufficient amends for their descending from such evil ancestors.

I am confident the new bishopricks founded among them by the piety and generosity of his Majesty's ancestors, as well as those of *Carolina, Barbadoes* and *Boston*, establish'd by himself, will greatly contribute to the reformation of manners and principles in our colonies, and to the keeping them firm in their allegiance to the crown. Besides, as [376] the severe ecclesiastical discipline settled there against all profaneness and scandalous immorality in both laity and clergy, and the encouraging those two noble colleges, erected there by *George* III. have gone a great way already in their civilizing and improving them; so I doubt not but a regular continuance of them, will fully amend what is yet wanting.

The melancholy prospect you have drawn, as to the corruption and debauchery of the *French* nobles, and the misery and excessive poverty of the lower people, must surprize every one, who considers the glory, virtue, and bravery of that nation in the last centuries, that cost her jealous neighbours such treasures of wealth and blood to prevent the universal empire she aim'd at in those days. It is true, one would not see so dangerous a rival restor'd to her former strength and vigour; but yet a generous enemy cannot see her present misfortunes, without some regret. However, a few years and a wise administration may by degrees resettle her affairs, and bring her out of that weak and languishing consumption that at present preys on her; but that deadly corruption and degeneracy of faith [377] and manners that infects her clergy and laity, seems of a more desperate malignancy, because it does not only prey on her vitals, but is also encourag'd and increas'd by those physicians, who are only able to undertake the cure. Certainly while the King and his Ministers find their account in imitating the maxims of *Venice*, keeping the interest of the clergy low, and their persons and character contemptible, Religion and the influence of the mitre will be utterly absorb'd in reason of state, and the power of the crown; and the subject must necessarily become equally sceptical in their belief, corrupt in their principles, and immoral in the conduct of their lives. Now tho' this will evidently lessen the unreasonable authority of the Pope and the Church with the nation; yet whether such measures will not at the same time unloose the sacred bonds, by which religion ties the allegiance of the people to the supreme magistrate, and make them bad subjects in proportion as they are bad christians, is worth the consideration of the mighty *Machiavels* of *France*.

Your Excellency, who is so well acquainted with the history of our own country, will be the better able to judge of such [378] consequences by the reign of *Frederick* III. in the 19th Century; when the miserable infection that had corrupted both the lives and faith of one part of our people, had almost driven the other to an absolute revolt in their allegiance and principles, to *Rome* and her superstitions. A consequence as natural in the politick, as a consumption to and old inveterate cough in the natural body; and if that wise Prince had not in time foreseen, how unsafe all foundations must be, that were not built on a pious, prudent regulation of the establish'd church, and by professing an abhorrence for libertinism and scepticism, and a zeal for our religion, by preferring and honouring none that were known to think meanly of it as to their opinions, or that dishonoured it by their lives, I know not if we had not now been bowing to images, and adoring the Pope. The struggles and convulsions which that looseness of principles we were infected with, produc'd in his father's reign, are known to every body, that does but cursorily look into the history of those times; and certainly, nothing but the piety and prudence of his son, could have restor'd our peace and happiness, whose calm and rational zeal for our [379] religion, in a few years wrought as great a change in the people, as ever happen'd on such an occasion since the days of *Constantine the Great*, when the sincere Christian triumph'd over the dissembling Pagan. But I will not follow this subject so far as it would lead me; and shall only say, that I heartily wish our neighbours in *France* may not find some consequences from the maxims they are pursuing, very different from what they expect; and that they are not tumbling into a greater, to avoid a lesser evil; like him who run into the water for fear of rain.

But let us leave these melancholy prospects for other nations, and let us reflect a little on the happy condition of our own country, and what it owes to that glorious Line of *Hanover*, that has adorned its throne with such an uninterrupted race of Heroes. What blessings have they not deriv'd on us, and our posterity, by their counsels at home, and their arms and courage abroad in the field; by giving us the best contriv'd and the best executed laws, and by raising the trade, wealth, power, and glory of our country to such heights, that our enemies may envy, but cannot lessen, and our friends may admire, but know not how to increase? [380] And certainly, as our ancestors used to say, when they were torn in pieces by their senseless and distracted factions, *That* England *could only be ruin'd by* England; so we may as truly maintain, that our happiness, and (that greatest of all our blessings) our Liberties, as now settled under our excellent Prince, can never be destroy'd but by Parliaments; and our Church, as it now stands fenced in by human Laws, and founded on the divine Law, can only be overturn'd by the Fathers of it the Bishops. As neither of those cases can be supposed possible, unless men should break thro' the most sacred trusts; and, in spite of the most solemn obligations that nature, religion, and honour, can bind them by, prove false to their Posterity, their Country, their King and their God; I think we may be justly secure of their continuance, and bid adieu to jealousies and fears!

I return your Excellency my thanks for your two manuscript treatises, which gave me much entertainment for three days, which I stole from the hurry of affairs in this restless town, to give to my gardens in my beloved retirement at *Windsor*. You have so high a relish for the true rational [381] pleasures of life, which are to be found in the silence and solitude of the country, that I shall easily persuade you to believe me, when I aver, that a debtor releas'd out of the City-*Marshalsea*, is not more transported with his liberty than I am, when I get loose from the crowd of importunate great beggars, (that besiege our chambers and anti-chambers, nay, our tables, and even our very beds, that should be sacred to peace and rest,) to breathe a little free air in that private retreat I am so fond of.

This was ever my way of thinking in my best health and vigor; but I must own, it grows much upon me of late, now that I am in the decline of life, and find the business of the world increase upon me, with the additional load of age and its infirmities. You will smile at me, may be, when I tell your Excellency, that I sometimes think seriously of retiring betimes, and living no longer, as I have done this thirty years, enslav'd to the world, and the wretched business of it, but to be at last possess'd of that delightful wish, *vivere sibi & musis*; or, to translate it into better *English*, to live to my self, and the great Author of all things.

[382] When or whether ever I shall be able to put this in execution, I cannot say; but if I do not tell you my fixt resolutions, I tell you at least my sincere desires, which lie nearer my heart than any thing else on this side of the grave; where, I think, I find many hints given me every hour, that I am soon to retire. I am sure the unreasonable fatigue I am forced to undergo at Court, will hurry me thither the sooner; and I often reflect on the remark in the *Talmud*, *That there is no prophet in the Old Testament*, (as they past their days without care) but they out-liv'd four Kings: and

that *Joseph* died before his brethren; *because,* says the *Talmudists, he was turmoil'd and barrass'd by being prime minister to* Pharaoh.

But these, you will say, are but the little fretful sallies of a mind sick of confinement, and thirsting after liberty; let us therefore leave them, without justifying them further with the least complaint of the malice, the envy, and ingratitude of the publick, which, (tho' perhaps not very successfully, yet still) we endeavour to serve; and return to the business of the world, and the worthy Creatures that make up the Crowd, and contribute to the noise of it.

[383] The best news I can send you from it (you see, my Lord, death and the grave are still in my thoughts) is the departure of sir *John Wingford,* the best lawyer, and the worst judge that ever appear'd in *England.* He was, at the bottom, extremely avaricious; he had long refus'd the place of chief Justice, which his Majesty had offer'd him, on account of his prodigious abilities, for the sake of the immense sums he got every year from the crowd of his clients. But as the severe act against lawyers exorbitant fees, and the infirmities of a bad constitution and a wasted body in the latter part of his life, at length oblig'd him to comply with the desires of his Majesty, and indeed of mankind, to accept of it; he did it with the worst grace imaginable, and as haughtily, as tho' he had sacrific'd the interest of his family to the good of the nation.

I must own, with shame for my ignorance, that I was no small instrument in settling that affair; and I can make no better atonement for it, than confessing that I have now reason to believe, this first and greatest of our lawyers, (whose memory and imagination, whose learning and judgment seem'd [384] by turns to outdo not only mankind, but themselves,) to the disgrace of human nature, prov'd the vilest and most corrupt of judges; and found the way, as I'm told, to make a comfortable balance between the bribes given his wife, and the fees of a private pleader at the bar. But he's gone to appear before the great Tribunal of his Maker, and therefore we shall leave him to stand or fall, as he pleases to determine; and I shall only add to the trouble I am giving your Excellency, since we are upon this subject, the death of a much honester judge, but a weaker man, my Lord Chancellor *Hoskins,* who died last week, a few days before him, of a fit of the apoplexy, which took him off in an instant.

Tho' his abilities were vastly meaner, yet his probity and honesty were infinitely superior to the others; but he had so perverse an integrity, that if any one attempted, or appeared to attempt, to lead or wheedle, or influence him in his decrees, he was sure to go the contrary way, where-ever it lead him. He carried this so far, that my Lord *D----* having a suit before him for a great Estate with Mr. *L----p,* in which he was sure to be cast, contriv'd to get a certain [385] great man, whom I shall not name, to recommend Mr. *L----p's* interest to him, with a kind of menace if the did not do him justice; by which single expedient he so turn'd the scales, that he run violently and headlong against Mr. *L----p*; and indeed against justice, and reason, and equity, to avoid the imaginary guilt of being influenc'd and biass'd.

It is true, some of his friends have attempted to make an apology for this weakness, by asserting, that on his being advanced to that bench, he had been misled in his judgment in one of the first causes he heard, by Mr. *P----l*, a near relation of his Wife's; and as he had been severely censur'd for it, like the scalded dog, he was afraid of the least shower of rain that threatned to fall on him: but surely this was but giving a stronger proof his weakness instead of excusing him, and shews more fully what vile and wretched creatures we are, when our poor scanty portion of reason is influenc'd by our passions or folly.

But I will quit this ungrateful subject for one that ought to be more agreeable to you and me; and that is, my sincere assurances, that as much as I have ever been attach'd to [386] the interest of your Excellency, and your noble family, I have never been biass'd by any other regard, than that evident merit and justice, which oblige me both by inclination and judgment to be, with the most reasonable passion and affection,

My Lord,
Your Excellency's, &c.

N----m.

My Lord,

Rome, Feb. 28. 1997.

By the last Courier by the way of *Lyons*, I was made happy in the receipt of your Lordship's of the 2^d instant, for which I return you my most sincere thanks; and as I hope I shall never forget the friendship and kindness you have express'd for me in it, so I shall make it the study of my life to deserve them more and more, by all the little services I am capable of rendring you and my royal Master.

I was favour'd with two dispatches of Mr. Secretary's the week before within six days of each other, to which I made the properest returns I could in the present state of things; and as they will be communicated to your Lordship, I shall not give you [387] the trouble of a needless repetition of them here. I have, since I made those answers, communicated the contents of them, and the advices and orders that occasion'd them to the Imperial and *French* Ambassador here; who seem very unanimous in entring into all his Majesty's measures, and express greater resolution and resentment against the Court, than I could have expected from the indifferent posture of their affairs at present.

They have given me such peremptory assurances of this kind, and of acting in concert with our Court, that I am fully convinc'd, if the Emperor's health continues to improve, we shall be able to give a greater blow to the ambitious views of this Empire of the *Vatican*, than she has receiv'd since *George* IVth oblig'd her forces to repass the *Alps*, and leave *France* in peace, and the *Swiss* in full possession of *Piedmont*, and that part of *Savoy* which they have ever since been masters of.

Your Lordship's reflections on the immeasurable growth of the Papal Power, and the weakness and blindness of those who contributed to it, are equally becoming your experience and knowledge as a statesman, and the honest zeal of a *Briton* and a Protestant [388]. If you express some resentment, it arises from a generous concern for the welfare and liberty of *Europe*, and the Honour of Christianity; both which have been in the most daring manner endanger'd, not to say destroy'd, by the insatiable ambition of this pretended Vicegerent of Heaven.

I am infinitely rejoic'd, that what I have hitherto been able to remit to you from hence, has been any ways agreeable to your Lordship; and shall therefore continue to send you such observations of the same nature, as I think may entertain you. This I am sure is a nobler use than any thing I am able to furnish you with can deserve to be applied to. The truth is, your Lordship has brought me so deeply in your debt by your last letter, that I fear all the diligence and means I can use, will be too little to balance accounts in any tolerable manner with you. However, I will depend on your goodness to accept of such inconsiderable payments as I am capable of making you. To begin some attempt this way, I must acquaint your Lordship, that since my last letters to Mr. Secretary, according to my instructions, in concert with the two Ambassadors, I demanded an audience of his Holiness the 20th instant; [389] to which I was immediately admitted, tho' he was that morning something indispos'd, by a cold he had got the day before, by walking too late in his gardens.

I found him in his great chamber hung with purple velvet, where he receiv'd me the first time I had audience of him; and as I perceiv'd by his smiling on me when I enter'd, and by the contenance he put on when I begun to speak to him, that he either was, or desir'd to make me think he was perfectly pleas'd with me, I resolv'd both to deliver the Memorial on the part of his Majesty in relation to the Inquisition; and also to lay before him, that in presenting it, I not only obey'd my Master's commands, but also in every line of it spoke the sense of the Emperor and his most Christian Majesty. Accordingly I acquainted his Holiness, that I had demanded that audience on an affair of the greatest importance to the reputation of the *Roman* See, the happiness of *France*, and the quiet of all her neighbours, who were deeply interested therein. That his Holiness, by the suggestions of men of unquiet and turbulent spirits, who were better understood than nam'd, had of late made several extra-ordinary steps to the setting up the Inquisition [390] in *France*, where his Predecessors had never once thought of establishing it; and as such an attempt will infallibly be accompanied by several ill consequences, I humbly besought him that he would, with that calmness and goodness which distinguish'd his character, allow me to lay before him those pressing reasons, which made it at all times improper, and at this time utterly impracticable. I observ'd he blush'd at these words; and rubbing his forehead with his hand, seem'd to be more than ordinarily mov'd; and as I expected he would have spoke, I stopp'd a little that I might frame what I had to say, as near as I could, to the temper he should put on; but as he only nodded to me, and bid me go on, I immediately proceeded.

That if those who press'd his Holiness to follow such counsels would consider the reasons that made such an attempt both now and at all times unadvisable, they would not shew such warmth and passion in carrying it on, as the manifestly had done. That these reasons were founded, First, on the natural temper of the *French*, who being of a free communicative disposition, and wearing their hearts as it were at their lips, would [391] be expos'd to a thousand accusations for words, that proceed from mere levity and gaiety of mind; rather than any guilt or wickedness of the heart, where heresy can only be feated.

That in the second place, it was notorious that there was no nation in *Christendom* where hereticks had been so effectually purg'd and driven out, even to the loss of many millions of subjects, as in *France*; and this both by open wars and private massacres, as well as the fiercest persecutions, tho' against the solemn stipulations of formal treaties, in which the honour of the Crown was constantly sacrific'd to its zeal for Religion, and its regard for this See.

That in the third place, as none of his Holiness's Predecessors had ever resolv'd on such an attempt before, it would be consider'd in *France* as the most violent outrage against the liberty of the subject, and the honour of the Crown, that could be contriv'd by the greatest enemies of both: and as *France* abounded with discontented people, and was still labouring under its late misfortunes, an innovation of that sort would be attended with such commotions and factions, as must end in an utter subversion of [392] the Royal, if the Inquisition should be establish'd; or if resisted by force, and succesfully oppos'd, of the Papal Authority. As I kept my eye fix'd on his Holiness, I plainly perceiv'd his colour come and go at these words, that shew'd an extraordinary emotion within; but as he put on a pretended smile, and endeavour'd to disguise it, by coughing two or three times, and stroaking his face with his handkerchief, and as I apprehended there was as much fear as anger in his contenance, I made no pause, but continued my remonstrances.

That, fourthly, as the power of the Clergy had of late years been carried higher than ever, and that at his Holiness had by the last treaty posses'd himself of two of the strongest places of *Dauphine*, and almost entirely master'd *Savoy*, and thereby, in effect, posses'd the keys of *France* as absolutely as those of St. *Peter*, this new attempt would be consider'd as setting up a Monarchy within a Monarchy, and opening the gates thereby to new violences, rapine and war.

That, fifthly, as some (and his Holiness best knew who) have and do obstinately maintain, that the Clergy are not subject to their secular Princes, nor oblig'd to obey [393] their Laws, whether contrary to the Ecclesiastical Estate or no, the least Princes could do, was to prevent their Lay Subjects being liable to imprisonment, corporal punishment, and even torture and death, from this terrible tribunal of the Clergy, especially since such power was expresly against the laws of the land.

That, in the sixth place, as there had been high disputes between the most Christian Kings and his Holiness's predecessors, concerning the privileges, rights and immunities of the *Gallican* Church, and the extent of the Papal Authority; the Tribunal of the Inquisition might be applied to extirpate such doctrines, and those who maintain them, as heresies and hereticks, to the endangering the power of the Crown and Church of that Nation. That moreover, as the Ecclesiastical Laws, establish'd in 1897. by *Paul* the IXth, had determin'd, that subjects might refuse tributes and taxes to their Sovereigns without sin, if they thought them unjust; and might disobey any other legally proclaim'd Law of their respective Princes, which they judg'd very inconvenient for them to submit to; and as all loyal subjects in *France* were generally of a different opinion [394], they might, on declaring their sentiments herein, be taken up and detained in the prisons of the Inquisition as hereticks, on account of their being loyal and good *Frenchmen*.

In the eight place, as to matters merely spiritual, since many doctrines are taught by certain divines (whom his Holiness highly esteem'd) as true, which the Christian Church have been so far from approving, that they have violently oppos'd them as false, and over-turning the very foundations of Christianity; if the Power of the Inquisition should be lodg'd (as it certainly would) in those very hands, the best Catholicks might be imprison'd and tortur'd by such as hereticks, for holding the real doctrines of Christianity; which possibly has been sometimes the case.

Here his Holiness, who had hitherto been entirely silent, was no longer able to conceal his impatience; but looking with a fix'd and stern contenance at me, ask'd me, if I had any thing further to offer to him? To which I thought it best to reply (cutting of two or three less agreeable remonstrances, that I should not too far incense him) that I had not. I have in command however [395], added I, to enforce all I have said to your Holiness, with representing it as the common sentiments of the Emperor, as well as his most Christian Majesty and my Master; in all whose names I humbly besought him to accept the Memorial I had in charge to deliver to him, (and therewithal I took it out of my breast, and in a very respectful manner presented it to him) beseeching his calm consideration and favourable answer to it.

He took it somewhat hastily, and put it into his pocket; and after a short pause answer'd me very calmly (being, as I conceiv'd by his mien and gestures, glad I had done) and told me, *imperatoria brevitate*, it should be fully consider'd, and as fully answer'd.

I saw evidently how disagreeable an entertainment I had given his Holiness; and being desirous, if possible, to smooth his temper, which I had ruffled too far by speaking more truth to him in half an hour, than probably he had heard in all his Pontificate before; I pulled out the Catalogue of our Nobility I had been favour'd with from your Lordship, very fairly copied and translated, and told him, in obedience to his commands, I had procur'd him the List of the *British* Peerage in the present Parliament.

[396] He seem'd glad to have the scene and the subject shifted; and taking it from me, and looking on the title, he ask'd me immediately how many Catholicks there were among them? To which I replied, after some hesitation, that in his Holiness's sense of things there was not one Catholick Peer in *Great Britain*; but that in our opinion, there was not one Heretick among the whole of our Nobility. He appear'd not a little surpriz'd, tho' he made me no answer; but look'd at me with an odd mixture of disgust and astonishment in his contenance, by which I plainly saw he was less acquainted with our affairs than I imagin'd. Immediately herewith, finding my attempt to remove his ill humour was likely to increase it, and conceiving my retiring would probably be the most agreeable compliment I could make him, (since I saw him not a little perplex'd and disturb'd) I put an end to my audience with the best looks and the best *Italian*, I could get together for the occasion.

I made not the least mention, as your Lordship sees, of the other articles relating to the *Swiss* Cantons, and our trade and fleet in these seas; because I judg'd it improper to insist on them now, when he appear'd in [397] none of the best dispositions to answer me as I could desire. I hope therefore you will approve of my delaying them for some happier hour, and the *mollia tempora fandi*, which I shall not fail to watch for, and take hold of, and give an exact account of the answers I receive thereon.

I know not whether it may not be agreeable, after entertaining your Lordship with this audience, to give you some account of the present Pope *Innocent* the XIXth; and though I doubt I shall draw his picture very unskilfully, I shall at least endeavour to avoid two great faults of Limners, and shall both give you a sketch that shall resemble him, and yet one that shall not flatter him. He is in his person a low, broad, strong-made man, and somewhat of the *staturâ quadratâ Suetonius* gives to *Vespasian*. He is of a saturnine complexion, and melancholy aspect, with large black eyes and a bottle nose, a well-shap'd mouth, but which appears with less advantage when he laughs, (which indeed is seldom) having very bad teeth; which however would shew better had he more of them. He is reckon'd perfectly chaste as to women, his chief pleasures being eating and drinking a little too [398] voluptuously, and using much exercise either by hunting or hawking when he rides, or walking long in his gardens. He is not however much given to his bed, seldom sleeping more than seven hours; and even in the heats of the summer avoids reposing himself in the day time. He seldom minds books any farther than to buy vast quantities of them, to crowd his favourite library; and, after the *Italian* taste, he is fond of filling it with vast collections of admirable pictures, busts and statues, being a passionate admirer of antiquity in all its branches, as his fine cabinets do plainly shew. However, he loves the company of learned men, but chiefly those of his own Order, by whom he is continually surrounded, and who would willingly exclude all others from his notice, as well as his favour.

He is about 52, and has been now six years Pope; and as he was chosen, as I may say, to the Pontificate before *Pius* the VIIIth his predecessor died, chiefly for his zeal for his Order, he has not, since he attained that dignity, given away one considerable Place, Abbey, or Benefice, but by the advice of the Cardinals in full Consistory.

[399] He had but one Nephew that he has ever shewn the least regard for, and to him he has only given the hat, and some benefices, which in all are worth but about 30000 *l*. sterling annual rent; but he is so very dissolute and debauch'd, and of such mean parts and abilities, (and especially since no Popes are elected till they are sworn not to lavish the wealth and preferments of the Church on their families) that it is thought he will do no more for him. All his other relations he is so cold to, whether in regard to his oath, or for want of natural affection, that he has not admitted them to come to *Rome* but once since his election, and that but for a few weeks, sending them home with very moderate presents.

He is a *Milanese*, of a pretty good family; his father Don *Mario Franzoni* having a considerable ancient estate in the neighbourhood of that city, to which his being heir, was the first occasion of his being entic'd by the Jesuits (with their usual policy) to enter into their Society, tho' they had conceiv'd great hopes of him for his talents and abilities, which were very extraordinary. When he grew up, he answer'd all their expectations; [400] and being made Secretary to the famous Cardinal of *Santineri*, who was employ'd in so many important negotiations, and afterwards as Nuntio at the Courts of *France* and *Spain* successively, (in the late wars between the two Crowns) he shewed what he was able to do, by gaining his esteem, who was one of the ablest and severest judges of men.

When his master was made Pope, he soon got the reward of his many and faithful services, being in two or three years time made Bishop of *Paua, Maestro di Camera* to the Pope, Archbishop of *Milan*, Legate of *Ferrara*, Nuncio to *Venice*, and at last Cardinal, with the title of *Santa Maria in Aquino*. In these posts he gained the love and admiration of all, both as an excellent master of Politicks, an upright Judge, and one whose prudence and wisdom knew how to influence every one, and be influenc'd by none. He has a great turn to business, is indefatigable in weighing and considering whatever he sets about, and finding out the best and easiest means to bring it to pass, determining nothing but on sure grounds, shewing the clearest head, and the firmest resolution in every thing he takes cognizance of, or sets himself to accomplish. There is [401] nothing too deep, too dark, or too weighty for the strength of his parts, having no defect but the want of learning, which he makes ample amends for, by that kind of knowledge which is most cultivated by his society, a perfect experience of affairs, and a thorough insight into the nature of mankind, who are the tools of their ambition and policy.

He is indeed somewhat apt to give way to passion, and to act with too little dissimulation with regard to others with whom he is offended; and especially in speaking against those whose follies, or irregularities in their conduct, displease him. This had like to have lost him the Pontificate; but as that was concerted in the late Pope's life, his enemies were not able to put him by; and indeed they could hardly have chosen a man likelier to serve the society, and preserve, if not enlarge their power, if it were possible to carry it further. His scheme to get himself chosen Emperor, is a manifest proof of this, the success whereof is but too likely, if his Imperial Majesty should relapse, before his design can be sufficiently countermin'd.

[402] He has few very intimate favourites, dividing his kindness equally among the ablest of the Cardinals, who are most capable and desirous to serve the society, which has been the inviolable maxim this See has observ'd ever since it became the inheritance of the Jesuits. But as I have taken up a great part of this dispatch with describing what I knew of this extraordinary person, I shall defer giving your Lordship the characters of the most considerable Cardinals who are chiefly employ'd by him in his weightiest affairs; and shall now pass to some other matters that deserve your notice.

And the first thing I shall mention is, the extraordinary Bull which his Holiness has just publish'd, in relation to keeping of *Lent* with less strictness than formerly. The original Bull in *Latin* is very voluminous, and therefore I shall content my self to send such an abstract, as shall take in the substance of the whole, only omitting such unnecessary forms as occasion its length.

It begins then with a sort of preface, in which his Holiness *Inno-cent* XIX. addressing himself to all true sons of the holy *Roman* church, takes notice of the universal [403] care of the faithful incumbent upon him, and the perpetual sollicitude he is under, both for the salvation of souls, and the ease and happiness of the christian world. He fervently exhorts all the faithful to exert their best endeavours to prevent the daily revolts and falling off of so many members of the catholick church, who in these evil, nay, worst of times, on whom the ends of the world are come, are deluded by hereticks, and led away by the Devil into the paths of error, and the dangerous infection of the northern schism.

After enlarging a good deal on this point, he proceeds to take notice, that whereas the severe discipline of the church, conformable to the zeal of the primitive times, concerning the abstaining from flesh in *Lent*, had been found to produce sundry great inconveniences to the scrupulous observers thereof; (all which are enumerated and enlarg'd on with very pathetick complaints:) Therefore, says the Bull, to lighten such burthens, which, like an heavy yoke, do gall the neck of our zealous catholick children; and, to make the observance of *Lent* less painful to them; we, by virtue [404] of the supreme authority committed to us from above, have thought fit to pronounce and determine, and by these presents do absolutely determine and decree, that all wild fowl, and more particularly and especially those which resort to and generally live on the water, and frequent rivers, ponds, lakes and seas, be from henceforth deem'd and taken as fish, and be used, understood, receiv'd and taken as such, by the faithful for ever.

Moreover, that no doubt, suspicion, or scruple herein may remain in the minds of all true catholicks, concerning the deeming, taking, using, understanding, receiving and eating the several kinds of fowl, for real and actual fish, as we have and hereby do pronounce and decree by our sufficient authority and determination; we have thought fit to annex and subjoin here-unto those cogent and weighty reasons and motives, that have determin'd our judgment in this matter, in which the salvation of souls, our great and chief care, is so deeply embark'd.

First then, whereas the original foundation of fish being appointed to be eat in *Lent*, was greatly built on the opinions [405] of those eminent physicians and philosophers *Galen, Hippocrates, Chrysippus* and *Erasistra-tus*, who maintain'd, that fish do not nourish any more than water, into which they are immediately turn'd, we do declare the same to be false and absurd, groundless and ridiculous. For tho' *Ariosttle*, in his fifth book, does maintain that opinion, whose great authority, with those afore-cited, did too far influence the piety of the church herein; yet it is found by constant experience, that those kinds, formerly only accounted as fish, do rather nourish the body more than those kinds, which we have, and hereby do allow to the faithful. It is also as vulgar and trivial an error, that those kinds of fish were appointed to be eaten in fast-days, and in *Lent* particularly, because in the Deluge the sea and all kinds of fish, escap'd the general curse that fell on other creatures, the earth and its productions; for it is certain, that curse fell equally on all.

But, secondly, our judgment hath been grounded on these other important reasons; first, because of the great and surprizing conformity between these two species of animals, the feathers of the one answering the scales [406] of the other, as the clearness, fluidity and brightness of the water, the element of the one, doth to the air, the usual element of the other; in both which elements also they do mutually live, as a sort of amphibious creatures, as the diving of waterfowl, and the flying of some fish, and the frisking and leaping out of water of all, do plainly manifest.

But further, this conformity is found also in the fins of the one corresponding to the wings of the other, and that they agree in that remarkable circumstance peculiar to them, of moving the lower eye-lid only, and that many of them have a kind of holes in their heads for eyes and ears which no other animals have; and, which is still more wonderful, neither of them have bladders, or do stale or urine like other creatures; and the very motion of the one in the air, (the tail serving as a rudder to both) is nearly resembling that of the other in the water. But there is still behind a yet more surprizing proof of this great conformity between them, and which has been of great weight with us; and that is, that the globules of their blood are both of an oval figure, which is found in no other [407] animals, as is evident every day to those who make use of microscopes, which put this point out of all doubt.

But, thirdly, what has mightily determin'd us herein, is the constant usage of all our predecessors in the *Roman* See, who have ever allow'd the sea-fowl call'd the *Macreuse*, to be deem'd, eaten and taken as fish; which is a plain Indication, that our present decrees and determinations are in all respects bottom'd on the same truths, and conformable to theirs. It is true, the learned *Naudæus* has pretended to prove that wild fowl, and especially the *Macreuse* aforesaid, cannot be reckon'd fish, because all animals that have necks, have lungs, and if lungs cannot be fish: But this is so vile and false a way of reasoning, that it deserves not be confuted, since both whales, and dolphins are fish, and yet have lungs, as the learned* *Scaliger* plainly proves against *Cardan*.

But, 4thly, we have made this decree also for the good of souls, because we continually find many, who, thro' the former severity, are alienated in their affection to holy catholick church, and fall off daily to the hereticks; or at least, if they do [408] not revolt from us, endanger their souls, by incurring our excommunication, and privately eating flesh, which is so expressly forbidden on that terrible penalty.

---

* Exercit. *p.* 224.

In the 5th place, we have consider'd the tenderness and delicacy of some constitutions, which are frequently endanger'd by being confin'd at that season from all sorts of flesh; and moreover, we find by experience, that there are fewer children got in *Lent*, which is much to be laid to heart in a church, which ever has, and we trust ever will, depend on her numbers. There is also less work and husbandry done then, from the same cause, men as well as beasts being then much weaker, by having been pinch'd by the bitterness of winter, and at the same time stinted in their food; many weaker husband-men being also killed by the change of diet. Nay, this evil extends to their very calves, kids and lambs, which are frequently starv'd, or at best stinted in their growth, by having little milk left to suckle them; all which are heavy grievances, and produce many ill consequences to our catholick children.

Lastly, we have been mov'd hereunto by two special reasons. The one is, because [409] while our faithful sons are thus pinch'd and burthen'd, hereticks thrive, and are fatted by their losses, keeping at least 9000 vessels in taking fish, which they extort great rates for from our people, to the great detriment of our church, and the intolerable increase of their naval power. But our other reason is no less considerable, and that is, that *Lent* is most unequally settled and appointed throughout the christian world; for while the faithful in *Europe* are thus bow'd down to the grave, by the severity of the church, others, in different regions of the world, have their *Lent* in so favourable a time of the year, that their fruits and gardens load them with all kinds of delights. Of this last point, *Chile*, and its fruitful country and climate, among many others, is a flagrant instance; and therefore it is but fit to bring all catholick christians herein upon a greater equality, and to prevent *Europe* from envying the advantages of the youngest daughter of the church, *America*.

For these therefore, and many other as important reasons, which it is needless, or improper to insert here; we, out of our paternal care of the faithful, have, and hereby [410] do decree, that all wild fowl, and especially all water-fowl aforesaid, be from henceforth deem'd, taken, re-ceiv'd, understood and eaten as fish by all catholicks, of whatever region, country or climate; and we also, in tender regard to the faithful, do allow all *English* and *Dutch* Brawn to be taken, eaten, receiv'd, deem'd and us'd as Sturgeon, as well because the fleshy parts thereof, are so macerated by the boiling, pickling, and long keeping, as to have less, and more wholsome nourishment in it, than any kind of fish; and also, because as it is entirely of heretick growth, it is probably less nutritive, than the poorest sort of viands in christian and catholick countries.

Lastly, for the greater ease, consolation, and satisfaction of all the faithful, and that their bodies may not be worse treated than those of schismaticks and hereticks, when their souls are so much better secur'd and provided for; we do further determine and decree, that as well on all fast-days, as throughout the whole of *Lent*, it shall be lawful to all our Nuncio's, Bishops, and parish-priests, and all proper officers duly authoriz'd by us to that end, to issue licenses to all sick people, or all that are afraid of being [411] sick, or otherwise incommoded, (or apprehensive of being incommoded in their health or strength by abstaining from flesh, when the allowance of such fowl or fish is not sufficiently agreeable to them) to eat all and every kind of flesh, that they shall judge to contribute more effectually, to the sustenance and comfort of their bodies, in their pilgrimage here. Provided always, that all such persons do regularly take out authentick licenses for the same, and pay, if rich, for such license, either for the whole *Lent*, or the year, the sum of twenty Scudi, or, if poor, the sum of two Scudi, and no more.

And to prevent, cut off, silence and confute for ever, all debates, cavils, disputes or objections hereon; we do hereby declare, that all and every person who shall in any wise oppose, contradict, argue against, or in any sort contravene this our decree, is, and shall be adjudg'd to stand excommunicated, and cut off, as a rotten member, from the body of the holy catholick church; unless by his full and ample submission, repentance and retractation, he shall be absolv'd for the same. Given under the seal of the Fisher, this 19th of *February*, 1998. and in the sixth year of our Pontificate.

[412] Thus, my Lord, I have perform'd my promise, and given you an abstract of their famous Bull, the political views of which will sufficiently employ your Lordship's thoughts. There is nothing more certain, than that this See has resolv'd on new modelling their church, finding by experience the absolute necessity there is for it. For altho' the power of the *Roman Vatican* is vastly increas'd, it is evident their interest with all catholick Princes is greatly sunk. Indeed they are almost on the wing to depart from her, if the vast height of that deluge of riches, strength and interest were but once so far abated; that, like *Noah's* dove, they could find a safe place for even the sole of their foot to retreat to, and not be oblig'd to return unto the prison of the ark, when they have taken their flight from it. The only hold this See has of them, is very different from that they had in antient times; for then she was reverenc'd as the real head of the christian church, arm'd with the divine authority; whereas she is now regarded as a temporal tyrant, who makes religion but the stalking horse to universal empire. How greatly this has shaken her authority among the Princes of *Europe*, and alarm'd [413] their jealousies, is perfectly known to your Lordship, as well as the vast increase of credit and reputation that the protestant faith hath obtain'd hereby in the world. And tho' reasons of state, and their jealousies of our trade and power, keep them too much estrang'd from us; yet such a crisis of affairs may come, as may unite them all with us so far, as to renounce the papal authority, and set up patriarchs of their own, and as probably reform the faith, as alter the government of their churches.

Indeed the ill success of the *French* King, in attempting this, had kept them greatly in awe, together with the vast power of the clergy in their respective Kingdoms. For the chief ecclesiasticks being entirely Jesuits, or their creatures, do their utmost to support the interest of the *Vatican*, and to watch every motion of their sovereigns, that looks like the least encroachment on the papal authority. In the mean time, all possible measures are taken at *Rome*, to prevent either the people of their sovereigns, taking new disgusts at her towring ambition. It is this probably has occasion'd the Bull I have sent you; which, as ridiculous as the pretences in it are, will please the people [414] extremely; and will also hurt our royal fishery, and lessen the numbers of our seamen, at the same time that it takes off one great burthen that lay on the good catholicks shoulders.

There is another point, which this See is as fond of correcting as the affair of *Lent*, and that is, the vast damage they receive from the celibacy of the Clergy, and the numbers of hands which are every year cut off from them, by shutting up such crowds in monasteries and nunneries. These might bring an incredible addition of strength to the Church and all popish Princes, if they had not, by such silly monastick institutions, made them useless to both. It is not to be denied, but that this method has produc'd great genius's in their Church, who, by brooding over their melancholy, and closely pursuing their studies, have made a great figure, either for piety, abstinence and charity, or for learning and knowledge, (especially in divinity); the ablest pens for the interest of this See having been pluck'd from the wings of the poor creatures that are fed, and shut up in these hen-houses. The Church has also found her account by encouraging celibacy, from [415] the great wealth many of those her unmarried votaries have left her heir to; but the scandal that has fallen on her by the irregularities many of them, unable to bear these restraints, have daily run into, have, in my opinion, largely over-balanc'd her Gains.

Besides, I am persuaded, for one great genius in piety or learning her monasteries and the celibacy of her Clergy have produc'd, they have lost and buried ten, that would otherwise have been serviceable to the Church or State: while, under a silly pretence of despising the world and its glory as vain and sinful, they have lull'd thousands of excellent persons asleep, and deadned them to all regard for their Country, or any ambition to excel in useful knowledge and practice of the Sciences, or employing themselves in the civil arts of peace and war, in which the good of society is so deeply concern'd. This is a prodigious damage done to the publick; but there is another that sits heavier on them, which they are more concern'd at; and that is, their occasioning and immense draw-back on their numbers, and in proportion diminishing their strength and their power.

[416] Let us consider this a little, my Lord, as to *France* and our own Country, since the antient reformation of religion among us; excluding all consideration of the damage to Christianity in general for so many

centuries before. As I know *France* pretty well, I think I have grounds to say, there were no less than 300000 churchmen and nuns under vows of celibacy at that time in that Kingdom; and probably not fewer than 120000 under the same denomination in *Great-Britain* and *Ireland*; the breed of all which numbers we have gain'd for 500 years, and that of all their descendants; and the *French* have lost, and consequently in propoortion, all other catholick Countries.

It is plain that this is of infinite service to one party, and of equal detriment to the other; and in a few centuries more, as their number must daily sink, and their trade, wealth and manufactures in proportion with them, it is easy to foresee that the balance will still be turning, and at last decide in favour of the Protestants; tho' the advantages of the evidence and truth of their doctrines, and the discovery of the faults [417] and errors of the Papists, should no way contribute thereunto.

I have seen computations that pretend to demonstrate, that by this single mistake in politicks, and cutting off the breed of such numbers, whose real abilities and bodies might have rais'd such powerful recruits to their cause; the Church of *Rome* has lost near 30 millions of souls, whose labour, trade and wealth, were they now in being, might have prov'd a vast over-balance of the protestant interest and power. At the same time, as tho' this was not enough, besides the tyranny of their Government and the Inquisition, they as it were strive to lessen their numbers still more; by almost daily fasts, pilgrimages, and annual *Lents*, and an unpardonable connivance at adultery and whoredom (not to mention the unnatural sin;) all which are vast draw-backs and discouragements to matrimony. As the Protestants have wisely avoided these faults, it is evident what advantages we have over them, if we make a right use of them. And yet after all, it is to be fear'd, that the perpetual policy, industry and application of this See, and the coldness and sleepiness of our people, may be so ill [418] match'd, as to give them too many occasions of breaking in on us, by our divisions and factions, and yielding them the victory, which we indolently rely on Providence for, and they, by so many plots, artifices, and engines of state, are perpetually contriving to obtain.

But as I acquainted your Lordship, that the Jesuits are very sensible of the inconveniences we have been remarking on, I must do them the justice to take notice of several remedies they have of late apply'd to this evil in *Italy*, and where-ever they have interest and power to put them in practice.

And in the first place, it is generally believ'd, that they indulge numbers of their Clergy in private marriages, who have not the gift of continence; but this is manag'd with great address and secrecy, and cannot bring in very large recruits to them. In the next place, they keep a severe hand on the admission of persons into their monasteries, allowing much fewer than ever to be harboured there, and only such as would be useless or troublesome to the world, if they were in it. Nay, I am assur'd, that two or three pious Bishops having left lately large [419] sums by their wills to the founding new monasteries; this Court order'd a stop to be put to them, and divided the money among the neighbouring poor; which shews their sentiments on this head. They have also of late made several laws, by one of which all unmarried laymen or women are oblig'd, if past forty, to pay one fifth of their income to portion poor virgins and young tradesmen who marry. By another they have reviv'd the *Roman Papian* law, by which all who were unmarried after twenty-five, are incapable of giving or receiving a legacy; and by a third they have re-establish'd the *Jus trium liberorum* of old *Rome*, by which parents who have three or more grown children living, are favour'd with an exemption from certain taxes. These have had extra-ordinary effects; nor have their allowing of divorces, in case of barren or very unhappy marriages, and obliging both parties to marry others, and of late punishing whoredom and adultery with great severity; and above all, their obliging mothers to nurse their own children, (by the neglect of hir'd nurses, thousands of infants being daily lost to the commonwealth) been of less benefit to [420] the filling their exhausted Country with its truest riches, numbers of subjects.

These, my Lord, are useful regulations indeed; but as they are but of late date, and come like the prescriptions of wise physicians in an old consumption, where the lungs are too far spent and wasted, it is very uncertain how far they may prove successful; and at worst, we have the pleasure to know, we have the benefit of them of a long time in *Great-Britain*, by the care of the wisest legislature, and the best of Princes that ever watch'd over the publick interests.

Before I conclude this subject, I cannot but acquaint your Lordship with an answer I once had from a zealous Jesuit in this city, who, discoursing on it with me, maintain'd that the Protestants, who glory in the increase of their numbers, do multiply merely from the curse of God upon them, that by a just judgment he might have the more victims, to pour down his vengeance on, for their heresies, wars, and numberless sins against the Church. For, said he, in the zeal of his heart, had they kept up monasteries and nunneries, God had wanted some millions of sacrifices, to suffer for [421] the sins of themselves and their parents. You see, my Lord, how conveniently the charity of the good society would dispose of us, tho' we increas'd faster than we do; they want but power sufficient to their wills, or they would enforce their opinions by real facts, and convince us abundantly, that Heaven had mark'd us out for vengeance. But I have enlarg'd too far on this subject already, and shall therefore increase your Lordship's trouble no further, by speaking to some other particulars mention'd in your last, which I shall chuse to reserve for another occasion; and shall trespass no longer on your patience, than to assure you of my best diligence, in answering the ends of my residence here, and my shewing my self with a heart fully sensible of all your favours,

My Lord,
Your Lordship's, &c.

Hertford.

My Lord,

London, Chelsea, April. 5. 1998.

Notwithstanding the pleasure I have ever had in your Excellency's correspondence, I am in pain to begin it today [422], with acknowledging, that tho' I have been honour'd with three of yours of *Nov.* 29th, *Jan.* 17th, and *March* the 8th, from *Mosco*; I have never yet been able to make my acknowledgments for them, except by a very short answer to the two first, which deserv'd a very different return. But the truth is, I have ever liv'd on such good terms, and with so entire an intimacy with your Excellency, that I am in less pain how to excuse my self to one, who hath ever lov'd even my faults; and will therefore the easier pardon any involuntary omissions of the respect which I owe you. I can the easier hope, to find your Excellency favourable in your construction of my long silence, when I tell you, I have had more perplexing and uneasy affairs on my hands of late, than I ever remember since I knew this Court.

As they are at last pretty well over, I hope I shall be able to prove a better correspondent now to your Excellency than I have been; by being for some time more than ordinarily engag'd, in endeavouring to be as faithful a servant to my royal master, as my infirmities and labours increasing together, would allow me. Besides, [423] not to accuse my self too far, I must plead in my defence, that I have ever had my share in the trouble of most of Mr. Secretary's dispatches to *Mosco*; so that my offences are only personal trangressions against your Excellency's goodness, and which is a great matter for a minister to have to say, I have at least no national guilt to answer for.

That I may atone for the faults I confess so sincerely, I must begin with my best thanks for your account of the state of our affairs at your Court; and as you have put our trade there on an excellent footing, I doubt not but our merchants will find their interest in it, as we may see already they do, by their having sent double the number of ships, on the account of the increase of that branch of our commerce, than they formerly us'd to do.

As his Majesty resolves to keep up the best correspondence possible with the Czar, and to have a Resident at least, if not an Ambassador, perpetually with him, to preserve a constant mutual intercourse of good offices between the two Crowns, and favour our trades thither all we can; so I believe nothing but your being wearied [424] of that employment, will incline him to recall your Excellency. I believ'd indeed by your long continuance in that Court as an Ambassador, you were almost chang'd into a perfect *Russian*; but I never expected to see your Excellency turn'd a downright *Laplander*, as one must almost suppose you, by the relation you give of one of the most incredible things, that ever this or any age before it, heard of.

For my part, I shall never dispute against absolute fact, and a fact your Excellency declares your self an eye-witness of; but I can assure you, his Majesty has not so strong a faith; and is of opinion, you have either a mind to laugh at us, or to make us laugh at you and your Sun-shine. I therefore beg in your next, you may inform us if you have heard or seen any thing more, of the handy-work of these Sun-drummers; tho' after all, they are only qualify'd to serve us poor people of the northern Regions, and can be of no sort of service to those who are burn'd up in the South; and whose prayers, like the old *Jews*, are all for rains and dews, and rivers and springs.

Your full and particular account of the intrigues of the Jesuits, in relation to the [425] *Greek* Church, and bringing it and *Russia* under the papal yoke, had the honour of his Majesty's notice and approbation; but (as the King observ'd in reading it) the Jesuits have been humble enough, to copy after some part of those excellent plans, which his Majesty and his royal Ancestors, put in execution long since here, to the infinite service of the *British* Churches.

For so long ago as the beginning of the last century, *Frederick* III. establish'd præmiums in our principal colleges, for those who gave the best proof of their scholarship; not to mention the royal college founded by him, and so nobly enlarg'd by new endowments by his successors, and particularly his present Majesty. Nay, the Jesuits have only imitated the zeal, of one of our best Princes in the same century, who at once raised 400 poor livings to 50 *l.* a year, by recommending their deplorable circumstances, to the care of the legislature; and we all know with how much nobler a munificence, our royal master has very lately taken care, of a provision for all the rest of his poor and distressed Clergy. But whencesoever they have borrowed their regulations, I am persuaded [426] of what your Excellency maintains, that the *Russian* Church must in a very little time, become a province of the *Roman* See, and embrace all her errors, superstitions, and idolatry, as the essential truths of Christianity.

But I shall not touch on this subject, which lies ever uppermost in my thoughts, and haunts my dreams, left I expatiate too far upon it; and therefore shall only add my sincere prayers, (and by God's blessing my best endeavours) that this over-whelming deluge that thus saps and privately undermines, or violently in a torrent breaks thro' all the mounds and banks, that human industry and wisdom would oppose to it, may not, when it swallows up and covers the rest of the Earth, rush over and subvert the sacred fences, of the Protestant church and religion in the world.

Your relation of the extraordinary improvements they have made in the practice of Physick, was extremely welcome to me; but, to say truth, many particulars in it are criticis'd by our most celebrated practitioners here, as less proper and useful than your Excellency seems to think them; but as you are no physician, and only report [427] such facts as you have been inform'd of, you are no way accountable, for any mistakes they may be liable to.

For this reason, I shall not send you any of their objections, which seem besides of less importance, than to deserve your notice; and shall rather chuse to return all the miracles of your Jesuits, (in physick among the *Russians*) with one that in my opinion exceeds them all, which *Great-Britain* has alone found out the secret of. Your doctors therefore must triumph no longer, that they cure the Gout, and dissolve the Stone, that they subdue Fevers, and restore and heal Consumptions as easily as we cure Agues, or that they have secret specificks for the Jaundice, Small-pox, Dropsies and Pleurisies; for we have a skill in physick superior to all their performances, in a distemper hitherto judg'd incurable by all. A distemper every one is as certain to labour under as the Small-pox, and yet subject to have several times in his life; a distemper (which can be said of no other) that generally does most harm to the noblest and worthiest spirits in the world; nay, a distemper which I have been told you have had some terrible fits of, [428] can your Excellency yet guess at it, my Lord, it is that fatal and desperate malady, violent Love!

I should not offer to mention this to you, if I was not as certain of the truth of it, as that I am now in my chamber writing to you; for I have actually known two of my intimate acquaintance, my Lord *L*----- and Sir *Thomas D*----- who were dangerously seiz'd with it, cur'd within these six weeks, and they are now perfectly well, as they have assur'd me with their own mouths. Nay, my Lady *B*---*y W*--- my wife's relation, who, after a long courtship (which was basely broke off) had engag'd her affections to my Lord *P*--- and was so irrecoverably gone in it, that she could neither eat or drink, or sleep, or even speak, but with him, and his conduct in her thoughts, was also in a little time so perfectly recover'd, that she made a visit to his Lady, without the least palpitation of heart; and is so indifferent to him, that she can even praise him. She is no longer splenatick or melancholy, but receives and returns the visits of her friends, goes to all publick places with the greatest gaiety and pleasure imaginable; and is so good [429] humour'd, that she has not turn'd off a servant these two months. Your Excellency sees I do not write these facts, from the general report that prevails here with every body, but as cases within my own knowledge and observation; so that you may depend on it, this art is arriv'd here to its utmost perfection, and that the cure of this terrible disorder is now become more infallible, than that of the Ague by the Jesuits Bark.

Doctor *Howard* is the person to whom the world is indebted for his admirable secret; and tho' by this Majesty's commands, he has entrusted the methods of cure, for fear of death, to three of the King's Physicians; yet they are sworn not to discover or make use of it, till he is safe in his grave. I cannot therefore pretend to give your Excellency the real secret of this prodigious art; but I shall tell you the method of his prescriptions, as far as some of his own patients have related it to me; by which it is plain, he treats it in the general, as they do several other chronical distempers, having ever an exact regard at the same time, to the particular constitution of the disorder'd person.

[430] The first thing the Doctor prescribes to them, is, the taking a little Pill thrice every day for three days, with a small paper of powders, which taste and smell like powder of Crabs-eyes; both which 'tis conceiv'd sweeten the blood, correct the acrimony of the humours, and chear and recreate the spirits extremely. After these three days, they bleed and blister them severely for about a week, as the case and the patient's constitution allows them; this done, they take the pills and powders again for two days, then they give them violent purgatives to 8 or 9 stools a-day for a week or longer, as the case is, with strong sudorificks to carry off redundant humours; all which is accompanied with drinking a kind of ptisan, and keeping to as low and emaciating a diet as the patients can allow, for at least ten days or longer, if they can bear it easily. This method (the chief secret of which, they say, lies in the pills and ptisan) constantly eradicates the disorder, in the most inflammable constitutions in a month's time; and in some much less will do, and especially where they are not naturally, of a very rank or robust constitution.

[431] I have already hinted, that the chief secret is conceal'd in the pills and ptisan, which alter the state of the blood and humours, and fortify the heart; while the regular evacuations calm the hurry of the spirits, cool the body, and discharge from it all the vicious morbifick particles separated from the habit, till at last that inflammable disposition is entirely remov'd, which is the great source of these kinds of disorders. It is certain, that ever since this method has been follow'd by Dr. *Howard*, the violent effects of this passion or possession, I know not which to term it, have never disturb'd the world as they used to do. For now whenever people find their passion is unsuccessful and desperate, withot hanging or drowning, shooting or poisoning, which was the usual method, they calmly send for Dr. *Howard*, who immediately puts them into the Love-course, as they call it, and so they get rid of it at once, and then very quietly go about their affairs; and as soon as they have recover'd the cure, (which, as in

most other cases, generally takes up as much time as the distemper) they chuse a more proper, or at least a less cruel person for their adorations. It is universally agreed, [432] that the sincere and tender hearts of the poor Ladies, are cur'd with much more difficulty than the Men; and some of them, as my Lady R----- particularly, died, after she had been given over for incurable; but this does not happen one time in a thousand.

This I take to be one of the happiest discoveries of this age; for tho' *Morison*, in his Itinerary,* assures us, that in this time the baths of *Baden*, were made use of with great success for the cure of this terrible distemper, hopeless love; yet I think he evidently took up that story on very insufficient grounds. For not to urge that if this were true, they would have been the most famous baths, and the most resorted to by all people and nations in the whole word, (which is false in fact); he overthrows his own assertion, by maintaining, a few lines after, they were of great service to women that were barren. Now without appealing to the experience of our Ladies and Gentlemen, who know very well on what account they frequent our Baths and Spaws; I leave it to common sense to judge, how it is possible these waters of *Baden*, could produce two such contrary effects, as curing Love and removing [433] Barrenness; and consequently, I think, we may allow Dr. *Howard's* prescriptions, to be a blessing to his fellow-creatures peculiar to this age, and utterly unknown to our ancestors.

I shall not trouble your Excellency, with many consequences with which this affair is, and will be accompanied in the world, but shall pass on to something more important; and that is, to return you my sincere thanks, for your noble present of the Czar's travels in sculpture, which have oblig'd me infinitely. However, as I think them too noble a present, for the library of a private subject, you will allow me, after professing my self deeply indebted to your generosity, to give them, in your name, to his Majesty, who is you know extremely fond of such curiosities.

As to the proposal you make, of the King's offering his mediation between the Czar and the King of *Sweden*, who are both making such preparations for war, I must acquaint your Excellency, that upon some private hints from the *Swedish* Ambassador here, his Majesty order'd me to feel the pulse of the Czar's Envoy at this Court; but he declar'd frankly, his master could [434] never think of a peace, or the least step towards it, while his enemies kept any part of *Livonia* in their possession. Thus this affair is desperate, unless the bravery of the *Swedes* this next campaign, (as I heartily wish) may reduce them to speak in a lower stile. I am very sorry I had not notice early enough, of the departure of the last caravan for *China*, because as the *Chineses* we formerly brought over, and who have taught our people here to be as good potters, and to make as fine vessels

---

* P. 26.

as any in *China*, are growing old and crazy; and as we would be the better, to have some more skilful hands from thence, I must beg your care to have twenty or thirty, of the best that can be hir'd at any expence, sent to us by the return of the first caravan. Our chief want is painters and bakers, tho' the truth is, we are already such masters in this art, that we export vast quantities of our manufacture for real China; and it is, in my opinion, only to be distinguish'd from it, by its being differently, and perhaps I might say, better painted.

I am now to acquaint your Excellency, that his Majesty has made a new regulation, as to that noble foundation of the three [435] Secretaries of the Embassy, which G. III. appointed to accompany all his Ambassadors at his own expence, (of 200 *l. per Ann.* each) in order to breed them up to a perfect knowledge in state-affairs, as you well know. The King is pleas'd to signify to all his foreign ministers, that he has resolv'd to add one to their number, and will allow no person to receive the salary of Secretary, who has not spent four years at one of the universities, and will not oblige himself to spend six years, at each Court the Embassy is sent to, and to write in his turn all dispatches sent the Crown, and take the oath of secrecy and fidelity usual in such cases.

Mr. Secretary writes this post, to have all these articles strictly observ'd and comply'd with, and an exact account transmitted to the Secretary, of these Gentlemen that are now with our Envoys, that any who do not come within these regulations, may be dismis'd, and new ones nominated by his Majesty in their places; in all which I doubt not, Mr. Secretary will find an exact compliance on your part.

[436] It is certain these are very useful improvements of that noble scheme; and as our Embassies have by these means, prov'd excellent nurseries to us for able Statesmen, and prevented our being the dupes and bubbles of other Nations, in matters of negotiation and treaty, as we too often were in the days of our ancestors; his Majesty and his Ministers abroad, cannot be too exact, in seeing his orders duly executed. There is also a particular article added to these instructions, which is, that if any one of the Secretaries of the Embassy, be ever known to be guilty of any indecency in his manners, or offends against sobriety, modesty, truth or honour in his conduct; he is immediately to be confin'd and displac'd, till his Majesty's further pleasure be known.

It is said, the famous Duke of *Cumberland*, so celebrated in our histories, who was son, or grandson, I forget whether, to that excellent Prince *George* the II^d, was the first inventor of this project, which has almost been as serviceable to our Country as ever his sword or counsels prov'd; and I am persuaded few of his many great actions, endear'd him more to his countrymen than this, tho' it was not actually put in execution [437], till *George* the Third's halcyon days.

As Mr. Secretary gave you a full account, of the dissolution of the last Parliament and the calling of this, I must now acquaint you, that they met last week, and are fallen to the dispatch of all matters recommended to them, with great diligence and application. As this was the first time of their sitting in their noble new Parliament-house in *Hide-Park*, I went with his Majesty there to see them; and indeed I think I have not beheld a nobler sight, than that beautiful room which has been built for their sitting in, and the august crowd of Lords and Commons, that met his Majesty in the house of Lords, which is no ways inferior to the other, except in size.

As the Peers were all in their robes, and the Commons in their *Venetian* Senators habits, you may imagine how glorious an assembly this was, with one of the greatest Princes at present in the Christian world, or which is more, of the royal Line of *Hanover*, speaking to them from the Throne, with all the spirit and elegance of *Cæsar* to his Senate, without his ambition and tyranny. For my part it mov'd me so strongly, [438] that I was a little able to hide my tears then, as to conceal the pleasure it gave me, from your Excellency now; and tho' I have seen the States of *Hungary*, the Parliament of *Paris*, the Diet of *Ratisbon*, and the Senate of *Venice*, they look'd in my thoughts like boys in a school or a college, to them. The *Venetian* habit, which *Frederick* the II^d introduced, gives a vast air of solemnity and gravity to the Commons; and certainly how venerable a figure soever the Parliaments of our ancestors make in our imaginations now, they must have made a very absurd appearance to the eye, that survey'd them in so many party-colour'd habits, white, black, red, blue, grey, and with as many other variable dies as the rainbow, as 'tis plain from history they used to wear in their debates. Some have imagined, they used this method to distinguish their particular divisions, parties, and leaders by, like the factions of the *Prasini* and *Veneti* of old among the *Romans*; and there are some passages in our ancient *English* Poets and Historians, and particularly one in *Pope* that looks a little this way; but yet it is certain there is nothing of truth in this conjecture; and that the different colours in their cloaths, proceeded [439] merely from the humour and caprice of every member. And tho' some late authors maintain, that 'tis ridiculous to suppose an assembly, that so often determined the fate of Empires and Nations, would meet together in such an odd variety of different coloured suits, (like a regiment of Train'd-Bands, that were not able to cloath themselves one way) unless there were some politick view and meaning in it; or, at least, that they designed to distinguish their several religions by their colours; yet I can produce very clear proofs that all this is entirely mistake and fancy, and that what I have asserted, is the real truth of the matter.

I am sorry that they have abrogated the good antient custom of printing their votes, and that they now keep their debates and resolutions, so private and secret as they do, or else I should have had the pleasure of sending them all to your Lordship. However, I shall tell you one remarkable part of their proceedings, and that is, their voting that no person shall sit in that house that is not past 25, nor against whose conduct any thing criminal, dishonest, or immoral, can be evidently proved before the Secret Committee, which is always appointed to examine into petitions [440] of this nature. At the same time to prevent the attacks of private malice, whoever petitions against a member on his account, is oblig'd to give security to prove his allegations, or be imprison'd for five years, as an infamous and scandalous informer. It two-thirds of the Committee vote the allegations duly proved, the member has his choice of having his case heard before the whole house; or, if he declines that, of withdrawing privately, and upon his non-attendance, his seat is declared vacated, and a writ is issued for electing a new member. Nay, they have bolted the doors of that house, against all who are engaged in many law-suits, or either distrest in their affairs, or involv'd in debt, or that have not been seven years possess'd of the estate that qualifies them to be elected, if the said estate be purchas'd by such members, and not descended to them. The reasons on which these important votes are grounded, are almost self-evident; and they have further added to them, that none shall be capable of sitting in that house, who is not at least two months of the year, resident in the Borough or Country that he represents; and who receives any pay or salary, of any kind or nature soever from the Crown; [441] both which are most useful and admirable resolutions concerning the elected; and indeed those concerning the members attendance in the house, on the great trust reposed in them by their country, are fully as important. These votes are, that any one absent one half of a sessions, without proof by affidavit of a proper cause approv'd by the house, vacates his seat; and every member who on the Speaker's circular letter, giving warning of an approaching weighty debate, presumes to absent himself without sufficient cause, shall be reprimanded on his knees by the Speaker. Nay, they have voted that any one who, during such debates, shall leave the house, or that shall presume to vote without hearing them, shall, at the bar, demand pardon of the house for the same.

To enforce these yet farther, they have resolv'd that the house shall be called over every *Tuesday* and *Friday*; and all that are absent twenty days in the session without leave, or sufficient cause shewn, and above all, when important matters are debated, shall be severely censur'd by the House for the first and second fault, and on a third commission of it, expelled. It is believ'd they will soon [442] order heads of a bill to be brought in, to make all those votes and resolutions pass into a law; and indeed it seems of great consequence that they should.

I must confess, as a publick minister, I am less fond of such severe regulations; for tho' the loyalty and tranquillity of these times, make them less to be feared at present, yet such divisions and discontents may arise hereafter, as may make them less favourable, not to say pernicious to the

328

interest of the Crown. But when I consider, as a friend to my country, of what infinite service they would be to the banishing corruption, and mean-interested servile hirelings from that house, that should be sacred to truth, honour, loyalty, and the love, the eternal love of our country, I cannot but incline to them.

I have a thousand times weigh'd the chief arguments, for and against this important point in my own mind, and I must own I have ever found the certain advantages, so much transcend the possible inconveniences, that the ballance has still turn'd in favour of such regulations. Indeed our House of Commons thus modell'd, would prove such a bulwark against rapacious or designing ministers [443], as well as against Princes of too enterprizing or ambitious spirits in future ages, and wou'd be such a security, to preserve the rights and prerogative of the Crown, and the privileges and liberty of the People, in the same equal channels in which they now run, pure and unmix'd; that I am persuaded his Majesty could not consult the happiness of, his successors or people more, than by turning these votes into a law. As the King seems to think in this way, possibly this may be done; and if not in this parliament, at least in this reign.

Your Excellency will be surpriz'd, after professing that these are my sentiments, when I tell you, that there is a numerous faction, started up already in this very parliament, to oppose all the measures I am taking for the publick good, and misrepresent the whole of my past administration. To mortify me the more (if such trivial changes in the most changeable of all things, the heart of Man, could mortify me) I find the faction is supported underhand by Sir J--- C--- and Mr. L. two persons that I little expected, and much less deserv'd such ungrateful returns from, after all I have done for them. In the mean time, as they keep behind the curtain, Mr. M---- is the person who leads the [444] faction; and indeed his great abilities entitle him to it, for as your Excellency well knows, 'tis with Men as with Deer, the best headed leads the herd. Yet this very Man have I favoured enough, to have tied him to my interest for ever; nor do I know any cause for his forsaking me, but that I have oblig'd him beyond a possibility of return; and when that is the case, *Tacitus will tell us the natural consequence. The great outcry is rais'd about the publick accounts, and I know not what millions that are clandestinely sunk and evaporated into air; as I doubt not I shall see all these clamours do, when I can properly clear myself, by laying my accounts before the house. Sir R----d B---- is as loud as any, and rails with his usual blundering eloquence, but he has not talents even to serve a good cause; and tho' his abusive tongue can bruise like a cudgel, it wants edge to wound his enemy; or, as *Du Hailan* the

---

* Pro gratiâ odium redditur.

French Historian said, he can blacken like an old cold cinder, but cannot burn.

In a few weeks, I shall see how far this blind and groundless malice will lead them, and shall give your Excellency an account [445] of what these worthy intrigues produce. In the mean time, let me speak it without arrogance, I am secure, and almost careless of what may happen; for, believe me, my Lord, I am more willing to return to Fortune the trifles she has lent me, and resign the mighty envied posts which they pursue me for, (if my royal Master would approve of it) than ever I was to receive them. It is long since I have learn'd in this school of the world, where so few are educated, without feeling severely the smarting corrections of their master's rod; that there is little to be got in it worth the pain and trouble, and above all, our virtue, which we generally pay for the knowledge and experience we lay up there. Judge therefore, if when one finds malice, and rancour, and envy, are constantly the returns which are made those who happen to succeed better in it; if one can avoid being weary and sick, of the silly pursuits we are so eagerly engag'd in there, and fond of retiring from its noise and hurry. This is not the language of the Courtier, but of the Man and the Friend, whom your Excellency has known a little too long to mistrust his professions, or imagine he can dote at this time of life on the silly fopperies of place, [446] preferment and power, which in the vigour and sun-shine of his days, he never put in balance with peace and retirement, with innocence and honour.

But I begin to grow grave, and therefore it is time I should take my leave of your Excellency, to whom I wish all the happiness, prosperity, and favour this world can give you. I wish them not to you as real solid blessings, but as pleasing imaginary satisfactions, and the best kind of appearances of happiness here, to blunt the edge of so many real evils as we continually labour under. Above all, I wish them to you because they now and then afford us, the substantial delight of doing good to others, of relieving wanting merit, pulling down the oppressor, stripping the prosperous villain of his spoils, drying up the tears, and defending the cause of innocence in misery.

May I live (for the few years I can yet live) to see this the chief employment and business of your life in this world; and may not the errors and sins of mine, prevent my seeing you crown'd with the glory of it in another. I am, my Lord,

Your Excellency's, &c.

N----m

[447] *To the Lord High Treasurer, & c.*

Paris, March 4. 1997.

My Lord,

I was honour'd with your Lordship's of *February* the 24th from *London* yesterday, which brought me new proofs, of that undeserved affection and regard, with which you have ever honour'd me. I know not whether to applaud most, your Lordship's care of our Country, or affection to your friends and my family, or to make my compliments to you as the best of Ministers or Patrons. But I hope you will believe me honest enough to wish, that our family should rather be depriv'd of your favour, than our Country should ever be robb'd of so able an head, or so sincere and zealous an heart, to consider and pursue her interest. If I do not deceive my self, I think I don't say this, with any little view to my brother's being made one of the Secretaries for foreign affairs (how greatly soever I am oblig'd by it) but from a real sense, of what the happiest Nation and the best of Princes owe you, for the labours of an illustrious life wasted in their service.

[448] But your Lordship's mind, and the obligations you lay on your friends as well as your country, are above the little returns of words and compliments; and therefore I shall take a method to pay you my acknowledgments, that will be more agreeable to you, by shewing you that I have endeavour'd to discharge the trust, you have repos'd in me here. Pursuant to your commands therefore, and my instructions from the Secretary by his letters of the same date, on *Tuesday* last I demanded an Audience of his most Christian Majesty; to which I was immediately admitted, tho' that morning the Pope's Nuntio, and the *Spanish* Ambassador were both put off, with excuses of his Majesty's indisposition. Upon account of these excuses, (as I suppose) his Majesty receiv'd me in his bed-chamber, where I found him accompanied with none but Mr. *Meneville*, his chief minister, who, as you know, leads him as he pleases. He receiv'd me, with a very great appearance of good humour and frankness; and as he had the memorial in his hand which I had given him the *Sunday* before, as he came from mass, he immediately cut off the formality of a prefatory introduction to what [449] I had to say, by telling me he had carefully read and consider'd with Monsieur *Meneville*, the memorial I had presented him with, on the part of his *Britannick* Majesty, my Master. He told me he was perfectly convinc'd of the terrible train of consequences which must attend the establishing the Inquisition in *France*; and as he well knew the motives that made the Pope press for it, were only to increase his power, and that of the Clergy who adher'd to him in his Kingdom, he was willing and desirous to take any measures he could to prevent it. That he conceiv'd those propos'd in the memorial were well concerted, and

would be of great service; but that he thought there was an omission in it, that was absolutely necessary to be supply'd, if we resolv'd to deter the Pope, from such a dangerous and insolent outrage on the honour of *France*, and the liberty of his subjects. As he spoke all this very quick, and with a good deal of action and emotion, as his manner is, he made a short pause here, and seem'd to expect my reply. Upon which I told him, that I was so confident of the King my Master's zeal, to lessen the unreasonable power of the [450] Empire of the *Vatican*, and at least, prevent any new encroachments, as to what regarded *France*, that I was certain his most Christian Majesty's proposals, for additional measures for that end, would be chearfully embrac'd. I would have gone on to desire that his Majesty would consider, that as all the extraordinary steps taken by my Master, were barely for the interest of *France*, I doubted not but all possible regard would be shewn, as to any further demands, to avoid unnecessary expence to *Great-Britain*' but he stopp'd me with his usual eagerness and quickness, to tell me, that the omission he complain'd of was, that of sending two Squadrons on the Coasts of *Italy*. I was so glad to find there was nothing further insisted on, that I told his Majesty, without hesitation, that he might depend on that assistance, whether matters came to an open rupture with the Pope or not. That his Majesty of *Great-Britain* seldom fail'd to send a small one into the *Mediterranean* every year for the protection of the trading part of his subjects; and that I doubted not but he would send two much stronger and earlier than ever, to any stations which should be [451] thought necessary for the service of *France*. He seem'd extreamly pleas'd with this declaration, and turning about to Mr. *Meneville*, he whisper'd him so loud, that I plainly heard him ask him, have I any thing more to say? To which the other having answer'd so low, that I could hear nothing; his Majesty instantly turn'd to me, and laying his hand on his breast, said, I am deeply indebted to his *Britannick* Majesty. He repeated these expressions at least thrice; and then, as I found he continued silent for some time, I pull'd out the last Memorial which I receiv'd in Mr. Secretary's dispatch, and told his Majesty, that I was commanded to present it to him on behalf of my Master; and to let him know, that it was a copy of the several heads of things which our Ambassador at *Rome* was charg'd with to represent to his Holiness, against the establishment of the Inquisition in his territories. He took it from me, and just looking over the title, he gave it into Mr. *Meneville*'s hands, saying, it is long; you must make an abstract, and report the substance of it to me; upon which words, Mr. *Meneville* [452] said nothing further, but put it in his pocket, whispering something into his Master's ear. His Majesty then turn'd to me, and ask'd me, whether our Ambassador at *Rome*, had already deliver'd that Memorial to his Holiness, and obtain'd a favourable answer to it; to which I could only answer, that I look'd on that as certain, but as yet I had no account of it; and that when I had, I should immediately acquaint his most Christian Majesty with my intelligence. To this he made no reply; but turning his discourse on the sudden to the ambition of the papal See, he said, with surprizing emotion to me, they think to make my Kingdom a Province to *Rome*; but, says he, striking his hand on his heart, not till I and half my Army are first cover'd with the sods of *Dauphine*; meaning, as I conceiv'd, that he would first die fighting on his frontier to *Savoy* and *Italy*. I told his Majesty, I hop'd neither of those unfortunate accidents would happen. I know not, said he, but I am sure one shall not happen without the other. If Providence had not disappointed all my best concerted projects, I had long before now secur'd the peace and honour of [453] *France*; but it so pleas'd Providence, that every thing went contrary to my just designs. I did my best, and used my utmost endeavours; but all was to no purpose. Every body knows the event; I can blame no body but Providence; Providence would have it so, and I was forc'd to submit to its decrees. I observ'd he dropp'd some tears with these last words, and as I saw him in a great deal of trouble and concern, and having nothing further to speak to him on; I only begg'd Mr. *Meneville* I might soon have an answer to my memorial, and put an end to my audience, and immediately withdrew. The complaints against Providence, that made up the whole of the latter part of my audience, seem'd to me something very extraordinary, and brought to my mind the behaviour of *Francis* I. a predecessor of this King's, about 450 years ago, in somewhat the like circumstances. For when he saw his rival *Charles* V. had taken St. *Disier*, and was resolv'd to besiege him in *Paris*, he broke out into violent complaints against Providence, repining at its decrees; and said to his wife, my Darling, (for so he used to call her) go pray to heaven, that if [454] against all justice *Charles* V. must be favour'd thus, that at least its partial providence, will allow me to die fighting in the field, before I live to be besieg'd in my capital. After all, these fine complaints of these mighty Lords of the world, that dare thus repine against and reproach the justice of their Maker, seem to me as impudent and silly, as the conduct of *Sorbiere's**[*] Abbe St. *Cyran*. That old Author tells us, the Abbe, as he was one day eating cherries in his room, endeavour'd still as he eat them, to throw the stones out of the window, which often hit against the bars, and fell on the floor; upon which he ever and anon flew into a fury, crying out, see how Providence takes a pleasure to oppose itself against my designs. And indeed, my Lord, the mightiest undertaking of these rivals of Heaven, are, in the eye of infinite power, neither greater or nobler than the good Abbe's cherry-stones, that he was directing with so much care and prudence. I have hinted enough to your Lordship of the weakness of this Prince in my former letters; and as in Princes more than in other Men, to be [455] weak, is to be unhappy; I believe there are few among his subjects, (as

---

[*] Sorberiana, *p.* 74.

wretched as the subjects in *France* are) who are more uneasy in all the chief circumstances of life than he is. Indeed, by what I have been able to observe of the world, and the mighty monarchs of it, whom we envy and admire so much; I am persuaded this is oftner the case than we are apt to imagine. Crowns are such weighty, troublesome ornaments, that there are but two things that can make them sit easy on the wearer's head; either an ardent desire of doing great and glorious actions, and deserving well of mankind; or the senseless vanity of seeing one's self so high above others, as to the fopperies of power, riches, palaces, high living, and all the little tinsel shew of pomp, pleasure and luxury.

The first of these are seldom found, but in a few great spirits, who appear now and then like comets, to the amazement of the world; and are to be excepted from the general rules that others move by. The other indeed is often to be met with; yet so high a degree of it, and good success with it, is necessary to [456] sweeten the cares of Princes; and so many disappointments and misfortunes in publick and private life befall them, and often such ill health, and other accidents, that level them with the rest of mankind; that we must believe them seldom at ease, tho' we should not take into the account the prodigious expectations they entertain, which are therefore the harder to gratify; and the violence of their passions with which they pursue them, which makes the least ill success the more insupportable.

However, this Prince has one good quality, which will make him serviceable to our present views, in spite of his weakness and unhappiness; and that is, a good degree of courage; which, with the help of two or three ill ones, much obstinacy, and a violent unforgiving temper, will probably cut out more work for his Holiness than he can easily manage. The whole Nation is in great expectation what the event of our councils will be; and I perceive the Jesuits are in prodigious apprehensions, seeing so terrible an alliance likely to be form'd against them, as *Great-Britain*, *France* and *Germany*. They set [457] all engines at work, to defame and asperse our sovereign and nation as hereticks and monsters, that are odious to God, and all good men; and they are as busy to expose and ridicule his most Christian Majesty, by spreading vile reports as to his personal frailties, and all the errors and mistakes imputable to him, as a Man or a King. They have writ two dangerous pamphlets lately, which are handed about in manuscript; one of them is a virulent satire against this King and his first Minister, *Meneville*: It is a sort of diary of his life for the last *Lent*, of which I shall transcribe you two days. First day of *Lent*. Got up betimes from Madam *Du Vall*, confess'd to Father *L* ----- a *Dominican*, and got absolution; forgot to go to mass, and eat my breakfast; dress'd by the Duke of *C*----- the Count of *D*----- and Mr. *P*----- went to Mr. *Meneville*'s, and ask'd leave to go to council; could get no answer, till he had consulted the *British* Envoy; got his consent, and went thither. Resolv'd on a war with the Pope, swore the ruin of the Church to the hereticks, past an arret against schools and colleges, as opening peoples eyes too much. [458] Another against popular preachers and zealous bishops; went to dinner as soon as Mr. *Meneville* was ready, eat till I was sick, drank till I was fuddled ---- Mr. *Meneville* swears the Pope is an heretick ---- deserves to be burnt, chain'd to *Trajan's* pillar, and make the Churches in *Rome* serve for faggots. Grew very merry, sent for Mrs. *Du Vall*; scolded her, forgot going to confession. Went to cards, my old luck, lost every thing I play'd for; cheated by mrs. *Du Vall*, bubbled by Monsieur *Meneville*, laugh'd at by every one, pitied by no body. Went to the opera, six foot-soldiers cried *vive le Roy*, pleas'd to see such proofs of my people's love. *British* Ambassador bowed very civilly. Several of my own servants carry'd with much respect to me. Very fine musick, and a world of company. Madam *Du Vall* the finest woman I could see there --- went home, supp'd upon flesh, got fuddled, threatned the Pope, swore heartily, commended the brave hereticks of *Great-Britain*, and their almighty fleets, talk'd over the great feats I would do when they help'd me, lost my tongue and my senses, sent for Madam *Du Vall*, and was carried to bed.

[459] Second day; made Madam *Du Vall* get up first ---- call'd for Father *L*----- the *Dominican*, confess'd, and absolv'd; heard mass in my chamber, while I eat my breakfast ---- sick in my stomach, my head out of order, drank some brandy, took the air at *New Marly*, at noon; out of sorts, took a cordial, ask'd Mr. *Meneville*'s advice, and took another cordial, grew better, got home, and din'd on flesh, could eat little, drank the more. The *British* Ambassador came to wait on me. The Pope a villain, Bishops rascals, Jesuits rogues, and Catholicks fools. The riches of the monasteries and convents, and the Lands of the Church, the best fund to maintain a war with the Pope ----- Monsieur *Meneville* will manage all. Mrs. *Du Vall* shall make the campaign with me, will give her an estate in church-lands; much pleas'd, heard a fine consort of musick, order'd a new tax upon *Guienne* to pay the band of musicians; saw Mr. *Le Blanc* dance; gave him a regiment for it; a great pity he's no soldier ----- *British* Ambassador went home. Call'd for supper, bad stomach, swallow'd wine enough, and eat some *Portugal* hams, to shew I was a good Christian, and no *Jew*. Made [460] Madam *Du Vall* sing, and Mr. *Meneville* dance. A fine gentleman, a faithful subject, and an able minister; might get his bread by dancing, better than *Nero* by his fiddling. Drank abundance, talk'd more; begun to think, grew dull and melancholy, fell asleep in my chair, dreamt I was drinking with the *British* Ambassador and the Devil; waken'd in a fright, carried to my apartment, sate on my close-stool, and rail'd at the world, went to bed, and ventur'd to lie alone.

The rest is all of the same nature, very malicious; and, like all true malice, very dull. For this reason, I shall not trouble your Lordship with any more than a few short hints of another; in which they pretended to prove his *Britannick* Majesty and his Parliaments are the publick incendiaries of

Europe. That his Majesty has erected the house of commons into a sort of grand prerogative-court, where the wills of all the crown'd heads of *Europe* are to be first duly prov'd and enter'd, with a *salvo jure magnæ Britanniæ Regum si illis aliter visum fuerit*; and the next heir is to be admitted or rejected, as best suits the convenience of the present state of things, [461] and the inclinations of the good people of *Great-Britain*. That no such will is to be deem'd authentick, unless the deceas'd takes care to have 100000 arm'd witnesses, to prove the validity thereof. That in case such will be pronounced valid, it shall not be construed to extend to bequeath to the heir, or his subjects, any foreign trade or naval power; but so far as they shall be dependent on, and subservient to, the interest and commerce of *Great-Britain*, ad no further. That in case any prince or potentate, nation or people, shall presume to construe it otherwise, the said prerogative-court do issue out a writ, call'd a *Classis major quæ scire faciat*; and settle all points of the said will thereby, as they judge proper; substituting a convenient decree and will of the said court, in the place thereof, of which the known rule is, *Salus Populi Suprema lex esto*. That the said court has pretended to compute, by their political arithmetick, that since the 16th Century to the 20th, the Princes of *Europe* have sacrific'd the lives of above 100 millions of the bravest of their subjects to Wars, begun and carried on for the most frivolous silly causes imaginable; [462] and sometimes, for little trivial piques of ministers and favourites against each other, for which an honest heretick would not turn off a footman. That therefore they have made a decree, that no monarchs in *Europe* shall presume to go to war till their quarrel is tried in the said court, and sentence presume'd there for war or peace, and to act accordingly. There is abundance of such aukward malice in the pamphlet, which is not worth repeating. I shall therefore omit it, to acquaint your Lordship with the resentments of a particular person, who may be able to do us more prejudice, with a few words to his master, whom he rules and governs as he pleases, than all the pens of the Jesuits, who think to govern the world.

I need not tell your Lordship, that I mean Mr. *Meneville*, who expostulated with me yesterday in a very calm and civil, but at the same time in a manner that shew'd a great deal of conceal'd resentment. He met me at court, and ask'd me to walk with him in the King's garden; he talk'd to me a little on the Memorial I had given his Master, and then began a long expostulation, that has made me apprehensive we [463] may have disgusted him too far. He told me, I very well knew the *French* sea-ports had never remain'd in our hands, or the last treaty of peace been sign'd between *France* and *Great-Britain*, but for him; which God knows, says he, I did not do for the sake of the pension then so solemnly promis'd me, or to provide for my family, but to serve my country, that was tearing in pieces. That your Lordship and I both knew he had not got it accomplish'd, if he had not ruin'd the Marquis of *M------* who was violently for carrying on the war with *England*; and persuaded the *French* King he was a pensioner of the Pope's, tho' he said Marquis was Mr. *Meneville*'s good friend, and as faithful and wise a minister as ever was in *France*. That three years after he had thus got the peace sign'd, his Majesty would have broke it again, but that he offer'd him a thousand arguments against it, and sav'd *Great-Britain* from that storm; and now he kept him firm to the scheme of our court, for humbling the Pope, and opposing the Inquisition; which last point, however, he insisted the less on, because it was the true interest of the Kingdom. That I very well knew how [464] ill his pension had been paid, ever since it was first promis'd him; that there was now two years and an half due, and not a penny offer'd him. That your Lordship, (you will pardon the freedom of reporting this) manag'd your master's treasures like a banker, rather than a prime minister; and that if the friends of *Great-Britain* in foreign Courts were always thus us'd, we would find the scene chang'd suddenly. I would fain have interrupted him here, but he would not let me; so he went on to say, that if he could think of deserting *Great-Britain*, he might find his account much better with the Pope's Ministers, where he had been offer'd near double what we contracted for; but his Master's honour, and the interest of his Country, were too near his heart. However, as the forgeting real services, and remembring small disobligations, often made the best friends enemies, he desir'd I would consider well of it, and without a useless waste of words and reasons; (which, says he, you are ready to give, and I will not receive) take care to answer these complaints, with the single argument, that can only justify your conduct to me. The instant he had said this, he left me [465] without allowing me time to reply; and as I have faithfully related the whole of his expostulations, I humbly recommend it to your Lordship's consideration, to have the arrears of his pension instantly paid him. I am persuaded, the Pope's Ministers would give him vastly more than we do; and tho' he must, to oblige them, run counter to his Master's inclinations, and the body of the people; yet he has such an ascendant over the King, that he is able to manage him, and every thing by him, as he pleases. I shall add no more on this subject, but to beg I may be instructed very suddenly how to answer Mr. *Meneville*, with something more than good reasons and great promises, or my credit here will be but short-liv'd. In the mean time, I am persuaded, if he be kept our friend, all will go well, and we shall probably mortify the Pope sufficiently. Indeed his most Christian Majesty, has so vastly improv'd the strength of his frontier towns in *Dauphine*, by their new-invented method of fortification, that the strongest places in *France*, fortified after the old manner, are not strong enough to keep sheep from wolves, or geese from foxes, when compared with them. All the [466] troops are ordered to be compleated without delay throughout *France*, and money is sent to *Swisserland* for remounting the cavalry; so that every thing here looks like preparations for war, and the Jesuits and their numerous party are evidently under great apprehensions of its breaking out. However, probably their interests in all Courts is so prodigious, and they have so many spies that lie within the bosoms of their enemies, that they will manage so, if possible, as to make all this storm blow over. A few months will clear up this matter, and I shall redouble my efforts to bring every thing to bear; being persuaded, such a crisis, when both *France* and the Emperor are warmly inclin'd to a rupture with the Pope, and to concert proper measures to curb his ambition, is not easily found.

In the mean time, my Lord, allow me to pass to less busy scenes of things, and to tell you, that after I parted with Mr. *Meneville* yesterday, I went to see the magnificent entry of the old Marquis *del Carpio*, Ambassador extraordinary from *Spain*. He had an infinite train of rich liveries, coaches and attendants, and made an appearance becoming that Monarchy in its highest splendor [467]; but as he is a violent enemy to *Great-Britain*, and will certainly serve the Jesuits, (whose creature he is) all he can, I heartily wish him and his fine shew in *Madrid*. I knew him when I was in *Spain* very well, his name is *Haro*, and he has very considerable estates in *Andalusia*; and is on that account, and his zeal and bigottry, much consider'd by the Jesuits; but otherwise, he is both in his person and understanding, infinitely despicable. This entry cost him a vast sum of money, which I suppose the Jesuits, whose errands I am sure he comes on, will answer for him. The very coach, which he rid in cost near 6000 *l.* and brought into my mind the rich shrines for relicks, (to say nothing of some great noblemens palaces) which are so glorious and splendid without; and yet within, contain nothing but the decay'd remains of some worthless creature, which must now be reverenc'd as sacred, and regarded almost with adoration by the crowd. I shall leave no stone unturn'd, to get as early intelligence as I can, from the best hands, of the design of this embassy, which I am sure are no ways auspicious to our present views; and shall give your Lordship notice of [468] them with all possible expedition. It is certain, that one part of his business is, to influence this Crown to give no sort of encouragement or assistance to the *Portuguese*, in the dispute which is arisen in *America*, between them and the *Spaniards*, and is likely to be carried on with prodigious violence. As the affair is perfectly new, and the whole of it sufficiently curious, I shall let your Lordship in a few words into so much of it, as I could learn at present. 'Tis a matter likely to be attended with prodigious consequences, and to engage both the pens and the swards of the two nations, with all the rage that either glory or profit, can stir up in them; for the quarrel is about nothing less than the bounds of their several Empires in the vast Continent of *America*. Your Lordship must remember to have read, how Pope *Alexander* VI. in the 16th Century, when the discovery of the new World was thought little of, divided it into two hemispheres, the eastern and western; the first of which he bestow'd on the *Portuguese*, and the last on the *Spaniards*. For the first three or four

Centuries, every thing was very calm and quiet, neither Nation having been able to penetrate [469] and discover, much less to plant and occupy, the inmost parts of that prodigious Continent. But as of late years, *America* is grown vastly populous, and the inhabitants for this last Century, by the help of the natives, have carried their colonies and plantations thro' the remotest provinces; it happen'd the *Portuguese* and *Spaniards* frequently met, and had furious contests and engagements, about the boundaries of their dominions. The *Portuguese* maintaining, that the *Spaniards* have intruded too far, and the others denying it, all the Geographers of each Nation, and the Mathematicians of *Europe*, have been engag'd of one side or other with the utmost fury and passion; and yet cannot agree about fixing the Longitude, differing, many of them, about 19 degrees. It will, in all probability, cost much blood and treasure, before this dispute be determin'd; and 'tis generally said, the Jesuits in *Paraguay*, who are jealous of them both, blow up the coals, and use all their arts to put things in a flame; which is no difficult task between two Nations sufficiently warm and resentful, and that have such vast tracts of a very rich fertile country, to contend about.

[470] The *Spaniards* have lost a great friend in the Duke *de Richlieu*, who died here last week, in spite of all the heaps of wealth he had rais'd, by cheating the Nation, and ruining 8 or 10000 families. However, he died very comfortably among his Jesuits, to whom he left 10000 *l.* out of near fifty times that sum, to pray his soul out of purgatory. It is currently reported here, my Lord, that he had violent disputes with his confessor, what the value of his sins might be computed at, and the masses requisite to pray his soul out of danger. Tho' he was much afraid of going there, and heartily superstitious; yet he lov'd his dear money so well, that 'tis said it was not without great uneasiness he inserted that sum in his will. After all, there are so many people who wish him at the Devil, that I am terribly afraid, they will be apt to out-vote a few priests, who endeavour to pray him into Heaven; and that the curses of those he has ruin'd, will probably drown the sound of the prayers, of these he had paid.

Your relation of the vast improvements in the royal Fishery and Plantation-companies, were extreamly agreeable to me, [471] on account of the advantages which our Nation, and the glory your Lordship's administration, will reap from them; but as to my private affairs, they were of no sort of benefit to them, having unluckily sold out about two months before. 'Tis incredible, my Lord, with what regard and honour you are consider'd in this Nation, upon the new regulations you have establish'd about those two companies, and in what terms they mention the whole of your ministry, and his Majesty's reign. As I am convinc'd, there never were praises better deserv'd, it gives me infinite concern to find your Lordship's stile so much chang'd from its usual spirit and force, and to hear you talk in so desponding a manner of the infirmities of age, your weariness of the world; and, which I fear is nearest your heart, the envy and malice of a generate race, and an unthankful age. But your Lordship's spirit is of a nobler turn, than to let your virtue be alarm'd from its own shadow, envy; which is so far from injuring, that it is ornamental, and a necessary help to it, and rather serves than hurts it. 'Tis true, your Lordship stands in need of such assistances; but in other [472] people, the fear of its lashes makes them watch over their frailties, and avoid running into a thousand mistakes, which otherwise they would fall into. By this means, 'tis so far from hurting virtue, that, like the clipping of the sheers to the hedge, it makes it grow thicker and stronger from its wounds. Your Lordship has been too long used to it, not to know that it accompanies the actions of the great; like the dragons, gryphons, and other beasts and monsters, which the heralds give them, not as blots and deformities, but for the ornaments and supports of their coats of arms.

May you live many years to triumph over the groundless malice of your enemies, and enjoy the well-deserv'd gratitude and praises of your friends; may your Lordship long continue to serve his Majesty and your Country; and at last, in a good old age, loaden with years and honours, retire to that grave, which you think of so often, and I hope will wait for so long; which is the sincere wish of, my Lord, your Lordship's, &c.

Herbert.

[473] *To the Lord High Treasurer,* & c.

Constantinople, May 1. 1998.

My Lord,

Since I wrote to you the 29th of *February*, and the 16th of *April*, in return to yours of the 29th of *November*, I have never heard the least account from you; which is owing, I am sensible, to a want of ships sailing to this port, and no neglect or disregard of your friends, of whom your Lordship is but too observant and careful. In a few days, I flatter my self, I shall be made happy in your letters; and to know what hopes you can give me, either of the chief Physician for the Grand Signior's own service, or the professors of Astronomy, for whose salaries and provision I became responsible. I therefore hope there will be no hesitation or delay in procuring some worthy Gentleman to come and settle in the *Grand Cairo* college, which is at last so happily establish'd by my interest with the Grand Signior.

It is incredible, with what zeal and expedition such things are dispatch'd, when the order is once issued by the Port; for [474] then all hands are at work, and in a few weeks they are able to raise very extraordinary structures. The College at *Grand Cairo*, and the Astronomy-school, I am inform'd, were entirely finish'd in this manner in a few weeks, tho' there are spacious apartments, two large halls, and a noble observatory built up, pursuant to the inclos'd plan I transmit to your Lordship.

I am impatient to hear something of the dogs I formerly wrote for to your Lordship; for I have been ask'd a thousand questions about them, their perfections, and their performances, by the Grand Signior, whenever he sees me; and he often sends for me, when they are the chief affair of state, he wants to settle with me. I am forc'd to answer him at random, as near as I can, to what I imagine will be the truth; and, as any disappointment would be intolerable and insupportable, I must conjure your Lordship, that all possible care to gratify his Highness, may be taken herein. I must repeat the same thing, as to a Physician, which is of vast importance: and may oblige, if complied with, considerably, and if neglected, may produce terrible consequences for so small a trifle. [475] Since I wrote last to your Lordship, I have been three or four times at the Seraglio with the Grand Signior, entertaining him with your tellescope, in which he takes more delight each day than other; and is grown so familiar with every one of the planets, that he visits them now by himself, without staying for any introduction of mine. Tho' he is not very fond of travelling upon the Earth, he frequently makes the great tour of the Heavens, and visits all the constellations in their turns; and begins to be confident, that in another age, we shall not only be able to see the inhabitants of the Moon, which would be useless, without any other benefit, but to invent engines to carry us thither.

I am so often sent for to the Seraglio on these accounts, that I am frequently call'd there the Sultan's Astronomer; but as I have made as many delightful excursions by Land and by Sea, as well as in the Air and the Heavens, your Lordship must allow me to describe some of them to you. One of the first I made this spring with him, was, to the Isles of *Papa-Adasi*, (as the *Turks*, or the *Princes*, as the Christians call them,) in a gilt barge, row'd by [476] eighty slaves; and as the barge was entirely built for rowing, it is incredible with what prodigious swiftness we flew along the water, going at least three or four leagues an hour. As we went to hawk and shoot on these lovely Islands, the Grand Signior had several other barges, with his fowlers, ostragers, and falkners, and a vast number of setting-dogs, spaniels, and many casts of hawks of all kinds, who followed us at some distance. The Sultan keeps several families on the great Island, who plow and sow entirely to feed the wild fowl, letting a vast many acres of grain rot every year on the ground, that they may make their haunts there; and it being death to shoot one of them, but when the Grand Signior is on the Island, it is incredible what prodigious quantities resort thither. There are of all sorts and kinds on it; for even those that are of a weak wing, and make short flights, as partridge, pheasant, quail, &c. and which could not easily fly hither, are by the Sultan's order carried there to breed. The Islands lie at the extremity of the *Propontis*, and tho' they are not many leagues round, have great variety of grounds. In the largest, towards the north, there is a sort of mountain; [477] and as all the plains and valleys, and even the mountain itself, abound with natural woods, mix'd with fine vineyards, and arable lands and pasturage, beautifully chequer'd, there is not possibly a lovelier scene to be met with.

We came there early, and they having had notice the day before, the Sultan's horses which were kept there, were all at the sea-shore, waiting for him and his attendants. We landed opposite to his magnificent hunting-lodge, with great silence, and in an instant we were all mounted, and the select band of his sportsmen, with their dogs, haws, and guns, attending us. When we were got up into the Country, this great band divided itself into eight or ten several parties, which were for different kinds of game, and then all fell to their sport with such agreeable confusion of entertainment and pleasure, as was perfectly surprizing. I am persuaded, both their falkners, fowlers, dogs and hawks, are infinitely more skilful than ours; for I saw not one that did not perform their parts to admiration all the while we were in the field; and tho' both at our own and the Emperor's Court I have been often delighted [478] with such sports, yet I never saw any thing comparable to these.

I will give your Lordship a short account of two or three passages, that gave me most pleasure that you may judge if I am unreasonable in applauding them so highly; and as you used in your youth to be fond of such entertainments, I hope it will still be agreeable to you, to hear of those of others.

I observe they use the same diversion as we do in *England*, of daring the larks with the Hobby, soaring over them aloft in the air, while the dogs rang'd the field till the nets are drawn over the poor birds that lie close to the ground, and are afraid to trust to their wings; but then 'tis their custom that the moment they are taken, they are carried in a cage to the Emperor, who immediately gives them their life and liberty. Their goshawks fly the river at mallard, duck, goose, or hern, and the several kinds of large water-fowl; and all the time we were in the field, I never saw them fail to kill them at *source*, as they call it. But what was more surprizing, was, a large kind of falcon, which is so couragious, that I saw them seize on the fallow deer and wild [479] goats, fastning between their horns, and flapping their wings in their eyes, till they run themselves dead, and the huntsmen come in and cut their throats.

But their fowlers are yet more extraordinary than their hawks: I saw one of them, call'd *Ibrahim*, who drove a covy of patridges into his nets, as our shepherds would drive sheep into a pinfold; which, as it was a method unknown to me, I shall describe to your Lordship. He had an engine made of canvass, exactly cut and painted, like an horse, and stuffed with feathers or hay; with his horse and his nets he went to the patridge-haunts; and having found out the covy, and pitch'd his nets below slopewise and hovering, he went above, and taking the advantage of the wind, drove downward. Then covering his face with long grass, and holding the engine so as to hide him, he stalk'd towards the patridges very slowly, raising them on their feet, but not their wings; and driving them just before him at pleasure. If they chanc'd to chuse a road contrary to the path he would have them take, he cross'd them with his horse, and by artfully facing them, forced them into the path that led to the nets, to my great surprize and pleasure.

[480] But I saw this same man with more delight, taking the whole eye of pheasants, both cock, hen, and pouts, to the great entertainment of the Sultan and my self, who observ'd him from the top of a neighbouring hill. He had an excellent pheasant-call, all the different notes of which he understood, and made use of with such perfect skill, that having pitch'd his nets in the little pads and ways of the wood, which they make like sheep-tracts in the places where they haunt; and taking the wind with him, and his canvass horse, for they still run down the wind, he drove the whole eye, or brood, into his snares, and brought them to the Sultan, who was much pleased, and rewarded him for his skill and diligence with a purse of money. It were a vain attempt, to think of describing the twentieth part of the diversion and sport we met with; but if your Lordship will represent to your self, a vast number of swallows in a summer's evening, on the bank of a lovely river, hunting for their prey, and pursuing with infinite swiftness and skill, the little flies and insects floating on the air or the water, or the tops of the grass, you will have a tolerable image of our sport, and the isles of *Adasi* this delightful day.

[481] After all, your imagination will fall vastly short, both of the numbers of the pursued and the pursuers, and the transports and delight of the beholders: All nature, not excepting the great Lord of Nature the Sun, labouring to pay its share of tribute and homage to the Grand Signior's pleasure. But as I never should have done, if I attempted to describe half the diverting scenes and adventures of that day, I will shut them all up, with giving you an account of one of the last of them; when the Sultan being wearied, retired to a noble tent that had been set up for him, where in the shade we continued to enjoy the prodigious prospect, (for it was open from the bottom a few feet) and to refresh ourselves with drinking sherbet, chocolate and coffee. His Highness immediately order'd all the game we had kill'd that day, to be laid in their several heaps before him;

deer, chamois or wild goats, on one side; and on the other, wild geese, duck and mallard, herns, cranes, pheasants, patridge, grouse, snipes, quails, rails, and a number of birds, that I know not how to name, being foreigners to our country, unless I make use of the *Turkish* language.

[482] But as the Grand Signior resolv'd to wait for the Visier, whom he had sent three days before, to inspect the Architects and Engineers he was employing in the island *Tenedos*; just as we had sufficiently, like true conquerors, refresh'd ourselves on the field of battel, possess'd ourselves of the plunder, and reckon'd the slain, the Grand Vizier came. He gave his Highness a very particular and agreeable account, of that strong and noble Arsenal and Magazine, which he is building with such vast expence, by that harbour. It is true, the Port is very ordinary; tho' even that is improving, by the vast mole he is running out into the sea, opposite to the ruins of old *Troy*. The Arsenal, when finish'd, will be of great importance, and put a bridle, as it were, on the mouth of the *Hellespont*, the *Propontis*, and *Thracian Bosphorus*; and will contribute a good deal to preserve the dominion of the *Archipelago*, that is, so much as our excellent Prince is pleas'd to allow him in those seas.

We had hardly receiv'd the Visier's relation of the fortifications there, when we were all order'd to embark in our several stations and barges, where our Galley-slaves receiv'd us with their usual salutation; and in [483] a little time, by the help of so many well-plied oars, brought us to *Constantinople*. However, as the night overtook us in the middle of the channel, and the wind blew very high, tho' without danger, I observ'd the sea-water perfectly seem'd to flash fire, with the violent motion against the sides of the barge; so that I read plainly by it, to my great surprize. It put me in mind of *Moses*'s expression in the first of *Genesis*, where he says *the Spirit of God mov'd on the face of the waters*; and then follows, *God said, Let there be light, and there was light*; and made me wonder some have not fancied, that as man was created out of the earth, so light was form'd out of the waters, and the divine motion given them, as suddenly and brightly as the flame starts out of gunpowder, when touch'd by the fire.

I forgot to take notice to your Lordship, that as the Visier brought with him the new plan of the *Dardanelles*, the Sultan bid me take notice of the *Romeli-iskissar*, (or the Castle that guards them on the side of *Europe*) which has been built up of late years very fine and strong, and fortified with the largest cannon in the world; and ask'd me, if I thought the ships of my King [484] would be able to batter down that, as they had done the old one in his great Uncle's time? I was a little surpriz'd at the question; but I avoided answering it directly, as civilly as I could, by saying, I doubted their being able, and was sure they would not be willing. But as we landed immediately at the Seraglio, the Sultan only answer'd me with a smile, and a courteous nod; and ordering the barge to convey me safely cross the water to *Galata*, I took my leave of this good-natur'd and generous

Sultan, who wants only our Education and Religion, to make a great figure in the world. I got to my lodgings about two hours after sun-set, much pleas'd with the magnificent variety of one day's diversions; and was hardly set down on my sofa to repose myself, after so agreeable a fatigue, when my old Druggerman or Interpreter, *Abraham*, a learned *Jew*, whose conversations often entertain my solitary hours, came to me with a good deal of surprize and amazement in his face. I immediately saw something extraordinary had happen'd, and enquir'd of him what was the matter? My Lord, says he, I bring you an account, which if it proves true, will make the enemies of my nation, and [485] the despis'd *Jewish* people, glad to lick the dust of their shoes. Here is Rabbi *Solomon* just come from *Tunis*, who is sent to warn our brethren, that the ten Tribes are discover'd in the middle part of *Africa*, where they retir'd in the days of their Captivity and affliction. He says they have a vast Empire there, and are very powerful, having near 50 millions of souls under their Kings, who are most observant of the Law, and have preserv'd their language pure and unmix'd, as well as their rites and ceremonies. The said Rabbi *Solomon* avers, that the great Messiah is risen among them, and hath chosen out an army of 500000 pick'd men, all as valiant as the *Maccabees*; that they have left all the strong holds of their Empire of *Gangara* and *Seneganda* well garison'd, and are in motion from the frontiers of those kingdoms, to cross the desarts of *Borno* and *Guoga*, and pass the *Nile*, seize on *Egypt*, and then the land of *Canaan* their Inheritance, and build up the fallen glories of mount *Sion* and *Jerusalem*. As I had a map of *Africa* in my room, I immediately search'd it for the kingdoms and desarts, my good Druggerman had settled his friends in, and found so far all was right; but desiring [486] to know what authorities he or Rabbi *Solomon* had for this report, he gave me two letters from the Synagogue of *Tunis*, directed to the faithful *Jews* of *Stamboul* and its Provinces, willing them to be on their guard, and behave like men, for the Kingdom was about to be restor'd to *Israel*. Along with these he communicated to me, under the solemnest promises of secrecy, the Messiah's Manifesto; in which he exhorts his subjects and brethren to prepare to rise, for the restoring both the sword and sceptre, into the hands of the faithful and chosen of heaven; and commands them to be ready, to depart for *Jerusalem* to the solemn sacrifice, so soon as they had certain intelligence from him, of his being possess'd of *Egypt* and *Grand Cairo*. I read them all over (that is, the *Turkish* translation of the *Hebrew*) with much admiration; and asking *Abraham*, if he believ'd these to be genuine letters? he answer'd me very hastily and angrily, as genuine as the Talmud; and that it was universally known to all the *Turks*, and the merchants in *Stamboul*, that these things were true; and it is certain, I had heard for several days, of some commotions in the inland parts of *Africk*, of a strange people. [487] I then ask'd him, what the *Jews* determin'd to do? Even, says he very eagerly, to obey the commands of their Messiah; and so soon as he hath conquer'd *Egypt*, to depart from the four winds under heaven, and be gather'd unto the brethren of the dispersion at *Jerusalem*, at the solemn sacrifice. He said this with tears in his eyes, and such emotion of heart, that I could not chuse but pity him, and his deluded people, who are as credulous as malice or love; and will probably, throughout this vast Empire, be standing with their ears prickt up, and, like birds, ready to take wing with all they can carry with them, if the news of this Revolution continues.

He had hardly done talking of this new-risen Messiah, when the Chiaus from the Grand Signior entred my apartment, with I know not how many slaves, loaden with part of the spoils we had taken that day, and which in his Master's name he presented me with, by his order. Your Lordship may believe, my thanks were not the only payment I made, in return for this prodigious favour; but I must own, it gave me so honest and reasonable a pleasure, to receive so extraordinary and publick a mark of the Sultan's [488] regard for me, that I thought it cheaply purchas'd. I made the Chiaus sit down by me; and, as if some revolution planets were risen on the world, he began to tell me, that since the Sultan had come to the Seraglio, the Grand Visier had told him two surprizing pieces of news. Upon this the Chiaus related *Abraham*'s story, very much in the same manner I have told it your Lordship; but with this addition, that the new Messiah was the strongest and most beautiful man upon earth.

The other account he gave me was, that according to a belief they ever have entertain'd in *Persia*, a great Prophet had lately appear'd there, who calls himself *Mahomet Mahadi*, the son of *Hossein* second son of *Ali*, who solemnly avers to the people, (who so many ages have been expecting him) that he lay hid all this while in a cave of the mountains of *Georgia*. He declares he is come from *Mahomet*, and is deputed and authorized by him to refute all errors, and reunite all in one belief, that there may be no more divisions and schisms, among faithful Mussulmen and true Believers.

He preaches on horseback, and made his first sermon in the city of *Maradel*; and [489] seiz'd on the horse, which for so many Centuries has been kept for him there at the publick cost, * ready saddled and bridled. The Chiaus, who told all this with the gravest air in the world, said that he was followed by great multitudes; and that it was expected the *Turks* and *Persians* might by his means be united in Faith and Doctrine; but that the Prince of *Basora* and he were like to have violent struggles. As I desir'd he would explain the occasion of their difference, he told me, that the Prince of *Basora*† had all along pretended to an hereditary succession in the good graces and peculiar favours of the holy Prophet *Mahomet*. That in virtue of that interest he had in him, the Prince and all his ancestors

---

* *Vid.* Ambass. Trav. in *Persia*.
† *Vid.* ditto Ambass. Travels.

had constantly, for such rewards and sums as they could agree for, given written assignments on the Prophet in heaven, for such places there, as the Prince recommended persons to him for. This privilege his ancestors and he, like our Popes, had posses'd undisputed, till now that unfortunately the new Prophet *Mahomet Mahadi* avers, that he is commission'd to declare, that the holy Prophet has abrogated the Privileges, formerly allowed to the Princes of *Basora*, they having recommended many unworthy [490] people to his best post in heaven; and that now the said privileges were entirely transferr'd to *Mahomet Mahadi*, the son of *Hossein*, the son of the blessed *Ali*. I ask'd the Chiaus, if these accounts were well vouch'd and confirm'd? He assur'd me they were; and that all men were alarm'd with them beyond imagination, expecting vast revolutions would attend them, unless some unforeseen accidents should intervene and prevent them. That the Grand Visier, by the Sultan's desire, had sent for the Mufti to consult with him hereupon; being apprehensive very dangerous commotions may arise on the side of *Persia*, if the utmost care be not us'd in it; and that it was believ'd the Grand Signior would be summon'd, to give an account before the new Prophet, of the fatal schism between the *Turkish* and *Persian* Mussulmen. The Chiaus having ended his extraordinary history, was pleas'd to withdraw; and as the good *Abraham* retir'd along with him, they left me to my own reflections on the amazing credulity, superstition and blindness of mankind. If either of these two accounts from *Africa* or *Persia* prove true, it is possible those populous territories, may be laid waste and [491] destroy'd in the flame they may kindle. But the *Jews*, my Lord, are above all other nations foolishly credulous; this *Abraham* my Truchman, is really more knowing and judicious than most of his Tribe, and yet he reads the *Talmud*, the *Misnah*, and all the fabulous mysteries of the *Cabbala*, with as much veneration as the Pentateuch. He is as much persuaded that our tears were not salt, till *Lot*'s wife was chang'd into a pillar of salt; that she has still her *Menses*; and that she was thus chang'd, because that out of malice she would not put down the saltseller on the table to the angels; as that *Sodom* was burnt. He believes stedfastly, that before the Decalogue was given the *Israelites*, God desiring it should not be confin'd to them, went to mount *Seir*, and offer'd it to the *Idumæans* descended from *Isaac*; but when they heard the sixth commandment, *Thou shalt not kill*, they got up and refused it; for that it had been said to their ancestors, (*Gen.* xxviii.) *By thy sword thou shalt live.* That upon this God offer'd it to the *Ishmaelites* descended from *Abraham* by *Hagar*; but when they heard the seventh, *Thou shalt not commit adultery*, read, they refus'd their obedience to that command, since they had receiv'd a contrary [492] one, namely, *Thou shalt increase and multiply*; upon which (he avers) God was forc'd to offer it the *Jews*, who took it without exception.

Nay, I've heard him maintain, that at his leisure hours in the sixth day, God created ten things privately; 1st, the earth that swallowed up *Corah*,

Dathan, and *Abiram*; 2dly, the whale that swallowed up *Jonas*; 3dly, the rainbow which he hid in the clouds; 4^{thly}, the ram which was sacrific'd for *Isaac*; 5^{thly}, the rod with which *Moses* wrought his miracles; 6^{thly}, the manna for the *Jews*' 7^{thly}, the stone of which the tables of the Law were made; 8^{thly}, the devil and his accomplices; 9^{thly}, hammers and pinchers, which men cou'd never have invented; and 10^{thly}, the head of *Balaam*'s ass. He has been still of opinion, (among a thousand other as absurd opinions) that as women cannot be capable of the covenant of circumcision, so they cannot be entitled to happiness in the next life; and that at the day of judgment, which will be on a *Friday*, *Adam* must be compleat, and therefore will reassume his rib, and so *Eve* will cease to be; and all women descended from her will be contracted into that rib, and be no more, and consequently not judg'd.

[493] But it were endless to reckon up the traditions he holds, and I only quote these few, to shew your Lordship the wild superstition and credulity of this people, who make a mock of our faith as absurd, and yet are capable of ruining the welfare of their country and families, by following the first Impostor that sets up for a Messiah, and begins a rebellion that for a few months appears successful.

But we will dismiss him at present, to speak on something more agreeable; and to acquaint your Lordship, that I here transmit you the names of such of the *Greek* Popes and Bishops, *&c.* as are averse to submit to, and unite to the Church of *Rome*, which they look on as a superstitious and idolatrous usurper; and who have join'd unanimously in the Remonstrance, to which their names are annex'd, in petitioning for his Majesty's powerful protection against her. As it is highly reasonable, to make some provision for the necessities, and even the ease of these deserving men, I do earnestly beg, that such a moderate stipend shall be annually settled on them, as may prevent their suffering too far, from the power and oppression of the Jesuits, for their maintaining the truth of [494] their doctrines, and the equality, if not the preeminence of their Church over *Rome*.

But your Lordship must accompany me with the Grand Signior, in another excursion we made by water, for fresh air and the diversions of the field, a very few days ago; which may possibly give you some amusement to read, as it gave me infinite delight while I was enjoying it. I was summon'd last *Tuesday* by the Sultan, to attend early at the Seraglio the next morning; when accordingly we got aboard the same barges, with all the Falconers and Fowlers, Guns, Dogs, and Nets, that were necessary to make our diversion fully compleat. Your Lordship has heard of that little wonder of the earth, for beauty and riches, the Grand Signior's new house of pleasure, known by the name of the *Fanari Kiosc*, which he has finish'd with such immense expence at the lovely Promontory near *Chalcedon*. 'Tis built something after the manner of the King of *France*'s house of pleasure at *New Marli*, but adorn'd with vast expatiating porticos of the finest pillars, and over them with close galleries of his Sultana's apartments. The whole is built in the middle of the finest garden, after the *European* manner, that is to be met [495] with in the world; cut out into regular plantations of fruit and forest, and parterres of flower-gardens, mix'd with so agreeable an extravagance, that is seems to strike the eye and the imagination of the spectator, with too forcible a suprize. For the extent of the gardens is so unbounded, the plantation of trees, both fruit and forest, are so numerous and so large, and the whole so skilfully interspers'd, with a vast profusion of parterres and compartments of flower-beds, fountains, cascades, vases, obelisks, temples, vistas, porticoes, walks and alleys; and all surrounded with so perpetual a serenity of the heavens, and fertility of the earth, that it looks like the Paradise, which God planted for the Lord of the world to dwell in. The gardens are so vastly extended, that they constantly allow deer to graze among them; but they are such as they breed up, and prepare for this purpose, by hamstringing them, so that they can't run fast; and gelding them when their heads are grown, so that they never herd with other deer, nor cast their horns, but still wander about the gardens; where they strike the fancy very agreeably, with seeing so unsual an inhabitant of the parterre, browsing among the knots of flowers. The prospect [496] from this great height is as astonishing, as all the other circumstances; for form hence we have a compleat view of the Grand Seraglio, its buildings and gardens, of the vast dome of *Sancta Sophia*, and the chambers of the Divan; the lovely Isles of the *Princes*, and the smooth glassy face of the *Propontis*, as well as the haven of *Chalcedon*; the beauteous bason and gulf of *Nicomedia*, and the rich hills and plains of fertile *Bythinia*, that lie below its view, in the finest irregular level that the eye can dwell on.

Nay, the whole city of *Constantinople* rising in its beauteous terrasses, street above street, and dome above dome, with all its gilded minarets and steeples, towers and cupolas, and mix'd with the surprizing verdure of the groves and gardens, and shades of cypress, and other ever-greens, which beautify the prospect of that city, lies perfectly under its command; with all the crowds of shipping, saicks, skiffs, boats and barges, that perpetually cover the face of the sea below it, and by their constant motion heighten the prospect extremely.

To this earthly paradise were we carried, my Lord, the *Bostangi Bassa* steering us, as [497] his office obliges him; and as it is not over four or five miles from the Seraglio, we flew there in our vast row-barge in an instant, and found it surrounded by a high wall of full twenty miles circuit. This extent of ground is kept entirely under all kinds of beasts, both of forest and chase, and all sorts of wild fowl; having vast natural lakes, and artificial canals and rivers, for those that delight in the water, and great ranges of plow'd fields sown, and woods and coppices cut into walks and avenues, for the other kinds. Being never disturb'd, but just on odd times when the

Sultan comes to hunt and fowl, the frequency and tameness of the game is surprizing; both birds and beasts starting and flying before you for a little space, and then stopping their flight, and standing at a gaze about you, till the murdering hawk or gun, or the treacherous dog, teaches them to avoid the arts and snares, that Man is contriving for their ruin. Nay, in all the noise and confusion of the field, when such numbers were hunting on the one side, hawking on another, setting in this field, and shooting in some adjacent one; yet the herds of the beasts, and the flocks of the fowl, never attempted to betake [498] themselves to the open country, but kept still within their belov'd confinement, and the delightful boundaries of the park-walls. Judge, my Lord, how lovely a scene this must make to one, who has so high a relish of the sports of the field, as the Grand Signior; where in every inclosure or coppice, you see new game rise before you, and find fresh employment for the faulkner, the huntsman, and the fowler. The truth is, we were marvelously entertained, for the three or four cooler hours of the morning; but as we wanted the delicious breezes of the *Papa-Agasi* Islands, and (besides the calmness of the day) there being not a cloud to be seen in the whole hemisphere, the Sun was so violently hot, tho' so early in the year, that one would have thought it had been in *July* or *August*, and made it impossible to move, under the violence of its rays, with any ease. We therefore retreated to the great *Salone* of the royal *Kiosc*, where in the fine porticoes to the north of the *Salone*, listning to the murmuring water-falls of one of the finest fountains in the World, we sate cool and undisturb'd by the Sun-beams. We staid a good while here, sitting on the *Sofas*, and [499] musing after the fashion of the *Turks*, without speaking to each other, but now and then a few monosyllables; when we were agreeably surpriz'd, with the *Bostangi-Bassa*'s approaching us with above 100 slaves, all loaden with different kinds of viands, the spoils of the field and the forest, the earth, the air, and the water. If there had been living creatures in the other element, the fire, as *Aristotle* pretends there are, I believe he had brought them too, and laid them as he did all the others, at the feet of his mighty Master. While we were at our sports in the field, the Bostangi Bassa had taken the slaves and barges, with all the nets, and had brought the tribute of the ocean for his part, mix'd with the spoils of the garden, in a great many baskets and dishes, loaden with cherries, strawberries, apricots, melons, and other of their early fruits. The Sultan was much pleas'd and as it was near dinner-time, he order'd they should get it ready with all expedition; and as the *Turks* live on the simplest kind of food, that is as easily dress'd as 'tis digested; in a very little time it was serv'd up, in the north portico of the great Salone, where we were sitting. The Grand Signior, with his usual [500] goodness, commanded me to dine with him; which I did with infinite pleasure, being delighted to receive every day, new proofs of his more than ordinary regard for me. Our meal, tho' it was chiefly rice, boil'd in the broth of different kinds of flesh, or else mix'd with bits of mutton, or the flesh of our pheasants and patridges, relisht very well; having the *Turkish* sauce to it, temperance, and heighten'd with (the more usual one of the Christians) exercise.

We had some dishes mix'd up with a sort of curdled milk, call'd Joghourt, and differently colour'd with saffron, or the juice of pomgranates and raspberries, and several other ingredients; and some fish and roast meats, or Kiabab (as the call it) of our venison and wild fowl, which we hardly tasted. To this we had the most delicious and wholesome drink, that ever the earth pour'd out of her breasts to her children, plain water, from the fountain we sate by, with a little fresh bread, (for they never eat it stale) to give it the higher flavour. Thus, without taking as many hours to it, as our gormandizing *Britons*, and other *Europeans* do, we finish'd our light, and therefore our pleasing and healthful repast; which, however, was a [501] little lenghtned out, with a lovelier desert of fruit, than I had ever seen so early in *May*.

And now I cannot but take notice to your Lordship, of a fashion that obtains here in all meals of fruit-kind, which I heartily wish were the mode in *Great-Britain*; and that is, the placing on the table a large *China* bowl, with a cover to it that slopes down into the vessel, with a wide aperture in the middle of the descent. Into this every body throws the melon-parings, the stalks and stones of the cherries, and the cores of pears and apples, the skins of gooseberries, and the stones of damsins, plumbs, &c. all which we Christians, in so odious and filthy a manner, take out of our mouths flaver'd with our spittle, and lay expos'd to every ones eyes, on our plates or the table: Whereas this neat and cleanly vessel hides all that vile filth, and hinders the eye from being shock'd and offended with such heaps of nastiness. They call it *Ordoma*, which I know no word we have to answer; but it signifies a pot or *Privy* for the *Mouth*; and it is so universal of late among them, that those who can't buy *China* ones, have earthen ones of common potters ware; the *Turks* [502] above all things, studying neatness and cleanliness.

But it is time, my Lord, to hasten to the sea-shore and our barges, whither the cool evening and the declining sun is calling us. Here you must now suppose us embark'd, and floating on the loveliest of all the basins in the earth, the smooth surface of the *Propontis*; flying with the incredible force of so many oars with vast rapidity on its crystalline bosom, unruffled with the smallest breeze. As we sate in the boat, I ask'd the Grand Signior, if the accounts of the *Jews* ten tribes being discover'd in *Africk*, and marching with their Messiah for *Egypt*, and of the Prophet *Mahomet Mahadi* appearing in *Persia*, were true. He seem'd a little suprize'd with the question; but as he had no mind to punish my curiosity with a harsh reply, he told me I must wait for the lame post, to be secure of the truth of such great events; by which I found plainly, there is more in those reports than

I imagin'd, tho' probably less than *Abraham*, my Interpreter, and the Chiaus would have me believe.

Imagine us now, my Lord, landed at *Constantinople*, and retir'd to our different [503] habitations, and the trouble of this letter shall last but a very little longer, than while I describe to you the exact figure and person, of one of the *Turkish* Santones or Dervises, as they are generally call'd. I found this extraordinary creature, sitting in my hall when I came home, from whence he would not retire by fair means, for all that my servants could say, till I came and gave him a piece of silver, to procure the favour of his quitting my territories. He was not one of those kinds of Monks, who live together in a particular community, under certain regulations; but a vagabond member, that counterfeited abstinence and sanctity, and a scorn for the World and all that was in it, in order to be admir'd and rewarded. He was a little creeping wretch, with a long red beard, that he continually stroak'd, and had cover'd his head with a tall sugar-loaf cap of blue linnen, with black strings and fringe sow'd to it, which hung down to his neck. He wore two sheep-skins for a coat, sow'd together like a sack, with two holes for his arms at the sides, and at the top and bottom for his head and feet: This he had tied about his middle, with a Buffaloe's tail, which was strung round with several [504] little rings of red and white marble. He had a bracelet of the same creature's hide about his arms, and in his right hand he carried a wand, with a piece of ivory at the end, like a saw, to scratch his back where he could not get at it to claw it with his nails; to which splendid equipage, he had join'd a long thick club, as a weapon of defence, and an horn that hung over his shoulders by a string, to sound upon occasions, and gather the good Musselmen about him. Behold, my Lord, the dress of religion run mad, or putting on the mask of hypocrisy! would to God she never look'd better when so disguis'd, and we should have fewer of the Jesuite tribe cloaking the wickedness of their actions, under the sanctity of their habits; and yet fewer, who out of a furious zeal against such disguises, would strip religion as naked as the Savages of *America!* I wait with impatience for your next letters, and am,

My Lord,
Your Lordship's, &c.

Stanhope.

[505] Preface the IIId.
By way of *Postscript* to the Criticks.

When I last parted with thee, my dear reader, with all the civility of a man that was in hopes never to meet thee again; I was just shutting up my defence, against all the objections that envy or ignorance cou'd bring, to hurt this inestimable performance. I little imagin'd then, that after having so entirely driven my enemies out of the field, they shou'd be able to bring any fresh forces against me. But, alas! I find that many-headed monster, an ingenious reader, is like the dreadful Hydra; and that no sooner an author, with the labour of an *Hercules*, has cut off one envenom'd head, and laid it groveling and senseless at his feet, but instantly a crowd of others, as poisonous and spiteful, rise up in its place to attack him. Accordingly I am assur'd, since I finish'd my second Preface, that there is started up one formidable objection, which I am oblig'd to answer, as it carries an air of truth with it, and is grounded on this; that these vast discoveries and improvements, these changes and revolutions of things below, which are mention'd in the subsequent letters [506], cannot possibly happen, nor consequently be true, many of them are so improbable.

To which I answer, in the first place, that for that very reason, because they are improbable and unlikely, I give credit to my good angel's prediction of them, and am confident they will come to pass. I will not say with *Tertullian, Certum est quia impossibile est*; but I will say, with all submission and modesty, that had my good genius design'd to impose on me in these matters, or I upon the wise, the judicious and wise reader, they would have been contriv'd with a greater approximation, (as the learned speak) and verisimilitude to truth. If they were mere fables invented to deceive, they would have been model'd, to as near a conformity as possibly they could, to the least disputed realities, and would have put on the dress of probability at least, in order to impose on the credulity of mankind. There is a vast extent in invention and imagination; and if falshoods were design'd to be obtruded on the world by these papers, they might easily have been cook'd up, in the common appearances and resemblances of such things, as are frequently found out, and discover'd every day.

[507] The small regard therefore that is shewn here, to such little tricks and subtilties, in many prodigious discoveries in arts and sciences, travels, revolutions and alterations of all kinds, and especially in the 4th and 6th volumes, ought to stand as an evidence of their truth; and that they are not forgeries and impostures, but real facts, which time will produce, and which are delivered to mankind with the carelesness and simplicity of an honest publisher; more sollicitous to reveal actual facts and events, as he receiv'd them, than to disguise them so craftily to the world, as to seem more likely to happen, and easy to be believ'd.

Were there occasion for it, and were I not apprehensive of enlarging this Preface too far, I could say a great deal here on that famous observation, *Aliquando insit in incredibili veritas, & in verisimili mendacium*; and convince my readers, how little weight any objection ought to have with him, that is bottom'd on this sandy foundation. But I hope I need not dwell much on this point; and indeed whoever are knowing and learned enough, to be acquainted with the infinite incredible verities in the world of science, the vast numbers of improbable [508] and unimaginable truths, to be met with there, and the heaps of plausible errors and delusive falshoods, that men are so usually led away with; will never consider the improbability of some relations in this work, as an argument for any thing, but their being more unseign'd and genuinely true.

But, 2*dly*, I have to answer, that there is nothing foretold here, which will really seem so very improbable, to those who know the infinite power of the great Source of all events below; who have consider'd the vast operations of nature, the force of our minds when set on work by ambition and emulation, and the strange changes and chances, the revolutions, alterations and improvements, which attend all things here; as well as the vast fields of art and knowledge, which the new world hath brought forth among us, by the labours of different voyagers. Let such ignorant objectors therefore, that are buried in the present state of the earth, and think it will continue in a manner unimprov'd and unalter'd, let them, I say, look back, if they know any thing of it in former ages. Let them consider how absurd and incredible it would have appear'd, if a man, for example, at the building of *Rome*, had (thus enlighten'd [509]) foretold the vast growth of that Monarchy, the overturning all others by that embryo state, the majesty of the pagan religion there, the birth and rise of the Christian, the breaking of the *Roman* Empire into several little scraps and pieces, which are now miscall'd Kingdoms; the spreading conquests of the Pope and his Monks, their disposing of crowns and sceptres, and temporal and eternal happiness at their pleasure, the reformation of Religion, and all the wars, factions and revolutions, which that spiritual Monarch occasion'd, to maintain his Empire on earth, and his interests and pretended alliances with heaven: Let them reflect, I say, if such a relation (or prediction) would not be receiv'd as more ridiculous and impossible, than those that are mention'd in these six volumes.

But the truth is, whoever knows any thing of the history of this globe, or the little wretches that crawl on it, and call themselves men and lords of it, would never raise so weak an objection. For what is it, but one constant scene of the most surprizing and incredible changes? How have the very face and features of it (if I may so speak) been perpetually torn and dismember'd, by deluges [510] and earthquakes, by vulcanoes, tempests and inundations? as every one knows, that is acquainted with geography, or natural philosophy, or that will read the accounts of such matters, in good authors.

Strabo particularly in his first book, and *Pliny* in numberless places,[*] will instruct us sufficiently on this point; not to omit *Diodorus Siculus*, and especially where he gives us the account, how the vast overflowing of the *Pontus Euxinus* laid the whole *Archipelago* under water, destroying all the inhabitants, tearing up the mountains by the roots, and forming a new world of islands, that here and there peer up their rocky heads, amidst the deluge.

As to the amazing alterations, in the manners and customs of particular nations, who is there that is ignorant, how power and politeness, how arts, and arms, and learning, have been, from age to age, changing their seats, and, like the ocean, gaining ground in one place, while it loses it in another? How is *Greece*, the seat of freedom and knowledge, philosophers and patriots, [511] become a nest of slaves and ignorants; and instead of those renowned Architects and Sculptors, that for so many ages crowded her cities with the noblest palaces, and taught her animated marbles almost to breathe and move, fill'd with rustick builders of clay cottages and huts, and cutters of saltsellers and mortars, as [†]*Tournefort* calls them? How is the mighty *Rome* grown the mother of superstition, cowardice and cruelty, who was once the chief nurse of the opposite virtues among men? In a word, not to dwell too long on so painful a subject; how has she fallen from her once exalted character, and exchang'd the generous sentiments and conduct of her ancient heroes, for the impious dreams of visionary Monks, the furious rage of Bigots, the little craft of Hypocrites, and the silly dotage of her mitred Monarchs?

As to the state of learning, to look no farther back than the last two ages; how is *Aristotle*, the father of science in former times, degenerated, in many respects, into the character of ignorance and infancy in this? How are the schoolmen, who gave laws to heaven and earth, depos'd and rejected, and [512] their wrangling doctors succeeded, by the great improvers of knowledge, who have made such important and successful discoveries, in this wide world of matter and life, which the others had so long kept us strangers to? Besides, if we consider how few years are past, since we improv'd Astronomy by a true system, verified by demonstration, and founded Philosophy on actual experiments, not on imaginary notions and opinions; since the compass and the needle trac'd out the mariner's unerring road on the ocean, and war join'd fire to the sword, or muskets banish'd bows and arrows; since the invention of printing gave new lights and aids to the arts; since musick and painting had a new birth in the

---

* *Vid.* Plin. lib. 2, 3, 4, 5, *and* 6. *See also* Reflessioni Geografiche del P. D. Vitale Terra Rossa à cap. 13. ad 22.

† *Vid.* Tournefort's Voyage, *Vol.* I, *p.* 156.

world; since regular posts were first invented, and set up by *de Tassis** in *Spain*, and trade and correspondence got wings by land, as well as by sea; since Physicians found out either new drugs or specificks, or even the secrets of Anatomy, or the circulation of the blood; since our own nations learn'd to weave the fleece of our sheep, or that even half of the earth had found out the other; and above all, if we reflect, that the small compass of [513] time, which all these great events have happen'd in, seems to promise vast improvements in the growing centuries; it will not appear surprizing, and much less absurd, that such discoveries and improvements are allotted to our posterity, in these volumes.

Even as to trade, riches and power, how has the new world prov'd the great nursery and prop of the old, which as so long a weak and sickly infant, hardly thought worth the rearing or owning, tho' it is now grown one great source, of the strength, wealth and prosperity of those kingdoms, who almost grudg'd its support? Nay, as to Politeness and Literature, and the arts of Peace and War, to look no farther back than our own doors, and our own homes; how is *Great Britain*, within a small space of time, tho' once so despis'd and neglected in *Europe*, grown, under the care of a few good Princes, the seat of trade, and power, and learning, and the glory and admiration of the whole earth, even at this present hour; to say nothing of that progress foretold in this work, which she will daily make, (except under some administrations and reigns, and certain years of reigns) and is now actually making, of growing still [514] greater and more considerable? Away therefore with these objectors of improbability, who deserve as little to be regarded, as those who insinuate that I have copied all this work, from the famous *Mazapha Einok*, or *Enoch*'s Prophecy, which *Ægidius Lochiensis* brought *Peireskius*† from *Æthiopia*, and which was supposed to contain the history of all things, to the end of the World; tho' I solemnly aver, I neither handled, nor saw, or even believed such a work was, or is in being, whatever some learned men, both of the *Jewish* and Christian persuasion, alledge for its existence.

The truth is, this last insinuation is so trivial, as well as false, that I had not thought it worth mentioning; but that I might omit nothing which my friends, (to whom I entrusted the communication of the manuscript to others) assur'd me, the most ill-natur'd of their correspondents, objected against it. As I have always thought, malice should never be disregarded, how blind or stupid soever it appears; so I have left none of the silly remarks, of my opposers unconfuted [515]; tho' if one takes a view of these objectors, the best of them will appear but like a child playing at blindman's buff, where the hood-wink'd trifler, catches at every thing he can, and runs about, the fool and jest of all around him, in a violent fume

---

* Strada de bello Belgico, Dec. 2. lib. 10.
† Vita Peireskii per Gassend. Lib. 5. *p.* 395.

and hurry; and after guessing wrong at whatever he blindly stumbles on, is forc'd to let it go, and then falls to again, with the same success, and lays hold on another.

Without attending therefore any longer, to the answering the stupid malice of objectors, I shall proceed to give my friends, the learned world and posterity, some cautions about this work, and so conclude, and let it take its fortune.

And the first caution I shall give them is, that tho' I am confident all things deliver'd in these six Volumes, will inevitably come to pass; yet left hereafter any base *attempts might be made*, on the lives, honours, or fortunes, of some illustrious persons mention'd in them, in order to overturn such predictions, as seem to relate to them; I do hereby forewarn posterity, not to entertain any designs, of destroying the [516] credit of these papers, by such indirect methods.

As I freely own, I chiefly intend this caution, for my dear friends the good fathers the Jesuits, who may be too free with their pens, or their penknives, with such views, I think it would be in vain to urge against them, the *Wickedness* of such a procedure; for their zeal and piety is so prodigious, that if they believe it for the good of the Church; that single argument, will sufficiently sanctify any measures, which Men less holy and religiously given, would foolishly boggle at. I therefore shall only put them in mind, of the *Folly* of attempting such an impossible project, as the removing privately out of the way the persons, or publickly stabbing the reputation of such people, as are doom'd and foretold here to be their enemies.

Let me then beg of them, and all that are capable of acting, with their honest and furious zeal or artful wisdom, to consider, that besides the vanity of fighting thus, against unavoidable events, I have also in many places purposely so disguis'd Mens actions and characters in this work, that it will be impossible for them, to discern the real [517] persons, till the very facts themselves, discover them to the World.

In the next place, I do hereby declare before-hand to *Posterity*, that if some things should seem, not to fall out exactly as they are foretold, that they, and not these incomparable productions, must bear the blame of it. Let them be assur'd, that those appearing failures, happen from one of these two causes. First, that either they do not understand what is or appears to be written, thro' the disguises I necessarily made use of, or that people may put, on their own or others actions, in order to elude such predictions; or, 2dly, Men are deceiv'd, either by reports of others, or their own fallacious senses, persuading them they have seen things happen otherwise, than they really have, and consequently the bare appearance of events, ought not to be set up in opposition, to the undoubted truths here discover'd to them.

I remember well, an impertinent objection of this nature, was once made by the Queen of *Poland*, to a very renown'd and illustrious Prophet of the 17th Century*, [518] who had dedicated to her an admirable work, in which he had foretold the ruin of the *Mahometan* Empire, by the arms of *Lewis* XIII. and *Urban* VIII; nor shall I forget the wise and judicious answer he gave her. For on his presenting his book to her Majesty, she pretended to censure one mistake he had run into, by not having known, that *both* the Heroes of his Prophecy, hapned to be some months dead, without having attempted what he foretold of them; to which the Author replied, (as I beg leave to do, to all silly objections of the like nature, which Posterity may raise against this Work) that pretended *facts*, are never to be set in competition, with unquestionable Predictions; and those that offer to do so, are not fit to be disputed with.

This therefore I request of them, in return for my labours in presenting them with these Volumes, that they fully assure themselves, that all I have or shall publish is true, and then let them depend on it, that whatever comes to pass, will in due time, (sooner or later) be accommodated to, and be found to tally with every thing, foretold in them.

[519] But I must go yet further with my cautions, and that I may conceal nothing from posterity, I shall own, that I am in much less pain, for the verification of any Predictions in these letters, than I am left the few copies I print of them, may thro' envy or folly, or an utter ignorance of their worth, be entirely lost or suppress'd, before those times, when their truth and value will be confirmed. I therefore beg all, into whose hands these Repositories of truth, these invaluable Anecdotes of history shall fall, to preserve them with care, till the days of which they speak shall appear, tho' like the Prophet *Micaiah*, they are kept ever so close prisoners, till their truth or falshood be manifested to all. Besides, as it is much to be fear'd, my dear friends the Jesuits, (of whom, like that ill-boding prophet, these papers, to my great concern, do never prophecy good, but evil) may buy them up at immense prices, in order to suppress them, I must beg of posterity, that some Law may pass, that authentick copies of them; may be safely preserv'd in our publick libraries, and, like the Sybilline oracles, the consulted on the emergencies of state; and that it may be death or banishment, [520] for any person to apply the leaves of them, either under pies or pasties, to pack up groceries, to line trunks, or cover bandboxes, or make use of them in any mean filthy office whatever.

As to the *imitatorum servum pecus*, the little tribe of copiers, who will endeavour to foist their spurious writings on the publick, for the sequel of this I have now honour'd the World with; I am not much in pain, for any damage their maim'd productions may bring, to these immortal Archives

---

* Vide *Bayle's* Dict. in the letter M on *Desmaretz*.

of futurity. The truth is, I look on this sort of writers in the same light, as those silly kind of birds called *Dotterels*, which Mr. *Camden*[*] tells us, by aping the motions and actions of the cunning Fowler, and imitating all he does, are soon caught hold of and destroy'd by *him*, whom they endeavour to mimick. Possibly the sublimity of that superior genius, which has enrich'd this nation with these treasures, may deter such creatures, from attempting so vile an insult; tho' alas when we hear the ingenious *Stephen Pasquier*,[†] complaining so gravely and judiciously to *Ronsard*, [521] that no sooner *Jeane la Pucelle*,[‡] push'd by a divine inspiration, and as it were delegated from Heaven, came to succour the arms of *Charles* VII. but immediately two or three impudent wretches started up in *Paris*, and pretended to be commission'd, in the same celestial manner as she was; how can I hope this performance, will not meet with the like treatment, from base counterfeits.

However, at the worst, I am prepar'd for this little misfortune, if it must be born; and tho' it is certain, that there seldom appear'd a glorious work, but it occasion'd a spawn of creeping plagiaries, to forge something as like it as they can; yet it is some comfort to consider, that the same thing which gives them birth, destroys these little abortions; and that like *Moses's* rod, it soon devours the false serpents, that pretend to imitate the miraculous product, of a superior power.

But really this sort of scriblers, does not alarm me half so much, as another race of impertinents, who are call'd Commentators, and pretend, (tho' with very different success) to improve books, just as Gardeners do their fruit-trees; upon which [522] they graft and inoculate, all that their silly taste and fancy can furnish them with, while the mother-stock is quite lost and hid in the exuberant growth, that too often converts all its wholsome juices, to feed a barren superfluity of leaves. As I have great apprehensions, the vast reputation of this work, will occasion several learned blockheads of that tribe, to attempt something of this nature upon it, I do hereby in the face of the World, enter my protest in form against such proceedings; and all notes, observations, remarks, explanations, constructions, castigations, emendations, or various readings, which these animals may pretend to affix, to the native simplicity of the original text, of these venerable volumes.

I am loth to be particular on this head, for fear of giving offence, by reflections that may look too national; and especially where a people honestly zealous for their country's liberties, and that have so long been our good and faithful allies, may seem ill-treated. But as it is too shamefully notorious, that the *Dutch*, above, all the Earth, have a most violent turn to

---

[*] In his account of *Lincolnshire.*
[†] Les Lettres d'Estienne Pasquier, *p.* 17. a Lyon. 1607.
[‡] The Maid of *Orleans.*

play the fool this way, I do hereby solemnly aver, let [523] what will be the consequence, if any man among them, like a new *Mezentius*, thinks to tie the dead carcase of his comment, to this living work, I shall give him reason to wish, that his hand, like *Scævola*'s, was on fire, when he employ'd it in such an attempt.

At the same time that I think it proper, to lay the world and them, under this severe restriction, I am ready to make them abundant amends, for my extraordinary sensibility in this point, by my easiness and condescension in another; and that is, by allowing a free liberty, for all nations and languages, not only in *Europe*, but the rest of the world, to translate it as often as they please, into their mother tongues, how rude or barbarous soever they may be. Far be it from me to wish, much less to endeavour, to confine that day-spring of knowledge, which by my means is about to rise upon the world, unto any particular corner of the earth, unto any little nation, sect, or tribe of people whatever! No! I have not such a narrow mind! Let it have its full course! Let all mankind make their best use of it! provided these two conditions be punctually observ'd: First, That some *Englishman*, who [524] understands *French*, and, like the rest of our country-men, can search to the bottom of things, may only be employ'd to translate it, for that superficial people of the other side the channel; and, secondly, That all judicious Catholicks do engage, (in return for my thus freely communicating it to them) that they will read it without bigotry or prejudice, or any silly fears of the Pope's authority, when he places it (as my good Genius has assur'd me he will) in the *Index Expurgatorius*, and prohibits the reading of it, under pain of lying half a century in the devil's* oven, or, which is much worse, in the prisons of the holy Inquisition, so justly rever'd by all good Christians.

And now, most dear Reader, (begging thou may'st not be afflicted at it) I must hasten to a conclusion of this *Geryon*-like monster of a Preface, which possibly, in such a nation as this, made up of Authors and Criticks, may never be read; or if it be, may have little weight with thee. Be that as it may, I cannot but wish, for thy sake, and what it introduces to thee, it were equal either to that of *Calvin* before his Institutions [525], or *Causabon*'s to his *Polybius*, or *de Thou*'s to his history, which are justly esteem'd the three master-pieces of all prefatory discourses.

I have ventur'd on the publick, and must stand to the sentence of that ever-changing Camelion, that lives only on what it catches with its tongue, to which I expect to become a prey. Yet am not I without hopes, that tho' some may be sufficiently ignorant and malevolent, to say this work I have given them, is like *Euclio*'s house in *Plautus*, *quæ inaniis oppleta est & araneis*; yet others, *quorum ex meliore luto finxit præcordia Titan*, whose

---

* *A new name, which my good angel has given Purgatory' in the originals of these Letters.*

minds are more enlighten'd, and capable of judging of the true value of things, will have nobler thoughts of it.

I have taken due precaution for its protection, by dedicating it to the service of the world, thro' the hands of that illustrious Person, who will one day prove an ornament to these nations in his life, and a blessing to mankind, in the Heroes that are to descend from him; and am resolv'd not to prostitute the subsequent parts to any but Patrons, that, like him, understand what a treasure I present with him; left I seem to copy the silly authors of this age, who dedicate [526] their books to such ungenerous and insensible creatures, that one would think they were imitating *Diogenes*, who us'd to beg of statues, to teach him to bear the coldness and neglect of those persons, to whom he applied for relief, protection and favour.

Nevertheless, I would not be thought in publishing this admirable performance, to have aim't at so poor an end, as making the great men of *Europe* pay court to me, for any advice of instructions I may give them; or to oblige those who sit on the thrones of the world, to pay me tribute and homage, as they us'd to do to the famous *Peter Aretine*. On the contrary, I declare beforehand, neither Kings or Queens, Princes or Princesses, Noblemen or Ladies, Knights or Gentlemen, Ministers of State or Merchants, must expect any favour from me, or directions for their future conduct, and true interests of their descendants, but as they shew themselves real friends to my native Country, and the civil and religious Rights, of these happy Nations.

To have done; As I appeal to Time, the great parent of truth, for the verification of all I publish, and to Posterity, (which, as [527] *Tacitus* speaks, *decus suum cuique rependit*) for that honour and deference, which I already behold them paying, to my faithful labours; so I appeal to all the sensible, the learned, the judicious and worthy spirits of the present age, from the judgment and censures, of the common herd and mob of mankind; that is, Lawyers without probity, Physicians without learning, Soldiers without Courage, Citizens without honest industry, Knights and 'Squires without common Sense, Clergymen without piety, Noblemen without honour, Senators without regard to their country, Patriots without integrity, and Scholars without genius, judgment, or taste!

FINIS.

Notes to the Text*

145

[**titlepage**] Μάντις [...] καλῶς: the best prophet is the one who guesses well. Simonetti, 'Who Is the Best Prophet?', p. 351.

[**titlepage**] **Bon Dieu!** [...] **de Propheties?:** La Mothe Le Vayer, 'Discours de l'histoire', p. 267.

[**titlepage**] **Hoc** [...] **motus:** 'Among us, too, reason has only recently found a reliable answer to these questions. (4) There will come a day when the passage of time and the efforts of a longer stretch of human history will bring to light things that are now obscure. One lifetime, even if it can be wholly devoted to astronomy, is not sufficient for the investigation of such important matters. [...] So it will take a long succession of people to explain these matters. (5) There will come a day when our descendants are astonished that we did not know such obvious facts. [...] The celestial bodies cannot stand still or be turned aside: they all move forward; they proceed just as they first began. Their motion will end only when they do. The movements of this eternal structure are unalterable [...]'. Seneca, *Natural Questions*, VII.4–5, p. 130.

146

[i] *Rothsay*: Rothesay.

[i] **Prince of Wales** [...] **Order of the Garter:** Frederick Lewis, Prince of Wales (1707–1751).

[iii] *the false Patriot's Love for his Country*: the sentence echoes the subtitle of the *Themistocles*.

[iii] *matrimonial* **Smithfield Bargains:** a marriage made for convenience, from the proper name of a renowned meat market in London.

---

* Editorial notes are keyed to the page number in this edition, original page number in square brackets, and lemma or relevant point in the text.

148

[vi] **Titus,** *the Delight of Humankind***:** the remark on the Roman emperor Titus Caesar Vespasianus (39–81 CE) echoes Suetonius's biography. Suetonius, *Lives of the Caesars*, II, book VIII.2. — 'The Deified Titus', I, pp. 306–07, 'Titus, of the same surname as his father, was the delight and darling of the human race'. A similar expression — 'the Favourite of Heaven and Darling of all good Men' — was a reference to George II in the Whig *London Journal* ('Cato's Political Letters'). Compare also to Swift, *Travels into Several Remote Nations of the World*, I, p. 59: 'Delight and Terror of the Universe' (a reference to the Emperor of Lilliput).

149

[x] *Hunc* [...] *prohibete***:** stand back, don't block the way of this young one who comes to save/a world in ruins. Virgil, *Georgics*, book I, lines 500–01.

150

[**Preface, 1**] *Don Quixote***:** Cervantes Saavedra, *El ingenioso hidalgo don Quixote de la Mancha*; Eng. trans.: *The Ingenious Hidalgo Don Quixote de La Mancha*, trans. by Rutherford.

[**Preface, 1**] *Thuanus* [...] **his History:** Jacques-Auguste de Thou (1553–1617); the reference is to de Thou's *Historia sui temporis* (1604-), perhaps in the English version: *Monsieur de Thou's History of his Own Time.*

[**Preface, 1**] *Malherb* [...] **for fear of the** *French* **Criticks:** ironic references to the French poet François de Malherbe (1555–1628) and to the man of letters and critic Jean-Louis Guez de Balzac (1597–1654). Both these authors, in different ways, are known for their influence on French literature along classicist lines, with an emphasis on compositional perfectionism.

[**Preface, 2**] **the** *Spaniard* [...] **Eyes in it:** Pedro Espinosa, 'El Perro y la Calentura: novela peregrina' (1625), attributed to Francisco de Quevedo in a number of editions, including *The Comical Works of Don Francisco de Quevedo*, 'The Dog and the Fever: An Unaccountable Novel or, A Rapsody', pp. 372–405, see p. 379. Cf. Fuller, *Gnomologia*, p. 109.

151

[**Preface, 5**] *De futuro [...] veritas*: lit. of the contingent future the truth is insofar as we determine it. The editor of *Memoirs* is claiming that the truth of the contingent future is determined by him.

[**Preface, 5, footnote**] **Mr. *Lintot***: Bernard Lintott, the publisher and bookseller mentioned in the text footnote, printed works by Pope and Gay among others and the choice seems consistent with the satirical, antiphrastic self-portrait of the narrator. On Lintott: McLaverty, 'Lintot [Lintott], (Barnaby) Bernard'.

[**Preface, 5**] **Cardinal *Berule***: Pierre de Bérulle (1575–1629), theologian and founder of the Society of the Oratory of Jesus (1611) dedicated to the reform of clerical education in France. Bérulle was a leading religious figure, influenced by the Neoplatonism of pseudo-Dionysius and Augustine, and known for both his mysticism and his intolerance of Protestants. Ablondi, 'Bérulle, Pierre De'.

152

[**Preface, 8**] *Num furis? [...] ede*: [Ulysses] — Are you mad? or do you purposely make fun of me with your dim oracle? [Tiresias] — O son of Laertes, whatever I say will or will not be; for prophecy is great Apollo's gift to me. [Ulysses] — But what means that story? Tell me, if you may. In the Latin text the modern reference edition reads 'Laërtiade' and 'quidquid'. 'Son of Laertes' is an epithet for Ulysses. Horace, *Satires*, II.v, lines 58–61.

153

[**Preface, 8**] **St. *Bridget***: Birgitta Birgersdotter, known as St. Bridget of Sweden (*c.* 1303–1373).

[**Preface, 8**] **Chancellour *Gerson***: Jean Gerson or de Gerson (1363–1429).

[**Preface, 10**] **Jesuit *Thyræus* [...] *de apparitione Spirituum***: Thyraeus, *De Apparitionibus Spirituum Disputatio Theologica*.

154

[**Preface, 11**] ***Ptolemy* [...] Circumstances**: Ptolemy, *Tetrabiblos*, fol. 365ʳ.

155

[**Preface, 16**] *Cevennes*: metonym for the Huguenots, French Protestants who settled in the mountain region of Cévennes, in southeast France. In 1685 the Edict of Fontainebleau revoked the Edict of Nantes and, with it, the freedom of worship, ushering in a century of persecution. McCloy, 'Persecution of the Huguenots in the 18th Century'.

156

[**Preface, 17**] *Chevalier*: James Stuart (1688–1766).

157

[**Preface, 18**] *Van Helmont's* **Condition** [...] **Sex:** van Helmont, *Ortus Medicinae*, 'Confessio Authoris', pp. 13–16.

[**Preface, 18–19**] *Pisander* [...] **Trick:** in Aristophanes' *Birds* Pisander pays a visit to the necromancer Socrates, who conjures spirits, asking to see his soul, which had deserted him while still alive.

[**Preface, 20 and footnote**] **as a** *Kircher* **told** *Schottus*: Schott, *P. Gasparis Schotti* [...] *Physica curiosa*, p. 524.

159

[**Preface, 25**] *Charles* **II** [...] **upon Earth:** in 1662 Charles II granted the royal charter that constituted the Royal Society as a corporate body. The charter expressed the King's desire to favour all forms of learning, with a preference for natural philosophy: '[...] but with particular grace We encourage philosophical studies, especially those which by actual experiments attempt either to shape out a new philosophy or to perfect the old', quoted in Peters and Besley, 'The Royal Society, the Making of "Science"', p. 227. During Charles II reign, the Royal Observatory was also founded. In 1675, a royal warrant established the role of the Astronomer Royal in a bid to resolve the challenge of calculating longitude at sea.

[**Preface, 26**] **satyrical Observers** [...] **Times to come:** an oblique reference to contemporary satirists, possibly but not exclusively the Tories united around *The Craftsman*, who, the narrator hopes, will turn their wits to the future described in *Memoirs* and lose sight of current affairs.

160

[**Preface, 27 and footnote**] *Somnia [...] negligebat*: he was not indifferent to his own dreams or to those which others dreamed about him. Suetonius, *Lives of the Caesars*, I, book II — 'The Deified Augustus', pp. 282–83. The quote comes in all likelihood from the edition Suetonius Tranquillus, *C. Suetonii Tranquilli Opera Omnia*, caput XCI, p. 220.

[**Preface, 27–28**] *moris [...] indicaret*: it was an ancient custom that a person who had received a dream concerning the state should make it public and describe its content either verbally by means of a crier or by means of a public notice.

[**Preface, 28**] *Jamaica [...]* **1692**: the earthquake that occurred in Jamaica on 7 June 1692.

161

[**Preface, 29**] **In** *petto*: a borrowing from Italian, lit. 'in the breast', 'in the hearth' (after the Latin *in pectore*), meaning privately, in secret. The *Oxford English Dictionary* records its use in English from the mid-seventeenth century onwards, and that one of the earliest occurrences was in Swift's *A Discourse of the Contests and Dissensions between the Nobles and the Commons in Athens and Rome* (1701). *Oxford English Dictionary Online* (hereafter OED).

[**Preface, 29**] *Arcana imperii*: secrets of the state.

[**Preface, 29**] *uti [...] Calchas*: so Calchas interprets the omens. Virgil, *Aeneid books I–VI*, book II, pp. 328–29, line 182.

[**Preface, 30**] *Alcoran*: Qur'an.

[**Preface, 31**] *Parcite [...] sequitur*: Forbear to resent me, my brothers, if now I do not tell you what follows. The expression may be from a secondary source, such as François Garasse, *La doctrine curieuse*, p. 731.

162

[**Preface, 31**] **the Adventure of the** *Bear* **and the** *Fiddle*: Reference to Samuel Butler's *Hudibras* (1662).

[**1**] **Captain** *Milton*: a 'Joseph Milton, Earl Milton' is mentioned also *infra*, on p. 275 of the text, in the list of the members of parliament in 1997.

163

[3] *Dunkirk* and *Calais*: the first letter opens the series commenting on British commercial success: a favourable treaty is almost concluded with the Ottoman Empire — thanks to which British producers and traders will no longer have to pay protectionist duties — while George VI has forced France, *manu militari*, to give up all its ports in the Channel (in an unspecified recent past). Back in London, The Lord High Treasurer has just been declared Prime Minister and Treasurer.

[5] *Mufties*: in the Ottoman empire, a Mufti was the official head of religion within the state or his deputy as chief legal authority for a large city, OED.

[5] *Grand Seignior*: lit. grand lord, a title given to the Turkish Emperor.

164

[5] *Janizaries* and *Spahies*: Janissaries and Sipahis were two professional cavalry corps in the Ottoman army; Boyar and Fleet, *A Social History of Ottoman Istanbul*, pp. 91–95.

[6] *Enthusiasts*: the term is used in a now obsolete sense to designate possessed or inspired persons. In the eighteenth century it was intended in a derogatory sense to describe someone who falsely claimed to be receiving divine communications, or whose views were fanatical, OED; Bailey, *An Universal Etymological English Dictionary, sub voce* 'Enthusiast'.

[6] *Hogies*: those who have completed a pilgrimage to the Mecca, one of the Islamic pillars, here used as a synonym of 'clerk of law', Percy, *William Percy's Mahomet*, ed. by Dimmock, p. 206.

[7] *Dervices*: early modern form for *dervishes*, OED.

[7] *Timariot*: formerly, in the feudal system of Turkey, the holder of a *timar*, a fief held by military service, OED.

165

[8] *Kuperlies*: possibly an epithet for Turk viziers that, when in conference, were called 'kubbe viziers' in reference to their meeting place, the Kubbealtı (under-the-dome) in Topkapı Palace. To be found in other coeval texts such as Knolles, *The Turkish History*, pp. 1, 2, 14, 23; [Jones], *A Compleath History of the Turks*, III, p. 31.

[9] **Bassa:** an earlier form of the Turkish title *pasha*, an officer of high rank, OED.

166

[11] **This has been chiefly owing [...] warlike Exercises:** A reference to the Ottoman practice of *devshirme* established in 1395: the periodic forced recruitment of young boys, particularly from the Christian Balkas, to form the Janissaries and serve as court or administrative officers. They received a Turkish education, and assumed Islamic names and identities. Esposito, ed., *The Oxford Dictionary of Islam*, pp. 67, 158.

167

[13] **Wallachia:** historical region in south-eastern Europe (part of present-day Romania), which acknowledged allegiance to the Ottoman Empire in the fifteenth century.

168

[17] **O Fortunati [...] Angligenæ!:** o progeny of England, happy beyond measure, could they but know their blessings! Variation on Virgil, 'O fortunatos nimium, sua si bona norint,/agricolas!': 'O farmers, happy beyond measure, could they but know their blessings!', Virgil, *Georgics*, liber II, lines 458–59. The ambassador to Constantinople rewrites the quote and uses it to refer to the fortunes of the British people (*Angligenae*, lit. people of English birth), who enjoy 'the best of Constitutions' and 'the best Princes'.

169

[19] **5 *l.* a Year:** here and henceforth the symbol *l.* is used as a currency sign for the pound. Derived from the Latin *L* for *libra*, the l in lower or uppercase continued to be used until the nineteenth century in printed texts, alongside its version with horizontal line or lines drawn through (£, ₤), introduced from the seventeenth century onwards. Houston, *Shady Characters*, pp. 45–46 for its use in the eighteenth century.

[20] **Iman:** Imam, the prayer-leader of a mosque; the spelling variant was not unusual in eighteenth-century texts, OED.

[20] **Cady:** *Cadi*, a civil judge, usually of a town or village; the spelling variant was not unusual in eighteenth-century texts, OED.

170

[23] *Cadelisker: cadilesker,* a chief judge in the Turkish empire, OED.

173

[29] *Civita Viechia:* Civitavecchia, a port city on the Tyrrhenian coast of Italy, northwest of Rome.

174

[31] *Aulæ nostræ [...] hominum:* the respect there is for this Court is only founded on men's opinion and on their patience. The text references a passage in [de Thou], *Historiarvm svi temporis,* p. 12, here the original sentence reads: 'fama si quidem & hominum patientia huius aulæ stat maiestas': the quote is likely from a secondary source, such as Naudé et Patin, *Naudæna et Patiniana,* p. 71. De Thou's memoirs were never translated into English; a French version was published in 1711 as *Mémoires de la vie de Jacques-Auguste de Thou.* In de Thou's text the cardinal is identified as 'Prosperum Sancta crucium', Prospero Santacroce (1514–1589). On de Thou see also *supra,* p. 10 of the text.

[32] *Millanese:* Milanese, the area around the city of Milan (Italy).

175

[34 and footnote] the *Moses* and *Aarons* [...] **Gods to Kings:** 'And the Lord said unto Moses, See, I have made thee a god to Pharaoh: and Aaron thy brother shall be thy prophet', Exodus 7.1. *The Bible,* ed. by Carroll and Prickett.

[35] *keys:* the keys of Saint Peter, a symbol of Papal authority, here used as a metonymy for the power of the Vatican.

176

[36] *Loretto:* given what the text is discussing, this is likely the town of Loreto, in central Italy, an important destination for Catholic, particularly Marian, pilgrimage.

[36] *he Wars:* read *the wars.*

177

[39] *Omnibus [...] Venter!*: all [the animals] alike have only sleep and food. Manilius, *Astronomica*, pp. 294–95, line 899. The modern standard text reads: 'omnibus una quies venter'.

178

[43] *per fas & nefas*: lit. 'by licit or illicit means', meaning regardless of legal or ethical implications.

180

[48] *Inquisition* in *France*: the English ambassador to Rome tells of the pope's plans to establish an inquisition in France and to assume the title of emperor by influencing the electors (who were princes of the Holy Roman Empire with the right to elect the emperor).

181

[50] *Ex traduce*: archaic expression, 'having origin from a parent stock' (from Latin *ex* — out of, *traduce* ablative of *trādux* — vine-layer, and *dūcĕre* — to lead).

182

[52] **the Pretender:** James Stuart (1688–1766), see also *supra*, p. 17 of the text.

183

[57] *Knez*: historical title among Slavonic nations, equivalent to prince, sometimes implying sovereignty. The *Oxford English Dictionary* records its use in English from the late sixteenth century onwards.

186

[63] *Kannus*: a decorated shamanic drum, used by the Sami people in magical ceremonies; Irving, 'Comparative Organography in Early Modern Empires'.

187

[68] *Scheffer [...] Lapland*: Scheffer, *The History of Lapland*.

189

[71] *propter metum Judæorum*: John 20.19, 'for fear of the Jews'.

[72] *Joannes Nider* [...] **the Storm:** a modern transcription of the passage alluded to is in: Franck, *Quellen und Untersuchungen zur Geschichte*, pp. 88–98. In the episode narrated by Nimer, the judge is called Peter von Greyerz (Gruyères) and the defendant Stedelen: the author mistakenly combines the names of the two protagonists.

192

[78] *Busbequius*: Busbecq, *Itinera Constantinopolitanum*.

[79] *Herodotus* [...] **Grave:** Perhaps a reference to Herodotus, *The Persian Wars*, book IV, paragraph 71.

193

[81] *Menage* [...] **pleases:** Menage, *Menagiana*, IV, p. 22. The collection of thoughts and mottos under the title *Menagiana*, first published in 1693, went through several editions in the 1690s and early 1700s: the anecdote could have been taken from any of these.

[82] *Ratio ultima Regum*: the last argument of kings.

194

[85] *Livy* [...] **them:** Livy, *History of Rome*, II, book III, part X.

195

[86] *Silphium*: a plant from the Mediterranean region, which has been variously identified as *Thapsia garganica* and *Narthex silphium*, yielding a gum resin or juice valued by the ancients as a condiment or medicine; the *Oxford English Dictionary* records its first mention in English in 1706.

[86] *Assa Fœtida*: a resinous gum, with a strong alliaceous odour, obtained from the *Narthex asafœtida*, used in medicine as an antispasmodic, and as a flavouring in cooking, OED.

[87 and footnote] *Fulvius Hirpinus* [...] *Escargatoire*: Pliny, *Natural History*, III, book IX, paragraph 82, pp. 280–81; Cato, Varro, *On Agriculture*, III.12, pp. 488–89, see also III.14, pp. 494–95.

[87] dr. *Frier* [...] **Travels:** Fryer, *A New Account of East-India and Persia*, p. 53.

[88] *Tacitus* [...] **Conqueror:** Tacitus, *Agricola*, ch. 24, pp. 166–67.

200

[100] *Vergerius* [...] *Italy*: Pier Paolo Vergerio (1498–1565), papal diplomat, nuncio to King Ferdinand in Germany in 1533, bishop of Capodistria (Koper), later religious exile and Protestant propagandist. Jacobson Schutte, 'Vergerio, Pier Paolo'; on Vergerio and the collection of relics: Paschini, *Pier Paolo Vergerio*, pp. 6–7.

201

[103] *Emptum Charovii*: acquired in Charovia. Here and henceforth, places of provenance in the list of relics are often indicated in Latin, with expressions such as *emptum* — bought, purchased — or by city names with locative endings, such as *Romæ* — in Rome. Here *Charovia* may be a misspelling of Charcovia or Charkovia (Kharkiv, in Ukraine).

202

[105] *emptum Cassini*: acquired in Cassino, a town in Southern Italy.

204

[111] *Romæ St. John Lateran*: the relic comes from the archbasilica of Saint John Lateran in Rome.

205

[112] *Xaintonge*: Saintonge, historical French province on the southwestern Atlantic coast, today part of the department Charente-Maritime.

[112] *Caveat Emptor*: lit. 'let the buyer beware', meaning the buyer concludes the transaction and purchase at their own risk.

205-06

[115] *Rivet* [...] **Sins:** Rivet, *Apologia pro sanctissima Virgine Maria*, liber II, caput IX, p. 292.

206

[115] **Quasillum:** wool basket.

[115] *Halae:* an ancient town in the Greek region of Locris.

[116] *magni Michaelis apud Carcassonenses: apud* is Latin for 'at', 'in the precincts of'. Cathedral of Saint-Michel, in the town of Carcassonne (France).

[116] **His Brain very well dried:** The source of inspiration for this detail and for the spirit of the whole listing of relics is Thumm's *Apodeixis theologica*, p. 114.

[117] *Quicquid [...] facinus:* whatever the truth might be, faith purges the crime. Caesar Baronius (1538–1607) was an ecclesiastical historian, he became cardinal in 1596 and Librarian of the Vatican the subsequent year. The quotation was repeated in several late seventeenth-century sources, and the author may have taken it, for instance, from André Rivet — whose 'Apology for the Virgin' was mentioned earlier in the text: *A. Riveti [...] Operum Theologicorum*, 'Tractatus secundus', p. 271; or perhaps from Patrick, *Reflexions upon the Devotions of the Roman Church*, p. 28; or Fuller, *The Historie of the Holy Warre*, liber III, ch. 12, p. 129.

208

[120] δυσνόητα: obscure matters, things difficult to understand.

[121] *noli me tangere:* touch me not. John 20.17, *The Bible*, trans. by Carroll and Prickett.

[123] *Testiculi eorum:* their testicles.

209

[125] *Gononus's Chronicon [...]* **under his Bed:** Gononus, *Chronicon SS. Deiparæ Virginis Mariæ*, p. 176.

[125–26] **St.** *Apollonia's* **Head [...] from** *Placentia* **in** *Spain:* the list of the relics of Saint Apollonia seems to be modelled on that in the work of the Church of England clergyman and religious controversialist Patrick, *Reflexions upon the Devotions of the Roman Church*, p. 233.

[126] *Volaterræ* in *Etruria*: Volterra in Etruria (Italy). Etruria was an ancient region in central Italy, corresponding approximately to modern Tuscany and parts of Lazio and Umbria.

[126] *Bononia*: Bologna, Italy.

[126] *Mechlin*: Mechelen, Belgium.

210

[126–27] **His Tongue [...] as the famous *Mendozius* tells us:** the source for the remarks on St Anthony's incorruptible tongue is in all likelihood Patrick, *Reflexions upon the Devotions of the Roman Church*, pp. 325–26.

[127] *populo*: people. Santa Maria del Popolo, a church in Rome.

[128] **Pere *Mabillon* writ [...] holy Church:** Mabillon, *Lettre d'un bénédictin à Monseigneur l'évesque de Blois*; on Mabillon and the cult of the holy tears of Christ: Hickey, 'Capturing Christ's Tears'.

211

[129] **as *Tacitus* assures us [...] 62:** Tacitus, *Histories*, book III, chs 60–63, pp. 616–23.

[130] *Homo [...] mendax*: man is a credulous and mendacious animal. Commonplace, notably used by Sorbière in his *Relation d'un voyage en Angleterre*, p. 188. Sorbière's caustic remarks on aspects of coeval British culture prompted the replay of Thomas Sprat; his *Relation* was translated into English and published together with Sprat's *Observations* in 1709: *A Voyage to England, Containing Many Things Relating to the State of Learning*, see here p. 78 for the Latin quote.

212

[132] **To the Lord High Treasurer:** the addressee of the letter contains a clerical error: the content is clearly that of a letter written by (and not addressed to) the Lord High Treasurer to the Ambassador in Constantinople, in reply to the one received on 3 November 1997 (see above pp. 1–28 of the text after the preface).

213

[134] **like *Esau*:** Genesis 25.29–34.

215

[139] *Mutatâ [...] Mores*: a change in the music generates a change in manners.

[139] *Curandum [...] retineatur*: care must therefore be taken to keep the music sombre and soothing. Cicero examines the connection between changes in music and the characteristics of a nation in *Laws*, II, chs 38–39 and III, ch. 32, discussing Plato, *Republic*, IV.424. The Latin tags quoted in the text come, however, from a secondary source, see Rose, *Musical Authorship*, pp. 163, 173 and n. 73.

216

[143] *Statical Hygroscopes*: an instrument which indicates (without accurately measuring) the degree of humidity of the air, OED; notably in 1673 Robert Boyle proposed his version of the instrument's design, see Boyle, *Works of Robert Boyle*, ed. by Hunter and Davis, VII, pp. 427–42.

[144] **Solar** *Maculæ*: sunspots.

218

[147] *Sheldon's* **Theatre**: the Sheldonian theatre, designed by the architect Christopher Wren and inaugurated in Oxford in 1669, was named after Archbishop Gilbert Sheldon, promoter and financier of the project. The theatre was used for academic ceremonies as well as anatomical demonstrations and the staging of plays. The spaces under the seating galleries were also used by the university press. Books bore the imprint 'At the Theatre', a custom that continued for many years even after the university press was moved to the Clarendon building (1712–1713). Downes, 'Wren, Sir Christopher'; Kilburn, 'The Fell Legacy', p. 120.

[147] *per ann.*: (abbreviated form of *per annum*), each year.

[148] **stinking of the Lamp**: an idiomatic phrase that sarcastically emphasises the fact that a book bears signs of great labour; a book smells of the lamp when the author has had to keep revising it until late at night by lamplight, in an attempt to remedy its flaws.

221

[154] *Venient Romani*: the Romans shall come. John 11.48, *The Bible*, trans. by Carroll and Prickett.

222

[163] **St. *Chrysostome*'s Homilies:** John Chrysostom (*c.* 347–407), Bishop of Constantinople and Doctor of the Orthodox Church. His vast production of homilies and sermons enjoyed great popularity from the late ancient and medieval periods onwards in many of the languages of Christianity including Latin and, in the early modern era, French and English. Bonfiglio, 'The Armenian Translations of John Chrysostom'.

223

[166] *Si qua [...] recede:* lit. 'if you sit on a seat and that seat is a comfortable seat for you, remain sitting on that seat', meaning if you are comfortable where you are, stay there, do not change places. A Latin proverb that is also used for practice in pronunciation and accent.

[167] *nec prece nec pretio:* neither by prayer nor by bribery. The Latin expression is found in Ovid's *Fasti* (11.805), but is commonly used to describe an incorruptible person or institution.

225

[171] *Matchiavels:* Intriguers, schemers (from Niccolò Machiavelli, 1469–1527, Florentine statesman and humanist), here derogatory, OED.

[171] *Engastromythick* **Divinity:** the deity of the stomach, meaning inspiration for these professors comes from the stomach, i.e. hunger or gluttony.

[172] *conditio sine quâ non:* a condition one cannot do without, an indispensable condition.

227

[177] *Morduites:* in *Hakluytus Posthumus*, this is the name of a people who, living in a border region between the Tartars and Russians, developed a hybrid religion, mixing Christian, Islamic, and Jewish elements; Purchas, *Hakluytus Posthumus*, I, p. 324.

[177] **the Dead Sea, as *Mandeville* describes it:** *The Travels of Sir John Mandeville*, pp. 67–68. This is a modern edition based on the 1725 English edition; purportedly authored by the English knight Mandeville, the *Travels* first appeared in France in 1357 and was translated into many European languages.

228

[**179 and footnote**] *James Mora* [...] **in his Travels:** Addison, *Remarks on Several Parts of Italy*, p. 40.

232

[**188**] *Janisarchi*: *kapalı çarşı*, lit. a covered bazaar, a market in Constantinople. The anglicised name and the subsequent description are similar to those given by Giovanni Francesco Gemelli Careri in his *Voyage Round the World*, p. 72.

235

[**197**] **disagreeahle:** read disagreeable.

[**198**] **like the *Chæroneans*** [...] **their Rulers:** Pausanias, *Description of Greece*, book XL, paragraphs 10–12, pp. 360–61.

236

[**198**] **Bassas:** see *supra*, note on p. 9 of the text.

[**199**] *Moses's* **great miracle** [...] **Land:** Exodus 8.16–19.

[**199**] **the Geese in the Capitol** [...] **slept:** Livy credited the geese of the Capitol of Rome, sacred to Juno, with saving the city from a surprise attack by the Gauls in 390 BCE with their gabbling and clapping. Livy, *History of Rome*, III, book v, pp. 158–59. The episode is also recounted by Plutarch in *Moralia: The Roman Questions*, question 98.

237

[**203**] *Res unius ætatis*: a matter lasting only one age, whose duration cannot exceed one generation. Florus, *Epitome of Roman History*, book I, paragraph 10, pp. 10–11.

238

[**205**] *De Gloria* [...] *De Exilio*: *De Gloria* (On glory) is a lost philosophical work by Cicero, composed around 44 BCE. In 1522 the Venetian printer and humanist Paulus Manutius accused Pietro Alcionio, classical scholar and translator, of plagiarising part of Cicero's work in his dialogue *De exilio*, and then destroying the only existing copy. According to the

version of the story mentioned in the text, Cicero's codex was owned by Bernardo Giustiniani, a member of an important Venetian family, who bequeathed his library to a monastery of which Alcionio was the physician. The historian of Italian literature Girolamo Tiraboschi later argued that the accusations were false: *Storia della letteratura*, p. 1065.

[206] **Historian *Trogus Pompeius* [...] *Augustus*:** Pompeius Trogus's *Historiae Philippicae* was a forty-four-volume history of the world, centered on Macedon under Philip II (hence the title meaning 'Philippic histories'). While this work, composed in the first century BCE, is lost, the tables of contents and an epitome survived in a later compilation by Justin, dated around the second or third century CE. Alonso-Núñez, 'An Augustan World History'.

[206] *Pharaoh's lean kine* [...] **fort:** Genesis 41.1–4.

239

[207] *Vocontii*: a Celtic people of Gallia Narbonensis, subjugated by the Romans in the first century BCE; *Narbon Gaul*: Gallia Narborensis, a Roman province in present-day southeastern France.

[207] *Sertorian* **War:** a war fought in the Iberian Peninsula in the first century BCE, between the opponents to Sulla's regime led by Sertorius and the government of Rome led by Sulla.

[209] *Pera*: a quarter of the Ottoman city of Galata, outside the city walls. During the seventeenth century and up to the eighteenth century it developed as an upper-class quarter where a number of wealthy Europeans built their residences. Çelik, *The Remaking of Istanbul*, p. 30.

[209] *Bumicilli*: the entry 'Bumicili' in Diderot and d'Alembert's *Encyclopedie*, authored by Edme-François Mallet, describes them as: 'a Mohammedan sect in Africa [...] great sorcerers. They fight against the devil, so they say, and run bruised, covered with blows, and all scared [...] they counterfeit a fight in the presence of everyone for two or three hours, with javelins or zagaies, until they fall down from weariness. But after resting for a while, they come to their senses, and walk about. It is not yet known what their rule is, but they are said to be very religious'. Similar descriptions are to be found in a number of earlier eighteenth-century French, English, and Dutch universal dictionaries and encyclopaedias.

240

[210] **Bedlamite:** rare for madman or lunatic, from the term for an inmate of Bedlam, Bethlem Royal Hospital in London, OED.

[210] **teople:** read people.

[214] *Hachìm Bachi*: the imperial head physician. Shefer-Mossensohn, *Ottoman Medicine*, p. 31, in other eighteenth-century sources there are the alternative spellings such as 'achim-bachi' and 'hekim bachi'.

242

[216] *Momus*: in Greek mythology, Momus was a deity of the ridiculous, of satire. As a challenger of authority and harbinger of scepticism, he had important revivals in early modern English culture. Momus is also expert in finding fault with the gods, a meaning established by one of Aesop's fables in which, when called upon to judge three different creations by three Olympian gods, he criticised all three. In this sense — as a caustic critic par excellence, or ur-critic — the figure of Momus also appears in Swift's *A Tale of a Tub* and *Battle of the Books*; see McClure, *Doubting the Divine in Early Modern Europe*. In the text there is a specific reference to Aesop's fable: the author compares his critics to the bull created by Poseidon, of which Momus had remarked that, having eyes under his horns, he is unable to aim his charge accurately. In this case, therefore, the author establishes a simile between himself and Momus, to denounce the blindness or misdirection of his critics.

243

[217] *Esau's* **Angel** [...] **Patriarch:** Genesis 32.

[217, **footnote**]: Bernard, *The Religious Ceremonies*, I, pp. 30, 40.

[218] *Mongir* **and** *Guavequir*: Purchas, *Hakluytus Posthumus*, vol. VIII, 'A Relation of a Journey begun, Anno Dom. 1610. written by Master George Sandys, and here contracted' (1615), p. 153. Mongir and Guave-quir also appear as characters in William Percy's *Arabia Sitiens, or A Dream of a Dry Year* (1601), see Percy, *William Percy's Mahomet*, ed. by Dimmock.

[219 **and footnote**] *Elementa Magica* **of** *Petrus de Abano*: Agrippa, *Henrici Cor. Agrippæ ab Netthesheym de occulta philosophia*, pp. 556–89. On Agrippa see also *infra*, pp. 226–27 of the text. The attribution of the *Heptameron* to Abano is considered spurious by current studies. On Peter of Abano (*c.* 1250–1316), natural philosopher, physician, astronomer, and astrologer see also *infra*, note on p. 231 of the text.

244

[220] ***Quod [...] ratione valet:*** what is valid by virtue of a prescription is also valid according to reason.

[220 and footnote] ***Hesiod*** [...] **Mankind:** Hesiod, *Theogony*, pp. 106–09.

[220] **Works of *Menander*** [...] **him:** *Poetae Comici Graeci*, VI.2 — *Menander*, ed. by Kassel and Austin, p. 282. Menander's fragment 500 was notably discussed by Plutarch, an author quoted elsewhere in *Memoirs*. Plutarch, *Moralia*, VI, 'On Tranquility of Mind', pp. 220–21. In early eighteenth-century Britain, the then known fragments of Menander were available in Latin translations printed in London, Cambridge, Paris, and Amsterdam, often collected together with the writings of other authors in volumes dedicated to ancient comic poetry or drama.

[220–21 and footnote] ***Pythagoras*** [...] ***Diogenes Laertius*** **tells us:** for a modern edition of Diogenes' lives of Plato and Pythagoras: Diogenes Laertius, *Lives of Eminent Philosophers*, I, book III — *Plato*, pp. 276–373; Diogenes Laertius, *Lives of Eminent Philosophers*, II, book VIII — *Pythagoras*, pp. 320–65. Entries from Diogenes' *Lives and Opinions of Eminent Philosophers*, already translated into Latin in the sixteenth century, were often included in the editions of works of the respective philosophers, such as in collections of Plato's writings. From the last decades of the seventeenth century, a number of editions and compendia appeared in English translation.

[221] ***Seneca's*** **hundred and tenth epistle:** Seneca, *Epistles*, epistle CX, pp. 264–75. The epistle is included in early English translations such as Seneca, *The workes of Lucius Annæus Seneca*, pp. 450–53.

[221–22] **To go no farther than the Patriarchs** [...] **matters:** cf. for example Bartolocci, *Bibliotheca magna rabbinica*, I, p. 213; Naudé, *The History of Magick*, p. 27.

245

[223 and footnotes] **As to the Philosophers** [...] **vain thing:** Plato, *Theages*, pp. 374–75, paragraph 128; Xenophon, *Memorabilia*, book I, paragraphs 2–3, pp. 8–9; Maximus of Tyre, *The Philosophical Orations*, orations

VIII and IX, pp. 67–83; Apuleius, *Apologia*, pp. 342–98; for Antisthenes' fragments: Prince, *Antisthenes of Athens*, pp. 374–76.

246

[225] *Kircher's* **good Genius** [...] *Iter Extaticum*: see *supra*, p. 20 of the text and editorial note.

[225–26 **and footnote**] *Franciscus Albertinus* [...] **single Man**: Albertini, *Libellus de angelo custode*, pp. 21–22, 74.

[226] *Officium Angeli Custodis*: see *infra*, Bibliography, *Officium angeli custodis*.

[226] **Mons.** *Launoie*: we are inclined to think that this reference is to Jean de Launoy (1601–1678), a Catholic prelate and theologian known for applying a critical method in the investigation of visions, apparitions, and miracles. Launoy, *Joannis Launoii, Constantiensis, Parisiensis Theologi, Socii Navarraei, Opera Omnia*.

[226] **the Jesuit** *Schottus* [...] **advantage**: Schott, *P. Gasparis Schotti* [...] *Thaumaturgus Physicus*, 'S. Francisco Xaverio Magno Indiarum Apostolo. Thaumaturgo. Auctor', pp. 2–3. On Schott see also *supra*, p. 20 of the text.

[226–27] *Cornelius Agrippa* [...] **Angel**: Agrippa, *Henrici Cor. Agrippæ ab Netthesheym de occulta philosophia*, pp. 367–69; see also *supra*, p. 222 of the text.

[227 **and footnote**] *Bartholomæus de Sybilla* [...] **our mother's good Angel**: Sybilla, *Speculum peregrinarum quaestionum*, 'Quaestio II. Cap. Qurti, Secundæ decadis. Quod unus, & plures Angeli ad hominum custodiam possunt assignari', p. 436.

247

[227 **and footnote**] **In another treatise** [...] **and not a guardian Angel**: here the text seems to be erroneously attributing a treatise by Andrea Vittorelli to Sibilla: *De angelorum custodia lib. II*, p. 107. The treatise was dedicated to the newly elected Pope Paul V, who, a few years later, approved the publication of the *Officium* mentioned above.

[228 **and footnote**] *Joannes Eckius* [...] **festival**: Tillotson, 'Sermon XXI'; Eck, 'Homilia VII'. In the footnote referencing Eck, *vide*: see; *in dicto* *locol* read *in dicto loco*, meaning in the above-mentioned place, i.e. Eck's homily that is referred to in the text.

[**229 and footnote**] *Lactantius* [...] **less burthensome to them:** Lactantius, *L. Coelii Lactantii Firmiani Opera quæ quidem extant omnia*, here see *Institutionum divinarum*, liber II, caput XV, 'De inquinatione angelorum, & duobus generibus demonum', pp. 139–43; the numbering of the chapters varies depending on the edition; for a modern translation: Lactantius, *Divine institutes*, trans. and with an introduction and notes by Bowen and Garnsey, pp. 158–60.

247-48

[**229-30 and footnote**] *Carlo Fabri* [...] *Bohemia*: Fabri, *Scudo di Christo*, pp. 237–38.

248

[**231**] **Peter d'Apono:** Peter of Abano, see also *supra*, note on p. 219 of the text.

[**231 and footnote**] **he had no less than seven** [...] **tells us:** Elich, *M. Philippo-Ludwigi Elich, Ex Marpurgo Hessorum, Dæmonomagia*, p. 204. For a similar discussion mentioning Elich on Abano cf.: Naudé, *The History of Magick*, p. 182.

[**231 and footnote**] **We shall place** *Cardan* [...] **one a-piece:** Cardano, *De propria vita liber*, pp. 261–69. On the concept of genius in Julius Caesar Scaliger (1484–1558) see Oosterhoff, 'Genius and Inspiration in the Early Modern Period'. Cf. Naudé, *The History of Magick*, pp. 143–64 for a discussion of tutelar spirits ascribed to Socrates, Aristotle, Plotinus, Porphyrius, Jamblicus, Chicus, Cardano, and Scaliger. Also drawing on Naudé: Beaumont, *An Historical, Physiological and Theological Treatise of Spirits*, pp. 21–59.

[**231 and footnote**] *Cardan,* **because even his father** [...] **thirty years:** Cardano, *De rerum varietate*, liber XVI, caput XCIII, pp. 629–30; the passage is notably also mentioned in Schott, *Physica curiosa*, p. 185.

[**231 and footnote**] *Boissard* [...] **Angel:** Boissard, *Tractatus posthumus Jani Jacobi Boissardi Vesuntini De divinatione & magicis praestigiis*, p. 49.

[**232 and footnote**] *Froissard* [...] **them:** Froissart, *Le tiers volume de l'histoire et chronique de messire Iehan Froissart*, caput XVII, pp. 63–66.

[**232 and footnote**] *Tasso* [...] **Genius:** Manso, *La vita di Torquato Tasso*, p. 147; *La Vie du Tasse*, pp. 193–94 (the prefatory letter is signed: 'D. C. D. D. V.', i.e. Jean-Antoine de Charnes, Doyen de Villeneuve, hence the reference in the text's footnote).

249

[**232**] *Bodin* [...] **sort:** Bodin, *De la démonomanie des sorciers*, pp. 7^r–14^r.

[**232 and footnote**] *Guy Patin* [...] **agree to:** Naudé et Patin, *Naudæna et Patiniana*, pp. 3–5.

[**233**] **the Manuscripts of the reverend Dr** *Richard Nepier:* Oxford, BL, papers of Dr Richard Napier (1559–1634); for a detailed list of manuscripts see Hadass, *Medicine, Religion, and Magic*, pp. 185–90; for an influential account published in the early eighteenth century: Lilly, *The Last of the Astrologers*, with notes and introduction by Briggs, pp. 49–50.

[**233–34 and footnote**] **Dr.** *Meric Casaubon* [...] **Reader:** Casaubon, *A True and Faithful Relation of What Passed for many Yeers Between Sr. John Dee and Some Spirits*; on Dee and Casaubon see Clucas, 'False Illuding Spirits & Cownterfeiting Deuills'.

250

[**235 and footnote**] *Sic enim* [...] *vates?:* for such complete details are given of the rivalry of the chief men, the faults of the leaders, the changes of government, that there is nothing that they do not make clear, and it may readily appear that Cicero's foresight was almost divination. For he not only predicted the events that actually happened during his lifetime, but, like a seer, foretold those which are now being experienced. Cornelius Nepos, *On Great Generals, Fragments*, xxv — 'Atticus', pp. 316–17.

[**235–36**] *Lycurgus* **pretended** [...] **Favours in:** cf. Naudé, *The History of Magick*, p. 25.

251

[**238**] *Dead Men's Candles:* another name for *ignes fatui* or will-o'-the-wisps. On their interpretation as a prognosis of death in Wales: Martin, *Description of the Western Isles of Scotland*, p. 313.

[**239**] **Mr.** *Martyn* [...] **Islands:** Martin, *Description of the Western Isles of Scotland*, pp. 300–35.

[239] *Æthobirius*: Mount Atabyrion or Attavyros, on the island of Rhodes. According to a scholium to Pindar's *Seventh Olympian Ode*, the sacred bulls lodged in the temple of Zeus Atabyrius roared whenever the city was threatened. Hamilton, 'The Bull of Phalaris', p. 10 and n. 17.

251-52

[240] **the prophetick Cow** [...] *Herodotus*: Herodotos, *Histories*, I, book II, paragraph 52, pp. 339–41; paragraph 69, p. 357; paragraph 153, p. 465.

252

[240] **the Ox** *Apis* [...] *Pliny*: Pliny, *Natural History*, III, book VIII, paragraph 71, pp. 128–31.

[240] **Telestick:** telestic, relating to religious mysteries; mystical, OED.

[240 and footnote] **at Mr.** *Stanley* **informs us:** Stanley, *The History of the Chaldaick Philosophy*; **at:** read as.

[240] **The learned** *Rabbi Kimchi* [...] **Spirit:** Stanley, *The History of the Chaldaick Philosophy*, p. 50.

[241] **Learned** *Selden* [...] *Syriis*: Selden, *De Diis Syriis Sintagmata*.

[241] **Learned** *Selden* [...] *Saul*: on Selden, Philo Judaeus, and teraphims see Gaffarel, *Unheard-of Curiosities*, p. 71.

[241] *Homer* [...] *Ulysses*: Homer, *Odyssey*, I, book XI, pp. 404–05.

[241] *Scipio* [...] **come:** Silius Italicus, *Punica*: in the poem a number of prophecies take place, in book XIII, Scipio descends to Hades, where the ghost of the Sibyl predicts the death of Hannibal, see vol. II, book XIII, lines 397–893; Statius, *Thebaid*, I: in book IV Tiresias performs a necromantic ritual summoning the spirit of Laius, who predicts the outcome of the war over the throne of the city of Thebes; Valerius Flaccus, *Argonautica*, book I, lines 788–822; Lucan, *The Civil War*: in book VI the Thessalian witch Erictho reanimates through a necromantic ritual the corpse of a dead soldier, who then predicts Pompey's defeat and Caesar's assassination.

[241–42 and footnote] **The famous** *Psellus* [...] **point**: the eleventh-century Platonist scholar Michael Psellos (or Psellus) gathered and commented on the scattered fragments of the *Chaldean Oracles*, a collection of verses purportedly handed down by the gods to Julian the Chaldean in the second century CE. They include the descriptions of rites to conjure deities — by vivification of statues or by binding the god to a human medium — who would then prophesy the theurgist: Majercik, *The Chaldean Oracles*, pp. 26–29, and 106 fragment 149. See also Stanley, *The History of the Chaldaick Philosophy*, p. 53.

[242] **as the Devil [...] death:** Samuel, 28.7–20. The spirit of Samuel in this biblical episode has been interpreted, by Luther for example, as the manifestation of a spectre or evil entity, Brann, *Trithemius and Magical Theology*, p. 165.

253

[243 **and footnote**] *Eusebius de Præparatione Evangelica*: Eusebius, *Eusebii Pamphili Evangelicae praeparationis libri*, III, tome I, book VI, 236a.

[243] **St *Austin*'s Treatise *de naturâ Dæmonum*:** Augustine, *De divinatione daemonum*, pp. 597–618; Eng. trans.: *Demonic divination*.

[243] *Marcus Antoninus* **observes:** Marcus Aurelius Antoninus, Μαρκοι Ἀντονινοι τονʼαγτοκροπος [...] *Marci Antonini imperatoris*, see for example book I, paragraph 16, pp. 4–6, book VII, paragraph 49, p. 65.

[244 **and footnote**] **the humble *Loyola* [...] Life:** Maffei, *Ignatii Loiolae vita*; the reference may also be to a subsequent edition, such as Maffei, *De vita et moribus B.P. Ignatii Loiolae*.

[245] *horresco referens*: I am horrified to report it.

254

[245] *ut omnes [...] defendere*: cf. the modern standard text 'ut omnis [...] aperte intellegat nihil in philosophos non modo vere dici, sed ne falso quidem posse confingi, quod non ex innocentiae fiducia, quamvis liceat negare, tamen potius habeant defendere': in that way, all this crowd, [...] may clearly see that nothing can be truthfully alleged against philosophers, or indeed falsely fabricated, that their trust in their own innocence would not allow them to defend, even though they might deny them. Apuleius, *Apologia*, XXVIII.2–3, pp. 76–77.

[246] **the people about Mount *Atlas* [...] them:** Herodotos, *Histories*, II, book IV, paragraph 184, pp. 386–89.

[246] *Furius Cresinius* [...] **Crops:** Pliny, *Natural History*, v, book XVIII, paragraph 8, pp. 216–17.

254-55

[246–48] **all the mysterious Arts of Divination** [...] **shew they are:** The divination techniques mentioned in the text are typically listed in early eighteenth-century compilations dedicated to the subject, such as those of the Lutheran moral philosopher and theologian Georg Pasch: *Georgii Paschii Gedanensis* [...] *De novis inventis*, p. 583; or the handbook of scholarship by Fabricius: *Jo. Alberti Fabricii* [...] *Bibliographia antiquaria*, pp. 412–22, see here p. 414 for *gastromantia* as divination by a vase full of water.

255

[249] *Hermolaus Barbarus* [...] Εντελεχεια: Hermolaus Barbarus's evocation is mentioned by a number of coeval encyclopaedic compilations, including Naudé, *The History of Magick*, p. 162; and Bayle, *Dictionaire historique et critique*, tome I, premiere partie A–B, *sub voce* 'Barbarus (Hermolaus)', pp. 458–62, see p. 458 note; on Naudé's *Apology* see also *supra*, editorial notes to pp. 222, 236 and *infra*, p. 250 of the text; on Bayle see also *infra*, p. 517 of the text. ἐντελέχεια: entelechy.

[249] **the learned Jesuit** *Cotton* [...] **Divinity:** Pierre Cotton or Coton (1564–1626) was a Jesuit controversialist. His inquiry into the possessions at Loudun are mentioned by a number of secondary sources, including Bayle, *Dictionaire*, tome premiere, seconde partie C–G, *sub voce* 'Grandier (Urbain)', pp. 1277–82, see 1282 note.

[250] *Heroës* [...] *annis*: renowned heroes born during better years.

[250] **that learned** *Frenchman's* **Apology:** Naudé, *The History of Magick*.

256

[250] **Celestial Alphabet** [...] **below:** Basnage, *Histoire des Juifs*, tome II, pp. 1025–33.

[250–51 **and footnote**] **the** *Jewish* **Doctors of note** [...] **World:** Cf. Basnage, *Histoire des Juifs*, tome II, p. 1026; Gaffarel, *Unheard-of Curiosities*, p. 392.

[251] *William Postell* [...] **Nature:** *Abrahami Patriarchae Liber Iezirah*, n.p., see 8 — 'Viginti duas literas fundamenti decrevit Effinxítue'; see also Postel, *Linguarum duodecim characteribus differentium alphabetum*, n.p. 'De Lingua Samaritana'; cf. Gaffarel, *Unheard-of Curiosities*, pp. 398–99.

[251] *Picus* [...] **true:** della Mirandola, 'Disputationes adversus astrologiam', pp. 411–731.

[251] *Sixtus Senensis* [...] *Bibliotheca*: Sisto da Siena, *Bibliotheca Sancta A F. Sixto Senensi*.

[251] *Plotinus* [...] **killing himself:** Gaffarel, *Unheard-of Curiosities*, p. 395.

[251–52] *Flud* [...] **as** *Postell* **himself:** see for example Fludd, *Utriusque cosmi Majoris scilicet*.

[252] **Mr.** *Vincent Wing*: Vincent Wing, astronomer, astrologer, surveyor, and mathematical practitioner (1619–1668).

257

[253 and footnote] *Gaffarell's Tables* [...] **Defence of them:** Gaffarel, *Unheard-of Curiosities*, pp. 335–82, see also 383–433.

[253] *Patridge* and *Gadbury*: astrologers and almanac-makers John Partridge (1644–1715) and John Gadbury (1627–1704).

[253–54] *The most marvellous Victories of Women*: Postel, *Les très merveilleuses victoires des femmes du Nouveau Monde*.

259

[260] *Bruta Fulmina*: lit. 'unfeeling thunderbolts', meaning empty threats.

260

[260] *Concio*: lit. 'assembly' or 'meeting', a public speech or harangue addressed to an assembly.

[261] *Religio* [...] *matrem*: religion brought forth wealth, and the daughter devoured the mother.

[262] *Paul* the third [...] *Gregory* the eighteenth: Paul III: Alessandro Farnese (1468–1549, pope 1534–1549), who was the first pope of the Counter-Reformation, calling the Council of Trent in 1545; Pius II: Enea Silvio Bartolomeo Piccolomini (1405–1464, pope 1458–1464), who was a humanist scholar and writer, sustained the papal supremacy over the general council, and tried to organise a crusade against the Turks; Gregory XVIII: a projection into the future of the sequence of popes. At the beginning of the eighteenth century, the last pope to have taken the name Gregory had been Alessandro Ludovisi, Pope Gregory XV from 1621 to 1623, who had founded the Congregation for the Propagation of the Faith, the first permanent body to control Catholic missionary work.

260-61

[262–63] *Peter the Hermit's Crusade* [...] Holy Ghost: the occurrence of the goose believed to be imbued with divine influence by the followers of Peter the Hermit in 1096 was reported by coeval chronicles, who emphasised the foolishness and dangers of popular credulousness; Walker-Meikle, 'The Goose that Went on a Crusade'.

261

[264] *Id* [...] *fabulas*: he believed that his only problem was to ensure that the plays he had created would win the approval of the public. Terence, *The Woman of Andros*, Prologus, pp. 1–2.

[264] *Gregory* the twentieth, and *Pius* the tenth: both Gregory X and Pius X are imaginary future pontiffs; the last pope to take the name Gregory was Pope Gregory XV, see *supra*, note on p. 262 of the text; the last Pius was Michele Ghislieri, on the papal throne as Pius V from 1566 to 1572, who had had an important role in the Counter-Reformation and in the persecution of heretics in Italy. He was canonised in 1712.

262

[267] as *Bosman* tells us [...] a fat one: Bosman, *A New and Accurate Description of the Coast of Guinea*. First published in Dutch in 1704, in the first decades of the eighteenth century the work went through a number of editions in Dutch (1709, 1719, 1739), French (1705), and English (1705, 1721); in the 1967 edition: 'New Introduction', pp. vii–xxi, see p. xix.

263

[270] **the excellent scheme proposed by Mr. *Abraham Cowley*:** Cowley, *A Proposition for the Advancement of Experimental Philosophy.*

266

[278] ***Apparent* [...] *Vasto*:** here and there are swimmers seen in the vast abyss. Virgil, *Aeneid books I–VI*, book I, pp. 270–71, line 118.

267

[279] ***Tantas conversiones* [...] *si vices rerum ævum putes*:** such are the changes due to mortal frailty or the fickleness of fortune. If you add up the years it would not seem very long, but it would be a lifetime if you count the changes of fortune. Pliny the Younger, *Letters*, book IV, letter XXIV — To Fabius Valens, p. 3.

[279] ***Quod potest esse documento* [...] *circumagi*:** this should be a warning never to lose heart and to be sure of nothing, when we see so many fluctuations of fortune following each other in rapid succession. Pliny the Younger, *Letters*, book IV, letter XXIV — To Fabius Valens, p. 7.

268

[281] ***mala stamina vitæ*:** bad constitution.

272

[292] ***Richlieu* or *Mazarine*:** Richlieu (read Richelieu) is Armand Jean du Plessis (1585–1642), cardinal and chief minister to Louis XIII (1624–1642); Mazarine is Giulio Mazarini or Mazzarino (1602–1661), French cardinal of Italian origins, who succeeded Richelieu as first minister in 1642 until his death.

[294] **like the Prophetesses of [...] Women:** Aristotle, *History of Animals*, book III.XI, pp. 204–05.

273

[296] ***inter arcana Imperii*:** among the secrets of the state.

274

[298–99] *Chinese* **Sect of Bonzes** [...] *Xin, Xin, Xin:* Borri, 'An Account of Cochinchina', p. 832.

[299] *Gli Infecondi:* an Italian academy, the name literally means 'academy of the infertile ones'.

277

[305] *Ex nihilo nihil fit:* from nothing comes nothing.

281

[317] **gerat:** read great.

[317] **Bassas:** see *supra*, note on p. 9 of the text.

286

[335, **footnote**] **racolti:** read *raccolti*, collected (Italian); **Ranusio:** read Ramusio.

287

[336] *In hoc signo Victor eris:* by this sign you shall conquer.

289

[340–41] *Nulla* [...] *caruisse:* there is no safer way to ensure one's health than being without a doctor. Cf. Petrarca, 'De audacia et pompa medicorum', p. 797.

291

[346] *Asclepiades:* a Greek physician, active in Rome in the first century BCE, renowned for administering simple treatments, based on diet and drink; Scarborough, 'The Drug Lore of Asclepiades of Bithynia'.

[347] *Da Guazzabuglio di medici:* [protect me] from the hodgepodge of physicians. Mainardi, *Facezie, Motti, Buffonerie*, p. 96.

[347] *Moly, Cynospastus,* **or Mandrake:** herbs credited with curative and magical powers, used in ancient and early modern medicine,

see for example Gerard, *The Herball or Generall Historie of Plantes*, pp. 182–89, 983, 351–53.

[347] *propter metum Judæorum*: see *supra*, note on p. 71 of the text.

292

[351] *Antidotum versus Cæsarem*: an antidote against Caesar. The reference is to an episode recounted by Suetonius as an example of the brutality of the Roman emperor Caligula's crimes and ways: Caligula, on the point of assassinating his brother, suspecting that he had imbibed antidotes for poison as a precautionary measure, exclaimed: 'What! an antidote against Caesar?'. Suetonius, *Lives of the Caesars*, I, pp. 462–63.

293

[352, footnote]: [Filmer], *Patriarcha, or the Natural Power of Kings*; defence of the divine right of kings, in which a number of passages have been interpreted as advocating the primogenitary right of English kings through direct descent from Adam.

[353] hehaved: read behaved.

[354] pnblick: read publick.

[354] Bedlam: Bethlem Royal Hospital, a psychiatric hospital in London, see also *supra*, note on p. 210 of the text.

296

[361] Monarchy of the *Solipsi*: reference to the anti-Jesuit satire *Lucii Cornelii Europæi Monarchia solipsorum*.

300

[370] poledavies: coarse canvases used for sailcloth, OED.

301

[374] *Tibiscus*: Tisza, a major river in central-eastern Europe; mentioned in eighteenth-century English sources also as Theiss or Teiss.

304

[381] *vivere [...] musis*: lit. 'to live just for oneself and the muses', meaning to lead a quiet and solitary life, devoting oneself to one's studies without meddling in worldly affairs.

308

[391] **feated:** suited (obsolete), OED.

310

[395] *imperatoria brevitate*: seeing brevity as a priority, meaning giving a brief answer.

[397] *mollia tempora fandi*: propitious times to talk, cf. Virgil, *Aeneid books I–VI*, book IV, line 293, 'quae mollissima fandi Tempora'.

[397] **Limners:** altered form of 'luminers', illuminators of manuscripts, OEC.

311

[397] *staturâ quadratâ*: (to be) well built; Suetonius, *Lives of the Caesars*, II, book VIII — 'The Deified Vespasian', ch. XX, pp. 298–99.

312

[400] *Maestro di Camera*: chief chamberlain.

313

[405] *Ariosttle*: read Aristotle.

314

[407] *Naudæus* **has pretended [...] fish:** Naudé et Patin, *Naudæna et Patiniana*, p. 14.

[407 **and footnote**] *Scaliger* **plainly [...]** *Cardan*: Scaliger, *Iulii Cæsaris Scaligeri Exotericarum Exercitationum lib. XV*, p. 706.

318

[416] **propoortion:** read proportion.

324

[432 and footnote] *Morison,* **in his Itinerary** [...] **grounds:** Moryson, *An Itinerary Written by Fynes Moryson Gent,* p. 26.

325

[436] **Duke of** *Cumberland***:** William Augustus, the second surviving son of George II. Speck, 'William Augustus'.

326

[438] *Prasini* **and** *Veneti***:** associations that acted as teams and fans in the context of chariot races, as well as social and political factions.

328

[444, **footnote**] **Pro** [...] **redditur:** the return is hatred instead of gratitude. Tacitus, *Annals,* book IV, ch. 18, pp. 34–35.

[444] *Du Hailan***:** Bernard de Girard Seigneur de Haillan (1535–1610).

332

[453] *Francis* **I** [...] **besiege him in** *Paris***:** Francis I (1494–1547), king of France from 1515 until his death. His reign was marked by rivalry against Charles V, who became the German Emperor in 1519, succeeding Maximilian I, and King of Spain. Charles V's ambitions kept the two kingdoms in a state of belligerence for almost thirty years. The reference to St Disier is to the 1544 siege of Saint-Dizier, during the Italian War of 1542–1546. Potter, ed., *Henry VIII and Francis I,* pp. 160, 166.

[454 and footnote] *Sorbiere's* **Abbe St.** *Cyran* [...] **against my designs:** Sorbière, *Sorberiana ou bons mots,* p. 74.

333

[455] **oftner:** seventeenth- and eighteenth-century spelling of often.

334

[459] *New Marly*: the name echoes that of the French royal residence of Château de Marly, palace of Marly, built north-west of Versailles during the reign of King Louis XIV.

335

[460] *salvo [...] fuerit*: without prejudice to the right of the Kings of Great Britain if they see fit to do otherwise.

[461] *Classis [...] faciat*: to make known which of the parties prevails.

[461] *Salus [...] esto*: the safety of the people shall be the highest law. Cicero, *On the Laws*, book III, part III, paragraph 8, pp. 466–67.

340

[475] *Papa-Adasi*: today Princes' Islands, an archipelago off the coast of Istanbul. In Turkish they are called Prens Adaları ('Adasi' is the singular for 'island').

341

[476] *Propontis*: today the Sea of Marmara, between the Black Sea and the Aegean Sea.

343

[483] *the Spirit of God [...] light*: Genesis 1.2.

[483] *Romeli-iskissar*: the name echoes that of the existing Rumelihisarı, literally 'Romeli fortress', a medieval castle on the banks of the Bosporus.

344

[485] *Gangara* and *Seneganda [...] desarts of Borno* and *Guoga*: territories that eighteenth-century maps located in central western Africa, north-east of today's Nigeria. See for example: *Atlas Manuale*, 'A Map of Zaara. Negroland. Guinea. & c.'.

345

[487] **Chiaus:** messenger (an imperfect adaptation of the Turkish word *chāush*), OED.

[489] *Basora:* today Basra in Iraq.

346

[491] *Misnah:* read Mishnah (from the post-biblical Hebrew word *mišnāh*), OED.

[491] *Lot's wife* [...] **salt:** Genesis 19.

348

[494] *New Marli:* see *supra*, note on p. 459 of the text.

[495] **unsual:** read unusual.

[496] *Nicomedia:* today Izmit in Turkey.

[496] **saicks:** sailing vessels common in the Levant; the singular is currently spelled saic (from the Turkish word *shāīqā*), OED.

[496] *Bassa:* see *supra*, note on p. 9 of the text.

349

[498] *Papa-Agasi* **Islands:** see *supra* note on p. 475 of the text.

350

[501] **damsins:** eighteenth-century spelling for damsons, small plums, OED.

352

[506] *Certum est quia impossibile est:* it is certain because it is impossible. Harrison, '"I Believe Because It Is Absurd"', p. 341.

353

[507] *Aliquando [...] mendacium*: sometimes there is truth in things that seem incredible, and falsehood in things that are plausible.

354

[510 and footnote] *Strabo* particularly [...] on this point: Strabo, *Geography*, I, books I–II, see for example paragraphs 10, 19, 20; Pliny's natural history includes numerous references to natural disasters (volcanic eruptions, floods, earthquakes); several paragraphs of the second book (81–86, 110) are notably dedicated to earthquakes and volcanoes. Pliny, *Natural History*, I and II. The reference to Vitale Terra Rossa in the footnote is to *Riflessioni geografiche circa le terre incognite*.

[510] *Diodorus Siculus* [...] deluge: Diodorus Siculus, *Library of History*, III, book V, paragraphs 47–48.

[511] as *Tournefort* calls them: Tournefort, *A Voyage into the Levant*, I, p. 156.

355

[512 and footnote] regular posts [...] *Spain*: Strada, *De bello Belgico*, p. 44.

[514 and footnote] *Mazapha Einok* [...] *Æthiopia*: Gassendi, *Viri illustris Nicolai Claudii Fabricii de Peiresc*, p. 269.

357

[517 and footnote] an impertinent objection [...] 17th Century: Bayle, *Dictionaire*, tome II, premiere partie H–O, *sub voce* 'Marests (Jean Des-)', pp. 550–54, see p. 554 n.

[519] Prophet *Micaiah*: 1 Kings 22.

[520] *imitatorum servum pecus*: the servile herd of the imitators. Cf. Horace, *Epistles*, I.XIX, line 19.

358

[520 and footnote] **Mr. *Camden* [...] mimick:** Camden, *Camden's Britannia*, p. 472.

[520–21 and footnote] ***Stephen Pasquier* [...] *Charles* VII:** Pasquier, *Les lettres d'Estienne Pasquier*, p. 17.

[521] ***Moses's rod:*** Exodus 4.2–5; see also Exodus 7.10–12.

359

[523] ***Mezentius:*** an Etruscan king, was portrayed in the *Aeneid* as a tyrant who inflicted cruel punishments, including binding live prisoners to corpses, 'fitting hand to hand and face to face'. Virgil, *Aeneid books VII–XII*, book VIII, pp. 94–95, lines 483–88.

[523] ***Scævola:*** in an episode recounted by Livy, Gaius Mucius Scaevola let his right hand burn in a flame in front of the Etruscan king Porsenna who was at war with Rome in 508 BCE, after having failed to assassinate him (the episode, in which the Roman showed Porsenna exceptional courage and resolution, convinced him to ask Rome for peace). Livy, *History of Rome*, I, book II, pp. 258–59.

[524–25] ***Calvin* before his Institutions, discourses:** Calvin, *The Institution of Christian Religion*; *Monsieur de Thou's History of his Own Time*.

[525] ***quæ* [...] *araneis:*** it's completely full of emptiness and cobwebs. Plautus, *The Pot of Gold*, pp. 266–67, line 84; cf. Naudé, *History of Magick*, p. 293.

[525] ***quorum* [...] *Titan:*** whose heart is fashioned by the Titan with generous skill from a superior clay. The quote is adapted from Juvenal, *The Satires of Juvenal*, satire XIV, pp. 460–61, line 35.

360

[526] ***Diogenes:*** Diogenes the Cynic (*c.* 400–325 BCE); Diogenes Laertius, *Lives of Eminent Philosophers*, II, book VI, 'Diogenes', paragraph 50, pp. 50–51.

[**526**] *Peter Aretine*: Pietro Aretino (1492–1556), who was a versatile author of plays, satires, dialogues, and devotional works. He was known for his influence on contemporary arts and politics, particularly after he went to Rome in 1517 and obtained the favour and patronage of Pope Leo X and later of Giovanni de' Medici; Campbell, ed., *The Oxford Dictionary of the Renaissance, sub voce* 'Aretino, Pietro'.

[**526-27**] **Posterity** [...] *rependit*: posterity pays the wage of honour to every man. Tacitus, *Annals*, book IV, ch. 35, pp. 62–63.

Bibliography

Manuscripts and Archival Sources

Belfast, Public Record Office of Norther Ireland (PRONI), *Madden Papers: Introduction* (November 2007)

Cambridge, Cambridge University Library, Department of Manuscripts and University Archives, The Cholmondeley (Houghton) Papers, Correspondence, Letters, MS 1507, Samuel Madden to Sir Robert Walpole, n.d. [after June 1729]

Cambridge, Cambridge University Library, Department of Manuscripts and University Archives, The Cholmondeley (Houghton) Papers, Correspondence, Letters, MS 3047, Samuel Madden to Sir Robert Walpole, 3 January 1740

Dublin, Dublin Society, Minutes of the Board

Dublin, Marsh's Library, Research, personal communication with the author, 28 June 2021

Dublin, National Library of Ireland, Genealogical Office Manuscripts Collection, Visitations of Ireland: Pedigrees and Arms of Noble Families Living in Ireland, 1568–1648

Dublin, Trinity College Dublin, Manuscripts & Archives, *Admissions Records, 1637–1725* (Entrance books), MS IE TCD MUN V 23/1

Dublin, Trinity College Dublin, Manuscripts & Archives, MS TCD MUNI P /I/ 680, 30 March 1731, Bond, Samuel Madden [...] to the Rt. Hon. Marmaduke Coghill

Dublin, Trinity College, Manuscripts & Archives, Genealogy, MSS 1212–1221 (volumes compiled by Dr John Madden relating to the principal Irish and English families in the sixteenth to eighteenth centuries)

Dublin, Royal Society of Arts archive, MS RSA/PR/GE/110/6/119, Guard Book III, p. 119, Madden to Shipley, 26 November 1757

Oxford, Bodleian Libraries, Ashmole Manuscripts, Medical and astrological papers of Dr Richard Napier (1559–1634)

Small full calf octavo volume, *c.* 1730–1798, Private collection; microform in Public Record Office of Norther Ireland, Madden Papers, D3465 /G/ 3

Primary Sources

Abrahami Patriarchae Liber Iezirah, sive Formationis mundi, Patribus quidē Abrahami tempora præcedentibus revelatus, [...] Vertebat ex Hebraeis, & commentariis illustrabat 1551. Ad Babylonis ruinam & corrupti mundi finem, Guilielmus Postellus, Restitutus (Parisiis [Paris]: Væneunt ipsi authori, sive interpreti, G. Postello. In scholis Italorum, 1552)

Addison, Joseph, *Remarks on Several Parts of Italy, &c. in the Years 1701, 1702, 1703* (London: Printed for Jacob Tonson, within Grays-Inn Gate next Grays-Inn Lane, 1705)

Agrippa, Cornelius, *Henrici Cor. Agrippæ ab Nettesheym de occulta philosophia lib. III. Item, spurius liber de ceremoniis magicis, qui quartus Agrippæ habetur. Quibus accesserunt, Heptameron Petri de Albano. Ratio compendiaria magiæ naturalis, ex Plinio desumpta. Disputatio de fascinationibus. Epistola de incantatione & adiuratione, colli suspensione. Iohannis Tritemij opuscula quædam huius argumenti* (Lugduni [Lyon, but possibly spurious]: per Beringos fratres, [1600?])

Albertini, Francesco, *Libellus de angelo custode R.P. Francisci Albertini Soc. Iesu Theologi In gratiam Sodal. Angel. latio donatus* (Coloniae [Cologne]: apud Ioannem Kinckium sub Monocerote, 1613)

——, *Trattato dell'angelo custode. Del R. P. Francesco Albertino di Catanzaro della Compagnia di Giesù* (In Roma [Rome]: nella stamparia di Bartolomeo Zannetti, 1612)

Alumni Dublinenses: A Register of the Students, Graduates, Professors and Provosts of Trinity College in the University of Dublin (1593–1860): New Edition with Supplement, ed. by George Dames Burtchaell and Thomas Ulick Sadleir (Dublin: Alex. Thom & co., 1935)

Apuleius, *Apologia*, in *Apologia, Florida, De Deo Socratis*, ed. and trans. by Christopher P. Jones, Loeb Classical Library, 534 (Cambridge, MA: Harvard University Press, 2017)

Aristophanes, *Birds*, in *Birds, Lysistrata, Women at the Thesmophoria*, ed. and trans. by Jeffrey Henderson, Loeb Classical Library, 179 (Cambridge, MA: Harvard University Press, 2000)

Aristotle, *History of Animals*, vol. I, books I–III, trans. by A. L. Peck, Loeb Classical Library, 437 (Cambridge, MA: Harvard University Press, 1965)

'Art. IV: rev. Samuel Madden', *The Irish Quarterly Review*, 3.2 (1853), pp. 693–734

Atlas Manuale Or, A New Sett of Maps Of All the Parts of the Earth, As Well Asia, Africa and America, As Europe: Wherein Geography is Rectify'd, By Reforming the Old Maps According to the Modern Observations, And the Coast of All Countries are Laid Down, Agreeable to Mr Edmund Halley's Own Map, Which is Not Done in Any Before Extant [...] (London: Printed for A. and J. Churchill in Pater-Noster-Row and T. Childe in St Paul's Church-yard, 1709)

Augustine, *De divinatione daemonum*, in Sancti Aureli Augustini, *De fide et symbolo. De fide et operibus. De agone christiano. De continentia. De bono coniugali. De sancta virginitate. De bono vidvitatis. De advlterinis coniugiis lib. II. De mendacio. Contra mendacium. De opere monachorum. De divinatione daemonum. De cura pro mortuis gerenda. De patientia*, ed. by Joseph Zycha, Corpus Scriptorum Ecclesiasticorum Latinorum 41 (Vindobonae [Vienne]: Tempsky, 1900), pp. 597–618; Eng. trans.: *Demonic divination*, in *The Works of Saint Augustine: A Translation for the 21st Century* (Hyde Park, NY: New City Press, 2005), vol. XI, trans. and notes Edmund Hill, Ray Kearney, Michael G. Campbell, and Bruce Harbert, intro. by Michael Fiedrowicz, ed. by Boniface Ramsey, pp. 204–21

Aulus Gellius, *Attic Nights*, vol. I, books I–V, trans. by J. C. Rolfe, Loeb Classical Library, 195 (Cambridge, MA: Harvard University Press, 1927)

'Aus Ireland', *Wienerisches Diarium*, 28, 6 April 1740, p. 293

Bacon, Francis, *New Atlantis* (1626), in *Three Early Modern Utopias: Utopia, New Atlantis, The Isle of Pines*, ed. with an introduction and notes by Susan Bruce (Oxford: Oxford University Press, 1999), pp. 149–86

——, 'Of Travel' (1625), in *Francis Bacon: A Critical Edition of the Major Works*, ed. by Brian Vickers (Oxford: Oxford University Press, 1996), pp. 374–75

Bailey, Nathan, *An Universal Etymological English Dictionary: Comprehending the Derivations of the Generality of Words in the English Tongue [...]* (London: Printed for E. Bell, J. Darby, A. Bettesworth [...], 1721)

Bartolocci, Giulio, *Bibliotheca magna rabbinica de scriptoribus, & scriptis Hebraicis ordine alphabetico Hebraice & Latine digestis. Cum indice rerum, nominum & locorum sacræ scripturæ locupletissimo. Auctore D. Iulio Bartoloccio* (Romæ [Rome]: Ex typographia Sacræ Congregationis de Propaganda Fide, 1675–1694), 5 vols

Basnage, [Jacques], *Histoire des Juifs depuis Jesus-Christ jusqu'a present. Contenant Leurs Antiquitez, leur Religion, leurs Rites, la dispersion des dix Tribus en Orient, & les persecutions que cette Nation a souffertes en Occident. Pour servir de Suplément & de Continuation à l'Histoire de Joseph [...]* (Rotterdam: Chez Reinier Leers, 1706)

Bassompierre, François de, *Mémoires du Maréchal de Bassompierre contenant l'histoire de sa vie* (A Cologne: Chez Jean Sambix, 1703), 4 tomes in 2 vols

Bayle, Pierre, *Dictionaire historique et critique* (A Rotterdam: Chez Reinier Leers, 1697)

Beaumont, John, *An Historical, Physiological and Theological Treatise of Spirits: Apparitions, Witchcrafts, and Other Magical Practices. Containing an Account of the Genii [...] With a Refutation of Dr. Bekker's World bewitch'd; and Other Authors [...] By John Beaumont, gent.* (London: Printed for D. Browne [...], 1705)

Bergerac, Cyrano de, *Histoire comique contenant les états et empires de la Lune* (Paris: Chez Charles de Sercy [...], 1657), Eng. *A Voyage to the Moon*, trans. by Archibald Lovell (New York: Doubleday and McClure Co., 1899)

Berkeley, George, *Life and Letters of George Berkeley Formerly Bishop of Cloyne; and an Account of His Philosophy [...]*, ed. Alexander Campbell Fraser (Oxford: At the Clarendon Press, 1871), 4 vols

Bernard, Jean Frédéric, ed., *Cérémonies et coutumes religieuses de tous les peuples du monde, représentées par des figures dessinées de la main de Bernard Picart; avec une explication historique, & quelques dissertations curieuses* (Amsterdam: Bernard, 1723–1743), 7 vols and 4 supplements

———, *The Ceremonies and Religious Customs of the Various Nations of the Known World [...]* [trans. by Daniel Bellamy the elder] (London: Du Bosc, 1733–1739), 7 vols

———, *The Religious Ceremonies and Customs of the Several Nations of the Known World: Represented in above an hundred copper-plates, designed by the famous Picart [...]* (London: Printed for Nicholas Prevost [...], 1731), trans. by John Lockman, 3 vols (incomplete)

The Bible: Authorized King James Version, ed. by Robert Carroll and Stephen Prickett (1998; Oxford: Oxford University Press, 2012)

Bodin, Jean, *De la démonomanie des sorciers. A Monseignevr M. Chrestofle de Thou Chevalier Seigneur de Coeli, premier President en la Cour de Parlement, & Conseiller du Roy en son privé Conseil* (A Paris: Chez Iacques du Puys Libraire Iuré, à la Samaritaine, 1580)

Boissard, Jean Jacques, *Tractatus posthumus Jani Jacobi Boissardi Vesuntini De divinatione & magicis praestigiis: quarum veritas ac vanitas solidè exponitur per descriptionem deorum fatidicorum qui olim responsa dederunt: eorundemque prophetarum, sacerdotum, phoebadum, sybyllarum & divinorum, qui priscis temporibus celebres oraculis exstiterunt; adjunctis simul omnium effigiebus, ab ipso autore e gemmis, marmoribus, tabulisq[ue] antiquis ad vivum delineatus: jam modo eleganter aeri incisis per Joh. Theodor. de Bry* (Oppenheimii [Oppenheim]: Typis Hieronymi Galleri, 1615)

[Bond, William], *The History of the Life and Adventures of Mr. Duncan Campbell* (London: Printed for Edmund Curll, 1720)

Bond, William, *The Supernatural Philosopher: Or, the Mysteries of Magick, in All Its Branches, Clearly Unfolded [...] All exemplified in the History of the Life and surprizing Adventures of Mr Duncan Campbell [...]* (London: Printed for E. Curll [...], 1728)

Borri, Christopher, 'An Account of Cochinchina', in *A Collection of Voyages and Travels, Some Now First Printed from Original Manuscripts. Others Translated Out of Foreign Languages and Now First Publish'd in English [...] With a General Preface, The Whole Illustrated with a Great Number of Useful Maps, and Cuts All Engraved on Copper [...]* (London: Printed for Awnsham and John Churchill, at the Black Swan in Pater-Noster-Row, 1704), 4 vols, II, pp. 787–838

Bosman, Willem, *A New and Accurate Description of the Coast of Guinea, Divided into the Gold, the Slave, and the Ivory Coasts. A New Edition with an intr. by John Ralph Willis and Notes by J. D. Fage and R. E. Bradbury* (New York: Barnes & Noble, 1967)

The Bowyer Ledgers: The Printing Accounts of William Bowyer Father and Son, with a Checklist of Bowyer Printing 1699–1777, a Commentary, Indexes, and Appendixes, ed. by Keith Maslen and John Lancaster (London: The Bibliographical Society and The Bibliographical Society of America, 1991)

Boyle, Robert, *Works of Robert Boyle*, ed. by Michael Hunter and Edward B. Davis (London: Pickering & Chatto, 1999–2000), 14 vols

A Brief Description of the Future History of Europe, from Anno 1650 to An. 1710. Treating Principally of Those Grand and Famous Mutations Yet Expected in the World, as, the Ruin of the Popish Hierarchy, the Final Annihilation of the Turkish Empire, the Conversion of the Eastern and Western Jews, and their Restauration to Their Ancient Inheritances in the Holy Land, and the Fifth Monarchy […] Out of that Famous Manuscript of Paul Grebner […] (n.p.: n.p., 1650)

Bulwer-Lytton, Edward, *The Coming Race* (Edinburgh: William Blackwood and Sons, 1871)

Burke, William, *The Armed Briton; or, the Invaders vanquished; a play, in four acts* (London: Printed by A. Seale […] For J. T. Hughes […], 1806)

Busbecq, Augier Ghislain de, *Itinera Constantinopolitanum et Amasianum ab Augerio Gislenio Busbequij, &c. D. ad Solimannum Turcarum Imperatorem C. M. oratore confecta […]* (Antverpiae [Antwerp]: Ex officina Christophori Plantini, architypographi regij, 1581)

Caleb D'Anvers [pseudonym used jointly by the contributors to *The Craftsman* Nicholas Amhurst, Bolingbroke, and William Pulteney], *Corruption in the British Government under Walpole, and Its Opponents Represented by Caleb D'Anvers: Seven Scenes*, engraving (London and Westminster: Sold by the printsellers of London and Westminster, 1731)

Calvin, John, *The Institution of Christian Religion, Wrytten in Latine by maister Ihon Calvin, and Translated into Englysh According to the Authors Last Edition […]* (London: Reinolde Wwolf & Richarde Harisson, 1561)

Camden, William, *Camden's Britannia Newly Translated into English, with Large Additions and Improvements; Publish'd by Edmund Gibson […]* (London: Printed by F. Collins, for A. Swalle […], 1695)

Campbell, Duncan, *Secret Memoirs of the Late Mr Duncan Campbel [sic], the Famous Deaf and Dumb Gentleman […]* (London: Printed for J. Millan […], 1732)

Cardano, Girolamo, *De propria vita liber. Ex bibliotheca Gab. Naudaei* (Parisiis [Paris]: Apud Iacobum Villery, in Palatio sub Porticu Delphiniali, 1643)

———, *De rerum varietate libri XVII: Adiectus est capitum, rerum & sententiarum notatu dignissimarum index* (Basileæ [Basel]: Per Henrichum Petri, 1557)

[Casanova, Giacomo, credited as translator], *Icosameron, ou Histoire d'Édouard et d'Élisabeth qui passèrent quatre-vingt-un ans chez les Mégamicres, habitans aborigènes du Protocosme dans l'intérieur de notre globe […]* (Prague: à l'imprimerie de l'école normale, 1787), 5 vols; partial Eng. trans. *Casanova's 'Icosameron'; or the Story of Edward and Elizabeth […]*, trans. by Rachel Zurer (New York: Jenna Press, 1986)

Casaubon, Isaac, Πολιβιοι [...] *Polibii Lycortae F. Megalopolitani Historiarum libri qui supersunt. Isaacus Casaubonus ex antiqui libris emendavit, Latinæ vertit, & Commentariis illustravit [...]* ([Hannover]: Typis Wechelianis apud Claudium Marnium & haeredes Iohannis Aubrij, 1609)

Casaubon, Meric, *A True and Faithful Relation of What Passed for many Yeers Between Sr. John Dee and Some Spirits: Tending (had it succeeded) to a general alteration of most states and kingdomes in the world: His private conferences with Rodolphe Emperor of Germany, Stephen K. of Poland, and divers other princes about it: [...] Out of the original copy, written with Dr. Dees own hand, kept in the library of Sir Tho. Cotton [...] with a preface confirming the reality (as to the point of spirits) of this relation, and shewing the several good uses that a sober Christian may make of all [...]* (London: Printed by D. Maxwell for T. Garthwait, 1659)

A Catalogue of the Genuine and Valuable Collection of Printed Books and Manuscripts of the Late Mark Cephas Tutet, Esq. Fellow of the Society of Antiquaries [...] ([London: for Mr Gerard], 1786)

A Catalogue of the Most Eminently Venerable Relicks of the Roman Catholick Church, Collected by the Pious Care of Their Holinesses the Popes, [...] Which Are to be Desposed of by Auction at the Church of St. Peter's at Rome, the 1st of June, 1753, by Order of the Pope [...] (London: printed for W. Owen near Temple-Bar, 1752)

A Catalogue of the Most Eminently Venerable Relicks of the Roman Catholick Church, Collected by the Pious Care of Their Holinesses the Popes, [...] Which Are to be Desposed of by Auction at the Church of St. Peter's at Rome, the 1st of June, 1753, by Order of the Pope [...], ed. by Josephus Tela (London: Printed for the proprietor, by Jas. Adlard and Sons, 23, Bartholomew Close; Published by J. Souter, 73, St Paul's Church-Yard [...], 1818)

'A Catalogue of the Most Sacred and Eminently Venerable Relicks', *The Baltimore Literary and Religious Magazine*, 3 (1837), pp. 89–92, 137–40

'A Catalogue of the Most Sacred and Eminently Venerable Relicks', *Gentleman's and London Magazine* (January 1784), pp. 573–76, 640–43

Cato and Varro, *On Agriculture*, trans. by W. D. Hooper and Harrison Boyd Ash, Loeb Classical Library, 283 (Cambridge, MA: Harvard University Press, 1934)

'Cato's Political Letters in the London Journal, Continued to the End of March 1721', *London Journal*, 25 February 1721, p. 29

Cervantes Saavedra, Miguel de, *El ingenioso hidalgo don Quixote de la Mancha* (1605–1612); Eng. trans.: *The Ingenious Hidalgo Don Quixote de La Mancha*, trans. by John Rutherford, with an introduction by Roberto González Echevarría (New York: Penguin, 2000)

[Cheynel, Francis], *Aulicus his Dream of the King's Sudden Comming to London* ([London]: n.p., 1644)

Cicero, *On the Laws*, in *On the Republic, On the Laws*, trans. by Clinton W. Keyes, Loeb Classical Library, 213 (Cambridge, MA: Harvard University Press, 1928)

Condorcet, Marie Jean Antoine Nicolas Caritat de, *Esquisse d'un tableau historique des progrès de l'esprit humain. Ouvrage posthume de Condorcet* (Paris: chez Agasse [...], L'an III de la République [1794–1795])

The Constitutions of the Society of Jesus and Their Complementary Norms: A Complete English Translation of the Official Latin Texts, general ed. John W. Padberg, based on the Eng. trans. by George E. Ganss (St Louis: Institute of Jesuit Sources, 1996)

Cornelius Nepos, *On Great Generals, On Historians*, trans. by J. C. Rolfe, Loeb Classical Library, 467 (Cambridge, MA: Harvard University Press, 1929)

Cotton, Robert, *An Abstract out of the Records of the Tower, Touching the Kings Revenue: and How They Have Supported Themselves* (London: Printed for C. Tomlinson, T. A. and A.C, [1642])

Cowley, Abraham, *A Proposition for the Advancement of Experimental Philosophy* (London: Printed by J. M. for Henry Herringman; and are to be sold at his shop at the sign of the Blew-Anchor in the lower-walk of the New-Exchange, 1661)

The Critical Review, Or, Annals of Literature, 49 (1780)

della Mirandola, Giovanni Pico, 'Disputationes adversus astrologiam', in *Opera omnia Ioannis Pici, Mirandulae Concordiæque comitis, Theologorum & Philosophorum, sine controversia, principis: Viri, sive linguarum, sive rerum, & humanarum & divinarum, cognitionem spectes, doctrina & ingenio admirando [...]* (Basileæ [Basel]: Heinrich Petri, 1557), pp. 411–731

de Thou, Jacques Auguste, *Illustris Viri Iacobi Augusti Thuani [...] Historiarvm sui temporis ab anno Domini 1543. usque ad annum 1607. libri CXXXVIII: quorum LXXX priores, multo quam antehac auctiores, reliqui vero LVIII, nunc primum prodeunt, opus in quinque tomos distinctum: accedvnt Commentariorvm de vita sva libri sex hactenvs inediti, tomus V* (Avreliani [Orléans]: apud Petrum de la Rouiere, 1620)

———, *Jac. Augusti Thuani Historiarum sui temporis* (Londini [London]: Excudi curavit Samuel Buckley, 1733), 7 vols; Eng. trans. *Monsieur de Thou's History of his Own Time: Translated from the Geneva Edition of 1620, by Bernard Wilson, A. M. Vicar of Newark upon Trent, and Prebendary of Lincoln [...]* (London: printed by E. Say, and sold by W. Meadows in Cornhil, B. Motte and T. Worral in Fleet-Street, J. Stagg in Westminster-Hall, T. Jackson in Pall-Mall, and B. Farnsworth at Newark, [1729]–1730), 2 vols

———, *Mémoires de la vie de Jacques-Auguste de Thou [...] ouvrage meslé de prose et de vers, avec la traduction de la Préface qui est au-devant de sa grande Histoire. Première édition traduite du latin en françois* (Rotterdam [Rouen]: R. Leers, 1711)

Dibdin, Thomas Frognall, *The Bibliomania; or, Book-Madness; Containing Some Account of the History, Symptoms and Cure of This Fatal Disease. In an Epistle Addressed to Richard Heber* (1809; London: Printed for the Author, 1811), 2 vols

Dickens, Charles, *A Christmas Carol. In Prose. Being a Ghost Story of Christmas* (1843; Chicago: J. G. Ferguson Pub. Co., 1965)

Diodorus Siculus, *Library of History*, vol. III, books IV.59–VIII, trans. by C. H. Oldfather, Loeb Classical Library, 340 (Cambridge, MA: Harvard University Press, 1939)

Diogenes Laertius, *Lives of Eminent Philosophers*, vol. I, books I–V, trans. by R. D. Hicks, Loeb Classical Library, 184 (Cambridge, MA: Harvard University Press, 1925)

——, *Lives of Eminent Philosophers*, vol. II, books VI–X, trans. by Hicks, Loeb Classical Library, 185 (Cambridge, MA: Harvard University Press, 1925)

Deß Europäischen Lucius Cornelius Monarchia Derer Alleigenen Oder sogenanter Selbst-Sonnen: An den vortreflichen Leo Allatius Welcher neulichst Ein Namenschlüssel beygefüget worden (Waremund [false place of publication], 1663)

Doddridge, John, *The History of the Ancient and Modern Estate of the Principality of Wales, Dutchy of Cornewall, and Earldome of Chester* (London: Printed by Tho. Harper, for Godfrey Emondson, and Thomas Alchorne, 1630)

Dryden, John, *Annus Mirabilis: Year of Wonders. 1666. An historical poem [...]* (London: Printed for Henry Herringman [...], 1667)

Eck, Johannes, 'Homilia VII in die sancti Michaelis archangeli', in *Homilarum clarissimi viri D. Iohannis Eckii, unici prope hoc secula catholicæ fidei assertoris, hæreticorumque omnium impugnatoris. Tomus III qui est peculiariter de Sanctis [...]* (Parisiis [Paris]: Apud Petrum Regnault in via Iacobea, 1542), pp. 356^r–358^v

Elich, Phillipo-Ludwigus, *M. Philippo-Ludwigi Elich, Ex Marpurgo Hessorum, Dæmonomagia; sive Libellus ερoτεματικός De Dæmonis Cacurgia, Cacomagorum et Lamiarum Energiâ. Dæmonium non habeo* (Francoforti [Frankfurt]: Prelo Richteriano, Impensâ verò Conradi Nebenii, 1607)

Eusebius, *Eusebii Pamphili Evangelicae praeparationis libri XV ad codices manuscriptos recensuit anglice nunc primum reddidit notis et indicibus instruxit [...]*, ed. and trans. by Edwin Hamilton Gifford (Oxonii [Oxford]: e Typographeo academico, 1903), 4 vols

Fabri, Carlo de, *Scudo di Christo overo di David. In tre libri distinto. Ne' quali si tratta de' nomi d'Iddio, di Christo, di Maria Vergine, de' Prencipi de gli Angeli, de' Demoni, dell'Antico popolo Hebreo e sua lingua, & altre materie, le quali nella seguente pagina sono notate. Opera non meno utile, che necessaria, cavata dalla Sacra Scrittura, e dottrina de' SS. Padri dal R.D. Carlo de Fabri da Mondolfo I.V.D. [...]* (In Bracciano: Per Andrea Fei stampator ducale, 1621)

Fabricius, Johann Albert, *Jo. Alberti Fabricii [...] Bibliographia antiquaria, sive introductio in notitiam scriptorum, qui antiquitates Hebraicas, Graecas, Romanas et Christianas scriptis illustraverunt* (Hamburgi et Lipsiae [Hamburg and Leipzig]: Impensis Christiani Liebezeit, 1713)

[Filmer, Robert], *Patriarcha, or the Natural Power of Kings [...]* (London: Printed for Ric. Chiswell in St Paul's Church-Yard, Matthew Gillyflower and William Henchman in Westminster Hall, 1680)

Florus, *Epitome of Roman History*, trans. by E. S. Forster, Loeb Classical Library, 231 (Cambridge, MA: Harvard University Press, 1929)

Fludd, Robert, *Utriusque cosmi Majoris scilicet et Minoris Metaphysica, Physica atque Technica Historia. In duo Volumina secundum Cosmi differentiam divisa [...]* (Oppenhemii [Oppenheim]: aere Johan-Theodori de Bry, typis Hieronymi Galleri, 1617–1621)

[Fontenelle, Bernard de], *Entretiens sur la pluralité des mondes* (Paris: Chez la Veuve C. Blageart [...], 1686), Eng. trans. *Conversations with a Lady, on the Plurality of Worlds [...]*, trans. by John Glanvill (London: Printed by J. Darby, for M. Wellington, 1719)

The Friendly Daemon, or the Generous Apparition Being a True Narrative of a Miraculous Cure, Newly Perform'd Upon That Famous Deaf and Dumb Gentleman, Dr. Duncan Campbel, by a Familiar Spirit [...] (London: Printed, and sold by J. Roberts [...], 1726)

Froissart, Jean, *Le tiers volume de l'histoire et chronique de messire Iehan Froissart. Reveu et corrigé sus divers exemplaires, et suivant les bons auteurs* (A Lyon: par Ian de Tournes, Imprimeur du Roy, 1574)

Fryer, Johannes, *A New Account of East-India and Persia, in Eight Letters Being Nine Years Travels Begun 1672 and Finished 1681: Containing Observations Made of the Moral, Natural and Artificial Estate of Those Countries Namely, of Their Government, Religion, Laws, Customs [...]* (London: Printed by R. R. for Ri. Chiswell at the Rose and Crown in St Paul's Church-Yard, 1698)

Fuller, Thomas, *Gnomologia: Adagies and Proverbs; Wise Sentences and Witty Sayings, Ancient and Modern, Foreign and British Collected by Thomas Fuller, M.D.* (London: Printed for B. Baker [...], 1732)

———, *The Historie of the Holy Warre* (3rd ed.; Cambridge: Printed by Roger Daniel, and are to be sold by John Williams, 1647)

Gaffarel, James, *Unheard-of Curiosities: Concerning the Talismanical Sculpture of the Persians; The Horoscope of the Patriarkes; And the Reading of the Stars. Written in French, by James Gaffarel and Englished by Edmund Chilmead, Mr of Arts, and Chaplaine of Christ-Church Oxon* (London: Printed by G. D. for Humphrey Moseley, and are to be sold at his Shop, at the Princes Armes in St Pauls Church-Yard, 1650)

Garasse, François, *La doctrine curieuse des beaux esprits de ce temps ou prétendus tels contenant plusieurs maximes pernicieuses à la religion, à l'Estat, & aux bonnes moeurs, combattue et renversée par le P. François Garassus de la Compagnie de Iesus* (Paris: Chez Sebastien Chappillet, 1624)

Gassendi, Pierre, *Viri illustris Nicolai Claudii Fabricii de Peiresc, senatoris Aquisextiensis vita, per Petrum Gassendum [...]* (Parisiis [Paris]: sumptibus Sebastiani Cramoisy [...], 1641)

Gemelli Careri, Giovanni Francesco, *A Voyage Round the World*, in *A Collection of Voyages and Travels, Some Now First Printed from Original Manuscripts Others Now First Publish'd in English [...]* (London: Printed by Assignment from Messrs. Churchill [...], 1704–1732), 6 vols, IV, pp. 1–572

Gerard, John, *The Herball or Generall Historie of Plantes. Gathered by Iohn Gerarde of London Master in Chirurgerie very much enlarged and amended by Thomas Iohnson citizen and apothecarye of London [...]* (London: Printed by Adam Islip Joice Norton and Richard Whitakers, 1633)

Gillray, James, *French Invasion -or- Buonaparte landing in Great-Britain*, etching (London: H[annah] Humphrey [...], 1803)

———, *Promis'd Horrors of the French Invasion, or Forcible reasons for negotiating a regicide peace*, etching (London: H[annah] Humphrey, 1796)

Godwin, Francis, *The Man in the Moone* (1638; Amsterdam: Theatrum Orbis Terrarum and New York: Da Capo Press, 1972)

Gononus, Benedictus, *Chronicon SS. Deiparæ Virginis Mariæ: In quo omnia vitæ eius acta & celeberrima miracula per totum orbem patrata, ad haec usque tempora, prolixiùs describuntur* (Lvgdvni [Leiden]: apud Ioannis Caffin, & Francisci Plaignard [...], 1637)

Grainville, Jean-Baptiste-François-Xavier Cousin de, *Le dernier homme: ouvrage posthume* (Paris: Deterville, 1805), 2 vols

[Hartlib, Samuel], *A Description of the Famous Kingdome of Macaria Shewing Its Excellent Government [...]* (London: Printed for Francis Constable, 1641)

Haywood, Eliza Fowler, *A Spy on the Conjurer: Or, a Collection of Surprising and Diverting Stories, with Merry and Ingenious Letters by Way of Memoirs of the Famous Mr. Duncan Campbell [...]* (London: Printed for W. Ellis [...], 1725)

Herodotos, *Histories*, vol. I, books I–II, trans. and ed. A. D. Godley, Loeb Classical Library, 117 (Cambridge, MA: Harvard University Press, 1975)

———, *Histories*, vol. II, books III–IV, trans. and ed. by A. D. Godley, Loeb Classical Library, 118 (Cambridge, MA: Harvard University Press, 1975)

Hervey, John, *Memoirs of the Reign of George the Second: From His Accession to the Death of Queen Caroline* (London: John Murray, 1848), 2 vols

———, *Some Materials Towards Memoirs of the Reign of King George II: Printed from a Copy of the Original Manuscript in the Royal Archives at Windsor Castle; and from the Original Manuscript at Ickworth: Edited by Romney Sedgwick* (New York: AMS Press, 1970), 3 vols

Hesiod, *Theogony*, in *Theogony, Works and Days, Testimonia*, ed. and trans. by Glenn W. Most, Loeb Classical Library, 57 (Cambridge, MA: Harvard University Press, 2018)

———, *Works and Days*, in *Theogony, Works and Days, Testimonia*, ed. and trans. by Glenn W. Most, Loeb Classical Library, 57 (Cambridge, MA: Harvard University Press, 2018)

Hogarth, William, *The Adventure of the Bear and the Fiddle* (London: Henry Overton and J. Hoole, *c.* 1725)

————, *Cunicularii or The wise men of Godliman in Consultation*, etching (London, 1726)

————, 'Hudibras Visiting Sidrophel', *Seventeen Small Illustrations for Samuel Butler's Hudibras*, no. 11, etching and engraving (1721–1726)

[Holberg, Ludvig], *Nicolai Klimii iter svbterranevm novam telluris theoriam ac historiam quintae monarchiae adhuc nobis incognitae exhibens e bibliotheca B. Abelini* (Hafniae & Lipsiae [Copenhagen and Leipzig]: Svmptibvs Iacobi Prevssii, 1741), Eng. trans. *A Journey to the World Under-Ground* (London: Printed for T. Astley [...], 1742)

Homer, *Odyssey*, vol. i, books i–xii, trans. by A. T. Murray, rev. by George E. Dimock, Loeb Classical Library, 104 (Cambridge, MA: Harvard University Press, 1919)

Horace, *Epistles*, in *Satires, Epistles, The Art of Poetry*, trans. by H. Rushton Fairclough, Loeb Classical Library, 194 (Cambridge, MA: Harvard University Press, 1942)

————, *Satires*, in *Satires, Epistles, The Art of Poetry*, trans. by H. Rushton Fairclough, Loeb Classical Library, 194 (Cambridge, MA: Harvard University Press, 1942)

Johnson, Samuel, 'Addison', in *The Works of Samuel Johnson, LL.D.* (Oxford: Talboys and Wheeler, and W. Pickering, 1825), 9 vols, vol. vii, *The Lives of the English Poets*, pp. 418–73

————, 'Swift', in *The Works of Samuel Johnson, LL.D.* (Oxford: Talboys and Wheeler, and W. Pickering, 1825), 9 vols, vol. viii, *The Lives of the English Poets*, pp. 192–228

[Jones, David], *A Compleath History of the Turks, from Their Origin in the Year 755, to the Year 1718. Containing The Rise, Growth, and Decay of that Empire, in its Respective Periods, under Their Several Kings and Emperors [...]* (London: printed by J. Darby [...], 1719), 4 vols

J[ones], S[tephen], *New Biographical Dictionary; or, Pocket Compendium [...]* (London: G. G. & J. Robinson, 1794), *sub voce* 'Madden (D. R. Samuel)'

Juvenal, *The Satires of Juvenal*, in *Juvenal and Persius*, ed. and trans. by Susanna Morton Braund, Loeb Classical Library, 91 (Cambridge, MA: Harvard University Press, 2004)

J. W. C., 'The Dramatic Writers of Ireland No. II [...]', *The Dublin University Magazine: A Literary and Political Journal*, 45 (1855), pp. 166–82

Kautsky, Karl, *Thomas More and His Utopia*, trans. by H. J. Stenning (1888; New York: International Publisher Co., 1927)

Kircher, Athanasius, *R.P. Athanasii Kircheri e Societate Jesu Iter extaticum cœleste, quo mundi opificium, id est, cœlestis expansi, siderumq[ue] tam errantium, quàm fixorum natura, vires, proprietates, singulorumq[ue] [...]* (Herbipoli [Würzburg]: sumptibus Joh. Andr. & Wolffg. Jun. Endterorum hæredibus, 1660)

————, *Athanasii Kircheri e soc. Iesu Itinerarium exstaticum quo mundi opificium. Id est cœlestis expansi, siderumque tam errantium, quàm fixorum natura, vires, proprietates, singulorumque composition & structura, ab infimo telluris globo, usque ad ultima mundi confinia, per ficti raptus integumentum explorata, nova hypothesi exponitur ad veritatem* [...] (Romæ [Rome]: typis Vitalis Mascardi, 1656)

Knolles, Richard, *The Turkish History from the Original of That Nation, to the Growth of the Ottoman Empire with the Lives and Conquests of Their Princes and Emperours* [...] (London: Printed for Robert Clavell [...], 1700)

Lactantius, *Divine institutes*, trans. and with an introduction and notes by Anthony Bowen and Peter Garnsey (Liverpool: Liverpool University Press, 2003)

————, *L. Coelii Lactantii Firmiani Opera quæ quidem extant omnia, videlicet Institutionum divinarum lib. VII, De ira dei lib. I. De opificio dei lib. I. Epitome librorum D. Institutionum. Phoenix. Carmen de dominica resurrectione. Accesserunt Xysti Betuleii* [...] *commentaria* [...] (Basileæ [Basel]: per Henricum Petri, 1563)

La Mothe Le Vayer, François de, 'Discours de l'histoire' (1638), in *Œuvres de François de La Mothe La Vayer. Conseiller d'État ordinaire. Troisième édition reveve, corrigée et augmentée* (A Paris: Chez Augustin Courbé [...], 1662), tome I, pp. 231–84

A Larum for London (1602; [Amersham]: The Tudor Facsimile Texts, 1912)

Launoy, Jean de, *Joannis Launoii, Constantiensis, Parisiensis Theologi, Socii Navarraei, Opera Omnia, ad selectum ordinem revocata. Ineditis opusculis aliquot, notis nonnullis dogmaticis, historicis et criticis* [...] (Coloniae Allobrogum [Geneva]: sumptibus Fabri & Barillot, Sociorum et Marci-Michælis Bousquet & Sociorum, 1732), 5 vols

A Letter to the Right Honourable Earl Temple: Upon the Probable Motives and Consequences of His Lordship's Conduct with Regard to Mr. Wilkes (London: Printed for W. Nicoll, 1763)

'Librorum manuscriptorum viri praeclari Joannis Maddeni Collegi Medicorum Dubliniensium Paresidis, Catalogus', in *Catalogi librorum manuscriptorum Angliae et Hiberniae in unum collecti* (Oxoniae [Oxford]: E Theatro Sheldoniano, 1697), II.2, pp. 57–60

Lilly, William, *The Last of the Astrologers: Mr William Lilly's History of his Life and Times from the Year 1602 to 1681*, reprinted from the second edition of 1715, with notes and introduction by Katharine M. Briggs (London: Folklore Society, 1974)

Livy, *History of Rome*, vol. I, books I–II, trans. by B. O. Foster, Loeb Classical Library, 114 (Cambridge, MA: Harvard University Press, 1919)

————, *History of Rome*, vol. II, books III–IV, trans. by B. O. Foster, Loeb Classical Library, 133 (Cambridge, MA: Harvard University Press, 1922)

————, *History of Rome*, vol. III, books V–VII, trans. by B. O. Foster, Loeb Classical Library, 172 (Cambridge, MA: Harvard University Press, 1924)

Lucan, *The Civil War (Pharsalia)*, trans. by J. D. Duff, Loeb Classical Library, 220 (Cambridge, MA: Harvard University Press, 1928)

Lucii Cornelii Europæi Monarchia solipsorum. Ad virum clarissimum Leonem Allatium (Venetiis [Venice]: n.p., 1645)

Mabillon, Jean, *Lettre d'un bénédictin à Monseigneur l'évesque de Blois, touchant le discernement des anciennes reliques, au sujet d'une dissertation de Mr Thiers, contre la Sainte Larme de Vendôme* (Paris: Pierre et Imbert de Bats, 1700)

Madden, Samuel, *Boulter's Monument: A Panegyrical Poem, Sacred to the Memory of that Great and Excellent Prelate and Patriot, the Most Reverend Dr. Hugh Boulter [...]* (London: Printed by S. Richardson, 1745)

[————], *A Letter from the Reverend Mr. M--d--n [Samuel Madden] to the Hon. Lady M---n---x [Lady Elizabeth Molyneux], on Occasion of the Death of the Rt. Hon. S-----l. M---n---x [Samuel Molyneux], Esq; Who Was Attended by M. St. A--d--e, a Fr--ch s--g--n [Monsieur Nathaniel St André, a French Surgeon]* (Dublin: Printed by G. Faulkner [...], 1730)

[————], *A Letter to the Dublin-Society, on the Improving Their Fund; and the Manufactures, Tillage, & c. in Ireland* (Dublin: Printed by R. Reilly for G. Ewing [...], 1739)

[————], *Memoirs of the Twentieth Century: Being Original Letters of State, under George the Sixth: Relating to the Most Important Events in Great Britain and Europe, as to Church and State, Arts and Sciences, Trade, Taxes, and Treaties, Peace, and War: and Characters of the Greatest Persons of those Times; From the Middle of the Eighteenth, to the End of the Twentieth Century, and the World. Received and Revealed in the Year 1728; and now Published, for the Instruction of All Eminent Statesmen, Churchmen, Patriots, Politicians, Projectors, Papists, and Protestants* (London: Printed for Messieurs Osborn and Longman, [...] 1733)

————, *Memoirs of the Twentieth Century Being Original Letters of State, under George the Sixth*, with an 'Introduction' by Malcolm J. Bosse (New York: Garland, 1972)

————, *Memoirs of the Twentieth Century*, includes Liam Gillick, 'Prevision: Should the Future Help the Past?' (1998) (n.p.: Halmos, 2010), electronic ed.

————, *A Proposal for the General Encouragement of Learning in Dublin-College [...]* (Dublin: Printed by G. Grierson [...], 1731)

————, *Reflections and Resolutions Proper for the Gentlemen of Ireland as to their Conduct for the Service of their Country [...]* (Dublin: Printed by R. Reilly, for George Ewing, Dame St., 1738)

————, *Reflections and Resolutions Proper for the Gentlemen of Ireland as to their Conduct for the Service of their Country [...]*, reprint (Dublin: For George Ewig, 1816)

————, *Themistocles, the Lover of His Country: A Tragedy. As It Is Acted at the Theatre-Royal, in Lincoln's-Inn-Fields* (London: Printed for R. King [...], 1729; and Dublin: Printed by S. Powell for George Risk [...], 1729)

Maffei, Johannes Petrus, *De vita et moribus B.P. Ignatii Loiolae qui Societatem Iesu fundavit, libri III* (Lugduni [Lyon]: Iuxta exemplar impressum Antverpiae, apud Ioannem champion, in platea Cambii, 1638)

—, *Ignatii Loiolae vita, postrema recognita* (Antverpiae [Antwerp]: ex officina Martini Nutij, ad insigne duarum Ciconiarum, 1605)

Mainardi, Arlotto de', *Facezie, Motti, Buffonerie e Burle del Piovano Arlotto [...] nuovamente ristampate* (in Firenze [Florence]: appresso Giunti, 1568)

Mallet, Edme-François, 'Bumicili', in *Encyclopédie, ou dictionnaire raisonné des sciences, des arts et des métiers, etc.*, ed. by Denis Diderot and Jean le Rond d'Alembert, tome II, p. 464; University of Chicago, ARTFL Encyclopédie Project (Autumn 2017 edition, based on the first printing of the Paris edition), ed. by Robert Morrissey and Glenn Roe, <http://encyclopedie.uchicago.edu>, [accessed 1 January 2023], *ad vocem*

[Mandeville, Bernard], *The Fable of the Bees: Or, Private Vices, Publick Benefits. The second edition [...]* (1714; London: Printed for Edmund Parker [...], 1723), 2 vols

Manilius, *Astronomica*, ed. and trans. by G. P. Goold, Loeb Classical Library, 469 (Cambridge, MA: Harvard University Press, 1977)

Manso, Giovanni Battista, *La vita di Torquato Tasso* ([In Roma [Rome]: Appresso Francesco Cavalli, 1634])

Marcus Aurelius Antoninus, Μαρκοι'Αντονινοι τον'αγτοκροπος *[...] Marci Antonini imperatoris, De rebus suis, sive de eis quae ad se pertinere censebat, libri 12. Locis haud paucis repurgati, suppleti, restituti: versione insuper Latina nova; [...] Studio operâque Thomae Gatakeri, Londinatis [...]* (Londini [London]: Impensis Edv. Millington, in Vico vulgò dicto Little Britain. Veneunt apud bibliopolas Londin. & utriusque Academiæ, 1697)

Maréchal, Sylvain, *Le jugement dernier des rois: prophétie en un acte, en prose* (Paris: de l'imp. De C.-F. Patris, L'an II de la République [1793–1794])

Martin, Martin, *Description of the Western Isles of Scotland: Containing a full account of their Situation, Extent, Soils, Product, Harbours, Bays, Tides, Anchor-Places, and Fisheries. The Antient and Modern Government, Religion and Customs of the Inhabitants; particularly of their Druids, Heathen Temples, Monasteries, Churches, Chappels, Antiquities, Monuments, Forts, Caves, and other Curiosities of Art and Nature: Of their Admirable and Expeditious Way of Curing most Diseases by Simples of their own Product. A Particular Account of the Second Sight, or Faculty of foreseeing things to come, by way of vision, so common among them. A Brief Hint of Methods to Improve Trade in that Country, both by Sea and Land. With a new Map of the Whole [...] The Second Edition, very much Corrected* (1703; London: Printed for A. Bell, at the Cross-Keys and Bible, in Cornhill; T. Varnam and J. Osborn in Lombard-street; W. Taylor. at the Ship, and J. Baker and T. Warner at the Black Boy in Paternoster-Row, 1716)

Maximus of Tyre, *The Philosophical Orations*, trans. by and with introduction and notes by M. B. Trapp (Oxford: Clarendon Press, 1997)

Menage, Gilles, *Menagiana, ou les bons mots et remarques critiques, historiques, morales et d'erudition* (A Paris: Chez la Veuve Delaulne, rue Daint-Jacques, vis-à-vis la rue des Noyers, à l'Empereur, 1729), 4 vols

[Mercier, Louis-Sébastien], *L'an deux mille quatre cent quarante. Rêve s'il en fût jamais* (Londres [London]: n.p., 1771); Eng. trans. *Memoirs of the Year Two Thousand Five Hundred*, trans. by William Hooper (Dublin: Printed for W. Wilson [...], 1772), 2 vols

———, *L'an deux mille quatre cent quarante. Rêve s'il en fût jamais; suivi de L'homme de fer, songe* (A Paris: chez Lepetit jeune et Gerard, [...], An X [1801–1802]), 3 vols

Mittié, Jean-Corisandre, *Descente en Angleterre, prophétie en deux actes et en prose* (Paris: [...] Chez Girardin [...], An VI — 1798)

Molyneux, William, *The Case of Ireland's Being Bound by Acts of Parliament in England* (Dublin: Printed by Joseph Ray [...], 1698)

La monarchia de Solessi tradotta dall'originale latino di Melchiorre Inchofer della Compagnia di Gesù con alcune note e diverse operette importanti sopra lo stesso argomento (Lugano [false place of publication]: n.p., 1760)

La Monarchia de' Solipsi tradotta dall'originale latino di Melchiorre Inchofer della Compagnia di Gesú colle note tradotte dal francese, e varj frammenti, ed opuscoli inediti sull'istesso soggetto (In Gallipoli [possibly false place of publication]: n.p., 1710)

More, Thomas, *Libellus vere aureus nec minus salutaris quam festivus de optimo reip. statu deque nova insula Utopia authore clarissimo viro Thoma Moro inclytae civitatis Londinensis cive & vicecomite cura M. Petri Aegidii Antverpiesis & arte Theodorici Martini Alustensis, Typographi almae Lovaniensium Academiae nunc primum accuratissime editus* (Lovanii [Leuven]: Theodorici Martini [...], 1516)

Morelly, Étienne-Gabriel, *Code de la Nature*, critical ed. by Stéphanie Roza (1755; Paris: La ville brûle, 2011)

Moryson, Fynes, *An Itinerary Written by Fynes Moryson Gent. First in the Latine tongue, and then translated by him into English: containing his ten yeeres travell through the twelue dominions of Germany, Bohmerland, Sweitzerland, Netherland, Denmarke, Poland, Italy, Turky, France, England, Scotland, and Ireland [...]* (London: Printed by J. Beale, 1617)

Mr. Campbell's Packet for the Entertainment of Gentlemen and Ladies (London: Printed for T. Bickerton, 1720)

Naudé, Gabriel, *The History of Magick by Way of Apology, for all the wise men who have unjustly been reputed magicians, from the Creation, to the present age. Written in French by G. Naudaeus [...] Englished by J. Davies* ([London]: Printed for John Streater, 1657)

———, and Guy Patin, *Naudæna et Patiniana ou singularitez remarquables, prises des conversations de Mess. Naudé & Patin. Seconde Edition revue, corrigée & augmenté d'Additions au Naudæana qui ne sont point dans l'Edition de Paris* (Amsterdam: chez François van der Plaats, 1703)

Nelson, Robert, *An Address to Persons of Quality and Estate: By Robert Nelson, Esq;
      To which is added, a Representation of the Several Ways and Methods of Doing
      Good [...]* (Dublin: Printed for Peter Wilson, 1752)

'News', *St. James's Chronicle or the British Evening Post*, 11 January 1766–1714
      January 1766, n.p. (but p. 3)

'News', *Owen's Weekly Chronicle*, 11 January 1766–1718 January 1766, n.p. (but
      p. 4)

Nichols, John, *Biographical and Literary Anecdotes of William Bowyer [...]*
      (London: printed by and for the author, 1782)

——, *Literary Anecdotes of the Eighteenth Century [...]* (London: Printed for the
      Author [...], 1812), 6 vols

Nider, Johannes, *Formicarium [...] In Quinque Libros Divisum; Quibus Christianus
      quilibet, tu[m] admirabili Formicarum exemplo, tum historijs pro re accommodatis,
      et ad parandam sibi sapientiam [...]* (Duaci [Douai]: Beller, 1602)

'Nouvelles Littéraires', *Journal des Sçavans*, December 1758, pp. 867–68

*Officium angeli custodis: Pauli V. Pont. Max. authoritate publicatum: In gratiam verò
      Congregationum B. Virginis Mariae nunc premium latinè simul & gracè eidtum
      opera Georgii Mayr è Societ. Iesu.* (Antverpiae [Antwerp]: Apud Hereds Martini
      Nutij, & Ioannem Meursium, 1617)

'On Monday the 9th of April will be Published, Price Six Shillings, Bound,
      Memoirs of the Twentieth Century', *Fog's Weekly Journal*, 31 March 1733, n.p.
      (but p. 2)

'On Monday the 9th of April will be Published, Price Six Shillings, Bound,
      Memoirs of the Twentieth Century', *Fog's Weekly Journal*, 7 April 1733, n.p.
      (but p. 2)

'On Monday the 9th of April will be Published, Price Six Shillings, Bound,
      Memoirs of the Twentieth Century', *London Journal*, 24 March 1732–1733,
      n.p. (but p. 3)

'On Monday the 9th of April will be Publish'd, Price Six Shillings, Bound, Memoirs
      of the Twentieth Century', notices in *London Evening Post*, 24 March 1733–27
      March 1733, n.p. (but p. 4)

'On Monday the 9th of April will be Publish'd, Price Six Shillings, Bound, Memoirs
      of the Twentieth Century', notices in *London Evening Post*, 27 March 1733–29
      March 1733, n.p. (but p. 4)

'On Monday the 9th of April will be Publish'd, Price Six Shillings, Bound, Memoirs
      of the Twentieth Century', notices in *London Evening Post*, 31 March 1733–
      3 April 1733, n.p. (but p. 4)

Ovid, *Metamorphoses*, vol. I, books I–VIII, trans. by Frank Justus Miller, rev. G. P.
      Goold, Loeb Classical Library, 42 (Cambridge, MA: Harvard University Press,
      1916)

[Paltock, Robert], *The Life and Adventures of Peter Wilkins [...]* (London: Printed
      for J. Robinson [...], 1751), 2 vols

Partridge, John, *Prodromus, or, An astrological essay upon those configurations of the celestial bodies whose effects will appear in 1680 and 1681 in some kingdoms in Europe: Which predictions are drawn for the opposition of Saturn and Mars in December, 1679, and the conjunction of Saturn and Mars in August, 1680, and these things considered, and compared with the nativity of the late damnable plot* (London: Printed for W. Bromwich [...], 1679)

Pasch, Georg, *Georgii Paschii Gedanensis [...] De novis inventis, quorum accuratiori cultui facem prætulit antiquitas, tractatus, Secundum ductum Disciplinarum, Facultatum atque Artium in gratiam [...]* (Lipsiæ [Leipzig]: Sumptibus Hæredum Joh. Grossi, 1700)

Pasquier, Etienne, *Les lettres d'Estienne Pasquier conseiller et advocat general du Roy en la Chambre des comptes à Paris* (A Lyon: Pour Paul Frellon, 1607)

Pasquillus ecstaticus [Celio Secondo Curione], *The Visions of Pasquin, or, A character of the Roman court, religion and practices together with an account of the arts of the Pope's nephews to get money, the tricks of the priests to fill the churches coffers by masses for the dead, the policy of the Jesuites to cully princes, and cheat Christendom, as also an exact description of purgatory and hell, in a dialogue between Pasquin and Marsorio, translated out of Italian* (London: Printed, and are to be sold by Richard Baldwin, 1689)

Patin, Charles, *Travels thro' Germany, Bohemia, Swisserland, Holland; and other parts of Europe [...]* (London: Printed for A. Swall and T. Child at the Unicorn in St Pauls Church-yard, 1697)

Patrick, John, *Reflexions upon the Devotions of the Roman Church, with the Prayers, Hymns & Lessons Themselves, Taken Out of Their Authentic Books: In Three Parts, This First Part, Containing Their Devotions to Saints and Angels, Also Two Digressions Concerning the Reliques and Miracles in Mr. Cressy's Late Church-History* (London: Printed for R. Royston [...], 1674)

Pausanias, *Description of Greece*, vol. IV, books VIII.22–X (Arcadia, Boeotia, Phocis and Ozolian Locri), trans. by W. H. S. Jones, Loeb Classical Library, 297 (Cambridge, MA: Harvard University Press, 1935)

P. B., *The Priviledges of the House of Commons in Parliament Assembled* (London: Printed for J. R., 1642)

Percy, William, *William Percy's Mahomet and His Heaven: A Critical Edition*, ed. by Matthew Dimmock (Aldershot: Ashgate, 2006)

Petrarca, Francesco, 'De audacia et pompa medicorum', in *Francisci Petrarchae [...] Opera quae extant omnia, in quibus praeter Theologica, naturalis, moralisq[ue] philosophiae praecepta [...]* (Basileae [Basel]: per Sebastianum Henricpetri, 1581), pp. 796–801

Plato, *Theages*, in *Charmides, Alcibiades I and II, Hipparchus, The Lovers, Theages, Minos, Epinomis*, trans. by W. R. M. Lamb, Loeb Classical Library, 201 (Cambridge, MA: Harvard University Press, 1927)

Plautus, *The Pot of Gold*, in *Amphitryon, The Comedy of Asses, The Pot of Gold, The Two Bacchises, The Captives*, ed. and trans. by Wolfgang de Melo, Loeb Classical Library, 60 (Cambridge, MA: Harvard University Press, 2011)

416 BIBLIOGRAPHY

Pliny, *Natural History*, vol. I, books I–II trans. by H. Rackham, Loeb Classical Library, 330 (Cambridge, MA: Harvard University Press, 1938)

——, *Natural History*, vol. II, books III–VII, trans. by H. Rackham, Loeb Classical Library, 352 (Cambridge, MA: Harvard University Press, 1942)

——, *Natural History*, vol. III, books VIII–XI, trans. by H. Rackham, Loeb Classical Library, 353 (Cambridge, MA: Harvard University Press, 1940)

——, *Natural History*, vol. V, books XVII–XIX, trans. by H. Rackham, Loeb Classical Library, 371 (Cambridge, MA: Harvard University Press, 1940)

Pliny the Younger, *Letters*, vol. I, books I–VII, trans. by Betty Radice, Loeb Classical Library, 55 (Cambridge, MA: Harvard University Press, 1969)

Plumard de Dangeul, Louis Joseph, *Remarks on the Advantages and Disadvantages of France and of Great-Britain with Respect to Commerce [...] Translated from the French Original* (London: Printed for T. Osborne, 1754)

Plutarch, *Lives*, vol. VII, *Demosthenes and Cicero, Alexander and Caesar*, trans. by Bernadotte Perrin, Loeb Classical Library, 99 (Cambridge, MA: Harvard University Press, 1919

——, *Moralia*, vol. VI, trans. by W. C. Helmbold, Loeb Classical Library, 337 (Cambridge, MA: Harvard University Press, 1939)

Poe, Edgar Allan, 'A Tale of the Ragged Mountains' (1844), in Edgar Allan Poe, *The Complete Works of Edgar Allan Poe* (New York: G. P. Putnam's sons, 1902), pp. 245–61

Poems, By a Young Nobleman, of Distinguished Abilities, lately deceased; particularly, the state of England, and the once flourishing City of London [...] the third edition with corrections and additions (London: Printed for G. Kearsly [...], 1780)

Poetae Comici Graeci, vol. VI.2 — *Menander. Testimonia et Fragmenta apud scriptores servata*, ed. by Rudolf Kassel and Colin Austin (Berlin: De Guyter, 1998)

Postel, Guillaume, *Linguarum duodecim characteribus differentium alphabetum, introductio, ac legendi modus longè facilimus. Linguarum nomina sequens proximè pagella offeret. Guilielmi Postelli Barentonii diligentia [...]* (Parisiis [Paris]: apud Dionysium Lescuier, sub porcelli signo, vico Hilario [...], [1538])

——, *Les très merveilleuses victoires des femmes du Nouveau Monde, Et comment elles doibvent à tout le monde par raison commander, & même à ceulx qui auront la Monarchie du Monde vieil [...]* (A Paris: Chez Jehan Ruelle [...], 1553)

Powell, Thomas, *Direction for Search of Records Remaining in the Chancerie Tower, Exchequer, with the Limnes Thereof* (London: Printed by B. A. for Paul Man, and are to be sold at his shop in Chancerie Lane, at the signe of the Bowle; or in Distaffe Lane, at the signe of the Dolphin, 1622)

The Priviledges and Practice of Parliaments in England: Collected out of the Common Lawes of this Land ([London]: [printed by B. Alsop and T. Fawcett], 1628)

The Proceedings of the Hibernian Society [...] (Dublin: Printed for G. Faulkner [...], 1758)

Ptolemy, *Ptolemy's Quadripartite; or, Four Books concerning the Influences of the Stars. Faithfully render'd into English from Leo Allaccius*, trans. by John Whalley (London: Sibly & Sibly, 1701)

———, *Tetrabiblos*, trans. by Frank E. Robbins, Loeb Classical Library, 435 (Cambridge, MA: Harvard University Press, 1940)

Purchas, Samuel, *Hakluytus Posthumus or, Purchas his Pilgrimes: Contayning a History of the World in Sea Voyages and Lande Travells by Englishmen and Others* (1625; Cambridge: Cambridge University Press, 2014), 20 vols

[Pure, Michel de], *Épigone, histoire du siècle future* (Paris: Chez Pierre Lamy […], 1659)

———, *Épigone, histoire du siècle futur*, modern ed. by Lise Leibacher-Ouvrard and Daniel Maher (Québec: Presses de l'Université Laval, 2005)

Quevedo, Francisco de, *The Comical Works of Don Francisco de Quevedo, Author of The Visions […] Translated from the Spanish [by John Stevens]* (London: Printed, and are to be sold by John Morphew […], 1707)

The Reign of George VI. 1900–1925: A Forecast Written in the Year 1763 (London: Printed for W. Nicoll at the Paper-Mill, in St Paul's Church-Yard, 1763)

Relation d'un voyage du pole arctique au pole antarctique par le centre du monde. Avec la description de ce perilleux passage, & des choses merveilleuses & étonnantes qu'on a découvertes sous le pole antarctique. Avec figures (Amsterdam: Chez N. Etienne Lucas […], 1721)

Rétif de La Bretonne, Nicolas-Edme, *L'an 2000* (1789; Strasbourg: J. H. Ed. Heitz — Heitz et Mündel, 1905)

Review of *A Catalogue of the Most Eminently Venerable Relicks of the Roman Catholick Church*, *The Monthly Review or Literary Journal*, 6 (1752), pp. 233–34

Rivet, André, *Apologia pro sanctissima Virgine Maria matre domini. Adversus veteres et novos Antidicomarianitas, Collyridianos & Christianocategoros […]* (Lugduni Batavorum [Leiden], 1639)

———, *Operum Theologicorum quæ Latine edidit tomus tertius. Continens opera polemica; quorum seriem sequens pagina indicabit […]* (Roterodami [Rotterdam]: ex Officina Typographica Arnoldi Leers, 1660)

The Romans of Partenay, or of Lusignan: Otherwise Known as The Tale of Melusine, ed. by Walker W. Skeat, Early English Text Society, 22 (London: Oxford University Press, 1866)

Scaliger, Julius Caesar, *Exotericarum Exercitationum lib. XV. De Subtilitate, ad Hieronymum Cardanum. In fine sunt duo Indices prior breviusculus, continens sententias nobiliores alter opulentissimus, penè omnia complectens* (Francofurti [Frankfurt am Main]: Impensis Claudii Marnii hæredum, Ioannis & Andreæ Marnii & Consortum)

————, *Iulii Cæsaris Scaligeri Exotericarum Exercitationum lib. XV. De Subtilitate, ad Hieronymum Cardanum. In fine sunt duo Indices prior breviusculus, continens sententias nobiliores alter opulentissimus, penè omnia complectens* (Francofurti [Frankfurt am Main]: Impensis Claudii Marnii hæredum, Ioannis & Andreæ Marnii & Consortum, 1576)

Scheffer, Johannes, *The History of Lapland Wherein Are shewed the Original, Manners, Habits, Marriages, Conjurations, & c. of That People. Written by John Scheffer, Professor of Law and Rhetoric at Upsal in Sweden* (At the Theater in Oxford: to be sold by George West and Amos Curtein, 1674)

Schott, Gaspar, *P. Gasparis Schotti […] Physica curiosa, sive Mirabilia Naturæ et Artis libris XII. Comprehensa, Quibus pleraq[ue], quæ de Angelis, Dæmonibus, Hominibus, Spectris, Energumenis, Monstris, Portentis, Animalibus, Meteoris, &c. rara, arcana, curiosaq[ue] circumferuntur, ad veritatis trutinam expenduntur: variis ex historia ac philosophia petitis disquisitionibus excutiuntur, & innumeris exemplis illustrantur* (Herbipoli [Würzburg]: Sumptibus Johannis Andreæ Endteri & Wolfgangi Jun. hæredum, excudebat Jobus Hertz […], 1662)

————, *P. Gasparis Schotti […] Thaumaturgus Physicus Sive Magia universalis naturæ et artis Pars Quarta et ultima, In VIII libros digesta, Quibus pleraq[ue] quæ in Cryptographicis, Pyrotechnicis, Magneticis, Sympathicis ac Antipathicis, Medicis, Divinatoriis, Physiognomicis ac Chiromanticis, est rarum, curiosum, ac prodigiosum, hoc est, vere magicum, summa varietate proponitur, varie discutitur, innumeris exemplis aut experimentis illustratur, solide examinaturr, & rationibus Physicis vel stabilitur, vel rejicitur. Cum figuris Æri incises […]* (Bambergæ [Bamberg]: sumpt. Joh. Martini Schönwetteri, bibliopolae Francofurtensis, 1677)

[Scott, Sarah], *A Description of Millenium Hall and the Country Adjacent Together with the Characters of the Inhabitants and Such Historical Anecdotes and Reflections as May Excite in the Reader Proper Sentiments of Humanity, and Lead the Mind to the Love of Virtue. By a Gentleman on His Travels* (London: J. Newberry, 1762)

Selden, John, *De Diis Syriis Sintagmata II editione novissima Adversaria nempe de Numinibus commentitiis in Veteri Instrumento memoratis […]* (1617; Lipsiæ [Leipzig]: Laurenti Sigismundi Cörneri, 1662)

————, *Jani Anglorum facies altera* (Londini [London]: Impens. Auctor typis T. S. procur. I. Helme, 1610)

Seneca, *Epistles*, vol. III — Epistles XCIII–CXXIV, trans. by Richard M. Gummere, Loeb Classical Library, 77 (Cambridge, MA: Harvard University Press, 1925)

————, *The workes of Lucius Annæus Seneca, both morrall and natural […] Translated by Tho[mas]. Lodge, D. in Physicke* (London: William Stansby, 1614)

————, *Naturales Questiones*, trans. by Harry M. Hine (Chicago: University of Chicago Press, 2010)

Shelley, Mary Wollstonecraft, *The Last Man* (London: Henry Colburn, 1826), 3 vols

Silius Italicus, *Punica*, trans. by J. D. Duff, Loeb Classical Library, 278 (Cambridge, MA: Harvard University Press, 1934), 2 vols

Sisto da Siena, *Bibliotheca Sancta A F. Sixto Senensi, ordinis Prædicatorum, ex præcipuis catholicæ ecclesiæ autoribus collecta, & in octo libros digesta; quorum inscriptiones sequens pagina indicabit […]* (Venetiis [Venice]: apud Franciscum Franciscium Senensem, 1566)

Sorbière, Samuel, *Relation d'un voyage en Angleterre: où sont touchées plusieurs choses, qui regardent l'estat des sciences, & de la religion, & autres matières curieuses* (A Paris: Chez Louis Billaine, at Palais, dans la grande Salle, à la Palme & au grand Cesar, 1664); Eng. trans. (with Thomas Sprat, *Observations on the Same Voyage*): *A Voyage to England, Containing Many Things Relating to the State of Learning, Religion, and Other Curiosities of that Kingdom. By Mons. Sorbiere. As Also Observations on the Same Voyage, by Dr. Thomas Sprat, Fellow of the Royal Society, and now Lord Bishop of Rochester. With A Letter of Monsieur Sorbiere's, Concerning the War between England and Holland in 1652: To All Which is prefix'd his Life, Writ by M. Graverol. Done into English from the French Original* (London: printed, and sold by J. Woodward, in St Christopher's-Alley in Threadneedle-Street, 1709)

———, *Sorberiana ou bons mots. Rencontres Agreables, pensées judicieuses, et observations curieuses, de M. Sorbiere* (A Paris: Chex la Veuve Marbre-Cramoisy, 1694)

[Sorel, Charles], *Histoire comique de Francion, ou les tromperies les subtilités, les mauvaises humeurs, les sottises et tous les autres vices de quelques personnes de ce siècle sont naïvement représentés […]* (1623; Paris: Chez Pierre Billaine […], 1626), Eng. trans. *The Comical History of Francion wherein the variety of vices that abuse the ages are satyrically limn'd in their native colours, interwoven with many pleasant events, and moral lessons* (London: Printed for Francis Leach, and are to be sold by Richard Lowndes […], 1655)

Southey, Robert, *Common-Place Book: Fourth Series. Original Memoranda, etc.*, edited by his son-in-law, John Wood Warter, B. D. (London: Reeves and Turner, 1876)

St André, Nathaniel, *A Short Narrative of an Extraordinary Delivery of Rabbets […]* (London: N. Blandford, 1726)

Stanhope, Philip Dormer, *The Letters of Philip Dormer Stanhope […] Edited, with Notes, by Lord Mahon* (London: Richard Bentley, 1845), 4 vols

———, *Letters Written by the Late Right Honourable Philip Dormer Stanhope […]* (Dublin: Printed for E. Lynch […], 1774–1775), 2 vols

———, *Miscellaneous Works of the late Philip Dormer Stanhope […] The Second Edition […]* (London: Printed for Edward and Charles Dilly, 1779), 4 vols

Stanley, Thomas, *The History of the Chaldaick Philosophy* (London: Printed for Thomas Dring, and are to be sold at his Shop at the George in Fleet-street neer Cliffords-Inn, 1662)

Statius, *Thebaid*, vol. I, books I–VII, ed. and trans. by D. R. Shackleton Bailey, Loeb Classical Library, 207 (Cambridge, MA: Harvard University Press, 2004)

Strabo, *Geography*, vol. I, books I–II, trans. by Horace Leonard Jones, Loeb
    Classical Library, 49 (Cambridge, MA: Harvard University Press, 1917)

Strada, Famiano, *De bello Belgico: The History of the Low-Countrey Warres Written in
    Latine by Famianus Strada; in English by Sr. Rob. Stapylton: Illustrated with
    Divers Figures* (London: Printed for Humphrey Moseley [...], 1650)

Suetonius, *Lives of the Caesars*, vol. I, *Julius, Augustus, Tiberius, Gaius, Caligula*,
    trans. by J. C. Rolfe, intr. K. R. Bradley (Cambridge, MA: Harvard University
    Press, 1914)

——, *Lives of the Caesars*, vol. II, *Claudius, Nero, Galba, Otho, and Vitellius;
    Vespasian; Titus, Domitian; Lives of Illustrious Men: Grammarians and
    Rhetoricians; Poets (Terence, Virgil, Horace, Tibullus, Persius, Lucan); Lives of
    Pliny the Elder and Passienus Crispus*, trans. by J. C. Rolfe, Loeb Classical
    Library, 38 (Cambridge, MA: Harvard University Press, 1914)

——, *C. Suetonii Tranquilli Opera Omnia, quæ extant, interpretatione et notis
    illustravit Augustinus Babelonius, jussu Christianissimi Regis ad usum Serenissimi
    Delphini* (Parisiis [Paris]: Apud Fredericum Leonard, Regis ac Serenissimi
    Delphini Architypographum, 1684)

Swift, Jonathan, *Travels into Several Remote Nations of the World. In four parts. By
    Lemuel Gulliver, first a surgeon, and then a captain of several ships* (London:
    Printed for Benj. Motte [...], 1726), 2 vols

——, *Volume VI of the Author's Works: Containing the Publick Spirit of the Whigs;
    and Other Pieces of Political Writings, & c. with Polite Conversation, & c.* (Dublin:
    Printed by and for George Faulkner, 1738)

——, *The Works of the Reverend Dr Jonathan Swift [...]* (Dublin: Printed by
    George Faulkner, 1762–1768), 19 vols

Sybilla, Bartholomeo, *Speculum peregrinarum quaestionum Fr. Bartholomaei
    Sybillae [...] In quo, De animabus, De cælo, Inferno, Purgatorio De Angelis bonis,
    ac malis, Deq[ue] hominibus, necnon de alijs scitu dignissimis (varijs
    Quaestionibus, per tres Decades) pertractatur. [...] Cum indice questionum, &
    rerum memorabilium, nuper emisso* (Venetiis [Venice]: apud Marcum
    Zalterium, 1587)

Tacitus, *Agricola*, in *Agricola, Germania, Dialogue on Oratory*, trans. by M. Hutton
    and W. Peterson, rev. by R. M. Ogilvie, E. H. Warmington, and Michael
    Winterbottom, Loeb Classical Library, 35 (Cambridge, MA: Harvard
    University Press, 1914)

——, *Annals books IV–VI, XI–XII*, trans. by John Jackson, Loeb Classical Library,
    312 (Cambridge, MA: Harvard University Press, 1937)

——, *Histories*, in *Histories books IV–V, Annals books I–III*, trans. by Clifford H.
    Moore and John Jackson, Loeb Classical Library, 249 (Cambridge, MA:
    Harvard University Press, 1931)

Terence, *The Woman of Andros*, in *The Woman of Andros, The Self-Tormentor, The
    Eunuch*, ed. and trans. by John Barsby, Loeb Classical Library, 22 (Cambridge,
    MA: Harvard University Press, 2001)

Terra Rossa, Vitale, *Riflessioni geografiche circa le terre incognite distese in ossequio perpetuo della nobiltà veneziana [...] Consecrate [...] dal P. D. Vitale Terra Rossa [...]* (In Padova [Padua]: Per il Cadorino, 1687)

'Theatre Royal England. In rehearsal, and meant to be speedily attempted a farce in one act, called The Invasion of England. Principal Buffo, Mr Buonaparte, Being his First (and most likely his Last) Appearance on this stage', *The Anti-Gallican: Or Standard of British Loyalty, Religion and Liberty* (1804), p. 16

Thumm, Theodor, *Apodeixis theologica: Ἀπόδειξις Pontificios esse Εικονο — Σταυρο — Σκελετολάτρας. Erroribus et corruptelis Roberti Bellarmini opposita, et ad disputandum proposita. Prside Theodoro Thummio [...] Respondente M. Christophoro Zellero [...]* (Tubingæ [Tübingen]: Apud Eberhardum Wildium, 1623)

Thyraeus, Petrus, *De Apparitionibus Spirituum Disputatio Theologica* (Moguntie [Mainz]: Casparus Behem, 1582)

——, *A Theological Discussion of the Appearances of Spirits* (Moguntie [Mainz]: Casparus Behem, 1582)

Tillotson, John, 'Sermon XXI. The Nature, Office, and Employment of Good Angels. Preached on the Feast of St. Michael', in *The Works of the Most Reverend Dr. John Tillotson, Late Lord Archbishop of Canterbury: Containing two hundred sermons and discourses, on several occasion: to which are annexed, prayers composed by him for his own use: a discourse to his servants before the Sacrament: and a form of prayer composed by him, for the use of King William: being all that were printed after His Grace's decease: now collected into two volumes: together with tables to the whole: one, of the texts preached upon: another, of the places of Scripture, occasionally explain'd: a third, an alphabetical table of matter: published from the originals* (London: Printed by Benjamin Tooke, John Pemberton, and Edward Valentine in Fleetstreet; Jacob Tonson in the Strand, and James Round in Exchange-Alley, 1722), 2 vols, I, pp. 152–61

Tiraboschi, Girolamo, *Storia della letteratura italiana del cavaliere abate Girolamo Tiraboschi [...] Dall'anno 1500 fino all'anno 1600*, vol. VII, part III (Venice: n.p. [but printed by Antonio Fortunato Stella], 1796)

Tournefort, Joseph Pitton de, *A Voyage into the Levant, perform'd by Command of the Late French King Containing the Antient and Modern State of the Islands of the Archipelago; as also of Constantinople, the Coasts of the Black Sea, Armenia, Georgia, the frontiers of Persia, and Asia Minor [...]* (London: Printed for D. Browne, A. Bell, J. Darby, 1718), 2 vols

The Travels of Sir John Mandeville: The Version of the Cotton Manuscript in Modern Spelling (London: Macmillan and Co., 1915)

The True Whig Displayed: Comprehending Cursory Remarks on the Address to the Cocoa-Tree [from a Whig by John Butler]: By a Tory (London: Printed for W. Nicoll, [1762])

Valerius Flaccus, *Argonautica*, trans. by J. H. Mozley, Loeb Classical Library, 286 (Cambridge, MA: Harvard University Press, 1934)

van Helmont, Jan Baptist, *Ortus Medicinae: id est, initia physiciae inaudita: progressus medicinae novus, in morborum ultionem, ad vitam longam* (Amsterodami [Amsterdam]: Apud Ludovicum Elzevirium, 1648)

——, *Van Helmont's Workes, Containing his Most Excellent Philosophy, Physick, Chirurgery, Anatomy; wherein the Philosophy of the Schools is Examined, the Errours therein Refuted, and the Whole Art Reformed and Rectified [...] done into English by J. C. [J. Chandler] [...]* (London: Printed for Lodowick Loyd [...], 1664)

Veiras, Denis, *L'histoire des sevarambes*, critical ed. by Aubrey Rosenberg (1677–1679; Paris: Champion, 2001)

——, *The History of the Sevarambians: A Utopian Novel*, ed. and with an introduction by John Christian Laursen and Cyrus Masroori (1675, 1738; Albany: State University of New York Press, 2006)

La Vie du Tasse Prince des Poetes Italiens (A Amsterdam: Chez George Gallet, 1695)

[Villars, Nicolas-Pierre-Henri de Montfaucon de], *Le comte de Gabalis, ou Entretiens sur les sciences secretes* (Paris: chez Claude Barbin [...], 1670)

[——], *The Count de Gabalis: Being a diverting history of the Rosicrucian doctrine of spirits, viz. sylphs, salamanders, gnomes, and dæmons [...]* (London: Printed for B. Lintott and E. Curll [...], 1714)

[——], *The Count of Gabalis, or, The extravagant mysteries of the Cabalists exposed in five pleasant discourses on the secret sciences done into English by P.A. Gent. [Philip Ayres] [...]* (London: B. M., printer to the Cabalistical Society of the Sages, at the Sign of the Rosy Crusian, 1680)

Virgil, *Aeneid books I–VI*, in *Eclogues, Georgics, Aeneid books I–VI*, trans. by H. Rushton Fairclough, rev. G. P. Goold, Loeb Classical Library, 63 (Cambridge, MA: Harvard University Press, 1916)

——, *Aeneid books VII–XII*, in *Aeneid books VII–XII, Appendix Vergiliana*, trans. by H. Rushton Fairclough, rev. G. P. Goold, Loeb Classical Library, 64 (Cambridge, MA: Harvard University Press, 1918)

——, *Georgics*, trans. by Peter Fallon, intr. and notes by Elaine Fantham (Oxford: Oxford University Press, 2004)

Vittorelli, Andrea, *De angelorum custodia lib. II. In quo altero angelorum ministeria, ex Sacris Litteris recensentur. In altero universum custodia argumentum explicatur* (Patavii [Padua]: ex officina Petri Pauli Tozzi, 1605)

Volney, Constantin-François de Chasseboeuf, *Les ruines, ou Méditation sur les evolutions des empires [...]* (Paris: Chez Desenne [...], 1791)

Wells, H. G., *The Time Machine: An Invention* (New York, H. Holt and Company, 1895)

[Witherspoon, John], *The History of a Corporation of Servants: Discovered a few years ago in the interior parts of South America. Containing some very surprising events and extraordinary characters* (Glasgow: printed for John Gilmour [...], 1765)

Xenophon, *Memorabilia*, in *Memorabilia, Oeconomicus, Symposium, Apology*, trans. by E. C. Marchant and O. J. Todd, rev. Jeffrey Henderson, Loeb Classical Library, 168 (Cambridge, MA: Harvard University Press, 2013)

Secondary Studies

Abbott, T. K., 'Preface', in *Catalogue of the Manuscripts in the Library of Trinity College, Dublin, to Which is Added a List of the Fagel Collection of Maps in the Same Library* (Dublin: Hodges, Figgis, & co.-Longmans, Green & co., 1900), pp. iii–vii

Ablondi, Fred, 'Bérulle, Pierre De (1575–1629)', in *The Cambridge Descartes Lexicon*, ed. by Lawrence Nolan (Cambridge: Cambridge University Press, 2015), pp. 65–67

Adas, Michael, *Machines as the Measure of Men: Science, Technology, and Ideologies of Western Dominance* (Ithaca, NY: Cornell University Press, 1989)

Alkon, Paul K., *Origins of Futuristic Fiction* (Athens: University of Georgia Press, 1987)

———, 'Samuel Madden's "Memoirs of the Twentieth Century"', *Science Fiction Studies*, 12.2 (1985), 184–201; reprinted in *Vintage Visions: Essays on Early Science Fiction*, ed. by Arthur B. Evans (Middletown, CT: Wesleyan University Press, 2014), pp. 25–46

———, *Science Fiction before 1900: Imagination Discovers Technology* (New York: Routledge, 2002)

Allan, D. G. C., '"Dear and Serviceable to Each Other": Benjamin Franklin and the Royal Society of Arts', *Proceedings of the American Philosophical Society*, 144.3 (2000), 245–66

———, *William Shipley: Founder of The Royal Society of Arts: A Biography with Documents* (London: Hutchinson, 1968)

Alonso-Núñez, J. M., 'An Augustan World History: The "Historiae Philippicae" of Pompeius Trogus', *Greece & Rome*, 34.1 (1987), pp. 56–72

Altaher, Amer, 'What Happened to Utopias in the Eighteenth Century?' (MPhil dissertation, University of Leicester, 2014)

Andersson Burnett, Linda, 'Translating Swedish Colonialism: Johannes Schefferus's *Lapponia* in Britain c. 1674–1800', *Scandinavian Studies*, 91.1–2 (2019), 134–62, <https://doi.org/10.5406/scanstud.91.1-2.0134>

Andersson, Jenny, *The Future of the World: Futurology, Futurists, and the Struggle for the Post-Cold War Imagination* (Oxford: Oxford University Press, 2018)

Aranda, Daniel, 'Le Jeu des temporalités dans les utopies et uchronies de Rétif de la Bretonne', *Temporalités*, 12 (2010), <https://doi.org/10.4000/temporalites.1333>

Armitage, David, *The Ideological Origins of the British Empire* (2000; Cambridge: Cambridge University Press, 2004)

Ashley, Mike, 'The Fear of Invasion', *British Library*, Discovering Literature: Romantics & Victorians, 15 May 2014, <https://www.bl.uk/romantics-and-victorians/articles/the-fear-of-invasion> [accessed 1 January 2023]

Austen Leigh, R. A., 'William Strahan and His Ledgers', *The Library*, s4–III.4 (1923), 261–87, <https://doi.org/10.1093/library/s4-III.4.261>

Avery, Emmett L., *The London Stage, 1660–1800: A Calendar of Plays, Entertainments & Afterpieces, Together with Casts, Box-Receipts and Contemporary Comment, Part 2: 1700–1729*, ed. with a critical introduction by Avery (Carbondale, IL: Southern Illinois University Press, 1960), 2 vols

Baczko, Bronisław, *L'utopia. Immaginazione sociale e rappresentazioni utopiche nell'età dell'illuminismo*, trans. by Margherita Botto and Dario Gibelli (1978; Turin: Einaudi, 1979)

Bailey, Michael D., *Battling Demons: Witchcraft, Heresy, and Reform in the Late Middle Ages* (University Park: Pennsylvania State University Press, 2002)

Balaudé, Jean-François, 'Daimôn', in *Dictionary of Untranslatables: A Philosophical Lexicon*, ed. by Barbara Cassin (Princeton and Oxford: Princeton University Press, 2017), *ad vocem*

Barnett, Eleanor, 'Reforming Food and Eating in Protestant England, *c.* 1560–*c.* 1640', *The Historical Journal*, 63.3 (2020), 507–27, <https://doi.org/10.1017/S0018246X19000426>

Beattie, John M., *The English Court in the Reign of George I* (London: Cambridge University Press, 1967)

Beckert, Jens, *Imagined Futures: Fictional Expectations and Capitalist Dynamics* (Cambridge, MA: Harvard University Press, 2016)

Beckett, J. C., Review of *Macmillan History of Literature: Anglo-Irish Literature* by A. Norman Jeffares, *The Modern Language Review*, 80.3 (1985), 685–86 <https://doi.org/10.2307/372901>

Beebee, Thomas O., *Epistolary Fiction in Europe, 1500–1850* (Cambridge: Cambridge University Press, 1999)

Beerden, Kim, *Worlds Full of Signs: Ancient Greek Divination in Context* (Leiden: Brill, 2013)

Bell, Duncan, *Reordering the World: Essays on Liberalism and Empire* (Princeton: Princeton University Press, 2016)

Beretta, Francesco, 'Melchior Inchofer et L'hérésie de Galilée: Censure Doctrinale et Hiérarchie Intellectuelle', *Journal of Modern European History/Zeitschrift Für Moderne Europäische Geschichte/Revue D'histoire Européenne Contemporaine*, 3.1 (2005), 23–49

Berndt, Katrin, and Alessa Johns, eds, *Handbook of the British Novel in the Long Eighteenth Century* (Berlin: De Gruyter, 2021)

Berry, Henry F., *A History of the Royal Dublin Society* (London: Longmans, Green and Co., 1915)

Biedermann, Hans, *Dictionary of Symbolism: Cultural Icons and the Meanings Behind Them* (New York: Meridian, 1992)

Biondi, Albano, 'A. Curione, Celio Secondo', in *Dizionario Biografico degli Italiani*, vol. XXXI (Rome: Treccani, 1981), pp. 443–49

Birkbeck Hill, George, 'Notes on I', in Jonathan Swift, *Unpublished Letters of Dean Swift*, ed. by Birkbeck Hill (New York: F. A. Stokes, 1900), p. 8

———, 'Notes on XXXIV', in Jonathan Swift, *Unpublished Letters of Dean Swift*, ed. by Birkbeck Hill (New York: F. A. Stokes, 1900), p. 147

Bleiler, Everett F., *The Checklist of Science-Fiction and Supernatural Fiction* (Glen Rock, NJ: Firebell Books, 1978)

———, with the assistance of Richard J. Bleiler, *Science-Fiction: The Early Years* (Kent, OH: Kent State University Press, 1990)

———, *Science-Fiction: The Gernsback Years* (Kent, OH: Kent State University Press, 1998)

Bleiler, Everett F., and David Langford, 'Hollow Earth', last updated 9 May 2022, in *SFE: The Encyclopedia of Science Fiction*, ed. by John Clute and David Langford, <https://sf-encyclopedia.com/>, [accessed 1 January 2023], *ad vocem*

Bode, Christoph, and Rainer Dietrich, eds, *Future Narratives: Theory, Poetics, and Media-Historical Moment* (Berlin: De Gruyter, 2013)

Bohak, Gideon, *Ancient Jewish Magic: A History* (Cambridge: Cambridge University Press, 2008)

Bonfiglio, Emilio, 'The Armenian Translations of John Chrysostom: The Issue of Selection', in *Caught in Translation: Studies on Versions of Late-Antique Christian Literature*, ed. by Madalina Toca and Dan Batovici (Leiden: Brill, 2019), pp. 35–63

Borghero, Carlo, *La certezza e la storia: Cartesianesimo, pirronismo e conoscenza storica* (Milan: Franco Angeli, 1983)

Bosse, Malcolm J., 'Introduction', in Samuel Madden, *Memoirs of the Twentieth Century Being Original Letters of State, under George the Sixth*, with an 'Introduction' by Malcolm J. Bosse (New York: Garland, 1972), pp. 5–9

Boswell, James, *The Life of Samuel Johnson, LL.D.: Including a Journal of a Tour to the Hebrides: A New Edition […]* (New York: George Dearborn, 1833), 2 vols

Boyar, Ebru, and Kate Fleet, *A Social History of Ottoman Istanbul* (Cambridge: Cambridge University Press, 2000)

Bradley, Mark, ed., *Classics and Imperialism in the British Empire* (Oxford: Oxford University Press, 2010)

Brady, Andrea, and Emily Butterworth, *The Uses of the Future in Early Modern Europe* (New York: Routledge, 2010)

Braida, Lodovica, *L'autore assente. L'anonimato nell'editoria italiana del Settecento* (Rome: Laterza, 2019)

————, 'Les almanachs italiens du XVIIIᵉ siècle: véhicules de "faux préjugés" ou "puissants moyens d'éducation"?', in *Les lectures du peuple en Europe et dans les Amériques (XVIIᵉ-XXᵉ siècles)*, ed. by Hans-Jürgen Lüsebrink, York Gothart Mix, Jean-Yves Mollier, and Patricia Sorel (Brussels: Complexe, 2003), pp. 259–70

————, *Le guide del tempo. Almanacchi piemontesi nel '700* (Turin: Deputazione Subalpina di Storia Patria, 1989)

Brann, Noel L., *Trithemius and Magical Theology: A Chapter in the Controversy over Occult Studies in Early Modern Europe* (Albany: State of New York University Press, 1999)

Brewer, John, *The Pleasures of the Imagination: English Culture in the Eighteenth Century* (New York: Farrar, Straus and Giroux, 1997)

Briggs, Asa, *A History of Longmans and Their Books, 1724–1990: Longevity in Publishing* (London: British Library and New Castle, DE: Oak Knoll Press, 2008)

Broadwell, Liz, 'Lions on the Clock II: Six Owners, Five Marks of Provenance, One Book (and Two Lawsuits)', in *Special Collections Processing at Penn*, blog of the Special Collections Processing Center (SCPC) of the University of Pennsylvania's Kislak Center for Special Collections, Rare Books and Manuscripts, March 17, 2021, <https://pennrare.wordpress.com/>, [accessed 1 January 2023]

Bross, Kristina, *Future History: Global Fantasies in Seventeenth-Century American and British Writings* (Oxford: Oxford University Press, 2017)

Browning, Reed, 'Hervey, John, second Baron Hervey of Ickworth (1696–1743)', in *Oxford Dictionary of National Biography*, 2008, <https://doi.org/10.1093/ref:odnb/13116>

Bruce, Susan 'Introduction', in *Three Early Modern Utopias: Utopia, New Atlantis, The Isle of Pines*, ed. with an introduction and notes by Susan Bruce (Oxford: Oxford University Press, 1999), pp. ix–xlii

Brückmann, Patricia, 'Pope's Shock and the Count of Gabalis', *English Language Notes*, 1.4 (1964), 259–60

Bucholz, Robert O., ed., 'Household of Frederick Lewis, Prince of Wales 1729–1751', in *The Database of Court Officers: 1660–1837*, <http://courtofficers.ctsdh.luc.edu/>, [accessed 1 January 2023], *ad vocem*

Bühring, Benjamin, *Die Deutsche Kanzlei in London. Kommunikation und Verwaltung in der Personalunion Großbritannien — Kurhannover 1714–1760* (Göttingen: Universitätsverlag Göttingen, 2021)

Bullard, Paddy, 'Rhetoric and Eloquence: The Language of Persuasion', in *The Oxford Handbook of British Philosophy in the Eighteenth Century*, ed. by James A. Harris (Oxford: Oxford University Press, 2013), pp. 84–103

Bunbury, Turtle, *Irish Diaspora: Tales of Emigration, Exile and Imperialism* (London: Thames and Hudson, 2021), electronic ed.

Burke, Bernard, *Genealogical and Heraldic History of the Landed Gentry* (London: Henry Colburn, 1849)

Burke, Peter, 'Foreword: The History of the Future, 1350–2000', in *The Uses of the Future in Early Modern Europe*, ed. by Andrea Brady and Emily Butterworth (New York: Routledge, 2010), pp. ix–xx

———, 'History, Myth, and Fiction: Doubts and Debates', in *The Oxford History of Historical Writing*, vol. III, *1400–1800*, ed. by José Rabasa, Masayuki Sato, Edoardo Tortarolo, and Daniel Woolf (Oxford: Oxford University Press, 2012), pp. 261–81

———, *A Social History of Knowledge: From Gutenberg to Diderot* (Cambridge: Polity, 2015)

Burns, William E., *An Age of Wonders: Prodigies, Politics, and Providence in England, 1657–1727* (Manchester: Manchester University Press, 2002)

Burrow J. A., and Ian P. Wei, eds, *Medieval Futures: Attitudes to the Future in the Middle Ages* (Woodbridge: Boydell, 2000)

Cagnolati, Antonella, 'L'utopia al potere: Il famoso regno di Macaria', *Annali dell'Università di Ferrara*, Sezione III, *Filosofia, Discussion Papers*, 57 (2000), retrieved from <https://www.researchgate.net/>, [accessed 1 January 2023]

Cahill, Patricia A., *Unto the Breach: Martial Formations, Historical Trauma, and the Early Modern Stage* (Oxford: Oxford University Press, 2009)

Cameron, Euan, ed., *The New Cambridge History of the Bible, Volume 3: From 1450 to 1750* (Cambridge: Cambridge University Press, 2016)

Campbell, Gordon, ed., *The Oxford Dictionary of the Renaissance* (Oxford: Oxford University Press, 2003)

Cannon, John, 'Lyttelton, Thomas, second Baron Lyttelton (1744–1779)', in *Oxford Dictionary of National Biography*, 2004 <https://doi.org/10.1093/ref:odnb/17310>

———, 'Stanhope, Philip Dormer, fourth earl of Chesterfield (1694–1773)', in *Oxford Dictionary of National Biography*, 2012 <https://doi.org/10.1093/ref:odnb/26255>

Capp, Bernard Stuart, *Astrology and the Popular Press: English Almanacs, 1500–1800* (Ithaca: Cornell University Press, 1979)

———, 'Wing, Vincent (1619–1668)', in *Oxford Dictionary of National Biography*, 2004 <https://doi.org/10.1093/ref:odnb/29731>

Caravale, Giorgio, *Forbidden Prayer: Church Censorship and Devotional Literature in Renaissance Italy* (London: Ashgate, 2012)

Cascardi, Anthony J., 'Don Quixote and the Invention of the Novel', in *The Cambridge Companion to Cervantes*, ed. by Anthony J. Cascardi (Cambridge: Cambridge University Press, 2002), pp. 58–79

Cazzola, Matilde, Edward Jones Corredera, Giulia Iannuzzi, and Guido G. Beduschi, *Imperial Times: How Europe Used Time to Rule the World (XVIII–XIX Centuries)*, monographic issue, *History of Historiography*, 77 (2020)

———, 'Introduction. Imperial Times: Towards a History of Imperial Uses of Time', *Imperial Times: How Europe Used Time to Rule the World (XVIII–XIX Centuries)*, monographic issue, *History of Historiography*, 77 (2020), pp. 11–26

Çelik, Zeynep, *The Remaking of Istanbul: Portrait of an Ottoman City in the Nineteenth Century* (Berkeley and Los Angeles: University of California Press, 1993)

'Chesterfield, Earl of Stanhope — ex libris', Downside Abbey, photo taken on 15 October 2015, published on Flickr, <https://www.flickr.com/photos/downsideabbeyarchives>, [accessed 1 January 2023]

Chuanacháin, Deirdre Ní, 'Utopianism in Eighteenth-Century Ireland' (Ph. D. dissertation, University of Limerick, 2013)

Cipolla, Carlo M., *Clocks & Culture 1300–1700* (1967; New York: Norton, 1977)

Claeys, Gregory, 'Chronology of Main Eighteenth-Century British Utopian and Anti-utopian Texts', in *Utopias of the British Enlightenment*, ed. by Gregory Claeys (Cambridge: Cambridge University Press, 1994), pp. xxix–xxxii

———, 'Introduction', in *Utopias of the British Enlightenment*, ed. by Gregory Claeys (Cambridge: Cambridge University Press, 1994), pp. vii–xxviii

Claeys, Gregory, ed., *Utopias of the British Enlightenment* (Cambridge: Cambridge University Press, 1994)

Clark, J. C. D., *Samuel Johnson: Literature, Religion, and English Cultural Politics from the Restoration to Romanticism* (Cambridge: Cambridge University Press, 1994)

Clarke, I. F., 'Before and After "The Battle of Dorking"', *Science Fiction Studies*, 24.1 (1997), 33–46

———, 'Future-War Fiction: The First Main Phase, 1871–1900', *Science Fiction Studies*, 24.3 (1997), 387–412

———, *The Pattern of Expectation: 1644–2001* (London: Cape, 1979)

Clarke, I. F., ed., *British Future Fiction* (2001; London: Routledge, 2016), 8 vols

Clavin, Terry, 'Molyneux, Daniel', *Dictionary of Irish Biography*, 2009, <https://dib.ie>, [accessed 1 January 2023], *ad vocem*

Clucas, Stephen, 'False Illuding Spirits & Cownterfeiting Deuills: John Dee's Angelic Conversations and Religious Anxiety', in *Conversations with Angels: Essays Towards a History of Spiritual Communication, 1100–1700*, ed. by Joad Raymond (Palgrave Macmillan, 2011), pp. 150–74

Clute, John, 'Madden, Samuel', last updated 12 September 2022, in *SFE: The Encyclopedia of Science Fiction*, ed. by John Clute and David Langford, <https://sf-encyclopedia.com/>, [accessed 1 January 2023], *ad vocem*

———, 'Ruins and Futurity', last updated 7 March 2022, in *SFE: The Encyclopedia of Science Fiction*, ed. by John Clute and David Langford, <https://sf-encyclopedia.com/>, [accessed 1 January 2023], *ad vocem*

Cooper, Thompson, 'Madden, Samuel', *Dictionary of National Biography*, ed. by Sydney Lee (New York: Macmillan and Smith, Elder & Co., 1885–1900), 63 vols, vol. xxxv (1893), pp. 296–97

Corfield, Penelope J., *Time and the Shape of History* (New Haven: Yale University Press, 2007)

Crane, Ronald S., , *English Literature, 1660–1800: A Bibliography of Modern Studies: Compiled for Philological Quarterly* (Princeton: Princeton University Press, 1950), 4 vols, vol. II, *1939–1950*

Cranfield, G. A., 'The "London Evening Post", 1727–1744: A Study in the Development of the Political Press', *The Historical Journal*, 6.1 (1963), 20–37

Croker, John Wilson, 'Sketch of the Life of Bassompierre', in *Memoirs of the Embassy of the Marshal de Bassompierre to the Court of England in 1626*, ed. and trans. by Croker (London: John Murray, 1819), pp. v–xx

Csicsery-Ronay, Istvan Jr., 'Science Fiction and Empire', *Science Fiction Studies*, 30.2 (2003), 231–45

Curry, Patrick, 'Partridge, John (1644–1715)', in *Oxford Dictionary of National Biography*, 2004 <https://doi.org/10.1093/ref:odnb/21484>

———, 'Gadbury, John (1627–1704)', in *Oxford Dictionary of National Biography*, 2004 <https://doi.org/10.1093/ref:odnb/10265>

Darnton, Robert, *Libri proibiti. Pornografia, satira e utopia all'origine della rivoluzione francese*, trans. by Vittorio Beonio Brocchieri (1995; Milan: Mondadori, 1997), pp. 120–40

Davidson, Gustav, *A Dictionary of Angels: Including the Fallen Angels* (New York: Free Press and Collier-Macmillan, 1967)

De Girolami Cheney, Liana, 'The Symbolism of the Skull in *Vanitas*: *Homo Bulla Est*', *Cultural and Religious Studies*, 6.5 (2018), 267–84, <https://doi.org/10.17265/2328-2177/2018.05.001>

DeMaria, Robert Jr., *The Life of Samuel Johnson: A Critical Biography* (1993; Oxford: Blackwell, 1994)

De Smet, Ingrid A. R., *Thuanus: The Making of Jacques-Auguste de Thou (1553–1617)* (Geneva: Droz, 2006)

Donaldson, Ian, 'Concealing and Revealing: Pope's "Epistle to Dr. Arbuthnot"', *The Yearbook of English Studies*, 18 (1988), pp. 181–99, <https://doi.org/10.2307/3508197>

Downes, Kerry, 'Wren, Sir Christopher (1632–1723)', in *Oxford Dictionary of National Biography*, 2004, rev. 2012, <https://doi.org/10.1093/ref:odnb/30019>

Eccleshall, Robert, 'The Political Ideas of Anglican Ireland in the 1690s', in *Political Discourse in Seventeenth- and Eighteenth-Century Ireland*, ed. by D. George Boyce, Robert Eccleshall, and Vincent Geoghegan (Houndmills: Palgrave, 2001), pp. 62–80

Ellis, Roger, '"Flores Ad Fabricandam … Coronam": An Investigation into the Uses of the Revelations of St Bridget of Sweden in Fifteenth-Century England', *Medium Ævum*, 51.2 (1982), 163–86 <https://doi.org/10.2307/43628648>

Esposito, John L., ed., *The Oxford Dictionary of Islam* (Oxford: Oxford University Press, 2003)

Eusterschulte, Anne, 'Pierre Bayle's *Dictionaire historique et critique*: Historical Criticism and Impartiality of Judgement', in *The Emergence of Impartiality*, ed. by Kathryn Murphy and Anita Traninger (Leiden: Brill, 2014), pp. 305–32

Evans, Mihail Dafydd, 'Madden, John (bap. 1649, d. 1703/4)', in *Oxford Dictionary of National Biography*, 2004 <https://doi.org/10.1093/ref:odnb/55487>

Fabricant, Carole, 'Eighteenth-Century Travel Literature', in *The Cambridge History of English Literature, 1660–1780*, ed. by John Richetti (Cambridge: Cambridge University Press, 2005), pp. 707–44

Fairclough, H. Rushton, 'The Art of Legacy-Hunting' (editor's introduction), in Horace, *Satires, Epistles, The Art of Poetry*, trans. by Fairclough, Loeb Classical Library, 194 (Cambridge, MA: Harvard University Press, 1942), pp. 196–97

Feder, Kenneth, *Frauds, Myths, and Mysteries: Science and Pseudoscience in Archaeology* (1990; Mountain View, CA: Mayfield, 1999)

Feiner, Shmuel, *The Jewish Enlightenment*, trans. by Chaya Naor (Philadelphia: University of Pennsylvania Press, 2011)

Findlen, Paula, 'Jokes of Nature and Jokes of Knowledge: The Playfulness of Scientific Discourse in Early Modern Europe', *Renaissance Quarterly*, 43.2 (1990), 292–331 <https://doi.org/10.2307/2862366>

Fitting, Peter, ed., *Subterranean Worlds: A Critical Anthology* (Middletown, CT: Wesleyan University Press, 2004)

Forbes, Thomas R., 'The Social History of the Caul', *The Yale Journal of Biology and Medicine*, 25.6 (1953), 495–508

Fox, Peter, *Trinity College Library Dublin: A History* (Cambridge: Cambridge University Press, 2014)

Fraioli, Deborah, 'Gerson Judging Women of Spirit: From Female Mystics to Joan of Arc', in *Joan of Arc and Spirituality: The New Middle Ages*, ed. by Ann W. Astell and Bonnie Wheeler (New York: Palgrave Macmillan, 2003), pp. 147–65

Franck, Johannes, *Quellen und Untersuchungen zur Geschichte des Hexenwahns und der Hexenverfolgung im Mittelalter* (Bonn: C. Georgi, 1901)

Fraser, A. M., 'The Molyneux Family', *Dublin Historical Record*, 16.1 (1960), 9–15

Friedrich, Markus, 'Genealogy and the History of Knowledge', in *Genealogical Knowledge in the Making: Tools, Practices, and Evidence in Early Modern Europe*, ed. by Jost Eickmeyer, Markus Friedrich, and Volker Bauer (Berlin: De Gruyter, 2019), pp. 1–22

——, 'Jesuit Organization and Legislation: Development and Implementation of a Normative Framework', in *The Oxford Handbook of the Jesuits*, ed. by Ines G. Županov (Oxford: Oxford University Press, 2019), pp. 23–43

Gallagher, Catherine, *Telling It Like It Wasn't: The Counterfactual Imagination in History and Fiction* (Chicago: University of Chicago Press, 2018)

Garland, Henry, and Mary Garland, eds, *The Oxford Companion to German Literature* (Oxford: Oxford University Press, 1997), electronic ed.

Gerrard, Christine, *The Patriot Opposition to Walpole: Politics, Poetry, and National Myth, 1725–1742* (Oxford: Clarendon Press, 1994)

Gerschel, Lucien, 'Sur un schème trifonctionnel dans une famille de légendes germaniques', *Revue de l'histoire des religions*, 150.1 (1956), 55–92 <https://doi.org/10.3406/rhr.1956.7143>

Gibson, R. W., *St. Thomas More: A Preliminary Bibliography of His Works and of Moreana to the Year 1750 Compiled by R. W. Gibson with a Bibliography of Utopiana Compiled by R. W. Gibson and J. Max Patrick* (New Haven: Yale University Press, 1961)

Gigerenzer, Gerd, Zeno Swijtink, Theodore Porter, Lorraine Daston, John Beatty, Lorenz Kruger, *The Empire of Chance: How Probability Changed Science and Everyday Life* (Cambridge: Cambridge University Press, 1989)

Ginzburg, Carlo, *The Night Battles: Witchcraft and Agrarian Cults in the Sixteenth and Seventeenth Centuries* (1983; London: Routledge, 2011)

Gliozzi, Giuliano, *Adamo e il nuovo mondo. La nascita dell'antropologia come ideologia coloniale: dalle genealogie bibliche alle teorie razziali (1500–1700)* (Florence: La Nuova Italia, 1977)

Goldie, Mark, 'The English System of Liberty', in *The Cambridge History of Eighteenth-Century Political Thought*, ed. by Mark Goldie and Robert Wokler (Cambridge: Cambridge University Press, 2006), pp. 40–78

Greenblatt, Stephen, *Renaissance Self-Fashioning* (Chicago: University of Chicago Press, 1980)

Gregg, Edward, 'James Francis Edward [James Francis Edward Stuart; styled James; known as Chevalier de St George, the Pretender, the Old Pretender] (1688–1766), Jacobite claimant to the thrones of England, Scotland, and Ireland', in *Oxford Dictionary of National Biography*, 2004 <https://doi.org/10.1093/ref:odnb/14594>

Güven, Suna, 'Displaying the Res Gestae of Augustus: A Monument of Imperial Image for All', *Journal of the Society of Architectural Historians*, 57.1 (1998), 30–45 <https://doi.org/10.2307/991403>

Hacking, Ian, *The Emergence of Probability: A Philosophical Study of Early Ideas about Probability, Induction and Statistical Inference*, 2nd ed. (1975; Cambridge: Cambridge University Press, 2006)

Hadass, Ofer, *Medicine, Religion, and Magic in Early Stuart England: Richard Napier's Medical Practice* (University Park, PA: Penn State University Press, 2019)

Hall, David, *Worlds of Wonder, Days of Judgment: Popular Religious Beliefs in Early New England* (Cambridge: Harvard University Press, 1989)

Halpern, Richard, *The Poetics of Primitive Accumulation: English Renaissance Culture and the Genealogy of Capital* (Ithaca: Cornell University Press, 1991)

Hamilton, John T., 'The Bull of Phalaris: The Birth of Music out of Torture', Working paper, Department of Germanic Languages & Literature, Harvard University, 2012, pp. 1–13

Harley, David, 'Explaining Salem: Calvinist Psychology and the Diagnosis of Possession', *The American Historical Review*, 101.2 (1996), 307–30 <https://doi.org/10.2307/2170393>

Harris, Michael, *London Newspapers in the Age of Walpole: A Study of the Origins of the Modern English Press* (Rutherford: Fairleigh Dickinson University Press, 1987)

Harris, Robert, 'The *London Evening Post* and Mid-Eighteenth-Century British Politics', *The English Historical Review*, 110.439 (1995), 1132–56

———, *A Patriot Press: National Politics and the London Press in the 1740s* (Oxford: Clarendon Press, 1993)

Harris-McCoy, Daniel E., *Artemidorus' Oneirocritica: Text, Translation, and Commentary* (Oxford: Oxford University Press, 2012)

Harrison, Peter, '"I Believe Because It Is Absurd": The Enlightenment Invention of Tertullian's Credo', *Church History*, 86.2 (2017), 339–64 <https://doi.org/10.1017/S0009640717000531>

Harvey, Karen, *The Imposteress Rabbit-Breeder: Mary Toft and Eighteenth-Century England* (Oxford: Oxford University Press, 2020)

Hazen, Allen T., *A Catalogue of Horace Walpole's Library* (New Haven: Yale University Press, 1969), 3 vols

Headrick, Daniel R., *Power over People: Technology, Environments, and Western Imperialism, 1400 to the Present* (Princeton: Princeton University Press, 2012)

Hedesan, Delia Georgiana, '"Christian Philosophy": Medical Alchemy and Christian Thought in the Work of Jan Baptista Van Helmont (1579–1644)' (PhD dissertation, University of Exeter, 2012).

Hellekson, Karen, *The Alternate History: Refiguring Historical Time* (Kent: Kent State University Press, 2013)

Hickey, Helen M., 'Capturing Christ's Tears: *La Sainte Larme* in Medieval and Early Modern France', in *Feeling Things: Objects and Emotions through History*, ed. by Stephanie Downes, Sally Holloway, and Sarah Randles (Oxford: Oxford University Press, 2018), pp. 58–71

Higgins, Ian, 'The Politics of *A Tale of a Tub*', in *Swift's Politics: A Study in Disaffection* (Cambridge: Cambridge University Press, 1994), pp. 96–143

Hobbins, Daniel, 'Jean Gerson', last modified 2012, in *Oxford Bibliographies*, <https://www.oxfordbibliographies.com/>, [accessed 1 January 2023], *Medieval Studies, ad vocem* <https://doi.org/10.1093/OBO/9780195396584-0032>

Holmes, Richard, 'English Whigs and Irish Patriots: Archbishop Boulter and the Politics of Party in Hanoverian Ireland', *Eighteenth-Century Ireland/Iris an dá chultúr*, 31 (2016), 73–91

———, 'Introduction', in *James Arbuckle: Selected Works*, ed. by Richard Holmes (Lewisburg: Bucknell University Press, 2014), pp. xv–xl

Hölscher, Lucian, *Die Entdeckung der Zukunft* (Göttingen: Wallstein Verlag, 2016)

Holt, P. M., 'The Study of Islam in Seventeenth- and Eighteenth-Century England', *Journal of Early Modern History*, 2.2 (1998), 113–23 <https://doi.org/10.1163/157006598X00126>

Hont, Istvan, 'The Early Enlightenment Debate on Commerce and Luxury', in *The Cambridge History of Eighteenth-Century Political Thought*, ed. by Mark Goldie and Robert Wokler (Cambridge: Cambridge University Press, 2006), pp. 379–418

Hope Nicolson, Marjorie, *Voyages to the Moon* (1948; New York: Macmillan, 1960)

Houston, Keith, *Shady Characters: The Secret Life of Punctuation, Symbols, and Other Typographical Marks* (New York: W. W. Norton & Company, 2013)

Hunt, Lynn, Margaret C. Jacob, and W. W. Mijnhardt, eds, *The Book That Changed Europe: Picard & Bernard's, Religious Ceremonies of the World* (Cambridge, MA: Belknap Press of Harvard University Press, 2010)

Hunt, William, *The Irish Parliament 1775: From an Official and Contemporary Manuscript*, (London: Longmans, Green, and co., 1907)

Iannuzzi, Giulia, *Geografie del tempo. Viaggiatori europei tra i popoli nativi nel Nord America del Settecento* (Rome: Viella, 2022)

——, 'Waging Future Wars: *The Reign of George VI*, Imagined Conflicts and the Birth of a Global Consciousness in the European Mind', in *Waging War and Making Peace: European Ways of Inciting and Containing Armed Conflict, 1648–2020*, ed. by Matthew D'Auria, Rolf Petri, and Jan Vermeiren (Berlin: De Gruyter, in press)

Iggers, Georg G., and Q. Edward Wang, with contributions from Supriya Mukherjee, *A Global History of Modern Historiography* (London: Routledge, 2013)

Imbruglia, Girolamo, *The Jesuit Missions of Paraguay and a Cultural History of Utopia (1568–1789)*, trans. by Mark Weyr (Leiden: Brill, 2017)

Irving, David R. M., 'Comparative Organography in Early Modern Empires', *Music & Letters*, 90.3 (2009), 372–98

Jacob, Margaret C., *The Secular Enlightenment* (Princeton: Princeton University Press, 2019)

Jameson, Fredric, *Archaeologies of the Future: The Desire Called Utopia and Other Science Fictions* (London: Verso, 2005)

Jeffares, A. Norman, *Macmillan History of Literature: Anglo-Irish Literature* (New York: Schocken Books, 1982)

Jettot, Stéphane, and Jean-Paul Zuñiga, eds, *Genealogy and Social Status in the Enlightenment* (Liverpool: Liverpool University Press, 2021)

'John Madden', Royal College of Physicians of Ireland, Heritage Centre, Lives of the Presidents, 1667–1699, <https://heritage.rcpi.ie/Projects/Lives-of-the-Presidents/>, [accessed 1 January 2023], *ad vocem*

Johns, Alessa, 'Feminism and Utopianism', in *The Cambridge Companion to Utopian Literature*, ed. by Gregory Claeys (Cambridge: Cambridge University Press, 2010), pp. 174–99

——, *Women's Utopias of the Eighteenth Century* (Urbana and Chicago: University of Illinois Press)

Johnson, Trevor, 'Guardian Angels and the Society of Jesus', in *Angels in the Early Modern World*, ed. by Peter Marshall and Alexandra Walsham (Cambridge: Cambridge University Press, 2006), pp. 191–213

Jones, Prudence, 'Ptolemy', in *Dictionary of African Biography*, ed. by Emmanuel K. Akyeampong and Henry Louis Gates Jr. (Oxford: Oxford University Press, 2012), electronic ed.

Jones, Tom, *George Berkeley: A Philosophical Life* (Princeton: Princeton University Press, 2021)

Kelly, James, 'Public and Political Opinion in Ireland and the Idea of an Anglo-Irish Union, 1650–1800', in *Political Discourse in Seventeenth- and Eighteenth-Century Ireland*, ed. by D. George Boyce, Robert Eccleshall, and Vincent Geoghegan (Houndmills: Palgrave, 2001), pp. 110–41

Kelly, Patrick, 'Berkeley's Economic Writings', in *The Cambridge Companion to Berkeley*, ed. by Kenneth P. Winkler (Cambridge: Cambridge University Press, 2005), pp. 339–68

Kilburn, Matthew, 'The Fell Legacy 1686–1755', in *The History of Oxford University Press*: vol. I — *Beginnings to 1780*, ed. by Ian Gadd (Oxford: Oxford University Press, 2013), pp. 107–37

——, 'Frederick Lewis, prince of Wales', in *Oxford Dictionary of National Biography*, 2004 <https://doi.org/10.1093/ref:odnb/10140>

Koselleck, Reinhart, 'The Eighteenth Century as the Beginning of Modernity' (1987), in *The Practice of Conceptual History: Timing History, Spacing Concepts*, trans. by Todd Samuel Presner et al. (essay collection; Stanford: Stanford University Press, 2002), pp. 154–69

——, *Futures Past: On the Semantics of Historical Time*, trans. by Keith Tribe (1979; New York: Columbia University Press, 2004)

——, *The Practice of Conceptual History: Timing History, Spacing Concepts*, trans. by Todd Samuel Presner et al. (essay collection; Stanford: Stanford University Press, 2002)

——, 'The Temporalization of Utopia', in *Timing History, Spacing Concepts*, trans. by Todd Samuel Presner et al. (essay collection; Stanford: Stanford University Press, 2002), pp. 84–99

Kramnick, Isaac, 'Corruption in Eighteenth-Century English and American Political Discourse', in *Virtue, Corruption, and Self-Interest: Political Values in the Eighteenth Century*, ed. by Richard K. Matthews (Bethlehem: Lehigh University Press and London: Associated University Presses, 1994), pp. 55–75

Kukkonen, Karin, *A Prehistory of Cognitive Poetics: Neoclassicism and the Novel* (New York: Oxford University Press, 2017)

Kupiec, Anne, '"Le Dernier Homme" de Grainville. Religion et Révolution', *Tumultes*, 20 (2003), 31–45

Landa, Louis A., '"A Modest Proposal" and Populousness', *Modern Philology*, 40.2 (1942), 161–70

Langford, David, David Pringle, Brian M. Stableford, and John Clute, 'Lost Races', last updated 11 May 2016, in *SFE: The Encyclopedia of Science Fiction*, ed. by John Clute and David Langford, <https://sf-encyclopedia.com/>, [accessed 1 January 2023], *ad vocem*

Langford, Paul, *A Polite and Commercial People: England 1727–1783* (Oxford: Oxford University Press, 1989)

Latimer, Bonnie, 'Alchemies of Satire: A History of the Sylphs in *The Rape of the Lock*', *The Review of English Studies*, new series, 57.232 (2006), 684–700

Leask, Nigel, 'Eighteenth-Century Travel Writing', in *The Cambridge History of Travel Writing*, ed. by Nandini Das and Tim Youngs (Cambridge: Cambridge University Press, 2019), pp. 93–107

Lees, J. C., 'The Religious Retinue of Leicester House: Chaplains of Frederick Louis, Prince of Wales, 1729–51', *Journal for Eighteenth-Century Studies*, 40.1 (2017), 89–109 <https://doi.org/10.1111/1754-0208.12388>

Le Goff, Jacques, *Time, Work & Culture in the Middle Ages*, trans. by Arthur Goldhammer (1977; Chicago: University of Chicago Press, 1980)

Leibacher-Ouvrard, Lise, '*Épigone, Histoire du siècle futur* (1659): première uchronie et politique-fiction nostalgique', *French Forum*, 25.1 (2000), 23–41

Lemarchand, Frédérick, 'L'idéologie moderniste et l'utopie', *Écologie & politique*, 3.37 (2008), 23–31

Léonard, Albert, 'Suétone', in *La collection ad usum Delphini*, II — *L'Antiquité au miroir du Grand Siècle*, ed. by Martine Furno (Grenoble: UGA Éditions, 2005) <https://doi.org/10.4000/books.ugaeditions.2985>

'A Letter from the Reverend Mr. M--d--n to the Hon. Lady M---n---x', entry in the National Library of Ireland catalogue, <https://catalogue.nli.ie/>, *ad vocem*

Long, Gerard, 'The National Library of Ireland', in *The Cambridge History of Libraries in Britain and Ireland*, vol. III, ed. by Alistair Black and Peter Hoare (Cambridge: Cambridge University Press, 2006), pp. 266–67

Lorenz, Chris, and Berber Bevernage, eds, *Breaking up Time: Negotiating the Borders between Present, Past and Future* (Göttingen: Vandenhoeck & Ruprecht, 2013)

Lunney, Linde, 'Skelton, Philip', in *Dictionary of Irish Biography*, 2009, <https://dib.ie>, [accessed 1 January 2023], *ad vocem*

Macaulay, Rose, *Pleasure of Ruins* (New York: Walker, 1953)

MacLean, Gerald M., *The Rise of Oriental Travel: English Visitors to the Ottoman Empire, 1580–1720* (Houndmills: Palgrave, 2006)

'Madden, Thomas — 1640', in University of Toronto Libraries, *British Armorial Bindings*, <https://armorial.library.utoronto.ca/>, [accessed 1 January 2023], *ad vocem*

Majercik, Ruth, *The Chaldean Oracles: Text, Translation and Commentary* (Leiden: Brill, 1989)

Major, Philip, ed., *Literatures of Exile in the English Revolution and Its Aftermath, 1640–1690* (London: Ashgate, 2010)

Malcolm, Noel, 'The 1649 English Translation of the Koran: Its Origins and Significance', *Journal of the Warburg and Courtauld Institutes*, 75 (2012), 261–95

Manning, Patricia W., *An Overview of the Pre-Suppression Society of Jesus in Spain* (Leiden: Brill, 2020)

Manuel, Frank E., and Fritzie P. Manuel, *Utopian Thought in the Western World* (Cambridge, MA: Belknap Press of Harvard University Press, 1979)

Margolis, Jonathan, *A Brief History of Tomorrow: The Future, Past and Present* (London: Bloomsbury, 2001)

Marshall, Peter, 'The Guardian Angel in Protestant England', in *Angels in the Early Modern World*, ed. by Peter Marshall and Alexandra Walsham (Cambridge: Cambridge University Press, 2006), pp. 295–316

——, and Alexandra Walsham, eds, *Angels in the Early Modern World* (Cambridge: Cambridge University Press, 2006)

Marsh's Library, *Catalogue*, <https://marshlibrary.ie/catalogue>, [accessed 1 January 2023], *ad vocem*

Maslen, Keith, *An Early London Printing House at Work: Studies in the Bowyer Ledgers: With a supplement to* The Bowyer ornament stock *(1973), an appendix on the Bowyer-Emonson partnership, and 'Bowyer's Paper Stock Ledger', by Herbert Davis* (New York: Bibliographical Society of America, 1993)

——, and John Lancaster, 'Introductory Commentary', in *The Bowyer Ledgers: The Printing Accounts of William Bowyer Father and Son, with a Checklist of Bowyer Printing 1699–1777, a Commentary, Indexes, and Appendixes*, ed. by Keith Maslen and John Lancaster (London: The Bibliographical Society and The Bibliographical Society of America, 1991), pp. xxviii–xxix

——, 'Checklist of Bowyer Printing, 1710–1777 (with works in the press 1777, completed 1778–1783)', in *The Bowyer Ledgers: The Printing Accounts of William Bowyer Father and Son, with a Checklist of Bowyer Printing 1699–1777, a Commentary, Indexes, and Appendixes*, ed. by Keith Maslen and John Lancaster (London: The Bibliographical Society and The Bibliographical Society of America, 1991), pp. 1–406

Matei, Oana, 'Gabriel Plattes, Hartlib Circle and the Interest for Husbandry in the Seventeenth Century England', *Prolegomena*, 11.2 (2012), 207–24

Matytsin, Anton, 'Historical Pyrrhonism and Historical Certainty in the Early Enlightenment', in *Pour et contre le scepitcisme: Théories et pratiques de l'Antiquité aux Lumières*, ed. by Élodie Argaud, Nawalle El Yadari, Sébastien Charles, and Gianni Paganini (Paris: Champion, 2015), pp. 243–59

Matytsin, Anton M., and Dan Edelstein, eds, *Let There Be Enlightenment: The Religious and Mystical Sources of Rationality* (Baltimore: Johns Hopkins University Press, 2018)

McBurney, William H., *A Check List of English Prose Fiction, 1700–1739* (Cambridge, MA: Harvard University Press, 1960)

McCloy, Shelby T., 'Persecution of the Huguenots in the 18th Century', *Church History*, 20.3 (1951), pp. 56–79

McClure, George, *Doubting the Divine in Early Modern Europe: The Revival of Momus, the Agnostic God* (Cambridge: Cambridge University Press, 2018)

McCoog, Thomas M., 'The Society of Jesus in the Three Kingdoms', in *The Cambridge Companion to the Jesuits*, ed. by Thomas Worcester (Cambridge: Cambridge University Press, 2008), pp. 88–103

McCready, Susan, 'Performing Time in the Revolutionary Theater', *Dalhousie French Studies*, 55 (Summer 2001), 26–30

McGuire, Brian Patrick, *Jean Gerson and the Last Medieval Reformation* (University Park, PA: Pennsylvania State University Press, 2005)

McKenzie Richmond, Ian, 'Deux œuvres rendues à l'abbé de Pure', *Revue d'Histoire littéraire de la France*, 77.2 (1977), 179–86

McKeon, Michael, *The Origins of the English Novel, 1600–1740*, with a new introduction by the author (1987; Baltimore: The Johns Hopkins University Press, 2002)

McLaverty, James, 'Lintot [Lintott], (Barnaby) Bernard (1675–1736)', in *Oxford Dictionary of National Biography*, 2004 <https://doi.org/10.1093/ref:odnb/16746>

Minois, Georges, *Storia dell'avvenire. Dai profeti alla futurologia*, trans. by Manuela Carbone (1996; Milan: Dedalo, 2006)

Minuti, Rolando, 'Oriental Despotism', in *EGO — European History Online*, published by the Leibniz Institute of European History, 2012, <http://ieg-ego.eu>, [accessed 1 January 2023], *ad vocem*

———, *Orientalismo e idee di tolleranza nella cultura francese del primo '700* (Florence: Olschki, 2006)

———, *Una geografia politica della diversità. Studi su Montesquieu* (Naples: Liguori, 2015)

Moore, Steven, *The Novel: An Alternative History 1600–1800* (New York: Bloomsbury, 2013)

Mueller, Judith C., 'A Tale of a Tub and Early Prose', in *The Cambridge Companion to Jonathan Swift*, ed. by Christopher Fox (Cambridge: Cambridge University Press, 2003), pp. 202–15

Mulcahy, Matthew, 'The Port Royal Earthquake and the World of Wonders in Seventeenth-Century Jamaica', *Early American Studies*, 6.2 (2008), 391–421

Nagel, Alexandra H. M., 'Marriage with Elementals: From Le Comte de Gabalis to a Golden Dawn Ritual' (MA dissertation, University of Amsterdam, 2006–2007)

Nahin, Paul J., *Time Machines: Time Travel in Physics, Metaphysics, and Science Fiction* (New York: Springer Verlag-American Institute of Physics, 1993)

Negley, Glenn Robert, *Utopian Literature: A Bibliography with a Supplementary Listing of Works Influential in Utopian Thought* (Lawrence: Regents Press of Kansas, 1977)

Nelles, Paul, 'Jesuit Letters', in *The Oxford Handbook of the Jesuits*, ed. by Ines G. Županov (Oxford: Oxford University Press, 2019), pp. 44–72

Nelson, Charles E., 'A Late 17th Century Irish Herbarium in the Library of Trinity College, Dublin', *The Irish Naturalists Journal*, 20.8 (1981), 334–35

Novotný, František, *The Posthumous Life of Plato* (The Hague: Martinus Nijhoff, 1977)

O'Brien, Karen, 'History and the Novel in Eighteenth-Century Britain', *Huntington Library Quarterly*, 68.1–2 (2005), 397–413 <https://doi.org/10.1525/hlq.2005.68.1–2.397>

Ó Ciardha, Éamonn, *Ireland and the Jacobite Cause, 1685–1766: A Fatal Attachment* (Dublin and Portland, OR: Four Courts Press, 2004)

——, 'Madden, Samuel Molyneux ("Premium Madden")', in *Dictionary of Irish Biography*, 2009, <https://dib.ie>, [accessed 1 January 2023], *ad vocem*

Øhrstrøm, Peter, and Per Hasle, 'Future Contingents', *The Stanford Encyclopedia of Philosophy*, Summer 2020 edition, ed. by Edward N. Zalta, <https://plato.stanford.edu/archives/sum2020/entries/future-contingents/>, [accessed 1 January 2023]

Oman, C[harles], 'The Editor's Preface', in *The Reign of George VI. 1900–1925: A Forecast Written in the year 1763*, Republished, with Preface and Notes by C. Oman (1763; [London]: Rivingstons, 1899), pp. vii–xxvi

Oosterhoff, Richard, 'Genius and Inspiration in the Early Modern Period', in *Encyclopedia of Early Modern Philosophy and the Sciences*, ed. by Dana Jalobeanu and Charles T. Wolfe (Cham: Springer, 2020) <https://doi.org/10.1007/978-3-319-20791-9>

Orr, Leah, 'Genre Labels on the Title Pages of English Fiction, 1660–1800', *Philological Quarterly*, 90. 1 (2011), 67–95

O'Shaughnessy, David, 'Staging an Irish Enlightenment', in *Ireland, Enlightenment and the English Stage, 1740–1820*, ed. by David O'Shaughnessy (Cambridge: Cambridge University Press, 2019), pp. 1–28

Osterhammel, Jürgen, *Unfabling the East: The Enlightenment's Encounter with Asia*, trans. by Robert Savage (2013; Princeton and Oxford: Princeton University Press, 2018)

O'Sullivan, William, 'John Madden's Manuscripts', in *Essays on the History of Trinity College Library*, ed. by Anne Walsh and Vincent Kinane (Dublin: Four Courts, 2000), pp. 104–15

Pagden, Anthony, *Lords of all the World: Ideologies of Empire in Spain, Britain and France c. 1500–c. 1800* (New Haven: Yale University Press, 1998)

Paglia, Camille A., 'Lord Hervey and Pope', *Eighteenth-Century Studies*, 6.3 (1973), 348–71 <https://doi.org/10.2307/3031690>

Papke, David Ray, 'The Communistic Inclinations of Sir Thomas More', *The University of the Pacific Law Review*, 48.29 (2016), 29–43

Parrinder, Patrick, 'Introduction', in *Learning from Other Worlds: Estrangement, Cognition, and the Politics of Science Fiction and Utopia*, ed. Parrinder (Durham, NC: Duke University Press, 2000), pp. 1–18

——, 'Revisiting Suvin's Poetics of Science Fiction', in *Learning from Other Worlds: Estrangement, Cognition, and the Politics of Science Fiction and Utopia*, ed. Parrinder (Durham, NC: Duke University Press, 2000), pp. 36–50

——, *Utopian Literature and Science: From the Scientific Revolution to Brave New World and Beyond* (London: Palgrave, 2015)

Parrinder, Patrick, ed., *Learning from Other Worlds: Estrangement, Cognition, and the Politics of Science Fiction and Utopia* (Durham, NC: Duke University Press, 2000)

Paschini, Pio, *Pier Paolo Vergerio il giovane e la sua apostasia: Un episodio delle lotte religiose nel Cinquecento* (Rome: Scuola tipografica Pio X, 1925)

Pavone, Sabina, 'Anti-Jesuitism in a Global Perspective', in *The Oxford Handbook of the Jesuits*, ed. by Ines G. Županov (Oxford: Oxford University Press, 2019), pp. 833–54

———, *Le astuzie dei gesuiti. Le false Istruzioni segrete della Compagnia di Gesú e la polemica antigesuita nei secoli XVII e XVIII* (Rome: Salerno, 2000)

———, 'Between History and Myth: The Monita Secreta Societatis Jesu', in *The Jesuits II: Cultures, Sciences, and the Arts, 1540–1773*, ed. by John W. O'Malley, Gauvin Alexander Bailey, Steven J. Harris, and Frank T. Kennedy (Toronto: University of Toronto Press, 2006), pp. 50–65

Pearl, Jason H., *Utopian Geographies and the Early English Novel* (Charlottesville: University of Virginia Press, 2014)

Pelli, Moshe, 'The Epistolary Story in Haskalah Literature: Isaac Euchel's "Igrot Meshulam"', *The Jewish Quarterly Review*, 93.3–4 (2003), 431–69

Perkins, Maureen, *Visions of the Future: Almanacs, Time, and Cultural Change, 1775–1870* (Oxford: Clarendon Press-Oxford University Press, 1996)

Pestana, Carla Gardina, *Protestant Empire: Religion and the Making of the British Atlantic World* (Philadelphia: University of Pennsylvania Press, 2009)

Peters, Michael A., and Tina Besley, 'The Royal Society, the Making of "Science" and the Social History of Truth', *Educational Philosophy and Theory*, 51.3 (2019), 227–32 <https://doi.org/10.1080/00131857.2017.141780>

Petitier, Paule, 'Le dernier homme et la fin de l'histoire: Grainville, Shelley, Michelet', *Écrire l'histoire* 15 (2015), 149–57 <https://doi.org/10.4000/elh.615>

Phiddian, Robert, *Satire and the Public Emotions* (Cambridge: Cambridge University Press, 2019)

'Philip Dormer Stanhope, 4th Earl of Chesterfield', in *Encyclopaedia Britannica*, last rev. by J. E. Luebering, last updated 18 September 2022, < https://www.britannica.com/>, [accessed 1 January 2023], *ad vocem*

Pickover, Clifford A., *The Girl Who Gave Birth to Rabbits: A True Medical Mystery* (Amherst, NY: Prometheus Books, 2000)

Pirri, Pietro, 'Albertini, Francesco Maria', in *Dizionario Biografico degli italiani*, vol. I (Rome: Treccani, 1960), *ad vocem*

Pohl, Nicole, 'Utopianism after More: The Renaissance and Enlightenment', in *The Cambridge Companion to Utopian Literature*, ed. by Gregory Claeys (Cambridge: Cambridge University Press, 2010), pp. 51–78

Pons, Alain, 'Sur la Dixième époque: Utopie et histoire chez Condorcet', *Mélanges de l'Ecole française de Rome. Italie et Méditerranée*, 108.2 (1996), 601–08 <https://doi.org/10.3406/mefr.1996.4457>

Porter, Roy, *The Creation of the Modern World: The Untold Story of the British Enlightenment* (New York: W. W. Norton, 2000)

Potter, David, ed., *Henry VIII and Francis I: The Final Conflict, 1540–1547* (Leiden: Brill, 2011)

Prieto, Andrés I., 'The Perils of Accommodation: Jesuit Missionary Strategies in the Early Modern World', *Journal of Jesuit Studies*, 4.3 (2017), 395–414 <https://doi.org/10.1163/22141332–00403002>

Prince, Susan, *Antisthenes of Athens: Texts, Translations, and Commentary* (Ann Arbor: University of Michigan Press, 2015)

Pringle, David, Brian M. Stableford, Peter Nicholls, and David Langford, 'Lost World', last updated 2 April 2015, in *SFE: The Encyclopedia of Science Fiction*, ed. by John Clute and David Langford, <https://sf-encyclopedia.com/>, [accessed 1 January 2023], *ad vocem*

Puttevils, Jeroen, 'Invoking Fortuna and Speculating on the Future: Lotteries in the 15th and 16th Century Low Countries', *Quaderni storici*, 3 (2017), 699–726 <https://doi.org/10.1408/90446>

Quintero, Ruben, ed., *A Companion to Satire: Ancient and Modern* (Malden: Blackwell, 2007)

Rabasa, José, Masayuki Sato, Edoardo Tortarolo, and Daniel Woolf, eds, *The Oxford History of Historical Writing*, vol. III, *1400–1800* (Oxford: Oxford University Press, 2012)

Raven, James, 'The Anonymous Novel in Britain and Ireland, 1750–1830', in *The Faces of Anonymity: Anonymous and Pseudonymous Publication from the Sixteenth to the Twentieth Century*, ed. by Robert J. Griffin (New York: Palgrave Macmillan, 2003), pp. 141–66

Reed, Annette Yoshiko, *Demons, Angels, and Writing in Ancient Judaism* (Cambridge: Cambridge University Press, 2020)

Reusch, Heinrich, 'Inchofer, Melchior', in *Allgemeine Deutsche Biographie*, 14 (1881), pp. 64–65, online <https://www.deutsche-biographie.de/pnd124293077.html#adbcontent>, [accessed 1 January 2023]

Richey, Rosemary, 'Madden, Samuel Molyneux [called Premium Madden] (1686–1765)', in *Oxford Dictionary of National Biography*, 2004 <https://doi.org/10.1093/ref:odnb/17754>

Rieder, John, *Colonialism and the Emergence of Science Fiction* (Middletown, CT: Wesleyan University Press, 2008)

——, 'On Defining SF or Not: Genre Theory, SF and History', *Science Fiction Studies*, 37.2 (2010), 191–209

Rife, Joseph L., 'Apollonius of Tyana', in *The Oxford Encyclopedia of Ancient Greece and Rome*, ed. by Michael Gagarin (Oxford: Oxford University Press, 2010), pp. 140–41

Roberts, Adam, 'The Copernican Revolution', in *The Routledge Companion to Science Fiction*, ed. by Mark Bould, Andrew M. Butler, Adam Roberts, and Sherryl Vint (London: Routledge, 2009), pp. 3–12

——, *The History of Science Fiction*, 2nd ed. (London: Palgrave, 2016)

Rose, Stephen, *Musical Authorship from Schütz to Bach* (Cambridge: Cambridge University Press, 2019)

Rosenberg, Daniel, and Anthony Grafton, *Cartographies of Time* (New York: Princeton Architectural Press, 2010)

Rowland, Ingrid D., 'Athanasius Kircher's Guardian Angel', in *Conversations with Angels: Essays Towards a History of Spiritual Communication, 1100–1700*, ed. by Joad Raymond (Houndmills: Palgrave Macmillan, 2011), pp. 250–70

Rubiés, Joan-Pau, 'The Jesuits and the Enlightenment', in *The Oxford Handbook of the Jesuits*, ed. by Ines G. Županov (Oxford: Oxford University Press, 2019), pp. 855–90

Sale, William Merritt, *Samuel Richardson: Master Printer* (Ithaca, NY: Cornell University Press, 1950)

Sambrook, James, 'Molloy, Charles (d. 1767)', in *Oxford Dictionary of National Biography*, 2008 <https://doi.org/10.1093/ref:odnb/18915>

Sayre Schiffman, Zachary, *The Birth of the Past* (Baltimore: Johns Hopkins University Press, 2011)

Scarborough, John, 'The Drug Lore of Asclepiades of Bithynia', *Pharmacy in History*, 17.2 (1975), 43–57

Schier, Volker, 'Birgitta of Sweden and the Birgittine Order', last modified 2018, in *Oxford Bibliographies*, <https://www.oxfordbibliographies.com/>, [accessed 1 January 2023], *Medieval Studies, ad vocem* <https://doi.org/10.1093/OBO/9780195396584–0255>

Schutte, Anne Jacobson, 'Vergerio, Pier Paolo', in *The Oxford Encyclopedia of the Reformation*, ed. by Hans J. Hillebrand (Oxford: Oxford University Press, 1996), 4 vols, vol. IV, pp. 228–29

Sebastiani, Silvia, *The Scottish Enlightenment: Race, Gender, and the Limits of Progress* (New York: Palgrave Macmillan, 2013)

Seeber, Edward D., 'Sylphs and Other Elemental Beings in French Literature since Le Comte De Gabalis (1670)', *PMLA*, 59.1 (1944), 71–83 <https://doi.org/10.2307/458845>

Shapin, Steven, *A Social History of Truth: Civility and Science in Seventeenth-Century England* (Chicago: University of Chicago Press, 1994)

Shaw, Matthew, *Time and the French Revolution: The Republican Calendar, 1789-Year XIV* (Woodbridge: Royal Historical Society-Boydell, 2011)

Shefer-Mossensohn, Miri, *Ottoman Medicine: Healing and Medical Institutions, 1500–1700* (Albany: State University of New York Press, 2009)

'Sibyl', in *Encyclopaedia Britannica*, last updated 4 July 2022, <https://www.britannica.com/topic/Sibyl-Greek-legendary-figure>, [accessed 1 January 2023]

Simoncelli, Paolo, 'Curione, Celio Secondo (1503–1569)', in *The Oxford Encyclopedia of the Reformation*, ed. by Hans J. Hillebrand (1996; Oxford: Oxford University Press, 2005), *ad vocem*

Simonetti, Elsa Giovanna, 'Who Is the Best Prophet? The "Manifold" Character of a Quotation in Plutarch', in *The Dynamics of Intertextuality in Plutarch*, ed. by Thomas S. Schmidt, Maria Vamvouri Ruffy, and Rainer Hirsch-Luipold (Boston: Brill, 2020), pp. 349–61

Simpson, Evelyn Mary, *A Study of the Prose Works of John Donne* (Oxford: Clarendon Press, 1962)

Singles, Kathleen, *Alternate History: Playing with Contingency and Necessity* (Berlin: De Gruyter, 2013)

Spadafora, David, *The Idea of Progress in Eighteenth-Century Britain* (New Haven: Yale University Press, 1990)

Speck, W. A., 'William Augustus, Prince, duke of Cumberland (1721–1765)', in *Oxford Dictionary of National Biography*, 2004, rev. 2008 <https://doi.org/10.1093/ref:odnb/29455>

Spini, Giorgio, *Ricerca dei libertini. La teoria dell'impostura delle religioni nel Seicento italiano* (Rome: Universale di Roma, 1950), pp. 217–46

Standish, David, *Hollow Earth: The Long and Curious History of Imagining Strange Lands, Fantastical Creatures, Advanced Civilizations, and Marvelous Machines Below the Earth's Surface* (Cambridge, MA: Da Capo Press, 2006)

Stephenson, Joseph F., 'A Mirror for London: The Geopolitics of *A Larum for London* at the Globe in 1599', *Parergon*, 30.1 (2013), 179–201 <https://doi.org/10.1353/pgn.2013.0047>

Stewart, Susan, *The Ruins Lesson: Meaning and Material in Western Culture* (Chicago: University of Chicago Press, 2020)

Suvin, Darko, *Metamorphoses of Science Fiction: On the Poetics and History of a Literary Genre* (New Haven, CT: Yale University Press, 1979)

Tarantino, Giovanni, 'From Labelling and Ridicule to Understanding: The Novelty of Bernard and Picart's Religious Comparativism', in *Through Your Eyes: Religious Alterity and the Early Modern Western Imagination*, ed. by Giovanni Tarantino and Paola von Wyss-Giacosa (Leiden: Brill, 2021), pp. 236–66

Thompson, E. P., 'Time, Work-Discipline, and Industrial Capitalism', *Past & Present*, 38 (1967), 56–97 <https://doi.org/10.1093/past/38.1.56>

Thornton Forster, Charles, *The Life and Letters of Ogier Ghiselin de Busbecq seigneur of Bousbecque* (London: C. Kegan Paul, 1881), 2 vols

Todd, Dennis, 'St André, Nathanael (1679/80–1776)', in *Oxford Dictionary of National Biography*, 2008 <https://doi.org/10.1093/ref:odnb/24478>

Tortarolo, Edoardo, 'L'eutanasia della cronologia biblica', in *La centralità del dubbio. Un progetto di Antonio Rotondò*, tome I.III, *Scritture, ragione e storia*, ed. by Camilla Hermanin and Luisa Simonutti (Florence: Olschki 2010), pp. 339–59

——, *The Invention of Free Press: Writers and Censorship in Eighteenth Century Europe* (Dordrecht: Springer, 2016)

Toulmin, Stephen and June Goodfield, *The Discovery of Time* (1965; Middlesex: Penguin, 1967)

Trinity College Dublin, Library, items acquired by the Library before 1872, Printed Catalogue Online, <https://www.scss.tcd.ie/misc/1872catalogueB/>, [accessed 1 January 2023], *ad vocem*

Turpin, John, 'The School of Design in Victorian Dublin', *Journal of Design History*, 2.4 (1989), 243–56

Urstad, Tone Sundt, *Sir Robert Walpole's Poets: The Use of Literature as Pro-government Propaganda 1721–1742* (Newark: University of Delaware Press and Associated University Press, 1999)

Vance, Norman, *Irish Literature: A Social History: Tradition, Identity, and Difference* (Oxford: Blackwell, 1990)

Vaughn, James M., *The Politics of Empire at the Accession of George III: The East India Company and the Crisis and Transformation of Britain's Imperial State* (New Haven: Yale University Press, 2019)

Ventura, Iolanda, 'Pietro d'Abano', in *Dizionario Biografico degli Italiani*, vol. LXXXIII (Rome: Treccani, 2015), pp. 437–41

Versnel, H. S., 'Daimon', in *The Oxford Classical Dictionary*, ed. by Simon Hornblower and Antony Spawforth (Oxford: Oxford University Press, 2005), *ad vocem*

Vieira, Fátima, 'The Concept of Utopia', in *The Cambridge Companion to Utopian Literature*, ed. by Gregory Claeys (Cambridge: Cambridge University Press, 2010), pp. 3–27

Vlassopoulos, Kostas, 'Imperial Encounters: Discourses on Empire and the Uses of Ancient History during the Eighteenth Century', in *Classics and Imperialism in the British Empire*, ed. by Mark Bradley (Oxford: Oxford University Press, 2010), pp. 29–53

Walker-Meikle, Kathleen, 'The Goose that Went on a Crusade', *The Medieval Magazine*, special issue *The Crusades*, 125, 5 May 2020, available online <https://www.themedievalmagazine.com>, [accessed 1 January 2023]

Walsham, Alexandra, 'The Pope's Merchandise and the Jesuits' Trumpery: Catholic Relics and Protestant Polemic in Post-Reformation England', in *Religion, the Supernatural and Visual Culture in Early Modern Europe: An album amicorum for Charles Zika*, ed. by Jennifer Spinks and Dagmar Eichberger (Leiden: Brill, 2015), pp. 370–409

'Wappen des C. J. Sullon', Herzog August Bibliothek, Wolfenbüttel, in *Kupferstichkabinett* <http://diglib.hab.de?grafik=exlib-berlepsch-18-1-00226>, [accessed 1 January 2023]

Wasserman, Ryan, *Paradoxes of Time Travel* (Oxford: Oxford University Press, 2018)

Watson, George, ed., *The New Cambridge Bibliography of English Literature: Volume 2, 1660–1800* (Cambridge: Cambridge University Press, 1971)

Watt, Ian, *The Rise of the Novel: Studies in Defoe, Richardson and Fielding* (Berkeley: University of California Press, 1957)

Webster, Charles, 'The Authorship and Significance of Macaria', *Past & Present*, 56 (1972), 34–48

Weinbrot, Howard D., *Eighteenth-Century Satire: Essays on Text and Context from Dryden to Peter Pindar* (Cambridge: Cambridge University Press, 1988)

Welburn, Andrew J., *Power and Self-Consciousness in the Poetry of Shelley* (Houndmills: Macmillan, 1986)

Welch, Robert, ed., *The Oxford Companion to Irish Literature*, assistant ed. by Bruce Stewart (Oxford: Clarendon Press, 1996)

Wilders, John, 'Introduction', in *Samuel Butler: Hudibras*, ed. by John Wilders (Oxford: Oxford University Press, 1967), pp. xiii–xliii

Wilford, F. A., 'ΔΑΙΜΩΝ in Homer', *Numen*, 12.3 (1965), 217–32 <https://doi.org/10.2307/3269447>

Williams, David, *Condorcet and Modernity* (Cambridge: Cambridge University Press, 2004)

Wilson, David, *The History of the Future* (Toronto: McArthur, 2001)

Wilson, Robert R., 'The Prophetic Books', in *The Cambridge Companion to Biblical Interpretation*, ed. by John Barton (Cambridge: Cambridge University Press, 1998), pp. 212–25

Winkler, Kenneth P., 'Introduction', in *The Cambridge Companion to Berkeley*, ed. by Kenneth P. Winkler (Cambridge: Cambridge University Press, 2005), pp. 1–12

Wisniewski, Robert, *Christian Divination in Late Antiquity* (Amsterdam: Amsterdam University Press, 2020)

Woolf, Daniel, *A Global History of History* (Cambridge: Cambridge University Press, 2011)

Worcester, Thomas, 'Anti-Jesuit Polemic', in *The Cambridge Encyclopedia of the Jesuits*, general ed. Worcester (Cambridge: Cambridge University Press, 2017), pp. 30–34

Wright, Jonathan, 'United Kingdom', in *The Cambridge Encyclopedia of the Jesuits*, general ed. Thomas Worcester (Cambridge: Cambridge University Press, 2017), pp. 795–97

Zimmerman, Everett, *The Boundaries of Fiction: History and the 18th British Novel* (Ithaca: Cornell University Press, 1996)

Županov, Ines G., ed., *The Oxford Handbook of the Jesuits* (Oxford: Oxford University Press, 2019)

Index

Page numbers in italics refer to figures, terms in quotation marks denote fictional characters and places.